Religion in
the Victorian Era

L.E. Elliott-Binns

James Clarke & Co.
Cambridge

Published by
James Clarke & Co.
P.O. Box 60
Cambridge
CB1 2NT
England

e-mail: **publishing@jamesclarke.co.uk**
website: **http://www.jamesclarke.co.uk**

ISBN 0 227 17074 1 hardback
ISBN 0 227 17073 3 paperback

British Library Cataloguing in Publication Data:
A catalogue record is available from the British Library.

First published 1936, reprinted 1946, 1953
by The Lutterworth Press
Reprinted 2002

Copyright ©1936 L.E. Elliott-Binns

All rights reserved. No part of this publication may be reproduced, stored in a retrieval system or transmitted in any form or by any means, electronic, mechanical, photocopying, recording or otherwise, without the prior permission in writing of the Publisher.

CONTENTS

	INTRODUCTION	*page* 7
1.	THE PRE-VICTORIAN ERA: POLITICAL CONDITIONS	11
2.	THE PRE-VICTORIAN ERA: THE CONDITION OF RELIGION	36
3.	THE EARLY YEARS OF VICTORIA	59
4.	EDUCATION TO 1843	79
5.	THE OXFORD MOVEMENT TO 1845	92
6.	THE ROMAN CHURCH IN ENGLAND	114
7.	THE DEVELOPMENT OF THOUGHT TO 1870	131
8.	RELIGION AND SCIENCE	153
9.	RELIGION AND HISTORY	172
10.	THE MIDDLE YEARS	193
11.	THE REVIVAL AND DEEPENING OF RELIGION	212
12.	THE OXFORD MOVEMENT: THE SECOND PHASE	226
13.	SOCIAL PROBLEMS	243
14.	THE DEVELOPMENT OF THOUGHT FROM 1870	271
15.	THE CAMBRIDGE SCHOOL	292
16.	EDUCATION FROM 1843	311
17.	THE PRESS	328
18.	LITERATURE AND ART	338
19.	WORSHIP	361
20.	THE CALL OF THE WORLD	375
21.	SOCIAL CHANGES	401
22.	NEW METHODS	420
23.	THE MINISTRY	446
24.	REUNION AND FEDERATION	468
25.	THE END OF AN EPOCH	490
	INDEX	513

CORRIGENDA (*see Preface*)

p. 57, l. 21 Strictly speaking there was no single founder of the Plymouth Brethren.

p. 329, ll. 24f. This was not so. Smith's suggestion was: "We cultivate literature on a little oatmeal". That adopted came from Francis Horner, who had found it in Publius Syrus.

p. 395, ll. 20ff. It must not be forgotten, however, that John West had started work on the Red River in 1820, and Bishop Mountain found a few churches and clergymen when he arrived there.

p. 457, l. 21 Regent's Park College is now at Oxford.

p. 479, Under efforts at co-operation mention should have been made of The World's Evangelical Alliance founded in 1846.

INTRODUCTION

The genesis of this volume is to be found in the suggestion, made considerably more than thirty years ago, by a friend of my father who discerned in me some literary ambition, that I should read Goethe's *Dichtung und Wahrheit*. I followed his advice; and set up a thirst for biography which has proved insatiable. Since that time my lighter reading has lain chiefly in this department of letters, and there is hardly a biography of any prominent figure of the last century, in the ecclesiastical sphere at least, which I have not read. Thus when I was asked to undertake a History of Religion in the Nineteenth Century, although the period was very remote from my usual range of studies, I received the suggestion with sympathy; for I had already a considerable knowledge of the necessary background.

The lives of the great men and women of the past century, and of many who were by no means deserving of the epithet, have been my chief authorities. And because I have had to deal with many minds and many diverse points of view, seeking fairness I have left them, in not a few cases, to use their own words. To have summarized their opinions and their descriptions of incidents and movements in words of my own would not have been a difficult matter; but I doubt if I could have preserved the nicety of their point of view, and certainly not the freshness of the original utterance. At all points I have tried to be as constructive as possible, and so have refrained from criticism. Each spokesman has been allowed to present his own case; and I hope that the Roman Catholic and the adherent of Keswick who may happen to pick up this volume will equally find matter of which they can approve. The faith which each represents, together with that of countless others, contributed its ingredient to that mixture of beliefs which must be included in the term Religion in the Nineteenth Century.

But the title of the volume is not a History of Religion in the Nineteenth Century, but in the Victorian Era which formed only a part of it. I made this modification after beginning my task as I came to feel that the Victorian Era offered a more

RELIGION IN THE VICTORIAN ERA

self-contained period for study. This feeling was reinforced by a passage which I happened to come across in Edward Armstrong's *Italian Studies*, in which he writes: "Centuries are even less satisfactory than reigns as lines of demarcation. A reign's beginning, or its end, may really cause or emphasize a change . . . whereas there is no personality in a year" (*op. cit.*, p. 177). The restricted era thus chosen is not itself entirely satisfactory, for it forms no clear-cut unit. Politically it began with the passing of the Reform Bill in 1832; from the point of view of the philanthropist, who loomed so large in the Victorian world, with the Anti-Slavery Agitation of the Eighteenth Century. None the less, there are certain phenomena, the manifestations in the religious sphere of general tendencies observable also elsewhere, which only came to maturity after the Queen's accession.

My work naturally challenges comparison with the recent volume by the Dean of Exeter, *Church and People, 1789–1889*. But it has certain quite definite differences from this excellent piece of work. Dr. Carpenter wrote with the Centenary of the Oxford Movement in his mind and he dealt primarily with the Church of England. I have taken a wider sweep, and have endeavoured to survey Christianity in England without regard to any particular Denomination. I have restricted myself to religion in England; but this has not meant that I have failed to realize that it was affected by many influences outside England. The reader, indeed, may perhaps be surprised that I have given so much space to secular events, and in particular to events beyond the frontiers of this realm. I have done so deliberately, for the history of a country, or its religion, cannot be studied in isolation. So, on the one hand, I have tried to trace out the actions and reactions of great forces—political, social, economic, intellectual, as well as religious—during the reign; and, on the other, to keep in mind not only the contemporary life of the nation, but, in addition, the shifting background of the general European world.

In his study of a by-gone period the historian often feels that he is trying to evoke phantoms from the irrecoverable years, or even to stir the ashes of forgotten conflicts; the figures are mere shadows, and the landscape against which

INTRODUCTION

they move cold and flat. But in studying an age so recent as that which forms the subject of the present volume this feeling cannot exert itself. The historian has materials so abundant that he is able to catch vivid details from a hundred different sources. So numerous are they, indeed, that his chief difficulty is selection and arrangement. There is so much that demands to be included, in its appropriate setting, in the vast panorama of the Victorian Age.

Some acquaintance with the history of religion in the immediate or not very distant past is essential for all those who would face the problems of the present. For such knowledge is not the slowly dying knowledge of an age which is itself dead; but the knowledge, made vivid by appreciation, of that which still abundantly survives, survives in us its children. There are those, of course, who affect a disdain for the Victorian Age which prevents their seeing anything of value in it. They are greatly in error in their attitude, and I would commend to them the admirable defence which Dr. Major set forth in the Introduction to his *Life and Letters of W. Boyd Carpenter*. "It is the fashion of our complacent Georgian idealists to regard the Victorian Age as a sort of Cimmerian chaos of competitive industrialism, scientific materialism, and smug hypocrisy, and to ignore the extraordinary amount of work the Victorians accomplished in the spheres of intellectual enlightenment and of political and social reform. The Victorians had their ignorances and their limitations, their sickly sentiment and their bad taste, and the age that follows them is highly sensitive to their defects. But the Victorians had great courage, great energy, and great kindness of heart" (*op. cit.*, pp. v f.).

No age can live on the hoarded gleanings of the past; it must earn the right to live under its own vine and fig-tree; none the less, that past has abundant lessons for those who have the insight and power of imagination to receive them. Of the lessons which we may learn of our fathers there is one which I feel to be precious above the rest—not to be ashamed of our aspirations. We must learn to believe that just as the acts of the individual who seeks to do the will of God are not merely fortuitous, but manifestations of eternal principles, so his aspirations are capable of being linked to something universal, that beneath the most exalted conceptions of the human spirit lie the ancient harmonies of heaven.

In conclusion I should like to express my gratitude to the Rev. R. Mercer Wilson and to the readers of the Lutterworth Press for a number of helpful criticisms and suggestions.

L. E. ELLIOTT-BINNS

CAMBRIDGE
The Conversion of St. Paul, 1936

PREFACE TO SECOND EDITION

I am grateful for various suggestions and criticisms made by a number of reviewers and correspondents, among the latter I should like to mention the late Bishop Knox, Canon H. G. G. Herklots, the Rev. G. W. Neatby and the Rev. F. G. Lowe. As, however, the circumstances in which the present edition is being produced restrict alterations to a minimum I have only been able to change one paragraph (on p. 323) and to revise the closing sentence of the volume which I had left in a rather ambiguous form. In addition a list of corrections will be found on p. 6. I have to thank the Theological Editor of the Lutterworth Press, the Rev. G. H. Gordon Hewitt, for his kind offices and help.

L. E. E.-B.

BUCKDEN.
Lent, 1946

I

THE PRE-VICTORIAN ERA: POLITICAL CONDITIONS

IF we are to understand the position and development of religion in the Victorian Era we must look back into the years which immediately preceded it; and above all we must take note of that great upheaval which released so many new forces and set in motion so many new movements—the French Revolution. We must also observe the effects of the wars to which it gave rise; for they too, by delaying reform, allowed measures intended to foster social progress to remain in abeyance, and had a considerable influence on the life of England in all its aspects, and not least upon the religious.

THE NAPOLEONIC WARS

The French Revolution had begun as a movement to free all peoples from the power of oppressive rulers and to proclaim the doctrine of equality. It ended in an internal despotism with France, all ideals lost in the lust for glory and power, as the oppressor of her neighbours. The course of events had justified the warnings of Burke rather than the raptures of Coleridge and Wordsworth.[1] Incidentally it had also disappointed many Anti-clericals who had fondly supposed that the abolition of priestly power and religious superstition would bring in the Millennium. To England the speedy deterioration of France was a challenge to the nation's way of life and a threat to its survival. The natural reaction which followed bound the nation into a close unity and national solidarity was a feature of the generation which fought the Napoleonic

[1] Both these poets changed their views as a consequence: see Coleridge *Ode to France* and Wordsworth *passim*. Views such as those which they had abandoned were to reappear in Swinburne, to whom Liberty was a religion, and the ardent advocacy of it which had marked the early stages of the French Revolution, a necessity.

Wars. There were exceptions to this solidarity, especially before the true meaning of the events in France had been revealed; some extremists even drew up plans for a Republic in England. To all such the government, and the mob also, was merciless; and measures of repression, harsh and undiscriminating, were soon enforced; freedom of speech and freedom of the press were both, for the time, abolished.

The difficulties and dangers of the Napoleonic Wars made England realize her dependence on Naval Power, and the advantage of those seas which Shakespeare had termed a "moat defensive." At the beginning of the century there was a brief moment of peace, but it was only a breathing space, and it was not until after the abortive attempt to confine Napoleon in Elba and the "hundred days" that there came the final relief of Waterloo. On "that loud Sabbath" the menace to the security of Europe was dispelled once and for all. The nations had leisure to inspect their wounds.

Napoleon had been a force so stupendous that nothing less than the combined energies of Europe sufficed to check him; his claims and assumptions so comprehensive as to partake of the godlike. Indeed on one occasion the Russian Ambassador had ventured to remind him that man proposes, God disposes. "I am he that proposes," Napoleon thundered back, "and I am he that disposes." No wonder that men saw in him the Beast of the Apocalypse and regarded his fall, when it came, as a portent. And a portent indeed it was.

The cessation of war seemed to promise a period of recovery and relief but it was such only in the negative sense of being free from strife. The Congress of Vienna in 1815 attempted to restore the ideals and conditions of the eighteenth century, to put Europe back to the pre-war period. But like the Congress of Versailles of our own day it failed to achieve this unnatural restoration. For just as Versailles set itself to make the world safe for democracy, and democracy at once began to die out in most European countries, so after 1815 the attempt to check the rise of liberal opinions had but partial success, and that not enduring, in spite of the so-called Holy Alliance. This project was the fruit of the eccentric brain of Alexander I of Russia stimulated by the exalted ideals which

PRE-VICTORIAN ERA: POLITICAL CONDITIONS

so often follow in the wake of a great war. The three emperors of Russia, Austria, and Prussia proclaimed to the whole world their determination to apply the principles of Justice, Christian Charity, and Peace to external and internal relations, and they recommended their peoples to strengthen themselves every day more and more in the principles and to exercise the duties which the Divine Saviour had taught mankind. The Holy Alliance was a high-sounding ideal. But it had behind it neither moral nor intellectual force, and once it was taken up by the cynical Metternich it quickly became an instrument for the suppression of liberty within the territories of the contracting powers. How far this fact lies behind the Antireligious feeling of Continental Socialism it would be hard to say. It must certainly have discredited religious "talk" amongst those who longed for Liberty.

For England the Napoleonic Wars had been a great epoch of strong determination, and it is perhaps not fanciful to see in the children born at that time something of its force and pain. They emerged as vital and considerable personalities. Many of them were admirable not only for intellectual genius, but for physical beauty, for strength of will and massiveness of frame.[1] It was indeed a great epoch and will bear comparison at most points with any other in British history. The splendid courage and endurance which finally wore down and conquered Napoleon; the signs already of commercial supremacy; achievements in literature, art, and science; all these lent to it a grand air.

To England, as to the rest of Europe, peace brought only disappointment. Taxation was still burdensome, and the National Debt had swollen to such proportions as to furnish a standard of vastness.[2] The hopes of a revival of trade did not at once mature, and a succession of bad harvests added to the miseries of the poor. The nation, at this juncture, found little to reassure or console it in the ruling house. George III, whose madness was varied by short fits of sanity which were still more devastating in their effects, since they allowed him

[1] Gladstone and Tennyson are obvious examples.
[2] Baron Stockmar used it of the love of Leopold of Coburg (later King of the Belgians) for his wife: see Lytton Strachey, *Queen Victoria*, p. 4.

to interfere in politics, died in 1820. Then came George IV —"mud from a muddy spring," said Shelley tersely. Under him the crown fell into open contempt, and a proud nation had to endure the spectacle of the consort of its sovereign publicly tried for adultery, with no attempt to conceal the sordid and revolting details which inevitably accompany such an action. When William IV followed ten years later, contempt was modified by amusement. For the "sailor-prince" affected the traditional manners of a boatswain on shore, and seemed to have a fair measure of hereditary insanity.

SOCIAL CONDITIONS

Accustomed as we are to a land whose main population lives in great towns, to a land which imports the bulk of its foodstuffs, the effort to visualize the condition of England in the early years of the nineteenth century requires to be determined and sustained. For England a hundred years ago was a land of small towns and villages, of country seats and their surrounding estates, a land whose vast potentialities for production of wealth were yet unexploited. It was, moreover, a self-sufficient land, at least so far as the essentials of life were concerned; everything that it imported, with the exception of sugar, was by way of being a luxury. It was also, thanks to the channel and the ships that guarded it, a land of peace and security, in spite of all the tumult and warfare of the continent. It was, on the whole, a contented land. Life might be strenuous, but it was full of interest and variety— for if the country as a whole was self-sufficient, so were its parts. Each community made its own tools, and produced all that it required for its own needs. The women were able to spin and to make clothes for themselves and their households. Food ample enough for the parish was grown within it, or near by; and there was no temptation to produce an excess for sale in the big towns, since such did not then exist. The hours of labour might be long, but the men were often their own masters, and in any case there was that personal dealing between producer and consumer which softens the hardships of toil. The people in each village kept largely to themselves;

they knew their neighbours and depended on them for social intercourse. To wander about was not attractive, for commercial requirements had not yet produced good roads, and movement beyond a small range was neither easy nor pleasant. For those who wished to travel long distances or to send off consignments of goods there were as yet no railways or canals. It was the age of stage-coaches, outside places, hurried meals, and thick great-coats; an age when the bugle of the passing mail gave a daily note of time to remote hamlets. Life was more stationary, less migratory, and restless. It was the last hour of the old "Merrie England."

There was another side to the picture, however, which must not be forgotten. Wages were low and there was unemployment. The end of the war and the discharge of soldiers made conditions of labour more difficult. It is true that the unrequired surplus of a small and voluntary army was in numbers paltry when compared with the millions who returned after 1918; but they were sufficiently large to affect the economic balance of 1816. The war had brought some increase of wealth to the countryside, but it was the few who reaped the benefit of it. Agriculture might flourish, but this meant dear food; for the landlords' Parliament by its Corn Laws took good care that the price of wheat did not drop. Underneath an outer crust of contentment forces were at work which were to bring alarm to the possessing classes, and in the end relief to the miserable and oppressed. The natural instincts of Englishmen, which make them love freedom and hate injustice, had been kept in check during the war, or rather they had been turned towards foreign affairs; after the peace they could no longer be diverted from conditions at home when once their true state was revealed. The credit for making them known belongs largely to one man—William Cobbett, whose *Political Register* and the descriptions contained in it came as a shock to many. A feeling of indignation was aroused which was to prove a powerful factor in bringing about reforms. There was indeed much for men's humanitarian instincts to take hold of and mould afresh. Much to alarm lovers of right and freedom. Justice itself was still unfair between class and class, and the punishments which were sanctioned and inflicted were brutal and harsh. In 1818 there were still more than two hundred crimes for which the death penalty could be imposed;[1] whilst transportation for life might follow such a slight offence as damaging a bridge. It was not until an efficient police-force had been established by Sir Robert Peel that such determents to crime could be abolished. But in general the chief business of the law was to protect property and to support the employer of labour. It had hardly as yet been grasped that the poor and weak had rights of their own, or even that attempts by labourers to improve their conditions were not criminal offences.

Over the agricultural civilization described above, in something approaching feudal splendour, presided the local landowners, the squires or lords of the manor. Above them the great nobles kept up almost royal state, travelling in huge, clumsy carriages escorted by outriders, and on great occasions by their mounted tenants. Their life was surrounded by magnificence, but the vast dwellings in which it was passed must have been extraordinarily uncomfortable in cold weather. To exaggerate the power and importance of the landlords in the eyes of their own people would be almost impossible. It can be gathered from the dying words of the farm bailiff, which suggested to Tennyson his *Northern Farmer: Old Style:* "God Almighty little knows what He's about a-taking me. An' Squire will be so mad an' all."[2] Although in the early years of the century the landed aristocracy was beginning to lose its hold of the political machine, its control of local affairs continued almost to the end of the Victorian Era.[3]

THE INDUSTRIAL REVOLUTION

Such was the civilization of England a hundred years ago. Based on and rooted in the soil, and firm, like one of its native oaks, to withstand every evil wind; and if, again like an oak,

---

[1] Up to 1790 burning alive was still a penalty recognized by the law: see Lecky, *England in the Eighteenth Century*, I, p. 506.

[2] *Alfred, Lord Tennyson*, II, p. 9. This anecdote recalls Monckton Milnes' remark on the poem itself that "people did not mind Tennyson's printing 'god' with a small letter since he kept the capital for 'Squire.'"

[3] See below pp. 406 f.

PRE-VICTORIAN ERA: POLITICAL CONDITIONS

it remained in one spot, that too was not without its advantages, it made for quiet and stability, for self-reliance and contentment. But that civilization, in spite of its brave appearance of solidarity, was already about to pass away. The tree might stand, but its roots were dead. During the single reign of George III (1760–1820) "new forces of machinery and capitalized industry worked their blind will upon a loosely organized, aristocratic society that did not even perceive that its fate had come upon it."[1] Regardless of the prosperity, or even the amenities of rural England, regardless of the suffering and rights of the masses, the Industrial Revolution pursued its way unhindered. The profit of the manufacturer and the trader was alike the compelling motive and the sole standard of value. And so, almost by haphazard, the greatest transformation that Western Civilization has so far experienced was brought about. It is possible that the intelligence of the eighteenth century might have been capable of guiding and controlling this strange offspring of its later years; but the war, as it prevented many much-needed reforms, prevented also the "rationalization" of the new invention of machinery and all the changes that came in its wake. This may have been so. But there are many who refuse to place the blame of this failure upon the disturbed political situation. Mr. Marvin, for example, affirms that "at the end of the eighteenth century . . . man's power of production and of controlling nature had outrun his moral powers and his social organization . . . the steam-engine worked more quickly to transform industry than man's mind worked to absorb its products and re-organize society. For the moment the machine controlled the man."[2] Thus a new epoch was already at hand, a new "age" in the history of humanity had dawned;[3] and, as always in such circumstances, man was unaware of it. The Factory System "with all its opulent triumphs and all its strange new

[1] G. M. Trevelyan, *History of England*, p. 507.
[2] *The Century of Hope*, p. 84. The same opinion was held by William Morris: see A. Clutton-Brock, *William Morris*, p. 222.
[3] "In thousands of years . . . the steam-engine, and the procession of inventions of every kind that accompanied it, will perhaps be spoken of as we speak of the bronze or of the chipped stone of prehistoric times: it will serve to define an age." Bergson, *Creative Evolution*, p. 146.

social perplexities" had come.[1] We must now enquire into its immediate effects upon the life of England.

The effects of the Industrial Revolution were many and various, for no department of human activity escaped them entirely. One consequence which did not reveal itself until the System had reached international proportions, and even then was not sufficiently distinct to be recognized at once, was the restoration of the unity which the passing of the Middle Ages had taken from Europe. It was to restore it, however, in an altogether different form and on a scale infinitely more vast. The unity of the Middle Ages had been cultural, a single world-wide language; it had been political, a single Empire; above all it had been ecclesiastical, one visible Church.[2] The new unity was not to be cultural, certainly not ecclesiastical; it was to be industrial and commercial. The world order which was slowly to draw into it all peoples and countries was to be based on commerce. In it the predominant place, for half a century at least, was to be taken by England. Thus the Industrial Revolution gave to England's greatness a new foundation, and added a new cause of assurance to her pride. The whole world looked to Lombard Street.

But England herself was changed in the process of becoming the mistress of the world's finances; she had to substitute the life of the fields for the life of the city, to become no longer predominantly rural, but urban. But in this urban stage of her development the memory of the long centuries in which she had been rural still worked in the blood of her children; and even in the narrowest town they love to live in small houses rather than, as do other urban peoples, in blocks of flats. These small houses represent "the desperate efforts made by a race reared in village communities to maintain in the urban aggregation some semblance of a home."[3]

The towns which sprang up all over England, with their

---

[1] Lord Morley, *Recollections*, I, p. 4.
[2] See Elliott-Binns, *The Decline and Fall of the Medieval Papacy*, p. 368.
[3] C. F. G. Masterman, *The Condition of England*, p. 101. It is this phenomenon which inspired a sympathetic German critic to repeat with approval the saying that London itself is but a large village: see Carl Peters, *England and the English*, p. 36.

Churchmen, of whom Lord Robert Cecil (later to be the third Marquis of Salisbury) was a type, this was its most objectionable feature, because, as he pointed out in a speech in Parliament, the more sincere a Jew was the more must he take a view "hostile to their whole body, and to all their institutions," —must he be "opposed to all in a religious sense that they were there to uphold."[1]

DEBT TO THE EIGHTEENTH CENTURY

Such was the condition of affairs, from the political and social point of view, when Victoria came to the throne, and such were some of the achievements, in the way of reform, which marked the period immediately before. It should, however, be noticed that the first thirty years of the nineteenth century were in many ways merely a continuation of the previous century; they saw the culmination of efforts which had arisen and gathered force within it. Among them were the agitation against slavery, the literary flowering of the Lake poets, and even the continued strength of the Evangelical party in the Church of England upon which we are about to comment. The new era began with the passing of the Reform Bill in 1832, and, in religion, with the rise of the Oxford Movement which almost coincided with it.[2] Before passing on it may be well to say a little more concerning the eighteenth century, since its achievements are so commonly belittled, and since the nineteenth century, and even the Victorian era itself, owed so much to it.

There are in history certain centuries which are badly placed, and because of this they have received but little justice. Such in the Middle Ages was the fourteenth;[3] such in modern times was the eighteenth. Coming as it did between the seventeenth and the nineteenth it has been regarded by many as "a time of relaxation, of moral and political depravity,

[1] Quoted by Lady Gwendolen Cecil, *Life of Robert, Marquis of Salisbury*, I, p. 126.

[2] This statement is subject to two qualifications at least—the foundation of the great religious societies, and the beginning of work overseas (or foreign missions as they were called) both belong, although arising in the previous generation, to the future rather than the eighteenth century.

[3] See Elliott-Binns, *The Decline and Fall of the Medieval Papacy*, p. 70.

There can be no doubt that the relief was, in part at least, the work of the Nonconformists. Up to 1828 their own grievances and the strong Protestant feeling which possessed them prevented their giving any support to a measure which would have placed the Roman Catholics in a more favourable position than themselves; the repeal of the Test and Corporation Acts, however, changed the whole situation. When the Emancipation Bill became law Daniel O'Connell, in the name of Ireland, expressed his country's gratitude "for the exertions on our behalf by our Protestant Dissenting brethren."[1]

Among others who had supported the movement was Sydney Smith; but the reasons which he gave for doing so, in the famous *Letters of Peter Plymley*, were calculated to cause uneasiness and chagrin in the hearts of those whom he professed to assist. Amongst other things he urged that if young Roman Catholics were admitted to Parliament they would speedily become "as totally devoid of morality, honesty, knowledge, and civility as Protestant loungers in Pall Mall"; they would, in addition, acquire a supreme contempt for their priests. He even ventured to express his surprise "at the madness of the Catholic clergy in not perceiving that Catholic Emancipation is Catholic infidelity."

Some disabilities still remained. Until the passing of the Marriage Act of 1837 Roman Catholics desiring a religious ceremony which had legal force were compelled to be married by a Church of England clergyman. It was not until 1880 that they were allowed to hold their own burial services.

Jewish Emancipation

The emancipation of the Jews followed more slowly. Robert Grant brought in a Bill for this end in the year following Catholic Emancipation, but it was not until 1858–1860 that they obtained full political rights. Many Christians felt, with Lord Shaftesbury, that if Jews chose to live in England they ought, if they desired to share in the government, to conform to the moral law of the country which was the Gospel. Supporters of the Bill urged in its favour that it was only the sincere Jew who was kept out of Parliament. But to many

[1] See Silvester Horne, *Nonconformity in the Nineteenth Century*, p. 39.

Tomline that he was determined to refuse office unless he was allowed again to bring the matter forward (see Lord Rosebery, *Pitt*, p. 222). But George III would not hear of further concessions, he had the belief, from which nothing could move him, that to allow emancipation would be to break his coronation oath. In 1807 he even refused to allow Roman Catholics to hold high command in the Navy and Army; an action which was approved in the subsequent election.

The end of the war and the fall of Napoleon had a discouraging effect on the movement for emancipation, for it left the Pope, in the minds of many, as the only suitable object for the application of a number of unpleasant Biblical prophesies. Canning noted in 1816 the growth of public opinion against emancipation (see Stapleton, *Life of Canning*, I, p. 117); and though a Catholic Relief Bill passed the Commons in 1821 it was thrown out in the Lords. But there was so much feeling in Ireland over the question, and it was so skilfully exploited by Daniel O'Connell, that civil war seemed the only alternative to granting relief. In spite of popular feeling in England both Peel and the Duke of Wellington at length gave way and lent their support to the measure (see Maxwell, *Life of Wellington*, II, pp. 237 and 240). When the Bill came before Parliament T. F. Buxton voted for it on the ground that the peace and safety of Ireland demanded its passage. In the House of Lords, however, Lloyd of Oxford was the only bishop to vote in its favour. Many people felt that the Roman Catholics were few and harmless and that this measure of relief could not injure the country. Some of those who voted for the Bill afterwards regretted it, and Sir William Palmer, writing fourteen years later, condemned it as having been responsible for breaking down "public principle, public morality, public confidence," and also as having dispersed the Tory party and led directly to the revolutionary happenings, for so he regarded them, of the Reform Bill period.[1] To Keble the Roman Catholic Emancipation Act was the beginning of the conflict of Church and State.[2] Some actually saw in the burning down of the Houses of Parliament in 1834 a divine punishment for its passing.

[1] *Narrative of Events*, etc., p. 96.   [2] W. Lock, *John Keble*, p. 26.

the British and Foreign Bible Society, the absence of any kind of religious ceremony was due to the impossibility of pleasing all its varied clientele. Dissenters objected to any set form of prayer, such as a collect, while Churchmen found the extempore effusions of some of their Nonconforming brethren a burden to the flesh; there were moreover the Quakers to be considered, they were generous supporters, but would hear of no set arrangements. It was not until 1857 that a better and more tolerant spirit prevailed and opening prayers were allowed.

The repeal of the Corporation and Test Acts in 1828 did much to improve the position of Dissenters of all classes, but there were still many grievances. The Protestant Dissenters had put out in 1833 a list of six restrictions under which they laboured;[1] the Roman Catholics, even when these Acts had been repealed, were still subject to political discrimination. They had not long, however, to wait for its removal.

Roman Catholic Emancipation

The Emancipation of the Roman Catholics in 1829 was the result of no sudden whim, none the less it was an unpopular measure. As long ago as 1778 a measure of relief had been granted, then as in 1791 with some support from the bishops; but the result of that Act was to arouse the fury of the mob which, under Lord George Gordon, actually besieged the Houses of Parliament and was only subdued with the help of troops. This outbreak had echoes in other parts of England. At Bath, for example, the Roman Catholic chapel and the house of the bishop were burnt down. The result was to terrify the Roman Catholics to such an extent that in some cases they suspended the building of new chapels. Much of the fury of the outbreak was due to feeling against the Irish rebels.

Pitt felt strongly in the matter and in 1801 wrote to Bishop

[1] The chief of them were: exclusion from Oxford and Cambridge; Church Rates and other payments; refusal of the right to use their own form of burial; the necessity of conforming to objectionable rites in the marriage service. As these restrictions were not to be removed until the reign of Victoria they will be left for consideration to a later chapter: see pp. 71 ff. below.

By it officers of corporations were compelled to swear adherence to the doctrine of passive obedience, to renounce the Covenant, and to receive the Holy Communion according to the rites of the Church of England at least once a year. The Test Act of 1673 extended the former Act so as to affect Roman Catholics. It made attendance at Holy Communion and a denunciation of transubstantiation a necessary qualification for holding any office. For some time Protestant Dissenters had occupied positions of trust and an annual Act of Indemnity had safeguarded them from any consequences to which they were liable under the above measures; none the less so long as the Acts remained on the Statute Book there was a feeling of injustice and inequality in their minds. Churchmen also had come to dislike them, for some Nonconformists made a practice of communicating yearly in their parish Church in order to qualify for office; this was in the eyes of the Churchman a disgusting piece of profanity. In any case their existence was recognized as tending to disunion and bitterness.[1] Both these Acts were repealed in 1828.

Actual restrictions on worship still existed. These, it is often forgotten, affected Churchmen as much as Nonconformists; both alike were in danger of exposing themselves to prosecution by experiments in worship which might prove to be violations of the law. The Conventicles Act allowed services in Churches and in Dissenting Chapels which had been duly licensed; other gatherings for worship were illegal. For long even the Missionary Societies did not dare to open their proceedings with prayer lest they should commit a technical offence and lay themselves open to prosecution if any ill-disposed person should care to denounce them. In 1826 the Society for the Propagation of the Gospel ventured to ignore the law, and it was followed in 1828 by the Church Missionary Society. These were, of course, both Church Societies, and as such less liable to have proceedings begun against them; hence their position as pioneers. In undenominational societies, like

---

[1] Pusey described them as "both in their means and end a disgrace and deterrent to religion," and as more than anything else perpetuating "the bitterness of party spirit among Christians": see Liddon, *Life of E. B. Pusey*, I, p. 133.

PRE-VICTORIAN ERA: POLITICAL CONDITIONS

The year 1834 saw an attempt to deal with poverty in the shape of the New Poor Law. It provided outdoor relief for the sick and aged only, the rest had to go to the workhouse where food and shelter were provided in return for labour. By its provisions the administration of the Poor Law was taken from the churchwardens and placed under elected boards with some central supervision. The measure met with much criticism. Barnes, who was in *The Times* creating a new standard of journalism, wrote a number of fierce leaders prophesying that it would sow the seeds of perpetual discord between the poor and the rich; whilst Carlyle was unsparing in his denunciations. "Let there be workhouses," he cried, "and bread of affliction there. It was a simple invention; as all great inventions are.... A still briefer method is that of arsenic. Rats and paupers can be abolished."[1] The results of the New Poor Law were not entirely bad. To its credit must be placed the ending of the vicious Speenhamland system, a system found in the South of England only, by which the labourers had their wages supplemented by outdoor relief. Thus the farmer paid insufficient wages, and the labourer was turned into a pauper. When a generation grew up which had not known such abuses a new spirit of independence and self-reliance was bound to emerge, and with it a spirit of thrift. But it is said that the more independent spirit of the North is due, in part at any rate, to its never having suffered under this system.[2]

THE REMOVAL OF RELIGIOUS DISABILITIES

At the beginning of the nineteenth century Dissenters from the Established Church, whether Protestant or Roman Catholic, were subject to a number of restrictions, not so much in the exercise of their religion, as on their activities as citizens. The chief measures under which they suffered were the Corporation and Test Acts. The former measure had been passed in 1661 and had been aimed at the Presbyterians in particular.

[1] *Chartism*, ch. iii. Quoted by F. S. Marvin, *The Century of Hope*, p. 107. The evils of the workhouses were also described by Charles Dickens in *Oliver Twist*, which was published in 1838.
[2] Probably it would be more true to say that the Northern labourer being more independent would never have tolerated the system at all.

moved to do this by the bad faith of their employers, who having solemnly promised, with the rector of the parish as witness, that they would give them the rates current in the rest of the county, i.e. 10s. a week, reduced them to 7s. Unfortunately the men in arranging the ceremonial of their branch imitated the Friendly Societies, and since Englishmen are great ritualists (except in religion), invented an elaborate order of initiation which included the taking of oaths. All unconsciously they thus rendered themselves liable, under an Act of Pitt's administration, to penalties for administering illegal oaths. They were accordingly arrested in February 1834, and sentenced to seven years' transportation.

There can be no doubt that this monstrous sentence for what was merely a technical violation of the law by ignorant and peaceable men, was a deliberate attack on the Trades Union Movement, whose rapid progress was arousing alarm, especially as in some places the Unions were already threatening a general strike. Attempts were at once made to get a reprieve; but Lord Melbourne, who was Home Secretary, refused to move. Probably he felt that the Whigs, having safely got their Reform Act, no longer needed the support of the working classes, and that all agitators were dangerous, especially if they were Methodists. The men were therefore sent to Australia to share the life of the vicious and criminal. Loveless himself had actually to work in irons with a convict on each side of him. Such conditions to respectable and religious men must have been unspeakably repulsive. At home their sympathizers continued to press for justice. Among the most prominent of them was Thomas Wakley, M.P. for Finsbury, and known in other circles as the founder of the *Lancet*. Circumstances soon proved favourable, for in 1836 Melbourne was succeeded by Lord John Russell. In the meantime the Trades Union movement was showing signs of collapse, even the Grand National Consolidated Union was no more, and the time for mercy had obviously arrived. The men were pardoned, brought back to England, and settled on farms, one in his native Dorset, the rest in Essex.[1]

[1] For fuller details see Marjorie Firth and Arthur Hopkinson, *The Tolpuddle Martyrs*.

Baptist preacher, Robert Hall, supported the Leicestershire farm labourers when their paltry wages were threatened with reduction.[1] For this he was bitterly attacked by William Cobbett.

The repeal of the Combination Acts in 1824 was followed by a number of strikes and an amending Act passed in the following year prohibited any person "doing any act or making any threat to induce any manufacturer to alter the rules of his factory, or any workman to accept or leave any employment, or to join any club."[2] Thus the liberty to combine for improved conditions was much restricted. And, indeed, any such attempts were regarded at this epoch as dangerous, and even the most innocent unions of members of the working classes aroused panic and condemnation. The London Mechanics' Institution was fiercely denounced in 1825 in the following terms: "A scheme more completely adapted for the destruction of this empire could not have been invented by the author of evil himself than that which the depraved ambition of some men, the vanity of others, and the supineness of a third and more important class, has so nearly perfected."[3] In spite of such denunciations there was a rapid spread of Trades Unions throughout the country. One of their chief advocates was Robert Owen, himself an employer of labour. He had been moved by the inhuman conditions which many of the workers had to endure in the early years of the century and determined to do what he could to improve them. The Union through which he worked had the very imposing title of The Grand National Consolidated Trades Union, and by 1833 it had a membership of half a million, a figure higher in proportion to the population than the entire membership of the Trades Unions in this country at the present day.

Among the associations entered into at this time was one which has become famous. A small group of six labourers in the Dorset village of Tolpuddle decided to combine under the leadership of George Loveless, a Methodist local preacher, in order to work for better conditions and wages. They were

---

[1] See Silvester Horne, *Nonconformity in the Nineteenth Century*, pp. 11 f.
[2] Spencer Walpole, *History of England*, II, p. 181.
[3] Quoted by A. W. Peel, *These Hundred Years*, p. 37.

The emancipation of the slaves did not, of course, affect Britain itself directly; but no account of Social Emancipation would be complete without it, for not only was the consent of Parliament necessary, but the movement had a strong reaction on the life of the nation. It created what Professor Coupland has called a "moral revolution," and "founded in the conscience of the British people a tradition of humanity and of responsibility towards the weak and backward black peoples whose fate lay in their hands."

Reforms at Home

We come now to efforts after emancipation and freedom for our own countrymen. This was a matter which unfortunately did not arouse anything like the same enthusiasm, especially in religious circles, and many who clamoured for the freedom of the black man abroad were quite blind to the conditions under which men, women, and children were compelled to live and work at home.

But if their betters refused to take steps for the amelioration of the hard conditions under which they laboured the working classes themselves had sufficient initiative to strive for improvement on their own account. Such efforts were a striking feature of the pre-Victorian era. Until Pitt's Combination Acts of 1799 and 1800 had been repealed in 1824 and 1825 any kind of corporate action was impossible. This repeal was due in the main to the unselfish devotion of Francis Place, the Radical tailor of Charing Cross. Whilst most men were concerned to make fortunes for themselves and to rise above the class to which they belonged, Place worked his way up from poverty with the deliberate object of gaining influence which might be used for the betterment of his fellows. The religious leaders, on the whole, shewed little sympathy with such aspirations. The clergy as a class were so closely connected with the landlords, in many cases they farmed their own glebe, that they were almost to a man on the side of the employers. Though they might do much to ameliorate the lot of sufferers, they were opposed to any efforts from below to alter conditions. The Nonconformists, not having landed connexions, were free from prejudices, and more ready and able to help. The famous

PRE-VICTORIAN ERA: POLITICAL CONDITIONS

to have arisen, as Hugh Stowell pointed out at the C.M.S. annual meeting in 1834. Wilberforce did not live to see the actual passing of the Bill—he died on July 29, 1833—but he had the satisfaction of knowing that it was already assured.

When the date of emancipation approached there was much apprehension, both on the part of the owners and the friends of the slaves, as to the effect of suddenly giving their freedom to eight hundred thousand men and women. Such apprehensions proved to have been needless. On the evening of July 31, 1834, the churches and chapels were thrown open everywhere and the slaves crowded into them. As midnight was about to arrive they fell on their knees and thus awaited the moment of their freedom. Twelve sounded. Then they sprang to their feet, free at last; and throughout the islands there rose to God a great burst of thanksgiving.[1]

Buxton himself, by his devoted and unceasing labours, ruined his health. In spite of an attack of apoplexy at the age of forty, he persisted in going on until at last a complete breakdown laid him aside. He died on February 9, 1845, at the age of fifty-nine and was buried in Westminster Abbey. Like Wilberforce before him religious faith was the mainspring of his efforts, and like Wilberforce again, prayer was among the chief weapons on which he relied.[2]

Thus the slaves were free. But for seven years a system of apprenticeship was allowed to continue. This gave to the bad type of master the chance of continuing what was practically the old system under another name. This evil was exposed by Joseph Sturge, the Quaker, who went to the West Indies in order to collect evidence at first hand. Parliament was convinced and in August 1838, although the system had still three years to run, it abolished it. This decision was greatly helped by the good conduct of the slaves themselves.[3]

---

[1] See *Life of Sir T. Fowell Buxton*, p. 296.

[2] It was at his suggestion that January 16, 1833, was set aside as a Day of Intercession for the Emancipation of the Slaves.

[3] Many people imagine that Slavery no longer exists; this is far from being the case as can be seen from Sir John Harris's valuable and interesting volume, *A Century of Emancipation*.

quite kindly people, that the whole agitation was a "radical, rapacious, or sentimental attack on a long-established industry."[1] The Churches were apathetic and seemed indifferent to human suffering so long as its victims were not of the white race. Even the early Evangelicals were not at one in condemning it. Whitfield himself was the owner of slaves, and, indeed, resented efforts made to restrict traffic in them; whilst John Newton seems never to have realized its harmfulness or to have offered a single word in defence of his having practised it. An evil implants itself so firmly in the life around, becomes so much a part of it, that even a sensitive conscience cannot always be relied upon to isolate and denounce it.

The Slave Trade was abolished in British possessions in 1807. There still remained the task of emancipating the slaves and abolishing the institution of slavery itself. This was undertaken seriously in 1823 when the Anti-Slavery Society was formed. Wilberforce lent the movement his invaluable support, but the leading figure was Thomas Fowell Buxton. In bringing a motion for its abolition before Parliament he described slavery as "repugnant to the principles of the British Constitution and of the Christian religion." But it was not everyone who was willing to accept such a statement and the effort to abolish slavery was opposed as strongly as the earlier attempt to destroy the Slave Trade. It was not until the passing of the Reform Bill had increased the number of those who were in its favour that it was finally successful.[2] The Bill passed the Commons on August 7, 1833,[3] and the Lords on the 20th of the same month. It was not to come into force until midnight on the following July 31st. By way of compensation to the slave-owners the sum of £20,000,000 was voted. The question of any compensation to the slaves themselves does not seem

[1] Harris, *A Century of Emancipation*, p. 2.

[2] The death in prison of John Smith, a missionary of the London Missionary Society, in 1824 did much to marshal Christian opinion against the institution, and was as "fatal to Slavery in the West Indies ... as the execution of John Brown was its deathblow in the United States."

[3] The Bill was supported in a notable speech by the youthful T. B. Macaulay: see G. O. Trevelyan, *Life and Letters of Lord Macaulay*, I, pp. 110 f.

to the evils which were afflicting their fellows. In the efforts to amend such evils the Evangelicals took a leading part. The awakening itself was not distinctively religious; it probably owed most to the French Revolution which aroused men from their indifference and revealed the intolerable conditions under which others were living. Even those who were opposed to the Revolution and deeply shocked by its methods were touched in heart and conscience; political sympathies and prejudices could not stand before such overwhelming wrongs. These wrongs had been there all the time and voices of protest had, here and there, been raised against them; but it required the flames of a great political combustion to light them up before men became fully aware of them and of the need for reform. The most famous and valuable expression of the new realization of social evils was found in the effort first to abolish the Slave Trade and then to Emancipate the slaves themselves.[1]

The Abolition of Slavery

To us slavery seems an evil so patent that we do not realize the extraordinary difficulties which postponed its abolition, and the widespread feeling which brought upon its opponents so much abuse and unpopularity.[2] This was not merely due to the immense vested interests which were involved, or even the danger of disturbing the relations of the mother-country and the colonies; but to the conviction on the part of many

[1] Though there were innumerable workers in this cause, including Granville Sharpe and Clarkson, the outstanding name is that of William Wilberforce: see Coupland, *William Wilberforce*. The early attempts to abolish the Slave Trade anticipated the outbreak of the French Revolution; but during the wars reforming zeal seems to have found its outlet in efforts on behalf of the slaves.

[2] Cf. Lord Nelson's outbreak: "I was bred in the good old school, and taught to appreciate the value of our West Indian possessions, and neither in the field nor in the Senate shall their just rights be infringed, while I have an arm to fight in their defence, or a tongue to launch my voice against the damnable doctrine of Wilberforce and his hypocritical allies." (Quoted by Lady Knutsford, *Life of Zachary Macaulay*, p. 258.) Alongside this may be placed Hurrell Froude's letter from Barbados in 1834 in which he expresses his dislike of the "niggers" and of Buxton's cant: see L. I. Guiney, *Hurrell Froude*, p. 139.

the Reform Bill of 1832. The lower classes, for some reason or other, had hoped for great things—hence their rioting in support of the Bill—but far from proclaiming the Millennium and putting an end to hunger, poverty, and distress, it merely shifted the power from one class that used the people for its own ends to another. The result was disillusionment and the feeling that political methods could bring but meagre results. Some were disposed to try more violent ways.

But if the lower orders were disappointed by the Act of 1832, to the aristocracy and the Church it seemed to promise the end of all things. They were unused to change of any kind and their opposition was bitter. It was an age when all differences, both in politics and religion, were taken seriously, and social consequences were not uncommon. The father of Dr. Pusey would speak of "Whigs and Atheists" as members of a single class, and opposed for years the marriage of his eldest son to Lady Emily Herbert solely because she was a member of a leading Whig family.[1]

The Whigs, although they stood for reform, had very clear ideas as to its limits; they might attack the Church, but they had no wish to destroy it; they might grant privileges to the middle classes, but they had no desire to disturb the balance which allowed power to remain with the holders of large estates. Although Sydney Smith himself could utter sweeping denunciations of ancient abuses he had no real wish for fundamental changes and did not hesitate to declare that the golden age would not be the immediate sequel of parliamentary reform.

When one examines the Bill in the calm atmosphere of present-day politics and with the cold eye of reason it is hard to understand that any great hopes could have been placed upon it. It is true that it removed abuses and corrected anomalies; but it went no further, and was lacking in any constructive ideas.

SOCIAL EMANCIPATION

The Evangelical Movement of the eighteenth century had coincided with an awakening on the part of men everywhere

[1] *Life of E. B. Pusey*, I, p. 2.

undoubtedly guided this preference, for no real dealing with social problems could be hoped for from the unreformed House of Commons.[1]

The great Revolution of 1688 had made no provision for adjustments of political representation which might become necessary owing to changes of population. At the beginning of the nineteenth century such adjustments were urgently required, as well as the abolition of nominated members. Out of a total of 658 members of the House of Commons only 234 were elected; in some cases the constituencies which they purported to represent had disappeared. On the other hand growing towns like Manchester and Birmingham were unrepresented. The whole situation was absurd. William IV was in favour of reform, but the Duke of Wellington and the Tory party, who were in power on his accession in 1830, refused to move and were in consequence driven from office. The new Whig Ministry (the first for twenty years) under the leadership of Lord Grey at once brought in a Bill for Reform which not only provided for the cancellation of "rotten boroughs" and for the distribution of their seats among the towns, but also established a £10 qualification for householders and gave votes to leaseholders and copyholders in county divisions. The Bill passed the Commons, but was thrown out in the Lords. There followed at once so widespread an outbreak of fury that the Lords had in the end to give way: the Bill became law on June 7, 1832.

The revival of the Whig Party was due largely to reaction against the restraints endured whilst the war was being carried on; the minds of Englishmen turned once again towards liberty, and the revival of a belief in the principle became a striking feature of the period.[2] Moreover the growing middle classes naturally lent their support to a party which promised them a measure of political enfranchisement. Their trust was not mistaken, and they were the only people to benefit from

[1] Wordsworth had regarded parliamentary reform as the great need of the day; an instance of prophetic insight. See Knight, *Life of William Wordsworth*, II, p. 130.

[2] The expulsion of the Bourbons from France in 1830 had given a great stimulus to liberal opinions, in both politics and religion. For the latter see Dean Church, *The Oxford Movement*, p. 49.

policy of encouraging commerce at the expense of agriculture involved the transfer of political predominance to the democratic and progressive party. In England the struggle began between the merchants and the landlords, and it was of epic character; for it represented the clash not only of opposing interests, but of distinct ways of life; it was the conflict of the dying spirit of feudalism with that of encroaching commerce.

All these changes and new conditions affected religion enormously and the Victorian Era inherited from the past a number of urgent problems. There was the question of providing for the spiritual needs of the new populations in the great towns; the growing separation of the classes; the difficulties which were to come from the glorification of wealth and the absorbing power of business. There was to be the question of education, especially as the workers gained more and more political power. There was also the expansion of the Church into lands overseas to be encouraged and guided alongside the growth of commerce and discovery. Behind it all was the rising tide of liberalism, both in thought and politics; the demand for the removal of restraints and for better social conditions and wider opportunities. All these problems the Victorian Age had to face as we in our turn are still facing them in many cases. Before going on to examine the manner in which Religion responded to the challenge contained in them, we must enquire into its state during the generation before Victoria herself ascended the throne. Before doing so, however, it will be well to consider in some detail the efforts that were made in that same generation to find remedies for some of the anomalies and disabilities which clung to certain of its aspects. The kindred subjects of Political, Social, and Religious Emancipation demand our attention.

POLITICAL REFORMS

It has already been pointed out that many necessary reforms had had to be abandoned owing to the nation's obsession with the Napoleonic Wars. But even when peace came, although the need for social reform and readjustment was pressing, such obvious problems were forgotten or set aside for the time; the chief field for reform was the political. A true instinct narrow streets and gloomy alleys, must have seemed veritable prisons to the swarms of country-bred folk who moved into them. To make the passage from country to town more facile, the old, cramping restrictions by which the movements of the wage-earners had been controlled were removed. Industry wanted "hands," and no effete apprentice system, no merely parochial outlook, was allowed to stand in the way of its obtaining them. So they crowded in, in most cases to endure with inarticulate suffering, degrading poverty, and to receive quite inadequate rewards. Helpless and hopeless they sank down into a state of sullen depression. These dumb multitudes can have found but little consolation in the thought that their labours and sufferings were bringing wealth and power to those who exploited their powers; or even that their old rulers, the squire and the landowner, were being forced to give place to them. For the old landowning class was already beginning to feel the encroachment of the growing class of wealthy merchants. Here and there in the country large estates would come into their hands, while on the outskirts of the growing towns their resplendent villas were an unescapable sign of their call for consideration.

The economic and social changes which followed in the wake of the Industrial Revolution were to involve ultimately changes political. The growing importance of the Factory, and the system based upon it, meant that those who were concerned in it, employers and workers alike, would one day put forward demands which could not be shirked. The one would require to have a larger share in the government of the nation; the other, at least some measure of enfranchisement as a step to fuller powers when the times should be propitious. The large and wealthy class of manufacturers was not likely to acquiesce in the monopoly of power held by the territorial aristocracy; the workers, in their turn, would not be content to see the middle classes only as the partners in that power. A similar change took place in Athens with the transformation of the community from an agricultural one to a commercial. Solon had looked upon the Athenian state as one based on agriculture, and the governing class as drawn from the conservative or aristocratic party; with Themistocles, and later Pericles, the

PRE-VICTORIAN ERA: POLITICAL CONDITIONS

after the strenuous efforts and glorious achievements" of its predecessor.[1] But this is not the whole story and a good deal needs to be remembered of its wise moderation and sanity, its serenity and confidence. It has been well called the age of balance and of reason.[2] Much of what made it seem like an era of decay was in reality preparation for what was to come. Beneath the surface the seeds of a new activity were slowly maturing; autumn and winter were but the heralds of a coming spring. Its own achievement was, moreover, considerable in itself, and not merely by way of preparation and of promise. It laid the foundations of a new commercial system, and saw the beginnings of the Empire of India and the Dominion of Canada. Its great men in science and philosophy, Newton and Locke, had been the preceptors of Europe.[3] Whilst already in the social sphere dim foreshadowings of the comfort and luxury of the new century were to be discerned.

[1] F. S. Marvin, *The Century of Hope*, p. 1.
[2] This age of reason was by a strange paradox also an age of superstition. Alongside Newton and Locke there were Cagliostro and Swedenborg, and, in our own land, Blake and his visionary mind open to influences which were not entirely healthy: see G. K. Chesterton, *William Blake*, pp. 119 ff.
[3] See further Creed and Boys Smith, *Religious Thought in the Eighteenth Century*.

2

THE PRE-VICTORIAN ERA: THE CONDITION OF RELIGION

At the opening of the century the state of religion in England seemed parlous. There was a widespread neglect of Christian duties and much indifference to Christian doctrine—so Bishop Horsley of Rochester complained in 1800. The "vicious ignorance" of the poor was balanced by the "presumptuous apostasy" of the wealthy; whilst among the growing class of industrial workers the writings of Tom Paine were finding an attentive audience. Even the Methodist Revival had brought little remedy, and in some places the Church services were at times not held for lack of any congregation. Sunday was little observed especially among the fashionable, for whom it was a favourite day for concerts and assemblies.[1] The undoubted spread of revolutionary ideas, both political and religious, among the masses shewed that the Church's hold upon them was not so firm as had been supposed; though during the war national and patriotic sentiment had rallied them to the Church as one centre of national solidarity. But such adhesion was too superficial to affect life or character.

FOUNDATION OF RELIGIOUS SOCIETIES

The occupation of the thoughts and energies of the nation with the carrying on of the war naturally told against religious activity; but in spite of it the period saw a sudden development in the direction of the formation of a number of voluntary societies for encouraging various religious and philanthropic objects.[2] Chief among them were those founded for work overseas. In fostering these associations religion, in the words of Mr. Warre Cornish, "left the closet and entered the com-

---

[1] The protest of Bishop Porteus against this profanation was made "at the risk of unpopularity and loss of court favour": F. Warre Cornish, *History of the English Church in the Nineteenth Century*, I, p. 101.

[2] The formation of such associations really goes back to the efforts of Wilberforce and his friends to abolish the Slave Trade.

mittee room."[1] Leaving aside for the time an account of the great Missionary Societies,[2] a short account may now be given of the foundation of some of the other outstanding organizations which date back to this period.

The oldest of these organizations is the Religious Tract Society. It owed much to the example of the Rev. George Burder of Coventry who had begun to print tracts on his own account as early as 1781. On May 8, 1799, a meeting of those interested in such a method was held and the society founded. Among its first supporters were Zachary Macaulay, Edward Bickersteth, and Legh Richmond, to name leading Evangelicals. The first secretary was Joseph Hughes, a Baptist minister of Battersea, who was later to be the first Nonconformist Secretary of the British and Foreign Bible Society. The Society was undenominational with its management shared equally between Churchmen and Nonconformists. From printing tracts it widened its activities to the production of magazines and other literature.

The British and Foreign Bible Society was in some sense the daughter of the Religious Tract Society, for it was in the Committee Room of the latter that it had its birth. This was in 1804. The circumstances which led to its formation are interesting. There had been in existence for the greater part of a century the Society for Promoting Christian Knowledge. But by this time, like its venerable sister, the Society for the Propagation of the Gospel, it had lost energy and vision, and when there was a sudden demand for Bibles in Wales, it failed to meet it. The famous story of Mary Jones of Tynoddol, a small Welsh girl who walked long distances to the nearest Bible in order to learn texts, and then had to tramp thirty miles when she had money enough to pay for a copy of her own, aroused much feeling. At the meeting which founded the new Society Granville Sharpe was in the chair; but the first president was Lord Teignmouth, a member of the Clapham Sect. The committee included Churchmen and Nonconformists as well as representatives of foreign Churches in England. Although it won the support of Bishop Porteus many Church-

[1] *Op. cit.*, I, p. 3.
[2] These will be considered in Chapter 20 below.

men looked upon it with suspicion, as "an evil and revolutionary institution, opposed alike to Church and State."[1] This came out when an attempt was made to form an auxiliary society at Cambridge. There was a violent dispute in which Isaac Milner, Dean of Carlisle and President of Queens', supported the Bible Society, Herbert Marsh, later to be Bishop of Peterborough, opposed it. Marsh's objections were that the Society for the Promotion of Christian Knowledge was capable of supplying the need of Bibles and that the Bible ought not to be circulated apart from the Prayer Book. The Dean had an additional grievance against the future Bishop for he was one of the very few Englishmen, at that time, who had studied in Germany, and his orthodoxy in Church matters was compromised by a willingness to speculate on Gospel origins. This last fact gave the controversy an interest which it might otherwise have lacked; but as a whole it was profitless to both sides and led to misunderstandings and divisions—the almost inevitable result of religious strife.

But strife on a wider scale was to follow the development of the Society's work and to lead to secessions and the formation of other agencies. The decision in 1811 to omit the Apocrypha, for example, caused the Bible Societies on the continent to cut themselves off. Twenty years later there was bitter controversy over the question of allowing Unitarians to co-operate in the work of the Society. Rowland Hill very sensibly put the case for their continued connexion by declaring that he would encourage even a Mohammedan who wished to help in the circulation of the Scriptures. But such an argument did not satisfy all, and when the society decided to make no alteration in its constitution a number of its supporters left it to found the Trinitarian Bible Society.

In 1809 was founded the London Society for Promoting Christianity among the Jews. This like the London Missionary Society and the Bible Society was undenominational in its start. The first committee consisted of two clergymen, two Nonconformist ministers, and fifteen laymen. Its earliest efforts were "on impracticable lines," but its earnest efforts succeeded in bringing the whole question of the position of the Jew

[1] Hodder, *Life of Lord Shaftesbury*, I, pp. 43 f.

PRE-VICTORIAN ERA: CONDITION OF RELIGION

before Christian people.[1] Later practical difficulties arose over the dual basis of the Society and in March 1815 it became exclusively a Church of England Society. During the rest of the century, and up to the present day, this Society has continued its difficult work both in England and on the continent, and its labours have not gone without their reward.

In February 1836 the Church Pastoral Aid Society was founded at a meeting held in the Committee Room of the Church Missionary Society. It owed a good deal to the efforts of godly laymen, prominent among whom were Robert Seeley, the publisher, and Frederic Sandoz of Islington. Its objects were, as the title suggests, to provide helpers for work at home and at first its members were drawn from all sections of the Church of England. W. E. Gladstone was a Vice-president and Dr. Pusey a subscriber. But the High Churchmen disapproved of the employment of lay-agents as they regarded them as likely to work under the direction of the Society rather than under ecclesiastical discipline, and in the end they withdrew to form their own Society now known as the Additional Curates Society.

THE CHURCH OF ENGLAND

From this brief consideration of Christian activity, as seen in the formation of various religious associations, we must now turn to examine the state of the denominations which co-operated in their formation. Naturally we begin with the Church of England itself as the oldest and largest.

At the beginning of the century the Church was quite unprepared to face the testing times which were coming upon it. The peace and security of the previous century had left it "soft." One of its gravest weaknesses was the prevalence of a low idea of the ministry and its responsibilities. The country clergy who formed the vast majority—we have a not unkindly picture of them in *The Vicar of Wakefield* and the novels of Jane Austen—were not vicious or corrupt, far from it. They were kind-hearted, careful of the bodily needs of their parishioners, but with an inadequate concern for their spiritual welfare. Some of them were scholars and in most cases they

[1] See Gidney, *History of the London Society*, etc., p. 39.

raised the tone of the life around them, especially as setting a high standard of family life, and formed valuable centres of culture and manners; but they differed but little from other country gentlemen. They were too much at home in the world, too much at ease in Zion.

There were, it must be confessed, many definite abuses. These were more dangerous as the prevailing spirit of the times, with its fear of all revolutionary ideas, disliked any change, even if it came as a means of reformation. So inveterate had many of these abuses become that they were taken as a matter of course. Perhaps the most common and most damaging abuses were the joint evils of plurality and non-residence—by which a parson held a variety of benefices at the same time and handed over the care of most, if not all, of them to poorly paid curates. Even a good man like Bishop Van Mildert held the Rectory of St. Mary-le-bow with that of Farningham, near Sevenoaks; while Copleston was Dean of St. Paul's and Bishop of Llandaff at the same time. Others less virtuous piled up livings and took little interest in them beyond anxiety to draw their stipends.

When the war ended life became more normal and interest turned once again to home affairs. The Church, with fresh support available, entered upon a stage of real advance, though it was some time before its effects became widespread. There had been, even during the first quarter of the century, a growing feeling of dissatisfaction in many hearts. There were ardent souls who could not away with the prevalent "slackness"; to them stagnation seemed to promise nothing but speedy decease. Such was Thomas Arnold, the famous Headmaster of Rugby and preceptor of liberal minds; such was John Keble, whose *Christian Year* first appeared in 1827;[1] such was John Henry Newman whose sermons at St. Mary's, Oxford, were calling men to a stricter and more holy life, to a deeper reality and moral earnestness. To this awakening there is abundant testimony; the Church was stirring at last and beginning to realize that it had duties and responsibilities

[1] Many of the poems had been written during a number of previous years. The volume was published anonymously and Hurrell Froude was afraid that people might take the writer for a Methodist: *Remains*, I, p. 184.

PRE-VICTORIAN ERA: CONDITION OF RELIGION

as well as emoluments and privileges. Southey observed in 1817 that both knowledge and zeal were reviving on all hands and seemed to recall the first fervour of the Reformation.[1] But the Church had yet to reap the harvest of the years of neglect and reliance on privilege. It is one of the ironies of history that an institution is often thus beset when making a genuine effort at reformation; perhaps because a common revival has given life both to the reformers and to the outside critics. Many chose to regard it as an obstacle to the progress of religion itself, as well as generally injurious. Joseph Hume took it upon himself to warn young men that if they chose to be ordained they must not expect to receive compensation at the coming disestablishment of the Church, they would enter it with their eyes open "when its charter (!) is on the eve of being cancelled by the authority which gave it, when it is admitted on all hands to be not useless only, but absolutely detrimental."[2] In the so-called *Black Book* of 1820 and the *Extraordinary Black Book* of 1831 the Church, together with the aristocracy, the Bank of England, the East India Company, and other established societies, was exposed in all the shame of its many abuses; for as such those responsible for the attacks regarded them. Some of the opposition was no doubt inspired by political feeling; owing to the attitude taken up by the Bishops in the House of Lords on the question of Reform. In the riots which followed the rejection of the Bill in 1831 they were offered not only insult, but personal violence. During the disturbances at Bristol in October of that year the Palace of the Bishop was burnt down. Among the spectators was Charles Kingsley, then a schoolboy at Clifton. It was his "first lesson in what is now called 'social science'"—Dean Church was also a schoolboy at Bristol at this time.[3] Such attacks were probably due to mere unthinking violence and cannot safely be taken as evidence of a wide and deep feeling against the Church. The noisy agitators of the towns were more than outweighed by the solid loyalty of the country districts.

[1] *Life and Corr. of Robert Southey*, III, p. 285. But about the same time Shelley denounced the prevailing religion as "Christless, Godless, a book sealed."   [2] Quoted in *The Christian Remembrancer* (1841), pp. 422 f.
[3] *Life of R. W. Church*, p. 10.

The Bishops and Clergy

The Bishops, being in the public eye, had thus to bear the blame of much for which they were not solely responsible. But so far as the weakness and neglect on the part of the Church was concerned they were directly and indirectly responsible. Here and there Bishops might be found who were doing their duty; but many of them were guilty of gross neglect of their proper functions. This comes out in the matter of the choice of candidates for the ministry and in their treatment of Confirmations.

The examination of candidates was often a mere farce. Bishop Moberly, who was ordained in 1826, for example, tells us that he did no more than read a few verses from the Greek Testament without being asked any questions on them (*Dulce Domum*, p. 25), while Dean Hook was examined five years earlier by his own father to whom he was to go as curate, and then ordained privately by the Bishop (Stephens, *Life of W. F. Hook*, p. 39). It is true that these were both exceptional men, perhaps already recognized as such; but there was much general carelessness. One very objectionable feature was that the examination was held immediately before the ordination itself, so that some of those who were prepared to be ordained would often be sent away before the service, even on the very day. The friends of the candidate, unless they were present, could not be certain that he was actually being ordained or not. As late as 1842 Charles Kingsley wrote to his future wife as he waited for ordination: "I would have written when I knew my success yesterday, but there was no town post" (*Life*, p. 27).

During the time of waiting for the ordination no attempt was made to supervise the candidates and nothing was done, beyond a charge from the Bishop, which might be quite formal, to arouse them to the seriousness of the step which they were taking, or to give them devotional help by the way. Sometimes, already, things were better. Dean Alford who was ordained at Exeter in 1833 says of the Bishop's charge: "Altogether it was the most solemn thing I ever heard. He talked to us most seriously for nearly two hours on the inward call, the ministerial duties, etc." Of the ordination itself he wrote: "the Bishop's manner was most solemn, and altogether all was most suitable and proper."[1]

Confirmations were held at infrequent intervals and then carried out in a most undignified manner. Archbishop Manners-Sutton, for example, simply stretched out his hands once over the crowd of candidates. The service, when taken with greater regard for the rubric that the Bishop should lay his hand "on the head of every one severally," was very long, lasting often enough five or six hours. As attempts to arrange the candidates were usually absent they had simply to fight their way to the chancel, and in the course of the struggle injuries to clothes and even persons were often received. Thus what is for the lay member of the Church of England the most solemn moment of his life was turned into an occasion for distressing and distasteful memories. Even in those days of neglect there were a few dioceses where things were better. Lincoln, Chester, and Winchester had a name for performing the rite "in a solemn and edifying way."[2]

The general position of the Bishops in the years immediately before our period has been well described by Lord Bryce in a letter to Thomas Hughes in which he comments on the change both in the Bishops themselves and in the attitude of the people towards them. "Forty or fifty years ago," he wrote, "they were usually rich, dignified, and rather indolent magnates, aristocratic in their tastes and habits, moderate in their theology, sometimes to the verge of indifferentism, quite as much men of the world as pastors of souls. Now and then eminence in learning or literature raised a man to the bench; there were the 'Greek play' bishops, such as Monk of Gloucester, and *The Quarterly Review* bishops like Copleston of Llandaff. . . . They were respected as part of the solid fabric of English society, more than for personal merits. But they were often a mark for political invective or literary sneers."[3]

When improvement came it was, as Dr. Carpenter has

---

[1] *Life of Dean Alford*, p. 91. The Bishop of Exeter was, at this time, the famous Henry Phillpotts, and from him a much higher standard was to be expected.
[2] See Canon Ollard in *Confirmation*, I, pp. 213 ff., for details.
[3] *Life of Bishop Fraser*, pp. 357 f.

pointed out, "mainly due to Evangelical Bishops" (*Church and People*, p. 253). It was some time, however, before any definite Evangelical was found on the episcopal bench. Henry Ryder, consecrated to Gloucester in 1815, was the first; and his appointment was severely criticized, amongst others by Archbishop Manners-Sutton. The next was Charles Sumner, appointed to Llandaff in 1826, but translated to Winchester in the year following. During his long episcopate of forty-two years he reorganized his vast diocese and set an entirely new standard of episcopal activity. His brother, John Bird Sumner, became Bishop of Chester in 1828, and displayed a like energy and ability. On one occasion, finding that many of the congregation were standing in the passages whilst a number of pews were empty, he stopped the service to enquire why they were not occupied. "The pews are private property," he was told, "and the owners have shut them up." "There can be no such thing," he said, "in the House of God. Send for a blacksmith to take off the locks. We will sing a hymn while he does it."

Another, this time not an Evangelical, who did much to restore the prestige of the Bishops, was Blomfield, Sumner's predecessor at Chester, and Bishop of London from 1828 to 1855, when he was succeeded by Tait, the future Archbishop. He was possessed of a great power of constructive work, being careful and thorough in all his undertakings. His capacity and vigour shewed that the Church had leaders who were aware of their responsibilities and able to undertake them. In the years following the Reform Bill, when there were many who desired to extend reforming activities to the Church, it was a factor of immense usefulness to have a Bishop like Blomfield occupying so prominent a position.[1]

With carelessness and neglect sitting enthroned in the highest offices of the Church it was not surprising that the same spirit was found in the stall of the incumbent of the parish. Perhaps the position can best be grasped by taking a single concrete example. The Rev. E. B. Ellman, a Sussex parson, tells us that in 1819 four clergymen after taking their morning services dined together one Sunday at Hurstmonceaux. The afternoon

[1] See Davidson and Benham, *Life of A. C. Tait*, I, pp. 196 f.

turned out to be wet, so, abandoning all thought of further duty, they spent it in playing cards. It is interesting to notice the names of those who were present. Robert Hare, Vicar of Hurstmonceaux, was the host; the others were, Edward Raynes, Vicar of Firle, and later Archdeacon; Harry West, Vicar of Wartling; and — Capper, Vicar of Wilmington, who is mentioned elsewhere as the only resident incumbent between Eastbourne and Lewes.[1]

In spite of the presence in it of idealists, such as Arnold, Keble, and Newman, and their fellows; in spite of the efforts of a few reforming Bishops, the Church as a whole before the rise of the Oxford Movement was undoubtedly tainted with Erastianism and much too ready to acquiesce in parliamentary interference, however high-handed. Many Churchmen were so frightened by the spirit of reform around them that they seemed to have lost all belief in themselves or in their Church. They were despairing and apologetic (in the bad sense), and regarded the situation as so menacing that they were glad to save anything from the coming wreck. To retain a remnant of their material privileges and possessions seemed well worth while even if it involved the sacrifice of the rest. The Church had lost its own heat and light, and possessed only "such mimic flame as neither lights nor harms." But there was, as we have seen, another side, and the Church's power was really much more considerable than many supposed. Had it been otherwise, so shrewd an observer as Leopold, King of the Belgians, would not have advised his niece on coming to the throne to cultivate it; "you cannot without *pledging* yourself to anything *particular*," he wrote, "*say too much on this subject.*"[2]

The Orthodox Party

From this general survey of the Church of England in the Pre-Victorian era we turn now to examine the position and prospects of the chief parties or schools of thought within it. The first to be considered must be the High Church or Orthodox party. Its members claimed to stand in the traditional Anglican

---
[1] See *The Recollections of a Sussex Parson*, p. 56.
[2] Quoted in *Letters of Queen Victoria*, I, p. 79.

ways and to look back to Hooker, and in a lesser degree to the Caroline divines, Andrewes, Jeremy Taylor, and Ken. Their aim, in the words of Bishop Copleston, was "to preserve the unity of our church, and to make (it) in effect as well as in name, a national church." They were men of a studious and sober fashion of mind, knowing what they believed and why they believed it, suspicious of enthusiasm and distrustful of novelties, both in faith and practice. Their own lives and doctrines were based on the broad, traditional faith which had been preserved much more widely than is often supposed. For this last statement support may be found in Pusey's declaration that he had learnt Church principles at his mother's knees (*Life*, I, p. 7); the assertion of the Kebles that they had absorbed their views in their father's vicarage;[1] or in the venerable figure of Routh, President of Magdalen, to whom Newman dedicated his *Lectures on the Prophetical Office of the Church* as to one "who has been reserved to report to a forgetful generation what was the theology of their fathers." But in this party there was, in the first years of the century, but little life; its members were in the position of those who guard potent weapons against a day when once again they may be called into use.

In this school of thought there were several prominent leaders whose names ought not to be forgotten. One of the chief was Sikes of Guilsborough, a man of retiring habits, but a real force in the background. His great desire was to see the phrase "the Holy Catholic Church" made into a reality; in this he was a forerunner of the Oxford Movement. He had originally been an Evangelical, but in reading the works of Thorndike his views underwent a change. Another was Jones of Nayland, who died in 1800, but by his writings, mostly in defence of the Church, his influence was still a living thing. Handley Norris of Hackney also deserves notice. He was perhaps the most prominent of the clerical members of the party. For the sake of preserving his independence he repeatedly refused high preferment and stood outside the ecclesiastical machine. These were all of the clergy. But alongside them there were devoted laymen who were worthy to be

---

[1] Keble's highest praise of any statement was: "It seems to me just what my father taught me": W. Lock, *John Keble*, p. 81.

PRE-VICTORIAN ERA: CONDITION OF RELIGION

compared with the Clapham Sect of the Evangelicals. There was William Stevens, a wealthy merchant, but a student of theology as well, who had a considerable knowledge of Hebrew. In 1800, seven years before his death, he founded a club called "Nobody's Friends" (Nobody was his own pseudonym)—qualification for membership included the holding of sound principles in "religion and polity."[1] Then there was Joshua Watson, a nephew of the redoubtable Archdeacon Daubeny, whose sister was the wife of Sikes. He lived at Clapton, which suggested the name of the Clapton Sect, sometimes given to this group. He certainly was a High Church parallel to Thornton and the other Christian business men of the Evangelicals. Watson was one of the founders of the National Society and did much to revive the Society for the Propagation of the Gospel.

The Liberals

Next we pass to the Liberal party, if party it can be called, for it is no uncommon thing for Liberal groups to consist mainly of leaders without followers; such in a manner was the Liberal Group in the Church at the beginning of the reign of Victoria. It was made up of a number of individuals who had a similar attitude to theological and ecclesiastical questions. In Church matters they were frankly Erastian and regarded the Church itself as a kind of government department; and organized religion as chiefly useful for preserving morals and supporting venerable institutions, as in fact the cement of the whole social structure.

The names of Paley, who died in 1805, and Samuel Parr, who lived nearly twenty years longer, belong to this group. But the great name which adorned it was that of Sydney Smith whose brilliant pen graced contemporary journalism with sparkling epigrams. His liberalism came out most prominently in attacks on the other parties in the Church. He frankly regarded his sacred calling as being merely one profession amongst others, and so, like a barrister or any other professional man, he had the right to be ambitious and to

[1] Dr. Carpenter by a slip says that the club was founded in his memory: *Church and People*, p. 68.

seek after positions of eminence and wealth. None the less he did his duty when the advent of the Whigs to power gave him promotion, and shewed activity and energy in administration when such things were sufficiently rare. He never became a Bishop, and put this failure down to the resentment aroused in Evangelical and Nonconformist quarters by his scathing attacks in earlier days.[1] A man of finer type than any of the above was Edward Stanley, Bishop of Norwich until his death in 1849, the father of a more famous son, the future Dean of Westminster. At Oxford there was a group of distinguished Liberals associated with Oriel College. Copleston was one of the most influential of this group, and Whately, later to become Archbishop of Dublin. The latter stood a little apart in his views from the rest and it was to him, strangely enough, that Newman owed his awakening to the idea of the Church as a spiritual body.[2] The best known of this group, however, was Thomas Arnold. His moral force and strong sense of duty exercised great influence, not only through Rugby and among Liberals, but outside and beyond. A High Churchman like Archbishop Benson could say that to him he owed his very soul.[3] Arnold was not really great intellectually and his thinking did not go deep enough; for this reason he often failed to realize the corollaries of some of his favourite theories. Such were some of the Liberals of the years around the coming of Victoria. Copleston, Whately, and Arnold all lived into her reign; as did the little Cambridge Group, Thirlwall, Julius Hare, and F. D. Maurice. With them we shall deal in a subsequent chapter.[4]

The Evangelicals

We come next and last to the most influential of all the parties in the Pre-Victorian Era—the Evangelicals. They

[1] See Hesketh Pearson, *The Smith of Smiths*, p. 66.

[2] See Newman, *Apologia pro Vita Sua*, p. 13: Newman also testified to his warmth and generosity in personal relations (*op. cit.*, p. 12).

[3] This was said during a visit to the Lakes in 1851 (see A. C. Benson, *Life of E. W. Benson*, p. 42). It is perhaps worth noting that he had already acknowledged a similar debt to his own Headmaster, Prince Lee (*op. cit.*, p. 18).

[4] See pp. 143 ff. below.

probably reached their highest point of purity and genuine power at the end of the eighteenth and the beginning of the nineteenth centuries. Certainly they had much to do with the general awakening of the Church at this time; for in zeal and diligence they far surpassed the members of all other schools. "The deepest and most fervid religion in England," wrote Liddon, "during the first three decades of this century was that of the Evangelicals." It seems certain that their influence in the Church and country was very considerable, and much greater than can be accounted for by their numbers, or by the positions of ecclesiastical importance which were held by members of the party. Such was their power, especially amongst the wealthy, that religion had become almost "the thing," and in consequence many pressed in who had no real sincerity of belief, members of "that ungracious crew that feigns demurest grace." Hypocrisy was an easy matter, for the Evangelical theology, since it consisted of but a few cardinal doctrines upon which the rest turned, was, for the superficial, simple of acquirement. The correct phrases, few in number, though far-reaching in depth, which to an earlier generation had been a means of conveying real experiences, had become a convention, almost a shibboleth, and, like all shibboleths, were capable of being imitated by the indolent and hypocritical.[1]

Popularity thus proved a danger, as so often to a religious party, and standards were lowered. The fashionable chapels were attended by congregations who had little intention of following the hard, upward path trodden by their fathers, and by degrees the preaching fell to the level of the congregations. A higher standard of life and ideals was preserved in the country districts where even as late as the thirties Evangelicals were in some districts still called upon to face much prejudice and petty persecution, "the insults of the poor and the ostracism of the wealthy."[2] But in general Evangelicals were sufficiently strong to be able to adopt an attitude of superiority and even of denunciation towards those who differed from

---
[1] The above paragraph is based on my volume *The Evangelical Party in the English Church*, p. 43.
[2] See *Life of Bishop Moule*, p. 3, where the experiences of his father, who became Vicar of Fordington in Dorset in 1829, are recorded.

them. They clung tenaciously to their influence and power and tried to extend it; there was, indeed, a distinct possibility of their dominating the Church of England (especially a little later when Lord Shaftesbury reached a position of great influence); and the desire, on the highest grounds, to do so, was not lacking. But such a dominance was never really possible. For one thing their impatience of opposition, the fruit of the belief that they were led by the direct inspiration of God, and that they alone knew His will,[1] united other parties against them and drove out some who might have been powerful agents.[2] Again they were suspected by the great Tory party, which had vast influence in the Church, as too friendly with the Dissenters, as unreliable in their political opinions, and as over-scrupulous and too much interested in the souls of other people.[3] Moreover there were certain weaknesses inherent in Evangelicalism itself which made it unfit to be the ruling party in the Church. It was at its best in evangelizing, both at home and abroad, but it had no adequate realization of the need for character training and it attached too much importance to the emotional side of religion.[4] These criticisms may not have been true of the leaders of the movement, but they applied to the rank and file, and at this epoch the supply of great leaders and preachers began to give out.

Thus when the Victorian Era began the Evangelicals had already lost something of their first love and become conventional for the most part. It is, however, easy to exaggerate the extent to which this had occurred and the bitter denunciations of Mark Pattison certainly require much qualifica-

[1] "When a man seeks divine guidance on every occasion, and is convinced of his own integrity, it is difficult for him to avoid the belief that he is inspired." F. Warre Cornish, *op. cit.*, I, p. 19. This was true also of Luther: see *Erasmus the Reformer*, pp. 39 f.

[2] Walter Kerr Hamilton, Bishop of Salisbury, had been a great Evangelical preacher, but left the party in disgust at its denunciations of others.

[3] G. M. Trevelyan, *History of England*, p. 600.

[4] See Overton, *The English Church in the Nineteenth Century*, pp. 138 ff. "The Evangelical preaching has been deficient in reverence because it has been deficient in depth" wrote Maurice (*Life of F. D. Maurice*, I, p. 335).

tion.[1] But it is admitted by Dr. Stock, for example, that they had become "too comfortable"—which meant, of course, a loss of appeal to ardent and romantic souls—and that from about 1827 onwards "a general spirit of disunion . . . spread in Evangelical ranks."[2] The growing power of newly established Puritan sects, such as the Irvingite Movement with its apocalyptic message and the Plymouth Brethren, tended to draw away the more adventurous and the more narrow; whilst within the party there was disputing over the question of Infant Baptism, and in some quarters a too curious interest in the mysteries of unfulfilled prophecy.

NONCONFORMITY

The rather critical attitude towards the Evangelical Revival, within the Church, finds a parallel in the attitude of certain Nonconformists towards the wider Methodist Revival, of which it formed a part. Dr. Dale, for example, considered that it had been weakened by "its failure to afford a lofty ideal of practical righteousness, and a healthy vigorous moral training" (*Life*, p. 221). He even went so far as to affirm that Congregationalism itself had suffered from and been diverted by the Revival (*op. cit.*, p. 349).

This may well be true, but the debt which Nonconformity in general owed to the Movement can scarcely be exaggerated —for Nonconformity, more than an established religion, suffers

[1] The opinion of Mark Pattison may be quoted in full as a type of what the more extreme opponents of Evangelicalism have said. But it has to be remembered that Mark Pattison was cynical and pessimistic about all things and not least about him'self. The following is the passage: "In 1833 Evangelicalism was already effete. The helpless imbecility of Evangelical writing and preaching; their obvious want of power to solve, or even to apprehend, the questions of which they are nevertheless perpetually talking; their incapacity to explain the Scripture, while assuming the exclusive right to it; their conceit of being able to arrive at conclusions without premises; in a word, their intellectual weakness, contributed very greatly to the fall of the Evangelical school before a better-informed generation" (*Essays*, II, p. 194). For a more balanced judgment we may turn to Overton, *The English Church in the Nineteenth Century*, p. 99, who wrote: "it is said that the Evangelical party grievously degenerated in the years immediately preceding the Oxford Movement; but I feel bound in common justice to add that I can find no traces of this degeneracy in the lives of its leaders."

[2] *History of the Church Missionary Society*, I, pp. 281 and 287.

from the ebb and flow of religious opinion. In the seventeenth century it had reached the high-water mark of power and influence; but in the years which followed the general decline of religion had left it so weak and feeble as almost to be in danger of extinction. From this state of stagnation it was rescued by the Revival. Now as another new century continued on its course it showed signs of vigorous growth. This can be seen in the number of those who left the Church of England. An example may be found in the parents of J. Guinness Rogers, both of whom had been brought up as Churchpeople, but both of whom had been drawn into Nonconformity, quite independently. "Like numbers besides, they became Dissenters, not because of any abstract preference for Dissent, but simply because they were attracted to the Churches where they had received spiritual benefit."[1] The parents of Robert Browning are another example of those who were drawn to Dissent by its vigorous life. His father had been a Churchman and his mother a Presbyterian; they compromised by both becoming Independents. No doubt the growth of Nonconformity in the beginning of the nineteenth century was due in part to the revival of democratic sentiments after the repression of the war years had been removed. There was a renewed claim for religious equality such as had been urged by Price and Priestley. This claim was necessary for Nonconformity still suffered from many disabilities; such as the political restrictions with which we have already dealt and the lack of opportunity which came from the almost complete exclusion of Nonconformists from the Universities and Public Schools of the country. This meant inevitably a loss of culture and dignity, in spite of the noble efforts of individuals, here and there, to rise superior to the limitations imposed upon them.[2] To this position of inferiority there was

---

[1] *J. Guinness Rogers, an Autobiography*, p. 3.

[2] The case of the Rev. Eli Cogan, a Unitarian minister, to whose school the youthful Disraeli was sent, may be cited in this connexion. Dr. Parr regarded him as the only Nonconformist who was a Greek scholar. Cogan complained in a letter to Isaac d'Israeli that he had "been obliged to acquire without assistance when a man what ought to have been communicated to (him) when a boy": see Monypenny and Buckle, *Life of Benjamin Disraeli*, I, p. 28.

PRE-VICTORIAN ERA: CONDITION OF RELIGION

one unexpected exception in the Quakers. They held a position in the social world, perhaps by the possession of great wealth, which was much higher than that of other Nonconformists. This can be illustrated at a little later period by the almost royal progress of Elizabeth Fry on the continent of Europe.[1]

These were disabilities which were soon to be removed, and served but to delay a process which was destined to continue in spite of them; for Nonconformity was setting out on that great career of influence and usefulness which is one of the most striking phenomena of the nineteenth century. Already two lines which it was to follow can be distinguished: the zeal for the application of the principle of individual right and liberty in the political sphere, and the insistence that Christian beliefs require a philosophical rather than a theological presentation, the insistence "that the old verities are capable of new statement, and that loss of dogma may be the gain of faith."[2] This second clause, as it stands, would have met with the approval of Erasmus; but to a Churchman its application would need to be rigidly controlled if disaster was to be averted.

In one field Nonconformity shewed its force and life; it had, in this era, almost a monopoly of popular preachers. The Evangelicals, for the moment, had few great preachers; whilst the other Church parties were too intellectual and too dry to win popular support. Sydney Smith speaks of them as "freezing common sense for large salaries . . . amidst whole acres and furlongs of empty pews." Some of these preachers were survivors from the previous century, some luminaries of a more recent dawning. Of the former it may suffice to mention Rowland Hill, perhaps the most popular preacher in London in the early years of the century,[3] and Robert Hall,

---

[1] See Gurney, *Elizabeth Fry's Journeys, 1840–1841*.

[2] Silvester Horne, *Free Church History*, p. 389.

[3] He was the son of a Shropshire baronet and had, after much difficulty, been ordained deacon in 1782. He built the Surrey Chapel where he ministered as an independent preacher for half a century. He always claimed to be a Churchman and was a supporter of the Establishment. He had a violent quarrel with the Methodists whom he described as a "ragged legion of preaching barbers, cobblers, tinkers, scavengers, draymen, and chimney-sweepers": Silvester Horne, *Free Church History*, p. 273.

the famous Baptist.[1] Among the latter class the great name is that of Edward Irving, who in the years between 1825 and 1833 literally took London by storm, drawing crowds of the highest society to the Scotch Churches in Hatton Garden and Regent Square. De Quincey called him "the greatest orator of our time."[2]

Having spoken of Nonconformity as a whole we must now, as in the case of the Church, turn to its various manifestations, both new and old. We begin naturally with Three Denominations, which, from their longer existence, may be called historic, the Independents, the Presbyterians, and the Baptists. Of the Congregationalists or Independents there is not much to say, they had perhaps derived the least benefit from the Methodist Revival (Dale as we saw regarded its influence as on the whole harmful). They stood for an intellectual, sane presentation of the gospel, as they understood it, and for the independence of each several Congregation. Already signs could be observed of a desire for more co-operation between the various congregations and a realization that independence might mean weakness. In 1831 the Congregational Union, an entirely voluntary body, had been established to meet this realized need; but on that more can best be said at a later point.[3] The Baptists had undergone struggles in the eighteenth century. At the famous Salters' Hall Conference in 1719 the General Baptists had been in favour of permitting Unitarian views in their pulpits, whilst the Particular Baptists had rejected the notion. During the last part of the century many General Baptist congregations became definitely Unitarian, The Baptists, even in the nineteenth century, seem to have been troubled with the antinomian tendencies which had been a mark of their Anabaptist forefathers in the sixteenth. The furious attacks which Robert Hall levelled against such views are a measure of their extent and influence.[4] This antinomian attitude may have been due to the Calvinism which most of the leaders still retained. There was, however, a striking exception in John

[1] Hall was the son of a Baptist minister and is chiefly associated with Broadmead Chapel, Bristol. He died in 1831.
[2] For the sect which developed out of his ministry see below, p. 57.
[3] See below, pp. 483 ff.   [4] See *Life of F. D. Maurice*, I, p. 375.

Foster (died 1843). His revulsion from Calvinism even took him in the direction of unorthodoxy. "I have discarded the doctrine of Eternal Punishment," he wrote, "I can avow no opinion on the peculiar points of Calvinism for I have none, and see no possibility of forming a satisfactory one. I am no Socinian, but am in doubt between the Orthodox and the Arian doctrine, not without some inclination to the latter."[1] Of the English Presbyterians more must be said, and this can best be done in a separate paragraph.

As a result of the teaching of Wesley and his fellow Arminians the rather barren Calvinistic orthodoxy of English Nonconformity had been, in spite of itself, considerably modified. Many of those who took part in the Methodist Revival were, of course, Calvinists—everyone knows of the bitter strife between them and the Arminians—but the whole trend of the Movement, with its emphasis on the freedom of the will and the universality of grace, was against Calvinism. The new and varied life which came with it therefore acted as a solvent of rigid Nonconformist Orthodoxy. There was, perhaps as a partial consequence, a tendency to look with less severity on the Socinian and Arian views which had prevailed so widely in the early years of the eighteenth century—gaining in some cases the partial approval even of Anglican divines. Since 1788 such views had been represented by a definite denomination—the Unitarians. By the beginning of the nineteenth century the great majority of the English Presbyterians had adopted this form of belief. These men must not be confused with the Scottish Presbyterians who remained rigidly orthodox; they were, many of them, the successors of those ejected in 1662 for conscience' sake, and, following the example of Chillingworth, author of the dictum "the Bible and the Bible only the religion of Protestants," they had become Unitarian. This explains a statement in Newman's account of his early life which is apt to be misunderstood by those who fail to realize this distinction. Looking back Newman declares himself grateful to God for having been born in the communion which afterwards he had left, for he adds "had I been born an English Presbyterian, perhaps I should never have known

[1] Quoted Ryland, *Life of John Foster*, p. 25.

our Lord's divinity" (*Apologia*, p. 382). The extent to which the Unitarians clung to the Bible led them into uses which to more Orthodox Christians seemed inexplicable. Michael Maurice, the father of F. D. Maurice, for example, always baptized in the name of the Trinity, since the New Testament so commanded. This drew from Robert Hall the comment: "Why, Sir, as I understand you, you must consider that you baptize in the name of an abstraction, a man, and a metaphor."[1] It should be explained that the doctrine of the Trinity was rejected because it is not explicitly stated in the New Testament. "Convince us that any tenet is authorized by the Bible," wrote C. Wellbeloved, the Principal of Manchester College in 1823, "from that moment we receive it."[2] The Unitarians at the beginning of the century shewed signs of aggressive activity, and in 1806 a Fund was started for purposes of expansion; but the older members were afraid that they might be degraded to the level of the Methodists and so little came of it.[3]

The Quakers were affected like other bodies by the rise of the Plymouth Brethren and lost a number of adherents. There was also a tendency on the part of the younger people to find the pecularities, to which the older people now clung all the closer, not a little irksome, and to dislike them as suggesting that Quakerism was a kind of superior Christianity.[4] The strict marriage regulations, by which unions outside the denomination were forbidden, also told against it. This had its good side from the standpoint of religion in general, for the distinctive contribution which the Quakers had to make was thus spread over a wider field; the children of those who conformed carrying it into another generation.

Among the Methodists the impetus of the original movement had not yet entirely died out; a vivid picture of what life amongst them could still mean can be found in the *Autobiographical Recollections* of Benjamin Gregory, where the earlier chapters tell of great activity in rural areas, and incidentally the burden of the move at the end of every three years in days when travelling and the transport of furniture was very

---
[1] Quoted in *Life of F. D. Maurice*, I, pp. 122 f.
[2] *Three Letters*, p. 51.   [3] *Memoirs of R. Aspland*, p. 198.
[4] See Louise Creighton, *Life and Letters of Thomas Hodgkin*, pp. 6 and 46 ff.

difficult. Two characteristics which were to mark them for the greater part of the Victorian era had already revealed themselves; the tendency to stand apart from other Dissenters, and the tendency to split up still further. The former characteristic was made deeper by the attitude of the older Denominations who looked upon them as upstarts and also by their own clinging to the services of the Church which they had abandoned. The latter tendency is illustrated by the rise of the Welsh Calvinistic Methodists in 1811 under the leadership of Thomas Charles of Bala, an ex-Church of England clergyman, and famous as the virtual founder of the Bible Society, for it was he who made widely known the need of Bibles in Wales.

Two new sects of outstanding importance arose in this period, to both of which reference has already been made, the Plymouth Brethren, and the Irvingites or Catholic Apostolic Church. The Plymouth Brethren really had their origin in Dublin in 1825. In some of their tenets, such as a deep horror of war, they resembled the Quakers; but they were unlike them in a strict observance of the sacraments—the breaking of the bread was observed every Sunday. They also took a great interest in the fulfilment of "prophecy." The founder was John Nelson Darby, who had resigned his curacy in the Church of England on account of what he regarded as its worldliness. His strong personality impressed itself deeply on the society; but coming into contact with a man of equally strong will, Benjamin Wills Newton, a split resulted in 1845. The narrow outlook of the Plymouth Brethren cut them off from other Nonconformists, made them self-contained and sadly crippled their influence. The Catholic Apostolic Church was founded in 1833 after Irving had been deposed by the Presbytery of Annan. Though it was made up of his followers, he himself was allotted but an inferior post in its elaborate organization; though later on he was given, in response to a message delivered by "tongues," the authority of an Angel. The society has lasted on into the present,[1] but it played very little part

[1] The last "Apostle," to name the chief rank, died in February 1901. The society is now ruled, I believe, by "Coadjutors," since, unlike the Primitive Church, it does not seem to possess the power of filling vacancies in the original twelve.

in the development of Victorian religion in England, being of too high-flown a nature to commend itself to English people, and having to face the greater attractions on the one hand of the revived Church life of the Oxford Movement, and of Spiritualism on the other.

3

THE EARLY YEARS OF VICTORIA

HOME AFFAIRS

To those of us who are well on into middle age it is solemnizing to realize that there are no longer any living who can remember the coming of Victoria to the throne. With their passing the whole early period of her reign seems suddenly to have become distant and far-off; it belongs no more to life, but takes its place, with the Stuarts and Hanoverians, as a part of history. The preconceptions which governed the thoughts and ideas of the period have become strange and unfamiliar, though our grandparents, and even our parents, had their share in them; we have, almost in a moment, lost the clue. Even their furniture and their buildings puzzle us—as Mr. Chesterton puts it, "the Crystal Palace is the temple of a forgotten faith" (*G. F. Watts*, p. 3).

The accession itself marked decisively the coming of a new era in more ways than one. Politically it severed our link with continental Europe, for whilst Victoria succeeded her uncle on the throne of England, Hanover passed to Ernest Augustus, Duke of Cumberland. The consequence of this separation it is impossible to gauge; what, for example, would have been Hanover's reaction to schemes for German unity had her ruler been also sovereign of Great Britain? More important for our purpose was the utter transformation of the crown and court. It was believed that when Victoria heard that she was queen of England her first words were: "I will be good," and though the Queen herself in after life denied that this was so, the words, in view of her whole history, might well have been a solemn vow. The world had become accustomed to seeing the British crown held by a succession of debauched and disreputable old men, "a melancholy succession of madness, and vice, and folly," Canon Scott Holland named them (*Personal Studies*, p. 5). Now their place was taken by a simple, unspoilt girl who was to raise the crown from the abasement and contempt into which it had fallen under her immediate predecessors.

Her first guide, in matters of serious import, was Lord Melbourne. But though the favourite reading of this statesman was theology and the Fathers of the Church, his usual conversation and manner of life would not have suggested it. But he was a faithful and loyal servant, and taught his sovereign many needful lessons of statecraft. Later there was to come her marriage with Prince Albert, and the entry of the great influence of her life. Even when he was dead it was by his ideals that she was to be guided. But that tragic death, which took place in 1861, brought to a close the early and the best years of her reign. From that moment, as Mr. Lytton Strachey has said: "She herself felt that her true life had ceased . . . and that the remainder of her days upon earth was of a twilight nature—an epilogue to a drama that was done" (*Queen Victoria*, p. 190).

Middle-Class Power

Politically the Victorian Era began, as already I have suggested, with the passing of the Reform Bill in 1832. That measure was the foundation of that middle-class dominance which was to be the chief characteristic of the reign on its political side. It must be admitted that the new possessors of power were, on the whole, worthy of the trust which such a possession involves. Their growth in power and riches was phenomenal, but they were amazingly free from corruption, and set a very high standard of public life. The middle classes were self-reliant, and valued their integrity too highly to allow practices which had been tolerated by their more highly born predecessors. At the same time they had their ambitions and their aspirations; "the Englishman loves a Lord," is a well-known saying, and this was true of the new class which was rising to power; they did not wish to level down those above them, but to rise to similar heights. This was an important factor in preserving the stability of the state and constitution; but lack of taste made their influence an unhappy thing in literature and art. It was, however, in the political sphere that their real contribution was made and in that sphere they found their chief means of self-expression. Above all they produced a statesman in whom the best type of middle-class ideal became incarnate.

Sir Robert Peel may be called the first of the modern type of statesman and the harbinger of the new aristocracy which was to be recruited from the magnates of industry. His services to England, both at home and abroad, can hardly be overestimated. At home he made possible the peaceful transition from the old political world to the new. This might easily have been accompanied by revolution and disorder. His government of 1842–1844, as Lord Morley has said, "laid the groundwork of our solid commercial policy, it established our railway system, it settled the currency." Abroad, to quote the same high authority, it "gave us a good national character in Europe as lovers of moderation, equity, and peace."[1]

Unfortunately these early years are stained by serious failures to realize the duty of a Christian people. The nation as a whole had no conception of the attitude which ought to be taken towards the weaker races of mankind. In practice they were held to be without rights, even the right to expect honest conduct. England behaved with scandalous bad faith towards Scinde, and forced on China in 1840 the disgraceful Opium War. Well might the great German publicist, Treitschke, regard our conduct as a revelation of England's greed and hypocrisy, which advanced to the conquest of an Empire with the Bible in one hand and the opium pipe in the other. But there were not wanting Christian politicians to make their protest; Lord Shaftesbury,[2] the Evangelical, and Mr. Gladstone,[3] the High Churchman, both shewed a true appreciation of the rights of the matter and were not afraid to make their opinions known.

REVOLUTION IN EUROPE

We now turn to the condition of affairs in Europe; for though only a brief survey is possible, such will help us to understand developments at home. In France the middle classes, as here in England, had gained supremacy; this they

---

[1] *Life of W. E. Gladstone*, I, p. 247.
[2] Hodder, *Life of Lord Shaftesbury*, I, pp. 44 ff., II, p. 11.
[3] Gladstone spoke out "heavily" and "strongly against the trade and the war" (*op. cit.*, I, p. 226) and in secret dreaded "the judgement of God upon England for our national iniquity towards China" (*op. cit.*, I, p. 227).

held under the "citizen king," as Louis Philippe loved to be known, from 1830 to 1848. But the middle class in France had not the same high sense of honour as that in England, and a series of grave scandals revealed the corruption of the politicians and robbed them of the confidence of the country just when the spread of the Industrial Revolution brought unrest and the need for adjustment. The result was a Socialist Revolution in February 1848 and the formation of the Second Republic. Louis Philippe found an asylum in England. This was but one of many outbreaks in the year 1848 during which Europe, as Dowden has said, was "like a sea broken by wave after wave of Revolutionary passion."[1] The convulsions, although they actually began in Palermo, had their real focus in Vienna, and it was in countries under Austrian rule that they mainly spread.[2] But within two years these movements were everywhere crushed and absolutism was once again supreme. In Italy Rome rose against the Pope, and the North against Austria. But after the defeat of Novara on March 23, 1849, all seemed lost. "The Pope," wrote Mazzini, "clutches the soul of the Italian nation; Austria the body whenever it shows signs of life."[3] In Germany these movements brought to an end a period of political stagnation, even if, for the moment, they were not highly productive. England itself in the year of Revolutions did not escape without its alarms; and it is well to remember all that was going on in the rest of Europe before we allow ourselves to be unduly scornful of the panic aroused over Chartism.

CHARTISM

Chartism was largely spontaneous in origin and growth and not definitely, amongst the greater part of its leaders, a revolutionary movement at all.[4] It came to birth with the realization

[1] *Life of Robert Browning* (Everyman Edition), p. 109.
[2] J. A. R. Marriott, *History of Europe, 1815–1923*, p. 141: see also a useful table of events, pp. 142 f.
[3] Quoted Marriott, *op. cit.*, p. 165.
[4] The movement "could not be explained as the work of professional agitators or as the outcome of mere sedition": Monypenny and Buckle, *Life of Disraeli*, I, p. 480.

by the workers that the great Reform Bill had left them much as they were before. That is why the leaders in their speeches attacked, not the aristocracy and the Corn Laws, but the middle classes and the industrialists.[1] The "Charter" itself, drawn up by William Lovett of the London Working Men's Association at the suggestion of Francis Place, makes purely political demands;[2] though no doubt it was hoped that these would open the way to social and economic changes, such as higher wages and better conditions of labour, the control of machinery, and, with some, increased facilities of education. There was nothing in it of Socialism, much less of Communism, and Place himself was an individualist. Meetings were held to arouse the workers to their wrongs and attendance at them was, in some cases at least, strictly limited to those who were actually manual labourers. Archbishop Temple, as a young man, presented himself at one of them, and before being allowed to enter had to show his hands. Thanks to his work on the family farm at Axon in Devonshire they were sufficiently rough to pass the test (*Frederick Temple*, I, p. 82). Here and there violent outbreaks occurred, partly stirred up by the sense of political wrong and helplessness, partly by the hard conditions of life during "the hungry forties." Then in 1848 the revolutions on the continent roused the workers to the possibility of pressing their own claims, and it was determined to present the Charter to Parliament backed by an overwhelming body of supporters. This scheme was enough to arouse the worst fears of the comfortable and settled, and on the appointed date, April 10th, some 200,000 special constables were enrolled,[3] and troops and artillery were held in readiness at strategic points. These military preparations were undertaken in all seriousness under the direction of the Duke of Wellington himself, who, with his staff, dressed in

[1] *Op. cit.*, I, p. 481.
[2] The six points of the Charter were: (1) Annual Parliaments; (2) Universal Suffrage (including Women); (3) Vote by Ballot; (4) The Abolition of property qualification for candidates; (5) Payment of Members; (6) Equal electoral divisions.
[3] These included the future emperor of France, Louis Napoleon, then a refugee in England.

plain clothes to avoid attention, surveyed the whole metropolis.[1] However, the whole thing "petered out." Rain came down, the workers were cowed by the vastness of the forces arrayed against them, and all passed off quietly. The movement seems to have suffered from defective leadership; not that the leaders were insincere, but they were incapable, being better at talking than at organizing.[2] The resulting depression gave to certain Christian leaders the opportunity of putting before the working men of England the claims of Christ and the hopes to be found in the proclamation and application of His teaching; from the Charter and its failure arose the Christian Social movement.

PERIOD OF CALM

With the failure of the various revolutionary movements on the continent and the collapse of Chartism in England Europe seemed to be entering upon a long period of peace and increasing wealth, for the possessing classes at least. In England, at any rate, some twenty years of prosperity served to blind men's eyes to the innumerable abuses and social evils which lay at the root of the nation's life. During that time much might have been done to prepare for the lean years which were to follow. But the continuance of prosperity seemed to be assured for an indefinite period, and it is to the belief in continued good times ahead and not to entire lack of foresight that the serious neglect to make provision for the future and to remedy the cruel injustices of the present must be attributed. Time, men thought with easy optimism, would solve all problems.

In the relations between nations there was an equally unjustified optimism, especially as to the effect of commerce. In all quarters during the years from 1848 to 1852 there was the expectation that an era of peace and freedom had begun; but

---

[1] See T. H. S. Escott, *Great Victorians*, p. 63. It was not only in London that apprehensions were aroused, but elsewhere; troops were sent, for example, to Liverpool to protect the shipping: see Jackson, *Ingram Bywater*, p. 3.

[2] Mr. Ramsay MacDonald considers that "The Chartist Movement shows not the dishonest leader, but the wind-bag, charlatan leader." *The Socialist Movement*, p. 205.

it was to be discovered that commerce instead of linking the peoples together would involve them in a desperate rivalry for markets, and that beneath the surface there were many irritations which in the end could but result in war and bitterness. But when the Great Exhibition was opened in 1851 it seemed to many that all was now to be well, and that the gigantic structure itself had an almost mystic meaning. To Kingsley, for example, it was "a sacred place, shadowing forth noble ideas of universal peace, and brotherhood, while displaying the achievements of Art and Physical Science" (*Life*, p. 112). All this on the eve of a series of desperate conflicts—the war over Schleswig-Holstein, the Crimean, the Mutiny, the wars in which Prussia, Austria, and France were to be involved. All the brave rejoicings over the achievements of Art and Science were to lead but to an age of scientific warfare, and even to conflict in the world of art itself.

RELIGIOUS CONDITIONS

The Church of England

The early years of Victoria saw a gradual but certain strengthening and revival of the religious life of the nation, and not least of the National Church. Religion in the forties had not been of a high quality. The standpoint of the majority of the men of that generation, especially among the governing classes, was that of the second Marquis of Salisbury, who is described by his granddaughter as having been "a Protestant to whom the Roman Catholics are idolators, a Churchman to whom Dissenters are merely rebels against the Establishment."[1] As F. D. Maurice surveyed, not only the governing classes, but the rest of society, he found little that was encouraging: "The upper classes became, as may happen, sleekly devout, for the sake of good order, avowedly believing that one must make the best of the world without God; the middle classes try what may be done by keeping themselves warm in dissent and agitation, to kill the sense of hollowness; the poor, who must have realities of some kind, understanding from their betters that all but houses and laws are abstractions, must make a grasp at them or else destroy them."

[1] Lady Gwendolen Cecil, *Life of Robert, Marquis of Salisbury*, I, pp. 100 f.

RELIGION IN THE VICTORIAN ERA

But things were really improving. Looking back from the vantage point of 1878 Dean Stephens considered the year 1850 "as marking an epoch in the history of the Church of England. The difference between her condition then, and her condition at the beginning of the century, was as great as the difference between the seasons of spring or early summer, and of winter. She was now abundantly fruitful in good works of every description. In all parts of the country, old churches were being repaired; new churches and new schools were being built; fresh life was pervading every department of parochial work: and was visible alike in multiplied services, and more frequent celebrations of Holy Communion; in the due observance of Holy Seasons, and Holy Days; in increased attention to Church music, and a decent and devout ceremonial; in the formation of guilds, sisterhoods, and all kinds of charitable associations. And while straining every nerve to do her work at home, and to keep pace with the rapid growth of the population, the Church had not been unmindful of her duty to foreign parts" (*Life of W. F. Hook*, p. 438). This was the conclusion, as I have said, of one who looked back after a lapse of more than a quarter of a century. To those living at the time and holding a similar moderate Catholic standpoint, the prospects did not appear nearly so hopeful nor the achievement so admirable. Moberly, then Headmaster of Winchester, wrote in his Journal in January 1851: "Never did so dark a year break upon the Reformed Church of England. The Government, the vast majority of lay people, and a considerable proportion of the clergy are bent on banishing the Catholic element from the Church of England. Meanwhile secessions take away our very heart" (quoted *Dulce Domum*, p. 94).

In this improvement, this "resuscitation of activity and zeal," all parties in the Church had their share. Dr. Stephens praises especially "the energy of individuals belonging for the most part to the old High Church party. Foremost among them must be placed the Vicar of Leeds (i.e. Hook), and Bishop Longley in the north of England, Archbishop Howley, and Bishop Blomfield in the south. And to these must be added ... Samuel Wilberforce, Bishop of Oxford" (*op. cit.*, pp. 438 f.)

at a slightly later date. The second great impulse, according to Dean Stephens, was to be found in the great Tractarian Movement. This was so important a feature of the life of the Church of England in the early years of the Victorian Era that it demands separate treatment and only the bare mention of its influence need here be specified.

These two impulses or forces in the eyes of Dean Stephens exhausted the cause of the renewal. But the Evangelicals must not be forgotten. They may not have been foremost in multiplying services and in forming guilds and sisterhoods, but their work was, in other directions, exceedingly fruitful. From the first they had made great headway in inland watering-places like Cheltenham, Bath, and Tunbridge Wells. In this period Francis Close, who afterwards became Dean of Carlisle, ruled Cheltenham with almost despotic power, whilst at Tunbridge Wells Edward Hoare carried on the godly succession. At Brighton also the saintly Henry Venn Elliott exhibited some of the characteristics of his grandfather, Henry Venn.

But in other, and perhaps more difficult, spheres Evangelicalism was exhibiting its power; in the slums of London and in the great cities its preachers were proving amazingly successful. Foremost among these was William Champneys, afterwards Dean of Lichfield, who went to Whitechapel in 1837. If in Charles Sumner we have the first of the modern type of Bishop, Champneys was the pioneer of the modern type of town parson. Whitechapel at this time was sunk in the lowest state, vice and crime were rampant. The Church life of the place was non-existent; one service on Sunday morning at which none of the parishioners were present had been the extent of its provision for the spiritual needs of the inhabitants. Champneys tackled his difficult problem with great energy and courage, and fortunately he had not to tackle it single-handed. Ten years before he went to Whitechapel the Church Pastoral Aid Society had begun its magnificent work as a home missionary agency, and by the aid of the Society he was able to obtain an active body of colleagues. So successful was the work, when once the effects of years of neglect had been overcome, that in 1851 there were present over 1,500 in the morning, over 800 in the afternoon, and more than

1,600 at night. Churches and schools were built and various experiments made in organizations. These are now common in every active parish; but Whitechapel under Champneys shewed the way.[1]

In the growing towns of the Midlands and the North also the Evangelicals had a firm footing. Among the more prominent were Hugh McNeile in Liverpool,[2] J. C. Miller in Birmingham, Hugh Stowell in Salford,[3] Atkinson in Leeds, and Robinson in Leicester. In one other important respect the Evangelicals were preparing the way to better things in the person of J. B. Sumner. As Archbishop of Canterbury (from 1848 onwards) he put an end to the old "prelate" type of Church dignitary, and made the beginning of the new, more human, shall we say, more Christian "Father in God." His simple manner of life was almost a scandal to the older Church and State Anglicans. Refusing to be driven about in his state coach, with outriders and armed guards, he would wander amongst his people with an umbrella under his arm. To those who complained of his lack of dignity he would reply "I cannot imagine that any greater reproach could be cast on the Church than to suppose that it allowed its dignity to interfere with its usefulness." Later there came Pelham of Norwich, Waldegrave of Carlisle, and Baring of Durham.[4]

An additional cause for the improvement in the Church's position may undoubtedly be found in the various measures of administrative reform which helped to rescue it from decay. An eminent Nonconformist historian considers that they "strengthened the Church's corner-stones, added buttresses

---

[1] The above paragraph is taken from *The Evangelical Faith*, p. 45.

[2] It was Hugh McNeile who once exclaimed: "Controversy! People object to controversy, but who can escape it out of Utopia. Controversy! you cannot live without controversy." Quoted by Major, *W. Boyd Carpenter*, p. 137.

[3] Stowell was Hook's rival for the living of Leeds in 1837: Stephens, *Dean Hook*, p. 201. What changes there might have been had the final decision of the Trustees been different.

[4] Bishop Creighton, who served under him as Vicar of Embleton, has testified in the *Dictionary of National Biography* to his good work, though he felt that there was not enough trust of his clergy, he would not even appoint Rural Deans.

to its walls, and gave it a new lease of continuance."[1] These reforms were part of the general movement of the times which challenged all privileges and endeavoured to expose all anomalies and abuses. Though they were carried out by Parliament and by the Ecclesiastical Commission which Parliament appointed there was no feeling of enmity against the Church behind them. On the contrary they made, as we have seen, for the greater efficiency of the Church.

It was in 1835 that Peel appointed a Commission to enquire into Ecclesiastical Duties and Revenues. This was the real origin of the permanent Ecclesiastical Commission. The original Commission made reports to Parliament which resulted in beneficial legislation, especially in the matter of the redistribution of revenues. By reducing the excessive revenues of some of the cathedrals, London and Durham in particular, a sum of £140,000 a year was ultimately set aside for the provision of new parishes and other needful measures.[2]

Nonconformity

Thus the Church of England was developing and arousing itself from the complacency which had, in earlier days, been a barrier to its true progress. Nonconformity likewise was growing and advancing; and with its growth there came an increasing realization of the disabilities under which it laboured. The older Dissenters, like the older Roman Catholics, had been thankful for toleration and quiet, they feared, by undue activity or prominence, to arouse unpleasant attentions; but a new, more aggressive tone now began to prevail. This change of outlook was bound, sooner or later, to provoke ill-feeling between the Church and Nonconformity.

Ill-feeling between Churchmen and Nonconformists was, of course, no new thing. In the previous era the Orthodox had disliked all Dissenters, and would have welcomed their complete disappearance. Even Nonconformist literature was objected to; Joshua Watson, for example, thought that the S.P.C.K. ought not to publish copies of the *Pilgrim's Progress*. On the side of Dissent there was even more bitterness; in this

---
[1] Stoughton, *Religion in England*, 1800–1850, II, p. 22.
[2] For fuller details see Mathieson, *English Church Reform, 1815–1840*.

Thomas Binney took a leading part. He it was who spoke of the Church of England as "a great national evil,"[1] and declared that it destroyed more souls than it saved. This provocative and paradoxical statement he endeavoured to justify, or excuse, by explaining that it only referred to the Establishment not to the Church as a spiritual agency or to its workers. Such a distinction was neither easy to grasp nor always convenient to remember.

The political developments of the period which saw the passing of the Reform Bill and all the agitation which preceded it gave to Nonconformists an opportunity of working against the Church and also of proving their own power and importance. The one thought of the political Dissenter was how he might "down" the Church; and Lord Grey is reported to have said "that the Dissenters had humbugged him; that they told him that they wanted the reformation of the Church, and that he found that they wanted its destruction."[2] The same type of Dissent was greatly encouraged by its successful part in the rejection of the education clauses of the 1843 Factory Act. Greville noted in his diary for November 29th of that year of the Nonconformists that "their success . . . has increased their notions of their own consequence, and nothing will satisfy them now but being put on a level with the Church." To the political Dissenter the Church was merely a vested interest, untrue to its high calling; a means for keeping down Nonconformity and not for Christianizing the country. There was much in past history to justify his attitude and he continued to flourish until the better feelings which existed between Churchmen and Nonconformity modified the bitter feeling between them. To-day one may say that mutual sympathy and understanding has led to the disappearance of the political Dissenter altogether.

The intervention of Nonconformists in politics was not, however, limited to attempts to "down" the Church. From the accession of Victoria onwards they began to play their part in the agitation against the abuses and injustices which affected their countrymen as a whole, quite apart from those

[1] See A. W. Peel, *These Hundred Years*, p. 27.
[2] Quoted by Liddon, *Life of E. B. Pusey*, I, p. 285.

which lay upon them as Dissenters. They had much to do with forming that public opinion which made possible the wealth of beneficial social legislation which was one of the great achievements of the era. Guinness Rogers considers that the prominent part taken by Nonconformist ministers in the Anti-Corn Law agitations marked the "starting point of the public life of the Free Churches. . . . For the first time the voice of Nonconformist ministers was heard in such strength upon affairs which seemed to lie outside their proper province" (*Autobiography*, p. 80).

With the extreme left of Nonconformity relations were more friendly, perhaps because it was not politically minded, and Churchmen of liberal mind were not averse to shewing practical sympathy. In 1838 Bishop Maltby of Durham went so far as to give a donation to a Unitarian chapel in his diocese and to subscribe to a volume of sermons by a Unitarian minister.[1] But such a course, one imagines, was not common.

For the most part Churchmen were content to ignore the attacks of Dissenters, and indeed to ignore them entirely. It is noteworthy that just as Dissent had grown through the neglect of the Clergy, so it tended to decay where the parish priest really tried to do his job in a human and a sympathetic manner. An example may be cited from the early life of Lord Tennyson who records a visit paid by his parents in 1852 to John Rashdall, Vicar of the Priory Church at Malvern, and father of a famous son, the late Dean of Carlisle. He writes: "Rashdall was a man so beloved by his parishioners and so simple and direct in his language from the pulpit that he had emptied the Dissenting Chapels for miles around" (*Alfred, Lord Tennyson*, I, p. 355).

Nonconformist Grievances

We noticed above that Nonconformists were conscious, as they grew in numbers and influence, of those disabilities which the legislation of the Pre-Victorian Age had failed to remove. Two

[1] Liddon, *op. cit.*, I, p. 20, n. 3. It may be well to recall that in the same year Queen Victoria, after consultation with Lord John Russell, agreed to accept the dedication of a Harmony of the Gospels by Dr. Lant Carpenter, a leading Unitarian. She had first to be assured that it was not of a specifically Unitarian character.

grievances stood out above all others—the necessity of paying Church Rates, and exclusion from the Universities. About each of these and the efforts made to remedy them something must now be said.

By the law of the land each parish was obliged to maintain the fabric of its church (apart from the Chancel when there was a rector). This was done by means of a rate, levied at the Easter Vestry and payable by all parishioners. To Nonconformists it seemed unjust and inequitable that they should be compelled to provide for the repair of a structure which they never used, except for marriages and burials, and then only under compulsion. The amount involved was, as a matter of fact, very small but the principle behind it was felt to be important. There were some who held that the charge should come out of the Tithe in spite of the custom to the contrary. In 1835 Lord John Russell's government had proposed to transfer the charge to the Consolidated Fund.

The only remedy which the Dissenters had was to outvote the Churchpeople at the Easter Vestry (which was, of course, open to all ratepayers) so that no rate could be fixed. As early as 1793 the Vestry of St. Peter's, Thetford, had refused to fix a rate. This method now began to be widely adopted.

The most famous case was that of Braintree where in 1837 no rate could be fixed. As the church was falling into disrepair the Churchwardens usurped the functions of the Vestry and themselves levied a rate. This action after much litigation was declared to be illegal. In 1841 the Churchwardens supported by a minority of the Vestry levied a rate; this also was declared illegal by the House of Lords in 1853. The law still held that a parish was responsible for the upkeep of its church, but it afforded no means of enforcing this responsibility if the necessary majority could not be obtained in the Vestry. Nothing remained but to fall back on voluntary effort. Thus the question of levying the rate solved itself. There still remained the case of individual Nonconformists living in parishes where the rate was actually levied. The notorious case again came from Essex, in the person of a cobbler, John Thorogood. This man having refused to pay his rate was in 1839 imprisoned for contempt of court. Several unsuccessful attempts to abolish Church rates altogether were made but it was not until Gladstone's Bill of 1868 that the matter was settled. This Bill permitted a Voluntary Rate to be levied, but allowed no legal power of enforcing payment from those who objected.

The other grievance was exclusion from the ancient Universities of the land which belonged to the Church of England and only members of that body had a right to use them. The Dissenters had a double grievance for their exclusion not only prevented them from having a share in the culture and education which the Universities existed to promote, but it also made it difficult for them to enter various of the learned professions which required a degree in those who practised them. The Nonconformist's only course was to go to a Scottish or continental University.

The exclusion of Nonconformists from Oxford and Cambridge was thus a very serious disability, for it made a cultural, as well as a religious, breach between them and the Church. This did not mean that Nonconformity was without its own culture; on the contrary there were many Nonconformist homes which were fit to be compared with the learned and cultivated country rectories in which the proud Anglican tradition of sound learning was still preserved. Such a one was the parsonage of the Rev. C. M. Birrell, pastor of Pembroke Baptist Chapel, Liverpool. Birrell was a man of rich endowments which he had nobly improved; his wide culture and conversational powers would have graced any Combination Room in Oxford or Cambridge. The home which produced Augustine Birrell, famous as a man of letters and a Cabinet Minister, could not have been lacking in culture. But it was a culture out of the main stream of life and tradition; and Augustine Birrell himself used to confess in later days that it required a great effort to be a Nonconformist, since it involved cutting oneself off, "not from the fountains of holiness, but from the main currents of secular life."[1]

But though this separation of culture and exclusion from the main stream was a serious handicap for many Nonconformists, it enabled the stronger minds to work out their own

[1] Quoted by Lord Morley, *Recollections*, I, p. 150.

fortunes. After the opening of the older Universities in 1871, the separate stream of culture which "for nearly two hundred years" had "flowed parallel to the main current of English scholarship" gradually merged with it. "To those who know them from the inside," wrote Mr. J. H. Wicksteed, "there is nothing insignificant in the Nonconformist backwaters where power was developed for the later fertilization of the great plain of twentieth-century thought."[1] One of the sources which fed this separate stream of culture came from the continent. England, as a whole, especially in the early years of the nineteenth century, remained in a state of comparative isolation from continental scholarship and philosophy.[2] But the Nonconformist who was eager for knowledge and culture, excluded from the public schools and Universities of his own land by the religious barrier, turned to the universities of Germany and Holland. Mr. Wicksteed writes of his father, who studied in Leiden under the great Dutch scholars of his day, and of Herford, who "served a similar apprenticeship in Germany" ; "Both men, throughout their lives, read freely in the literatures of Western and Southern Europe, and turned their critical insight from their own to other literatures, almost unconscious of the passage." [3]

The continued exclusion of Nonconformists had not been accepted without protest even before the Victorian Era, and numerous attempts had been made, even by Churchmen, to gain for them admission. In 1772 a petition was presented to Parliament, signed mainly by graduates of Cambridge,[4] begging that subscription to the Thirty-nine Articles should no longer be required as a condition of matriculation. In the debate which arose over this petition the arguments used on either side were, as F. Warre Cornish has observed, precisely those which were to be advanced in all subsequent discussions of the question until the final abolition of all tests in 1871. They were "the triviality of the Dissenters' grievance, the rights of

[1] In the foreword to C. H. Herford's *Philip Henry Wicksteed*, p. x.
[2] See pp. 132 f. below.
[3] *Op. cit.*, p. x.
[4] Among them were Paley, and Watson, later the notorious non-resident Bishop of Llandaff.

the Church, and the danger to religion; and, on the other side, the inefficiency of the Articles as a system of theology, the absurdity of requiring subscription from boys of fifteen and sixteen, the right and duty of private judgement, the dangers involved by attaching emoluments to the profession of opinions, the duty of enlarging the borders of the Church."[1]

In Cambridge from 1772 onwards Nonconformists had been admitted as students, but before proceeding to a degree they had to sign the Articles.[2] They were not admitted to scholarships or fellowships. At Oxford subscription remained a condition of matriculation, so Nonconformists were entirely excluded.

In March 1834 a body of resident Cambridge graduates, including a future Archbishop of York (Musgrave), a future Bishop (Thirlwall), and a future Dean (Peacock), petitioned Parliament for the removal of all tests before taking degrees. It was followed by a counter-petition with a much more influential backing. Even Cambridge was not yet ready for toleration. In Oxford, from which no petition had ever come, opposition to the admission of Dissenters was very fierce.[3] The same year saw the introduction of a Bill into Parliament to remove tests for degrees. Its supporters recognized that the right to vote, to fellowships and headships of houses, belonged to the Church of England, and would not be claimed by Nonconformists. Its opponents, with deeper insight, held that they would not be content until these too were made available. The Bill passed the Commons after furious and disorderly debates, but it was rejected in the Lords.

Church Building

In order to end this chapter on a note less acrimonious and distasteful than that of controversy over disabilities, we will now consider that remarkable sign of renewed life which could

[1] *History of the English Church*, I, p. 173.

[2] The well-known case of F. D. Maurice is an illustration. He completed his terms but could not, at that stage of his career, decide to accept the Articles. Later, when he became an Anglican instead of taking his Cambridge degree, he went to Oxford and started afresh.

[3] The real cause of the persecution of Hampden (see below pp. 96 f.) was the fact that in 1834 he had challenged Oxford exclusiveness by his *Observations on Religious Dissent*.

be observed in Churchmen and Dissenters alike in this period —the erection of innumerable new places of worship. The Churches a hundred years ago were faced with the same problem as faces them now when huge housing schemes are suddenly launched—the provision for the spiritual needs of the new populations. Then the growth was due to the rush to the towns from the countryside in consequence of the industrial developments. It was not unobserved by religious bodies, but nothing adequate was done. In the reign of George III not a dozen churches were erected in London, whilst the buildings which did exist were greatly neglected.[1]

In May 1814 Howley, Bishop of London, drew the attention of some of the "Orthodox" Churchmen to the grave need of fresh accommodation. In some parts of London there was not seating for one in ten of the parishioners. In the following year John Bowden, a member of this group, approached Lord Liverpool, then Prime Minister, hoping, vainly as it turned out, that Parliament would do something in the matter. Then in 1818 real progress began to be made. The Church Building Society was formed at a meeting in the Freemasons' Tavern under the inspiration of Archdeacon Daubeny and Joshua Watson. It laid down very sound principles for the government of its grants; they were to meet private efforts and not more than a quarter of the total cost was to be given. Schemes providing for free seats were especially encouraged. The same year Parliament provided the sum of £1,000,000 for new churches and allowed parishes to be divided and new ones to be created where necessary. The grant was made partly to counteract Dissent, as Lord Liverpool openly stated;[2] partly on the principle which Gibbon attributed to the Roman magistrates,[3] that religion is useful for the preservation of order. For the Church to receive grants in such circumstances probably retarded its real influence; for religion at once

---

[1] When in 1813 Henry Venn Elliott made a pilgrimage from Cambridge to Yelling, the scene of his grandfather's labours, he found the church almost in ruins, the walls overgrown with creepers, and everything in a state of desolation: Bateman, *Henry Venn Elliott*, pp. 25 ff.

[2] *Parliamentary Debates*, XXXVIII, p. 710.

[3] *Decline and Fall of the Roman Empire*, I, p. 28.

becomes suspected when it is regarded as a sort of "policeman" by those responsible for the government. The workers, for their part, at once dismiss its ministrations as "dope," intended to keep them quiet.

The money provided by the State for new churches was, however, but a small proportion of the total sum raised; between 1813 and 1833 voluntary effort accounted for at least £6,000,000.[1] In some cases the money was unwisely spent in erecting pompous and costly edifices in which little provision was made for those who were unable to rent a pew. When Bishop Blomfield came to London he did great things in the way of getting new churches built in the poorer districts such as Bethnal Green, Islington, and St. Pancras. His expenditure was marked by greater wisdom, though he had a reasonable regard for the beauty and dignity of the buildings which he sanctioned.

Church extension in this period was not confined to the Establishment. The early years of the nineteenth century were a time of chapel building also. The congregations of London and the big towns were quite accustomed to visits from wandering preachers who besought their alms towards some new building scheme. In 1839 J. Angell James urged the Congregationalists to attempt the erection of new chapels as he felt that the Church of England was likely "to build *down* and build *out* Nonconformists."

It is interesting to notice the figures of seating accommodation and of places of worship belonging to the Church and to the two leading Nonconformist denominations according to the Census of 1851. The Church had 14,077 places of worship with sittings for 5,317,915; Methodists of all kinds 11,007 places of worship with 2,194,298 sittings; whilst the Independents had 3,244 places of worship and 1,067,760 sittings. Thus there was a good deal of accommodation available in most districts. But in many cases the new buildings thus erected were but poorly used; they had something of the nature of missionary centres for the education and conversion of the people around them. It is said that of the working men of England in 1856 only 6 per cent went to any place of worship in the country,

[1] F. Warre Cornish, *op. cit.*, I, p. 81.

whilst in the towns the figure was as low as 2 per cent. A not entirely unsympathetic observer has written of this period: "There was much building of new churches in London and elsewhere. . . . But the misery and crime to be dealt with were not of a kind to be remedied by a provision for worship, and it was observable that while the existing churches bore a very small proportion to the population of their districts, they yielded more room than was occupied. Churches come of religion, but religion does not come of churches."[1]

[1] Harriet Martineau. Quoted by F. Warre Cornish, *op. cit.*, I, p. 82.

4

EDUCATION TO 1843

THE subject of Education is so important that it deserves to be considered next in order. On the continent and in Scotland the Reformation had been followed by the creation of a system of elementary schools. In England it had no such sequel and all education remained in the hands of the Church and was given only to those who wished to take advantage of it, so far that is as it could be considered to be available. But it was indeed not very available to most of the poor, and the schools were often ill-managed and really quite unserviceable; but such as they were the Church provided them. In the Middle Ages the Schoolmaster was a kind of minor ecclesiastic; after the Reformation, if he lost his clerical status, he still remained a kind of ecclesiastical official.

In order to complete the survey of Education before 1843, when the idea of a comprehensive national system and the responsibility of the State to provide it first came effectively above the horizon, it will be well, not only to consider elementary education, but that provided by the Universities and the Public Schools.

THE UNIVERSITIES

Since the two Universities of England, Oxford and Cambridge, were open to members of the Church of England only, and, with some few exceptions, those who held teaching offices were compelled to take Holy Orders, the history of these bodies is really part of the history of the Church. And, it may be added, it is a history which does not add to the Church's credit. At the same time it ought to be recognized, that at the beginning of the century the Universities like everything else were suffering from war conditions. The number of students had gone down seriously and desires for reform, which were by no means absent, were for the time held in abeyance.

It may be said that Oxford, to speak of the two institutions separately, touched the lowest depths of inefficiency in the eighteenth century. In it, according to Overton, "professors who never lectured, tutors who never taught, students who never studied, were the rule rather than the exception."[1] But in the very first year of the new century a measure was passed which contained the seed of better things; this statute introduced Public Examinations and was followed by the institution of the Class system by which honours could be obtained by such as were qualified to receive them.[2]

In the years immediately following the end of the war there were great improvements. These came mainly as the result of the efforts of two colleges, Oriel under its Provost, Eveleigh, and Balliol under its Master, Parsons. Cyril Jackson, Dean of Christ Church, also had a hand in bringing about a better state of affairs. Thus from an academic standpoint things began to look up. In religion, which one would have expected to have played a prominent part, there was little to arouse enthusiasm or even approval. The Churchmanship of Oxford was mainly of a political type and was much more concerned to preserve the privileges and possessions of the Church than to use them as a means of promoting spiritual life.

At Cambridge things were certainly better than at Oxford, whether viewed from the academic or the religious standpoint. Cambridge had begun to reform herself earlier than Oxford, and there was a much higher level of religion there owing to the power of the Evangelicals. Men like Isaac Milner, President of Queens' and Dean of Carlisle, Charles Simeon, Fellow of King's and Vicar of Holy Trinity, Professors Farish and Jowett, these made a real impression on the young men who came under their care and influence. Other schools of Churchmanship were also active in the University. There were, among the High Churchmen, Herbert Marsh (later Bishop of Peterborough), Christopher Wordsworth, Master of Trinity, and Hugh James Rose, later to become, for the brief remainder of his life, a leader among the Tractarians. The Liberals were represented by an earnest group under the leadership of Julius Hare, and they included Whewell, afterwards Master of

[1] *English Church in the Nineteenth Century*, p. 219.
[2] For the changes involved see Brodrick, *History of the University of Oxford*, pp. 192 ff

Trinity, R. C. Trench, the future Archbishop of Dublin, and F. D. Maurice. But even in Cambridge the college services were only perfunctorily carried on and were thoroughly unattractive. What was worse, in such circumstances, was that they were compulsory. From the academic point of view Cambridge studies, in all subjects except Mathematics, were greatly handicapped by the absurd regulation that all those who wished to take honours had first to do so in Mathematics. In spite of violent criticism, both within the University and from without, this regulation remained in force until 1850.[1]

Thus both Universities, in the period before the Reforming Commissions of 1850, may be looked upon as "static" rather than "dynamic" in spite of some efforts after reform. Someone once described them, to the delight of Sydney Smith, as "enormous hulks confined with mooring-chains, everything flowing and progressing around them." Sydney Smith himself did not conceal his opinion of the standard of efficiency reached by the two Universities and in a letter to a friend declared that "If men had made no more progress in the common arts of life than they have in education, we should at this moment be dividing our food with our fingers and drinking out of the palms of our hands."[2]

The two Universities were, as we have said, confined to members of the Church of England. They were also, with a few exceptions, for the use of the moneyed classes only. England had nothing to correspond to the opportunities offered to the poor student by the Universities across the border in Scotland, where there was no college system and the students lived in their own lodgings. The summer vacations were long and enabled them to earn money, either by teaching or even by manual labour, to support them during the single session lasting from November to April, which made up the academic year.

Before the accession of Victoria something had been done to provide a cheaper University education and one moreover that was free from any kind of religious test. In 1828 University College, London, was opened. It was a partial realization of

[1] See J. Bass Mullinger, *History of the University of Cambridge*, pp. 188 ff.
[2] See Hesketh Pearson, *The Smith of Smiths*, p. 27.

Bentham's dream of a purely secular education and no provision was made for religious teaching;[1] and not only were there to be no tests for the students, but the professors and lecturers were to be equally unrestrained.[2] Among its supporters were Lord Brougham and Campbell the poet; whilst the council included Zachary Macaulay, Grote, and James Mill. The exclusion of religion from this new foundation led to the formation of King's College, as a place where the young men of London might be brought up under Church principles.[3]

The new establishment in London was not regarded favourably by Oxford, and in 1834 the University petitioned against any charter being granted to it. Brodrick confesses that "the instinctive hostility of Churchmen to a non-religious academical body was quickened by a less honourable jealousy of a rival institution to be invested with the power of granting degrees" (*History of the University of Oxford*, p. 189).[4] But the advocates of the new University were strong and determined and the rejection of the University Tests Bill had finally disappointed their hopes that Dissenters might after all be allowed to have a share in the ancient Universities. The charter was granted in 1836. The new University of London was to be an examining body with the power to grant degrees, but the teaching was to be undertaken by the colleges. The recent foundations, University College and King's College, were now incorporated in it.

In the North provision for the higher education of the people began to be made by the Church, and in 1831 a scheme for employing some of the vast revenues of the see of Durham for this purpose was drafted under the inspiration of Bishop Van Mildert. It is worth noticing that Cromwell had contemplated, in 1657, using the Castle for a University, but the opposition of Oxford to the scheme had proved too strong.

[1] When Owens College was founded in Manchester in 1845 one of the conditions was that no religious instruction was to be given within its walls.
[2] See Leslie Stephen, *The English Utilitarians*, II, p. 32.
[3] Lord Shaftesbury regarded it as "erecting an embankment against the overflow of irreligion": see Hodder, *Life and Letters*, I, pp. 102 f.
[4] Sir Charles Wetherell declared that the scorn and contempt of mankind should prevent the new University from granting degrees: T. H. S. Escott, *Great Victorians*, p. 28.

If a University had been founded in the North before railway travel had been invented, it might have become quite strong: but facilities for reaching the older Universities robbed Durham of some of those who might have adorned it. None the less it soon made a position for itself and Routh tried to compensate for the past opposition of his University by leaving to it his Library in 1855. One of the objects of the new University had been to provide clergymen for the North; but with unusual insight the promoters had also made provision from the very inception for courses in mining and civil engineering.

THE PUBLIC SCHOOLS

In these too the Church of England had a monopoly of religious influence, but as in the case of the Universities no worthy attempt was made to use the opportunity.[1] In most schools "religion was treated as a necessary propriety rather than as a living influence."[2] The actual teaching of religious truths was strangely neglected and even Sunday worship was often confined to attendance at the local parish church. The day of School Chapels was not yet.[3]

From the point of view of scholarship things were not very much better. The public schools did, as a matter of fact, produce good scholars; but they were the exception. Gladstone said of the Eton of his own schooldays: "a boy might learn much, or learn nothing; but he could not learn superficially."[4] They also produced a succession of great men to serve God in Church and State, as the bidding prayer has it. But the public schoolboy was perhaps too fond of keeping to the broad highway and of leaving pioneering and originality to those who had not had his advantages. Sydney Smith, although he

[1] "At the beginning of the century," wrote Liddon, "the Church had no adequate idea of the splendid opportunities which Divine Providence still offered her in the public schools of this country." *Life of E. B. Pusey*, I, p. 17.
[2] *Op. cit.*, I, p. 11.
[3] Arnold was delighted that Rugby was an exception to this. On the religious conditions of the two leading public schools of the country see H. C. Maxwell Lyte, *History of Eton College*, p. 370, and P. M. Thornton, *Harrow School and its Surroundings*, pp. 241 ff. When Lord Shaftesbury was at Harrow no boy ever thought of attending the Holy Communion.
[4] See G. W. E. Russell, *Fifteen Chapters of Autobiography*, p. 312.

was a Wykhamist and had had a not undistinguished school career, hated public schools and "never missed an opportunity of pointing out the criminal abuses and absurdities of public school life."[1] He challenged even their ability to produce eminent men, claiming that the leading names in every art and science, from Shakespeare to Dr. Johnson, were those of men who had received their education in other ways. The same statement, in a different form, has more recently been made by Lord Bryce, who says: "In England it has become the fashion to assume that nearly all the persons who have shone in public life have been educated in one of the great public schools, and that they owe to its training their power of dealing with men and assemblies. Such a superstition is sufficiently refuted by the examples of men like Pitt, Macaulay, Bishop Wilberforce, Disraeli, Cobden, Bright, and Cecil Rhodes" (*Studies in Contemporary Biography*, p. 4). Probably the public schools were, before the reforming movement associated with the name of Arnold of Rugby, in much the same state of inefficiency as the Universities. Life in them was very rough and even vicious, though Lord Shaftesbury found Harrow in 1813 a vast improvement on the private school where he had spent his earlier years. "It was the beginning of a new life to him; whatever might happen now in vacation time he would at least be able to look forward with pleasure to his return to school."[2] The number of subjects studied was very restricted and consisted mainly, if not entirely, of the ancient classics of Greece and Rome. But this "large, legendary literature" as Mr. Chesterton has called it (*G. F. Watts*, p. 34), supplemented as it was in the early years of the century by the novels of Walter Scott,[3] did produce, in spite of Sydney Smith's opinion, a surprisingly large number who achieved greatness.

The public school, as known to the later nineteenth century, was really a new creation, and owed itself largely to economic causes, to that industrial revolution which created the new type of aristocrat, the industrial magnate. It was to provide

[1] Hesketh Pearson, *The Smith of Smiths*, pp. 23 f.
[2] Hodder, *Life and Work of the Seventh Earl of Shaftesbury*, I, p. 43.
[3] Ruskin loved to call himself "a violent Tory of the old school; Walter Scott's school, that is to say, and Homer's." See *Praeterita*, I, p. 1.

education for the sons of this class that it sprang into new life. None the less Arnold led the way. In 1827, the date of his appointment to Rugby, the spirit of criticism which was being turned on all existing institutions was being applied amongst others to education, and no doubt the prediction of Hawkins, the Provost of Oriel, that if appointed Arnold would change the face of education in England[1] weighed heavily in his favour even with so conservative a body as the school governors. To reform their establishment was a necessary way of preserving it.

The prediction was fulfilled to the letter. For not only did Arnold reform Rugby but he inspired other great headmasters to undertake similar tasks; sometimes in more difficult circumstances, because faced as Arnold had not been by old and deep-rooted traditions. Moberly's work at Winchester was confessedly so inspired. For he had examined Rugby and recognized what was being done "in raising the tone, religious and moral, of a great public school."[2] We cannot here enter into Arnold's methods and changes; they are described in that life which an eminent educational authority, Sir Joshua Fitch, regarded "as the most solid and enduring contribution to educational literature produced in England in the nineteenth century."[3] It was a great achievement, but perhaps a little hard on those who had to undergo the experiment; for his own intensity was apt to be a heavy weight on youthful shoulders and to introduce them too soon to a consciousness of vast outside responsibilities. Professor Sellar once remarked to Matthew Arnold, who had been a contemporary at Rugby: "What a good man Walrond is!" "Ah," sighed back Matthew Arnold, "we were all so good at Rugby." "Yes," returned Sellar, "but he kept it up."[4]

Thus the condition of higher education, so far as the public schools were concerned, was no better than that of the Universities. It has even been suggested by some observers that it had never reached lower levels from the days of King

---

[1] Stanley, *Life of Arnold* (Teachers' Edition), p. 49.
[2] C. A. E. Moberly, *Dulce Domum*, p. 31.
[3] See Preface to the Teachers' Edition of Stanley, *Life of Arnold*, p. v.
[4] Quoted in Lewis and Campbell, *Life of Benjamin Jowett*, II, p. 354, n. 1.

Alfred.[1] The other secondary schools of the country were just as little qualified to meet the needs of the growing generation. There were a number of ancient endowed Grammar Schools; these quite often were poorly attended and the endowments went to swell the income of non-resident masters. In not a few cases they were run as a side-line by incumbents or their curates. In some cases similar schools were started by Nonconformist ministers as a means of supplementing their income or as their sole occupation. With some exceptions they attracted only an inferior type of master and were often rough, even more so than the public schools of their day, with much bullying and cruelty. They justified Crabbe's condemnation:

"Oh! there's a wicked little world in schools,
 Where mischief's suffered and oppression rules;
 Where mild, quiescent children oft endure
 What a long placid life shall fail to cure."

There were also a number of Nonconformist Academies of a more official standing, attempts to provide secondary education for children from better class Nonconformist homes, and also nurseries for future ministers.[2] A great step in meeting the needs of the growing class of wealthy Nonconformist families was the foundation in 1807 of Mill Hill, a public school for Nonconformist boys which was started by the Congregationalists with some co-operation from the Baptists.

ELEMENTARY EDUCATION

Before the nineteenth century the only means of education for the poorer classes were Charity schools, most of which were provided by the Church. In the first fifty years of its existence the S.P.C.K. had founded no less than 2,000, and it is said that in the century following the death of Queen Anne the number of people who could read and write increased

---

[1] Cf. F. S. Marvin, *A Century of Hope*, p. 204.

[2] For a description of life in such institutions see Benjamin Gregory, *Autobiographical Recollections*, pp. 77 ff., and J. Guinness Rogers, *Autobiography*, pp. 36 ff.

fifty-fold.[1] Education received a slight stimulus from the system of a certain Dr. Bell, who in 1797 introduced into this country methods which he had worked out in Madras. Under his system the older children were used to teach the younger, and so great economies were possible. About the same time the same method began to be employed by a young Quaker, Joseph Lancaster, in a school which he started in Borough Road, Southwark. Lancaster apparently did not know of Dr. Bell and his system when he began his work; later on hearing of it he applied for advice and guidance, going down to Swanage, where Bell had been Rector since 1801, for this purpose.

Lancaster's work, perhaps from its more romantic surroundings and greater accessibility, attracted much more attention than that of Dr. Bell—it was even taken into royal favour by George III. But unfortunately his attitude towards religious teaching—he advocated what was later to be known as the undenominational brand—and his egotism led to serious controversy. In the end the advocates of Lancaster's system founded a society (in 1808), the British and Foreign School Society;[2] those of Dr. Bell followed with the National Society in 1811, in order as it was said to check "the Goliath of the Schismatics."

The founders of the National Society included Joshua Watson and Norris. They carried on their work with an efficiency and power of organizing which the Evangelicals, whose special forte it was, could hardly have bettered. By this and other means the responsibility of providing education was brought home to many of the clergy, and they rose to meet it. A Roman Catholic writer has admitted that any stigma which attached to the Church of England for its neglect of education up to 1800 was removed by the efforts of the following years.[3] The subject of educating the poor was not one which commended itself to the laity; many of them would have agreed with Lord Melbourne that it was futile if not positively dangerous.[4] The

[1] *History of British Baptists*, p. 262.
[2] Its name up to 1814 was the Royal Lancastrian Society.
[3] Murphy, *The Catholic Church in England and Wales*, p. 69.
[4] See Strachey, *Queen Victoria*, p. 55.

country gentlemen and the farmers in particular were of this opinion, and some, I believe, are still. In spite of apathy or opposition, steps began to be taken for making a more adequate provision than seemed possible by merely voluntary efforts, although there was for some time no suggestion that education should be made compulsory.

In 1802 the Factory Bill of Sir Robert Peel had required that children working in factories should receive instruction in reading, writing, and arithmetic. Five years later Whitbread got a Bill through the Commons which would have provided free education for all poor children in England. It was thrown out in the Lords by a majority which included fifteen bishops,[1] partly because its provisions for religious education were considered unsatisfactory, partly because the scheme itself was held to be inadequate.

If the nobility and country gentry considered that education was not necessary or even advisable for the poor, another school of thought was growing up in the early years of the century which held views exactly the opposite. This school of thought, the best known of whose leaders was Lord Brougham, believed that the great disease was ignorance; like Socrates they tended to identify knowledge and virtue and saw in education a solution for all the problems that beset the race. For a time they had great influence, but they were lacking in imagination and people began to tire of the cry of "march-of-mind";[2] whilst the secular tone of the movement naturally alienated Churchmen. It was from this school, however, that the first attempt to secure a comprehensive scheme of national education was to come. In 1820 Brougham himself introduced a Bill to this end. Its provisions were based on the findings of a Select Committee—incidentally he gave high praise to the clergy for their co-operation in providing the necessary information. It was to be essentially a Church system, the teachers were to be Churchmen, and to be licensed by the incumbent who was to supervise the curriculum; as a sop to Dissenters the catechism was not to be taught. This Bill although it aroused some interest was dropped after its first

---

[1] Romilly, *Memoirs*, II, p. 222.
[2] See Morley, *Life of W. E. Gladstone*, I, p. 156.

reading. A more successful effort followed in 1833 when Roebuck, at that time a Benthamite, with the support of Grote, the famous banker-historian, brought in another Bill. It was more successful in so far as the government of the day, through Lord Althorp, the Chancellor of the Exchequer, was stirred to do something. This took the form of a grant of £20,000 from public funds which was divided between the British and Foreign School Society and the National Society.[1]

The next important event was the creation, in 1839, of the Education Committee of the Privy Council. This Committee was to have its own staff of officials, and may be regarded as the first step towards establishing government supervision of education. There was at the time no suggestion that there should be a uniform type of school or that the State should itself provide education; but it was a step on the way towards such provision, especially as it was accompanied by the ruling that all schools receiving government grants were to be open to government inspection.

One weakness of all the schemes advanced during the first forty years of the century was the meagre notions held by their promoters of the qualifications necessary in those who should be entrusted with the instruction of the young. Even Tom Paine, an advanced thinker in so many directions, seems to have supposed that a few old people in each village, apparently without any special training, would suffice for this purpose.[2] The need for the proper training of teachers was first grasped by the National Society which in 1839 decided to establish Training Colleges. The first College, for men teachers, was St. Mark's, Chelsea, opened in 1841; while a College for women, at Whitelands, followed very soon. This example was taken up in many parts of England, usually on a diocesan basis, and some thirty training colleges were eventually built. The task of training the future teachers was, at this stage, a very arduous one, for many of those who offered had themselves first to be educated. The remuneration offered for teachers in elementary schools was so low that those already

---

[1] The National Society, which had nearly 700 schools, received £11,000; the British and Foreign Schools Society, which had less than 200, had the other £9,000.   [2] *The Rights of Man*, p. 132.

educated were not attracted to the profession. The candidates came as a rule from the small shopkeeping and labouring classes.

The next advocate of national education was Lord Ashley, later famous as the seventh Earl of Shaftesbury. He moved a resolution in February 1843 begging the Queen to "take to her instant and serious consideration the best means of diffusing the benefits and blessings of a moral and religious education among the working classes of her people."[1] At this time more than a million children were receiving no education at all, and their state of ignorance was appalling. When Disraeli published *Sybil* in 1845 he based his description of the condition of the poorer classes on the evidence of Blue Books: and it may be taken as authentic, although in the form of fiction. Even the famous case of the wretched girl who prided herself on the belief "in our Lord Pontius Pilate who was crucified to save our sins, and in Moses, Goliath, and the rest of the Apostles"[2] had many counterparts in real life. The need for training in moral and religious principles was brought home to the general public by the risings in Lancashire and Yorkshire when the mob gained temporary control and revealed the brutish ignorance of the lower classes.

In response to Lord Ashley's appeal the Queen gave her gracious consent, and on March 8th of the same year Sir James Graham introduced a Factory Bill which contained educational clauses. By these every factory was to have a chaplain, and the catechism and the litany were to be taught. The priest of the parish was to be the principal trustee, and teachers were to be approved by the Bishop. These proposals were vigorously opposed by the Dissenters as giving public money to support denominational teaching and they held a number of meetings in the large towns. The Roman Catholics also objected to the Bill, whilst an attempt to meet the wishes of the Nonconformists alienated many Churchmen. In the end the education clauses in the Bill were allowed to drop.

None the less the need was more clearly recognized and the Church at once began the attempt to provide more schools;

---

[1] See Hodder, *Life of Lord Shaftesbury*, I, p. 452.
[2] *Sybil* (Bradenham Ed.), p. 194.

EDUCATION TO 1843

a subscription list was opened, headed by the Queen and Sir Robert Peel.[1] The Nonconformists for their part raised large sums. Public opinion was not yet ripe for a compulsory system, but many children remained uneducated, especially in the towns, in spite of the increased efforts under the voluntary system. The difficulty of the latter was to raise funds for the ordinary running expenses; an emergency could generally be met, and schools built, but the training and payment of teachers and the upkeep of buildings was another matter.

In concluding this chapter a few words ought to be added on the subject of the Nonconformists and education. It was for them a real difficulty. On the one hand their resources were strained to keep up their chapels and to pay for their ministers; on the other there was a real difference of opinion among them on the subject of accepting government grants. At the beginning of the reign they were for the most part sending their children to the British schools, where such were available; but already the feeling was growing that something more definite should be done. In 1840 Dr. Matheson put forward the ideal of a day-school for every chapel. There was as yet no welcome for any kind of government scheme of education—probably because the control of the Church was feared—and in 1843 a Conference of Congregationalists affirmed that it was not the duty of the State to educate its citizens. This resolution was followed up by strenuous efforts to continue the voluntary system, and by 1846 the denomination had built a hundred new schools and adapted nearly fifty others. But the difficulties were too great. It was not merely a matter of providing buildings, teachers had to be found and trained as well. Although the Baptists and Congregationalists might hold out against government grants the British and Foreign School Society was already receiving them, and its schools were being used by Nonconformists up and down the country; whilst the Methodists, in this as in other things different from their fellow Nonconformists, were quite willing to accept such aids. The whole subject was, in the coming years, to be faced again and definite conclusions reached. But these must be reserved for a later consideration.[2]

[1] See *Frederick Temple*, I, p. 74.   [2] See Chapter 16 below.

5

THE OXFORD MOVEMENT TO 1845

THE story of this great Movement has often been told, and, after the mass of new literature which was generated by the Centenary celebrations in 1933, it may be perhaps unseemly once again to describe it. But its importance was so great, and its effects so widespread, not merely within the Church in which it arose, but on religion in England in general, that the attempt must be made.

Newman always dated the beginning of the Movement from Keble's Assize Sermon on July 14, 1833. But he himself had done much to prepare the way by his sermons in St. Mary's. These had been exceedingly effective in creating an atmosphere in which the new teaching could grow and thrive. In July 1833 he had just returned from a tour with Hurrell Froude to the Mediterranean, and the thought had come to him, as he mused on the unsatisfactory state of religion in England and the weakness of the Church, "that deliverance is wrought, not by the many but by the few, not by bodies but by persons," and, as a sequel, that he himself "had a mission."[1]

THE EARLY LEADERS

John Keble, to whose sermon the origin of the Movement was traced, was a very remarkable man. He went up to Oxford with a scholarship to Corpus Christi when only fourteen years old. Five years later he was a Fellow of Oriel. His character was distinguished by intensity and by the possession of unshakable convictions. Modest and retiring in things concerning himself, he was zealous and even arrogant when first principles were at stake; and, like Hurrell Froude, was not afraid to press such principles to their conclusions. He owed much to his father, who had not only educated him until his going

---

[1] *Apologia pro Vita Sua*, p. 38 (Pocket Edition). For the thought, cf. Creighton's statement that religion is always decaying amongst the many and being revived by individuals.

to Oxford, but had instilled those Church principles from which he was never to waver. Keble was a natural conservative, being in this the opposite of Newman, and was averse to change of any kind. Liddon said of him that "his faith in God's presence and guidance made all high-handed self-willed action on man's part appear more or less irreverent."[1] Had he found life in the Church of England impossible he would not, like Newman or Manning, have gone over to Rome, but, like Ken, have retired into isolation.

Newman had begun life as an Evangelical, and to the end he had a strong Evangelical strain in his outlook. There was in him a kind of double strand which can be seen from his basing his belief in God upon direct apprehension, and yet regarding religion as dogma. Thus experience and tradition stood side by side. He readily admitted even in his Roman days that "he almost owed his soul" to Thomas Scott, and that it was from Milner's *Church History* that he had obtained his first knowledge of the writings of the Fathers, and even that the doctrine of Baptismal Regeneration had come to him after studying a work by Archbishop Sumner. For a time Newman gave himself up to the influence of the acute minds of the Oriel common-room—he had been elected a Fellow in 1822—until he awoke with a start to find himself drifting into Liberalism. His first contact with the Movement, or rather with those who were preparing the way for it, came about through Hurrell Froude, a pupil of Keble. Froude was so remarkable a person and exercised so potent an influence over both Keble and Newman that more must be said of him.

According to Newman he was "a bold rider, as on horseback, so also in his speculations" (*Apologia*, p. 136). This was certainly true, and his audacious and uncompromising utterances attracted much attention and served to make the Movement known. He was not so much a leader himself—his delicate health, for one thing, was against this—but an inspirer of others, a gad-fly to sting into action. The Journals which he left behind him suggest a morbid and unhealthy temperament, but as in the case of Henry Martyn, whom he resembled in not a few ways, this must be modified by the testimony of

[1] *Life of E. B. Pusey*, II, p. 29.

contemporaries to his bright and lovable nature.[1] Perhaps the most striking estimate of his character came from the skilful pen of J. B. Mozley; it deserves quoting for its own sake. "His intercourse with earth and nature seemed to cut through them, like uncongenial steel, rather than mix and mingle with them. Yet the polished blade smiled as it went through. The grace and spirit with which he adorned this outward world, and seemed to an undiscerning eye to love it, were but something analogous in him to the easy tone of men in high life, whose good-nature to inferiors is the result either of their disinterested benevolence or sublime unconcern. In him the severe sweetness of the life divine not so much rejected as disarmed those potent glows and attractions of the life natural; a high good temper civilly evaded and disowned them. The monk by nature, the born aristocrat of the Christian sphere, passed them clean by with inimitable ease; marked his line and shot clear beyond them, into the serene ether, toward the far-off light, toward that needle's point on which ten thousand angels and all heaven move."

Froude differed from the other leaders as from Newman himself in his early days by his more sympathetic attitude towards the Church of Rome. One of his last letters to Newman, before his death in 1836, contained the following advice: "I must enter another protest against your cursing and swearing. What good can it do? And I call it uncharitable to an excess."[2] Had he lived (the question has often been raised), would he have followed, or preceded, his friend to Rome, or would he have remained loyal to the Church of England? The point is one of interest, but, in the circumstances of the case, hardly capable of any satisfactory solution; each man will prefer to treat it according to his own special predilections.[3]

THE DEVELOPMENT OF THE MOVEMENT

Having given some slight idea of the personalities of the earlier leaders, we must now turn back to trace the course of

[1] So sane a Christian as E. L. Hicks, late Bishop of Lincoln, was moved by reading Froude's Journals to start one of his own: see J. H. Fowler, *Edward Lee Hicks*, p. 11.   [2] Quoted Newman, *Apologia pro Vita Sua*, p. 136.
[3] For an interesting account of his life see L. I. Guiney, *Hurrell Froude*.

events. Keble in his Assize Sermon had condemned State interference as a sign of National Apostasy. Before the end of July 1833—a month in which Newman, full of energy and conscious of a divine mission, had returned from abroad—a conference had met at Hadleigh, the Suffolk rectory of Hugh James Rose. Out of the meeting, which Keble and Newman had not attended—they had little faith in such gatherings—arose an Association of Friends of the Church. Though this had the support of the leaders it came to very little; it was too cold and official, and its resolutions and motions were not calculated to arouse enthusiasm. This, however, could not be said of the Tracts which began to appear in the following September. These came, for the most part, from the pen of Newman himself, including the first and the fatal last one, and his spirit, though not his style, gleams through them all. They were intended to alarm and startle, as one might arouse those living in a burning house; and they succeeded in their purpose. Later, when Dr. Pusey joined the Movement,[1] they took on a more serious character, and some of them were long theological treatises.[2] Those which aroused the most criticism, before No. 90, were 80 and 87. Their subject was "Reserve in Communicating Religious Knowledge," and they were the work, not of an extremist, but of Isaac Williams, a man of a poetic and gentle nature. His arguments would nowadays be accepted by most thoughtful people; for reserve in religious teaching has continually to be practised, and the method seems to be accepted by our Lord Himself when He told the disciples that He had many things to tell them which they

---

[1] It snould be remembered that Pusey did not come into the Movement until it was well on its way. He then gave to it, in Newman's words: "a position and a name" . . . for he was a Professor and Canon of Christ Church, and had much influence from his family connexions. From 1840 onwards the name "Puseyism" became the popular title of the Movement, and took the place of "Newmanism," or "Newmania" as cynical opponents called it: see Liddon, *Life of E. B. Pusey*, II, p. 139.

[2] How far they converted outsiders to their views cannot, of course, entirely be known. But the case of Robert Gregory, a member of a leading Nonconformist family, who became a Churchman through reading them (later to be Dean of St. Paul's), must by no means have been unique: see *Autobiography of Robert Gregory*, pp. 4 f.

were not yet ready to receive (John xvi. 12). That these Tracts should have been picked out for an attack of peculiar virulence is a strange and revealing fact. In the prevailing atmosphere of ignorance and suspicion they excited fierce opposition. Nos. 80 and 87 were published in 1838. Three years later came the epoch-making No. 90.

Before going on to consider this Tract and its effects mention must be made of two earlier events which stirred up antagonism against the Tractarians and prepared for them a determined body of opposition. These events were the Hampden Case of 1836 and the publication of Froude's *Remains* in 1838.

The former case arose over the appointment of R. D. Hampden to be Regius Professor of Divinity in 1836. Four years before he had delivered a course of Bampton Lectures of some obscurity and ambiguity. But no one had taken any notice of them. For some of his information he had gone to Blanco White, an ex-Roman priest well on the way towards the Unitarianism which he was later to adopt.[1] When Hampden became Professor, however, these Lectures were examined by a few ill-disposed persons, Newman among them, and extracts published of what seemed an heretical character. Hampden's real offence was that he had written in favour of the relaxation of subscription, and though the Tractarians took a leading part in opposing him, they were by no means alone. In between the Lectures and the appointment to the Chair of Divinity Hampden had been Professor of Moral Philosophy and it had seemed natural to Lord Melbourne, with whom the appointment rested, to prefer him. He had been assured of his orthodoxy by Thirlwall, Bishop of Llandaff.[2] One important fact about the earlier professorship has not, I think, received the attention which it deserves. Hampden only came forward at the last moment as a candidate and up to his appearance it seemed as if Newman was certain of the post.[3] One is tempted to ask what would have been the future of Newman had he been elected and given himself up to the duties of this professorship? What also if the protest against Hampden had never

---

[1] He had some influence on James Martineau: see J. Estlin Carpenter *James Martineau*, p. 162.
[2] *Letters of J. B. Mozley*, pp. 52 ff.   [3] *Op. cit.*, pp. 38 ff.

been required? As it was, this last action was quite ineffective, but it left bad feeling behind it and the Liberals were only too ready to seize an opportunity for retaliation.[1]

The trouble over Froude's *Remains* was due to a lack of judgement on the part of Keble and Newman which was almost the only mistake which they made. Although the Journals of Henry Martyn had been published in 1837 England was not yet in a position to welcome the exposure of spiritual strivings and self-questionings. Moreover, there was a vast difference between the two books. Both might seem to be the productions of morbid and over-scrupulous minds; but whereas Martyn's views were essentially such as his countrymen would approve, those of Froude were startling, and subversive of existing ideas. Even Gladstone, who might have been expected to welcome them, was annoyed by "the rash intemperate censures pronounced upon the Reformers."[2] What was perhaps more damaging to Tractarian prestige was Froude's strange lack of any sense of humour, or perhaps the lack of that commodity in those who allowed some of his remarks to appear in print. The world made merry over his penitence and contrition for having glanced to see "whether goose came on the table for dinner." Samuel Wilberforce, who had been the editor of Henry Martyn's Journals, notes in his diary for March 17, 1838: "Read a little of Froude's Journals. They are most instructive to me; will exceedingly discredit Church principles, and show an amazing want of Christianity, so far. They are Henry Martyn unChristianized."

THE ROMEWARD DRIFT

To its original leaders the Oxford Movement had been a rallying to the defence of the Church against the aggressions of the State, and an attempt to revive doctrines which were part of the Church's heritage, but obscured and neglected in its actual life and teaching. Such doctrines were to most of them

---

[1] Hampden was condemned by the University or, rather, his writings. Many of those who voted in the majority (494 against 74) had never even read what they condemned; the whole thing was the result of panic and made many on reflection feel ashamed of their gullibility; this feeling did the Tractarians no good. [2] Morley, *Life of W. E. Gladstone*, I, p. 61.

nothing novel, for they claimed to have learned them from the lips of their parents. As the Movement developed, however, souls more ardent and reckless than Keble and Pusey were drawn in and brought with them doctrines which were much more akin to Roman accretions on the Catholic Faith than to the teaching, for example, of the great Caroline divines. The glamour of the Mother-Church of Western Christendom blinded their eyes to the humble virtues of the Church of their baptism, and even, one is afraid, to the claims of loyalty and common honesty.

Newman himself has noted this development. He says: "A new school of thought was rising, as is usual in doctrinal enquiries, and was sweeping the original party of the movement aside, and was taking its place.... These men cut into the original movement at an angle, fell across its line of thought, and then set about turning that line in its own direction" (*Apologia*, p. 181).

Among these newcomers was W. G. Ward. Ward had come up to Oxford a disciple of Arnold and a keen radical; but soon after his election to a Fellowship at Balliol in November 1834—Tait, the future Archbishop, was elected on the same day—he came under the influence of Newman. Thomas Mozley says that he retained "the intellectual force, the irrefragible logic, the absolute self-confidence, and the headlong impetuosity of the Rugby school" (*Reminiscences*, II, p. 5). It was not, however, until the autumn of 1838 that he openly came out as a Newmanite. His adhesion coincided with that of a number of other Roman sympathizers.[1] Two of the more advanced of these wilder spirits wrote to the *Univers* in April 1841: "We love with unfeigning affection the Apostolic See. We are destined to bring many wandering sheep back to the knowledge of the truth. Let us remain quiet for some years, till by God's blessing the ears of Englishmen become accustomed to hear the name of Rome pronounced with reverence." While Ward himself "felt bound to retain his external communion with the English Church because he believed that he was bringing many of its members towards Rome, and to unite himself with the Church which he loved, if by so doing he

[1] *W. G. Ward and the Oxford Movement*, p. 136.

thwarted the larger and fuller victory of the truth, seemed a course both indefensible and selfish."[1]

Newman was greatly influenced by these younger men, although, at the command of his Bishop, he did his best to restrain them. It was partly in order to induce them to remain loyal to the Church of England that his famous Tract 90 was written. In it he tried to show that the Thirty-nine Articles were "patient of a Catholic interpretation." It contained the following passage: "That there are real difficulties to a Catholic Christian in the ecclesiastical position of our Church at this day, no one can deny; but the statements of the Articles are not in the number, and it may be right at the present moment to insist upon this."

Immediately there was a protest from four tutors including Tait of Balliol and H. B. Wilson of St. John's. This protest brought matters to a crisis.[2] Newman himself, although he felt that he had been misunderstood, never complained of their action which he regarded as honest and likely, on the whole, to be beneficial. But the tutors were followed by the Bishops. Bagot of Oxford requested Newman to stop the issue of further Tracts, thus No. 90 was the last of the series. Other Bishops were more alarmed and less considerate; Phillpotts of Exeter, who was a stout Churchman, condemned its tone as "offensive and indecent and absurd . . . as well as incongruous and unjust" (*Charges*, pp. 31 f.).

To the Movement, as a whole, the publication of the Tract was a disaster, for it revealed plainly to the Church and Nation the real direction in which it was travelling. Outsiders were not at pains to distinguish between the various groups within it and thenceforward the Tractarians "came under an official ban and stigma."[3] For Newman himself the blow was overwhelming and his confidence in the Church of England, already weakening, began to desert him. If the Catholic faith was inconsistent with the Articles where was he?

The Movement received three further blows in quick suc-

[1] *Op. cit.*, p. 356.
[2] "The four Tutors did but lay a match to the tinder which had been long preparing." Davidson and Benham, *Life of A. C. Tait*, I, p. 83.
[3] Church, *The Oxford Movement*, p. 296.

cession. In January 1842 Isaac Williams, who was the obvious successor to John Keble as Professor of Poetry, had to withdraw his name owing to Anti-Tractarian prejudice. There followed, in May 1843, the suspension of Pusey from preaching within the University for two years on account of the views expressed in a sermon on the Eucharist. The censure and degradation of Ward on February 13, 1845, ought perhaps not to be reckoned as a Tractarian defeat,[1] for Ward was so obviously Roman in sympathy, and his reception into the Roman Church soon after his condemnation was the natural end to his career as an Anglican.[2] In the course of the proceedings in Convocation Ward made an eloquent defence in English. As he walked away afterwards with Tait, the latter ventured to express his admiration for the peroration in particular. Ward made the candid, but unexpected reply: "I am glad you liked it. These rhetorical efforts are out of my line, but Stanley said there should be something of the kind. He wrote it for me."[3] At the same meeting of Convocation an attempt was made to condemn Tract 90. It was, however, rendered abortive by the veto of the proctors, and, very significantly, was never renewed.[4]

NEWMAN

In what is perhaps the most moving and sincere of all religious autobiographies since St. Augustine wrote his *Confessions*, Newman has recorded his gradual alienation from the Church of his baptism. By means of a number of arresting images he tells how the happy confidence of his early years was gradually overcast by doubt and suspicion. Although he

---

[1] Dean Church, however, regarded it as "the final defeat and conclusion of the first stage of the movement." *The Oxford Movement*, p. 393.
[2] Ward gave public notice of this event a month before it happened in order "not to take people by surprise." See *Letters of J. B. Mozley*, p. 166.
[3] *Life of A. C. Tait*, I, p. 130.
[4] Tait, who was now Headmaster of Rugby, had written a pamphlet in which he deplored this attempt. If successful, he affirmed, it would operate to the exclusion of the best, because the most conscientious, men, and unduly narrow the Church of England. *Op. cit.*, I, p. 128. Other Liberals, Stanley, Lake, etc., were in agreement with him.

might shake them off for the moment, like the man who has seen a ghost he was no longer the same. Then at the end of 1841 began that lingering "death-bed" which was to culminate in his reception into the Roman Church in October 1845. On September 18, 1843, he resigned the living of St. Mary's, Oxford, and on the following Sunday preached at Littlemore his last sermon as an Anglican. This sermon, one of the most pathetic ever delivered, he called "The Parting of Friends." The concluding apostrophe to the Church of his birth gave utterance to the perplexity and sorrow that filled many hearts at that critical moment. "O my mother," he cried, "whence is this unto thee, that thou hast good things poured upon thee and canst not keep them, and bearest children, yet darest not own them? Why hast thou not the skill to use their services, nor the heart to rejoice in their love? How is it that whatever is generous in purpose, and tender or deep in devotion, thy flower and thy promise, falls from thy bosom and finds no home within thine arms? Who hath put this note upon thee to have 'a miscarrying womb and dry breasts,' to be strange to thine own flesh, and thine eye cruel towards thy little ones? Thine own offspring, the fruit of thy womb, who love thee and would toil for thee, thou dost gaze upon with fear, as though a portent, or thou dost loathe as an offence—at best thou dost but endure, as if they had no claim but on thy patience, self-possession and vigilance, to be rid of them as easily as thou mayest. Thou makest them 'stand all the day idle,' as the very condition of thy bearing with them; or thou biddest them be gone, where they will be more welcome; or thou sellest them for nought to the stranger that passes by. And what wilt thou do in the end thereof?"[1] Dean Gregory, who was present, has told us that there was not a dry eye in the church; Pusey, Morris (who was to follow Newman), and others sobbed unrestrainedly. When the sermon was ended "Newman descended from the pulpit, took off his hood, and threw it over the altar rails, and it was felt by those present that this was the mark that he had ceased to be a teacher in the Church of England."[2] So ended the Anglican

[1] Quoted by Liddon, *Life of E. B. Pusey*, II, p. 375.
[2] *Autobiography of Robert Gregory*, pp. 28 f.

career of one who has been described as "the real founder of nineteenth-century Anglo-Catholicism, the movement which he created and then tried in vain to destroy."[1] Pusey always said that Newman's great mistake had been to rely too much on the Bishops, so that when they withdrew their confidence he had nothing left upon which to lean. Pusey himself had looked to God's Providence acting through the Church.[2] It is significant that none of Newman's sisters, to whom he was greatly devoted, ever followed him, and that his brother, F. W. Newman, took a far different course, and even to the end questioned his sincerity.[3]

Whatever opinion one may hold upon Newman's religious view and changes, it cannot be denied that he was one of the great outstanding figures of the century whose romantic and tragic career has aroused the curiosity and interest of almost all his cultivated fellow countrymen. As a preacher, a writer, and a religious leader his fame is bounded only by the frontiers beyond which the English language has never penetrated. As a thinker perhaps more reservations are necessary; for though his mind was exceedingly logical and acute, considerations of the heart were apt to influence it in advance and to affect the result. He certainly had more foresight than other early leaders of the Tractarian Movement, for his mind was open to the desire for change, which he saw was inevitable and must, instead of being opposed, be turned to good account.

The career of Newman as a Roman does not concern us in this chapter; but one later incident may perhaps here be recalled. In 1868 Canon Irvine, the then Vicar of Littlemore, has recorded seeing an old man, broken by grief, sobbing over the lych-gate of his church. The collar of his old shabby overcoat was pulled up to hide his face—but in spite of this he recognized John Henry Newman.

[1] Inge, *Outspoken Essays*, I, p. 173.
[2] See Liddon, *op. cit.*, II, p. 57, and compare Newman, *Apologia pro Vita Sua*, p. 207.
[3] Newman was the only contributor to the Tracts who went over to Rome. All those who followed the same course had been, like him, Evangelicals, or Liberals, like Ward, by upbringing.

THE OXFORD MOVEMENT TO 1845

CHARACTERISTICS OF THE MOVEMENT

At this point a few general observations may well be made on the Movement as a whole, its characteristics and effects. It should first be realized that the Oxford Movement did not stand alone; it was part of a general and widespread revival of the "corporate," as against the "individual" spirit, which shewed itself in all departments of life as the nineteenth century advanced. If that century began with the emancipation of individuals, its characteristic developments were to be the Trade Unions, the Co-operative Societies, and even the Joint-stock Companies.[1] It was an age of societies and we have seen already the numerous religious associations which came into being at its very inception. The ancient and venerable society which men named the Church was bound to be affected by such a spirit of reviving co-operation.

The eighteenth century in England had looked upon the Church as a useful institution for promoting order and good morals; almost as a department of the State. The new Movement reacted strongly from such a conception; it tried to show, in Newman's words, that "there was something greater than the Established Church, and that was the Church Catholic and Apostolic, set up from the beginning" (*Apologia*, p. 35). On the continent the Catholic idea had already begun to revive and gain fresh strength, in part owing to political changes, but more owing to a reaction from the extreme individualism of the previous age. It is true that it had to work against much opposition and amid many difficulties, but from the beginning of the century it had made progress in France before crossing over to England. The Catholic revival came late to these shores, just as in the sixteenth century the Reformation had taken time to extend its influence here. There was also a movement in Germany towards greater co-operation during the same period. Outside the Church the same spirit can be seen at work, not only in the formation of religious societies, but in the strange experiments of the Irvingites.

One man there was whose influence in this direction had counted for much—S. T. Coleridge, the poet and philosopher.

---

[1] Cf. Bartlett and Carlyle, *Christianity in History*, p. 567.

He held his own conception of what the Church should be, and it was a noble and lofty conception which emphasized its spiritual and divine character; for he held that the Church was not dependent upon the will of man, but of God. Any merely human power or prestige which it might have acquired he held to be unessential, and even dangerous. Views such as these found a ready soil in the hearts of men who were determined to uphold a similarly high idea of the Church as against the predominant and popular view of it as almost State-controlled. They believed that the question which had to be fought out was "whether the whole idea of the Church, as a real and divinely ordained society, with a definite doctrine and belief, is not a delusion, and whether Christianity, whatever it is, is addressed solely to each individual, one by one, to make what he can of it."[1]

The Romantic Revival

This Catholic revival was influenced and reinforced by the parallel revival taking place in literature which is called the Romantic Movement. It is interesting to notice that among the early leaders of the Oxford Movement, in particular Keble and Newman, were men of poetic insight and power. It certainly looked to the past and tried to disinter the remains of Christian antiquity; not merely because it was dissatisfied with the present, and suffering from that nostalgia for the past which is so often the result of an inward conflict of the soul in warfare with its environment, but as containing definite teaching which was being forgotten. The Tractarians were practical and sensible men, even in their attitude to the past; it was only the lesser men who belonged to the school which only sees the Middle Ages by moonlight—to adopt Mr. Chesterton's phrase (*Blake*, p. 51). These mostly went over to Rome.

This romantic atmosphere in which Tractarianism was to find itself so much at home undoubtedly owed much to the novels of Sir Walter Scott, as well as to the romantic tales of Southey; but behind it there were deeper influences. Wordsworth in his poetry had done much; for underlying it

[1] Church, *The Oxford Movement*, p. 163.

there was profound philosophical teaching, and teaching of such a nature as readily to lead on to that of the Oxford School. But for the deepest influence we must look to Coleridge. It was not only his idea of the Church which had weight, but his whole demand for a more profound religious philosophy, as well as for a more worthy setting for religion; he "made trial of his age, and succeeded in interesting its genius in the cause of Catholic truth."[1]

A Reaction against Liberalism

Thus the Movement was part of a general awakening of the human mind and soul to the value of the past and a reaction against a too insistent individualism. It was also a reaction against liberal and radical views in both politics and religion. Men had been alarmed by the riots connected with the Reform Bill and other causes, and began to feel the need of some effective safeguard for morality and social order. They desired to preserve the bonds of society against such dangers, and they saw in a strongly ethical and authoritative religious system the best means of doing so. In the intellectual sphere also, Liberalism was a danger. It should be observed that by Liberalism was meant, not the reverent search after truth, but an aggressive and narrow rationalism which tended to prefer intellectual to moral excellence, and "in general the anti-dogmatic principle."[2] This spirit had been best seen in "the encyclopedist or negative temper which had preceded and created the great French Revolution."[3]

Newman, and those who with him realized the danger of this temper in social and intellectual matters alike, hoped to transform the Church of England into a compact and organized society by means of which the enemy could be driven out. But they had first to expel Liberalism from the Church itself. This was the great task to which they set themselves. It was indeed a heavy one, for latitudinarian

---

[1] Newman, *Apologia*, p. 107. Strangely enough Newman, in his old age, claimed that neither he, nor Froude, nor Pusey, nor Keble ever "read a word of Coleridge": see W. Barry, *Newman*, p. 30.

[2] Newman, *op. cit.*, p. 54.

[3] Liddon, *Life of E. B. Pusey*, I, p. 253.

ideas were widespread. Attacks on the use of the creeds in public worship were not unknown, whilst even bishops were supposed to wish to make changes in the Prayer Book! The mad cry for reform which rose on all sides seemed likely to overwhelm the Church; and behind it there seemed to be no principle, merely the vague feeling that change meant progress. The teaching of Dr. Arnold on the Church was held to be amongst the serious dangers; for he, following the ideas of the previous century, looked upon it as a human institution, necessary indeed, but not without its disadvantages. The only safeguard to membership which he postulated was acceptance of the Divinity of Christ. Like Milner before him, he saw in the history of the Church the repeated attempts of the genuine nucleus to free itself from the official Catholic Church.

But there was another enemy, this time without, who had to be faced—the reviving Roman Communion in these islands. The attitude of the Movement can be seen in the advertisement to the first volume of the Tracts, and Dean Church himself had stated quite definitely that it "started out of the Anti-Roman feelings of the Emancipation time. It was Anti-Roman as much as it was Anti-Sectarian and Anti-Erastian. It was to avert the danger of people becoming Romanists from ignorance of Church principles" (*op. cit.*, p. 241). The late Dean of Winchester (Dr. Hutton) said of Pusey: "Everything Catholic that Roman theologians taught, he independently accepted; but what was Roman and not Universal found hardly an entrance, by the tiniest loophole, into his beliefs." (In *The Future of the Church of England*, p. 18.)[1]

A Completion of Earlier Movements

Thus the Oxford Movement was a reaction against Liberalism and a turning back to distant ages of the Church. But it was also a kind of completion of parties existing in the Church of England at the time. In particular it carried on the ideas and principles of "Orthodoxy." It may indeed be regarded as a revival of that party, which in some obscurity had been

---

[1] Monckton Milnes once told Aubrey de Vere that he had been prevented from becoming a Roman Catholic by the rise of the Oxford Movement (*Life*, I, p. 118).

holding fast to the conception of the Church characteristic of the great Caroline divines. In *The British Magazine*, and especially in the poems appearing in its pages—afterwards to be collected into *Lyra Apostolica*—can be seen the stirring of the minds which were to bring the Movement to birth.[1]

In another direction the Movement claimed to be a completion and extension of the Evangelical Revival, a movement from which, no doubt, it had itself derived some measure of quickening power. The extent to which it continued and extended the principles of the earlier Revival is a matter for dispute; the answer depending on the presuppositions of those who consider the question. It is possible to argue that the Tractarian Movement was a perversion of the older Revival, a harking back to things which had definitely been abandoned at the time of the Reformation. The former opinion is, naturally enough, that of Liddon, for he believed that the Evangelical Movement, to quote his own words, "partly in virtue of its very intensity, was, in respect of its advocacy of religious truth, an imperfect and one-sided movement. It laid stress only on such doctrines of Divine Revelation as appeared to its promoters to be calculated to produce a converting or sanctifying effect upon the souls of men. Its interpretation of the New Testament —little as its leaders ever suspected this—was guided by a traditional assumption as arbitrary and as groundless as any tradition which it ever denounced. The real sources of its 'Gospel' were limited to a few chapters of St. Paul's Epistles . . . understood in a manner which left much else in Holy Scripture out of account; and thus the Old Testament history, and even the life of our Lord Jesus Christ, as recorded by the Evangelists, were thrown comparatively into the background. The needs and salvation of the believer, rather than the whole revealed Will of Him in Whom we believe, was the governing consideration. As a consequence, those entire departments of the Christian revelation which deal with the

---

[1] Even in poetry there was a developing tradition. "Keble was the expression of the Oxford Movement in its earlier phases, the popular and prosaic link between the quainter and more spiritual fabric of George Herbert and the more exquisite and intense devotional work of Christina Rossetti." *F. York Powell*, II, p. 180.

corporate union of Christians with Christ in His Church and with the Sacraments, which by His appointment are the channels of His grace to the end of time, were not so much forgotten as unrecognized."[1]

On the other side may be quoted the opinion of Bishop Moule, sane, and allowing to those who differed from him a full measure of consideration, and of credit for sincerity and high intention. "I for one," he says, "cannot think that the memorable Oxford group of the thirties consciously combined to prepare a complete counter-Reformation, though certainly one of them, Hurrell Froude, avowed a harsh and narrow animosity against the Reformers. To many of them, assuredly, a vision of the Church was present in which the best elements of patristic, medieval, and English theology appeared blended in a golden haze. Nevertheless, I cannot but maintain that their theory of the Body of Christ, and of the way of salvation, was not so much a development as a really new thing in the main stream of our post-Reformation theology. Certainly their teaching on the vital necessity of Episcopacy, on Justification, on Regeneration, and on the nature of the Eucharistic presence, was not that of Hall, nor even of Andrewes and Laud, nor of Beveridge."[2]

Self-denial and Holiness of the Leaders

The Movement owed its progress to the revival of certain almost forgotten doctrines; but there was also certain characteristics in its leaders giving it an attractive power which to certain temperaments was almost irresistible. These characteristics were in part the result of the Movement itself, in part the reasons for its existence. From the doctrine of the Church came a recognition of the place of authority and tradition; this led to a stern self-repression and a note of severity. From the doctrine of the Sacraments came a new realization of the importance of worship and of orderliness and dignity in its public conduct, which in turn led to a note of holiness in those who were to partake in them. These two notes were certainly prominent—severity and holiness.

[1] *Life of E. B. Pusey*, I, pp. 255 f.
[2] *The Evangelical School*, etc., pp. 28 f.

The severity shewed itself in various ways. In the individual life there was what Bishop Paget has called an "inner sternness of thought and will," a "hidden austerity which guards from softness and degeneracy the bright hopefulness and kindness of the 'peaceable temper.'"[1] It was this side of the Movement which attracted the youthful Frederick Temple. Writing to his brother in 1841 he compares "the free and easy religion of the Wesleyans, who generally think religion to consist in rapturous emotions" and "the severe, stern, self-watching and self-denial" of Newman. He expresses his conviction that the latter is the "religion of the Bible."[2] The basis of this severity was a realized sense of the divine presence which led to deep self-abasement and stern self-discipline. This self-abasement even extended to the avoidance of positions of prominence. "Those whom it (the Oxford Movement) influenced looked not for great things for themselves, nor thought of making a mark in the world."[3] Death found both Keble and Pusey in the positions which they had held when the Movement was first proclaimed.[4] This self-repression and severity came out also in their teaching, which derived its force from inner conviction and sober self-restraint rather than from the outward aids of rhetoric or emotional appeals. The vulgar may have been alienated and put off by this method; but it undoubtedly had a subtle power of attracting the finer souls, those especially who were weary of the superficial and shallow teaching of the more popular exponents of the gospel. At the same time this severer teaching had to cope with the Englishman's traditional dislike of theology; as Newman once said, it is very difficult to wind an Englishman up to a dogmatic level. The leaders themselves derived immense confidence from their principles, and there was a sweep and hopefulness about the Movement which drew to it innumerable sympathizers. Many must have felt that if only the truth could be presented

[1] Quoted *Life of Francis Paget*, pp. 317 f.
[2] *Frederick Temple*, II, p. 441.
[3] Church, *op. cit.*, p. 128.
[4] The same is true of Wesley and other leaders of the Evangelical school of thought—Simeon, for example. Those who become leaders of a party tend to lose that interest in the domestic affairs of the Church which is one of the surest ways of obtaining promotion.

to the nation it would embrace Catholic ideas and a new age would be brought in.

THE EFFECTS OF THE MOVEMENT

Before going on to consider the permanent achievement of the Oxford Movement, it will be well to pause to consider its immediate effects upon the Evangelicals within the Church of England and on the Protestant Nonconformists without.

In considering this matter of the effect upon the Evangelicals, it has first of all to be remembered that their original leaders were loyal Churchmen, otherwise they would have gone with the stream, and on the death of Wesley have drifted into Dissent. The depth of their Churchmanship is so little realized that it needs to be supported by evidence. Daniel Wilson, Bishop of Calcutta, wrote thus of one of the greatest of the early leaders: "Mr. Simeon neither verged towards the great error of over-magnifying the ecclesiastical polity of the Church and placing it in the stead of Christ and Salvation, nor towards the opposite mistake of under-valuing the Sacraments and the authority of an Apostolic Episcopacy."[1] Whilst Daniel Wilson himself, when Vicar of Islington, took the unusual step of establishing "an early Sacrament at eight, in addition to the usual Celebration."[2] He also used words which perhaps he might have avoided in view of later teaching, speaking of "the altar of our Eucharistic sacrifice,"[3] and "Blessed Lord, I am now about to partake of Thy Body as broken, and Thy Blood as shed for me."[4] Another Evangelical, on the eve of his ordination to the priesthood, wrote as follows: "It will be a source of unmixed gratification to me if I am spared to administer the Holy Sacrament of the Body and Blood of our Blessed Saviour to the many devout and faithful worshippers who are wont thus to approach the Lord."[5]

What was felt to be a dangerous emphasis laid on certain

[1] Carus, *Memoir of Simeon*, p. 845.
[2] The custom had never died out as is sometimes supposed: see Wickham Legg, *English Church Life, etc.*, p. 50.
[3] Bateman, *Life of Daniel Wilson*, p. 157.
[4] *Op. cit.*, p. 284.
[5] Quoted by G. W. E. Russell, *Short History of the Evangelical Movement*, pp. 19 f.

doctrines by the devotees of the Oxford Movement led many Evangelicals, who were convinced Churchmen, first to refrain from teaching such doctrines because they might be misunderstood, and then gradually to abandon them because so easily perverted. The Oxford Movement had thus the effect of driving the Evangelicals into the arms of the Low Churchmen with whom they are commonly identified. It must further be remembered that the outcry against Tract 90 was led by Broad Churchmen like Tait and Arnold, or old-fashioned High Churchmen, like Golightly, not by Evangelicals. It was only as the struggle became more acute that the greater energy and importance of the Evangelicals made them take the leading part and absorb the real Low Churchmen into their ranks.

If the effect of the Oxford Movement upon the Evangelicals was thus to drive them into opposition, even more did the Nonconformists react from it. As the Movement progressed it became increasingly definite in its doctrines and unwilling to make concessions. It inherited the attitude of the older "Orthodox," to many of whom the continued existence of voluntary societies (for as such they regarded the various Nonconformist bodies) seemed to exalt schism into a principle. The natural result was a wider separation between Dissent and the Church, and for some waverers the definite adoption of Dissent. Dr. Inge recalling early days when he lived in his grandfather's parish in Yorkshire, says: "There was a small Wesleyan chapel in the village; but half of the Methodists came to Church once on Sundays.... The stiffer Churchmanship of the next generation drove all such pious waverers into unmitigated Nonconformity."[1] The emphasis which was placed on the priesthood was another dividing line, for though a Nonconformist minister might appropriate the term "parson" (which strictly speaking is reserved for the incumbent of a parish), he would never think of calling himself a priest. Incidentally the stress on the sacerdotal side of Churchmanship was welcomed by some Nonconformists, who had always regarded the teaching of the Church and the language of its formularies as being Catholic and therefore objectionable. They now felt themselves justified for their separation. Others—

[1] *Assessments and Anticipations*, p. 15.

these, however, came later—felt that their dissent was not from the Church of England as such, but from the Establishment. They took up the position that the welfare of the Church of England was the concern of all Christian men and women in the country, and that they had, as such, the right to express an opinion on any matter which affected its doctrine or teaching. An outstanding example of this type was Andrew Fairbairn. According to Dr. Selbie, he "honestly believed that the claims put forth in the Catholic revival were disastrous to the highest welfare of the English Church."[1] A similar conclusion was reached by Thomas Hodgkin, the Quaker, whose sympathetic spirit and wide knowledge of the early centuries could not save him from regarding the Oxford Movement as "the greatest spiritual misfortune of our country in the nineteenth century—it was essentially a turning back into the darkness of the Middle Ages, it gave fresh vigour to the claims of the priesthood, and fixed attention on the 'childish things of Christianity.'"[2]

THE ACHIEVEMENTS OF THE MOVEMENT

Such were some opinions from great Nonconformist leaders and thinkers of the doctrines of the Oxford Movement; but even they did not, as we shall see later, refuse to recognize that it made very definite contributions to the religious life of the country and produced men and women of high spiritual attainments. A movement which had as its fruits saints like Dean Church and Bishop King, which inspired the scholarship of the *Lux Mundi* group and the devoted labours of a Father Dolling, must have been of God. These instances belong to the second and later generations of the Movement. But it was the first generation which set the standard that inspired them. They have been well described by Miss C. A. E. Moberly from the recollections of her childhood. "The eyes of our elders were fixed on the holiest realities of the Spirit, and in the services of the English Church they found the atmosphere in which they breathed most freely. Theology was to them a thrilling interest, and they moved and spoke and thought with

---
[1] *Life of A. M. Fairbairn*, p. 209.
[2] Quoted by Louise Creighton, *Life and Letters of Thomas Hodgkin*, p. 351.

THE OXFORD MOVEMENT TO 1845

unseen presences round them . . . as realizing the angels about the Throne and the solemn awe of the Throne. . . . Though no words about the Vision were suffered in our hearing out of church but with hushed voices and almost bated breath, yet the troops of children by whom they were surrounded did not miss the significance. The knowledge of the centre round which their thoughts revolved was an open secret, and an infinite nuance for holy things was the first lesson burnt into us by the demeanour of our leaders" (*Dulce Domum*, pp. 7 f).

This chapter may well be brought to a close by citing the testimonies of two further witnesses, neither of whom can be accused of prejudice in favour of the Movement. Dr. Inge considers that: "It lifted the religion of many Englishmen from the somewhat gross and bourgeois condition in which the movement found it, to a pure and unworldly idealism. And, unlike most other religious revivals, especially in this country, it has remained remarkably free from unhealthy emotionalism and hysterics" (*Outspoken Essays*, I, p. 186). Whilst Lord Morley reports the following opinion of J. S. Mill. He "used to tell us that the Oxford theologians had done for England something like what Guizot, Villemain, Michelet, and Cousin had done a little earlier for France; they had opened, broadened, deepened the issues and meanings of European history; they had reminded us that history is European; that it is quite unintelligible if treated as merely local. He would say, moreover, that thought should recognize thought and mind always welcome mind; and the Oxford men had at least brought argument, learning and even philosophy of a sort, to break up the narrow and frigid conventions of the reigning system in church and college, in pulpits and professorial chairs. They had made the church ashamed of the evils of her ways" (*Life of W. E. Gladstone*, I, pp. 163 f).

6

THE ROMAN CHURCH IN ENGLAND

In the early years of the nineteenth century the Roman Church in this land had reached a very low estate. Its members were regarded by most Englishmen as followers of an obscure foreign religious sect, and its priests, who often dressed as laymen,[1] as aliens, and undesirable at that. The vastness of the Roman communion, and even the very idea of a universal Church, had no meaning to their insular minds. Newman once spoke to a Roman congregation of the state of their Church in his own early days; there were, he said, but "A few adherents of the old religion, moving silently and sorrowfully about, as memorials of what had been," whilst J. A. Froude described it (c. 1830) as "a dying creed, lingering in retirement in the halls and chapels of a few half-forgotten families."[2] These old Catholic families were content to maintain their ancestral faith for themselves and their dependents. Many of them were landowners and they lived a self-contained life, not wishing to interfere with the religion of their neighbours, thankful, it may be, to be left in peace themselves, and a little fearful of doing anything which might attract attention and revive Anti-Catholic agitation.

Controversy between the Church of England and the Romans had lapsed with the death of Stillingfleet, Bishop of Worcester, at the end of the seventeenth century; though there must have been a good deal of discussion still going on as Tindal's reconversion was said to have been due to arguments which he heard in the coffee-houses. Its revival had been anticipated, if not provoked, by Bishop Barrington, who in 1806 publicly declared the Roman Catholics to be idolaters. Charles Daubeny, the famous Archdeacon of Sarum, from 1813 onwards habitually referred to the danger of Roman aggression

---

[1] A. W. Hutton wrote of this period: "The four Catholic bishops there were then in England would meet in lay attire at some out-of-the-way country inn, and there discuss and decide details of Church government over churchwarden pipes and a pot of beer." *Cardinal Manning*, p. 106.

[2] Quoted G. W. E. Russell, *Dr. Pusey*, p. 38.

in his charges. In 1819 he became increasingly urgent. "Time was," he says, "when any cry of alarm on the score of popery in this country would have been considered too ridiculous to have merited the attention of a thinking man. But I have lived to see a wonderful change of public opinion on this subject."[1] A few years later, as if to justify his alarm, appeared two volumes by Roman Catholics attacking the Protestant position. They were Bishop Milner's *End of Religious Controversy*[2] and Charles Butler's *Book of the Roman Catholic Church*.[3] Among those who rushed to the defence was Henry Phillpotts, later, as Bishop of Exeter, to win fame in other fields of controversy.

ROMAN CATHOLIC REVIVAL

From time to time individuals would go over to "the Papists," but their action was regarded as due to eccentricity, and their numbers were not sufficient to arouse alarm in the bosoms of the Anglican authorities; whilst the Catholics themselves were not too pleased by the proselytizing zeal which these newcomers often showed. One of the earliest was Kenelm Digby, the author of *The Broad Stone of Honour*, in 1823. In the following year a more important convert was Ambrose Phillips, a Leicestershire country gentleman. It was owing to his influence, in part at any rate, that the fanatical and eccentric George Spencer became a Roman.[4] George Spencer, the son of Lord Spencer, was a Cambridge man and had taken high honours; the attractions of the Papal system first came upon him in the somewhat unlikely atmosphere of the Paris Opera House during a performance of *Don Juan*. After being received he went to Rome to prepare for the priesthood, and there met Wiseman, whom he inspired with the possibility of the conversion of England. He himself, on his return thither, set about his part of the task with tremendous zest. He even succeeded in

---

[1] Quoted by Overton, *The English Church in the Nineteenth Century*, pp. 199 f.

[2] It is interesting to note, in view of later developments, that the good Bishop recognizes that the Church of England "has better pretensions to the marks of the Church than any other Protestant Society" (*op. cit.*, p. 125).

[3] Butler, who was a layman, also wrote a *Life of Erasmus*, which had considerable vogue until superseded by more adequate accounts.

[4] See the recent study, *Life of Father Ignatius Spencer*, by Urban Young.

gaining permission to address the future Queen Victoria. "She listened with great attention to everything I had to say, and maintained a respectful silence," he naïvely reported, "because she sat beside her mother." Spencer organized a great crusade of intercession, in conjunction with Ambrose Phillips, for the conversion of England. But the Roman authorities were embarrassed by such "enthusiasm"; and in other quarters he was rebuffed, for even Pugin, the architect who had become a Roman in 1834, criticized his taste in vestments.

The new life in the Roman Church soon came to be noted, not without dismay, in various quarters. A Congregational minister, for example, reported, in May 1830, that in his district the Romans were making "great, united, and persevering efforts";[1] while Arnold of Rugby wrote to Bunsen in August 1834 that the Roman Catholics were increasing rapidly: "Lord Shrewsbury and other wealthy Catholics are devoting their whole incomes to the cause, while the tremendous influx of Irish labourers into Lancashire and the West of Scotland is tainting the whole population with a more than barbarian element."[2]

THE TRACTARIAN MOVEMENT

We have already seen (p. 106 above) that one of the primary motives of the Tract writers was to oppose Roman Catholicism, none the less the rise of the Tractarian Movement gave to some Romans the hope that the Church of England was about to return to Catholic unity;[3] but such a hope was premature and unduly optimistic. It is true that Vol. I of the Tracts, issued in November 1834, saw in "the ever-multiplying divisions of the religious world the prelude to the extension

[1] See A. W. Peel, *These Hundred Years*, p. 45.

[2] Stanley, *Life of Dr. Arnold*, p. 338. The fact that Irish labourers came over to England in large numbers accounted for a good deal of the increase in the Roman Catholic population. That their standard of living was much lower than that of the English labourer and that they were willing to work for much less wages aroused against them a good deal of prejudice which was naturally extended to their religion, thus confirming the Englishman's inherited dislike of "Papacy."

[3] Cf. *Life and Letters of Ambrose Phillips de Lisle*, I, p. 199.

of Popery"; but there does not seem to have been any considerable spread of Romanism in this country before 1836. Then controversy revived, probably because Rome was becoming more active and there were reports of its progress. Newman wrote in January 1836 that Roman Catholics were "said to be spreading and strengthening on all sides of us, vaunting of their success . . . and taunting us with our inability to argue with them" (Tract LXXI, p. 1). The new life in the Roman communion in England was due to the arrival of Dr. Wiseman. A course of lectures which he gave in 1836 on "The Principal Doctrines and Practices of the Catholic Church" gave heart to his fellow-religionists and impressed many outsiders. In 1840 Wiseman was made Bishop of Melipotamus, a title which caused some amusement, and President of Oscott, a seminary near Birmingham, which under his rule became a centre of intellectual activity. Although Wiseman was a member of an old Catholic family, he was not really trusted by the English Roman Catholics. He had, for one thing, been educated mainly in Italy, and he was, moreover, suspected of great leanings towards the Jesuits. About this time he began to see that the Oxford Movement might be made to serve the purposes of Rome and launched a vigorous campaign of proselytizing.[1]

In January 1840 George Spencer came to Oxford for the purpose of interesting members of the Movement and any others who would listen to him in his schemes for Reunion. Newman avoided his company and in a letter to Pusey described him as "a gentlemanlike, mild, pleasing man, but very smooth."[2] At this time he seems genuinely to have been alarmed at the possibility of people going over, for in the same month he wrote to J. W. Bowden that "The danger of a lapse into Romanism . . . gets greater daily. I expect to hear of victims."[3] Probably his alarm was not well founded; at any rate, when he came to write his *Apologia* in 1865 he seemed to think that the Tractarian Movement had not helped the Roman cause, except negatively by causing Catholic doctrines

[1] Liddon, *Life of E. B. Pusey*, II, p. 151.
[2] *Op. cit.*, II, p. 127.
[3] Anne Mozley, *Life and Letters of J. H. Newman*, II, p. 297.

to be denied by the Church of England in the persons of its leaders. "There were no converts to Rome till after the condemnation of No. 90" (*op. cit.*, p. 156).

Meanwhile the progress of the Movement, especially in its relation to Rome and its potentialities as a nursery for providing converts, was attracting attention abroad and not least in Germany. Döllinger wrote to Pusey in September 1842 that the eyes of all Germany, "of Protestants as well as of Roman Catholics, are turned in fear or hope towards Oxford."[1] Evidence of the activity of the Romans comes also from a different source; Frederick Temple, the future Archbishop, noted in a letter of April 14, 1843, that lukewarmness was the last vice that could be attributed to them (*Frederick Temple*, I, p. 70).

THE ANGLICAN REPLY

Meanwhile the taunts and aggression of the Romanists were not allowed to go without reply. We have seen already that Hurrell Froude disliked Newman's "cursing and swearing" against them and implored him to give it up. His reproof seems to have had no effect, for in 1837 we find Newman describing the Roman Church as "a church beside herself... crafty, obstinate, wilful, malicious, cruel, unnatural as most men are—or rather she may be said to resemble a demoniac—possessed with principles, thoughts and tendencies not her own; in outward form and in natural powers what God made her, but ruled by an inexorable spirit who is sovereign in his management over her, and most subtle and most successful in the use of her gifts. Thus she is her real self only in name, and till God vouchsafes to restore her, we must treat her as if she were that evil one who governs her" (*Prophetical Office of the Church*, p. 101).

Manning, while still an Anglican, made a violent attack on the Church of Rome in a sermon preached on the Commemoration of Gunpowder Plot before the University of Oxford. Soon afterwards he called on Newman, then at Littlemore awaiting the end. But Newman would not see him,

[1] Quoted Liddon, *Life of E. B. Pusey*, II, p. 295.

and the task of receiving, and mollifying, the Archdeacon fell to his then disciple, James Anthony Froude.[1]

It is no mere coincidence that the fiercest attacks on Rome by Tractarian leaders should thus come from the two most famous for their subsequent change of allegiance. It was a sign, although perhaps an unconscious one, that confidence was being undermined. Pusey, on the other hand, was enabled, owing to his entire and unshakable belief in the English Church, to be more charitable than others who were less certain; he had "no deep horror of the Popish system" and his general attitude made some regard him as an unintentional "decoy bird" to Rome.[2]

Among the Evangelicals it was natural that there should be continual attacks on Rome; they had been a marked feature of the less intelligent members of the school ever since Catholic Emancipation in 1829 had reawakened them to the possibilities of harm from that quarter. Dean Church, when a schoolboy at Bristol, was taught to look upon Romans (and also Socinians) "with a kind of awful curiosity and dismay"; he even went so far as to buy a copy of the Canons of the Council of Trent for study in case he had "to confound possible Popish controversialists, who at that time were in the softening and minimizing mood."[3] A similar experience befell Liddon, who was a schoolboy in the years immediately before Newman's secession. We are told that: "The only religious instructions which he received were the vigorous and impressive anti-Roman discourses with which Dr. Hodges, the vicar of Lyme, tried to protect his flock each week from one of the least imminent of their dangers."[4]

THE SECESSIONS

It is interesting to notice the various causes which led to secessions when they actually came. Pusey held that these were two: the belief that the Church of England had lost the note of

---

[1] Kegan Paul, *The Century*, XXVI (1883), p. 129. Pusey also wished that Manning's charge of 1845 had shown "more love" for the Roman Church: see *Life of E. B. Pusey*, III, p. 286.
[2] *Op. cit.*, III, p. 308.
[3] *Life and Letters of Dean Church* (Eversley Edition), pp. 8 f.
[4] J. O. Johnson, *Life of Henry Parry Liddon*, p. 5.

Unity—Catholic minds refused to consider the doctrine of the Church Invisible; and the uncertainty of its teaching (*Life*, III, p. 299). This latter reason weighed with many. Manning wrote to Hope-Scott, after the Gorham Judgement and just before their joint "going over": "It is either Rome or licence of thought and will."[1] The same reason, in more recent times, accounted for Mrs. Warre Cornish's joining the Roman Church (and for many others who desired "certainty"). A friend wrote of her: "I don't think she could conceive of certainty as something gradually distilled from experience; it had to be wrenched at a moment of insight from life, and then held by the will as a possession."[2] Behind all other reasons there was—at once the great stumbling-block and the great attraction—the Papal Supremacy. This it was which chiefly decided the course of R. I. Wilberforce, as he explained in his *Principles of Church Authority*,[3] a work which played in his career the part which the *Essay on the Development of Doctrine* played in that of Newman. W. G. Ward had to find more original causes for secession, or at least some more original way of stating them. He went over because he found in the Roman Church a greater recognition of the supernatural element in religion; because it denounced the doctrine of Justification—he held that "careful and individual moral discipline is the only possible basis on which Christian faith and practice can be reared"; because of the heroic self-sacrifice of the saints. As to the last, it seemed hardly necessary to look to Rome to find it.

When men a century ago went over to Rome the step involved them in a more serious breach than it would normally do to-day. Passions ran high and religious opinions, especially those separating the Church of Rome from other religious bodies, were held more tenaciously. To go meant often to sever the friendships of a lifetime. When Newman seceded he remained on at Oxford for a few months, during which he still saw something of his intimates; then he left Oxford and saw them no more for many years. Dean Church who was at the time one

[1] Quoted A. W. Hutton, *Cardinal Manning*, p. 77.
[2] Quoted by A. C. Benson, *Memories and Friends*, p. 181.
[3] See in particular pp. v. and 284.

of his most devoted friends and disciples did not resume intercourse with him for fourteen years, even by letter;[1] whilst Pusey and Keble he did not see again until September 1865, less than a year before the death of the latter.[2] Those going over made it a practice to write letters of farewell to their friends as from a death-bed. The difference of religious views was enough to form a barrier, and though kindly and loving thoughts might continue on both sides, intercourse could no longer be continued on the old terms of intimacy, and, as a rule, simply lapsed without any definite breach. In some cases, of course, there was unpleasantness. Dean Gregory, who was a young man in the late forties, tells how he was accosted in Parker's shop at Oxford by someone whom he did not recognize at the time, and the only reply he could make to a hearty handshake was to say: "You have the advantage of me, might I ask your name?" The stranger, who turned out to be a Mr. Estcourt, who had been curate of Cirencester and had just gone over to Rome, turned away in a huff, saying: "Oh, that is it." Gregory had acted quite innocently, but on telling the incident to his vicar, Thomas Keble, the latter was much pleased and said: "That is the way you should always treat those fellows."[3]

Some of the converts, especially from among the clergy, probably deserved such treatment. Their defects were noticed at the time by acute observers. "The eagerness of certain clerical converts to parade their emancipation from the restraints of Anglican orders was an irritating feature of the day. In my correspondence ladies described with a sort of loathing encounters with old acquaintances whom they had known in all the decorum of clerical black, now garbed in showy waistcoats, or as one letter specifies in 'blue neckties and ginger-coloured trousers.'"[4] There was also a tendency, even among some of the best of those who went over, to emphasize the differences between their new beliefs and those of the Church they had abandoned. This was unfortunate, from

[1] *Life and Letters of Dean Church*, pp. 68 f.
[2] W. Lock, *John Keble*, pp. 186 f.
[3] *Autobiography of Robert Gregory*, p. 38.
[4] *Letters of J. B. Mozley*, p. 207, note 1.

their point of view, because it prevented them from gaining or preserving a true Catholic perspective; and, moreover, came between them and those who were Romans by birth. The latter were much less anti-Protestant and more English.

Converts must have found it hard to decide what was to be their relationship with those they had left behind. Were they to attempt to persuade them to follow, or were they simply to leave them as they were? Many took the former course, and Mark Pattison complains that "the converts never left you any peace" (*Memoirs*, pp. 221 ff). For those who had had parochial charges the matter was especially difficult. To Anglicans there seemed something a little underhand for a priest who had gone over to Rome to remain behind in his former parish and attempt to proselytize. But there was much to be said for it. When in the unfortunate parish of St. Saviour's, Leeds, all the staff, save one, became Romans, they remained on and tried to gain converts. What is perhaps harder to understand, in view of Dr. Pusey's close connexion with the parish, is that Newman himself went to Leeds to be present at their reception and preached a sermon in which he argued that the Roman Church was of God because of "the apprehension which it inspired, and by its success in spite of opposition."[1]

There is, however, another side. Some of those who went over seem never to have forgotten the benefits they had received in the Church of their baptism, as certain pathetic incidents tend to prove. We have already noticed Newman as an old man weeping at Littlemore; it is not so widely known that something of a similar nature occurred in the life of Manning. When he lay on his death-bed he handed to Cardinal Vaughan a small worn volume, saying: "I leave it to you. Into this little book my dearest wife wrote her prayers and meditations. Not a day has passed since her death on which I have not prayed and meditated from this book. All the good I may have done, all the good I may have been, I owe to her."[2]

[1] See Liddon, *Life of E. B. Pusey*, III, p. 364.
[2] See von Hügel, *Selected Letters*, p. 256. This authentic account of Manning's attitude to his dead wife should be compared with the imaginary statements of Lytton Strachey in his *Eminent Victorians*. It is difficult to be "clever" without seeming to be malicious. But no one has the right to give currency to damaging statements unless he knows them to be true.

THE ROMAN CHURCH IN ENGLAND

THE CATHOLIC REVIVAL

The early years of the century had seen a vigorous revival of Catholicism in France. It began with the publication of Chateaubriand's *Génie du Christianisme* in 1802; "the most superb rainbow that ever rose in a storm-beaten sky" as Lord Morley called it (*Recollections*, I, p. 186). From the day of its appearance Catholicism began to recover its power in France, and even to become fashionable. Other writers rushed in where he had led, the most prominent being De Maistre, whose *Du Pape* appeared in 1819, and Lamennais. The latter had an extraordinary influence, not so much among the laity and the fashionable, as with the younger clergy. He gave them a new message, and his writings moulded a whole generation.[1] But a reaction followed. The Papal Encyclical *Mirari vos* in 1832, which denounced liberty of conscience and the freedom of the press, also condemned Lamennais, and his services were lost to the Catholic Church. Henceforward he developed those democratic ideals which had already appeared in his teaching and gave himself up entirely to the service of the people. Into his tragic and influential course we cannot enter further; the important thing to notice is the new life which he and others brought to Catholicism in his native country.

The position of Roman Catholics in this country was becoming daily more considerable. They shared in the general revival of Catholicism which had been so noteworthy in France; their numbers were being added to by the immigration of Irish labourers; and, in another stratum of society, by converts from Anglo-Catholicism. No doubt the opening of diplomatic relations between the British government and the Papal See, which followed the passing of the Bill of 1848, did much to increase their prestige and to make them less suspect.

In July 1850 the new cathedral of St. George, Lambeth, was consecrated, and in the same month Dr. Wiseman was recalled to Rome. His own impression, apparently, was that he would not return to England; but Providence, and Pius IX, had decided otherwise. On September 30th, Cardinal Wiseman, as he had now become, was appointed Archbishop of West-

[1] See Dean Church, *Occasional Papers*, I, pp. 319, 321.

minster with twelve bishops under him. In a letter issued from "the Flaminian Gate" the new archbishop declared that "Catholic England had been restored to its orbit in the ecclesiastical firmament." The act of the Pope, which cancelled the Vicarates Apostolic, divided England into a number of dioceses, was hailed with exultation by the Roman Catholic press. Carried away by its feelings, it ventured on exaggerated and even absurd forecasts as to the consequences. There was even in more sober minds the hope, and, perhaps, the expectation, that the days were near in which England would return to the Papal fold. This led to a grave mistake in policy on the part of the Romans; instead of filling the country with numerous mission chapels, the erection of large churches and cathedrals was undertaken. The result was that by the end of the century many churches and chapels remained unconsecrated (and therefore unavailable for Sunday mass) because there were debts upon them.[1]

ANTI-PAPAL FEELING

Such views naturally aroused the anti-papal feeling which is latent in the hearts of so many Englishmen. There was nothing underhand or concealed about the objective of the new Archbishop and his suffragans; this was quite definitely to re-establish and to extend the Catholic faith in England. From their point of view it was a perfectly legitimate and praiseworthy undertaking; to the "man in the street," and even to his rulers, it appeared in the light of a dastardly conspiracy to rob England of its freedom and bring it under a foreign Power.

On the face of it there was undoubtedly some discourtesy on the part of the Pope in carrying through such a scheme without informing the British government; but apparently he thought that Lord John Russell understood what was being done, and in any case there were precedents in Ireland and the Colonies. To the popular mind the whole thing seemed like a deliberate challenge to the Crown and Parliament. There was an outbreak of resentment which found some outlet in the formation of new societies—such as the Protestant Alliance.[2]

[1] See T. Murphy, *The Catholic Church in England and Wales*, pp. 5, 101.
[2] See Davidson and Benham, *A. C. Tait*, I, pp. 183 f.

In some quarters it was vaguely suspected that a mysterious foreign Power was behind the move, and that in some unknown manner Cardinal Wiseman would be able to regain possession of Westminster Abbey and celebrate High Mass there. The Cardinal, in response, issued a very dignified letter in which he quietly made fun of the British public for its alarm. He promised to leave the Dean and Chapter to "range undisturbed," though he proposed to continue his habit of visiting "the venerable old church . . . and the shrine of good St. Edward." The Westminster he coveted consisted of the "concealed labyrinths of lanes and courts and alleys and slums, nests of ignorance, vice, depravity, and crime."

Disraeli, who can hardly have shared the popular alarm and indignation, speaks jestingly of the peasants fearing that the fires of Smithfield were to be revived.[1] His jests certainly represented the wild fears of many of the people. Even among the old Catholic families there was disapproval and apprehension. Lord Beaumont, with whom the Duke of Norfolk was in agreement, felt that such an "ill-advised measure" offered to Catholics "the alternative of breaking with Rome or of violating their allegiance to the constitution of these realms."[2]

Such a state of panic is simply inexplicable to the present day;[3] and things were made worse by a letter written by Lord John Russell to the Bishop of Durham in which he condemned the Pope's action, and, at the same time, took the opportunity of hitting at the "Puseyites." This perverse letter (as Lord Morley called it) was taken up by the press and became what would now be called a "stunt." One editor who was very forward in running it told Greville that he "thought the whole thing humbug and a pack of nonsense."[4] But that

[1] Monypenny and Buckle, *Life of Disraeli*, I, p. 1086.
[2] Quoted by A. W. Hutton, *Cardinal Manning*, p. 80.
[3] It was, however, typical of the singular lack of a sense of proportion which flourished in the middle years of the nineteenth century. The same period saw denunciations of the Great Exhibition which were equally foolish. "Agitated Nonconformists declared that the Exhibition was an arrogant and wicked enterprise which would infallibly bring down God's punishment upon the nation": see Strachey, *Queen Victoria*, p. 126.
[4] *Memoirs*, Pt. II, vol. iii, p. 369.

did not deter him from adding fuel to the flames. Some of the liberal supporters of the government soon began to perceive that the Prime Minister's attitude was really inconsistent with the principles of civil and religious liberty which the party professed to uphold. John Bright in particular was stern in his condemnation of the reckless disregard of consequences which had marked the Durham Letter.

In 1851 a Bill passed through Parliament, entitled the Ecclesiastical Titles Bill, by which the use of the new titles was forbidden. It was, however, ignored by the Roman Church and never enforced by the State. Twenty years later it was repealed.[1] The Prime Minister had spoken great words about conspiracies to undermine the liberties of Europe, and then produced nothing but this ineffective measure. *Punch* hit off the situation with its usual skill in a cartoon representing Lord John as a small boy chalking "No Popery" on Cardinal Wiseman's door, and then running away.

The agitation over what was called Papal Aggression was shared by Nonconformists, many of whom were just as clamant as the Churchmen who were more directly concerned. There seemed some inconsistency in those who demanded State action. But Guinness Rogers, who took up this line, defended himself: "Because I was opposed to all action of the State in matters of religion, I did not see that I was justified in allowing one Church . . . to act as if it was entitled to allocate the people of England into a number of dioceses ordained by the authorities of Rome."[2] The truth was that the Nonconformists feared that Rome might again become triumphant in England, to their own grave detriment and even danger. A leading Nonconformist historian has compared the Romans with the Moslems in their grasping at power: "Politically it is a constant experience that Catholics and Moslems are never content with mere equality, but on principle, always aim at superiority. And their widespread geographic adherents give them political

---

[1] Just before the repeal Cardinal Wiseman was prosecuted by a certain Mr. Cobbett for using the title Archbishop of Westminster. He lost his case, however, on a technical point; for he had failed to get the consent of the Attorney-General before bringing it.

[2] *J. Guinness Rogers*, p. 94.

means which they are seldom averse to use, to the detriment of both civil and religious liberty."[1]

The attempt to gain adherents was meanwhile going on with some vigour. Newman had lectured in 1850 on "Anglican Difficulties" and had "ridiculed the Church of his earlier vows with all the refined cruelty of which he was the master."[2] It was in this year that Westcott heard him in Birmingham and, whilst admiring his rhetorical powers, regarded his use of humour as "utterly irreverent, utterly unbecoming a Christian minister." Though he was grieved at Newman's attitude towards the Church "in which he so long ministered," he felt that he was not to be feared as an opponent; his arguments and sneers were so cheap, and the very applause with which the audience greeted them seemed to him to be reassuring.[3] Newman's bitterness, which cannot be denied, was probably partly due to his own inward struggle with the circumstances in which he found himself. He was not happy in the Roman Church, and continued to believe in it (as undoubtedly he did) in spite of irritation at its methods and his own inconsiderate treatment.[4] Manning was never bitter; but he was, for that very reason, from the Anglican standpoint all the more dangerous.[5] Newman had no real wish to attack the Church of England, but he was impelled to do so; later he recognized its value in the work to which he felt himself especially called —opposition to the widespread outbreak of infidelity and unbelief which he saw approaching. When Pusey's *Minor Prophets* came out, he congratulated him, and expressed his belief that such works were among the best means of meeting the growing scepticism.[6] Manning had no such hopes, and

[1] Whitley, *History of British Baptists*, p. 285.
[2] Inge, *Outspoken Essays*, I, p. 175.
[3] *Life and Letters of Brooke Foss Westcott*, I, pp. 163 f.
[4] The reaction of a convert of our own times, George Tyrrell, was different. Though he still had no desire to leave the Church of Rome, he could break out into regrets: "Church of my baptism! Church of Westcott, Hort, Lightfoot, Church, Liddon, Taylor, Leighton, Coleridge! Church of better-than-saints, why did I ever leave you?" Quoted Duncan Jones, *Ordered Liberty*, p. 75.
[5] See A. W. Hutton, *Cardinal Manning*, p. 227, where there are quotations from the writings of the two ex-Anglican cardinals.
[6] See *Letters of J. B. Mozley*, p. 259.

when Pusey in his *Eirenicon* of 1866 stated that many devout Roman Catholics recognized and rejoiced in the working of the Holy Spirit in the Church of England and regarded it as "the bulwark against infidelity" in the land,[1] he repudiated such ideas and accused the Church of England of "floating before" infidelity, declaring that its piety had "ever been more dim and distant from the central light of souls" than that of the Dissenters.

CARDINAL MANNING

For many years the Romans in England were divided into two distinct camps, the older Catholic families and the converts. The former regarded the latter, as we have already seen, with suspicion and even alarm; they were so active and so "Roman." This was especially true of "God's county"—Lancashire—and the rest of the North, where the faith had been held continuously from the Middle Ages. Mr. Stead, many years afterwards, described them as "a highly respectable, intensely conservative, utterly sterile set of citizens. From any point of view beyond that of the blameless discharge of their religious duties, and the preservation of their families intact from the incursion of modern thought, they are almost as useless to the Church as they can be. They are the fossils of the Church."[2] The appointment of Manning, the ex-Anglican archdeacon—regarded by many as "an aspiring refugee from a hostile camp"—to be Archbishop of Westminster in the place of Cardinal Wiseman in 1865 was accepted with real disfavour and resentment. His later activities, in particular his advocacy of the Temporal Power and Papal Infallibility, only increased their dislike and distrust. But he did a great work for his adopted Church and in the end overcame even the prejudice of the old Catholic families. Furthermore, he allayed the suspicions of the English people by his patriotism and by the prominent part which he took in moral and philanthropic enterprises. He succeeded, in fact, in gaining a measure of

---

[1] In his *Apologia* (p. 382), Newman writes: "Doubtless the National Church has hitherto been a serviceable breakwater against doctrinal errors more fundamental than its own."

[2] *Review of Reviews*, June 1890.

popularity with the crowd, especially in London, such as few ecclesiastical dignitaries have ever enjoyed.

A. W. Hutton has ventured to prophesy that the "historian of the future may mark the period of Manning's Cardinalate (1875-92) as that of the zenith of the Catholic revival in England. Within this may be taken the years (1879-90) during which Newman held the same exalted rank; if a culminating point is to be indicated in that period of some twelve years, it would be the day (April 25, 1884) when Manning and Newman were both assisting as Princes of the Church at the opening of the new church of the Oratory in London. No doubt, on some future occasion, two or more cardinals may be got together, but never again two such striking and memorable figures, appealing by their almost romantic past, and by their great but very different abilities, to the attention and respect of all Englishmen."[1]

Manning was essentially a statesman and a diplomatist. This can be illustrated by his attention to Mr. Gladstone. We know from his biography that Mr. Gladstone regarded "the proselytizing agency of the Roman Church in this country . . . as one of the worst of religious influences of the age";[2] yet when he visited Rome in 1866, Manning was careful to write to his friends there that "Gladstone does not come as an enemy, and may be made friendly, or he might become on his return most dangerous."[3]

It was, however, over the question of Papal Infallibility that Manning made his great mark. This concerns us here, not as it affected the Roman Church as a whole, but for the reaction to it in England. The "Papal Aggression" of 1850 had followed on the unfortunate experiences of Pius IX in Rome; his assertion of spiritual authority was perhaps intended to console him for the realization that his temporal authority was not so stable as he had imagined. An exactly parallel succession occurred in 1870, when the complete loss of the temporal power was the prelude to the assertion of complete and unlimited power in the spiritual sphere. This assertion

[1] *Cardinal Manning*, pp. 254 f.
[2] Morley, *Life of W. E. Gladstone*, II, p. 188.
[3] *Op. cit.*, II, p. 215.

was made at the Vatican Council of 1870. Into the story of that strange gathering when—in spite of the most strenuous opposition, and quite possibly in face of a majority of Catholics,[1] the decree of Infallibility was accepted—we cannot enter.[2] It is no doubt with a feeling of grateful confidence that the pious Roman reflects on the comfort of having such a weapon in the Church's armoury; but in point of fact it has never been brought out and used. There has never been a single Papal utterance which is unanimously accepted by Roman experts as fulfilling all the necessary conditions, though some think that the condemnation by Leo XIII of Anglican Orders was an infallible utterance.[3] This event, which took place in 1895, came as a great disappointment to a number of sanguine English Churchmen, like the late Lord Halifax, who had hopes of some kind of reunion with Rome. In the Apostolic Letter *Ad Anglos* no room is left for such hopes.[4] The sequel might have been another series of secessions like those in 1845 or 1851, of those who felt that the Papal condemnation of Anglican orders rendered all sacraments null and void; but there was, in spite of the expectations of Cardinal Vaughan and others, no such sequel. The effects of the Letter, according to Bishop Creighton, were to reinforce Protestantism and to make the position of Anglicanism more definite.[5]

[1] Three opposition bishops, those of Cologne, Paris, and Cambrai, representing between them five million Catholics, had but three votes; while the Papal States, with a population of less than a million, had sixty-two bishops present to swell the affirming vote.
[2] Those who wish for further information should consult Abbot Butler, *History of the Vatican Council*, and Dr. G. G. Coulton, *Papal Infallibility*; and on the general question, Salmon's *Infallibility of the Church*.
[3] See Butler, *op. cit.*, II, p. 223.
[4] A full account of the whole matter will be found in A. C. Benson, *Edward White Benson*, pp. 488 ff.
[5] See *Life and Letters of Mandell Creighton*, II, p. 206.

7

THE DEVELOPMENT OF THOUGHT TO 1870

IN this chapter, as in Chapter 14 which is its sequel, nothing more will be attempted than a brief survey dealing with the most prominent movements only. It would no doubt have been well to trace out the permutations of thought down to their last home, in the hearts of the common people; but such a task is beyond the power of the historian, he can only take note of the changes which are registered in the writings and systems of formal thinkers. None the less, he must ever remember that the thought of the common people ultimately responds to the changes higher up the stream; though it takes at least a generation for such changes to be grasped by them, longer still for them to be assimilated so as to affect deeply their attitude towards man and the universe. Yet these changes are the most important of all those that can come upon them; for as Goethe has said: "The deepest, nay the unique theme of the history of the world, to which all other themes are subordinate, is the conflict of faith and unbelief."[1] In this conflict there are often no clear-cut divisions; men, especially such as have had no training in logic, are capable of having interests in both camps, of holding, at one and the same time, totally inconsistent views. Ultimately, as logic is applied and such discordant views are pressed, their inconsistency becomes so obvious that one set or the other has to be abandoned. That is a process which requires time, and, in addition, a change in the climate of thought itself. This climate of thought, which is made up of the intellectual prejudices of the age, has inevitably a profound effect on the theological conceptions of those who live in it; and theology itself has a habit of taking its colour from the fundamental philosophies of its day; or to use yet another figure, "It ebbs and flows, not by its own laws, but in sympathy with the tides of other seas."[2] Hence in considering the mental attitude of the first half of the Victorian Era I have made a

[1] Quoted by Edward Caird, *Lay Sermons and Addresses*, pp. 84 f.
[2] Mark Pattison, *Essays*, II, pp. 184 f.

wide sweep and paid less attention to purely theological thought and more to philosophical; though I trust that I have never forgotten that this attitude is itself but the background for action, that the history of the period is no mere procession of ideas divorced from events. For our purpose indeed the ideas are mainly valuable as they took form in actions. It is therefore with the effects of the various systems of thought rather than with their contents that we are primarily concerned.

ISOLATION OF ENGLISH THOUGHT

At the beginning of the nineteenth century thought in England was out of touch with the continent, and, following its own path, gave little heed to what was going on elsewhere.[1] For this state of isolation there were several reasons, quite apart from the difficulties of communication brought about by the Napoleonic wars. The thought of France was suspect; had not the teaching of Voltaire and Rousseau been responsible for the Revolution and all its dreadful consequences? But from Germany too there was isolation. This came from dislike of the Kantian criticism of the intellect. It cut across the traditional English trust in the senses as a sure guide to knowledge and was therefore unwelcome.

The effects of this isolation from continental thought were various. For one thing there was no alliance between theology and philosophy, as in Germany; for another, when German influences did come in, they came like a flood and carried all before them in many quarters. But this hardly took place until the Victorian Era was ended, especially in Biblical Studies where the work of the Cambridge school held them up— though signs were not wanting of the breaking through which was to follow. There were, of course, thinkers here and there who were in touch with Germany, and a few scholars actually went over to German Universities—Coleridge and Carlyle are examples of the former, Herbert Marsh and Pusey of the latter—whilst through novelists and poets, if not through formal

[1] Europe, in its turn, had in the previous century practically ignored Bishop Butler, most typical of English thinkers. Ueberweg, in his *History of Philosophy*, does indeed give him three lines, but they are full of errors. The Encyclopaedias never go beyond a mere mention.

thinkers, German and other continental influences crept in almost unperceived. Isolation was not complete, as indeed it never can be, and in the great scientific discoveries which were to mark the century, co-operation was a commonplace.[1]

When the century began, the spirit of Rationalism was rampant, both here and on the continent, though already its limitations were becoming manifest. Under the form of Deism it had tried to subject religion to its own laws; only to demonstrate, once for all, that religion demands a God who is alive and active. It denied any revelation, since it was felt that natural religion could provide all that man required. This denial led to much shallow thinking, and because the emotions were ignored, man's truest and deepest needs found no provision. The result was to paralyse speculation and to make ready for the reaction against Liberalism which arose about 1830. "Reason had done its best, and that best was obviously insufficient."[2]

Dr. Pusey, although acquainted with Rationalism mainly through his German visits, traced it back to English influences, to "the hypocrisy of degenerate Puritanism or the licentiousness of the Cavaliers."[3] From this country it travelled to the continent, where ultimately two separate strands revealed themselves. There was an open and complete rejection of the whole Christian system because certain elements in it were felt to be indefensible, this was typical of France; and there was the German type of infidel who, without any rejection of Christianity as a whole, gradually reduced it, by devouring criticism, to a mere caricature of its former self. German thought was marked by a superb self-confidence which felt itself capable of finding solutions for every problem; by a superior spirit which made it unwilling to learn from its neighbours; and, above all, by an entirely artificial conception of man and his needs. The pathetic thing was that it had its origin, not among the opponents of Christianity, but among its defenders. Once on its way it received no effective resistance from the traditional Lutherans, nor from the Pietists, who were

---
[1] Storr thinks that scientific co-operation led the way: see *Development of English Theology*, p. 135.
[2] Storr, *op. cit.*, p. 26. [3] Liddon, *Life of E. B. Pusey*, III, p. 116.

akin to the English Evangelicals.[1] In England Rationalism had not yet come to such depths, and the Liberal Movement, although superficial in its methods and shallow in its thinking, by having a more limited objective certainly achieved much in the way of dissolving superstition and opening the door to new freedoms.

UTILITARIANISM

During the first quarter of the century Utilitarianism was, as Mr. Chesterton has put it, "The philosophy in office." Its great exponent was Jeremy Bentham,[2] and its motto was the "greatest happiness of the greatest number." Bentham, who was born in 1747, died on January 6, 1832, the day before that on which the Reform Bill received the royal assent. As a young man, in order to gain admission to Oxford, he had signed the Thirty-nine Articles without believing them. This piece of deception seems to have rankled in his mind, and led, not merely to an active disbelief in religion, but to a real hatred of it and of the Deity Himself. Bentham, and another Utilitarian leader, the banker-historian, George Grote, actually regarded Christianity as responsible for the social evils which they desired to remedy. The attitude of James Mill, who may be taken as forming the third member of the Utilitarian triumvirate, was not so violent (he had indeed been a minister of religion), but he reacted from what he regarded as the crude conceptions of Christian theology and desired its disappearance. The Utilitarian leaders seem to have been quite incapable of understanding Christianity, and their thoughts and plans were confined entirely to material things. Like the Stoic lawyers of the age of the Antonines they did good service in promoting social reforms and engendering a more humanitarian outlook. In other ways the Utilitarians resembled the Stoics, for they endeavoured to suppress the emotions and to bring them entirely under the control of the reason. In fact reason was not merely a crowned monarch, but a tyrant absolute.

The system, intensely earnest, narrow, and lacking in humour and grace, naturally laid itself open to caricature and gibes.

[1] *Op. cit.*, I, pp. 174 f.
[2] It can be traced further back to the influences of Locke.

THE DEVELOPMENT OF THOUGHT TO 1870

The youthful Disraeli, in his skit *Popanilla*, describes with great glee the effects of the appearance, through a shipwreck, of a library of Utilitarian volumes among a simple-minded people. In the end the King, under pretence of opening up relations with other peoples as a preliminary to starting the system, ships off the unfortunate Popanilla, who was its principal advocate, in an open canoe, assuring him that although he had never been to sea before he would speedily, by the aid of a treatise or two, make a consummate naval commander.[1]

But there were more serious reactions to Benthamism, as some called it, and even those who had been among its supporters began to see its serious limitations. One of such was James Martineau. His critical attitude did not take place until the posthumous publication of Bentham's *Deontology* in 1834. He then began to see the futility of emphasizing the consequences rather than the motives of actions. In 1837 in a sermon on John v. 30, which he entitled "Out of self we can produce nothing," he declared his separation.[2]

In spite of its limitations, however, and their realization by those who tried to follow out the system, Utilitarianism, as modified and humanized by John Stuart Mill, was destined to be an important influence in English thought during the first half of the Victorian Era. Mill's own departing from the straitest sect of Benthamism was revealed in an article in the *Westminster Review* of March 1840. In it he expresses his doubts as to the ability of Utilitarianism to provide a real philosophy of society or of history, and suggests that it needs supplementing by the deeper thought of Coleridge.[3] This last must have been a heavy blow to the "orthodox" follower of Bentham; but Mill elsewhere couples the names of Bentham and Coleridge together as "the two great seminal minds" of their age and country. But Mill was right and others were soon to perceive

---

[1] *Popanilla and Other Tales* (Bradenham Edition), p. 23.

[2] See J. Estlin Carpenter, *James Martineau*, p. 172.

[3] In post-war days the underlying theory of Benthamism has been attacked by Aldous Huxley. In *Brave New World* he suggests that happiness is not the Sovereign Good, but that there is a goal "somewhere beyond, somewhere outside the present human sphere," and that the purpose of life is "not the maintenance of well-being, but some intensification and refining of consciousness, some enlargement of knowledge" (*op. cit.*, p. 209).

that "happiness" was not an adequate test of utility, and that the idea that the interests of the individual and the community were identical was not a platitude, but a paradox. Mill also realized that his old leader had no adequate idea of the value of a sense of humour or of the love of beauty. There was between them a still more fundamental difference. Mill had a profound regard for the freedom and rights of the individual; Bentham, had it been possible, would willingly have sacrificed both in order to make people happy by compulsion!

John Stuart Mill is one of the most pathetic figures of the century, the victim of the mistaken zeal of a devoted father.[1] The elder Mill had brought up his son without any knowledge of religion, and he was never able to shake off the effects of his early training; that he was naturally religious is shown, I cannot help thinking, by his efforts in later life to get on more friendly terms with it and even, in his *System of Logic* (1843), actually to approach a kind of theism. His writings reveal one who was transparently honest, but whose mind was continually on the stretch; it is, of course, the mind of one who was never allowed to be a child or to relax. His fearless love of truth made him long to get to the ultimate cause of things; whilst his regard for his fellow men made him an ardent reformer, an advocate of freedom of thought, and a pioneer of the rights of women. His influence was very considerable and had "a profound effect upon the body of political thought which underlay and determined practical action in his own day and later times."[2] In English thought, and particularly in the philosophical teaching at Oxford, he was for a long time the supreme influence, only receding before the advance of the Hegelian school, led by T. H. Green.[3]

COMTE

Among the teachers who influenced Mill, though only in part, in his reaction from the pure form of Benthamism was Auguste Comte, his contemporary. This philosopher and religious founder had so much influence on English thought

---

[1] In his exceedingly interesting *Autobiography* he has described his education and upbringing.
[2] Sir Arthur Salter in *Great Victorians*, p. 309.   [3] See below, pp. 273 ff.

in general that something must be said about him and the strange system which was the product of his genius. Its whole basis was an enthusiasm for humanity, *le grand être* he called it, which had for him the value of God.[1] His social teaching was valuable from the emphasis which it placed on the social origin of wealth and the importance of order as a factor in any advance which hoped to prove permanent. In many ways his outlook was limited and his powers inadequate to the task which he had undertaken. His knowledge of history was only superficial, hence some of his mistaken theories; whilst in science he would not venture beyond the solar system, and limited research to external phenomena, thus ignoring psychology. "I wonder whether Comte was proof against the spring!" once wrote P. H. Wicksteed, an English thinker who understood him well.[2] This was typical of his limitations. None the less, he exercised great influence. His outlook was very much that of Ruskin, as Frederic Harrison has observed, though perhaps there was no direct borrowing; but on Westcott he certainly exercised a profound effect which the latter was glad to acknowledge.[3] This was, of course, only on the social side; but his "religion" was also taken up in this country and drew to it some of the most brilliant men of the day. The names of Congreve, Beesley, and Frederic Harrison are guarantees of this. There was a meeting for the worship of humanity in Fetter Lane, with, as some witty person once said, three persons and no God.[4] In fact, as a French writer of the present century has pointed out, Comte had a much bigger following in England than in his native land.[5] But its influence soon began

[1] Cf. Feuerbach: "God was my first thought, reason my second, and man my third."   [2] C. H. Herford, *P. H. Wicksteed*, p. 40.

[3] See *Social Aspects of Christianity*, p. xii, where Comte and F. D. Maurice are coupled together. The same pair had a great influence on Canon Barnett. Another who was affected by Comte was Charles Booth, the wealthy shipowner, who was responsible for the famous survey of the *Life and Labour of the People of London*.

[4] See R. F. Horton, *An Autobiography*, p. 31.

[5] "C'est en Angleterre, bien plus que dans son pays, qu' Auguste Comte a trouvé des disciples convaincus. . . . Même aujourd'hui, la doctrine positiviste, à peu près oubliée en France, éveille dans plus d'une âme anglaise, une foi vivante et comme un enthousiasme religieux." Emile Boutmy, *Psychologie politique du peuple anglais au XIX*ᵉ *siècle*, p. 61.

to wane in face of attacks from without and differences within. Probably Huxley had as much to do with its loss of influence as anyone when with his devastating skill he dubbed it: "Catholicism *minus* Christianity." Internally a serious split followed the publication in 1875 of the English translation of the *Politique Positive* by which the system was considerably modified.[1]

THE REVOLT FROM RATIONALISM

The reaction against Liberalism which took place at the beginning of the reign of Victoria was only partial since its protagonists were themselves, in many cases, Liberals. It was dissatisfaction with the limitations of the predominant school, rather than a complete disagreement with its underlying principles, which led to reaction. Liberalism in the early years of the century had been concerned mainly with outward practical things, reforms and philanthropic efforts and the destruction of privileges; it needed supplementing by something deeper and more positive. In the meantime germinal ideas were slowly coming to life under the soil, to appear above the surface with the new reign. It was in the 'fifties and 'sixties that men began, on a wide scale, to give recognition to the thought of a previous generation; that prophets like Carlyle and Maurice, and philosophers like Mill, began really to be taken seriously. But even in the earlier period there had been those who reacted. Some, like Wordsworth and Coleridge, had in their own youth abandoned the old faith and institutions and "set their faces to the wilderness, and after sojourning for a season there, came out on the other side, and found peace, having, after long soul-turmoil, discerned a meaning in the old truths they had not divined before."[2] Coleridge himself never ceased to be in a sense a Rationalist; but as he distinguished the Reason from the Understanding, including conscience in it and allowing

[1] See C. H. Herford, *op. cit.*, pp. 184 ff.

[2] J. C. Shairp, *Studies in Poetry and Philosophy*, p. xviii. In Hare's dedication of his *Mission of the Comforter*, occurs the following passage: "To the honoured memory of Samuel Taylor Coleridge, the Christian philosopher, who, through the dark and winding paths of speculation, was led to the light, in order that others, by his guidance, might reach that light without passing through the darkness."

that it could receive divine illumination, he was a Rationalist with a difference. But he never went so far as to be able to accept either an infallible Church or an infallible Bible. The real guide was the Spirit of God working in the Church and in the soul of man. Thus he stood for freedom of thought, and against any religion based solely on authority.

We come next to Thomas Carlyle. His reverberating voice rang in the ears of all who came within his influence; the young especially found it enthralling and their talk was apt to be full of his phrases. Of his influence there have been many contradictory estimates; some have even gone so far as to say that if you took away the Scotch accent and the insolence there was very little left. But this is to ignore his real achievement which, in spite of the "Everlasting Yea," was mainly negative and destructive. Against shams, or what he took to be such, he waged unceasing warfare; but in bringing them to the test of reality he sometimes forgot that venerable beliefs, if held by simple and sincere souls, should be treated with respect and tenderness. To refer to the Old Testament as Hebrew old clothes and to call for an exodus from Houndsditch was surely unjust, not to say unwise. Carlyle was apt to be lacking in sympathy with anything established and traditional, and his dislike of Orthodox Christianity was extended to all philosophical systems and even to Natural Science. "If Adam had remained in Paradise," he once said, "there had been no anatomy and no metaphysics."[1] None the less, he had his good side, and his insistence on the dignity of human life and the high worth of honest labour was a testimony needed in his day, as in ours. Moreover, his outlook was not limited to this world; he had a vivid realization of the unseen and witnessed to the spiritual nature of reality in an age of growing materialism. Carlyle had a firm belief in the devil and was greatly angered to find that Emerson did not share this conviction. In order to change his views Carlyle took his friend through a succession of the horrors of London—gin shops and so forth—ending up with the House of Commons! At each successive change of scene he ejaculated, "Do you believe in the devil noo?"[2]

[1] Quoted by J. Estlin Carpenter, *James Martineau*, p. 139.
[2] See J. W. Cross, *George Eliot's Life*, I, p. 214.

With Carlyle is often grouped his contemporary, the American Emerson, whose "transcendentalism" carried away many who were left unaffected by the more rugged teaching of the other. The extent and variety of his influence in England was truly remarkable. It was one of the causes of Stopford Brooke's breach with the Evangelicalism in which he had been nurtured;[1] it was to inspire the future Baptist leader, John Clifford, to struggle for culture and independence;[2] whilst Robertson Nicoll testifies to the mighty force which it exercised on young men in Scotland in the early 'sixties.[3] There were, it is true, others who disliked his teaching intensely; York Powell, for instance, saw in it nothing more than "sandy inconsequence and vague culture."[4] But it had a power of inspiration which was hardly excelled even by that of Carlyle. This inspiriting force was latent in the philosophy which he held and advocated. Martineau testifies that his tomes "recalled natural faiths which had been explained away, and boldly appealed to feelings which had been struck down; they touched the springs of a sleeping enthusiasm, and carried us forward from the outer temple of devout science to the inner shrine of self-denying duty."[5]

Emerson accepted no merely traditional religious system; he appealed to present experience and held that the "fountain of inspiration was still flowing." The creeds of the orthodox he rejected on the ground that the world was too young for a system, and, with an irony gentler than that of Carlyle, he talked of "rose-water theology," and "the cabinet keepers of our doctrinal museums." But Emerson was not merely denunciatory, he had his own positive ideas, and indeed his condemnation of orthodoxy was on the grounds that it was inadequate and kept men back from higher truth: "When the half gods go the gods arrive." One eccentric belief he had —that a prophet was about to come to lead mankind; "a

[1] Jacks, *Life of Stopford Brooke*, p. 42.
[2] Marchant, *John Clifford*, p. 12. Dr. Clifford had a copy of Emerson's *Essay on Self-Reliance* given to him by his Sunday School teacher. He constantly re-read it to the end and regarded Emerson as "the most potent force in shaping my life."
[3] *Letters of a Bookman*, p. 26.
[4] *F. York Powell*, I, p. 152.   [5] J. Estlin Carpenter, *op. cit.*, p. 174

Messiah was due from God." This belief led him to seek his "Messiah" in some extraordinary quarters; but this falling off is not of importance for us, except as a warning. What is important is to realize the attractive power of all this forward-looking teaching, even if it was based on no certain foundation. It had the effect of plunging young men in a ferment of mind; even if they did not end by accepting Emerson as a teacher, it led them to question all things.

RELIGIOUS THOUGHT

In the religious world there was also a ferment of thought as the various elements strove with one another. All three of them, Puritan, Catholic, and Liberal, can be found already by 1850 in Browning's *Christmas Eve and Easter Day*.

The Puritans were by this time beginning to realize that the special foundation of their own type of Christianity, the Bible, was to suffer change. The Evangelicals, timid and narrow in their thinking, were apt, as was natural, to become obscurantist in the face of attacks which they felt were difficult to meet. From sympathizers outside the Church of England they had some support; but among them, and especially among the Congregationalists, a great struggle over the limits of freedom of opinion was taking place. This came to a head in what was known as the "Rivulet" controversy.

In November 1855 T. T. Lynch, a London Congregational Minister, published a volume which he called *Hymns for Heart and Voice: The Rivulet*. At first it was well received; then came a series of violent attacks from Dr. Campbell, a well-known Minister of the same denomination, a man with an extraordinary gift for journalism, and the editor of several periodicals, including the *British Banner*. It was in the pages of this journal that the attacks took place. The unfortunate *Rivulet* was condemned as unchristian and unspiritual; a condemnation which received additional gravity by the supposed discovery that it had been inspired by the rational theology of Germany. A furious strife, by word and pen, at once broke out which ended by drawing in, on the one side or the other, many leading Congregationalists. Angell James, who was revered by both sides, tried vainly to soothe it in his *Tract for the Times, On*

Speaking the Truth in Love. The dispute, which was made more bitter by the successful attempt about this time to expel Samuel Davidson from Lancashire College for unorthodox teaching, came to an end when Dr. Campbell severed his connexion with the *British Banner* and started a rival, the *British Standard*. Thus the battle for some measure of freedom of thought was fought out and permanently won in one denomination at least.[1]

So much for the Puritans. We come next to the Catholics, as represented by the Oxford School in the Anglican Church. Their attitude was much the same as that of the Evangelicals; they were equally alarmed, as we shall see, by the publication of *Essays and Reviews*. One dangerous tendency amongst them, a tendency which marked the Medieval Church and called forth the condemnation of Erasmus,[2] was a desire for too narrow definitions of the lesser matters of the faith. But even here a better spirit was manifesting itself, a spirit which in the end would lead to *Lux Mundi*. It was R. W. Church who saw the danger of the desire completely to define all things; he came to this conclusion in connexion with the dispute over Baptismal Regeneration. At the time of the publication of J. B. Mozley's *Primitive Doctrine of Baptismal Regeneration* he wrote to a friend: "In the Middle Ages, and much more in the early times of the Church, there was infinitely more free speculation than seems compatible with Church views now. I think it must be we who are wrong. The nature of things seems more in favour of the old way than of ours." Shortly afterwards he wrote to Mozley himself: "I am very glad you worked the point well about ignorance. I never should be a metaphysician; but the way in which assumptions excite no question, and people go on spinning arguments, as if the whole invisible world was as easy to be understood as the theory of the steam-engine, has long been one of my standing wonders. The idea of perfect and absolute knowledge, which is involved in so much of what is said and taught on all sides, becomes daily more and more unendurable to me."[3]

[1] See A. W. Peel, *These Hundred Years*, pp. 221 ff.
[2] See Elliott-Binns, *Erasmus the Reformer*, p. 6.
[3] *Life and Letters of Dean Church*, pp. 173 f.

THE GROWTH OF LIBERAL IDEAS

This objection to fresh definitions of Christian doctrine was strongly upheld by the Liberals; many of whom, indeed, would gladly have dispensed with Christian dogma and tradition almost entirely, though anxious to preserve its religious and ethical elements.[1] At both Oxford and Cambridge the fundamentals of the faith were being explored by the reviving spirit of enquiry which was stirring them to renewed mental activity. In Oxford, Oriel and Balliol were the centres of such menacing efforts; whilst at Cambridge Thirlwall and Julius Hare, who had been prominent in the days immediately before 1837, had still a potent influence. Thirlwall had been a barrister before his ordination in 1827, when he returned to Trinity. His stay was cut short in 1834 by a quarrel with Wordsworth the Master over compulsory chapels and the admission of Dissenters to the Universities. From 1840 to 1874 he was Bishop of St. David's, where he gained the goodwill and admiration of his people. There is one striking testimony to the respect in which he was held, from an unexpected source. Dr. John Hughes, the grandfather of Hugh Price Hughes, although a strong Nonconformist, "was only known to take his hat off to one person, the bishop of the diocese . . . for whose learning and character he had a profound respect."[2] Thirlwall and Hare had together translated Niebuhr's *History of Rome*, whilst the former had also made available in English Schleiermacher's *Essay on St. Luke*. Julius Hare had been made Fellow of Trinity in 1818 and later took the family living of Hurstmonceaux. This was a step to the Archdeaconry of Chichester. He was famous for his large library and the number of German books which it contained. Though he was in many respects sympathetic to the Evangelicals his views on Inspiration and the Atonement were more liberal. He was strongly opposed to the "mocking-bird" of Tractarianism as he called it.[3]

[1] Liberals were urged to be cautious in expressing their views, "as a condition of real usefulness," as Jowett wrote in 1861 to the notorious Mr. Voysey: *Life and Letters of Benjamin Jowett*, I, p. 402.
[2] *Life of Hugh Price Hughes*, p. 4.
[3] *The Mission of the Comforter*, I, p. ix. I owe the reference to Storr, *Development of English Theology*, p. 338.

Among his pupils at Trinity was one of the most remarkable men and one of the greatest influences of the century, Frederick Denison Maurice.

Frederick Denison Maurice was in part a disciple of Coleridge[1] and had the distinction of being almost the only Anglican of the period[2] with a really adequate metaphysical training and a knowledge sufficient to give him a right to an opinion on philosophical subjects. His great achievement was to make men realize that eternity was not time extended, but time abolished. By learning to know God men come to share in Eternal Life and at the same time to surrender their individual lives "to that universal Energy which is the very life of God." His religion was founded on the nature of God and not in man's notions concerning Him: so he claimed.[3] He therefore rejected the Evangelical theory by which "the sinful man, and not the God of all grace," is made "the foundation of Christian theology." He regarded the Church as the source and inspiration of human fellowship; as human society rescued from the abnormality of the world, and restored to communion with God. Man's own dissatisfaction and despair come from his inability to be satisfied with the temporal and from his slavery to selfish objects. "Anything is better than this dark self," he bursts out, in a passage which has a strangely close parallel in the works of Tagore.[4] "I cannot bear to be dogged by that, night and day; to feel its presence when I am in

---

[1] At a later time when there was a liberal revival after the collapse of the Oxford Movement, Maurice "nobly upheld the torch of Christian idealism, and carried on the Coleridgean tradition of a more spiritual philosophy." Storr, *op. cit.*, p. 3.

[2] As Coleridge died in 1834 he belongs to the pre-Victorian Era, though his influence persisted in many quarters in the later period.

[3] C. F. G. Masterman, *F. D. Maurice*, p. 19. This central doctrine, that man partakes of the divine nature, is found also in Coleridge: e.g. *The Statesman's Manual*, p. 265.

[4] "I came out alone on my way to my tryst.
But who is this that follows me in the silent dark?
I move aside to avoid his presence, but I escape him not.
He makes the dust arise from the earth with his swagger;
   he adds his loud voice to every word that I utter.
He is my own little self, my lord, he knows no shame;
   but I am ashamed to come to thy door in his company."

company, and when I am alone; to hear its voice whispering to me—'Whithersoever thou goest, I shall go. Thou wilt part with all things else, but not with me.' "[1]

Maurice is often regarded as a Broad Churchman. This was not the case; he was, as C. F. G. Masterman has said, "A dogmatist to the backbone, and repudiated all advocacy of vague and watery creeds" (*op. cit.*, p. 172). He was classed as such because he fought the same opponents, and men are often divided up thus "rather than through their own affirmations" (*op. cit.*, p. 221). He would nowadays, I suppose, be called a Liberal Catholic; though he would himself have refused that, or any other party badge. Certainly the vague, undogmatic religion which the man in the street finds so attractive, if not for himself, at least for other people, would have aroused his scorn. As to the Broad Churchmen, he could say: "Their breadth seems to me to be narrowness. They include all kinds of opinions. But what message have they for the people who do not live on opinions?"[2]

There was a widely held idea, in Maurice's own day, that his thinking and language alike were "muddy"; certainly many failed to fathom his thought and found his language obscure. But there were others, perhaps moved by closer sympathies, who had no such difficulties. His influence worked in countless minds and perhaps above all in Kingsley and Hort.[3] Robertson of Brighton with whom we are now to deal also owed much to him.

The contribution which Robertson made to the thought of his day was mainly negative, since having destroyed the old "forensic," Evangelical scheme in which he himself had been brought up, he never really found anything to replace it. His chief merit, and the faculty which gave his preaching such power, was a deep sympathy with the difficulties and problems which beset the men of his generation. There were, of course, certain ideas which he promulgated, such as the need for

---

[1] *Theological Essays*, p. 19.
[2] Quoted C. F. G. Masterman, *op. cit.*, p. 28.
[3] The case of Kingsley is too well known to require references: for Hort, see *Life and Letters of F. J. A. Hort*, I, p. 42.

emphasizing the "perfect" humanity of our Lord;[1] and he was a pioneer in what is now a commonplace demand, that all aspects of life, social, individual, and national, should be subdued to the teaching of Christ. Had he lived longer he might have found some more complete and satisfactory system; as it was the service he rendered consisted in the exposure of what he held to be unworthy ideas of Christianity and the insufficiency of mere catchwords.

ESSAYS AND REVIEWS

The growth of liberal ideas within the Church had been going on for some time and the leaders of both the Evangelicals and the Tractarians had regarded them with apprehension; but until 1860 there had been no public alarm. In that year, which it may be remembered was the one following the publication of the *Origin of Species*, appeared a volume of *Essays and Reviews* dealing with religious subjects.[2] The volume itself was part of a series of similar productions though it differed from them in being concerned with theological subjects only. Within this limitation the topics were miscellaneous and the treatment, with the exception of Mark Pattison's essay on "Tendencies of Religious Thought in England, 1688–1750," neither weighty nor learned; the tone, which varied in the different essays,[3] was mildly rationalistic and, on the whole, too negative.[4] In some the object of the writer seemed essentially to be destructive, and undue emphasis was laid on the imperfections of the Bible to the ignoring of its positive merits.[5] Much of the contents of the volume would

[1] Henry Drummond says that Robertson taught him that Christ was not only God—but also man. From him he got his "first glimpse of liberty in the intellectual life."

[2] The contents of the volume are no longer of sufficient importance to require detailed discussion; for such, see Hunt, *Religious Thought in the Nineteenth Century*, pp. 199 ff., and Storr, *op. cit.*, pp. 429 f.

[3] Such was the opinion of Lord Morley: see *Life of Gladstone*, II, p. 163. The first essay, "The Education of the Human Race," by Frederick Temple, was the most moderate though it caused its author much trouble in later years.

[4] Stanley criticized it on this ground, *Life*, II, p. 33.

[5] It is claimed that Jowett's contribution, "On the Interpretation of Scripture," had been moderated on the advice of Tennyson: see *Alfred, Lord Tennyson*, I, p. 472.

now be regarded as mere commonplace; but when it appeared, and appeared as the work of clergymen of the Church of England, it seemed to many to be an act of deliberate and calculated treason.[1] The fiery Dean Burgon, for example, spoke of "the immoral spectacle of six ministers of religion conspiring to assail the faith which they outwardly professed"; others, adding the one layman among the contributors, called them the "Septem contra Christum."

The challenge of *Essays and Reviews*—and in the minds of its promoters it was definitely intended as a challenge to the "unwholesome reticence of the clergy"—was speedily taken up. Three courses of procedure were adopted: (*a*) a Declaration; (*b*) the prosecution of some of the contributors; (*c*) various attempts at a Reply. The Declaration was really a failure, in spite of the union of Evangelical and Tractarian leaders, their mutual antagonism for a moment forgotten, in its support. It is true that about half of the "Clergymen of the United Church of England and Ireland" declared their faith in "The Inspiration of the Word of God and the Eternity of Future Punishment"; but to be effective the manifesto required a much larger proportion. New views had spread much more widely among the clergy than many had suspected. Two of the contributors, Rowland Williams and H. B. Wilson, were prosecuted. The latter was one of the four tutors who had protested against Newman's Tract 90. Here too failure had to be acknowledged; for though the Court of Arches condemned them, its judgement was set aside by the Privy Council. On the various attempts to meet the statements in the volume a little more needs to be said.

Two collections of refutations were published, *Aids to Faith*, edited by William Thomson, the future Archbishop of York, then Bishop of Gloucester and Bristol; and *Replies to Essays and Reviews*, edited by Samuel Wilberforce.[2] The former included contributions by H. L. Mansel, F. C. Cook, Professor Rawlinson, Professor Harold Browne, and Dean Ellicott: the latter

[1] It was noticed by Frederic Harrison in the *Westminster Review*, which first aroused attention to the volume: he welcomed it as a sign that Christianity was adopting a more rationalistic outlook.

[2] For the contents of these volumes see Hunt, *op. cit.*, pp. 211 ff.

included E. M. Goulburn, Professor Heurtley, A. C. Haddon, Christopher Wordsworth, and J. W. Burgon. All these men were famous in their day and were to proceed to high office in the Church, if they did not already hold it. But their efforts were futile or worse. Westcott, although he did not care for *Essays and Reviews*, regarded the action against it as "more perilous than scepticism," and was shocked by the shrieking of the Bishops, including his own beloved Headmaster, Prince Lee.[1] Hort felt that many of those who attacked the volume had a much smaller love of the truth than the essayists themselves and feared that their object was to drive out of the Church all who loved truth above mere orthodoxy.[2] The thought of combining in a reply came to Westcott, Hort, and Lightfoot themselves; but they wisely abandoned the project.[3]

The publication of *Essays and Reviews* had very impressive consequences which "invested the volume with an importance out of all proportion to its real power";[4] for it familiarized the great body of educated people with the problems which were arising in the field of religion and theology. This was all to the good, as an enlightened Conservative, G. H. Wilkinson, had the ability to perceive; for it was a valuable quickening force to the laity who for the most part had "a sort of stupid historical faith, very vague and seldom strengthened by any reflection."[5] Further, it definitely showed that Liberal views had a legitimate place in the Church of England, and they were so far met that the form of subscription to the Articles was relaxed so as to express merely a general agreement with their contents. The storm which arose was but the beginning of a long period of unrest and dispute; for in the year after the publication of *Essays and Reviews* there appeared Colenso's *Commentary on Romans*; but Bishop Colenso and his views on both the Old

[1] See *Life of B. F. Westcott*, I, pp. 212 and 214.
[2] *Life and Letters of F. J. A. Hort*, I, pp. 428 and 440. It is interesting to notice that Hort himself had been invited to contribute to the volume. His refusal to do so had been based on his High Church views which were not those of the other writers: see *op. cit.*, I, pp. 399 f.
[3] See *Life of Westcott*, I, p. 214, *Life and Letters of F. J. A. Hort*, I, p. 37.
[4] James Martineau in the Introduction to J. J. Tayler, *Religious Life of England*, p. 14.
[5] Mason, *Memoir of George Howard Wilkinson*, I, p. 82.

THE DEVELOPMENT OF THOUGHT TO 1870

and New Testaments and their practical consequences can best be postponed to a future chapter when we come to deal with Biblical Criticism in more detail.[1]

AN AGE OF UNCERTAINTY

The period of doubt and disputing, which thus began, had its origins in a much earlier generation, although for the most part such ruminations had gone on beneath the surface. For the spirit of certitude which marked the Victorians[2]—it was incarnate in Macaulay—did not extend to religion and philosophy. Already in *In Memoriam* we have an echo of the unsettlement of the times. The poem has been well described as a work which, though it exhausted no problems, yet "intimated many of the deepest of them, and lent the voice of pathetic music and exquisite human feeling to the widening doubts, misgivings, and flat incredulities of the time."[3] It is, however, in the secret records of the minds of many who afterwards became the leaders of Christian thought and life that the extent to which doubts and misgivings prevailed can be ascertained—and also the faith that overcame them. Doubt was in the air and religious men breathed in an atmosphere permeated by it; they might resent it, but they could not evade it. Hence the large number of those who suffered from its attacks. The crisis which they had to face was in part intellectual and in part emotional; the mind and the heart were often opposed.[4] In many cases the problem was thrust upon them prematurely, before a deeper knowledge of life and wider experience had given them the necessary material for its

[1] It may be worth noting that in 1870 a second volume of *Essays and Reviews* was contemplated which was to include contribution from some of the original writers, including Wilson and Jowett. The illness of the former and the succession of the latter to the Mastership of Balliol, however, prevented its realization.

[2] Cf. D. Willoughby in *Great Victorians*, p. 270: "A spirit of certitude, wonderful to us who live in an age which has taken the note of interrogation as its emblem, impregnated the great Victorians."

[3] Morley, *Recollections*, I, pp. 14 f.

[4] In a letter to Channing in 1840 James Martineau traced "a simultaneous increase, in the same class of minds, of theological doubt and of devotional affection."

RELIGION IN THE VICTORIAN ERA

solution. The danger to thoughtful minds was all the greater because rival systems were offered to them as substitutes for the faith of the gospel. Strauss, for example, attempted to find in the theory of evolution, supplemented by a superficial optimism, a new religious conception of the universe. The age was thus compelled to make an inventory of its resources, to strengthen its bulwarks, to tell its towers and battlements.

Among those who were attacked by doubts were Thomas Arnold, Charles Kingsley, and Westcott; all men whose robust and serene faith was in later years to bring life and encouragement to their struggling fellow Christians. Arnold in his difficulties had gone to Keble and received the advice "to pause in his inquiries, to pray earnestly for help and light from above, and to turn himself more strongly than ever to the practical duties of a holy life."[1] His doubts do not seem to have gone down to fundamental things, but to have been concerned with certain articles only of the Christian faith. This was true also of Kingsley, who wrote of himself in 1840: "An atheist I never was; but in my early life I wandered through many doubts and vain attempts to explain to myself the riddle of life and this world, till I found that no explanation was so complete as the one which one had learnt at one's mother's knee" (*Life*, p. 14). "Faith was born of doubt," he wrote later, "it is not life but death when nothing stirs" (*op. cit.*, p. 133). Westcott, too, had to go through similar experiences. One of the results of his thinking things out was *The Gospel of the Resurrection*.[2]

The epoch was well represented by A. H. Clough, the poet, who was described by Northcote as "busily taking all his opinions to pieces and not beginning to put them together again."[3] It must be confessed that there was about Clough something a little morbid, a kind of detached enjoyment of his mental sufferings. This also was true in part of the age itself, for the influence of Rousseau still persisted in many quarters—

[1] Stanley, *Life of Arnold*, p. 19.
[2] See *Life of B. F. Westcott*, I, pp. viii, 46, 51, and 249. Other records will be found in *Life of R. W. Dale*, p. 66, *John Clifford*, p. 24, and even in *Bishop Handley Moule*, p. 33.
[3] See Morley, *Life of W. E. Gladstone*, I, p. 329.

a kind of sentimental Deism, as Huxley, who disliked it intensely, used to call it. He traced it in "the theosophic confectionery" of Channing, as well as in the ideas of Voysey, the founder of the Ethical Church.[1]

THE UNITARIAN ATTACK

Much of the unsettlement was no doubt due to the writings of various Unitarian thinkers of considerable ability. These writings were not intended to be anti-Christian, but to clear away what were regarded as accretions on the original faith. Their effect, however, was to increase the uncertainty which was beginning to arise. Such attacks were conducted along far different lines than those which carried the spiritual teaching of great Unitarian leaders like Channing himself and Martineau, to whom "moral perfection was the essence of God and the supreme end for man." The tendency to become intellectually arrogant was indeed condemned by Martineau, who pointed out that there was "a complacency of disbelief no less than of belief; a pride in detecting the fallacies of other men's creeds; a piety that never prays without hinting at the highly rational character of its worship."[2]

The chief agents in the Unitarian attack—their names are now no longer remembered—were Charles Hennell and his brother-in-law, Charles Bray. Bray published in 1841 *The Philosophy of Necessity*, which denied all human freedom; whilst three years before Hennell, in his *Inquiries concerning the Origin of Christianity*, had treated Jesus as a purely human teacher and rejected all stories of miracles. It was through reading this latter book that George Eliot gave up the evangelical beliefs in which she had been brought up.[3] So much was she influenced by this school that she began to spread the new ideas, mainly by means of translations from the German.[4] Another figure who deserves

[1] See Mrs. Humphry Ward, *A Writer's Recollections*, p. 309.
[2] *National Duties and Other Sermons* (1836), p. 152.
[3] A very touching and not unattractive picture of religious development and of the Hennells and Brays will be found in J. W. Cross, *George Eliot's Life*.
[4] The best known is the first form of Strauss's *Life of Jesus*. She also translated Feuerbach's *Essence of Christianity*, the only volume incidentally which she ever published under her own name—Marian Evans.

mention is Francis Newman, the brother of the Cardinal. His book, *The Soul, its Sorrows and its Aspirations* (1849), had once a wide circulation which was shared by his *Phases of Faith* published in the following year. Newman was an attractive figure, but his undogmatic, mystical faith was not of a quality sufficient to stand the strain of real life.

8

RELIGION AND SCIENCE

ALTHOUGH the question of the relations of religion and science persisted right through the Victorian Era, and still confronts us with its problems, it will be convenient to deal with it at this early stage; for it was in the middle of the century that it first became important, and it was in this period that the boundaries of science were most definite. Since then they have become less distinct, and indeed in our own day it is almost impossible to say where science ends and philosophy begins. I propose to deal with the subject under three main headings: The History of Scientific Discoveries; Their Effects; The Conflict between Religion and Science which resulted from them.

THE HISTORY OF SCIENTIFIC DISCOVERIES

In the seventeenth century men had chiefly been interested in physics and mechanics; but in the eighteenth they began to turn their attention to those departments which are more concerned with living beings, and with the idea of development. But even then, in England at any rate, biology, according to Darwin, "was wholly neglected" (*Life and Letters*, I, p. 4). In spite of the heritage of Bacon and Newton science was only beginning to shake off the swaddling clothes of medieval times, and it was not until the foundation of the Royal Institution in 1797 that any real advance was made. But when it came the advance was definite and certain. Not only were fresh discoveries made, but new methods of research were evolved; there was also an attempt to co-ordinate scientific studies as a whole. With the coming of the new century the advances made are wellnigh inconceivable. It will be useful to glance briefly at them.

In the first place came Thomas Young's discovery of the undulating character of light (1801) and then two years later Dalton's atomic theory. This last was important since it was a return to that interest in the minute in physics which had been almost non-existent since the days of Lucretius: the gigantic, in the form of the heavenly bodies, was so much more apparent and, superficially, so much more impressive. Then in 1826 Liebig shewed the importance of organic chemistry. But the great year was 1830. It saw the publication of Herschel's *Discourse on the Study of Natural Philosophy* which, with Whewell's *History of the Inductive Sciences* (1831), was to do so much to make scientific ideas better known, and the foundation of the British Association, the first completely satisfactory attempt to organize scientific research in England and to give it a "platform."[1] But most noteworthy in it there appeared Lyell's *Principles of Geology*. Lyell was the pupil of Buckland, who from about 1823 had been putting forth revolutionary ideas about geology, although his own treatise *Geology and Mineralogy* was not to be published until 1836. The suggestion that the earth had been evolving during vast ages was certainly startling to the religious mind. But the responsibility for spreading such ideas did not stand in the way of Buckland's advancement in the Church, for Sir Robert Peel made him Dean of Westminster in 1845. Lyell was, of course, a layman, and he had a further bombshell to explode. At first he had been anxious to show that his ideas could be reconciled with Genesis—an impossible and, as we now see, an unnecessary task.[2] Further, when Darwin's theories had first come in he had received them with suspicion. But in 1863 (to anticipate the course of events) he published his *Evidence of the Antiquity of Man* which accepted Darwin's theory of the origin of species, and gave to man an existence upon the earth which far exceeded anything that had hitherto been supposed. In 1865 there came E. B. Tylor's *Researches into the Early History of Mankind*, the first of a series of studies which raised the problems of anthropology and comparative religion.

[1] Though much work had been done by individuals the volume of English achievement had not been realized, and France had been regarded as the leader in scientific studies: see Merz, *History of European Thought in the Nineteenth Century*, II, p. 751.

[2] Nowadays people try and reconcile Genesis with Geology. For fuller details see T. G. Bonney, *Charles Lyell and Geology*.

Turning back, we may notice the discovery of the cellular structure of plants by Schleiden of Jena in 1838, and its extension by Schwann, who saw that in animals too the cell was the unit. In 1842 the translation of Müller's *Elements of Physiology* was a prelude to great advances in the study of that science. As Müller regarded everything as purely material—even the senses worked according to mechanical rules—the effect upon religion was not happy. Then in 1844 came the famous anonymous volume *Vestiges of the Natural History of Creation*, which denied special creation of species although admitting the possibility of a gradual development under divine guidance.[1] But it was in 1859 that the epoch-making work appeared in Darwin's *Origin of Species*.

So modest were Darwin's anticipations for his volume that the first edition consisted of 1,250 copies only. These were sold out on the day of publication. The book succeeded because it made audible and systematic the thoughts in many minds.[2] It not only collected a vast amount of evidence in support of evolution, but also suggested a possible method, that of Natural Selection, through which it might work. These two ideas, Evolution and Natural Selection, should be kept quite distinct when thinking of Darwin's achievement. The former had been known in classical times and was the basis of Hegel's philosophy; even in science it had been anticipated by Goethe and Schelling. All that Darwin did was to make it popular and to give illustrations of its application. But the suggestion that Evolution works by Natural Selection was a truly original idea. Both Aristotle and the Bible assumed that distinctions of species were original. But Darwin pointed out that varieties of plants and animals were continually being produced through selective breeding; why should not Nature have employed the same methods to produce the species we know? Darwin further suggested that Nature's test was survival value in the struggle for existence. His suggestion was made easier by the fact that the discoveries of geologists by giving vast aeons of time

---

[1] The volume was actually by R. W. Chambers: see Storr, *English Theology in the Nineteenth Century*, p. 364.

[2] "The world was weary of unquestioning faith in Genesis, and was hungry for explanations": G. P. Wells in *Great Victorians*, p. 159.

provided the necessary duration for endless varieties to be produced.

The doctrine of Natural Selection suited the age in which it arose, that "age of unchecked industrial competition, when the devil, or the workhouse, was waiting to take the hindmost."[1] Its importance, if the importance of an idea is to be estimated by the changes in thought which it effects, can hardly be exaggerated. Romanes, indeed, considered it as "the most important idea that has ever been conceived by the mind of man."[2] All the same it required time in which to spread and to overcome the natural prejudice of those who could not separate what they regarded as revealed truth from the revelation which came up from the earth around them. It was long before science got anything like a footing in educated thought in England, in spite of the noble achievement of English scientists. This was perhaps due in part to the control of higher education by the clergy who may have felt, by a kind of instinct, that its teaching was dangerous; still more to the predominantly classical tone of such studies. Science has always been regarded as an upstart and its whole external history "is a history of the resistance of academies and universities to the progress of knowledge. The first discoverers have always been the heretics, and often the martyrs of science."[3]

Amidst the spirit of resistance to the spread of scientific ideas and as an exception to the general tone of depreciation—Newman, for example, objected to the "vulgarity" of the language used by some scientists—a welcome was given to the new ideas in quite an unexpected quarter. It came from certain of our poets who thus showed their prophetic insight, as well as their wide sympathies. It can be found in the Preface to the second edition (1800) of Wordsworth's *Lyrical Ballads*; but it became really active in Shelley, as later in Tennyson. Shelley, especially in *Prometheus Unbound*, reveals himself as the prophet of the new Scientific Era, of which Prometheus was the pioneer. The Earth itself is compelled to admit the supreme power of man:

[1] Inge in *The Modern Churchman*, XIV, pp. 219 f.
[2] *Darwin and after Darwin*, I, p. 257.
[3] Mark Pattison, *Essays*, II, p. 203.

"The lightning is his slave; heaven's utmost deep
Gives up her stars, and like a flock of sheep
They pass before his eye, are numbered, and roll on!
The tempest is his steed, he strides the air;
And the abyss shouts from her depth laid bare,
Heaven, hast thou secrets? Man unveils me ; I have none."

Tennyson's interest in Natural Science and his anticipation of future discoveries were almost uncanny. When *The Vestiges of Creation* appeared in 1844, he at once got a copy; but the sections of *In Memoriam* which show so profound a sympathy with scientific discovery were already written and in circulation among his friends.[1] Two of the earliest lines which he wrote were:

"The rays of many a rolling central star,
Aye flashing earthward, have not reached us yet."[2]

THE EFFECTS OF THE DISCOVERIES ON RELIGION

Since science deals with the relations of God and the world which He has made, it naturally comes into conflict with the old crude religious ideas of a pre-scientific age, and in particular with the idea that God is seen in the abnormal and the unaccountable rather than in the usual. Such an idea is really a kind of Deism, and regards God as a great architect standing outside the world. In this and other respects science has been what Baron von Hügel has called the purgatory of religion; it has cleansed it from much that was really unworthy. The doctrine of Evolution gave a final blow to the Deism of the eighteenth century; and by its suggestion of belief in the Divine immanence pointed to a vital element in the Christian doctrine of the Incarnation.[3] But in doing so it increased vastly the territory of the natural at the expense of the "supernatural," as indeed Newman had already foreseen.[4] Not only so but it suc-

[1] See especially Cantos CXVIII and CXXIII.
[2] See *Alfred, Lord Tennyson*, I, p. 20.
[3] Cf. H. H. Gowen, *A History of Religion*, p. 41.
[4] "I frankly confess that the present advance of science tends to make it probable that various facts take place, and have taken place, in the order of nature, which hitherto have been considered by Catholics as simply supernatural": *Apologia*, p. 335.

ceeded in penetrating the very studies by which religion, on its historical and theoretical side, had been accustomed to maintain itself. All regions of thought are now permeated by the scientific outlook, and its methods have been adopted in every department of scholarship, and even, in some respects, of literature.

The result of this acceptance of the scientific method has been not only to transform scholarship; it has also, in many cases, affected the individual thinker, driving him back from the spiritual, and compelling him to find only in material things any kind of certainty. This effect, however, was characteristic of science in its earlier stages. We are now in a position to see that materialism itself finds no real support in natural science; but in the nineteenth century in the full flush of discovery men did not perceive this. Those who were thus driven back from the spiritual to their great loss, came to limit their thoughts and aspirations to things of this world only. "World-worship," as Santayana has said, "is the expedient of those who, having lost the soul that is in them, look for it in things external, where there is no soul." Moreover, the practical application of scientific discoveries made the world more and more comfortable and diverting; for the improvements in industry were accompanied by homely discoveries, such as the lucifer match and the possibilities of amusement opened up by photography. So much then for the general effect of scientific discovery and invention in permeating and transforming the whole atmosphere in which religion and the religious man had to breathe. We turn now to a more detailed consideration of its results.

One of the great lessons of the new science was that Nature was a unity. This, incidentally, was really implied already in the Creation story of Gen. i, since a single Creator requires that His work should be a unity. Following on this the older distinction, used for example in the quotation from Newman just cited, between the natural and the supernatural, broke down. It was, as Aubrey Moore pointed out, "misleading. There are not, and cannot be, any Divine interpositions in Nature, for God cannot interfere with Himself. . . . A theory of 'supernatural interferences' is as fatal to theology as to science."[1]

[1] *Science and the Faith*, p. 225.

This admission seemed to take away the evidential value of what were called miracles, for in a single creation ruled by natural law they must be regarded either as a "breach" of such law, or as a confession by the Creator of imperfection in His work. But the crude appeal to miraculous events to support spiritual truth was never really Christian, certainly not on the lines of our Lord's methods; and the Christian regards them as acts done in co-operation with Nature rather than as interferences, as acted parables rather than compelling signs.[1] The presence of Natural Law everywhere seemed also to threaten the Christian habit of Intercessory Prayer; but this again was only threatened in its cruder forms, in the idea that the main object of prayer is to persuade God to do our will rather than to enable us to find out His will and gain strength to do it. Natural Law also tended to limit the field of man's free will even if it did not actually exclude it altogether. The discoveries of physicists in more recent times have certainly gone in the direction of lessening the force and rigidity of Natural Laws; for them such "laws" represent not the certainty of the nineteenth-century scientists, but rather something more akin to probability. Science no longer insists that human actions are completely determined.

The story of Creation in Gen. i is quite consistent with and even presupposes the Unity of Nature; but can it be reconciled with the modern conception of creation, not as an act, but as an evolution? Probably it can, if details are not pressed. But it must be remembered that the ideas of creation held by most people in the nineteenth century were derived not from Genesis, but from Milton. There is a vast difference between the restraint and vagueness of "God said 'Let the earth bring forth, etc.,' " and the quaint details supplied by *Paradise Lost*. Take, for instance, the following:

> "The grassy clods now calved; now half appeared
> The tawny lion, pawing to get free
> His hinder parts, then springs as broke from bonds
> And rampant shakes his brindled mane; the Pounce,

[1] On this see F. L. Cross, *Religion and the Reign of Science*, pp. 26 ff. Storr, *op. cit.*, pp. 140 f.

The libbard, and the tiger, as the mole
Rising, the crumbled earth above them threw
In hillocks: the swift stag from the under ground
Bore up his branching head;"[1]

The idea that each separate species was created specially is not involved in the account in Genesis, and its demolition by the theory of evolution was not a blow aimed at revelation. Nor did the fact that evolution seemed to take the force out of what was called the argument from design really matter; what was affected was not the evidence for design but merely the manner in which the design was executed.[2]

The argument from design is as strong as ever, in the sense that Nature seems to be working towards some end; but we have, from observation of the processes of Nature, no clue to what that purpose is, nor even that it is benevolent. In other days, Paley could find evidence for the goodness of God from the existence of the little apparatus in the throat by which we are saved from being choked by our food. "Consider a city-feast," he exclaims, "what manducation, what deglutition, and yet not one Alderman choked in a century!"[3] But this no longer concerns us. In any case these are but unimportant outworks of the faith; but there were certain more fundamental doctrines which seemed seriously to be threatened by the theory of evolution; in particular those of the Fall of Man and of the Incarnation.

It is quite true that evolution is not consistent with the traditional story of the Fall in the Garden of Eden; but the important part of that doctrine was the fact, known to all from experience, that man is actually a fallen creature and unable, in his own strength, to do what he knows to be right. This is not affected by evolution, which as a matter of fact "establishes more firmly than ever what was always the chief religious

---

[1] *Op. cit.*, VII, lines 414 ff. In Book V a view of creation more on the lines of evolution is set forth.

[2] Cf. F. Temple, *The Relations between Religion and Science*, p. 114.

[3] Quoted Hastings Rashdall, *Philosophy and Religion*, p. 60. His comment is worth adding: "Such arguments look at the matter from the point of view of the Alderman: the point of view of the turtle and the turkey is entirely forgotten" (*op. cit.*, pp. 60 f).

element in the doctrine of the Fall."[1] So too in regard to the Incarnation. Under the traditional theory of creation this seemed to be almost an intrusion into a fixed system. With the acceptance of evolution the sense of intrusion is taken away and we have instead "the full self-manifestation of Him who was guiding and manifesting Himself in all the process." This self-manifestation "initiates a new evolutionary phase."[2]

Thus the theory of evolution need have caused no alarm in the minds of religious leaders and teachers had they but grasped its real significance, and the real significance of much of what was held to be part of the faith. But with the method by which evolution works, that of Natural Selection, things were different. This method involved a terrible waste, so it seemed, and immense suffering. Nature was "red in tooth and claw," and if Nature was God, how could this be reconciled with His love? It was a truly difficult problem and one calculated to arouse the alarm of Christian men and women. Henceforth, though there might be a firm belief in the omnipotence of God and in His love, the old view of Nature was no longer possible. No one could write as Paley had done: "It is a happy world after all. The air, the earth, the water teem with delighted existence. In a spring noon, or a summer evening, on whichever side I turn my eyes, myriads of happy beings crowd upon my view. 'The insect youth are on the wing.' Swarms of new-born flies are trying their pinions in the air. Their sportive motions, their wanton mazes, their gratuitous activity, their continual change of place without use or purpose, testify their joy and the exultation which they feel in their lately discovered faculties. . . . The whole winged insect tribe, it is probable, are equally intent upon their proper employments, and under every variety of constitution, gratified, and perhaps equally gratified, by the offices which the author of their nature has assigned to them."[3]

Such were some of the effects of biological discoveries on the ideas of God and Creation which were held in the nineteenth

[1] W. Temple in *The Future of the Church of England*, p. 37.
[2] *Op. cit.*, p. 40.
[3] *Natural Theology*, pp. 370 f. Quoted by Aubrey Moore, *Science and the Faith*, pp. 194 f.

century. These theories also affected the position of man himself; for they shewed that he was part of Nature, that, as Archdeacon Storr has said, "whatever may be man's peculiar spiritual endowment, his physical nature looks back to an ancestry which begins with the dawn of life."[1] But there were discoveries in other departments of science, in geology and astronomy, which still further took from man's dignity and importance, seeming to make his position in the universe very insecure and to rob his life of apparent significance. Such discoveries, in so far as other, spiritual values were set aside, left man bowed down with the sense of his own impotence in the face of the awful vastness and rigidity of Nature and its laws.[2]

The new knowledge of the sixteenth and seventeenth centuries had altered the position of the earth in relation to the universe and robbed it of its supposed central position. But even so the belief persisted—Dr. Inge would have it that it still persists—"that Christianity asserts the existence of a geographical heaven and hell." But "Hell is not beneath our feet; volcanic eruptions are not caused, as the schoolmen suggested, by overcrowding in the infernal regions; and heaven is not a place which could be reached by an aeroplane if we knew the way."[3] This took from man and his earth its importance in space. The discoveries of the nineteenth century took from them their importance in time. John Lightfoot, a famous Cambridge scholar of the seventeenth century, calculated that the creation of man took place at 9 a.m. on October 23rd in the year 4004 B.C. But geology made the idea that the earth was but some 6,000 years old childishly impossible; and then astronomy stepped in to show that the universe of which the earth formed so trifling a portion had existed for thousands of millions of years. Thus vast spaces of time lay behind man and his evolution; and presumably vast spaces of time lay in front of him in which he still might evolve; the opportunity for enormous improvement, or for enormous degradation, for science could give him no guarantee one way or the other.

[1] *Development of English Theology*, p. 131.
[2] This feeling was not entirely new. George Fox had felt it, "the elements and the stars came over me," he says.
[3] *Outspoken Essays*, II, p. 36.

All this was very unsettling, and the more so because it suggested that the whole universe was in a state of flux with nothing central or permanent about it. The difficulty was met in part by the doctrine of the immanence of God; but that doctrine may easily become pantheism in those who see nothing but an evolving universe.

THE CONFLICT BETWEEN SCIENCE AND RELIGION

With science advancing views of such immense revolutionary force, and advancing them often enough in a spirit of arrogance, is it to be wondered that even sincerely religious men regarded it as the instrument of the powers of evil to be fought and denounced at every turn? Religion clung to its obsolete ideas and feared to allow any relaxation. On the other hand, men of science felt that for too long science had been kept in leading strings by theology. It was now conscious of its power and of the restraints placed upon it. So science broke away. Theology struggled to bring it back under control; science fought for its freedom from all dogmatic restrictions and presuppositions—and in particular from the idea that the Creator was in the habit of suspending His own laws, a theory which made any science of Nature quite impossible.

The conflict waged most fiercely during the second half of the century, but it had earlier beginnings. Miller in his Bampton Lectures for 1817 on *The Divine Authority of Holy Scripture Asserted from its Adaptation to the Real State of Human Nature*, had warned science of its limitations. There had also been trouble over the relations of Geology and Genesis, as we have seen; but it was not until after the appearance of *The Origin of Species* that the battle was really joined. The first serious clash was at the meeting of the British Association at Oxford in 1860, when Samuel Wilberforce received rough handling, and deservedly so, from Thomas Huxley. Later, in his dramatic speech in the Sheldonian Theatre on November 25, 1864, Disraeli took the opportunity of making it clear that on the question whether man was an ape or an angel, he was on the side of the angels. This speech, which at times suggests that its brilliant author had his tongue in his cheek, was of a type to antagonize the earnest seeker after truth; but it did not stand alone, the defenders of religion were very prone to make appeals to sentiment. One frantic defender of the old ways ended an impassioned discourse with the words: "Leave me my ancestors in Paradise and I will allow you yours in the Zoological Gardens."

There was undoubtedly, on the part of the narrowly orthodox, a considerable panic; and when people are in a fright they are apt to behave, as Dean Church said, "more like old ladies than philosophers" (*Life*, p. 184). There certainly was a lack of dignity about the religious, or those who took it upon them to speak for religion, and Aubrey Moore, a clear and able thinker on the Christian side, could not forbear to apply to the situation some words of Dr. Whewell who had affirmed "that every great scientific discovery went through three stages. First people said, 'It is absurd.' Then they said, 'It is contrary to the Bible.' And finally they said, 'We always knew it was so.' "[1]

There were, however, even in the early stages of the conflict Christian men who kept their heads and were prepared to give to the claims of scientists a fair hearing. One of the earliest of these was Dr. Pye Smith, the tutor of Homerton Independent College, who was not afraid to claim that science was a revelation from God and to challenge the common assumption that Genesis taught that the age of the world is less than 6,000 years.[2] Dean Church himself when Darwin's book appeared, though he wished that it had been more explicit, condemned the "shortness of thought" which would at once "treat the theory itself as incompatible with the ideas of a higher and spiritual order" (*op. cit.*, p. 184). From Hort, too, it received a welcome. "In spite of difficulties," he wrote to Westcott in March 1860, "I am inclined to think it unanswerable. In any case it is a treat to read such a book."[3] Kingsley, in this as in many another matter, was in advance of his age. To him science was the voice of God and the only proper position of those who heard it, the reply "Speak, Lord; for Thy servant heareth" (*Life*, p. 318).

---

[1] *Science and the Faith*, pp. 83 f.
[2] See Hunt, *Religious Thought in England*, etc., pp. 82 f.
[3] *Life and Letters of F. J. A. Hort*, I, p. 414. A month later he wrote: "Whatever may be thought of it, it is a book that one is proud to be contemporary with" (*op. cit.*, I, p. 416).

In the preface to his *Westminster Sermons* he expressed the wish that every ordinand should be required to pass "in at least one branch of physical science, if it be only to teach them the method of sound scientific thought."

I have thought it well to give these instances in some detail because it is often supposed that the attitude of religious men was one of unbroken opposition. This was far from being the case. At the same time, even those who took up such an attitude were faced by scientists who were similarly obtuse to any good in those to whom they were opposed. The arrogance of some of them and the exaggerated claims which they made for their own department of learning had much to do with the bitterness with which the conflict was waged. If religious men tended to forget the charity which should have distinguished their treatment of "enemies," the men of science, once they strayed away from their own special topic, often left the scientific method behind them and allowed prejudice to control their judgement. There was indeed much to be said for them. Science seemed to be sweeping all before it, and in the intoxication of success it seemed capable of explaining all things. In the minds of many there was the conviction that a new age was about to dawn; that man by his unaided powers was about to triumph over all obstacles to happiness and progress. As for God and religion, there would no longer be any need of them. It was the "very flood-tide of materialism and Agnosticism—the mechanical theory of the Universe, the reduction of all spiritual facts to physiological phenomena" being taken as proved.[1]

Science was arrogant because judging things by its own standards it had made so measurable an advance over previous ages, and its votaries were almost prepared to take on their lips the words of the sirens: "We know all things that take place in the much nourishing earth."[2] It must be remembered that the man of science was not only a discoverer, he was a creator also. This gave to him an immense confidence and a prestige in other fields, which in the smaller minds slipped over into arrogance. For it was amongst the smaller men that the note of arrogance and dogmatism was most clearly heard in those first years of strife, amongst the rank and file, not

[1] *Bishop Moule*, p. 34. [2] *Odyssey*, xii, p. 186.

amongst the leaders. In those who may be called the campfollowers (i.e. the anti-religious propagandists who picked up the odd scraps of scientific knowledge) it was still more strident.

But even the leaders made calm assumptions that appeared to their opponents to be as arrogant as ill-founded. For a time Huxley and Tyndall appeared to dominate thought, and to take it for granted that their ideas and methods would never again be challenged by men of intellect. Looking back we marvel that such claims could ever have been made; but in the latter years of the nineteenth century it was not an unnatural mistake, and indeed we escaped by only a small margin the establishment of a despotism of science, with a new orthodoxy based on its findings, and having as its Aquinas the venerable figure of Mr. Herbert Spencer.[1]

Men were thus carried away by the vast achievements of Natural Science. And indeed its achievements were very great. But they were also exaggerated.[2] Life, by scientific discoveries and inventions, had been made safer (chemical warfare and aeroplanes lay still in the undiscovered future), comforts and luxuries had been multiplied; but it could hardly be claimed that it was nobler or even happier. Besides, in making its conquests science, like every other conqueror, had had to destroy much; and it was doubtful whether what had been destroyed was not ultimately of more value than its successor. "Your scientist," says one impassioned critic, "like a jerry-builder, erected structures which serve his doubtful purpose for a short time only, but which deface the beauty which has preceded them, for ever."[3] The achievement of science was

---

[1] Here and there attacks were made on the new science by those who had no religious motives. One of the most bitter was Samuel Butler, who attacked orthodox religion and orthodox science with equal violence and considerable skill. His contemptuous tone, however, did him much harm, and as a *dilettante* he was never taken seriously by scientists; but in some of his criticisms he was nearer the truth than his opponents.

[2] It is curious that whilst the truths of theology are criticized, scientific discoveries are at once taken as true by those equally untrained in either subject. "It is difficult to exaggerate the amount of faith involved in the ordinary man's acceptance of the conclusions of science": Will Spens, *Belief and Practice*, p. 12.

[3] John Collier in *Great Victorians*, p. 511.

confined to the material sphere; it had no contribution, save in the devoted lives of scientific men, to offer in the moral sphere. "Evolution," as Scott Holland once wrote, "yields no categorical Imperative."[1] In the minds of many its effects in the moral sphere were, indeed, to be disastrous, for it suggested that sin itself was nothing more than an animal survival or an ancestral failing handed down to individuals who might outgrow it, but could hardly be blamed for its presence. Thus the sense of sin and of responsibility was weakened.

Science thus had no message to the highest side of man's nature. It had, also, nothing to tell him about the things that mattered most; its discoveries were limited to material things. When it tried to explain the universe, usurping the functions of philosophy, it did so only by leaving man himself (regarded as a thinking being) out of account; by conceiving of him purely as an animal. Well had Keble, in his poem on Hooker, called on that judicious mind to "teach proud science where to veil her brow." But the warning was unheard or unheeded, and some of the best of scientists seemed to cherish the curious and ingenuous belief that they could find God and the soul, if indeed such existed, by means of the microscope or the telescope; thus making arithmetic and geometry the measure of all truth.

But science, by its absorption in material things, unfitted its votaries for discoveries in the higher realms of thought,[2] and even robbed them of all power to appreciate what lay beyond the border of their special studies. The notorious case is, of course, that of Darwin himself. As a young man he delighted in poetry and art, and was sufficiently convinced of the truths of religion to contemplate ordination (*Life and Letters*, I, p. 171). But with his growing interest in scientific research these passed away, to his intense regret. "It is an accursed evil," he wrote to Hooker in 1858, "to a man to become so absorbed in any

---

[1] *Personal Studies*, p. 173. Cf. Baron von Hügel's opinion that "Science cannot directly furnish us with a purpose and an ideal for our lives": *Selected Letters*, p. 118.

[2] Incidentally it may be noted that the genesis and development of man's highest powers receive no explanation from the doctrine of Natural Selection since they have no "survival value."

subject as I am in mine" (*op. cit.*, II, p. 139). And in a passage which has often been quoted he declared that if he had to live his life over again he would make it a habit to read some poetry and hear some good music at least once a week.[1] The loss of interest and even belief in religion which marked him and other men of science can, I think, be partly if not wholly explained by their absorption in material studies. In Darwin's own case the loss was gradual and indeed almost unobserved. "The rate was so slow that I felt no distress," he has recorded (*op. cit.*, I, p. 309). It must be remembered that he was never an atheist "in the sense of denying the existence of God" (*op. cit.*, I, p. 304).

The scientists of the Victorian Era had no desire to be materialists, or to attack religion save in self-defence. Darwin affirmed that he "never published a word directly against religion or the clergy" (*op. cit.*, II, p. 289), whilst many of the earliest scientists were men of deep religious feeling. Dalton the chemist was a Quaker, as was Young the physicist; whilst Davy joined in the outcry against geology as dangerous to religion, and Faraday was a devoted member of an obscure sect. The founders of the British Association in 1830 had numbered among them several clergymen, including Sedgwick, Whewell, and Buckland. It was in attacking a "supernaturalism" which they regarded as superstitious and obscurantist that "naturalism" became material. Such is its constant danger, for it tends to interpret the higher in terms of the lower, and to forget the ideal and the transcendental; nature itself, if interpreted by the senses alone, ceases to have any spiritual meaning. The end is "a sense-bound age, rejoicing in a mechanical philosophy."[2] Science, in effect, has created a new civilization with ideals and standards of its own; lofty and exacting, it may be, but different from those which have animated mankind for the long centuries of its past. No longer does the devotee of science look to Athens or Jerusalem for guidance as once he did; though Rome for a time, it may be, retains a diminishing authority.

[1] *Op. cit.*, I, pp. 102 f. His loss of faith was subsequent to the collection of the facts for *The Origin of Species* (*op. cit.*, III, p. 236).
[2] J. C. Shairp, *Studies in Poetry and Philosophy*, p. xvi.

The truths of Natural Science, so far as they have been ascertained, are absolute; they are the same for all individuals.[1] The truths of religion, on the contrary, are in a sense relative; they are conceived of differently by different individuals and can be known, unless received blindly on authority, only by a personal effort of the mind and will. Thus Science has a superficial advantage over Religion. It has a similar advantage in another respect, for its achievements are tangible and easily recognized; for this reason they make a deeper impression on the minds of those who are not accustomed to abstract thought, or whose spiritual powers are dim and weak. Religious impressions, from their very nature, are less stable and tend to be forgotten. It was the recognition of this fact which led Newman to place such emphasis on the need for a visible Church to give depth and permanence to impressions which otherwise might fade away.[2] But though the impressions of Natural Science may seem to be permanent, or more permanent than those of religion; they bring satisfaction only to man's lower desires. The higher are left hungry and disappointed.[3]

The coming of a new century saw the end of the conflict, or the promise of the end. Science and religion began to see that each had need of the other and that concessions had to be made and toleration exercised. The foremost religious minds have a growing appreciation of the value of the scientific outlook, and the foremost leaders of science have become humbler and more appreciative of the value of religion. Above all, the tendency to stray into each other's territory has been curbed. Churchmen now recognize that their panic was unjustified,

---

[1] The "quarrels" of biologists, as revealed, for example, at the meeting of the British Association at Norwich in September 1935, perhaps suggest that the field of certainty is, in some branches of science, not quite so wide as is often thought.

[2] Cf. W. Ward, *Last Lectures*, p. 28. "In one of the Dublin lectures he describes in a striking passage the evanescent quality of religious impressions in the individual mind, and their contrast in this respect to our inevitably vivid consciousness of the visible and palpable truths of physical science: and then he appeals to the visible Church as the only efficient practical force which can give depth and permanence to religious impressions."

[3] "Materialism's sun sets in a sea of disappointment," wrote W. James, *Pragmatism*, p. 108.

that the discoveries of Natural Science have not had that destructive effect on religion which was once feared; moreover, the lapse of time and further research has shown that such discoveries were in any case true whatever their effect. Perhaps they have remembered the teaching of Bishop Butler that "Revelation could never be strengthened by being isolated from Nature. What God is in Nature that He is in Revelation."[1] Scientists have become more humble because they recognize more adequately the difference between a hypothesis and a fact, and have to admit the failure of many theories which once were held to be safely established.[2] The fond belief once held that science worked automatically for progress was broken for ever by Huxley in his Romanes Lectures on *Evolution and Ethics* in 1893. To him the cosmic process seemed almost a power of evil. Further, it has become clear that science has nothing to say about origins, that its proper function is to deal with processes. This being so, there is less danger of a clash with religion or philosophy both of which concern themselves with ultimate things. In April 1892 Bishop Westcott wrote, perhaps with undue optimism: "Physicists are beginning, I think, to recognize that they deal only with abstractions, and that such a fact as the Incarnation is alone able to give reality to human knowledge" (*Life*, II, p. 88). Theologians and religious leaders, for their part, began to recognize that they had no right to impose limits upon genuine intellectual enquiry or to insist beforehand that its results shall conform to their own standards. With this recognition the quarrel is ended.

The end of the conflict and the growing understanding between religion and science is a mark of the last phase of the Victorian Epoch; but as such it was largely confined to this country. In other lands where the quarrel has been more bitter, and the Church has stood too strenuously for that which is old and traditional, no such understanding has yet been achieved. "When I have talked with men of science in other countries," observed Bishop Creighton, "I have found that

---

[1] See H. Scott Holland, *Personal Studies*, p. 54.

[2] "The progress of science is just as much strewn with the remnants of discarded theories as in the progress of philosophy": J. S. Haldane in *The Modern Churchman*, XIV, p. 281.

they considered it impossible for a man who is a thinker to be in any sense whatever in friendship with the Church; that this is not the case in this country makes me most hopeful for England and for the mission which she has in the world" (*Life*, II, p. 336).

So long as religion and science are in conflict there is an ever-present danger that thought may ultimately be divided up into water-tight compartments; that, as certain thinkers of the Middle Ages held, two standards of truth may be adopted, one for religion and one for science. Such a course means inevitably the loss of intellectual honesty by the Church and a disastrous diminution of its prestige and influence. Men of genuine religious faith are alienated,[1] whilst others are driven into open opposition to an agency which seems deliberately to preserve exploded superstitions. Though there may be a recognition that science has nothing to say on certain fundamental questions, there are still many left on which both science and religion are entitled to give an opinion. They must overlap and the disputes between them "can no more be closed by inventing 'religions of culture,' than the boundary quarrels of nations by setting up neutral provinces in the air."[2] But when science and religion are at one and working together in harmony, even though there may not be complete agreement, then we have the promise of new revelations, of fresh light on the problems which beset us both in life and thought.

[1] It was said of Sir James Paget, the famous surgeon, and the father of two Bishops in the Church of England, that "Religion was not to him a field in which the intellect might stand at ease while the emotions went through their evolutions or conflicts." Quoted in *Francis Paget*, p. 313.

[2] Martineau, *A Study of Religion*, I, p. 11.

9

RELIGION AND HISTORY

CHRISTIANITY is a historical religion in a twofold sense. Not only does it look back to certain historical facts; but also it holds a definite theory as to the meaning of history itself. It not only believes that Jesus Christ was God and man, but that the Incarnation is the clue to the meaning of the world process. Thus the question of the relation of religion and history may be said to be vital for the Christian believer.

Archdeacon Storr has claimed, and claimed rightly, that the growth of a feeling for history was perhaps "the most marked characteristic of the intellectual development of the last hundred years."[1] This growth arose by way of reaction from the neglect and even distrust of history which had marked the later years of the eighteenth century. The ideas then prevalent of an ideal primitive society and of a social contract which was the result of deliberate action, were "the negation of history." "The French Revolution defiantly turned its back on the past."[2] Already in those years, however, Lessing and Herder in Germany were manifesting the new spirit, and it spread to other lands in due season.

The revival of the historic spirit was helped by the new interest in the doctrine of evolution; for obviously, if past developments are to be traced, their history must be known. The philosophical form which it took in the works of Hegel exalted history, since he regarded it as no mere succession of events, but as "the actual unfolding of the nature of mind or spirit."[3] So too the growth of the Oxford Movement with its interest in the past helped on the new spirit for, as Pusey wrote, a Catholic Church must not only be a student of Scripture like a Reformed Church, but must add to it the knowledge of "ecclesiastical antiquity."[4]

---

[1] *Development of English Theology in the Nineteenth Century*, p. 1.
[2] G. P. Gooch, *History and Historians in the Nineteenth Century*, pp. 10 ff.
[3] C. C. J. Webb, *History of Philosophy*, pp. 224 f.
[4] Liddon, *Life of E. B. Pusey*, I, p. 336.

ENGLISH HISTORIANS

In England the rise of a succession of historians was a feature of the revived study of this branch of learning. In spite of the world-wide fame of Gibbon, Robertson, and Hume, appreciation of history had failed to develop in England before the coming of Macaulay. Macaulay made history interesting; but he was a party writer, and a great story-teller, rather than a scientific historian The same may be said of Carlyle, who shares with him the credit of awakening the feeling for history in Englishmen. Buckle, who had some kind of belief in God, in his unfinished *History of Civilization in England* (1857) tried to reduce history to a scientific system; but the real founder of new methods of study was Bishop Stubbs.

William Stubbs was born at Knaresborough in 1825 and the rich legacy of the past aroused in him from his earliest years a deep interest. "I was born," he tells us, "under the shadow of the great castle in which Becket's murderers found refuge during the year that followed his martyrdom, the year during which the dogs under the table declined to eat their crusts. There, too, as customary tenants of the Forest, my forefathers had done suit and service to Richard, King of the Romans, and after him to Queen Philippa and John of Gaunt, long before poor King Richard was kept a prisoner in the king's chamber. My grandfather's house stood on the ground on which Earl Thomas of Lancaster was taken prisoner by Edward II, on the very site of the battle of Boroughbridge; he, too, was churchwarden of the chapel in which the earl was captured. The first drive that my father ever took me led us across Marston Moor; one great-grandfather lived in an old manor-house of the monks of Fountains; another had a farm in the village where Harold Hardrada fell before the son of Godwin" (*Lectures on Medieval and Modern History*, p. 474). After a time at Oxford he settled down to lay the foundations of his great learning in the small parish of Navestock on the borders of Epping. There he remained until recalled to his university as Professor in 1866. With Stubbs must be remembered his friend and ally E. A. Freeman, a man of private means, who was thus enabled to devote all his time to the study which he made his own. With them also the poor town parson with brilliant gifts of narrative, though hardly so high a standard of accuracy, J. R. Green. Between Freeman and Green there was a real contrast in outlook. To the former history was "past politics, and politics present history"; he found his chief interest in wars and changes of government. The latter first shewed that the really important subject of history is the people itself; that kings and statesmen, soldiers and diplomatists, for all their dazzling exploits, fill but a secondary place. Freeman's great adversary, J. A. Froude, must not be forgotten; for if he was apt to rely too freely on a not very retentive memory, yet he set a standard of research which had never before been known in England. Another Oxford historian was only robbed of attaining to equal, if not greater heights, by being called to take a lead in more practical affairs. Mandell Creighton found his Navestock at Embleton beneath the clear skies of Northumbria and under the shadow of Dunstanborough. There he began his great *History of the Popes*, and made a reputation which caused him to be chosen as the first Dixie Professor of Ecclesiastical History in the University of Cambridge. His rival and successor, Henry Melville Gwatkin, I shall notice in a later chapter.[1]

England thus produced some great historians; but they all suffered from one great weakness: none of them had received an adequate training in theology. Their treatment of Church history was in consequence too external and objective. In dealing with men and movements, with politics and diplomacy, they were excellent; but when they came to touch on religious and doctrinal ideas they were never quite at home. Perhaps the greatest ecclesiastical historian of them all was J. B. Lightfoot; but the name of theologian is denied even to him (in spite of his great commentaries on some of the Epistles of St. Paul) by Armitage Robinson.[2]

[1] The lives of these great scholars form fascinating reading to anyone who is interested in their special studies. See Hutton, *Letters of William Stubbs*; Stephens, *Life and Letters of E. A. Freeman*; Leslie Stephen, *Letters of John Richard Green*; Herbert Paul, *Life of J. A. Froude*; Louise Creighton, *Life of Mandell Creighton*. Nor must Trevelyan's *Life of Lord Macaulay* be forgotten.
[2] *Lightfoot of Durham*, p. 127.

ARCHAEOLOGY

The awakened sense of history not only evolved new methods of study (these were worked out largely in Germany by great teachers such as Ranke), it also stimulated the search for fresh materials. Libraries were ransacked, expeditions were fitted out to visit new peoples, and even the soil itself was investigated for remains of ancient civilizations.[1] It is well to be able to record that the soil has yielded up to the skill and patience of the archaeologist a rich harvest of buried treasures of bygone ages. This harvest has affected every department of knowledge and the student of classics owes as much to it as the student of the Bible. It has brought to light vast, forgotten civilizations, and enabled scholars to fill up many gaps in their knowledge of the past, as well as to gain an entirely new perspective. "We now know that Greece and Rome, far from standing near the beginning of recorded history, were the heirs of a long series of brilliant civilizations. Our whole perspective has been changed. The ancient world ceases to be merely the vestibule to Christian Europe, and becomes in point of duration the larger part of human history."[2] For the student of the Bible, and in particular of the Old Testament, a similar revolution in thought and outlook has been carried through. The isolation of the people of Israel has been ended; they are now seen to be in the stream of world history; in race, language, and even in religion, they were not so distinct from their neighbours as a partial survey of their records had led men to suppose. This is all to the good, for as Professor S. A. Cook has said: "Ancient history becomes ultimately of purely antiquarian significance unless Biblical history forms an integral part of it; and the Bible runs the risk of being merely an object of superstitious veneration unless it is reinterpreted as part of a history which reaches to our own age" (In *The Modern Churchman*, XXIV, p. 483).

[1] Stanley Casson, in his fascinating volume *Progress of Archaeology*, p. 8, considers that archaeology became popular as a direct consequence of the Industrial Revolution and the new interest in geology. Railway cuttings and tunnels turned up fossils and curios and so led to a new interest in what was old.   [2] G. P. Gooch, *op. cit.*, p. 496.

Interest in early Egypt was aroused as early as 1798, when Napoleon took with him on his campaign a number of men of learning; something of the civilizations of Mesopotamia was also known in the early part of the nineteenth century; but little of the centuries prior to 1000 B.C. Then in 1874 came the epoch-making discoveries of Schliemann, whose *Trojan Antiquities* appeared in that year. Schliemann was not a trained scholar and he made many mistakes, but as a pioneer all honour is due to him. Not only did he excavate the site of Troy, but at Mycenae he revealed a vanished civilization. It is curious to remember that the ruins which he excavated had been known to Plato and his contemporaries, but no interest had been taken in them; of the still older Minoan civilization they were probably quite unaware. Thus the scholar of to-day knows far more of the ancient world than did the greatest of the Greeks or Romans.

The student of the Bible received help, both direct and indirect, from the discoveries of classical archaeologists; those in Egypt, for example, were naturally of profound interest in view of the sojourn there of the Israelites. But it was in Mesopotamia that the most important discoveries were made as a result of the deciphering of the masses of inscriptions which were there preserved. The story of the discovery of the meaning of the signs and the language which they represent is one of the most fascinating pages in the history of human endeavour; it tells how scholar after scholar laboured, each handing on to his successors a little more knowledge, until in the present day the majority of inscriptions, if they are undamaged, can be read with absolute certainty by the expert.

The highest value of the discoveries of the archaeologist is to be found, not as the Fundamentalist would have us believe, when they confirm statements in the Bible (as in many, but by no means all cases they undoubtedly do); but when they supplement and illustrate them. This they do in a variety of ways. First of all we have an assured basis for calculating the dates of events, for the chronology of the Biblical writers was not very exact or careful, and in the opinion of so conservative a scholar as Professor Sayce it must give way to the more accurate lists of the Assyrians.[1] Then again a comparison of the Biblical records and the monuments tells that the former are in the main historic, but that we must not expect accuracy of detail "nor apply to them a different standard from that which we apply to the earlier records of Greece and Rome." From this generalization the compiler of Chronicles ought to be excluded, for "archaeology makes it clear that his statements are not always exact. We cannot follow him with the same confidence as that with which we should follow the author of the Books of Kings. His use of the documents which lay before him was uncritical, the inferences he drew from his materials was not always sound, and he makes them subserve the theory on which his work is based."[2] Again, places and people mentioned in the Bible and not hitherto known elsewhere, have been discovered in the inscriptions. A well-known instance is Sargon, who appears in Isaiah xx. 1 as King of Assyria. Until his actual palace was discovered and excavated nothing was known of him beyond this reference. The insight of critics such as Eichorn, Gesenius, and Ewald had already anticipated the discovery and assigned to him a place between Shalmanesar and Sennacherib: he was, as a matter of fact, the father of the latter.

Although nothing beyond a few fragments written in the Hebrew language have been discovered, the study of that language has been greatly advanced by the work of the archaeologist, for he has shown that it is closely related to Assyrian and still more to the language of what is known as the Moabite Stone. This has led to a more exact knowledge of the meaning of Hebrew words and the usages of Hebrew grammar.

COMPARATIVE RELIGION

Before going on to consider in more detail the growth of Biblical Criticism it will be useful to notice very briefly the new light which came to Biblical research and to the study of religion in general by the much greater knowledge of Non-Christian

---

[1] See *The Higher Criticism and the Monuments*, pp. 318 and 406; and for lists of dates, Rogers, *Cuneiform Parallels to the Old Testament*, pp. 199 ff.

[2] Sayce, *op. cit.*, p. 462.

religions which was a mark of the period under review; the period which saw the rise of the science of Comparative Religion. This science was really one manifestation of a general interest in origins which also shewed itself in work such as that of the brothers Grimm in investigating the light thrown on primitive society and its ideas by folk-lore and fairy tales. The provision of a mass of new material at the same time stimulated its analysis and comparison. This material was collected by the archaeologist, the anthropologist, and the missionary. The latter, at first, was not encouraged in such activities. An early missionary who wrote an account of the gods of South India was reproved by the society which he represented on the ground that he "was sent to India to destroy the gods and not to write about them."[1]

Some interest in comparative religion there had, of course, always been. In the eighteenth century, for example, Conyers Middleton in his *Letter from Rome* had pointed out the numerous parallels between the religious practices of classical paganism and the contemporary Roman Church. But there was no widespread realization of its importance. The study probably had its real beginning when on May 8, 1840, Thomas Carlyle delivered his lecture on Mahomet, afterwards printed in *Heroes and Hero Worship*. It was something new to have a sympathetic account of the founder of a religion which was a dangerous rival to Christianity. Next may be noted F. D. Maurice's Boyle Lectures in 1846 on *The Religions of the World*, a comprehensive account of other faiths with the object of shewing that in Christ is to be found the fulfilment of all the desires which they express. It is interesting to notice that he commended this line of approach to the missionary in foreign lands. In this same year there came to England from Germany the man who above all others was to lay the foundations of the science in this country, Max Müller. His researches and publications, and perhaps above all his editorship of *The Sacred Books of the East*, had a profound effect on religious thought in England. Max Müller's work was based on the study of Sanscrit and of the religions of the Far East; the work of W. Robertson Smith was to expound the Semitic religions and to demonstrate

[1] Quoted by H. H. Gowen, *A History of Religion*, p. 5.

their close connexion with the religion of the Old Testament, which hitherto men had thought to be a thing by itself.

One result of the study of Comparative Religion was the realization that religion itself was universally diffused, and that it went back to the earliest days of the human race, a fact which impressed Herbert Spencer with a conviction of its truth. Some, indeed, tried to explain this fact by suggesting that fear of the unknown was natural and that magic was an obvious means of coping with it. But religion cannot be accounted for in such a way; had fear and magic been all there was in it, long ago it would have disappeared from civilized peoples. Aristotle's great principle that the end explains the beginnings can surely be applied here. Religion must be considered in its highest, not its lowest, manifestations if any really sound judgement is to be reached. The tracing out of its gradual evolution is considered by Mr. Marvin as "among the greatest of the conquests of the nineteenth century."[1]

Once the existence of high ideas of religion among non-Christian people had been recognized, through a more sympathetic study of their writings and ceremonies, a number of views at once became obsolete. For example, it could no longer be held that heathen religions were the debased survivals of the primitive revelation to Adam;[2] nor that they were impostures invented by a designing priesthood. Even St. Augustine's suggestion that the very virtues of the pagans were but *splendida vitia* had to be given up. The lesson in toleration had already been set out, with much less actual knowledge to support it, in Lessing's famous drama *Nathan der Weise*; but men had been slow to receive its teaching. Though Newman himself had admitted that "there is something true and divinely revealed in every religion."[3]

All this new knowledge could not fail to arouse in many minds a whole series of disquieting questions. Was Christianity after all the final Religion? It might be true that it was the

---

[1] *The Century of Progress*, p. 220.
[2] According to Van Mildert this debasement was due to "a wilful corruption of Sacred Truth": see *Historical View of the Rise and Progress of Infidelity*, p. 433.
[3] Quoted by F. S. Marvin, *op. cit.*, p. 217.

best religion yet known, but might not the future bring forth a faith even better? (Such questions shew the rather static idea which was then almost universal concerning Christianity.) The believer might be convinced that, in the words of a twentieth-century historian and apologist, "alike in basis and nature, in motive and method, in ideal and result the Christian faith differs from all its rivals far more than it resembles them."[1] But others might not agree. The situation was complicated and perplexing, and there were even those who found themselves drawn to the newly discovered Eastern religions as knowledge of them became more common. The fact that such religions were ancient and widespread as well as more romantic and mysterious (so it was thought) than the everyday religious teaching of the Churches, made them an attractive alternative to Christianity for those who wished to find something more satisfying than the scientific materialism which so widely prevailed. In just such a way the Oriental religions had appealed to the jaded Romans of the late Republic and the Empire. This attitude of mind was perhaps more common in the United States than in England; but it was not unknown.

There was, however, a darker side to the picture. Most of the religions other than Christianity, especially if they were ancient, revealed their all too human origin by the fables and obscenities which had been allowed to find a place, and that an honoured place, in their systems. They were expressions of man's need for power and knowledge and his utter inability to achieve them without divine aid. None the less, Comparative Religion had its contribution to make to the deeper understanding of the things of God and of the religious strivings and attainments of men. God had spoken to others in their darkness and His message had to be considered in any comprehensive theology. This was a truth which our fathers knew not. For as Storr has written: "A theology which seeks its material only in the revelation contained in the Bible will both fail to understand fully that material itself, and will make the part the standard of the whole" (*Development of English Theology*, p. 14).

[1] J. N. Figgis, *The Gospel and Human Needs*, p. 66.

RELIGION AND HISTORY

BIBLICAL CRITICISM

The new methods, both of writing history, and of testing such history as had already been written, were applied on all sides to the records of the past; naturally enough the writings collected in what we call the Bible were not exempt from this general review, and, like every other ancient literature of any importance, they had to submit to a criticism which in some cases must be ranked as distinctly hostile. But this was by no means common; most of those who undertook the task were men of sincere religious faith. To them it was no longer possible to preserve water-tight compartments in their minds, or to throw off habits of thought and criticism when they approached the Scriptures.[1] This meant a change of outlook from the old way of looking upon inspiration and the authority of the Bible in general. To our fathers the twin pillars upon which inspiration rested were miracles and prophecy. The progress of Natural Science altered entirely the evidential value of miracles;[2] that of Historical Criticism the value of prophecy. It came gradually to be realized that the real worth of the prophets lay in their spiritual and moral leadership, rather than in any supposed ability to forecast, in minute detail, the course of future events. Pioneers in freeing men from the older, mechanical idea of prophecy were Davison, whose *Nature and History of Prophecy* was published as early as 1819, and Thomas Arnold. With the adoption of the historical standpoint, revelation "ceased to be regarded as a mechanical thing operating from without at one uniform level, but was thought of as a progressive unfolding of the divine purpose."[3] Thus the Bible, as Coleridge had demanded,[4] came to be treated like any other book; and thus treated it shewed its difference, because unlike any other book it was capable of satisfying the deepest needs of the soul.

[1] Cf. T. R. Glover, *From Pericles to Philip*, p. 148. "Certain ideas depend on our thinking in compartments; and the removal of the dividing wall is criticism."
[2] See above, p. 159.
[3] Storr, *op. cit.*, p. 180.
[4] In his posthumous volume published in 1840, *Confessions of an Enquiring Spirit*.

German Influences

The chief leaders in the process of applying the new methods to the Bible were to be found in Germany. Mark Pattison, indeed, regarded the rise of German Theology in the eighteenth and nineteenth centuries as the coming of a fourth period of Doctrinal Development; the others being the Greek of the fourth and fifth centuries; the Latin of the twelfth and thirteenth; and the vernacular of the Reformation age. He admired its energy and earnestness which succeeded, so he affirmed, in bringing back the ideas of religion again within the orbit of human interest (*Essays*, II, pp. 150 f.). But as we saw above,[1] in spite of the work of Julius Hare, Arnold, and a few others,[2] German thought was suspected in England. In 1841 Thirlwall roundly declared that the English Church journals deliberately ignored everything emanating from Germany;[3] and as late as 1857 R. W. Church, whose views on the subject had been greatly modified by reading a *Memoir of Perthes*, the German bookseller, confessed that "strong dislike and condemnation" had been taught to him as the only correct attitude towards German thinkers (*Life*, pp. 176 f.).

Among Nonconformists there was an entirely different attitude, for many of them were in the habit of going to German universities to obtain that culture from which they were debarred at home. In Scotland, indeed, a few terms in Germany were a regular feature of a university course. Martineau went to Germany in 1848 and the following year; it was for him "a new intellectual birth," so he confessed.[4] Whilst W. F. Moulton wrote in his journal on December 10, 1856, that he had resolved to make German his main study during the vacation, with special reference to its usefulness in Biblical studies (*Life*, p. 43). It was therefore quite natural that when in 1865 A. M. Fairbairn, a young "Evangelical Union" pastor at Bathgate, found that the Augustinian theology of the Westminster Confession, even when modified

[1] See pp. 132 f.
[2] In 1825 Hare advised Arnold to read Niebuhr. He did so and "a new intellectual world dawned on him": see Stanley, *Life of Arnold*, p. 39.
[3] Perowne and Stokes, *Letters Literary and Theological of Connop Thirlwall*, p. 175.   [4] *Types of Ethical Theory*, I, p. xii.

by the less rigid teaching of his leader Morison, no longer satisfied him, and that the whole foundation of his faith had collapsed; it was natural for him to resign his charge for the time and go to Berlin to begin his studies all over again in an attempt to recover his lost faith. There under the influence of Dorner and Hengstenberg, and in a philosophical atmosphere permeated by Hegel, he found a new and higher faith.[1]

Suspicion of the new developments in German Theology was not unknown in Germany itself, where the pious looked on with unconcealed alarm. As early as 1817 Claud Harms, with strange prophetic vision, foretold that Lutheranism would be progressively reformed back to heathenism;[2] but the great shock came with the publication of Strauss's *Leben Jesu* in 1835.[3] This, the first edition of the book, was intended for scholars only, and it was written from the philosophical standpoint which divorced the idea from the fact. "The supernatural birth of Christ, His miracles and ascension remain eternal truths, whatever doubts may be cast on their reality as historical facts." So Strauss himself had written.[4] As we have seen, it was translated into English by George Eliot in her new-found zeal for liberal ideas; but she found much of it repulsive, especially his "dissecting the beautiful story of the crucifixion." She could only endure to continue her task by gazing at a cast of Thorwaldsen's figure of the risen Christ (*Life*, I, p. 112). In a later edition, published in 1865, Strauss re-wrote and modified his work in order to make it popular; but it was never received by the general public even in Germany, and after a quarter of a century it was almost entirely forgotten.

About the same time there arose what was called the Tübingen School, of which Baur was the leader. Baur regarded the conflict between St. Paul and the Judaisers mentioned in his Epistles as the key to the history of the Church up to the middle of the second century. He held that the earliest form

---

[1] Selbie, *A. M. Fairbairn*, pp. 36 ff. W. G. Elmslie was also in Berlin a few years later: see W. Robertson Nicoll, *Life of W. G. Elmslie*, pp. 49 ff.

[2] Quoted by Farrar, *History of Interpretation*, p. 413.

[3] Tholuck wrote in great alarm to Pusey: see Liddon, *Life of E. B. Pusey*, I, pp. 322 f.; but Bunsen was scornful and critical: see Stanley, *Life of Arnold*, p. 426.   [4] *Leben Jesu*, p. xxx.

of Christianity was a kind of Ebionite Judaism and that St. Paul transformed it. St. Peter he regarded as the leader of those who opposed St. Paul. This thesis was set forth in a number of weighty publications in the years between 1831 and 1847 and it gained a considerable following. But like the theories of Strauss it no longer commends itself nor receives serious attention.

Amongst those who had been influenced by Strauss's first *Leben Jesu* was a young French Oriental scholar now known to fame as Ernest Renan. In 1845, the year in which Newman joined the Roman communion, he had left it for "cultivated infidelity." Renan by no means agreed with Strauss's mythical theories, and probably the reaction aroused in his mind was in part responsible for his own *Vie de Jésus*. This work was begun in 1860 when its author was in Syria, and it owes much to the background of Eastern life amidst which it was written. It finally appeared in 1863 after the death of Renan's beloved sister and collaborator and his own return to France. Renan had spent a year in toning down what he felt to be the exuberance of the first draft;[1] but even in its present form it is highly emotional and sentimental, and much more like the work of an imaginative novelist than of a competent scholar such as Renan undoubtedly was. The picture of our Lord is that of a gentle teacher surrounded by female devotees, and the book has been not undeservedly described as a "Gospel in Dresden china." None the less, it had a considerable vogue and even to-day is still widely read, as witness the edition in Everyman's Library. No doubt the literary skill and grace of Renan's pen, preserved even in a translation, is the real cause of this survival which stands in strong contrast to the neglect of Strauss. But as a serious study of the life of Jesus it is of no account.

When Renan's work first appeared there was much scandal among the orthodox. Even a scholarly, though conservative, Churchman like Stubbs shared in it, as is shewn by his own account of the way in which he "robbed" J. R. Green, on their first meeting, of an unread copy.[2] Another story, also

[1] *Souvenirs d'Enfance et de Jeunesse*, p. 355.
[2] Hutton, *Letters of William Stubbs*, p. 68.

with its amusing side, is not so well known. An English lady travelling in Italy records that there was a three days' demonstration in the cathedral at Genoa "to purge the town from the guilt of Renan's infidelity." Its chief effect was to advertise the work, and in consequence "all the French copies of the book were sold and two Italian editions before the end of the week."[1]

Two years after Renan's volume there appeared in England an anonymous work entitled *Ecce Homo*, which attracted a good deal of attention. It was quite obviously not an attack upon orthodox Christianity; but the emphasis which it laid on our Lord's manhood was regarded in some quarters as very dangerous. Lord Shaftesbury went so far as to describe it as having been "vomited from the jaws of Hell."[2] The writer, as it soon became known, was Seeley, the historian.[3]

The 'sixties were indeed a trying decade for the Orthodox, for not only did it see the birth of the two volumes just mentioned, but Darwin's views (the *Origin of Species*, it will be remembered, was published in 1859) were being everywhere discussed, and *Essays and Reviews* were causing widespread alarm. In addition there was the notorious Colenso episode.

The Colenso Case

Colenso, who had been a Cambridge mathematician, was Bishop of Natal, where he had done good work in protecting the natives and in trying to teach them the elements of the Christian faith. It was their naïve questioning which led him to embark on his somewhat radical criticism.[4] In 1861 he had published a Commentary on the Romans for which he anticipated a hostile reception,[5] but it was around his work

---

[1] *Miss Wynn's Memorials*, p. 316.

[2] Hodder, *Life and Works of the Earl of Shaftesbury*, III, p. 164. It ought to be added that the expression was used in a public speech, and that Lord Shaftesbury recognized that it was perhaps injudicious, although he never doubted that it was true.

[3] The first person to discover the authorship was H. B. Swete, who knew Seeley intimately. Although a conservative in outlook Swete always spoke of the book with respect: see *Henry Barclay Swete: A Remembrance*, p. 17.

[4] See G. W. Cox, *Life of Colenso*, I, p. 483.

[5] *Op. cit.*, I, p. 126.

on the Pentateuch, which appeared in the year following, that the storm gathered. Colenso dealt freely with its authorship and unity, and as a mathematician he found the figures most unreliable, and proceeded to demonstrate their impossibility. Samuel Wilberforce, with his usual wit, explained that, of course, the Mathematical Bishop could not forgive Moses for having dared to write the Book of Numbers.[1] But the effect on the religious public was immense owing to the writer's position as a bishop. The English bishops, except Thirlwall,[2] demanded his resignation: the South African, under the vigorous leadership of Gray of Cape Town,[3] excommunicated and deposed him. Colenso refused to notice their action and was supported by legal decisions which gave to him the control of Church property in Natal. The result was a schism; for the other bishops, without any State permission, eventually elected a successor to what they regarded as the vacant see. Although Colenso died in 1883 and his party failed to get a successor consecrated, the schism went on until the resignation of his rival, Dr. Macrorie, in 1891. It was then agreed to submit the matter to Archbishop Benson, who appointed the Rev. A. Hamilton Baynes, Vicar of Christ Church, Greenwich, who had been his domestic chaplain, and so brought about agreement.[4]

Colenso's work on the Pentateuch, if the mathematical parts were his own, depended mainly for the rest on the researches of German scholars. There had already been an outcry against their methods when they first became widely known on the publication of Milman's *History of the Jews* in 1830. Dean Stanley has recorded "the horror created in remote rural districts by the rumour that a book had appeared in which Abraham was described as a 'sheikh.' "[5] But his work was really of a very mild character. Stanley himself in his *Lectures*

---

[1] See Bateman, *Life of Henry Venn Elliott*, p. 230.
[2] Thirlwall, however, did not agree with his views: see C. N. Gray, *Life of Bishop Gray*, II, pp. 46 f.
[3] Bishop Gray was the son of the Bishop of Bristol, whose palace had been burnt down in the Reform Bill riots of 1831.
[4] A. C. Benson, *Life of Edward White Benson*, p. 464.
[5] *Essays on Church and State*, p. 576.

on *the Jewish Church*, the first volume of which was published in 1862, made popular in England the ideas of Ewald, but these ideas also were comparatively mild. It may be said that Old Testament criticism, as it is now understood, both in Germany and England, dates back to the Dutch scholar Kuenen (1869-70) and to Wellhausen, whose *History of Israel* appeared in 1878. Wellhausen made use of earlier work on the Old Testament, especially of Reuss and the Hegelian Vatke, but his own achievement was considerable. The important point in his theory was not so much the dividing up of the Pentateuch, but that the Prophets were earlier than the Law. The new views were expounded by Robertson Smith, whose trial for heresy in Scotland in 1875 had already caused a sensation. In later lectures on *The Old Testament in the Jewish Church* and *The Prophets of Israel* he popularized the new views. He died in March 1894 at the early age of forty-seven; he was then Professor of Arabic in the University of Cambridge.

The majority of those who adopted critical views and spread them by their writings and lectures were men of real religious feeling and conviction. But to the ordinary churchgoer and even to his leaders they seemed little better than infidels. In the *British Review* Vaughan had spoken of "Rugby men, who take the free principles of their master in Biblical interpretation to an extent which allies them more with German Rationalism than with English Orthodoxy."[1] Whilst even Dean Church felt that questions of Biblical Criticism had been left too much "to be dealt with by a cruel and insolent curiosity, utterly reckless of results, and even enjoying the pleasure of affronting religion and religious faith" (*Life*, p. 412). To people in the later part of the nineteenth century there seemed to be something profane in the attempt to treat the Bible like any other book; just as in the Reformation age Erasmus was attacked because by correcting errors which had arisen in the text of the New Testament he made the Holy Ghost conform to the rules of grammar. The panic was largely due to ignorance,[2] but the results which certain scholars claimed to have reached

[1] Quoted by A. W. Peel, *These Hundred Years*, p. 221.
[2] Cf. Davidson and Benham, *A. C. Tait*, I, p. 276.

by the use of the new methods did not tend to the reassurance of the faithful. There was thus much to explain such an attitude of mind; but it was soon perceived that religion had nothing to fear from a reverent and careful criticism even when applied to the sacred narrative itself, and that the new methods and the new knowledge properly understood only added to the wonders of God's revelation. In all ages Christian people have been faced by the same problem—the combining of new knowledge with the old. The policy of rejecting what is new because at first sight it seems to conflict with the old, is surely a lack of trust in our Lord as the Truth.

Some pious souls had the insight to perceive that there were degrees of truth in the Bible and that slight inaccuracies in scientific or historical matters did not rob it of its spiritual value. When George Pilkington was a boy he refused to accept some of the miracles of the Old Testament, and on going to his mother with the question: "Is every word in the Bible absolutely true?" he received the very wise and helpful reply: "The Bible is intended to teach you to serve God; read it for that purpose, and in that sense every single word of it is perfectly true."[1] This attitude of mind, with its insistence on spiritual and moral values, was not everywhere found, and many of the leaders of Christian thought in attempting to defend the Bible chose to meet their opponents on ground chosen by the latter. This was perceived by Church, who confesses that the orthodox "apologetic and counter criticism has let itself be too much governed by the lines of attack ... we have not adequately attempted to face things for ourselves and in our own way, in order not merely to refute, but to construct something positive on our own side" (*Life*, p. 412).

The Conservative Reply

It must not, however, be imagined that conservative scholars allowed the matter of Biblical Criticism to go by default. Soon after Newman's secession Pusey had taken in hand the preparation of a Commentary intended to cover the whole Bible and to make use of all the aids of contemporary scholarship and the results of criticism which seemed to be well established.

[1] See C. F. Harford-Battersby, *Pilkington of Uganda*, p. 4.

Nothing, however, was to be included which was not "in accordance with Primitive and Catholic faith."[1] A number of scholars promised their help and Pusey drew up lists of proposed contributors. Then came the Gorham judgement and other troubles, and to Pusey's grief the matter fell into abeyance. In later years, Liddon tells us, he "lamented the failure of this—the most cherished project of his life."[2] It is probable that the early Tractarians were not really interested in criticism, that they shared Charles Marriott's view that the utmost it could do was to prepare a correct text "for the reading of the spiritual eye."[3] As is well known Pusey himself took up the Minor Prophets and completed his solitary task between the years 1860 and 1877. But it was all that ever saw the light,[4] and can hardly have done much to stay the progress of critical advance; for it was, as Frederick Temple once wrote, "a mass of learning without criticism."[5] Even at this late date Pusey hoped to revive his plan, and Liddon was persuaded to edit the Pastoral Epistles. He collected a good deal of material for the project, which later he used in his lectures, and an analysis of 1 Timothy was even published after his death.[6] Later he laid this aside in order to work on Leviticus, but he made little progress, much to Pusey's indignation.[7]

The truth of the matter is that all such attempts to reconcile modern scholarship and what is regarded as the Catholic Faith in the end defeat themselves and are seen to be of little real value; for the former is made to submit to the latter and no progress towards real understanding results. One is reminded of the comment of a witty Frenchman on Père

[1] See Liddon, *Life of E. B. Pusey*, III, pp. 149 ff. The originator of the scheme was the Rev. G. Forbes of Burntisland in Scotland.
[2] *Op. cit.*, III, p. 157.
[3] Randolph and Townroe, *The Mind and Work of Bishop King*, p. 142.
[4] A fragment on Romans by Keble was published after his death: see *Studia Sacra*, pp. 45 ff.
[5] *Life of Frederick Temple*, I, p. 56.
[6] J. O. Johnson, *Life of Henry Parry Liddon*, p. 50.
[7] On January 2, 1864, Liddon notes in his diary: "Called on Dr. P., who was very sharp about my having done nothing with the Commentary. ... He contrasted my idleness with Kay's promise to finish Genesis within the year." Quoted by Johnson, *op. cit.*, p. 69.

Didon's *Jésus Christ*: "He has brought rational criticism onto the sacred soil merely to slay it more solemnly."[1]

Pusey's well-known volume on *Daniel* was not part of the projected Commentary. It had a much more polemical tone and was definitely intended to expose the shortcomings of the critical school. It appeared in 1864, and had a strange fate; for in the panic of the ensuing years it came itself to be regarded with grave suspicion as a Germanizing work.[2] Lord Shaftesbury had a truer appreciation of its standpoint and was sufficiently optimistic to believe that it had, in conjunction with Payne Smith's *Isaiah*, permanently broken up the critical offensive, leaving not "a single scrap of reasoning, a single shred of fact" to be pleaded in its behalf (*Life*, III, p. 209). His commendation of a work by Pusey and his praise of the High Church leader as unsurpassed for intellect, attainments, and true piety, caused some offence to his fellow Evangelicals (*op. cit.*, III, pp. 209 and 254 f.).

Spread of the New Views

The new critical views remained for long the property of scholars and the more highly educated ministers of religion. The latter were chary about spreading views which they felt might cause unrest among the lay-people whose acquaintance with them was connected with notorious cases such as *Essays and Reviews* and Bishop Colenso. But rationalist and infidel writers and speakers were not slow to make use of the new knowledge and to spread it among the working classes as a means of discrediting Christianity. This aroused the more enlightened to the need for giving instruction to their own people; but the attempt was hazardous. Moderate criticism was really more alarming to the timidly orthodox than its more extreme form. So long as it was a weapon of anti-religious teachers, or those who were regarded as such, men did not take it seriously; it seemed so obviously the work of an enemy. Its spread among those who were orthodox Christians was an

---

[1] Anatole France, *On Life and Letters*, IV, p. 99.

[2] Other works which drew upon them the same unwarranted suspicion included Conybeare and Howson, *Life of St. Paul*, Alford's *Greek Testament*, and Perowne, *On the Psalms*.

ominous sign. This spread was foreshadowed in an address delivered to the Congregational Union in May 1864 by Dr. Allon. In it occurred the following significant passage: "Some of the most damaging assaults upon the Divine authorship of the Bible have really been assaults upon untenable theories of inspiration, which a more justifiable position utterly disables. . . . It is only by fully and fearlessly recognizing the human element in the authorship of Scripture that we can understand it, and find reality in it."[1]

An exceedingly interesting and valuable account has been left by R. F. Horton of his efforts in 1887 to acquaint the members of his congregation at Hampstead with the results of what he regarded as moderate and sane criticism. He gave a course of addresses to explain the true nature of Inspiration as revealed in the Scripture itself. Some of his hearers received so much help from them that they urged their publication. The result was a volume entitled *The Inspiration of the Bible*, which appeared in the following year, after some difficulty had been experienced in finding a publisher who was sufficiently bold to undertake the risk. It immediately aroused a fierce storm and the writer not only lost some of his own people, but came to be regarded as a heretic and an outsider.[2]

In other quarters there had already been resistance to the spread of the new ideas within the Church. There was a long controversy in 1878 over two volumes published by the Society for Promoting Christian Knowledge, a *Manual of Geology* by the Rev. T. G. Bonney and *The Argument from Prophecy* by the Rev. Brownlow Maitland.[3] Lord Shaftesbury felt so strongly on the matter that he severed his connexion with the Society and wrote a letter of denunciation to the Archbishop of Canterbury (*Life*, III, pp. 383 ff.). As late as 1888 Bishop John Wordsworth, himself a scholar of distinction in textual criticism, could prophesy that "should the accepted date and authorship of the Pentateuch be abandoned, public faith in the Gospel

---

[1] See A. W. Peel, *These Hundred Years*, p. 243.
[2] See R. F. Horton, *An Autobiography*, pp. 84 ff.
[3] The Society had already in 1867 suppressed a tract by Westcott on "The Resurrection as a Fact and a Revelation," because one of its Episcopal referees thought it heretical: see *Life of B. F. Westcott*, I, p. 256.

would fail."[1] In spite of such attempts to keep back the incoming tide it proved irresistible, and before the end of the century the newer outlook had been firmly established among scholars and the great bulk of the clergy and ministers. If one were to seek for a landmark to shew the rise of the tide one could, I think, find it in the publication of Sanday's Bampton Lectures on *Inspiration* in 1893 and Driver's *Introduction to the Literature of the Old Testament* two years previously. Its acceptance by the lay-people receives testimony from the following statement by Dr. C. A. Berry in *The British Weekly* contributed in 1896: "While it is too early to say how far the results of the higher criticism have affected our congregations, I can discern a real difference in their attitude. I believe that, apart from literary and technical criticism, the school of higher criticism has voiced the general sentiments of our average intelligent lay-men, and has relieved them from the sense they once had of disloyalty to the Bible. It has given our people a more rational and satisfying belief in the great truths of Scripture."[2]

[1] Watson, *Life of Bishop John Wordsworth*, p. 189.
[2] Quoted by J. S. Drummond, *Charles A. Berry*, p. 247.

10

THE MIDDLE YEARS

FOREIGN AFFAIRS

ON the continent of Europe and in America the years between the death of the Prince Consort in 1861 and the Jubilee of 1887, which we may call the middle period of the reign of Victoria, were regarded, not as the middle of a period, but as the beginning of a new era. This difference of outlook was due to the earlier development in Great Britain of the Industrial System. By this time it had come to be accepted in this country as a normal thing, although the problems to which it had given rise still sought a solution. In other lands the Industrial System had a later start and it was only now becoming really important. But quite apart from industrial development the period was one of vast changes in Europe. The great dividing point was the year 1871, a year which has been well called the *annus mirabilis* of modern history. In it Germany and Italy both attained to national unity. The way for both had been that of war; but the one had been helped, the other opposed by Napoleon III of France. France itself suffered severely and Paris above all; for after the first siege and capture, there followed a desperate Communist insurrection against the National Government, and for six weeks the French army had to besiege its own capital. When the troops forced their way in the horrors of the Revolution were repeated; and the rebellion was crushed to the accompaniment of massacres and conflagrations.

The Franco-Prussian War had involved the withdrawal of French troops from Rome, which was thus left open to the national forces. On September 20, 1870, the troops of Victor Emmanuel entered and the Temporal Power of the Papacy came to an end. An opportunity was given to the Romans to express their wishes in the matter of government. The reply was quite unequivocal: 40,788 voted for the King, a mere 46 for the Pope. The same year found the Pope, in the face of loss of political power, declaring, with the aid of a Council, his own Infallibility. "The decree of Papal Infallibility was the cordial which the Roman Church administered to itself in the hour of defeat, its defiance of the modern world, its protest against the sacrilege of Italian patriotism."[1]

Whilst wars were going on between the great European nations Great Britain was choosing a better way. The year 1871 saw the settlement of the *Alabama* dispute by diplomacy and arbitration, when the rising tide of national feeling on either side might easily have led to a conflict. This country paid heavy compensation for its negligence in allowing the *Alabama* to escape from its ports to the damage of American shipping. Mr. Gladstone thought that we had been harshly treated; but he rejoiced over "the moral value of the example set." His biographer rates it as "the most notable victory in the nineteenth century of the noble art of preventive diplomacy."[2]

HOME AFFAIRS

Political Changes

Turning now to home affairs we have to notice the profound political and social changes which marked the era. The early years of Victoria may be described as the era of upper middle-class influence; politically that influence came to an end, or was considerably modified, by the Reform Act of 1867, when a larger electorate was brought into partnership. Although the Act of 1832 had been intended by its promoters to set a limit to Parliamentary Reform, it had been obvious for long that it had failed to do so. The question of reform was already urgent in the early years of the 'sixties, but the deep interest which this country took in the American Civil War of 1865 postponed it; moreover, the strife in America shocked some of the most ardent supporters of reform; for it shewed dis-

---

[1] H. A. L. Fisher, *Bonapartism*, p. 4. In addition to the Franco-Prussian War of 1870-1, there had been war between France and Austria in 1859; the various other successful, if incomplete, attempts to gain Italian freedom; and the Seven Weeks' War of 1866 in which Prussia defeated Austria. There were also troubles in the Balkans culminating in the Russo-Turkish War of 1877-8.

[2] Morley, *Life of Gladstone*, II, p. 413.

ruption at work in "that ideal community which Bright and his friends had constantly held up for imitation."[1] In 1866 Gladstone brought in a Bill which would have increased the electorate by some 400,000 voters; but in spite of his appeals and warnings the Bill was thrown out and his government defeated.[2] The Conservatives then took office, but without any effective majority. The question of reform, however, was still urgent, and the Queen herself pressed it upon Disraeli.[3] In the end he brought in a Bill with a much wider programme. This passed in 1867, and by adding a million new names to the register it doubled the constituency. The extension of the franchise was opposed by many great and good men on the ground that the vote should be regarded not as a right, but as a trust. They would have reserved it for the thrifty and honest working men who were willing to save money enough to buy their own houses.[4] Lord Derby called the Conservative policy in 1867 "dishing the Whigs." It was in reality an early example of what Asquith was later to regard as the function of the Tory party—to forestall inevitable changes (*Life*, I, p. 102). A further reform in 1872 established voting by ballot —a measure which had long been urged on the House of Commons by Grote and others.[5] In the previous year a Bill had passed the Commons and been thrown out in the Lords. Finally, so far as this period is concerned, a Bill in 1884 enfranchised the agricultural labourer.

By this series of electoral reforms the people of England, without any violent revolution, but by constitutional development, found itself possessed of the powers which had been the ideal of the continental revolutions of 1848. The upper middle classes, and indeed the middle classes as a whole, had now to share their power with the classes beneath them. The older governing class had long ceased, from the days of the 1832 Act, to possess the almost unlimited power which had once been theirs. In this connexion it is important to notice the

[1] Monypenny and Buckle, *Life of Benjamin Disraeli*, II, p. 136.
[2] For details see Morley, *Life of W. E. Gladstone*, II, pp. 125 ff.
[3] Monypenny and Buckle, *op. cit.*, II, p. 295.
[4] See Hodder, *Life and Works of Lord Shaftesbury*, III, p. 220.
[5] John Stuart Mill rather strangely had opposed the ballot. He regarded the vote as a trust, and therefore something to be exercised openly.

reaction on their part to this loss of power. They did not, as in many foreign countries, give up politics entirely; instead, like the Patricians in the Roman Republic, they took their place in the new system. There was no vague plotting and conspiracy to recover supremacy, but a wise and determined effort to retain prestige, not by privilege, but by definite service and achievement. Incidentally the same attitude was adopted by the Church of England, or recommended to it by its Primate, in the face of undoubted loss of political power —for one of the obvious effects of extending the vote to the lower classes was greatly to increase the power and importance of the Dissenters. Archbishop Benson wrote in June 1883: "The Church of England has to be built up again from the very bottom. It is the lower and lower-middle classes who must be won.... Our claims must be our work" (*Life*, p. 273). The new power and importance of the Dissenters meant the emergence of a new Liberalism, far different from what had passed under that name at an earlier epoch, and having for its leaders men of deep religious feeling and conviction, such as Mr. Gladstone, the High Churchman, Richard Cobden, also a Churchman, and the Quaker, John Bright.[1] The older Dissenters had been Liberals for the sake, mainly, of gaining their own liberty; the newer generation, a large measure of liberty having been attained, could find in Liberalism an inspiration and a channel for social influence.[2] With their support Mr. Gladstone was able to push through a number of domestic reforms which for their day were noteworthy and the promise of still further legislation to come.[3] That much of it would be the achievement of Conservative governments did not then seem so likely as it did a few years later.

[1] "Bright was an insular Englishman with the stern conscience of a Quaker. To understand Cobden's place in history it is necessary to see what he had in common, not with Bright, but with Gladstone." J. L. Hammond in *Great Victorians*, p. 145.

[2] Even the Methodists were brought in at last: see D. Price Hughes, *Life of Hugh Price Hughes*, p. 51.

[3] The following are enumerated by D. Price Hughes in *Hugh Price Hughes*, p. 111: the Irish Land Bill, the Formation of School Boards, the Abolition of Purchase in the Army, the Ballot, the Abolition of University Tests, and a Bill in favour of Trade Unions.

That a party whose main strength consisted in a large following of Nonconformists should have been led by a rigid High Churchman like Gladstone, is at first sight anomalous. But though the conjunction involved many difficulties and some disagreements, there was so much in common between them that its strangeness ceases on a little investigation. Gladstone's sincere religion and its expression in politics was such, in spite of differences in detail, as to make him the natural leader of men whose religion was also sincere, and who sought in politics an outlet for their ideals. Gladstone's career as a politician and his standpoint as a democrat all go back to his religion. It was because he held the fundamentally Christian view that all souls, in the eyes of God, are equal, that he was a democrat; this his Nonconformist supporters could understand: it was because he was a religious man that he gave himself up, having been thwarted by parental disapproval from pursuing his original intention of taking Orders, to serve his country as a statesman. It is interesting to read the testimony of one of the chief of his lieutenants, himself not a professing Christian, on this point. "All his activities," wrote Lord Morley, "were in his own mind one. That is the fundamental fact of Mr. Gladstone's history. Political life was only part of his religious life."[1] This was a thing which godly Nonconformists could understand and appreciate.[2]

Although the Conservatives had given votes to so many thousands of new electors, they reaped no benefit from their act, for in 1868 when they next appealed to the country they were defeated. However, six years later tlay were again in power, this time with a clear and workable majority. The result was due in part to the emergence of a number of Labour candidates who, in three-cornered contests, split the Progressive vote and let in the Conservative; in part to a strange alliance between the old Tory aristocracy and the newly enfranchised working man against the middle-class domination of the

[1] *Op. cit.*, I, p. 200.
[2] "Who is Mr. Gladstone, father?" asked the children of Hugh Price Hughes. "A man who says his prayers every morning," was the reply (*op. cit.*, p. 119).

Manchester school. Included amongst the elected members, a sign and portent had it been recognized, were two Labour members, Alexander Macdonald and Thomas Burt.

Social Legislation

The domestic and social reforms which the previous government had carried through had done a little to meet a growing demand for such improvements. The new government was by no means averse to meet this demand and in a single session in 1875 it passed Bills which improved the relations of masters and men, encouraged saving among the poorer classes, and by a housing measure began that long and arduous conflict with slum dwellings the end of which, so we hope, is now at last in sight. These reforms were largely the work of the Home Secretary, Richard Cross, a shrewd Lancashire lawyer and business man.[1] The days were days of much social unrest and had the Conservatives shewn signs of being obstructionist, disaster might have followed. The works of Henry George were being read, and all over Europe socialistic ideas were spreading; the Fabians in England were propagating them in one class, while the Social Democrats were doing the same in another. The public conscience was wakening up to the conditions of the country, and exposures such as Mearns' *Bitter Cry of Outcast London* were widely read. The work of Charles Booth in revealing the conditions of life and labour in London was being undertaken, although the first of his many volumes did not see the light until 1889. In England a much more friendly spirit prevailed than on the continent, owing no doubt to the Englishman's superior political training and his confidence that sooner or later he would get his way by peaceful means. Elsewhere things were not so happy. Bismarck told Disraeli in 1878 that whilst in Germany anyone riding a horse was the object of bitter comment, in England the more horses a nobleman had the more popular was he. He foretold that England was safe from Socialism so long as racing flourished.[2]

[1] Monypenny and Buckle. *Life of Benjamin Disraeli*, II, pp. 704 f.
[2] *Op. cit.*, II, p. 1203.

World-wide Expansion

If this epoch saw the beginnings of that social legislation which has become so prominent a feature of the present century, it saw also the beginnings of the world-expansion which is equally characteristic. The reasons for this were many. The new industrialism demanded raw materials; this gave a new value to lands which had been considered of little use. It also manufactured surplus products, for which new markets were sought in lands overseas. The increase of population and its concentration in big towns meant, especially in England, which from this time ceased to be self-supporting, the importation of foodstuffs. There was also the need for colonies to receive the surplus populations and to give an outlet for those who in their various home countries had found insufficient scope for their powers. In this world-expansion England took a leading part. This was due to the Englishman's natural instinct for colonization, the fruit of his island situation and his history; and also to the fact that England was already, at the beginning of this epoch, much more highly developed industrially than her neighbours. She possessed, too, in Disraeli a statesman who was capable of taking a world-wide view. He had sufficient imagination to perceive that a new epoch was dawning and skill enough to prepare his countrymen to take their part in it. Men might smile at his grandiloquent ideas, for so they seemed, such as making the Queen Empress of India, but he had a sound instinct and great business ability. This last was shewn when in 1875 he carried through, with money borrowed from the Rothschilds, the purchase of the controlling interest in the Suez Canal. Another great statesman also saw it coming, but he was unwilling to allow his country to take part in it. To Bismarck the expansion of the 'seventies was matter for regret and the colonial expansion of Germany not to be encouraged. But England rose to meet a new set of responsibilities, though the members of the governing classes, who had studied their Thucydides in the class-rooms of Eton and Harrow, knew only too well that Empires can only be maintained at a high cost; and the difficulty of combining the imperial spirit with generous feelings or even common honesty.[1]

[1] Cf. Thucydides, II, 63, and III, 40.

RELIGION IN THE VICTORIAN ERA

Lights and Shadows of the Period

Looking back on the generation which filled the years between 1860 and 1890 Lord Morley described it as "animated, hopeful, interesting, and on the whole happy" (*Recollections*, I, p. 26). Probably most people would accept his description, though now we are able to see that much of the hope was ill-founded, because based on ignorance of the true conditions. There was a pathetic confidence, on the political side, in an uninstructed democracy, and a belief in the potency of the ballot box to bring in the New Jerusalem. The earlier Victorians, with their craze for education and the diffusion of useful knowledge, had surely been wiser. Men had yet to learn that liberty is not a gift to be bestowed, but a privilege to be earned; that it is easier to give a people freedom than to build them up in the ways of profitable citizenship. In years to come the *New Worlds for Old* of Mr. H. G. Wells was to demonstrate that Utopia would not be brought about by merely dreaming about it; even when the catastrophe, beloved of the Marxians, by destroying the old civilization had left a cleared ground for its erection. There would still be need for trained and devoted administrators, for clear-sighted leaders, and for patience and unselfishness among the rank and file. But even in the actual period itself, quite apart from its over-optimistic outlook on the future, there was much to cause disquiet and unhappiness. The retirement of the Queen under the crushing blow of her premature widowhood cast a gloom over the country; whilst the wars on the continent and the Civil War in America had their repercussions at home. The last in particular brought about a serious cotton famine in Lancashire. At the end of the 'seventies there was much economic depression; cheap food was beginning to come in from overseas; but this, in combination with several bad harvests, was a severe blow to agriculture. Wages were low and disputes between masters and men caused uneasiness and loss. The high stage of development which the country had attained made it all the more sensitive to disorders in the body politic. Abroad a succession of unexpected reverses and disasters dimmed the lustre of our arms and lowered the nation's prestige, even if their magnitude was not sufficient to endanger its position as a world power. We need but name Isandhlwana where a British force was overwhelmed and wiped out by a Zulu army in 1879; Maiwand, where a brigade met with disaster at the hands of the Afghans in the following year; then Majuba in 1881;[1] four years later the Fall of Khartoum and the death of Gordon. None of these was enough, as we have said, to inflict serious damage to the nation's life; but their cumulative effect must have been disquieting. That British diplomacy should have scored a victory at the Congress of Berlin in 1878, and succeeded in imposing its will on Russia, was something on the other side; even though it involved the breach of the good understanding between Russia and Prussia which was one of the causes of the Great War; for that congress was, indeed, as Lady Gwendolen Cecil has said, "a point of vital departure in the history of the world."[2]

The years which followed the first Boer War saw the Victorian Age pass its zenith; though the rejoicings over the Jubilee of 1887 concealed it from the eyes of the multitude, and the reign had many achievements of which it was rightly proud.[3] But the older people were becoming pessimistic, both in politics and religion. Lord Shaftesbury, approaching the close of his own long day of unselfish service, turned to Jeremiah for light on the times in which he found himself.[4]

[1] It is perhaps worth while to recall that the Zulu War of 1879 was fought to save the Boers, who had trekked from Cape Colony, after it had been purchased by the British from the Dutch, and had found themselves in danger of annihilation from the native tribes. After the disaster of Majuba Hill (which involved only a scanty force of British) the government granted the Boers a self-governing Republic, whilst retaining some inadequate and ill-defined suzereinty for the Crown.

[2] *Life of Lord Salisbury*, II, p. 297.

[3] The achievements of the reign up to 1887 were recorded in an impressive series of essays under the editorship of Mr. Humphry Ward with the title of *The Reign of Queen Victoria*.

[4] Hodder, *Life and Works of Lord Shaftesbury*, III, p. 454. The same thought occurred to Westcott some years later: see the notice to the second edition of his *Epistle to the Hebrews* published in 1892. He wrote: "The more I study the tendencies of the time in some of the busiest centres of English life, the more deeply I feel that the Spirit of God warns us of our most urgent civil and spiritual dangers through the prophecies of Jeremiah and the Epistle to the Hebrews" (*op. cit.*, p. x).

But in reality he was depressed unduly, at least as regards the state of religion. The last years of the reign were to see unparalleled expansion in the Mission Field, renewed activity at home, and, though this might have added to his gloom, new and important developments in the Oxford Movement.

THE CONDITION OF RELIGION

The Church of England

We come now to a general survey of the condition of religion in these middle years, leaving to separate chapters the more detailed consideration of special points. In the Church of England it was perhaps most remarkable for the emergence of a new type of bishop, sign of the new place which that Church was to take in the nation's life, of a new attitude towards its own claims and the methods of obtaining recognition for them.

The type of bishop which emerged was not, of course, entirely new. We have already noticed the unconventional conduct of Archbishop Sumner, who was Primate from 1848 to 1862. Another example of devoted work was Walter Kerr Hamilton, Bishop of Salisbury (1854-69); and Samuel Wilberforce, Bishop of Oxford (1845-69) and Winchester (1869-73) is often regarded as setting a new standard of episcopal activity. The newer bishops had, on the whole, less learning than their predecessors, but more energy and, in many cases, more genuine piety and desire to be true pastors of the flock. In James Fraser, who succeeded Prince Lee in 1870 in the see of Manchester, there was a still further move in the direction of the popular and somewhat unconventional, but exceedingly energetic type of bishop who is so common in the present century. Fraser made a habit of speaking out on current topics, not always, it must be said, entirely advisedly. He mixed freely with all classes of society in his diocese, and shewed friendly feelings towards the Dissenters, though he both regretted and disliked Dissent itself. Although his words received weight and attracted attention from the position which he occupied, he never used that position in order to press his views. Consideration came to him for his own merits, rather than because he was a bishop.

Under Palmerston, from 1855 onwards, much influence was exercised by Lord Shaftesbury in the appointment of bishops. This meant that Evangelicals were usually selected. It is hardly correct to say, as has often been done in the past, that men of inferior powers were, for party reasons, thrust on the Church as its bishops, by this influence; Longley, Tait, Thomson, Harold Browne, Ellicott, Trench, Alford, and Jeremie were none of them Evangelicals; whilst Baring, Waldegrave, and Jeune had had distinguished careers before being raised to the bench. But some were passed over who might well have been promoted. Even in the lesser patronage Shaftesbury exerted his influence to keep out men whom he considered to be dangerous; an example is the exclusion of R. W. Church, although he had the support of Gladstone, from the chair of Ecclesiastical History at Oxford in 1864.[1] In later years, when patronage was in the hands of Gladstone himself, Lord Derby, and Lord Salisbury, all of whom were High Churchmen, the balance was redressed.[2] Disraeli's appointments are so interesting, or rather his attitude towards them, that a little ought to be said on the subject. Among his papers was found a memorandum on Church Appointments written in 1863 in which he notes: "no more Low Church Bishops to be appointed. That vein has been overworked. Some of the last appointments in that way had been mean and insignificant" (*Life*, II, p. 103). In his first appointments he was almost shameless in his regard to political consequences. In order to obtain the support of the extreme and militant Protestants he made Hugh McNeile Dean of Ripon in 1868. Even the Queen, who had strong Protestant sympathies and was seldom critical of her favourite Minister, was shocked, and only consented to the appointment with reluctance.[3] Later he learned more wisdom and made some appointments which shewed greater consideration for the good of the Church, and less for

---

[1] See *Life of Dean Church*, pp. 200 f., and Morley, *Life of W. E. Gladstone*, II, p. 328. A. P. Stanley, another future dean, was the chosen candidate.

[2] The Church suffered not only from party appointments, but also from the fact that religious leadership was divorced, among High Churchmen, from the episcopate; that is so long as Pusey and Liddon were alive.

[3] Monypenny and Buckle, *Life of Benjamin Disraeli*, II, p. 401.

the promotion of the interests of the Conservative party. Gladstone, it need hardly be remarked, appointed strong Tories, such as Stubbs, to Bishoprics if he thought that they were the best men available for the office. Perhaps Disraeli's most successful appointment was that of Benson to Truro; in this he was inspired by Gathorne Hardy.[1] He thus gave the opportunity to one who was to be a great figure in the Church of the Victorian Era and not the least successful of its Archbishops. Like Tait, his predecessor, and Temple, who followed him, he had been a schoolmaster.

When Benson went to Truro he received a letter of good wishes from R. W. Church in which the following interesting passage occurs: "I hope you may be permitted to add in Cornwall another to the many victories which the revived English Church has achieved, and which, in spite of disasters and menacing troubles, make it the most glorious Church in Christendom."[2] Six years later, when Benson was made Archbishop of Canterbury, by Gladstone, there can be no doubt that Church would have been appointed had he so desired; but Gladstone knew that he had no wish for the office, and so no offer was ever made to him (in spite of statements to the contrary); Morley says quite definitely that his name was not even considered (*Recollections*, II, p. 71). Church himself hailed Benson's appointment, as he had done that to Truro, with unfeigned delight.[3] In truth their belief in the Church of England and their hopes for its future were so similar that this can easily be understood. Another has described Benson as "inspired with hope [for the Church of England] and fired with visions for her future still greater than her past."[4] This was the true spirit of the leader, and stands in marked contrast with the pessimism of Lord Shaftesbury recorded above.

But Lord Shaftesbury's pessimism was probably due to the decay of the Evangelical party in which he was supremely interested. The tendency to split up, which had marked all the bodies which had emerged from Wesley's teaching, had

---

[1] *Op. cit.*, II, p. 969.
[2] *Life and Letters of Dean Church*, p. 306.
[3] *Op. cit.*, p. 368.
[4] See Watson, *Bishop John Wordsworth*, p. 38.

become even more marked, although it did not, as in the case of the Methodists, involve any outward schism. "All confidence has ceased," Shaftesbury wrote in 1856, "and people, from a variety of causes, take up their opinions, and let them fall, entirely in reference to themselves or their particular sections."[1] In 1869 he speaks of "the coldness and insincerity of the bulk of the Evangelicals, their disunion, their separation in place and action."[2] Finally in 1885 at the close of his life, he said: "Although . . . I stand fast by the teaching of the Evangelicals, I do not hesitate to say that I have received, from the hands of that party, treatment that I have not received from any other. High Churchmen, Roman Catholics, even infidels have been friendly to me; my only enemies have been the Evangelicals."[3] There seems in this period to have been a general opinion that the glory of the Evangelical party had become disastrously dim. Mark Pattison writing in 1863 could even say that it "merely covers the ground with its ruins. The ranks of the Evangelical clergy are being thinned yearly. Their social ascendency has departed" (*Essays*, II, p. 195). But these criticisms and forecasts were really beside the mark; Evangelicalism was to shew that it still had enormous vitality and was as capable as ever of playing a part in the religious life of England.

The Church and Dissent

If the Evangelical party within the Church of England was thus inclined to split up, at the same time the breach, political in its origin, was growing between them and the Nonconformists with whose views they had much sympathy and with whom they had for long worked amicably in great philanthropic efforts and in support of the religious societies. The breach was in part the result of the celebration on St. Bartholomew's Day, 1862, of the bicentenary of the expulsion of Richard Baxter and other divines from the cures into which

---

[1] Hodder, *Life and Works of Lord Shaftesbury*, III, p. 3. On pp. 255 and 451 he expresses the opinion that the Evangelicals had ceased to be a party and that Evangelicalism had become a mere theological expression of doubtful meaning.
[2] *Op. cit.*, III, p. 254.   [3] *Op. cit.*, III, p. 255.

they had been intruded during the Commonwealth. Considerable feeling was aroused among Churchmen by the manner in which the celebrations were conducted; though many who took part in the anniversary had no wish to use it for controversial ends, but merely to pay their tribute to those who had so nobly obeyed their consciences. In this feeling the Evangelicals were at one with the High Churchmen. There had been no commemoration of the expulsion of the incumbents of these same benefices under Cromwell—though their sufferings had been quite as great, if not greater—probably because the expulsions had not all taken place on a single date and therefore did not seem so romantic or spectacular.

A few years later, in spite of the Gorham judgement allowing the Evangelical interpretation of the doctrine of Baptismal Regeneration, the great Baptist preacher C. H. Spurgeon suddenly attacked the Evangelicals and accused them of perjury in subscribing to the Prayer Book, which clearly taught the doctrine. "I impeach before the bar of universal Christendom," he exclaimed, "these men, who, knowing that baptism does not regenerate, yet declare in public that it does." Spurgeon, it should be remembered, was very fond of interfering in other people's affairs; on this occasion he was severely rebuked by Lord Shaftesbury, who turned on him with tremendous violence. Had such an accusation been made to him he would have replied, "Sir, I believe you are very ignorant; to say the truth, you are a very saucy fellow, and if you think that you represent the great and good Nonconformists of former days . . . or even that you have anything akin to the good, sound, and true religious Nonconformists of the present day; you are just as much mistaken as you would be, if you thought you were well versed in history, or had even been initiated in the first elements of good breeding or Christian charity."[1] Further misunderstanding followed the disestablishment and disendowment of the Church of Ireland in 1869, which was thought to be but a prelude to a similar

[1] From a speech at the Church Pastoral Aid Society's Meeting on May 8, 1862: quoted Hodder, *Life and Works*, etc., III, p. 160. It should be added that in later years the two men were great friends and allies.

dealing with the Church of England, and the Nonconformists were very aggressive and triumphant. Finally, many Dissenters, following the lead of the Birmingham Education League, desired to banish all religion and even the reading of the Bible from the schools of the country. With such attacks on the Church and on the teaching of all religion the Evangelicals were entirely out of sympathy, and for some years the feelings between them and those who would have co-operated with them so readily were too acute to allow of such a beneficent course.

The bicentenary of the Ejectments of 1662, to which reference was made above, had consequences more fortunate than the widening of the breach between Churchmen and Nonconformists; for from it flowed a revived interest in building new places of worship. Many new chapels were definitely planned, and Churchpeople, for their part, were not behind in providing for the ever growing populations. Dr. Carpenter records much activity and quotes from the Calendar of the English Church for 1872 that in the previous year ninety-six churches were reopened after restoration or reconstruction and seventy-eight new ones built (*Church and People*, p. 387).

Growth of Liberal Theology

It was in this period that the life of the Churches began to be disturbed by the growth of Liberal views and the efforts of those who disliked them to put a term to their advance. We have already seen the effect on thought of the new views of Biblical Criticism and the controversies over *Essays and Reviews* and Bishop Colenso. In spite of them the Liberals continued to make progress both within the Church of England and among Nonconformists. For the Liberal Churchmen a great landmark was the publication in October 1865 of *The Life and Letters of F. W. Robertson*, the work of a young Irish clergyman, later to obtain a widespread fame for himself—Stopford Brooke. The appearance of this book at this epoch was momentous, for it revealed a great character sustained and nourished by the views which many held to be suspect, if not definitely unorthodox. Four years later came the opposition to Temple's election to the Bishopric of Exeter on account of his share—a comparatively harmless one—in *Essays and Reviews*. The opposition, although it was led by some whom he respected on other grounds, drew from Church words of strong condemnation. In a letter to his American friend, the famous botanist, Dr. Asa Gray, written in November 1869, he describes it as "most unjust, and in its violence very discreditable . . . seeing a man learned and religious as Pusey is, so blindly unjust and intemperate, is a heavy blow against that which is more to Pusey than life" (*Life and Letters*, pp. 219 f).

There was also a famous controversy among the Congregationalists in 1877 and the year following; for this more justification could be urged, since J. Allanson Picton and those who thought with him urged that religious communion should no longer depend on theological agreement. Picton himself was really a Unitarian who regarded dogma and even the historicity of Christianity as of little moment. The Conference of 1878 rejected this proposal and affirmed the need for a common doctrinal basis.[1] It was some ten years later that Spurgeon launched his celebrated attack on what he called "Down-Grade" theology. The Baptist Union demanded evidence in support of his statements and the names of those whom he looked upon as affected by it; these he was either unable or unwilling to supply. The result was that the Union declared that the attack was quite unjustified and ought never to have been made.[2]

When one surveys Mid-Victorian religion as a whole the impression is not too favourable.[3] There was too great a consciousness that the growing prosperity of the country, the leaping figures for exports and imports, the rapidly growing empire, were all the Divine recognition of the worthiness of Britain and its inhabitants. Religion itself was regarded almost in the light of an investment. There was something in pro-

---

[1] A. W. Peel, *These Hundred Years*, pp. 266 ff.

[2] The whole incident is described by Marchant, *John Clifford*, pp. 156 ff.

[3] Even a Liberal like Dean Stanley seems to have despaired. Not long before his death he uttered the sad complaint that: "This generation is lost; it is either plunged in dogmatism or agnosticism. I look forward to the generation to come" (*Life*, II, p. 11).

ductive labour which deserved a more than earthly reward. Dr. Inge, who sees in Calvinism and Quakerism "the genuinely religious basis of the modern business life," finds this gospel preached in such books as those of Samuel Smiles, and in Clough's poem beginning "Hope ever more and believe, O Man" (*Outspoken Essays*, I, p. 256). In a further passage he condemns the selfishness which underlies the whole religious conception of much of the preaching and the popular thought of the day. "If I desire a future life," he writes, "because I have made certain investments in good works, on which I hope to make a handsome profit, in the words of the hymn—

> 'Whatever, Lord, we lend to Thee,
> Repaid a thousandfold will be;
> Then gladly will we give to Thee,
> Who givest all'—

that has no more to do with religion than if I invested my money on the faith of one of the very similarly worded prospectuses which I find on my breakfast table" (*op. cit.*, II, pp. 34 f.).

This Deuteronomic or "commercial" religion found its *reductio ad absurdum* in the British Israelite theory, that the English are the descendants of the Ten Lost Tribes and therefore the "Chosen People." Such a theory which is contradicted by history and science can obviously appeal only to the imperfectly educated and ultra-sentimental; but unfortunately such classes abound, and though they may not be taken seriously at home, the foreigner sees in their views another instance of the overweening egotism of the English race.[1] The theory might easily cause offence to a friendly nation like the Danes, for since they are held to be the descendants of Dan, having reached their country via the Danube, they are, of course, with all other members of that tribe excluded from the New Jerusalem.[2] So far as I know, the only other peoples who make a similar claim are the Afghans and the Abyssinians,

---

[1] Carl Peters, who really ought to have known better, devoted some pages to British Israelitism as an example of British megalomania in his sympathetic volume, published just before the war, on *England and the English*.

[2] See Rev. vii. 5–8.

the latter taking to themselves all rights in the tribe of Judah, which is not, of course, one of the "Lost Tribes" at all, and whose descendants ought more properly to be sought among the Jews. So long as British Israelitism exists, English people cannot, in any fairness, express their amusement at the "Nordic" imaginings of their German cousins.

Such eccentric "religionists" bring discredit on their orthodox brethren, and the supporters of so useful and sane an institution as the London Society for Promoting Christianity among the Jews are often supposed by the ignorant to share their queer beliefs. This society has always had to fight against ignorance and prejudice, as is witnessed by a somewhat amusing incident in the career of Lord Shaftesbury. He was serving as Chairman of a Commission on Lunacy when a dispute arose over the sanity of a certain lady. A medical man crept up to his chair and whispered confidentially: "Are you aware, my lord, that she subscribes to the Society for the Conversion of the Jews?" "Indeed!" replied Lord Shaftesbury; "and are you aware that I am President of that Society?" (*Life*, III, p. 139).

Another class of religious persons was that which consisted of those who, with a never discouraged confidence, persisted in the face of repeated disappointments, in forecasting the exact date of the Second Advent. Such forecasts brought only confusion to the simple, terror in not a few homes to the children who chanced to overhear the discussions of their elders, and an occasion for scoffing to the ribald.

The wide prevalence of eccentric types of Christianity among the imperfectly educated of all classes, and the predominance of the "commercial" spirit, were undoubtedly responsible in part for the vigorous Secularist offensive of the 'seventies and 'eighties. This attack had immense effect especially among the younger, thinking men and women of the working classes. Bradlaugh and others went about the country delivering lectures in which the Bible and the cruder teaching on the doctrine of the Atonement were openly ridiculed.[1] Much of their attack was directed against imperfect and warped ideas of the Gospel, and the best of such antagonists were inspired

[1] A good description of this propaganda and the efforts made to check it will be found in F. G. Bettany, *Stewart Headlam*, pp. 47 ff.

by quite noble, if highly mistaken, motives. Stewart Headlam, who fought them, "tooth and nail," once wrote: "How much nearer to the Kingdom of Heaven are these men . . . than the followers of Moody and Sankey" (*op. cit.*, p. 50). One of the greatest tragedies of the nineteenth century was the fact that to many came across only perverted or incomplete forms of Christianity, and so were compelled to reject it. Edmund Gosse's self-revelation in *Father and Son* is typical of such cases.

Bradlaugh himself became notorious for his refusal to take the oath when elected Member of Parliament for Northampton in 1880 on conscientious grounds. This eventually led to his imprisonment. One of the most striking incidents in connexion with the case was the telegram which Stewart Headlam, his opponent on the religious platform, sent to him. "Accept my warmest sympathy. I wish you good luck in the name of Jesus Christ, the Emancipator, whom so many of your opponents blaspheme" (*op. cit.*, p. 60). One very sensible view of the case was that of Guinness Rogers, who pointed out the illogicality in punishing a conscientious, intellectual atheist, whilst tolerating the far worse practical atheism in the hearts and lives of other members of the House.[1]

[1] *J. Guinness Rogers*, p. 132. Details of the case can be found in Morley, *Life of Gladstone*, III, pp. 11 ff.

II

THE REVIVAL AND DEEPENING OF RELIGION

REVIVALS

WHATEVER may be one's own particular attitude towards revivals and the methods adopted by those who conduct them, it is impossible to deny their significance in the life of the Church in the Victorian Era and especially during its middle years. This was recognized at the time by men of every school of thought, even Canon Liddon, who cannot be suspected of undue favour, publicly testified to the good done by Moody and Sankey in their mission to Oxford in 1875. What he commended above all was their courage and the example of evangelizing which they had set.[1]

There can be little doubt that Moody and Sankey and their followers and imitators were responsible, under God, for the general quickening of religious life in England in the 'seventies. That such a quickening took place is abundantly clear from the records of the time; "it was felt," writes an acute observer, T. H. Darlow, "for the time being, almost like a change of religious climate." Hort noticed it at Cambridge soon after he returned there in 1872. In a letter to Westcott he describes a service in Great St. Mary's and ends up: "Assuredly the springs of life are strangely breaking forth anew" (*Life*, II, p. 197). Henry Drummond, who was himself profoundly touched by the visit of Moody and Sankey, is perhaps not so detached a witness; but his testimony will be accepted by any unprejudiced mind from his known sincerity and truthfulness. It has a particular value, not only because he speaks as an eye-witness and fellow labourer, but also because he affirms that much of the work was permanent, and that it bore fruit in many different fields. Twenty years after the first great campaign, looking back, he could write: "It was the writer's privilege, as a humble camp-follower, to follow the fortunes of the campaign personally, from town to town

---

[1] See the sermon "Influences of the Holy Spirit," in *University Sermons*, II.

and from city to city, throughout the three kingdoms, for over a year. And time has only deepened the impression, not only of the magnitude of the results immediately secured, but equally of the permanence of the after effects upon every field of social, philanthropic, and religious activity."

Every section of the Church in this land benefited from the religious awakening. If the High Church Anglicans did not enrol many new adherents they themselves were quickened into imitation and their own great missioners, much as they differed from the Americans in method, drank from the same source of inspiration. It was naturally the Free Churches who reaped the largest harvest for, as Silvester Horne has said: "Religious revival produces Nonconformists as inevitably as the spring calls the trees into foliage. New thought, new faith, new method are the creation of a spirit of awakening, and must have liberty in which to realize themselves" (*Free Church History*, p. 253). In the Church of England it was the Evangelicals who welcomed, after some hesitation, the movement, and it was they who recognized its usefulness. Lord Shaftesbury, the lay-spokesman of the party, although he felt that Moody was lacking in eloquence and even in ordinary skill in delivery, declared that he would "do more in an hour than Canon Liddon in a century" (Quoted Hodder, *Life of Lord Shaftesbury* III, pp. 358 f.).

Their Dangers

The Movement, then, was one of deep significance on account of the variety and depth of its influence. It was none the less accompanied by serious dangers. Fortunately its own leaders were, on the whole, aware of these dangers and on their guard against them. Bishop McIlvane, an American sympathizer who knew the Revival Movement in its home land, was eager to make others realize that a time of revival was a time for increased watchfulness. "You can no more advance the growth of religion in the soul by excitement," he wrote, "than you can promote health in the body by throwing it into a fever."[1]

Probably the earlier movement of 1859 was marked by emotional appeals more than the later, Moody and Sankey,

[1] Carus, *Life of Bishop McIlvane*, p. 82.

crusades. The Quaker historian, Thomas Hodgkin, was certainly much perturbed by the "spiritual intoxication" of 1859,[1] and the accounts of its first successes were subject to "painful and large discounts." Many Evangelical leaders, as we shall see, held aloof from it; they dreaded the excitement, and even the type of hymn that was in use. "I cannot think," wrote Henry Venn Elliott, "that souls get to heaven by exciting or marching music."[2] On the other hand, the great Unitarian, James Martineau, defended the Movement; declaring that men must have "faith in the action of the spirit of God upon humanity."[3]

Among some of those who were touched by the Movement spiritual excitement led to sensual; this was especially true among the Celtic peoples. E. W. Benson, who went into Cornwall as Bishop of Truro in 1877, wrote to A. J. Mason soon after his arrival: "The confusion of sensual excitement with religious passion is awful. The immoralities of Revival simply appalling."[4] As spiritual excitement led in some cases to immorality, so in others it led to spiritual pride. This sometimes had its humorous side, as in a case which Benson records of the vicar of a parish being called in by the mothers of two young women who were quarrelling over "which had most grace." "They scratched each other, tore out each other's hair, and positively fought."[5]

Even when no definitely harmful results followed Revival meetings the Movement in general was not without drawbacks, for it was apt to make people, especially the young, impatient with the Church's ordered rotation of festival and fast. The natural man is ever tempted to see God in the unusual and the catastrophic; and to miss His influence in the usual and the commonplace.

Some of the harmful results of revival preaching were due to the defective and inadequate theology of the evangelists.

[1] Louise Creighton, *Life of Thomas Hodgkin*, p. 67.
[2] Bateman, *Life of the Rev. H. V. Elliott*, p. 214.
[3] J. Estlin Carpenter, *James Martineau*, p. 406.
[4] A. C. Benson, *Edward White Benson*, p. 170. Benson continued to be appalled by the fact that the people were religious, but that their religion seemed to have no power to control their lives and impulses: see *op. cit.*, pp. 171 and 201.
[5] *Op. cit.*, p. 189.

They were often men of fervent religion and deep spiritual experience, but apt to deviate into wild doctrines and eccentric conduct. Some of them caused much havoc and alarm by proclaiming the doctrine of "sinless perfection"; whilst many of them were very "shaky" in their theology, and in less tolerant times would have been burnt at the stake for heresy. It was no doubt ignorance of theology, which is, of course, the result of an incomplete and one-sided knowledge of the Bible, that led some of the speakers into irreverence and distressing familiarity. They forgot the majesty of the Most High. This failing was very evident to Thomas Hodgkin, although it was not sufficient to obscure the more attractive elements in the message. "Sankey's hymns," he wrote in 1873, "were always sweet to me. Moody's bad grammar, his comic bits, his familiar and irreverent way of speaking of the Everlasting God, repelled me, but his power and his wonderful pathos attracted me still more."[1]

History of the Movement

Having made these general remarks it will be of service to tell in outline something of the history of the Revival Movement. Revivals on a small scale and affecting only a limited area seem to have been comparatively frequent in the early years of the nineteenth century; they were a kind of continuation of the Methodist Revival and were largely carried on by the followers of Wesley.[2] But with the beginning of the second half of the century there came a series of movements on a scale which was almost world-wide. The first of these began as a consequence of a small prayer meeting held in New York in 1858. During the course of the next few years this revival covered the greater part of the United States and its course was marked by impressive spiritual achievements. Then like a great tidal wave it spread to the West Indies, and in 1859 leapt the Atlantic, touching even the ships as it passed, and appeared in Northern Ireland. Thence in the same year it was carried to England. The agents of its propagation were

[1] Louise Creighton, *Life of Thomas Hodgkin*, p. 86.
[2] For some examples see *The Autobiography of Benjamin Gregory*, pp. 12 f., 105 f., 233 f.

for the most part free-lance evangelists who recognized no outside authority. Some of its features were undesirable; there was much emotionalism, and outbursts similar to those which accompanied the Methodist Revival were not uncommon. Evangelicals were divided in their attitude: some of the leading men received it gladly—included amongst them were the younger Henry Venn, Canon Hoare, and William Pennefather; but some, like Henry Melvill of St. Paul's, were scornful. That the majority of Evangelicals should hold aloof from the Movement and even regard it with suspicion was not really surprising. Such movements were a novelty and some of its features were objectionable, and, after all, the ethos of the Church of England is such that its best work is done, and always will be done, by quiet, steady labours in the parish rather than by co-operating in big efforts of an undenominational character. In some Evangelical parishes, however, it found a welcome and among them in Fordington, near Dorset, where one who was to be greatly used by God had his first experience of such a Divine awakening. Handley Moule, the son of the Vicar, was then a boy of seventeen and he "saw the church thronged to overflowing and the large schoolroom packed night after night. No great preacher was there. The very simplest means carried with them a heavenly power. The mere reading of a chapter was enough. Hundreds before his very eyes were 'awakened, awed and made conscious of eternal realities.' The Revival passed, but the results remained. A great social uplifting followed; a vigorous movement for temperance and thrift arose spontaneously among the people and it was fostered and organized by the Vicar and his friends."[1] Two things stand out in this simple account. The almost spontaneous character of the whole proceeding and the presence on the spot of those who were willing and able to take charge of the newly awakened souls. Revivals fail, when they do, or succeed, very largely as such following-up efforts are made or not.

Moody himself came to England for his greatest triumph at the invitation of William Pennefather, for some years Vicar of St. Jude's, Mildmay Park. During his time as incumbent

[1] Harford and Macdonald, *Bishop Handley Moule*, p. 14.

THE REVIVAL AND DEEPENING OF RELIGION

Mildmay "became a centre of spiritual power which was felt to the ends of the earth." His secret was a simple one; "he was a man who walked with God, who simply asked his Heavenly Father for whatever was needed for this or that project according to that Father's will, and who found these childlike requests granted. He was the George Müller of the Church of England; and though his career was much shorter and (if one may so say) less sensational than that of the founder of the Orphan Homes, his influence upon the Evangelical circle has been incomparably greater."[1] During a visit to this country in 1872 the American evangelist went to a Conference at Mildmay and there his outstanding gifts as a missioner were recognized by the experienced eye of Pennefather. Accordingly, in conjunction with Cuthbert Bainbridge, he invited Moody to return to England in the following year to conduct a series of meetings.

It was whilst Moody was over here in 1872 that there occurred that amazing example of the power of persistent and believing prayer which has become classical. It is told in Moody's own biography; but perhaps the most impressive account is that given in *The Practice of Prayer* by Dr. Campbell Morgan. He himself knew the chief figure in the incident, Marianne Adlard, who was afterwards a member of his Church in New Court, London.

"There are saints of God who for long, long years have been shut off from all the activities of the Church, and even from the worship of the Sanctuary; but who, nevertheless, have continued to labour together in prayer with the whole fellowship of the saints. There comes to me the thought of one woman, who to my knowledge since 1872 in this great babel of London has been in perpetual pain, and yet in constant prayer. She is to-day a woman twisted and distorted by suffering, and yet exhaling the calm and strength of the secret of the Most High.

"In 1872 she was a bedridden girl in the north of London, praying that God would send Revival to the Church of which she was a member, and yet into which even then she never came. She had read in the little paper called *Revival*,

[1] Stock, *History of the C.M.S.*, III, pp. 21 f.

which subsequently became *The Christian*, the story of a work being done in Chicago among ragged children by a man called Moody, but (*sic*) putting that little paper under her pillow, she began to pray: 'O Lord, send this man to our Church.'

"She had no means of reaching him or communicating with him. He had already visited this country in 1867, and in 1872 he started again for a short trip without any intention of doing any work. Mr. Lessey, however, the pastor of the Church of which this girl was a member, met him and asked him to preach for him. He consented, and after the evening service he asked those who would decide for Christ to rise, and hundreds did so. He was surprised, and imagined that his request had been misunderstood. He repeated it more clearly, and again the response was the same. Meetings were continued throughout the following ten days, and four hundred members were taken into the Church. In telling me this story Moody said, 'I wanted to know what this meant. I began to make enquiries, and never rested until I found a bedridden girl praying that God would bring me to that Church. He had heard her, and brought me over four thousand miles of land and sea in answer to her request.'"

So much for Moody's visit in 1872. When he returned in the following June, bringing with him his equally famous colleague, Sankey, they were met, on landing at Liverpool, with the disastrous news that both of those who had invited them were dead and that no plans of any kind had been made for their reception or use. But they were not thus to be turned aside. It happened that in America Moody had come across a York tradesman of the name of Bennett; and he had told him to remember just two words if ever he came to England, York and Bennett. Moody took the man at his word and immediately telegraphed to him announcing his plight. Mr. Bennett, on receiving the message, consulted his pastor, the Rev. F. B. Meyer, and they at once invited the evangelists to visit York. Thus began a connexion between two men, not at all of the same type, who were to do mighty things for God in the work of evangelization and of deepening the spiritual life.

The beginnings at York were not very encouraging—there were only eight persons at the first meeting, but on moving on into Scotland a really impressive work was begun. An invitation to London soon followed, and in March 1875 they succeeded in filling the Agricultural Hall at Islington with a crowd of some 14,000 people. Every class of society soon began to feel their effects, from working men to the wealthy and leisured, and not the least service that Moody and Sankey did was to raise up other missioners, amongst whom was Henry Drummond. Some of the work done at the meetings was undoubtedly transitory and its effects soon passed away, but much of it stood the test of time and the harsh buffeting of experience.

In 1882 Moody and Sankey made the great experiment of a visit to the University of Cambridge. Their beginning was almost disastrous. Moody had certain quaintnesses of pronunciation, and he had unfortunately chosen Daniel the prophet as the subject of his first address, and his constant references to "Dannel" aroused much derision among the undergraduates. These same gentlemen persisted in regarding Mr. Sankey as an entertainer, and loudly applauded his efforts, and even called for encores. The unfortunate start was soon forgotten, however, and lasting work was done; among those who were converted was the rowdiest of the leaders, and it has been surmised that no other mission of eight days has ever had such wonderful results.[1] Moody himself seems to have been overwhelmed by the success of the mission. Handley Moule once told a company of Ridley men how he was kneeling next to him on the platform at the closing meeting when all who were conscious of having received definite blessing were asked quietly to stand up while the rest kept their eyes closed. He says that as the men rose Moody, who alone could see them, said under his breath, "My God, this is enough to live for."[2] Some of the results were undoubtedly bad, being due to the effect of novel methods on not over-strong characters; one young man actually set out, without any training and quite without support, to convert China, his only

[1] Harford and Macdonald, *Bishop Handley Moule*, p. 115.
[2] *Op. cit.*, p. 116.

equipment being a pocket Bible;[1] a foolish enterprise no doubt, but perhaps nearer to the mind of the first Apostles than some more modern methods. Wild schemes were initiated because men's hearts had been deeply stirred: the fervour and zeal were there; what was needed was, in addition, patience and the controlling hand of older and wiser friends. This need was met to a large extent by the efforts of John Barton, the Vicar of Holy Trinity, and Moule, who was then Principal of Ridley Hall. The most sensational result of the mission was, of course, the going out of the famous Cambridge Seven for service with the China Inland Mission. The leaders of this enterprise were C. T. Studd,[2] the cricket captain, and Stanley Smith, the stroke of the 'Varsity boat. They in their turn, before leaving England, conducted a great crusade to try and reach other University men and were extraordinarily successful. Henry Drummond has recorded the results of their efforts in Edinburgh University. In general their obvious sincerity and earnestness, backed up by Drummond's own scientific attainments, were especially effective in bringing back medical students who had given up the faith of their childhood owing to the apparent inability of the Church to assimilate the new scientific knowledge.

Before leaving this account of the Revival Movement, associated above all with the names of Moody and Sankey, it will be worth while to give the impressions of a great religious leader who was, by temperament, not unduly prejudiced in their favour. When Dale first came across the Movement he was apprehensive and a little suspicious of its probable effects. Later he became, on fuller knowledge and further observation, a steady supporter. The thing which most impressed him in the methods of the leaders was the use of "after-meetings," without which, so he concluded, "the preaching . . . would not have accomplished one-fifth of its results" (*Life*, p. 319). Dale felt that the later visits, although Moody was as vigorous

---

[1] Even G. L. Pilkington, who took a first class in the Classical Tripos in the year that Miss Ramsey headed the list, seemed to find such an enterprise admirable and almost worthy of imitation: see *Pilkington of Uganda*, p. xiv.

[2] Studd was not actually converted at the Cambridge meetings.

and impressive as ever, were not so successful. This he put down to a change of emphasis in the preaching by which repentance was no longer regarded as a change of outlook, but as "a doing of penance . . . a self-torture, a voluntary sorrow, a putting on of spiritual hair-shirts" (*op. cit.*, p. 530). This may have been so, but more probably the fact that Moody gave the same addresses as ten years before accounted for the reduced effect. This seems to have been the opinion of R. F. Horton, who was never so enthusiastic a supporter of the Revivalists. He felt that they "excited the people by drawing vast multitudes, and left a reaction . . . which weakened rather than strengthened the Church" (*Autobiography*, p. 69). Thus both Dale and Horton were not so much impressed by the big public meetings; the one seeing in their sequel the really effective means of influence, the other regarding them as probably dangerous rather than helpful.

CONFERENCES

The intention of the Revivalists was to arouse those outside the Church to an appreciation of their real state, and thus to lead them to their Saviour; in other words, the end was conversion. In this they were exhibiting the Church as a body still possessed of power, for as Sir John Seeley, perhaps an unexpected witness, has said: "Surely this Article of Conversion is the true *articulus stantis aut cadentis ecclesiae*. When the power of reclaiming the lost dies out of the Church, it ceases to be the Church. It may remain a useful institution, though it is most likely to become an immoral and mischievous one. When the power remains, there, whatever is wanting, it may still be said that 'the tabernacle of God is with men.' "[1] But alongside conversion, there was need also of the deepening of spiritual life in those who had already experienced it. This was supplied by what were known as Conferences.

Conferences were, of course, no new thing. The great Assemblies of the Nonconformist bodies, from the Congregational Union to the Methodists, had borne this name; whilst more akin there had been the Conference associated with the name of Islington. About this last something more must here

[1] *Ecce Homo* (5th Edition), p. 258.

be said. It grew out of a small meeting of clergy called together by Daniel Wilson on January 4, 1827, at his vicarage. In the earlier years different clergymen were elected as chairmen, but after the Rev. J. W. Cunningham, Vicar of Harrow, had held the office from 1834 to 1859, the Vicar of Islington, unless prevented by illness, has been president *ex officio*. For more than a hundred years the meeting has served as a centre for the Evangelical clergy, and has given them guidance and confidence in the face of loneliness and perplexity. The Conference is now held in the Church Hall, Westminster, having outgrown the Hall at Islington, but it still preserves its original character and performs its original function.

One striking sign of the realization of the need both for the conversion of the sinner and for the deepening of the lives of those who were already Christian was the giving up, at the Church Congress in 1870, of a whole session to the discussion of "Agencies for the Kindling and Revival of Spiritual Life": among those who spoke were Canon Body and Father R. M. Benson of Cowley, both famous Missioners of the High Church school. About the same time William Pennefather, who was to invite Moody to come to England, was founding the Mildmay Conference as a meeting place for all Christians without regard to office, denomination, or sex. In 1870 the great Hall to seat 2,500 was built; but Pennefather died in 1873 to be followed, as Chairman of the Conference, by Stevenson Blackwood. From about this time onwards the conviction was steadily growing in the minds of many that by faith deliverance, not only from the punishment of sin, but also from its power, was possible. Those who held such views were guilty in some cases of excesses, teaching perfectionism, and for this reason many Evangelicals regarded the whole movement with disfavour. Some, however, were willing to take their part, and amongst them may be mentioned H. W. Webb-Peploe and Evan Hopkins. Several Conferences between the differing schools were held, in particular one at Oxford, and another at Brighton, and amongst those who were influenced was T. D. Harford-Battersby. Harford-Battersby was a man of a wide and generous culture. In his early days he had fallen under the spell of J. H. Newman, but later came to be strongly affected by

THE REVIVAL AND DEEPENING OF RELIGION

F. W. Myers, whose curate he was, and the Bunsens. Having realized the value of a "resting faith," as it came technically to be called, he determined to spread the teaching which had been of so much blessing to himself. Accordingly in the summer of 1875 he called together a convention in a field belonging to his parsonage at Keswick, and thus began an enterprise which was destined to grow into one of the most famous and important of modern religious movements. Harford-Battersby himself never knew that the Convention which he had established was to be so widely used, for he died in 1883 when it was still an object of suspicion to many Evangelical leaders. This suspicion, which was very natural in view of the eccentricities of some of the teachers of similar doctrines, was not overcome until H. G. Moule in July 1886, having himself overcome such feelings through personal experience, took his place among the recognized speakers.[1] But if the older Evangelicals succeeded in overcoming their suspicion, men of other schools of thought still retained them. Dr. Dale, in spite of his support of Moody and Sankey, found much that was objectionable in such Conventions. "The unsound and uncritical use of Scripture, the passion for allegory by which the plain sense of the Bible was distorted . . . the incessant use of luscious and sensuous imagery derived from the language of human passion seemed to him fraught with the gravest moral peril" (*Life*, p. 329). But alongside this condemnation of the methods and the language used must be placed a long record of experiences of help received, even by men of intellectual gifts, and at the hands of some of the teachers who offended most in the way of language and imagery.

In 1875 at a Conference in Brighton conducted by Mr. and Mrs. Pearsall Smith, Quakers from America of much theological ignorance, Hugh Price Hughes received a blessing which sustained him to the end of his busy and over-occupied life and was proof against all but momentary periods of disappointment and depression. They taught that sin was no necessary condition of the Christian even in this life. This brought to Price Hughes a new sense that "his will" is "our

[1] See Harford and Macdonald, *Bishop Handley Moule*, pp. 126 ff.

peace" and a peace that was joy.[1] The triumphant faith which the message proclaimed at Keswick could bring may be illustrated by the experience of F. B. Meyer in 1887. It came to him before he first spoke at the Convention to which he had been invited on account of the wonderful spiritual influence which he was exercising in Leicester. The experience can best be given in his own words: "Before I first spoke on the platform I had my own deeper experience, on a memorable night when I left the little town with its dazzling lamps, and climbed the neighbouring hill. As . . . I walked I said, 'My Father, if there is one soul more than another within the circle of these hills that needs the gift of Pentecost it is I; I want the Holy Spirit but I do not know how to receive Him and I am too weary to think, or feel, or pray intensely.' Then a Voice said to me, 'As you took forgiveness from the hand of the dying Christ, take the Holy Ghost from the hand of the living Christ, and reckon that the gift is thine by a faith that is utterly indifferent to the presence or absence of resultant joy. According to thy *faith* so shall it be unto thee.' So I turned to Christ and said, 'Lord, as I breathe in this whiff of warm night air, so I breathe into every part of me Thy blessed Spirit.' I felt no hand laid on my head, there was no lambent flame, there was no rushing sound from heaven: but by *faith*, without emotion, without excitement, I took, and took for the first time, and I have kept taking ever since.

"I turned to leave the mountain side, and as I went down the tempter said I had nothing, that it was all imagination, but I answered, 'Though I do not feel it, I reckon that God is faithful.' "[2]

Finally the experience of R. F. Horton must be added; for Horton was a man of great intellectual powers, a Higher Critic, and not in the least likely to be led away by any merely emotional appeal. In 1890 through the agency of Reader Harris he felt that he had been brought to know that Christ was a Saviour not only from the punishment due for sin, but from the power of sin itself.[3]

---

[1] D. Price Hughes, *Life of Hugh Price Hughes*, pp. 105 f.
[2] Quoted by W. B. Fullerton, *Life of F. B. Meyer*, pp. 65 f.
[3] See *An Autobiography*, pp. 105 ff.

THE REVIVAL AND DEEPENING OF RELIGION

Before leaving the subject of Conventions and Conferences for the deepening of Spiritual Life something must be said of those held at "Broadlands." "Broadlands" had been the home of Lord Palmerston and after the death of his widow it came to her son, by a former marriage, William Cowper-Temple. Cowper-Temple, from the midst of a worldly home, had become a zealous, if somewhat unusual, Evangelical and with his wife spent much of his energies in striving to bring others into a like peace. In 1874 he began a series of Conferences which lasted, with only one break, annually until his death in 1888. The first Conference was attended by the Pearsall Smiths to whom Hugh Price Hughes owed so great a debt. Later there came as speakers or guests as varied a collection as ever graced a religious gathering; even convinced followers of the Tractarians, like Bishop Wilkinson and Charlotte Yonge, were to be found there. Mr. G. W. E. Russell recalls among the speakers "a Jew who had been converted by studying the Law of Sacrifice, a negress who had been a slave, and a retired schoolmaster who taught that sin was a disease. The discussions were animated, amiable, and desultory. No one kept to the prescribed subject. Everyone had his own gospel and preached it. Everyone agreed immensely with the last speaker, and forthwith proceeded to launch some entirely different theory of his own. There was no quarrelling and the mutual admiration was perfectly sincere. . . . And yet, though it was so very easy to laugh at them, these Conferences had a real value. They brought together earnest people who certainly would never have met elsewhere. They enabled Ritualists to understand the vital element of Evangelical religion. They showed Evangelicals that Ritualists were not necessarily slaves of the husk and the letter. They opened the eyes of orthodox believers to the mysterious workings of the Spirit of Truth in regions far beyond the precincts of all organized religion" (*Basil Wilberforce*, pp. 64 f.).

12

THE OXFORD MOVEMENT—THE SECOND PHASE

THE secession of Newman and those who, swayed by his influence or example, made the same perilous venture, left the Oxford Movement and its adherents shaken and discredited. At St. Mary's where once the subtle and mournful spell of Newman had exercised its all-but-resistless charm Charles Marriott maintained the feeble flame that still dimly burned there; otherwise the Movement seemed to have been stamped out in the place of its birth. Pusey was silenced, Newman himself had disappeared. But there were other facts to be considered. Pusey might have been silenced, but he was still loyal; and so too was Keble in the background; whilst James Mozley, as Church has put it, "shewed that there was one strong mind and soul still left at Oxford."[1] Even in its weakness it was yet capable of attracting men of great gifts to itself; for it was in 1848 that Robert Cecil, later as Marquis of Salisbury to be among the foremost of British statesmen, went up from a home where religion, if taken for granted, was strongly Protestant and unsympathetic towards anything which savoured of Rome. He almost at once embraced the principles which seemed so signally to have been defeated, and held them tenaciously to the end of his long life.[2] Some strength and life there must still have been to win so valuable a convert.

The Oxford Movement had begun, as someone has said, by being a chapel in the great unfinished cathedral of the Romantic Revival. Driven from Oxford it lost its academic flavour, and something, for the time at least, of its Romantic element. Full of zeal its adherents carried the appeal into the country. Just as the persecution at Jerusalem drove the early

---

[1] *Life and Letters*, p. 388.
[2] See Lady Gwendolen Cecil, *Life of Robert Marquis of Salisbury*, ?, pp. 24, 100 f. The strength of Lord Salisbury's Churchmanship was such that he determined to remove his sons from Eton when some rearrangement of school hours threatened to stop their going weekly to Communion, "then a rare eccentricity at Eton" (*op. cit.*, p. 120).

Christians to spread the faith in other cities, so now was the fire scattered to spring into flame in new centres—in fashionable West End parishes and the dark and awful streets of the growing cities. It thus exhibited for the first time what became its characterestic power—the ability to adapt itself to new circumstances. Even in Oxford this power was to be shewn; and, in a later generation, one who had felt and responded to the attraction of the Movement, but had afterwards turned from it almost as from an evil dream, could look back from his attitude of cynical detachment and note how the honey from the new Hegelian school was going into the Ritualist hive.[1] The whole history of the Movement since has been marked by this power of absorbing into itself elements from the air around it.

It was at this stage, at least in the eyes of Nonconformists, "truculent, ill-informed, and polemical"; attacking things which they held dear and condemning their most cherished leaders as "pestiferous heretics or wilful schismatics." So Dale judged it.[2] Later in a calmer air he modified the harshness of this judgement and distinguished the good in it from the bad—that is by Nonconformist standards. "The blessing of God was in it, though we did not see it, and in a form they did not understand; in the lives and in the devotion of these men a new endowment of the Holy Spirit came into the life of England" (*Life*, p. 699).

THE GORHAM CASE

The Movement thus began to settle down, and the Church to recover from the disaster of Newman's secession. But within a few years another blow of equal severity was to befall it. This arose in connexion with the Gorham Case. An Evangelical clergyman of that name was refused institution to the living of Bampford Speke by Bishop Phillpotts of Exeter as being unsound in the faith. The question in dispute was the meaning of Baptismal Regeneration. This was no new subject for controversy. One view had been expressed by Archbishop Laurence in his Bampton Lectures for 1804; only to be contradicted by Bishop Mant eight years later. Even the

[1] Mark Pattison, *Memoirs*, p. 167.
[2] A. W. W. Dale, *Life of R. W. Dale*, p. 699.

Methodists were involved in the matter, for some of them were afraid that the doctrine was sanctioned by certain expressions in Wesley's letters.[1] There is no doubt that the question was, and is still, difficult and abstruse. On the one hand the High Churchmen held that after Baptism the infant was different, that he had been made a child of God; on the other hand the Evangelical feared that the doctrine made "conversion" unnecessary.[2] Hort, while willing to allow a place in the Church for those who held similar views to Gorham, expressed the opinion that they would not have been tolerated in the early Church.[3]

Gorham was a learned and subtle disputant, but probably too nice in his definitions, and the Court of Arches on August 2, 1849, sitting under Sir H. Jenner Fust, upheld the Bishop, and declared that the Church of England taught the spiritual regeneration of infants in Baptism. An appeal to the Judicial Committee of the Privy Council followed. Here the Evangelicals relied, and relied successfully, on the great learning and sane judgement of William Goode. They were able to prove that the views which they held were also those of great teachers of the Church like Jewell, Ussher, Hooker, and Jeremy Taylor. In March 1850 the previous judgement was reversed, and Mr. Gorham's right to institution upheld. This decision had far-reaching effects, as it was the signal for a number of further secessions to Rome; among them two archdeacons, Manning and Wilberforce. Another strange sequel was the admission by James Mozley, one of the greatest of the Tractarians, after four years' hard study of the question, that the Evangelicals were entirely justified in holding their position.[4] In spite of

---

[1] Cf. Benjamin Gregory, *Autobiographical Recollections*, p. 222.

[2] This opinion was quite incorrect, and could be held by "no Christian instructed in the first principles of the faith": see Liddon, *Life of Pusey*, III, p. 236. Dr. Carpenter, *Church and People*, p. 200, n. 1, cites the opinion of R. I. Wilberforce (one of those who seceded on the decision): "The absolute necessity of conversion . . . in nowise interferes with the reality of the gift of regeneration, which is conferred in Baptism" (*The Doctrine of Holy Baptism*, p. 50).

[3] *Life and Letters*, I, p. 148.

[4] See *Letters of J. B. Mozley*, p. 227, and his later volume, *Review of the Baptismal Controversy* (1862).

the decision the Bishop of Exeter still refused to institute and even threatened excommunication to the Archbishop of Canterbury. The terms of the threat are sufficiently interesting to be reproduced: "We, Henry, Bishop of Exeter, do solemnly protest and declare, that any Archbishop, who shall institute Charles Cornelius Gorham to the cure and government of souls, will thereby incur the Sin of supporting and favouring heretical doctrines, and we do hereby renounce and repudiate all communion with anyone, be he who he may, who shall so institute the said Charles Cornelius Gorham." None the less the institution was carried out on August 6, 1850, by Sir H. Jenner Fust under a *fiat* of the Archbishop of Canterbury.

The Tractarian leaders had again a difficult task to keep their followers loyal. Keble seems to have contemplated some kind of suspension of communion, but Pusey addressing a great meeting in London made a distinction between the work of politicians and the Apostolic Faith which the Church itself had not renounced (*Life*, III, pp. 250 f.). The same line was taken by Bishop Wilberforce when Liddon hesitated about ordination after the decision was announced. He "did not consider the Church of England compromised by the decision ... as he should still consider the law of treason the law of the land if a guilty man had been acquitted."[1]

Those who rejoiced over Gorham's acquittal did so, not because they shared his views—Tait went so far as to state that no one agreed with him[2]—but because they did not wish to have the formularies of the Church of England interpreted in too narrow a sense. The views of Mr. Gorham might be extreme, but many held them in a less extreme form and to exclude them would have been the height of folly. The judgement was really a condemnation of narrow views.

THE REVIVED USE OF RITUAL

We come now to a subject which in the minds of many is so closely connected with the Oxford Movement as to be almost typical of it—the subject of Ritual. At first sight it might seem that not much space ought to be given to its consideration as being not of supreme importance save for the historian of the

[1] *Life of H. P. Liddon*, p. 27.   [2] *A. C. Tait*, I, p. 319.

Church of England in this era; but the interest aroused by it was so widespread that it cannot be regarded merely as a domestic affair. There were many outside the Church who felt that they had a right to notice what they regarded as an attempt to compromise the Protestant character of the National Church. The story of the revival of Ritual is not only important as revealing the amount of feeling in the country, as shown by the press notices, as well as by the ignorant and perverse attitude of the mob, but as demonstrating the difficulty of enforcing ecclesiastical authority. In this case such authority was repeatedly defied; and even when the law of the land was invoked the results were lamentable.

The revival of Ritual was a manifestation of that general feeling for the past of which the interest in archaeology, and indeed the whole Catholic Movement itself, were other signs. There was a widespread awakening to the value and interest of the past, and ecclesiastical as well as other antiquities had their share of attention. In 1838 the Oxford Architectural Society was founded and in the following year the Cambridge Camden Society. It was the latter that led the way in reviving the interest in Ritual,[1] though later on, as Liddon noted, the Cambridge High Churchmen were not so anxious for aesthetic innovations as their fellows at Oxford.[2]

One beneficial effect of the revived interest in antiquities was to promote a greater care for the structures of the churches as well as for their internal decoration and arrangement, and for the ornament and vestments which might find a place within them. There had been much neglect of the rubrics in performing the appointed services of the Church, and when in 1842 Bishop Blomfield endeavoured to get the Prayer Book more closely observed he met with opposition not only from the Evangelicals—the vigorous parish of Islington was to the fore among them—but also from High Churchmen who had

[1] See S. Gaselee, "The Aesthetic Side of the Oxford Movement," in *Northern Catholicism*, pp. 424 ff. Fuller details may be found in H. W. and I. Law, *The Book of the Beresford Hopes*, pp. 128 ff. Prominent members, in addition to Alexander Beresford Hope, were J. M. Neale and Benjamin Webb, the father of C. C. J. Webb.

[2] See Johnson, *Life of H. P. Liddon*, p. 35. This led to moderation in the chapel at Cuddesdon.

been alienated by his refusal to sanction innovations which they desired.

That the Movement in its efforts to revive neglected doctrine should make use of ritualistic acts and vestments as symbols of theological truths was but natural. The desire also to emphasize the continuity of the Church of England made it expedient, so many felt, to demonstrate that continuity by copying the services and ritual of the medieval Church. The fact that much of this ritual was associated with certain doctrines concerning the eucharist was not ignored, either by those who welcomed such ceremonial revivals, or those who resented them. The question was not merely one of outward usage but of doctrine. The "Ritualists" who began by restoring the ceremonial of the pre-Reformation Church in these lands soon combined with it, in their lust for novelties, an imitation of Roman observances which were of much more recent date, and in some instances suited to the mentality of Latin rather than Teutonic peoples.

This urge towards Roman rites met with little sympathy from those who had themselves left the English Church for that of Rome. Newman wrote to Henry Wilberforce in 1849: "When you propose to return to *lost* Church of England ways you are rational, but when you invent a *new* ceremonial which never was, when you copy the Roman or other foreign rituals, you are neither respectable nor rational."[1]

Manning, also, in his Roman days was highly disgusted with the lawless vagaries of the "Ritualists." "Ritualism," he wrote, "is private judgement in gorgeous raiment, wrought about with divers colours. It is, I am afraid, a dangerous temptation to self-consciousness.... Every fringe in an elaborate cape worn without authority is only a distinct and separate act of private judgement; the more elaborate, the less Catholic; the nearer the imitation, the further from the submission of faith."[2]

The extraordinary thing to be noticed is that Pusey himself and the early leaders had no sympathy with such antiquarian motives, and in particular always deprecated the unnecessary revival of disused vestments. To the end of his Anglican career

[1] W. Ward, *Life of Newman*, I, pp. 236 f.
[2] Quoted by A. W. Hutton, *Cardinal Manning*, pp. 226 f.

Newman celebrated facing south, the position adopted by Pusey himself until quite late in life.[1] More than one overzealous young priest found himself severely rebuked. One such was told, as early as 1839, that he had not been called "to preach a system, much less the externals of a system, but to tend [his] Master's sheep and lambs."[2] Pusey felt, again to quote his own words, that "to begin with outward things seems like gathering flowers, and putting them in the earth to grow."[3] Later on Liddon, in his turn, always tried "to restrain illegalities of ceremonial and doctrine, even with men over whom he had little direct influence."[4]

The truth was that the best men of the first two generations of Tractarians were not interested in such matters. Looking back on his childhood days Dr. Inge says that "ecclesiastical millinery was totally neglected; I do not think that my grandfather [Archdeacon Churton—a friend of the early leaders] ever wore a cassock."[5] While it is actually said that Pusey did not know what a cope was and had to ask Bloxam for information.[6]

When Robert Gregory, the future Dean of St. Paul's, was curate to Tom Keble at Bisley in 1844, he always celebrated standing in front of the altar, as he thought that the rubric ordered such a position. His vicar admitted that this was probably correct, though he himself had never adopted it, and he added: "Take care to let the people see you break the Bread and elevate the Cup. English people dislike the appearance of mystery."[7] They also disliked change, as Gregory himself records, citing the case of a certain country parson who had always preached in a surplice, but when the agitation against surplices began he dropped it for the more normal black gown. He was, as a result, mobbed by the congregation as a Puseyite![8]

---

[1] Liddon, *Life of Pusey*, IV, p. 211.
[2] *Op. cit.*, II, p. 145.
[3] *Op. cit.*, III, p. 369.
[4] Johnson, *Life of Liddon*, p. 182.
[5] *Assessments and Anticipations*, p. 15.
[6] Quoted in *Northern Catholicism*, p. 26.
[7] *Autobiography of Robert Gregory*, p. 35.
[8] *Op. cit.*, p. 47. Westcott records that as late as 1874 the clergy who attended the funeral of Mr. Perceval in surplices were held to be engaged in "a vast conspiracy to subvert the principles of the Reformation": *Life and Letters*, I, p. 324.

Popular Outbreaks Against "Ritualism"

The clergy who adopted ritualistic practices were, for the most part, men of deep earnestness and zealous in their parishes; but they were not always wise or tactful, and once set out in their course were difficult to restrain. The Bishops who attempted to curb them were frankly regarded as Erastian, and their recommendations ignored and their authority often defied. The practices which were introduced were many of them such as are now customary in the majority of Anglican churches; preaching in a surplice, singing the services, a robed choir, the use of the eastward position in the Communion Service, coloured frontals to the altar, and flowers upon it. But this mild Ritualism was taken to be another instance of papal aggression during the No-popery agitation of 1850, and the mob in many places decided to take a hand in stopping it. At the same time Bishop Blomfield was making a further charge against Roman innovations in his diocese.

The chief centres of disturbance were, in the West End of London, St. Paul's, Knightsbridge, and its daughter church, St. Barnabas, Pimlico, where W. J. E. Bennett was rector; in the East End, St. Peter's and St. George's. The police and magistrates made but feeble attempts to protect the churches from outrage and violence or to punish the rioters;[1] and for a number of years, Sunday by Sunday, most disgraceful outbursts were permitted to continue. Bennett himself resigned his living in May 1851 at the request of the Bishop, and moved to Frome. His successor, the Hon. Robert Liddell, although he made some slight concessions, did not succeed in placating the opposition. Two legal actions were commenced against him in 1854 for the removal of the stone altar, the cross, and candlesticks upon it, and for the cessation of coloured frontals, in St. Paul's and St. Barnabas[2] respectively. These were successful, but Liddell appealed and the case (Liddell v. Westerton) came at last to the Judicial Committee of the Privy Council which

---

[1] The Home Secretary declared in the House of Commons that it was not the duty of the police to mount guard in a church.

[2] In the case of St. Barnabas all these had been in evidence when Bishop Blomfield consecrated the church in May 1850. Like other bishops he did not care to discourage a keen man.

in March 1857 gave its judgement. It affirmed the distinction between an altar and a table, and insisted that a movable structure was necessary by law; that a cross, although lawful (and herein distinguished from a crucifix), must not be attached to or placed on the Communion table; that embroidered linen and lace might not be used in Holy Communion though an embroidered cloth was allowed.

St. George's, which was the scene of the disorders in the East End, was an exceedingly degraded parish in the Docks. Vice reigned almost unchecked and unashamed; the whole neighbourhood was given up to plundering the seamen who landed in its midst and to pandering to their vices. To a population of some 40,000 people the rector ministered single-handed. At this time he was Bryan King, a rigid High Churchman of serious and deep religious life, but, as he himself admitted, quite the wrong type to tackle the seething mass of sin and evil around him. He tried to observe the Prayer Book in its fulness and paid no heed to the protests of the congregation which grew smaller and smaller. In 1856 he actually adopted vestments. This was the signal for open violence in which the disorderly elements of a most disorderly neighbourhood found a glorious opportunity for indulging their lust for violence and rioting; the very boys and girls took a prominent part.[1] Things came to a climax on Easter Sunday 1860 when the rioting and sacrilege exceeded all bounds. King went away for a year whilst Bishop Tait, who was then Bishop of London, put a curate in charge. Finally he resigned and became Vicar of Avebury, a sphere more suited to his gifts than a London slum. In the meantime a vigorous mission work had been begun, with King's permission it need hardly be said, in the worst part of the parish. It was in 1856 that Charles Lowder, together with a group of like-minded helpers, began his labours. They invaded the worst streets with open-air meetings and by their unselfish lives and loving service began to make some headway. Those whom they collected to their mission church had no prejudices against "Romish" practices to overcome; the colour and warmth of the services was a welcome relief in their drab

[1] This would have shocked Polybius as did the part played by the children of Carthage and Alexandria in riots in those cities.

THE OXFORD MOVEMENT—THE SECOND PHASE

lives, and the missioners carried on their work undisturbed by the mobs which attacked the parish church, and even by Bishop Tait, who for once shewed a kindly inconsistency.

For some time it was left to the mob to attempt to stop the practices of the Ritualists, and no official steps were taken to check them beyond appeals and vain orders by individual bishops. The first people to invoke the aid of the law were not the opponents of Ritual but its sympathizers and that, of course, not in connexion with Ritual as such. After the founding of the English Church Union in 1856[1] the High Churchmen became aggressive, and such harmless practices as holding mission services in theatres proved especially obnoxious to them. They even tried, in another sphere, to prosecute Bishop Waldegrave of Carlisle for heresy. Finding itself powerless because of the state of the law the E.C.U. tried to get legislation in 1862 by which the bringing of priests to trial for heresy and breaches of Church discipline might be facilitated. It is very important to remember that the first attempts to invoke the aid of Caesar were made, not by Evangelicals or Broad Churchmen, but by the successors of the Tractarians. To counteract the aggression of the E.C.U. the Evangelicals in 1865 formed the Church Association, and a series of prosecutions soon followed. The object of many of these cases was simply to discover the state of the law, whether certain practices were legal or not, a subject upon which there was much uncertainty. In 1874 Tait, who had behind him the whole episcopate, brought in the Public Worship Regulation Bill.[2] The Bill was not intended to deal with matters in dispute,

[1] Its objects were:
To defend and maintain unimpaired the doctrine and discipline of the Church of England.
To afford counsel, protection, and assistance to all persons, lay and clerical, suffering under unjust aggression or hindrance in spiritual matters.
In general, so to promote the interests of religion as to be, by God's help, a lasting witness for the advancement of His glory and the good of His Church.

[2] Disraeli, remembering the fiasco of the Ecclesiastical Titles Bill of 1851, wished to avoid legislation; though averse to the "high jinks" of the Ritualists. The Queen, who was strongly opposed to such practices, urged the government to act. See Monypenny and Buckle, *Life of Disraeli*, II, pp. 654 ff., and cf. pp. 632 f.

235

but to hasten the processes by which they might be settled. A large number of prosecutions of leading Ritualists followed during the next few years, in four cases imprisonment being the result. The most notorious case was that of Mr. Green of Miles Platting, who remained in Lancaster Gaol for nearly two years. The result of these prosecutions was disastrous for those who initiated them. Of the last Stock says: "Probably no one event in the history of the past half-century has done so much to foster the Romanizing movement, and to injure the Evangelical cause, as the imprisonment of Mr. Green" (*History of the C.M.S.*, III, p. 6).

The system of prosecutions was certainly unwise, and caused public sympathy to go over to the Ritualists. In 1883 the Islington Conference protested against "the disastrous policy of attempting to stay error by prosecution and imprisonment." The last of the prosecutions was the trial of the saintly Bishop King in 1889, and ended in the famous Lincoln judgement. Henceforward the Evangelicals adopted the line of witnessing to the truth of their doctrines by trying to make their parishes as efficient as possible. This course was suggested by the Rev. A. J. Robinson, Rector of Holy Trinity, Marylebone, in a letter to *The Record* of August 12, 1892. The comments of the editor on the proposal are worthy of being repeated. "The wise course lies plainly before us. It is by doing good, rather than preventing evil, that the Evangelical body exerts a real influence in the Church. The repression of illegal practices is the duty of the authorities; their responsibility will be more readily recognized and more easily discharged when it is not attempted to be shared by volunteers. But, on the other hand, Evangelical work is heaped up around us waiting to be done. It would be a satisfactory and logical result of the judgement if the C.P.A.S. were to find its resources suddenly reinforced."[1]

Before leaving the Ritual Controversy it may be well to point out two deplorable consequences or features in it. There was the resort to mob violence on the one side; but on the other there was the disquieting spectacle of insubordination, a sad and unexpected failing in members of a Church which

[1] The above two paragraphs are taken from *The Evangelical Movement in the English Church*, pp. 58 f.

looked back to Hooker as one of its greatest teachers. This insubordination was the failing of high-principled men caught in a conflict of loyalties. But it cannot be denied that they defied authority and in most cases outraged the feelings of their flocks. This last distressed Pusey, whose name became a byword in connexion with the dispute. He wrote to Tait on April 26, 1860, expressing his sorrow "at the crude way in which . . . ritual has been forced upon the people, unexplained and without their consent."[1]

VARIED ACTIVITIES

The Ritual Revival was but one sign of the manifold activity which inspired the second generation of the Tractarians, as indeed it had inspired their fathers. But in other ways also it was recognizable. The restoration of Convocation in 1854, for example, was an instance of that renewed corporate life of which the Oxford Movement was a manifestation and a cause; so also were the starting of the Church Congress by Archdeacon Emery in 1861 and the Lambeth Conference of 1867.

On all sides the new life was recognized by observers so different and equally unprejudiced in its favour as Lord Shaftesbury and John Morley. The former wrote in 1877 that "All zeal for Christ seems to have passed away. The Ritualists have more of it than the Evangelicals" (*Life*, III, p. 383). This is an interesting admission, for its author regarded Ritualism as a kind of death-watch beetle eating away the life of the Church. Much later, in the days of *Lux Mundi* and the Christian Social Movement, Lord Morley could speak of the Anglicans at Oxford, the scene of the Movement's first days and of its disastrous defeat, as "trying to capture science, criticism, philosophy, and the new social spirit" (*Recollections*, I, p. 289). Some years before Mark Pattison, aroused by the report of the Church Congress meetings at Oxford in 1862, had attacked the Movement because its adherents were careless of learning and neglectful of the social problems which he felt they ought to be facing. This was, from his point of view, a strange mischance, for within a generation both reproaches were to be

[1] Davidson and Benham, *Archibald Campbell Tait*, I, p. 249.

removed by the activities which had come to a head in the days of Morley's observation.

The origin of *Lux Mundi* has been disclosed by its editor, Charles Gore, in the Preface to the first edition. It came from a group of Oxford men (with the addition, as in the case of *Essays and Reviews*, of a Cambridge man) who in the years 1875–85 found themselves "engaged in the common work of university education; and compelled for their own sake, no less than that of others, to attempt to put the Catholic faith into its right relation to modern intellectual and moral problems. Such common necessity and effort led to not infrequent meetings, in which a common body of thought and sentiment, and a common method of commending the faith to the acceptance of others, tended to form itself." The volume was one result of their co-operation. The writers were men of mature thought and life, not simply a group of young dons; and Illingworth thought that this had led to dulness, that there was about the volume a tone of "fortyness," as he put it (*Life of John Richard Illingworth*, p. 159).

Lux Mundi, when compared with *Essays and Reviews*, is remarkable for its constructive spirit. When any attempt is made to explain away beliefs which had been held by an older generation, there is with it an attempt to show that the new is better and more Christian. Such changes were indeed necessary, for the earlier Tractarians had ignored science and the new knowledge which was coming in like a flood on every side. The writers, like the Schoolmen in the height of their prime, now faced it. Indeed, they took the offensive and went out into the open, striving to meet the thought of their day on its own ground. The Church, in them, showed that it was no longer content to remain on the defensive; it was the beginning of a new type of apologetic. The sub-title, "A series of studies in the religion of the Incarnation," gives the clue to the point of view of the contributors; they desired to restate the dogmas of the Christian faith in the light of that doctrine, as itself illuminated by modern knowledge.

Illingworth contributed two essays, on "Pain," of which he had and was to have much first-hand experience, and on "The Incarnation and Development." These essays, except for a few sermons already published, were the first-fruits of a life of quiet meditation and study on God, the world, and man in the light of the great doctrine which formed the key-note of *Lux Mundi*. Few writers of philosophy have ever enjoyed so wide a circulation for their books as Illingworth; though now they no longer enjoy their first popularity. Like Aubrey Moore, who wrote on "The Doctrine of God," he had a wide and deep knowledge of the methods and ideals of modern science. Other doctrinal essays were R. C. Moberly's "The Incarnation as the Basis of Dogma," the first piece of writing of a great theologian, in which he showed the value of dogma in an age which was beginning to question it; Walter Lock on "The Church"; and Francis Paget on "The Sacraments." Of these nothing need be said, save that they are well-written essays by able men, but without anything dramatic or novel in their contents. The same may also be said of Talbot's "Preparation in History for the Incarnation." Albert Lyttelton's "Atonement" was perhaps the least successful essay in the volume, in spite of the fact that he had had to rewrite it.[1] In all these essays there was nothing to disquiet the conservative mind; they exhibited a quiet confidence in the faith and were of unimpeachable orthodoxy. What aroused alarm was the essay on "The Holy Spirit and Inspiration" by the editor Charles Gore.

Illingworth, to whom we owe a good deal of the "secret history" of the volume, tells us that the essay was an afterthought, as it was felt by the other contributors that the volume would seem incomplete without anything on the Holy Spirit. But it was, in a sense, to this "after-thought" that the beginning of the Liberal Catholic School in the Church of England can be traced; it showed that Biblical Criticism had at last penetrated into the innermost shrine, and been there welcomed. Especially obnoxious was the admission, although some of the early fathers of the Church were here followed, that our Lord was definitely ignorant of certain matters, that He really "grew in wisdom," and that the various statements in the Gospels (e.g. Mark xiii. 32, John xi. 34, Luke ii. 52) were intended to be taken literally, and referred to actual, not feigned, ignorance. This caused a great outcry and came apparently without any

[1] *Life of J. R. Illingworth*, p. 153.

previous warning of the writer's standpoint. To this we must return in a moment.

All the essays have now been mentioned save the first and the last two. The first came from the vigorous and lively pen of Henry Scott Holland and was a plea for "Faith," not merely as an intellectual thing, but as an act of the whole personality, "an energy of the basal self, by which it pledges itself to Christ, the same yesterday, to-day, and for ever." The last two dealt with the practical considerations which seemed to arise out of a belief in Christianity mainly as the religion of the Incarnation. W. J. H. Campion dealt with "Christianity and Politics" and R. L. Ottley with "Christian Ethics"; both subjects upon which there was much to say from their previous neglect, and which must be judged as pioneer efforts only. Campion boldly claimed that the ultimate authority in the moral sphere lay with the Church, which speaks in the name of God. To make this claim needed courage in an age which was becoming increasingly democratic, but was all the more necessary. Ottley's contribution has been described by Dean Carpenter as "rather a dry essay. But it was the right end of the volume. It rounded off the careful position which had been given to the Christian faith, and it enormously enlarged for most readers of that date the field of the Christian life" (*Church and People*, p. 560).

To the older Tractarians *Lux Mundi*, with its Liberal views, came as a severe blow, especially as Gore, the chief offender, was librarian of Pusey House. The greatest of them, Liddon, regarded the volume as "a proclamation of revolt against the spirit and principles of Dr. Pusey and Mr. Keble" and when he was offered the bishopric of St. Albans in 1890 made it one of the grounds of refusal. "It shows," he wrote in a statement which he left among his papers, "that I could not depend on the sympathy and support of the young High Churchmen, as I could not in any case have that of the Low and Broad; I should be practically without friends."[1]

It has been said by one who was behind the scenes that it was only through the offices of Dean Church that a definite

---

[1] *Life of Henry Parry Liddon*, p. 377. For an account of the whole controversy, so distressing to both sides, see pp. 360 ff.

split in the High Church party on the question of Biblical Criticism was avoided.[1] But some of the rank and file would not allow their consciences to be quietened, and the Church Congress at Birmingham in 1893 was scandalized by the scene which Father Ignatius created by holding up a copy of *Lux Mundi* and demanding that Gore should not be allowed to address the Congress.[2]

But if Liddon and the older High Churchmen were disgusted by the Liberal views of Gore and his fellow contributors, in other quarters it was felt that they had not gone far enough. Jowett, for example, was definitely disappointed.[3] Outside the Church of England the opinion of Fairbairn may be taken as typical of the views of the more enlightened and tolerant Nonconformist. Although he had always been deeply perplexed by "the contrast between the real piety of the men who represented the Oxford Movement, and their apparent insensibility to the finer and higher moralities of the mind," he hailed *Lux Mundi* as "a new and welcome departure in Anglican theology, and as being but the legitimate outcome of tendencies which had been long maturing."[4]

We noticed above Mark Pattison's jibe, to the effect that all T. H. Green's honey was going into the ritualistic hive; this was true in the sense that his right-wing pupils, as opposed to "left-wingers" like Nettleship and Ritchie, and later Bosanquet and Bradley, were many of them High Churchmen. Illingworth, Aubrey Moore, Scott Holland, and Gore, of the *Lux Mundi* group, were actually pupils of his at the same time. It was not, however, in philosophy only that Green's influence was felt; that interest which he took in social affairs, especially as viewed from a religious or ideal standpoint, also became theirs. Scott Holland tells us that he used to speak "of the spiritual value of political institutions, of the realization of our moral manhood by its expansion into national organizations" (*Personal Studies*, p. 188). Together with that of Green the influence of Maurice and of Westcott can be traced. It was indeed

---

[1] H. Scott Holland, *Personal Studies*, p. 235.
[2] See *Bishop Handley Moule*, p. 147.
[3] *Life of Benjamin Jowett*, II, p. 377.
[4] A. M. Fairbairn, pp. 203 and 214.

to Westcott's preaching at Harrow that Gore owed his first determination to tackle the social problem.[1] It was no accident which made Francis Paget, in his essay on "The Sacraments" in *Lux Mundi*, dwell on their social aspect; nor that the two closing essays of that volume should deal with Christian Politics and Ethics. The religion of the Incarnation must interest itself in all that concerns the life of man, and apply to it the principles which Christ Himself handed down to His followers. So these later Tractarians set themselves to the task of meeting the difficulties which beset both Church and State owing to social inequalities and injustices. By their efforts and the heroism and self-sacrifice which they exhibited, they brought the Church into close touch with others who were working for this same end. Bernard Shaw wrote in 1898 that: "Religion was alive again, coming back upon men—even clergymen—with such power that not the Church of England itself could keep it out."[2] With these efforts, however, we can best deal in a separate chapter, devoted to the subject as a whole, not merely as part of the Catholic Revival.

[1] See Prestige, *Life of Charles Gore*, pp. 9 f.
[2] Quoted by Ruth Kenyon in her essay, "The Social Aspect of the Catholic Revival," in *Northern Catholicism*, p. 392. Those who are interested in this subject ought not to neglect reading this valuable piece of work.

13

SOCIAL PROBLEMS

Although the adherents of the Oxford Movement took a leading part in the endeavour to remedy the evil social conditions which disgraced England in the last century, they had by no means a monopoly in such action. On all hands there was growing up a feeling of impatience at the persistence of these evils and a realization that their presence in a land which claimed to be Christian was an anomaly and a challenge.

THE CHALLENGE

In a previous chapter I described the state of society in England at the beginning of the century. With the development of the Industrial System conditions grew rapidly worse. In February 1839 Thomas Arnold wrote that "the state of our railway navigators [i.e. navvies] and cotton operatives is scarcely better than that of slaves, either physically or morally, and is far more perilous to society" (*Life*, p. 502). A few years later the hardships of the English working classes were held up as a warning to their fellows on the continent, where the evils which follow industrial development were beginning to manifest themselves.[1] Even the slave-owners were shocked by what they heard of the conditions under which labour in England was carried on. A striking example of this has been reported by Oastler, the great agitator for reforms. He was once in company with a West Indian slave-owner and three Bradford spinners. They began discussing their different labour systems, and the slave-owner was astounded. "Well," he said, "I have always thought myself disgraced by being the owner of slaves, but we never in the West Indies thought it possible for any human being to be so cruel as to require a child of nine years old to work twelve and a half hours a day, and that, you acknowledge, is your regular practice."[2]

---
[1] Engels, *The Condition of the Working Class in England* (1844).
[2] Quoted by Marchant, *Dr. John Clifford*, p. 6.

If the conditions under which people had to labour verged on the intolerable, so also did the houses which served as their homes. In the country the green fields and the fresh air are some compensation for insanitary and inconvenient dwellings; in the town there are not such advantages and the poor victims suffer from all "the deformities of crowded life." Their health is undermined both from lack of pure air and from under-nourishment.

In contrast to this abject poverty there went, on the part of the vulgar "new-rich," whose fortunes had been made largely by those who were forced to submit to it, a degree of wanton display and wasteful luxury which recalled the worst days of the Roman Empire. For society in England in the middle years of the Victorian Era, like that society and the Hellenic civilization which went before it, was based on the theory that there should be misery and oppression for the many that the few should be able to live lives of culture and ease. There were, as Disraeli has put it in his brilliant way in *Sybil*, that amazing *tour de force* drawn from the strange abyss of his own fancy and "smoky with reminiscences of lost Blue Books and vanished *Keepsakes*" (Philip Guedalla), there were really Two Nations, the rich and the poor. This unequal division of the good things and even the necessities of life was, though in a different manner, harmful to both sections of the community. One class was hardened and degraded by the conditions under which they were compelled to live; the other was softened and degraded by its senseless pursuit of pleasure. It has been well said that William Morris hated luxury "because it could not be really enjoyed, and he despised the luxurious because they did not know what real pleasure was."[1]

Such a condition of things constituted a definite challenge to the followers of Jesus Christ, though it took them much time to realize it as such. Many indeed, so obtuse was Victorian self-complacency, actually regarded their civilization as approximating to the Christian ideal.[2] But the challenge was even wider than it seemed, for in addition to the problems arising from economic causes, evil social conditions, and so

[1] A. Clutton-Brock, *William Morris*, p. 231.
[2] Cf. Christopher Dawson, *Religion and the Modern State*, pp. 103 f.

forth, there were others which affected all classes of the people alike; questions of drunkenness, gambling, and immorality.

In the early years of the Victorian Era drunkenness was still rife among the upper classes. The disgraceful scenes to which it gave rise are no longer remembered. They were such that forgetfulness is perhaps the best way of treating them. Lord Frederick Hamilton tells us that in his mother's girlhood at Woburn Abbey "it was the custom for the trusted old family butler to make his nightly report . . . to the drawing room. 'The gentlemen have had a good deal to-night; it might be well for the young ladies to retire,' or 'The gentlemen have had very little to-night,' was announced according to circumstances by this faithful family retainer. Should the young girls be packed off upstairs, they liked standing on an upper gallery of the staircase to watch the shouting riotous crowd issuing from the dining-room" (*The Days before Yesterday*, p. 299).

But things began quickly to improve; the Queen's own opposition to after-dinner drinking did much to stop it;[1] as later her son was still further to check it, by means of the exorcizing power of the cigarette.[2] Among the poorer classes drunkenness had greater excuse; it was so often the only means of escaping from the drab and horrible conditions under which they were compelled to live. The quickest way out of Manchester, it used to be said, is through the door of the public-house.

So too in regard to that other great social evil, gambling; it ever attracts those whose ordinary lives are dull and lacking in excitement or constructive effort. Its true nature is often forgotten by the respectable; but Machiavelli had the insight to recognize it, and in his recommendations to those who would build up, without regard to moral or other considerations, a strong State, he advised them to encourage it in the territories of their enemies, but to put it down, by military force if need be, in their own.

Immorality is a strange and difficult phenomenon to account for in its spread or decline. No doubt social conditions have

---

[1] See Lytton Strachey, *Queen Victoria*, p. 61.
[2] G. W. E. Russell, *Fifteen Chapters of Autobiography*, p. 174.

much to do with it; but still more has public opinion and the standards accepted by any particular community. In the 'sixties illegitimacy was very common in the Northern counties of Westmorland and Cumberland and amounted to 10 per cent of all births. Much of the evil was undoubtedly due to the "hiring" system by which men and women were publicly "bought" like sheep in a market and "engaged without knowledge, or reference, or character."[1] The attention of the country was aroused to the extent of the evil by John Percival, Headmaster of Clifton, a schoolmaster of the type of Arnold who did not regard his responsibilities to society as ending with his schoolboys. A series of his letters to George Moore the reformer was published in *The Times*. But, as Creighton found in his parish at Embleton, bad conditions are not always accompanied by a low moral standard;[2] whilst careful training, if it is not supported by a high standard, may be quite inadequate as a check on bodily impulses. Some years ago an enquiry was made concerning the girls who had left a certain London workhouse to go into service; it was found that after a short time every one of them, without exception, was on the streets.[3]

Spiritual Effects of Bad Conditions

Turning back to the effects of social injustice and unfair conditions, it must be realized that their evils are not limited to the body; it is not merely that their victims are cut off from their share of land and air and other material things of life; but the character itself suffers, save in the few noble souls who thrive by means of the very straitness of their surroundings. Such there are, who rise to the challenge of their disabilities; but for the vast majority, especially for those who engage in trades where most of the work is done by machinery, the challenge is too severe, they become hardened and dulled, with the whole nature degraded. This has been well put by Austin Freeman in *Social Decay and Regeneration*,[4] where he says: "Mechanism by its reactions on man and his environment is

---

[1] See Samuel Smiles, *Life of George Moore*, p. 142.
[2] *Life and Letters of Mandell Creighton*, I, pp. 152 f., and 157 n.
[3] *Life of J. B. Paton*, p. 188.
[4] Quoted by Inge, *Outspoken Essays*, II, p. 248.

antagonistic to human welfare. It has destroyed industry and replaced it by mere labour; it has degraded and vulgarized the works of man; it has destroyed social unity and replaced it by social disintegration and class antagonism . . ; it has injuriously affected the structural type of society by developing its organization at the expense of the individual; it has endowed the inferior man with political power which he employs to the common disadvantage by creating political institutions of a socially destructive type."

In addition to the deadening effect of the processes of the employment on the souls of the workers, there is that perverted point of view which is almost inevitably engendered in those who must struggle to gain even the necessities of existence. To them material things are bound to loom large, to seem indeed the only things worth striving for. The leaders may have vision and ideals, but the rank and file—taught by the examples of their betters—are "out" for what they can get. Such an attitude of mind, excusable as it may be, cannot lead to any real improvement; for selfishness can flourish in a Socialist State, just as readily as in one organized on a capitalist basis. Merely economic change can bring no moral relief, a fact which is recognized by the best minds in the Socialist Movement itself. Mr. George Lansbury, the late Leader of the Parliamentary Labour party, for example, has declared that "in a mere fight for bread and butter, without having an ideal in front of you, and without having the religious fervour and enthusiasm that religion gives, it is quite impossible to hope for the reformation of the world."[1]

On the continent the early leaders, men like Karl Marx and Engels, were moved to bitter contempt by the vulgar and selfish elements in their following. They only remained within the Movement from a sense of dedication, nourishing a vision and a hope of better things, of ultimate happiness and security for the whole race. Others who have had the vision have found the methods of Socialism unacceptable and have tried to realize its ideals in their own way. Thus it was said of P. H. Wicksteed that he "rejected the methods, as he embraced the ideals of Socialism. . . . His immense intellectual and moral

[1] Quoted in *The Modern Churchman*, II, p. 209.

energy was devoted less to bettering existing conditions than to equipping men with the spiritual viaticum which lightens the toil of the journey and makes its goal clear."[1]

But even the leaders and those who approach social problems with religious inspiration are in danger of loss of spiritual power through too emphatic an absorption in material problems. So much in these evils, and in the efforts to remedy them, is concerned so entirely with the external life of man that the emphasis is apt to become too material, and the only standard of life to be placed in the external world. "There is real danger," so Christopher Dawson has warned us, "that English religion, at least English Protestantism, may allow itself to be identified with an enthusiasm for social justice and reform which is hardly distinguishable from the creed of secular humanitarianism. . . . We find masses of well-meaning people who have never even begun to think announcing their intention of never ceasing from mental strife till they have built Jerusalem in England's green and pleasant land. . . . There are, it is true, quite a number of different Jerusalems: there is the Muscovite Jerusalem which has no Temple, there is Herr Hitler's Jerusalem which has no Jews, and there is the Jerusalem of the social reformers which is all suburbs: but none of these is Blake's Jerusalem, still less that city which the Apostle saw 'descending out of heaven like a bride adorned for her husband.' All these New Jerusalems are earthly cities established by the will and power of man" (*Religion and the Modern State*, pp. 108 f.). The Kingdom of God cannot be established by political or economic devices.

Some, when they become aware of the horrors and consequences of the conditions under which so many of their fellow men and women are living, are simply driven to a melancholy isolation, perhaps after some feeble efforts to ameliorate them. Conscious "of the great stream of human tears falling always through the shadows of the world," they are by temperament and training unfitted to do anything effectual to stem it; they become, as was said of Heine, symbols "of the vast, inwardly dissonant, tragic generation of the nineteenth century." Others build imaginary worlds, Utopias

[1] C. H. Herford, *Philip Henry Wicksteed*, p. 146.

in which all is well. But such Utopias are apt to look a little dull even when sketched by enthusiastic exponents; J. S. Mill himself was appalled by the lack of interest in a perfect world, until he happily recollected that man could there give himself up to the study of Wordsworth.

Denunciations

The nineteenth century had reached its middle years before there was any adequate recognition, by all but a few public-minded philanthropists, that such things as social problems existed, and that protests against their continuance began to be made. It took still longer for this recognition to become widespread and for serious endeavours at readjustment and reform to be made.

It was an individualistic age, and when the social order began to show fissures the only means of coping with them was to adopt "the recipes of a moral and social atomism, the salvation of the isolated soul or the maximum pleasure and profit of the private citizen." Moreover, any kind of interference with the liberty of the subject was at once resented. The evils, too, were sanctified by time and the whole system, of which they were a part, seemed justified by its success. Those who suffered under it were paying the necessary price of progress,

"Things like that, you know, must be
At every famous victory."

The victims deserved sympathy and assistance—but that was all; there was nothing wrong with the system, so men argued, so far as they had time to give the matter thought or consideration. Those of them who claimed to be religious would doubtless have felt it was part of the divine dispensation, for men in all ages have sought to explain such unpleasant phenomena at the expense of Providence. There was thus a kind of dual morality—one standard for the individual and another for society. The latter, and especially the business world, was under inflexible economic laws against which it was quixotic to rebel: the former, it was hoped, would do nothing to outrage, at any rate in public. the accepted moral standards. In this regard we have travelled far since the age of

Victoria—and it will be well to make the point. Now we realize that social problems are the result of misdirected human efforts and we feel the responsibility, by human wisdom and goodwill, of seeking remedies. Social and economic laws are looked upon, not as inevitable and compelling—so that to introduce such considerations as humanity, fellowship, and freedom would be folly—but as subject to man's control and guidance. They are recognized, in Dean Bate's words, as "spheres of our opportunity rather than masters of our fate" (in *The Future of the Church of England*, p. 175).

Amongst the first to agitate for a better state of affairs was Coleridge. His demands for social reform are often forgotten; but the truth was, as Maurice put it in the closing words of his Dedication of *The Kingdom of Christ*, that though thought to be a "theorist and dreamer [he] was in truth labouring to procure the most practical benefits for his country and for mankind." Another more vigorous voice was also early raised, not indeed against the system, for Thomas Carlyle was an individualist and had no trust in the people or in democracy in any shape or form, but against its evils. Believing as he did that man was capable of great advances and development, he attacked social conditions because they were robbing so many of their chance to progress. On similar but more definitely religious grounds Maurice and his group of Christian Socialists, about whom more will be said later, also made their protest. Though these men were hardly Socialists in the political sense, their influence tended in that direction.[1]

Among those inspired by Carlyle was John Ruskin, that great lonely figure, tormenting himself to the verge of insanity over the "terrific call of human crime for resistance and of human misery for help." Ruskin, who was born in 1819, lingered on to the beginning of the twentieth century; becoming, it is true, a little querulous before the end. He has been

---

[1] Cf. the opinion of W. Robertson Nicoll: "The influence of Carlyle and Maurice was nothing less than socialistic. Those who at twenty-one pored over *Sartor Resartus*, *Past and Present*, and *Chartism*, became distinct socialists, not such gentry as bawl the gospel of destruction and break club windows, but socialists of the higher type to whom nothing of humanity is common or unclean": *Letters of a Bookman*, p. 154.

well described as "the figure which best represents the spirit of social reform as it struggled to life after the depression of the Napoleonic Wars, found expression in the middle of the century, and became dominant at its close."[1] He came to see, after a time, that to help the miserable was not enough; the whole system upon which industry and society itself was based needed changing. A series of papers setting forth his ideas was accepted by the *Cornhill Magazine*, then newly established under Thackeray's editorship. Three of them appeared in the numbers from August to October 1860 and then he was told, with all politeness and regret, that the series must stop. The reading public was not yet ripe for the new economics. A similar attempt, two years later, in *Fraser's Magazine*, was equally unsuccessful, in spite of the sympathy of J. A. Froude the editor.[2] But there were some, even then, who began to recognize the fundamental truth and justice of his demands. Erskine of Linlathen wrote to Carlyle in August 1862 expressing his thankfulness "for any unveiling of the so-called science of political economy according to which avowed selfishness is the Rule of the World. It is indeed most important preaching—to preach that there is one God for religion . . . and another God for buying and selling—that pestilent polytheism has been largely and confidently preached in our time, and blessed are those who can detect its mendacities, and help to disenchant the brethren."[3]

Later there came the strangely attractive figure of William Morris, poet, craftsman, and artist, with his violent reactions against the same system and its evils. Because of his sane and healthy vigour he carried his readers away until humanity and its limitations were forgotten, and all that makes it impossible for such ideal schemes ever to be realized on this sorry earth. They shared his burning indignation with its brave anger against all that is mean and small; and unlike so much that is angry were raised by it; so selfless and heroic was it, with no

---

[1] F. S. Marvin, *The Century of Hope*, pp. 292 f.

[2] These papers were later reprinted as *Unto This Last* and *Munera Pulveris* respectively.

[3] Quoted by W. G. Collingwood, *Life of John Ruskin* (1911 edition), p. 162.

sense behind of cherished grievances. The medium he used were those moving poems in which the artist's insight into human relationships and all that they ought to mean is wedded to the scorn of the social reformer who knows that so many are robbed of their right to realize them. There is as an example the beautiful passage in "Mother and Son" in *Poems by the Way* which everyone ought to know:

> "Lo amidst London I lift thee, and how little and light thou art,
> And thou without hope or fear, thou fear and hope of my heart!
> Lo here thy body beginning, O son, and thy soul and thy life;
> But how will it be if thou livest, and enterest into the strife,
> And in love we dwell together when the man is grown in thee,
> When thy sweet speech I shall hearken, and yet 'twixt thee and me
> Shall rise that wall of distance, that round each one doth grow,
> And maketh it hard and bitter each other's thoughts to know?"

So fierce was Morris's indignation against the condition of things that he would gladly have seen the whole social fabric brought to ruin if thereby the regenerating forces, which he believed to be imprisoned within it, might be set free. Not even the fear of civil war would have prevented his pressing economic changes if the possessing classes refused to give up their property.[1] Well might Clutton-Brock declare that "with him the immense complacency of the Victorians came to an end."[2]

One thing which had marked Morris, and indeed the Christian Socialists and Ruskin also, was that he did not merely raise a voice of protest against the sufferings and miseries of mankind and of denunciation against the system which he held to be responsible for them; he tried to show the way to

---
[1] See A. Clutton-Brock, *William Morris*, pp. 149 and 236.
[2] *Op. cit.*, p. 147.

SOCIAL PROBLEMS

better things; to demonstrate that there were other methods and that a new conception of economic and industrial life was possible. It is time that we too turned to definite attempts to remedy the social evils which disgraced the community and brought dishonour on all those who professed to be its religious leaders and guides. Such attempts at finding remedies may conveniently be divided into three classes—those emanating from the victims themselves; those involving government action; and those which depended solely or mainly on voluntary efforts.

ATTEMPTS AT REMEDIES

(a) *By the Victims Themselves*

It would have been thought that the victims themselves and those who claimed to be their leaders would have taken the foremost place in the endeavour to find remedies for the system and its evils. This was by no means the case, and certain of the political and economic guides of the people were averse to such a course. For example, Karl Marx and his followers deprecated any attempt to ameliorate conditions; the worse they became, the more eagerly would those who suffered under them react when opportunity arose; and in any case "tinkering" was no good, a drastic reorganization of the entire social fabric was needed. This doctrine proved too high for the British working classes, and when opportunities for improvement were present they were too practical to neglect them. They were not sufficiently interested in abstract economic theories to allow themselves to sink deeper and deeper in order to gratify those who proclaimed them. Marx himself was the son of a Hebrew Christian, and his ideas were those of a Jewish prophet—with the proletariat in the place of oppressed Israel and the prosperous bourgeois in that of the Gentile. Even the catastrophic Day of Jehovah was not wanting.[1]

We have seen already[2] that attempts were made by the workers to protect themselves and to improve their conditions before the coming of Victoria to the throne. During her reign such efforts, having once been begun, continued to be made.

[1] See Dawson, *Religion and the Modern State*, p. 88.
[2] See pp. 26 ff. above.

At first Trade Unions were for the highly skilled only, but gradually the less skilled learned also to combine. There can be no question that the right of labour to combine is quite a legitimate one owing to the weakness of the individual workman in face of Capital; but it becomes a menace to society if the combinations attempt to enforce their own terms or to create a monopoly. The weapon by which Labour attempts to enforce its terms is, of course, by the withdrawal of its services to the community, or what is generally called a strike. As early as November 1838 Arnold of Rugby was expressing alarm at the efforts of agitators in Yorkshire and Lancashire to rouse the men to act and remedy the unequal rewards of Labour and Capital (*Life*, p. 405). Later came the grave troubles in connexion with the strike in the iron and engineering trades in the winter of 1852, when the industrial world was shaken to its foundations; and again a few years later the Trade Unions in Sheffield brought about a crisis by trying to gain control over the methods of production in the cutlery trade.[1] These attempts at violent action found little favour with the country as a whole and probably did much injury to the cause which their instigators hoped to promote. There were indeed suggestions that the Unions should be abolished, but in 1875 Disraeli's Act settled matters for the time.

(b) By Government Action

At first any kind of government interference was resented, as I have already pointed out, as trespassing on the rights of the individual. Men were divided in their minds on the subject and their perplexity is reflected in the works of Charles Dickens: they were equally ready on the grounds of humanity to denounce all who left things alone, and on the grounds of liberty all who tried to make them better. In spite of this perplexity government interference came increasingly to be invoked (an anticipation of the present century), and by 1877 Goschen actually declared in the House of Commons that "Political Economy had been dethroned in that House and Philanthropy had been allowed to take its place."[2] But the

---

[1] See C. H. Herford, *Philip Henry Wicksteed*, p. 48.
[2] A. D. Elliott, *Life of Lord Goschen*, I, p. 163.

legislation was not entirely inspired by motives of philanthropy —there was a certain rivalry between the County and the Factory which led the landowner to denounce the condition under which industry was carried on, and the manufacturer to make public the hardships of the agricultural labourer.[1] Lord Ashley had to face enormous difficulties in his campaign for better conditions owing to this quarrel. The mill-owners were represented by John Bright, who denied that there was any case to be made out for factory reform, and violently attacked the working men who supported the Ten Hours Bill. His speech has been described as "perhaps the most vindictive towards the working classes ever used in the British Parliament" (see *History of Factory Legislation*, p. 75). He went on to accuse Lord Ashley of ignoring the condition of the agricultural labourers in his own Dorsetshire. This last accusation, which was frequently made, was both inaccurate and unjust, for Lord Ashley had been so insistent that something should be done for these workers that he had quarrelled with his own father.

The mention of Lord Ashley, or, as he later became, the Earl of Shaftesbury, brings on the stage one who cannot be allowed to pass without further comment. The realization of his responsibility for others had been aroused in his mind, as the inscription at Harrow records, while yet a schoolboy, by the sight of a pauper funeral. From the attainment of manhood he took his place as the natural successor of Wilberforce and Foweil Buxton as the great Evangelical lay-leader, and like them he dedicated to the service of God and humanity all the numerous talents, whether they were personal or arising from his birth and connexions, which he possessed. Though his outward manner was cold and forbidding in its austerity, his heart was full of a constraining passion to save both the souls and the bodies of those around him. The long list of beneficent Acts of Parliament, beginning with the Ten Hours Act of 1847, represented but a small portion of his labours; for he was one of those whom Bacon has described in his divine saying: "The nobler a soul is, the more objects of compassion it hath." Shaftesbury thus forms a natural bridge from this section to that which follows; for he was one who laboured to remedy

[1] See Monypenny and Buckle, *Life of Benjamin Disraeli*, I, p. 631.

the evils of his times by legislation, and also by the encouragement and organization of voluntary effort. To the day of his death he gave himself up entirely to such activities, and even in passing to another world his thoughts were still turned to this, with a consciousness of all that was left undone: "I cannot bear to leave the world with all the misery in it." On his monument in Westminster Abbey there are but two words by way of a motto—"Love. Serve."

(*c*) *By Voluntary Efforts*

These followed a double course; in part they attempted to relieve suffering; in part they attempted to improve manners and habits of life. In this a certain amount of interference was necessary in the affairs of others, and like government interference though on a smaller scale, was resented by many; even if the circumstances of their lives did not allow them to voice their indignation. The amount of such efforts was undoubtedly vast, if one thinks of the numerous societies and organizations, as well as the regular routine work which centred in the churches and chapels of the land. One of the earliest pioneers had been John Howard, the Congregationalist, whose attempts to reform the prison system, both here and on the continent, had been so striking a feature of the last quarter of the eighteenth century. His work was continued by Elizabeth Fry, and she left an imperishable name, not least for all that she accomplished for the prisoners of her own sex in Newgate.

One great disadvantage of all voluntary social work is that those who take part in it may be suspected, sometimes indeed quite justly, of a desire to interfere in the lives of other people, and even to rob them of their pleasures. So Macaulay felt that the Puritans had hated bear-baiting "not because it gave pain to the bear, but because it gave pleasure to the spectators"; while another Whig, Sydney Smith, suggested that the Society for the Suppression of Vice, which flourished in his day, was inspired by class feeling and the love of interfering. The way of the philanthropist is indeed hard, and he must himself continually examine his motives if he is to avoid the many pitfalls which beset it. An attempt to put voluntary work on a more satisfactory basis was the Charity Organisation Society, founded in 1869. It tried to apply the methods of observation and experiment to the conditions of the people and to enlist the services of their wealthier fellow citizens. Among those who took part in its direction were Octavia Hill, Samuel Barnett, W. H. Fremantle (later Dean of Ripon), and C. S. Loch, its Secretary for nearly forty years. It flourished greatly in the 'eighties and undoubtedly did good work; but it was a little too "cut and dried," and many objected to the organizing of the Christian virtue of Almsgiving. It was also a little "superior" and by it: "The simple, warm-hearted and thoughtless benevolence of former ages was held up to reprobation."[1]

In the earlier years of the reign religious motives were at the bottom of nearly all the efforts to relieve distress and to improve conditions. Towards its end this series of motives was supplemented by others in which it was not so much the service of God as the love of man that was fundamental.[2]

Much of the work which was done by voluntary effort was concerned not with the conditions of labour or even of housing, all of which required legislation to alter them; but was limited to the realm of private life, and dealt with such evils as drunkenness and impurity. In connexion with the latter the names of Ellice Hopkins and Josephine Butler will not lightly be forgotten; nor the occasional but deeply self-sacrificing labours of W. E. Gladstone. The efforts to combat drunkenness were on so immense a scale and bulked so large in the public eye that more must be said about them.

The Temperance Movement

The attitude of the Christian world in the last century towards intoxicating liquors and even towards efforts at preventing their excessive use was by no means uniform. Lord Shaftesbury fully recognized the evils of drunkenness and continually preached up temperance; but he was never a total abstainer and even, in suitable surroundings, commended the moderate use of wine as a stimulant to sociability. "I am

[1] Beatrice Webb, *My Apprenticeship*. p. 222.
[2] Cf. *op. cit.*, p. 143. "I suggest that it was during the middle decades of the nineteenth century that, in England, the impulse of self-subordinating service was transferred, consciously and overtly, from God to man."

worse than a drunkard," he would say playfully, "I am a moderate drinker" (*Life*, III, pp. 323 f.). While Elizabeth Fry—and what better example of a Christian woman could be cited?—on her exacting Evangelistic journeys had continual resource to beer as a means of keeping up her strength.[1] To others strong drink was anathema and its avoidance almost a necessary part of the Christian profession. So fanatical were some Christians in this matter that even an innocent connexion with the Drink Trade was condemned.[2]

Among Nonconformist pioneers in the Temperance cause were Joseph Livesey, Robert Rae, and John Henry Raper. In 1832 the young men of Livesey's Adult School began a Temperance Society of their own. But in 1835 two American visitors to England were surprised at the little which was being done by Nonconformity. The Established Church and the Quakers were said to be the principal supporters of the British and Foreign Temperance Society.[3] Some of the early Teetotallers were over-enthusiastic and cases of expulsion from their societies for this offence were not unknown.[4] Whilst the whole Movement was condemned as "unscriptural, and likely to lead to monkish austerities."[5] It was not until 1874 that the Congregational Total Abstinence Association was formed.[6]

Much the same feelings prevailed among Churchpeople. G. W. E. Russell says of his parents: "Teetotalism was looked upon with suspicion, if not with disfavour. It was regarded as being a subtle form of works, and tending to self-reliance and self-righteousness."[7] But the Evangelicals supplied at least one prominent advocate of the Temperance Cause in the person of

---

[1] Her niece records (Hamburg, August 14, 1841): "We are also constantly applying to Uncle Buxton's Bottles. I tell Aunt that with them as Carnal and her Bible as spiritual food she might travel over the Arabian deserts": Elizabeth Gurney, *Elizabeth Fry's Journeys*, p. 137.

[2] Guinness Rogers records that a man refused to attend church when ıe preached because of his relationship to the brewers: see *J. Guinness Rogers, an Autobiography*, pp. 57 f.

[3] Peel, *These Hundred Years*, p. 106.

[4] Silvester Horne, *Free Church History*, p. 400.

[5] Peel, *op. cit.*, p. 107.

[6] *Op. cit.*, p. 282.

[7] *A Short History of the Evangelical Movement*, p. 135.

SOCIAL PROBLEMS

Close, the autocratic vicar of Cheltenham, later to be Dean of Carlisle. He it was who helped to form the Church Temperance Reform Society in 1862, and was president of the Church of England Temperance Society in 1873. The later fortunes of Temperance in the Church of England and beyond it can be read in the *Life of Edward Lee Hicks*, pp. 193 ff., the eager scholar and reformer who ended his days as Bishop of Lincoln. It should be noticed that as the century passed on and greater experience was gained, new and more adequate methods of dealing with the drink problem began to emerge. It became apparent, for example, that it was not enough merely to get men and women to sign the pledge; they had to be helped to keep it by the provision of substitutes for the public-house, of places where the weary and lonely could find fellowship and refreshment in suitable surroundings, and also a chance of recreation.[1] There are, of course, many who have been driven into poverty by excessive drinking: but intemperance, as Ramsay MacDonald has pointed out, "is not the cause of social poverty. Its chief effect is to select the victims of poverty."[2]

IMPROVED CONDITIONS AND THEIR EFFECTS

These various efforts to improve conditions were exceedingly productive, a fact to which few of those who lived in the later years of the era gave sufficient attention; conditions in their own day seemed so bad that the progress already made was ignored. This was well brought out by Lord Shaftesbury at a banquet at the Mansion House in 1884, when he told his hearers that it was only their ignorance of what things had been like in the early part of the century which prevented their realizing the enormous improvement, material, social, and moral, which had taken place.

Legislation had been slow and cautious; but advance had been certain, and along the whole front. There was not an industry which had not been affected, nor an aspect of social life which had been forgotten. At the beginning of the reign millions of the Queen's subjects had been compelled to live

[1] See J. L. Paton, *John Brown Paton*, p. 214.
[2] *The Socialist Movement*, p. 33.

in conditions of debasing poverty, a scandal to a civilized people and a potential danger to society. By its end cellars had given place to houses, wages had been raised substantially, the hours of labour had been curtailed, temperance and self-help had increased, opportunities of education had been multiplied, habits and customs had improved. In particular, hardships affecting women and children had been removed.

This improvement was due to both political parties; though the Conservatives, owing to their predominance in the House of Lords, were responsible for most of it. After the split in the Liberal party over Home Rule the magic of Chamberlain's name and his avowed interest in social reform carried over to their opponents a large accession of working-class votes. The Conservatives also gained adherents from the natural sequence of events; for every successful reform immediately transfers whole legions from the attacking to the defending army. "Even the Labour leader, if successful, tends to become conservative, to despise the material he once organized, the masses of unskilled labour, as scattered dust or crumbling snow."[1] Again ideas which at one time were regarded as extreme are accepted, and become commonplaces; those who supported them refuse to advance further; thus bringing upon them the condemnation of more advanced reformers who fail to realize that their moderation is the result not of cowardice or wavering, but of a reasoned and consistent policy.

The removal of hardships has often the effect of weakening the character of those who need no longer struggle against them; there are those who suspect that excessive governmental care robs the people of self-reliance and the feeling of responsibility. This suspicion has recently been put into words by Mr. J. B. Priestley in his study of post-war England:

"I cannot help feeling," he says, "that this new England is lacking in character, zest, gusto, flavour, bite, drive, originality, and that this is a serious weakness. Monotonous but easy work and a liberal supply of cheap luxuries might between them create a set of people entirely without ambition or any real desire to think and act for themselves—the perfect subjects for an iron autocracy."

[1] C. F. G. Masterman, *The Condition of England*, p. 285.

THE CHURCH'S PART

How far, it may be asked, was the Church responsible for these improvements, and what had been the response of organized religion to the double challenge of the evil conditions themselves and the soul-destroying environment which they created and fostered? Before attempting an answer to this question, a little may conveniently be said as to the two parts of the challenge.

In the first place the mere fact that so large a number of people were allowed to live, in a nominally Christian State, in conditions so intolerable was in itself an affront to the name of Christ, and deprived the faith of much of its force, since it seemed a mere theory which did not deserve to be taken seriously. The need of meeting this challenge was sternly insisted upon by R. W. Dale and his belief in the Lordship of Christ has been well summed up by his son as follows: "If at any point in the domain either of thought or of action, Christ's authority is not asserted—whether in art, literature, commerce, or politics—the failure to assert it is criminal, and must be retrieved" (*Life of R. W. Dale*, p. 398).

But there was another side to the challenge, and by it reforms were demanded, not only because of the sufferings and hardships which were involved in the conditions, but mainly because they kept men from realizing their true end as immortal souls. As F. R. Barry has said: "In an ill-organized social system no man can become what he is meant to be. He cannot become a completely harmonious self" (*The Relevance of Christianity*, p. 249). The importance of the social, political, and economic environment in which men spend their lives is enormous; but I think that Mr. Lionel Curtis exaggerates it in his recent book, *Civitas Dei*, when he declares that: "The claim of churches and schools to be answerable in the first degree for forming the character of a people, a claim supported not seldom by politicians and public officials, is a dangerous fallacy. The most potent factor in raising or lowering the character of a people, in increasing or diminishing their sense of duty to each other, is the structure of the society in which they live."

On the other hand it is not enough simply to affirm that if all men were Christians there would be no "social problems"; for the conditions which give rise to these problems are the shrewdest stumbling-block in the way of making society more Christian. There is here a vicious circle which the power of God, showing itself through inspired leadership, alone can remedy. In the meantime all the Church's efforts are based on an unselfish policy, for as Dr. Figgis has pointed out, social amelioration will not make her task any lighter; it is the "weary and heavy-laden" who respond to the call of Christ, not the secure and comfortable.

The Church's Neglect

In the early years of the reign the Church shared in the almost universal idea that social evils, as the product of inflexible laws, were inevitable. The Church indeed was definitely advised not to interfere. "In the huge and hideous cities," as Scott Holland put it in his vivid way, "the awful problem of industry lay like a bad dream; but Political Economy warned us off the ground. We were assured that the free play of competitive forces was bound to discover the true equipoise."

Maurice and his friends had held a different view, but their effort was premature and soon spent itself, and though voices here and there were raised in protest, the Church as a whole refused to stir. The work overseas captured the imagination of the more daring and energetic spirits, and acquiescence remained the normal attitude of Christian people, and a reliance on the old remedies which dealt with individuals only and left the system untouched. More churches, more schools, an insistence on authority and obedience; these were the only means suggested. The Church's leaders were blind to the real condition of the people and unaware that the whole social structure was unsound. To us such an attitude is difficult to understand and the change in outlook has been enormous: but, as C. F. G. Masterman wrote in 1907, before the Great War had brought still further ruin, "The ruins of a world occupy the intervening age" (*F. D. Maurice*, p. 111).

The Church, moreover, was part of the old order of things which was, in some measure, responsible for the conditions requiring a remedy. In its teaching the emphasis had been too much on what may be called the negative virtues, and to many who longed for social reform it seemed more concerned to defend existing rights than to abolish existing wrongs. The sins denounced were mostly those against good order and private property; the sins of the spirit—pride, anger, and malice—seem to have received less attention. If the votes cast by the Bishops in the House of Lords are examined they do not suggest that the Church was at all eager to improve conditions, and many felt that it was definitely unsympathetic. That was perhaps why many Social Reformers were anti-Christian, though to nothing like the same extent as on the continent. But by failing to apply the root principles of Christ to the community and to every relationship of life the Christian Church certainly lost the allegiance of many whom it might have won, and caused grave doubts to arise in the minds of the working classes as to its sincerity and value. And this loss of allegiance was not limited to the Church at home. At a Conference of the Student Movement some years ago a speaker, after referring to the presentation of Christianity to the Arab, went on as follows: "It is idle to invite him to know and love a God who entered our life to share and save it, so long as we interpret that salvation without reference to what in his experience are the most important functions of human life."[1]

Thus the tendency of the Church, in the person of its leaders, was to regard such fundamental problems as the existence of poverty, bad housing, and unjust conditions in general, as outside its sphere of action. At the same time it did not forget that its own birth had been in poverty and that for much of its early history it had been associated with poor men. If the problem was ignored, the symptoms were not; and many attempts were made to deal with the victims of the social system. This was really, though men did not see it at once, to reduce the Church to an ambulance corps in the army of progress (I owe the figure to Höffding), instead of placing it, as the pillar of fire and cloud, at its head. St. Augustine, in a moment of rare insight, had taught that God allows the wicked to partake of temporal riches, and the virtuous to suffer

[1] In *Christ and Human Need* (1921), p. 87.

temporal evils, in order to show the comparative unimportance of material conditions.[1] But to such heights the poor were not capable of rising, and the Church's message of consolation was rejected by many, as it is to-day, as "dope" intended to keep them quiet under intolerable conditions. The promise of future recompense was especially suspect; for the working man, as Dr. Inge has said, "is apt to think that the preacher is trying to put him off with cheques drawn upon the bank of heaven, the solvency of which he greatly doubts, in order to persuade him not to claim what he conceives to be his rights here and now" (*Outspoken Essays*, II, p. 33). All the same the gospel can only be presented in a very much reduced form if this aspect of it is ignored; the purpose of Christianity is not to make this world more comfortable by bringing about social amelioration, but to give men a new sense of values and to redeem their souls.

The Work of Individuals

Thus officially the Church took no open steps to improve conditions. But this did not mean that her members, as individuals, remained quiescent. When the Church's failure to act is denounced, this must be remembered in her favour—that she taught some of her children to see in the improvement of social conditions a definite piece of Christian service. Amongst these children one of the greatest was Lord Shaftesbury. His work for Factory Reform was taken up as a matter of practical Christianity, as were all his other efforts to make the lot of the poor and helpless more tolerable. His life set up a new standard of unselfish devotion, and his example inspired many others. After his death the Duke of Argyle proclaimed publicly that "the social reforms of the last century . . . have been mainly due to the influence, character, and perseverance of one man—Lord Shaftesbury." A tribute that was endorsed by the late Lord Salisbury.[2]

Alongside great men like Lord Shaftesbury there were many others whose names are unknown, who in the limited sphere of their own towns or parishes were taking a deep interest in the

[1] *De Civitate Dei*, I, p. viii.
[2] See Hodder, *Life of Lord Shaftesbury*, III, pp. 520 f.

material welfare of their fellows, and who both laboured to improve conditions and fearlessly denounced, on religious grounds, all social abuses. An example may be cited in Henry Moule, the saintly vicar of Fordington, and father of the late Bishop of Durham. He was the inventor of new and effective methods of sanitation which are still widely used.[1]

Other individual Christians, whilst not neglecting opportunities for "ambulance" work or for attempts at improving conditions, made it their business to denounce the prevailing economic and industrial system as fundamentally unchristian and to endeavour to change it. F. D. Maurice held that Christianity itself was degraded unless it rose to the task, that it was unsound so far "as men have ceased to connect it with the whole order of the world and of human life, and have made it a scheme or method for obtaining selfish prizes which men are to compete for, just as for the things of the earth." The study of history suggests that Christianity must in the long run conquer any civilization in which it arises or that civilization will perish. During the struggle, however, Christianity itself becomes corrupted by its antagonist to the extent that it fails to overcome it.

The true task of Christianity is to redeem both the individual and society, and for this philanthropy is not enough. The social and industrial system must be permeated and transformed, and redemption achieved "through the exercise of a common Brotherhood in the equalities of free service."[2] When Hort had to preach the sermon at the consecration of his ally and friend, Westcott, as Bishop of Durham, he described him as "one to whom the Christian society is almost a watchword, and who hears in every social distress of the times a cry for the help which only a social interpretation of the Gospel can give."[3] This is the true Christian attitude which must recognize the evil of a system based on Competition, and yet the necessity of a new heart and outlook, as well as new conditions. This same attitude was well brought out by Percival, later to be Bishop of Hereford, in a sermon preached in the famous church

[1] Harford and Macdonald, *Bishop Handley Moule*, p. 4.
[2] H. Scott Holland, *Personal Studies*, p. 66.
[3] *Life of Brooke Foss Westcott*, II, p. 101.

of St. Andrew's, Plymouth, in June 1886. At a time when the industrial system was taken for granted (the denunciations of the Christian Socialists having been forgotten), he spoke out openly of the evils of Competition and exposed its essentially unchristian character, declaring it to be "antagonistic in its very essence to the principles of Christianity . . . rooted in anti-Christ." But he was careful to warn his hearers against what he felt to be the weakness of Socialism and every other attempt to reform outward conditions apart from Christianity: "You cannot create a new world except by creating a new heart and a new purpose in common men."[1]

The Work of Associations

The work of the individual reformer, unless he is possessed of great influence or is content to limit his activities to a small sphere, is bound to suffer from his weakness. To remedy this he must associate himself with those who are like-minded. In the fight for more Christian conditions in England this was soon realized and the famous group of so-called Christian Socialists was the forerunner of numerous similar combinations of religious social reformers. Amongst the leaders, in addition to Maurice and Kingsley, were Ludlow, Vansittart Neale (who provided most of the money), and Tom Hughes. Their endeavour was to apply to the political and social ills of the times the principles of Christ, in whom they believed as the Incarnation of God Himself. After discussing matters with a number of the workers they eventually decided to start workshops, run, not on competitive but on co-operative lines. The object of these workshops was to demonstrate that "working men can release themselves, and can be helped by others to release themselves, from the thraldom of individual labour under the competitive system; or at least how far they can at present by honest fellowship mitigate its evils." Unfortunately the workers under co-operative principles proved themselves to be just as greedy and selfish as under competition. The promoters lost much money by their experiments and at length lost heart also and they were abandoned. The workers were in some cases not exactly skilled and those who supported

[1] Quoted by W. Temple, *Life of Bishop Percival*, p. 82.

them had much to endure. Canon North Pindar, writing of Oxford in 1848, says that "Christian Socialism was taken up ardently by the few, who for a testimony were content to wear strange patterned and ill-fitting trousers, made in the workshops of the C.S. tailor."[1] This humorous and unsuccessful side was prominent to many and no doubt the experiment was premature and ill-directed; none the less, the Christian Socialism of 1848 was, as G. W. E. Russell has testified, "one of the finest episodes in our moral history."[2]

At this point something may well be said of the Co-operative Movement. Its real founder was Robert Owen, who in 1821 began a series of experiments, not very successful, but pointing the way to better things. Then in 1844 came the "Equitable Pioneers" of Rochdale. The most important development, however, was that referred to already, of the Christian Socialists. Their two chief contributions to the Movement were to break down existing prejudices and by their efforts in getting the Industrial and Prudential Societies Acts of 1852 and 1862 through Parliament to gain for the Movement legal recognition and protection. In 1864 a new stage in the Movement was reached with the foundation in the North of England of a wholesale agency (known since 1873 as the Co-operative Wholesale Society), to be followed four years later by the Scottish Wholesale Society.[3]

The next combination to deserve notice is the Guild of St. Matthew, founded in 1877 in the parish of St. Matthew's, Bethnal Green, of which Stewart Headlam was then vicar. It had originally three objects:

(1) To get rid, by every possible means, of the existing prejudices, especially on the part of Secularists, against the Church, her sacraments and doctrines, and to endeavour to "justify God to the people."

(2) To promote frequent and reverent worship in the Holy

---

[1] See Abbott and Campbell, *Life of Benjamin Jowett*, I, pp. 135 f.
[2] *Fifteen Chapters of Autobiography*, p. 343.
[3] For the history of this important Movement and its principles and methods see G. J. Holyoake, *History of Co-operation*, and B. Potter (Mrs. Sidney Webb), *The Co-operative Movement in Great Britain*. Canon Raven has dealt with it in *Christian Socialism, 1848–1854*.

Communion, and a better observance of the teaching of the Church of England, as set forth in the Book of Common Prayer.

(3) To promote the study of social and political questions in the light of the Incarnation.

The Guild never had a large membership but it included some prominent Churchmen, such as C. W. Stubbs (Dean of Ely and Bishop of Truro), W. E. Moll, A. L. Lilley, C. E. Osborne, Conrad Noel, Percy Dearmer, J. G. Adderley, and F. L. Donaldson. Its chief usefulness was in providing a link between the Church of England and the promoters of the Labour Movement. The extreme views of many of its members, however, prevented its ever becoming really effective and the foundation of the Christian Social Union in 1889 was in the nature of a death-blow. It survived, however, until 1909.[1]

The Christian Social Union, which was a Union for Churchmen only, was founded at a meeting in the Chapter House of St. Paul's on June 14, 1889. Its first president was Westcott, and Scott Holland its first secretary. The declared objects were three in number:

(i) To claim for the Christian Law the ultimate authority to rule social practice.
(ii) To study in common how to apply the moral truths and principles of Christianity to the social and economic difficulties of the present time.
(iii) To present Christ in practical life as the Living Master and King, the enemy of wrong and selfishness, the power of righteousness and love.

The Union endeavoured to carry out these objects in a variety of ways: by compiling "white lists" of approved traders, by denouncing cases of overwork and bad wages, by examining the conditions in dangerous trades; above all perhaps through its literature and meetings by which public opinion was aroused.[2] Bishop Gore considers that it contributed "very largely to the change in the whole attitude of society and the Church towards the social question."[3]

---

[1] See F. G. Bettany, *Stewart Headlam*, pp. 79 ff.
[2] See Stephen Paget, *Henry Scott Holland*, pp. 169 ff.
[3] In Paget, *op. cit.*, p. 249.

SOCIAL PROBLEMS

Westcott, its first president, as we have seen, had been moved to the study of social problems, or at least had received guidance in their study, by reading Comte's *Politique Positive* and Maurice's *Social Morality*,[1] and his influence was extraordinarily high amongst those who were out of touch with organized religion. In 1895 he was actually asked to preside over a Demonstration of the Unemployed in Trafalgar Square.[2] In many ways Westcott was in advance of his time, and in April 1889 a Conference of Christians of various denominations was held in his house at Westminster which in his name as Chairman issued a letter to the press calling attention to the great danger from the growth of armaments.[3] The London *Echo* made the following significant comment on it: "The Canon says 'a war of despair seems to be the natural issue of an indefinite period of continuous mistrust and increasing burdens.' These words are important when addressed by a Church dignitary to the leading representatives of Christian Churches. The wonder is that the Churches have not moved long ago. The wonder is that men who profess to be followers of the Prince of Peace have maintained silence in the face of menacing facts so long."[4]

Thus the work of the Church in combating the evils of unjust and evil conditions was waged in the nineteenth century through the labours of individuals;[5] there was, as yet, little conception of the Church exercising, as it had done in the Middle Ages, the power of direction in all departments of life. The vast majority of Christian people would have agreed with the attitude of one who took a great lead in political and municipal life—R. W. Dale. It has been stated on the highest authority that "he was convinced that the Church was in its very essence a religious institution established for religious ends; that social and political reforms, however desirable, were not the objects of its activity; and that so to regard them would be to degrade the Church into a political organization."

[1] See the introduction to his *Social Aspects of Christianity*.
[2] *Life of Brooke Foss Westcott*, II, p. 194.
[3] *Op. cit.*, II, pp. 16 ff.
[4] *Op. cit.*, II, p. 21 n.
[5] The Lambeth Conference of 1888 had urged Churchmen to study urgent social questions.

Furthermore, to quote his own words: "The churches should do all they can in the power of the grace and truth of Christ to renew and sanctify all whom they reach; and that then Christian men—as citizens, not as members of churches—should appear in the community to discharge their duties to it, under the control of the spirit and law of Christ" (*Life*, pp. 648 f.). But there was another point of view, a point of view which was to grow in strength in the years which followed the Victorian Era. Those who held it were convinced that the Church had entirely mistaken its function; which was, not to provide opportunities of spiritual enjoyment for the select few, but to be God's instrument in bringing in the Kingdom of Heaven on earth.

14

THE DEVELOPMENT OF THOUGHT FROM 1870

THE later years of the Victorian Era formed a period of fermentation during which, beneath the surface, different tendencies were struggling together for expression and mastery. Thought during the period failed to attain unity, because the two opposing principles of reform and reaction in the air around were never reconciled. The application of modern methods had resulted in "a systematic attempt to analyse human experience into facts and beliefs, and to avoid confusion between these two constituents of our knowledge."[1] But such an analysis could only result in a conflict between the forces of tradition and advance. During the century the rising flood had been beating against traditional barriers which strove vainly to hold them back: here and there, the barriers had broken down under the pressure; here and there, the waters were held until they rose high enough to flow over the barriers. But in this there was gain as well as loss, and attempts at reconstruction were not wanting. In a paper read as early as 1879 James Ward, the distinguished Cambridge philosopher, had proclaimed his faith that all would yet be well. "The tide that seems to have overwhelmed the legends of the church and the dogmas of the school will I verily believe turn out to have left the essence of religion purer and plainer than before."[2]

Mr. F. S. Marvin has found two great characteristics in the thought of the age: A recognition of the "force of science, of organized knowledge, in framing and inspiring life" and of "the goal of human thought and activity, the community of all human beings conspiring to a common end by diverse means" (*The Century of Hope*, p. 55). As to the latter, one may see in it a following after Condorcet's ambitious notion of the perfectability of humanity; and in the former the way to materialism. This materialism was both speculative, as seen

[1] Oliver Quick, *Liberalism, Modernism, and Tradition*, p. 1.
[2] *Essays in Philosophy*, p. 108.

in Natural Science, and actual, in the growth of comfort and luxury. It undoubtedly led to a serious preoccupation with the things of the senses and the eternal background of life was lost. This loss was "very precariously supplied . . . by the idea of progress, the secular faith of the nineteenth century."[1]

A previous age had sought for stability in its thought, but now progress and change were the order of the day. This involved a clash between those who hailed reason and free enquiry as heralds of emancipation, and those who dreaded the "probing, progressive mind" as a destructive and solvent force. The new belief in progress was, no doubt, largely due to the emergence of evolution. It is notable that no one seemed to be curious as to what progress meant and whither it was tending; evolution was so evidently from the less to the more perfect that such an enquiry was unnecessary. Hence a species of optimism, based on natural development, began to possess men's minds; until at last the idea of God became a luxury. But by the end of the century a vast change had taken place, and this spirit of optimism was giving way to a growing pessimism; a pessimism due not to the spread of the teaching of Schopenhauer, or indeed to any metaphysical cause, but to that Natural Science which had built it up and was now to be the instrument of its collapse. The hand which dealt the blow was that of Huxley, who shewed that belief in the idea of mechanical progress was not justified. The change involved can be seen by comparing Herbert Spencer's *First Principles* and his *Principles of Sociology*; the difference between them, the loss of enthusiasm, and the growing dulness, is not to be explained only by the writer's decaying force; it corresponded to a real change in the mental atmosphere.

PHILOSOPHY

In Philosophy the first half of the Victorian Era had been characterized by a contempt for the study of metaphysics; Lord Bowen had even gone to the length of describing it as the search of a blind man, in a dark room, for a black cat

[1] Inge, *Vale*, p. 107.

that wasn't there.[1] Part of this antipathy was perhaps due to Carlyle, part to the intensely practical outlook of the age. This "pragmatic" attitude can further be illustrated from its conception of the function of religion. The most part regarded it as useful in keeping society together; they had, however, little interest in the question of its truth. But because its practical value was recognized, any attempt to expose the foundations upon which it rested was resented, and still more anything which might disturb them. Hence the fear and dislike of Bradlaugh and his fellows, and even of the efforts of critical students of the Bible. It is possible that Huxley invented the term "agnostic" to shew that he did not hold with such aggressive and opinionated atheism.

Revived Interest in Metaphysics

A little before 1870 signs were not wanting of a new awakening to the value of philosophical speculation among those who were not themselves professional teachers of the subject. The formation of the Metaphysical Society in 1869 by Tennyson and others was one of them.[2] This revived interest in metaphysics was soon followed by the beginning of the decay in what may be called the moderate rationalist school. This school reached its highest point of influence in the 'seventies; for though John Stuart Mill died in 1873 his writings still had power, especially in Oxford; and the rationalistic outlook had another powerful focus in *The Fortnightly Review*, of which John Morley was the editor from 1867 to 1882. Rationalism was too critical and too much a matter of the intellect long to retain its supremacy, and the last quarter of the nineteenth century saw a gradual, but continuous, waning of its influence. In the universities, and among them Oxford and Glasgow in particular, its place was taken by the followers of Hegel.

The teacher who was responsible for the spread of Hege-

[1] This can be compared with Bradley's condemnation, in more recent times, of its office as being to find "bad reasons for what we believe upon instinct": but this was the product of a cynical moment and hardly typical of either the man or the age.

[2] See *Alfred, Lord Tennyson*, II, pp. 166 ff.

lianism in Oxford, and through it in England, was T. H. Green.[1] This great teacher and leader, by his advocacy of a more spiritual philosophy, broke the predominant power of J. S. Mill, and brought fresh hope to those who held the Christian position. Green himself, although he would not have disclaimed the name of Christian, was hardly an orthodox believer. Reading between the lines of his letter to Scott Holland in 1870, one can see his real attitude, for he bids the latter "keep in view the distinction between what is temporarily edifying and what is true; between the eternal ideas on which the religious life rests, and theological dodges."[2] His sermon on "Faith" delivered in 1877 was a landmark. Green died in 1882 at the early age of forty-six; but after his death his power, in Oxford especially, continued to grow. He left behind him a noble band of enthusiastic disciples, many of whom belonged to the young High Church School. But Hegelianism, even in the form in which Green taught it, was no real help to the Christian faith; it tended too much to minimize the historical side of religion. In Ritschl, and still more in the Ritschlians, the process was carried further and "values" exalted at the expense of "facts" to an alarming extent. The Ritschlians, however, unlike the Roman Catholic Modernists, held firmly to the Historic Christ and His teaching.

That Hegelianism ever attained to so much influence in England is surprising, for both in method and content it is really alien to the English mind. This was perceived quite early by James Martineau, who agreed with Schopenhauer that Hegelianism was the *reductio ad absurdum* of metaphysics, and could never understand its notable popularity, especially the enthusiasm of the young High Churchmen [3] The vogue for Hegelianism in Britain came late, in fact after it had been given up in its native land; an illustration of the belief that Oxford is the place to which good German philosophies go

---

[1] It had been known before Green's days, of course, and had aroused the concern of Mansel: see Storr, *English Theology, etc.*, p. 403.
[2] Quoted by Stephen Paget, *Henry Scott Holland*, p. 52. Green appears as Henry Grey in Mrs. Humphry Ward's *Robert Elsmere*.
[3] See J. Estlin Carpenter, *James Martineau*, pp. 535 ff.

when they are dead. Towards the end of the century there was a strong reaction against any system of absolute idealism.[1]

The philosopher who nexts calls for notice is Herbert Spencer, who died in 1903 at the advanced age of eighty-three. His great merit was that he insisted on the recognition that our knowledge is limited, though not—it need hardly be explained—as Mansel had done, in order to postulate the need of revelation. Among philosophical teachers Spencer was remarkable for his neglect of the work of those who had gone before him;[2] hence, though much of his philosophy was the result of his own thinking, no single idea was really new. Huxley put it in a paradoxical way by saying that he was "the most original of thinkers, though he never invented a new thought."[3] For a time he had an amazing, though totally undeserved, influence. The explanation of this was that he appealed to those who desired a complete and logical system, but who were not themselves trained thinkers. From the first keen-eyed critics saw his weaknesses and, as it has been said, he was abused by philosophers, but taken by non-philosophers for a great thinker.[4] Bryce wrote to Fairbairn that, although he was not qualified to judge of his scientific work, "his contributions to the historical and sociological side of philosophy seem to me valueless.... Jowett once said to me of his work, 'All rubbish!' "[5] In later life his influence and reputation gradually declined, much to his own chagrin, for he was extremely sensitive, and he suffered much mental misery and even lost confidence in himself. The progress of natural science and especially of physics worked against his optimistic imaginings.[6] For one thing, however, he must be given credit: he was among the few thinkers in the latter years of the nineteenth century who had the insight and the courage to foretell the coming reaction against democracy which was so striking a feature of the years between the two world wars.

[1] Storr, *op. cit.*, p. 145.
[2] The same was true of Vico, the Italian philospher of two centuries ago.
[3] Quoted by Beatrice Webb, *My Apprenticeship*, p. 28.
[4] Matheson, *Hastings Rashdall*, pp. 110 f.
[5] Quoted by W. B. Selbie, *A. M. Fairbairn*, p. 412.
[6] See Beatrice Webb, *op. cit.*, pp. 36 f. and 90.

Ethical Studies

Last of all, a few words must be said of F. H. Bradley,[1] who was a disciple, although with definite limitations, of Hegel. Bradley is important because he was utterly and mercilessly opposed to the easy-going agnosticism which tended to flourish in the latter part of the century, and because, in defiance of a predominant and blatant materialism, he insisted that the real was the spiritual. His *Ethical Studies*, published in 1876—and never reprinted in his lifetime[2]—marked an epoch. In them he attacked the theory that any system of morality could be based on the belief in a future world. His view was that the moral ideal is self-sufficient and requires no reinforcement, and is, indeed, betrayed by the introduction of the question of rewards and punishments. At the same time he recognized that religion has its place in ethics, averring that "Reflection on morality leads us beyond it. It leads us, in short, to see the necessity of a religious point of view."[3]

The combination of morality and religion, for which Bradley stood, was typical of his age. The nineteenth century was austere and earnest, full of ideals; and because its faith was weak it clung all the harder to Christian ethics. It believed, with Kant and his disciples, that religion gave some kind of metaphysical guarantee of the victory of the moral sense. Another figure to be noticed in this connexion is Henry Sidgwick, like Green a Yorkshireman by birth and his contemporary at Rugby. In him the conflict between doubt and faith was never resolved. He confessed himself a theist; but though he looked upon Christianity as "indispensable and irreplaceable" from the sociological point of view, he could not make up his mind to accept it; and indeed resigned his fellowship at Trinity, Cambridge, on religious grounds. His great contribution to

---

[1] There is an illuminating little study of Bradley by T. S. Eliot, *For Lancelot Andrewes*, pp. 67 ff.

[2] In a note in *Appearance and Reality* (1893), Bradley justified his refusal to allow a reprint: "I feel," he wrote, "that the appearance of other books, as well as the decay of those superstitions against which largely it was directed, has left me free to consult my own pleasure in the matter."

[3] Quoted by T. S. Eliot, *op. cit.*, p. 83.

the study of morality was *Method of Ethics*, which appeared in 1874, two years before Bradley's masterpiece.

But already, before the close of the nineteenth century, the religious basis of ethics was beginning to be questioned. In every generation the religious problem takes a different form, and now the conflict was being carried into the region of conduct and action. Doubt here may have terrifying consequences; for without religious sanctions the masses of the people, who have no intellectual interest in ethical questions and little moral training, may so easily lose their grip on morality, and with it the sense of truth and honesty. The modern idea of subjective freedom, then gaining force, can provide no secure basis for man's moral life, or even for his intellectual being.

THEOLOGY

The years immediately preceding 1870 were full of warring tendencies in theological and religious thought. "One and the same epoch produced," wrote Dowden, "the sermons of Spurgeon, the *Apologia pro vita sua* of Newman, and the *Literature and Dogma* of Matthew Arnold" (*Life of Robert Browning*, p. 325). This note of warfare and divergence continued to characterize the period with which we are now to deal.

As a result of the conflict there was a tendency for the old groups, based on ecclesiastical rather than theological conceptions, to break up; certainly the newer divisions cut sharply across them. In the course of the last years of Victoria thought began to separate up into three groups, though naturally the dividing line between them was faint and shifting. There were the Conservatives, with what would now be called a "Fundamentalist" wing; there were the Liberals, with a Radical wing, tending to stray outside organized religion altogether; and there were those whose views were definitely "Agnostic."

The Conservatives held to the literal truth, with some few and unimportant exceptions, of the Bible. All the obscurities or seeming contradictions contained in the sacred narrative they put down to man's imperfect knowledge, or possibly to corruptions in the text. They failed to see that new knowledge imposes upon the Church the duty of facing it and of adjusting beliefs to meet the new conditions which it has brought about. In their obstinate clinging to the old they illustrate the tendency, often to be observed in religious societies, to congeal and to crystallize. Probably they merited the attack which Fairbairn, in an address to the Congregational Union in 1883, made upon them. "There is no worse foe," he said, "to his faith than the man who hates rational thought as if it were the invention of Satan, rather than the gift of God; there is no man who so little understands faith as the man who thinks devout feeling or an inspired heart the whole of religion" (*Studies in Religion and Theology*, p. 89).

The Liberals accepted the new knowledge, as contained in the discoveries of Natural Science and Biblical Criticism. They remained in communion with the Church and claimed the right to interpret its formularies in ways which would certainly not have been accepted by those who had originally drafted them. Some indeed felt that they could not stoop to this method, and accordingly went outside—such was Stopford Brooke. But others felt that their duty was to remain and purge the Church of old-fashioned ideas. When Brooke seceded in 1880 Haweis wrote to the *Daily News*, condemning his action as an "anachronism." This brought into the field J. R. Green, the historian, who in a letter to Brooke put it aside as "too flippant and insolent to waste a thought on, and . . . as immoral and base as it is insolent."[1]

The Agnostics were those who still felt an interest in religious questions and, in the best of them, a sadness at their loss of faith (a subject to which we shall return); they tried to make up by a stern endeavour to carry out their duties so far as they were able to discern them. Many of the Conservatives felt, and this excused their timid and rigid attitude, that negation, though it might be obscured in the case of individuals by their previous religious impressions, was the natural goal of all religious Liberalism.

Liberalism in the Church of England

In the Church of England there was an influential group of Liberal theologians; or perhaps one had better call them

[1] Quoted Jacks, *Life and Letters of Stopford Brooke*, p. 326.

religious teachers, for their theology was not of any great depth. Dale once said of Dean Stanley that he was utterly lacking in any theological sense, quite "colour-blind" indeed in the domain of theology.[1] While Jowett was probably stronger in the realms of practical things than in theological learning, he was certainly deficient in the knowledge of past theology, and often quite mistaken in what he regarded as its meaning. "In the story of English theology Jowett's truest title to fame is his championship of liberty of thought"—concludes Archdeacon Storr[2]—and anyone who is acquainted with the developments of that theology cannot fail to agree with him. His stern determination not to go beyond the facts as he saw them was an example which inspired others with a like restraint. Bishop Gore, as a young man, had his portrait on his study wall (he had been Jowett's pupil at Balliol), and when he felt that he was pressing an argument too far a glance at it was enough to pull him up (*Life*, pp. 38 f.). One work produced by an extreme Liberal had for a time an immense vogue. This was *Supernatural Religion*, which appeared in three volumes in 1872. It was anonymous, and by some extraordinary freak the name of Thirlwall got attached to it. The writer made an immense parade of learning, using in particular the numerous apocryphal Gospels which were not then so well known as they now are and going out of his way to accuse so great a scholar as Westcott of intentional deceit. All this made a profound impression. But the pretentious and inadequate nature of the author's scholarship was exposed by Lightfoot in a series of articles in the *Contemporary Review*—and the bubble was pricked.[3]

As preached from pulpits and proclaimed in lecture rooms, however, Liberal Theology had a great influence, in spite of its nebulosity. Creighton, as a young don at Oxford, listened

---

[1] *Life of R. W. Dale*, p. 215.
[2] See *Development of English Theology*, pp. 452 ff.
[3] The Dean of Lichfield was told by a well-known bookseller that the collapse of the demand for this volume constituted "the most remarkable phenomenon in the publishing trade that he had ever known or heard about . . . its sale was so rapid that the publishers could hardly produce it . . . fast enough to meet the demand." On the publication of Lightfoot's articles, immediately it became "a glut in the second-hand market": *Lightfoot of Durham*, pp. 9 f.

to Stanley preaching in the University pulpit, and he wrote to his future wife: "There was a certain amount of general moral enthusiasm, to the intent that it was desirable to be good rather than bad; but I had previously gathered that from other sources" (*Life and Letters*, I, p. 92). Young Oxford can always be rather biting—but the criticism was just. Some years before R. W. Church had already pierced through to the weakness of the whole position in spite of its great claims and the charm and influence of those who preached it. "What is this nineteenth-century religion for which all things have been preparing, and to which all good things, past and present, are subservient and bear witness?" he wrote to J. B. Moziey in 1865. "He (Stanley) seems to me in the position of a prophet and leader, full of eagerness and enthusiasm and brilliant talent, all heightened by success—but without a creed to preach. I suppose he would say that testifying for liberty and the love of truth and tolerance is a sufficient creed. But at any rate it can be only to intellectual people, and the world in general is not of that sort."[1]

If Liberalism, in spite of the ardour of some of its exponents, was only a vague force within the Church, it can claim certain definite achievements, for it was mainly responsible for giving to common men and women a more worthy idea of God. Tennyson wrote in 1869 that "The general English view of God is as of an immeasurable clergyman; and some mistake the devil for God" (*Alfred, Lord Tennyson*, II, p. 90). That this view has largely passed away, though not, unfortunately, entirely, was in the main due to the work of the Broad Churchmen. In particular they succeeded in modifying two doctrines in a more Christian direction—those concerning the Future Punishment of the wicked, and the Atonement. Looking back over a period of a generation Jowett, from the vantage ground of 1888, could write: "Our problems are not so serious as those of thirty or forty years ago. Then men thought they had to receive as a revelation from God that which conflicted with

[1] *Life and Letters of Dean Church*, pp. 202 f. As a comment the opinion of Hugh Price Hughes—that the Broad Churchmen had built excellent tabernacles for the few, they had not built them for mankind—may be quoted. See Dorothea Price Hughes, *Life of Hugh Price Hughes*, p. 96.

their sense of justice, and puzzled themselves with trying to reconcile God's goodness with the doctrine of eternal punishment" (*Life*, II, p. 305).

The first shot of the conflict over the question of Eternal Punishment was fired by the Council of King's College, when in October 1853 they forced F. D. Maurice out of his professorship on the grounds that his teaching on "the future punishment of the wicked and the final issues of the Day of Judgement" were "of dangerous tendency, and calculated to unsettle the minds of the theological students." There were in this conflict many misunderstandings, and those who condemned Maurice failed to comprehend his point of view. He stood for the truth that Eternal and Everlasting are not the same thing, or to use his own words, that Eternity "has nothing to do with time or duration" at all. In spite of the condemnation as A. W. Benn, who apparently thinks that Eversley is in Somerset, has pointed out, his disciple Kingsley "continued to preach his gospel unmolested to rural congregations" (*Modern England*, p. 321).

Meanwhile, indignation was rising in many minds, and Stopford Brooke, a short time before his secession, declared that "That intolerable doctrine ought to be clean swept out of the English Church. Not only would religion be the better for its destruction, but society, and government, and literature and art" (*Life*, p. 305). Much of the opposition to the doctrine came from the popular idea which quite misrepresented it, and even those who claimed to attack it as scholars were not so fully competent as they imagined. This came out in the controversy between Pusey and Farrar in 1879, when the latter was sufficiently candid to confess that he had not a sufficient knowledge of the views either of the early fathers or of his antagonist—in particular on such important points as the notion of material tortures and the idea that the greater part of humanity is damned.

The doctrine of the Atonement was an even more serious matter, for it stood so central in the Evangelical gospel. Into the various theories of the Atonement which have been held and propagated we cannot, of course, enter here;[1] but it will,

[1] A good account is contained in J. Kenneth Mozley, *The Doctrine of the Atonement*.

I think, be admitted that many of them, and these very widely held, were quite unworthy of the Gospel of Love. They suggested the Zeus of Aeschylus rather than the God and Father of our Lord Jesus Christ, and the lonely figure on Calvary might well have said with Prometheus:

"Mercy I had for Man; and therefore I
Must meet no mercy, but hang crucified
In witness of God's cruelty and pride."[1]

The revolt was against these crude theories and not so much against the doctrine itself; a violent objection to reducing a spiritual mystery, that of man's redemption in Christ Jesus, into a formula. Many would, no doubt, have agreed with Figgis when he wrote: "It were better to accept the crudest and most forensic doctrine of substitution rather than surrender the truth it is intended to set forth" (*The Gospel and Human Needs*, p. 60). There were also those who felt that it was possible to give the Atonement so prominent a place that other doctrines tended to be neglected. F. D. Maurice, for example, learned from Erskine of Linlathen's *The Brazen Serpent* that the Incarnation and not the Atonement was the central doctrine of Christianity and that a true gospel for humanity could not rest upon human sinfulness and the Fall.[2]

Amongst Liberal theologians within the Church of England mention must be made of Matthew Arnold. In his last poem, *Obermann Once More*, written in 1867, he gave up orthodox Christianity as a fond but beautiful dream; none the less, he clung to the Church and to the end of his life conformed. Like so many of his contemporaries he had a high regard for religion as an ethical force, although he could not longer receive its dogmas. In his theological writings, *St. Paul and Protestantism* (1870) and *Literature and Dogma* (1873), he attempted to shew that the really essential parts of Christianity were independent of its doctrines. Although he had not the full equipment of a theologian, his work still has value. Professor Percy Gardner, writing in 1911, declared that the former

[1] *Prometheus Vinctus*, 241-3 (Gilbert Murray's translation).
[2] *Life of Frederick Denison Maurice*, I, pp. 108 and 121.

volume contained "the best account of the Pauline theology" that he knew, adding, "so greatly does insight surpass learning."[1] Many of his ideas were made popular through the novels of his niece, Mrs. Humphry Ward.

The Sadness of Unbelief

A few pages above I referred to the sadness with which men of the Victorian Age gave up their belief in the faith of their childhood. This sadness is reflected in the writings, and especially the poems, of Matthew Arnold, who has been well described as the prophet of a generation "distracted between the intense need of believing and the difficulty of belief."[2] The change between that day and this is so vast that I feel justified in bringing in a series of rather long quotations to illustrate it. Then "differences of belief were taken gravely, as a tragedy, which now are taken lightly, as a comedy."[3] They were, indeed, often, as in the case of Lord Morley's father, taken as "a personal affront."[4]

The first quotation is from John Addington Symonds, of whom it has been said by one who knew him well, that "Emotionally he desired the warmth of a personal God, intellectually he could conceive that God under human attributes only, and found himself driven to say 'No' to each human presentment of Him."[5] In 1867 Symonds himself wrote: "In spite of myself the infinite tormented me: in spite of myself I kept looking skyward, sighing for illumination." And he adds, referring to his attempted description of his own religious history: "The sensation of God disappeared from me without the need of God being destroyed. But this is not a merely personal history, it is the history of the age in which we live, of the age of disintegration of old beliefs" (*op. cit.*, p. 315). Alongside this testimony of a historian and literary man, such as was Symonds, we may place that of a

[1] *The Religious Experience of St. Paul*, p. vii.
[2] Lord Acton in "George Eliot's Life," reprinted in *Historical Essays and Studies*, p. 303.
[3] Stephen Paget, *Henry Scott Holland*, p. v. Dr. Figgis is profoundly illuminating on this subject: see *op. cit.*, pp. 3 ff.
[4] Lord Morley, *Recollections*, I, p. 5.
[5] H. F. Brown, *John Addington Symonds*, p. xiv.

man of science. In *A Candid Examination of Theism* published anonymously in 1878 G. J. Romanes, for the work was really his, wrote as follows: "For as much as I am far from being able to agree with those who affirm that the twilight doctrine of the 'new faith' is a desirable substitute for the waning splendour of 'the old,' I am not ashamed to confess that with this virtual negation of God the universe to me has lost its soul of loveliness; and although from henceforth the precept to 'work while it is day' will doubtless but gain an intensified force from the terribly intensified meaning of the words that 'the night cometh when no man can work,' yet when at times I think, as think at times I must, of the appalling contrast between the hallowed glory of that creed which once was mine, and the lonely mystery of existence as now I find it—at such times I shall ever feel it impossible to avoid the sharpest pang of which my nature is susceptible" (*op. cit.*, p. 114).

These examples are drawn from those who reluctantly severed themselves from organized religion, or remained on as merely nominal members of religious bodies. Their testimony is valuable as revealing the natural affinity of the human heart for God, and the void which is left when belief in God seems no longer possible; a void which no merely human philosophy can ever fill for those who have known something higher. Even to-day when, as Figgis has said, "men give up Jesus and are glad," there is still a widespread feeling that all is not well, a growing recognition that man is not sufficient "for the spiritual tasks on which the value of his existence depends."

These cases call for much sympathy and profound regret that men so worthy found it impossible to conform and believe. Still more sad are those cases where men stayed on and perhaps attained to high position in their religious denominations when all the time they were tormented by doubt and lack of faith in the very things they had to preach and teach. Of these one example will be enough. Dr. Marcus Dods was a man of vast learning and wide influence in the Free Church of Scotland, yet he seems never to have had any full experience of the power of God's grace. He confessed in 1904 that he could not understand cases like that of Colonel Gardiner, "in which men never felt any temptation to old sins after conversion" (*Later Letters*, p. 154) and that his whole experience of prayer had been one of disappointment so much so that he only continued to use it "not because my own experience gives me any encouragement, but only because of Christ's example and command" (*op. cit.*, p. 29). In one pathetic letter he write : One who can believe in God should be very thankful. Very often, I may say commonly, I cannot get further than the conviction that in Christ we see the best that our nature is capable of, and must make that our own. And I am doubtful whether in this life much more is needed. ... I think I'd be absolutely and jubilantly joyful if I clearly, firmly, and unquestioningly believed in God—I won't say *and in immortality*, because the one carries the other" (*op. cit.*, pp. 101 f.). His whole life had been spent in the search after truth and at last he began to feel that "although the craving for truth is unquenchable and ineradicable, the attainment of truth is beyond us" (*op. cit.*, p. 22). He found the "worrying at the details of the Gospels" harmful and sickening and wished that "somebody would stop the stream of criticism and say something convincing about the existence of a personal God" (*op. cit.*, p. 87).

This widespread spirit of doubt and uncertainty had a twofold effect; it led to a greater tolerance, but also to attempts to find substitutes for Christianity in all kinds of obscure and even foolish cults. Certainly there is much more tolerance now than in the days of our fathers, and men are more content to find the things upon which they agree, even if they are but few, and, in company with one another, to attempt to express them, than to concentrate on their many points of divergence. As to the second effect; man's need for something outside himself takes strange forms when it ceases to find satisfaction in what the Christian believes to be the revelation given by God Himself. An age of unbelief is notoriously an age of superstition.

[1] This finds a parallel in the case of a well-known theologian who confessed to a Conference before beginning a paper on "Creative Prayer" that he was no adept and that what he was to say came from a "theorist rather than a practitioner": see *The Modern Churchman*, XIV, p. 347.

SPIRITUALISM

One of the most attractive of such superstitions was the cult of what is known as Spiritualism. This appealed to many of the finer souls, who, like Mrs. Browning, were "inclined to knock round at every door of the present world to try and get out."[1] It appealed also to John Ruskin, in a time of great sorrow, and, also be it said, of loss of mental balance.[2] But in Spiritualism there was so much that was vulgar, so much that was fraudulent, that few persisted in their following of this way of escape. Dowden condemns the whole movement as representing "a phase of nineteenth-century materialism and moral grossness, which cannot extinguish the cravings of the soul but would vulgarize and degrade them with coarse illusions" (*op. cit.*, p. 161). The noble words which Sir William Gairdner, the father of Temple Gairdner, addressed to a number of university men soon after the death of a son, should not be forgotten. "I do not envy," he said, "the man to whom the spiritual world is so shut that he must needs have a materialized ghost to make it palpable."[3]

Different from the vulgar craving after marvels was the work undertaken by serious scholars through what is known as Psychic Research. An early beginning of it was the "Ghostly Guild" founded in Cambridge in 1851 by Hort, Westcott, Henry Bradshaw, Benson, and others. Most of them eventually gave up the subject as doubtful of the good that would come from their investigations.[4] Later there came (in 1882) the Psychic Research Society and the investigations of men like Henry Sidgwick, Frederick Myers, and Edmund Gurney. It may truly be said that the publication of Myers's *Human*

---

[1] *Letter to Miss Mitford*, quoted by Dowden, *Life of Robert Browning*, p. 157. The views of Mrs. Browning were considerably modified "by the discovery that she had been duped by a friend in whom she had blind faith" (R. Barrett Browning in *Times Literary Supplement* for December 5, 1902). Browning himself discovered the famous medium Home in a vulgar fraud and refused him the house. His experience was useful to him in *Mr. Sludge the Medium*, written in Rome, in 1859–60.

[2] See Collingwood, *Life of John Ruskin*, pp. 240 f., 253.

[3] Quoted Padwick, *Temple Gairdner of Cairo*, p. 5.

[4] An account of this Guild will be found in *Life and Letters of Brooke Foss Westcott*, I, pp. 117 ff., including the circular sent round asking for material.

THOUGHT FROM 1870

Personality and its Survival of Bodily Death in 1901 marked an epoch. But that lies outside our period, as do the sincere if mistaken researches of Sir Arthur Conan Doyle.[1]

RELIGION AND PSYCHOLOGY

Before leaving the subject of Thought in the last generation of the Victorian Era something must be said of the development of the study which gave to it a special character—that of Psychology. An interest in Psychology had always been typical of English philosophy but progress had been held up by belief in what is known as "faculty" Psychology. Newman's *Grammar of Assent*, with its enquiries into the meaning of faith and the part played by the mind and the feelings in its construction, must have aroused a good deal of interest in the relations of Psychology and Religion. It was, however, in 1855 that two works appeared which seemed to threaten war between the two. Alexander Bain's *The Senses and the Intellect* emphasized the close connexion between the mind and the brain, whilst Herbert Spencer's *Principles of Psychology* looked to evolution for an explanation of the development of the human mind. From this it required but a few steps to find in Psychology a complete explanation of Religion itself and the idea of God. It is so simple to see in the latter an apotheosis of the "group-spirit" or the race, or even explain it away as due to auto-suggestion. The belief in a future life is obviously a "compensatory hallucination" intended to supplement the present! What those who look to Psychology as a means of getting rid of Religion fail to grasp is that it deals only with processes; it may in certain cases and within certain areas make probable suggestions as to how opinions have grown up; but it has no standard by which to test such opinions. It may put this or that down to "auto-suggestion," but it does not ask itself what "auto-suggestion" really is, or seem aware that the self which "suggests" needs explanation.[2]

---

[1] See further F. L. Cross, *Religion and the Reign of Science*, pp. 62 ff., and the article, "Psychic Research," in the *Encyclopædia Britannica*.

[2] See further Cross, *op. cit.*, pp. 52 ff.

CHRISTIAN MYSTICISM

The end of the century saw the sudden emergence of a new and more intelligent interest in Christian Mysticism. This interest, which in the present century was destined to develop immensely, owes its rise mainly to the Bampton Lectures in 1899 delivered by W. R. Inge, later to become the famous Dean of St. Paul's and one of the greatest religious forces of his time. During the greater part of the century mysticism had been suspected as hazy and dangerous. In Germany it had often been allied with theosophy, as in the case of Schelling, but there was not enough contact between German and English thought at that time to account for the general suspicion which prevailed here. This suspicion is found in many different quarters; Newman's treatment of the articles in Tract 90 was denounced as "mystical" by Mark Pattison in 1840 (*Essays*, II, p. 222); while a little later Charles Kingsley began to study mystical writers in order to be able to eradicate asceticism and mysticism from his message (*Life*, p. 22); whilst as late as 1888 Aubrey Moore could speak of "the dangerous haze of mysticism" (*Science and the Faith*, p. 56).

On the philosophical side this revived interest in mysticism probably owes much to the theory of T. H. Green, derived ultimately from Hegel, that a developing self-consciousness is the key to religious progress. The same kind of teaching, it is worth noting, was found in Frances Power Cobbe. But the spread of interest was fostered not a little by the literary revival, and in particular by the writers of the Celtic school, such as Fiona McLeod (William Sharp), and by Theodore Watts-Dunton, whose essay on "The Renaissance of Wonder" marked an epoch.[1] A mystical feeling has been characteristic of our greatest English poets; it is found in Blake, in Coleridge, and in Wordsworth; whilst in the writings of Emily Brontë it is very marked.

The most famous work on mysticism in general before Inge's Lectures was R. A. Vaughan's *Hours with the Mystics*. This volume was the fruit of vast labours; the author even learnt

[1] Watts-Dunton's novel *Aylwin* was published in 1898, the year before Inge's *Christian Mysticism*; it undoubtedly did much to arouse interest in the subject of mysticism generally.

Spanish and Dutch for its sake, but it is deficient in real sympathy. Inge himself has told us that he began the study of the mystics in 1888 on his going to Oxford as tutor of Hertford. Believing that the testimony of the saints and mystics had a much higher evidential value than was commonly supposed, he tried to find in Christian Mysticism a sound intellectual basis for his religious belief (*Vale*, p. 31, and cf. p. 39).

That mysticism has its dangers none will deny who has studied the writings of the mystics at first hand; it may foster morbidity, the feeling that one is but an exile here on earth, and, as in the case of Emily Brontë, a delight in the sense of frustration and a love of suffering which is hardly healthy.[1] It requires to be balanced, as indeed it was in the best mystics, by a regard to the outward world and the duties which it demands. Inge has defined mysticism as involving "an immediate contact real or supposed between the human soul and the Soul of the World or the Divine Spirit ... who in Christian theology is identified with the Logos-Christ." He goes on to specify the four stages of the mystic's progress as, (1) the punctual and conscientious discharge of his duties to society; (2) purification from all worldly and carnal lusts; (3) illumination; (4) a more immediate and ineffable vision of the Godhead (*Outspoken Essays*, I, pp. 230 f.).

It is probable that many more Christian people have mystical experiences than is commonly supposed, certainly such experiences have come to some of the least likely people. Bishop Moorhouse of Manchester was one of them. He describes himself as "a most sceptical person, not given to imagining things," yet amongst his papers after his death was found the description of an experience which came to him as a young man and was, in some sense, the controlling experience of his life. He had been going through a time of doubt and depression, and prayed earnestly one night for a sign of God's presence to encourage and guide him. "I awoke," he writes, "during that night filled with the most marvellous happiness

---

[1] Cf. her saying: "I would lose no sting, would wish no torture less"; *The Complete Poems of Emily Jane Brontë*. edited by Clement Shorter and C. W. Hatfield, p. 16.

in such a state of exultation that I felt as though a barrier had fallen, as though a door had suddenly been opened and a flood of golden light poured in upon me, transfiguring me completely. . . . I was filled with the sense of God's infinite love for all creatures and for myself; and not only that, but I felt so full of it myself I could have done anything . . . as an expression of my feelings. . . . People talk of the happiness of heaven; if such happiness as I felt can continue for ever it would indeed be bliss. I *was* in heaven. I felt so full of love to everybody that the words of the Sermon upon the Mount, 'Love your enemies, do good to them that hate you,' not only seemed *possible*, but they seemed the natural outcome of my state of mind. I have never experienced anything in the least like it; but the words of St. Paul were actually true, 'I live, yet not I, but Christ liveth in me.' I was possessed by the personality of Christ. . . . This state of mind continued about a fortnight. I could hardly go about my ordinary work, I felt so changed. I felt very much tempted to speak of it to somebody, but I never did. I *couldn't*. I said to myself, 'It is no doing of mine, if I speak of it I shall lose it.' " Bishop Moorhouse adds: "This is the foundation of my firm belief which underlies everything—belief in the infinite love of God to me and all creatures; and this has given me strength to stand up and fight battles for the truth."[1]

The Bishop's reserve is probably often imitated, and doubtless there are many recipients of such revelations, but a like delicacy of feeling, rightly or wrongly, restrains them from sharing their experiences with others. There certainly is grave danger of talking about them or of relying too much upon them. F. B. Meyer when once asked to repeat a description of an experience of his own, refused, saying, "You cannot live on an experience."

In the Moberly family such experiences seem almost to have been a regular thing and more than one member of the family

---

[1] Edith Rickards, *Bishop Moorhouse*, pp. 15 ff. Miss Rickards adds: "The narrative carries more weight, because though capable on rare occasions of strong emotion, he was not generally what would be called an emotional man, nor of easily excited imagination. His clear head, strong common sense, and perfect sincerity are vouchers for the truth of the account of the revelation which he declares had been granted him."

had them.[1] Perhaps the best known is that which has been enshrined in the small volume, *An Adventure*, first published anonymously in 1911, but now openly acknowledged as having come from Anne Moberly and Eleanor Jourdain, successive Principals of St. Hugh's Hall, Oxford.[2]

[1] See C. A. E. Moberly, *Dulce Domum*, pp. 71, 146, and 224 f.
[2] In the new edition (Faber & Faber, 1931), with a preface by Edith Olivier and a note by J. W. Dunne.

15

THE CAMBRIDGE SCHOOL

WHEN we speak of the Cambridge school, immediately our thoughts go to the three distinguished theologians who dominated the reign of Queen Victoria—Westcott (1825–1901), Lightfoot (1828–89), and Hort (1828–92). The position which they occupied, both at Cambridge itself and by their influence throughout the rest of the country, was unique. There was something almost romantic about them and their work; due perhaps to the close ties of personal friendship which held them together, due perhaps to the stories which grew up around them.

EARLY CAMBRIDGE THEOLOGIANS

But Cambridge theology did not begin with Westcott, Lightfoot, and Hort. Hort himself felt that "since the days of Fisher and Lady Margaret" it had reflected "in great measure the various movements within the Church of England" (*Life and Letters*, II, p. 430); whilst it is no difficult task to trace the succession to the Cambridge Platonists. "The chain is almost unbroken," wrote Inge, "from them to Coleridge, Wordsworth (especially in the *Prelude*), Erskine of Linlathen, and Westcott" (*Vale*, p. 46).[1] But men seem to have forgotten the Cambridge Platonists, in spite of the efforts of Dr. Inge himself and others to revive interest in them. And the Church has undoubtedly suffered for this neglect. Professor Pringle-Pattison once wrote to Hastings Rashdall: "The surprising thing is that in the great Church of England there is so little of the leaven of thinking Christianity. And it has so good a historical title to exist in the Anglican Church, with its Cambridge school of Christian Platonists and other groups."[2]

Coleridge undoubtedly exercised great influence on Cambridge in the early part of the century and his influence had a way of persisting. Of this we have odd traces; such as the

---

[1] Westcott was much interested in Benjamin Whichcote, on whom he wrote a paper republished in *Religious Thought in the West*.

[2] Quoted by Matheson, *Hastings Rashdall*, pp. 92 f.

notice by J. B. Mozley in February 1835 that "The Cambridge undergraduates have subscribed and made up a prize for the best account of Coleridge's system of Philosophy, open to the whole world" (*Letters*, p. 46). Hort, who was probably attracted by the combination of intellectual interest and spiritual earnestness (traits of Cambridge theology, by the way, at its best) to be found in Coleridge, contributed an essay on him to the *Cambridge Essays* of 1856.

Of theologians in a narrower sense there was no lack in the early years of the century. Herbert Marsh, Fellow of St. John's, Lady Margaret Professor, and Bishop in succession of Llandaff and Peterborough, is perhaps the most prominent. Marsh had been to Germany and at Göttingen had studied under Michaelis, whose works he brought to the notice of English readers. Then there was Thirlwall, who translated Schleiermacher's *Critical Essay* on St. Luke in 1825; and also Julius Hare, the teacher of F. D. Maurice, who, like Marsh, was in touch with German thought. Hunt says of him, that "as a theologian he strove to prevent the divorce of the spiritual from the intellectual, and to restore the true relation of the Tree of Knowledge to the Tree of Life" (*Religious Thought in England*, p. 186).

Coming down to the actual Victorian Era there was Alford, who ended his days as Dean of Canterbury. But though a deeply religious man, and not without insight, his work was hardly up to the standard which Cambridge demands from its sons. "Gwatkin used to say that when he began to take pupils he bought a copy of Alford to see where all their mistakes came from," Armitage Robinson tells us (in *Lightfoot of Durham*, p. 124). While Swete, with gentler kindness, expressed the hope, on the appointment of Alford to the Deanery of Canterbury, that greater leisure would enable him to give more care to his volumes (*Henry Barclay Swete*, p. 18). Of greater effectiveness was Ellicott, Lady Margaret Professor and then Bishop of Gloucester and Bristol. Mention must also be made of the famous pair, Conybeare and Howson.

THE TRIUMVIRATE

If we wish to discover the germ from which the Cambridge school really grew we shall probably find it in the class-room of Prince Lee, Headmaster of King Edward's School, Birmingham.[1] There Westcott, and, later, the two life-long friends, Lightfoot and Benson, gratefully accepted ideals of learning which in after life they were to realize. Prince Lee always insisted on exact scholarship, and attached great importance to the meaning of words as also to the significance of style. There can be no doubt that from him Westcott and Lightfoot gained their first love for research and in particular for the Greek Testament. The real triumvirate ought to have been Westcott, Lightfoot, and Benson. But the latter, although he remained in close touch with the other two Birmingham men, followed his own line—he even refused the chance of returning to Cambridge in 1875[2]—a line that led him in the end to the Primacy of the Church of England. It was, however, not at Birmingham but at Trinity that the link was forged which united them. The younger men were pupils of Westcott; and another pupil of his, Hort, who had come up from Rugby, there took the place which might have been Benson's. Thus Westcott was the uniting force behind the Cambridge school. Strangely enough he had at first thought of going to Exeter College, Oxford[3]—the college, incidentally, to which Maurice had gone on his decision to take Orders in 1830. It would be interesting to speculate on what might have been the future of the two Universities and of theology in England if Westcott had found himself in the home of Tractarianism in 1845. A subject of equal interest and mystery is provided by the fact that Newman nearly went to Cambridge.

Lightfoot

But if Westcott gave the impulse to the Cambridge school, as later he was to organize the harvesting, the middle period was dominated by Lightfoot. Westcott left Cambridge in 1852 for a mastership at Harrow, where he was to remain (with eyes often wistfully cast towards his old University) for eighteen

---

[1] His success as a headmaster was extraordinary. In a period of nine years on five occasions pupils of his were senior classics at Cambridge, and in the same period gained eight fellowships at Trinity.

[2] *Life and Letters of B. F. Westcott*, I, p. 386.

[3] *Op. cit.*, I, p. 31.

years. Lightfoot stayed on at Trinity. In 1861 he became Hulsean Professor, an appointment which Hort regarded as critical for Cambridge (*Life and Letters*, I, p. 448), and his lectures were attended by crowded audiences which included quite a number of senior men. In 1875 he took the Lady Margaret Professorship, having refused to be considered for the Regius in 1870 in order to allow Westcott's election, but he held it for a few years only as in 1879 he became Bishop of Durham. Although his episcopate was extraordinarily successful, especially when his lack of experience of practical work is considered, it will always be an open question whether it would not have been better for the Church and for religion in England if he had remained.[1] Dean Church in a letter to Benson written on January 23, 1879, after calling Lightfoot "the first scholar of England" goes on to affirm that "to be the foremost teacher of Christian learning at Cambridge at such a time as this is to hold a critical post, which is, in its way, alone and without its fellow, even in the highest places of the Church" (*Life and Letters*, p. 325). Although Lightfoot, by almost superhuman labours, did succeed in keeping up his scholarship, the amount which he produced was necessarily limited and his comparative silence was, as Dale said, an additional argument against episcopacy.

In spite of the long row of commentaries which stand to his name Lightfoot was not really a theologian, for he lacked those mystical and philosophical gifts which Westcott and Hort respectively possessed so abundantly.[2] In his commentary on *Galatians* he left the doctrinal questions on one side, intending, so Hort tells us (*Life and Letters*, II, p. 35), to discuss them in a commentary on *Romans* which was never written. The postponement was really typical and revealed his main interests. Such comments on doctrine as were included Hort found too "Protestant" and felt that Lightfoot had made no real attempt to fathom St. Paul's own mind (*op. cit*, II, p. 79).

---

[1] Westcott has told us that his leaving Cambridge was "a kind of martyrdom," but "when the change was once made, Cambridge was forgotten in the wider activities of Durham": Introduction to Lightfoot's *Historical Essays*, p. vii.

[2] See Armitage Robinson in *Lightfoot of Durham*, p. 127.

His considered conclusion was that Lightfoot was "not speculative enough or eager enough to be a leader of thought" and that his "mental interests lay almost exclusively in concrete facts or written words" (*op. cit.*, II, pp. 89 and 410). These criticisms are probably just, and Lightfoot must be judged primarily as a historian rather than as a theologian.[1] Harnack, in spite of his professed inability to understand the kind of picture which Lightfoot had made for himself of the sub-apostolic age, regarded him as "the most learned and the worthiest representative of the conservative critical school in England," and without any peer in the "conservative camp" in Germany for "range and accuracy of knowledge."[2]

Westcott

The appointment of Westcott as Regius Professor in 1870 was welcomed by Hort in a letter of prophetic insight to Maurice. "If Westcott has but life and strength given him, I cannot but think this will be the beginning of a new time for Cambridge" (*Life and Letters*, II, p. 143). He himself returned with unshaken faith in the possibilities of the work that lay before him, though he was a little disappointed in his failure to induce Maurice, then nearing the end of his long and strenuous life, to co-operate in arousing interest in social problems (*Life and Letters*, I, pp. 367 ff.).

The conjunctions of these two great names is an opportunity for investigating a matter which has often been misunderstood —the influence exercised by the older on the younger scholar whose ideas were so similar to his own. In an article contributed by Dean Moore Ede to *The Modern Churchman* (XXIII, pp. 527 ff.), he declares that Westcott himself specifically denied that there had been any such influence, and maintained that his own ideas had come to him quite independently. The matter is of sufficient interest and importance to quote the Dean's own account of what took place. "One evening when the Bishop was staying with me, as he often did, and we were chatting over the fire, I happened to say that I thought that the man who most profoundly influenced the thought of the Church

---

[1] See Headlam in *Lightfoot of Durham*, pp. 136 ff.
[2] *Theol. Literaturzeitung* (1890), coll. 297 ff.

of England was neither Keble, nor Newman, nor Pusey, but Frederick Denison Maurice. People did not realize this, because few of them read Maurice's writings, as he did not write in a popular style, but his ideas came to others through his disciples, such as Kingsley, and, I nearly added, yourself. To this Westcott replied, 'I am surprised at what you say, but perhaps I am not a fair judge; I never read Maurice.' 'What,' I exclaimed, 'you never read Maurice?' 'No,' said Westcott. 'I did read one thing he wrote,[1] and I purposely never read any more, for I felt that his way of thinking was so like my own that if I read much of Maurice I should endanger my originality.' 'Well,' I said, 'I think I ought to tell you the one complaint your friends make about you is that you never acknowledge your indebtedness to Maurice.' " Dr. Moore Ede then goes on to ask: "How can we account for the resemblance of the theological ideas of these two contemporaries? The reason is that they both of them drew their inspiration from St. John, both wrote commentaries on the Fourth Gospel, and under the influence of Johannine thought they both regarded the Incarnation as the central fact in the life of the world, the fact that the World, the Mind, and the Thought of God became flesh and tabernacled among us full of grace and truth."

[1] The "one thing" to which Westcott refers is no doubt Maurice's *Social Morality*, for in the Preface to his own *Social Aspects of Christianity* he writes: "Few books can teach nobler lessons, and I should feel it hard to say how much I owe to it directly and by suggestion." In 1892 he wrote to one of his daughters, calling it "one of my very few favourite books" (*Life and Letters*, II, p. 160). At the same time I think that Westcott's memory did not do full justice to the amount of Maurice's influence in his earlier life. In his diary for May 8, 1846, he refers to "Maurice's new lectures" (*op. cit.*, I, p. 224) and to his views on the Atonement (*op. cit.*, I, p. 229). In 1852 Hort wrote to him expressing his satisfaction that Westcott had bought *The Kingdom of Christ* (*Life and Letters of F. J. Hort*, I, p. 222); but we do not know whether the latter read it or not, for in July of that year he wrote: "at present Maurice is unread" (*Life and Letters*, I, p. 224). But if there had been a slightly greater perusal of the works of Maurice than the interview with Dr. Moore Ede would suggest, its substantial truth cannot be questioned. In fact Westcott was not fully aware until Maurice's *Life* was published how close was the affinity in their thoughts and ideas: see letter of March 1884 to Llewellyn Davies (*op. cit.*, II, p. 37).

Hort

We come now to the third member of the Triumvirate— F. J. A. Hort. Hort came, as we have seen, from Rugby where his youthful Evangelicalism had been considerably modified under the teaching of Arnold, and his successor Tait, the future Archbishop. After gaining a Fellowship at Trinity he followed the example of Westcott and "went down," taking a country living in 1857. This he held for fifteen years until he was recalled to Cambridge by the offer of a Fellowship at Emmanuel, a college originally intended by its founder for the especial cultivation of divinity. This appointment was a tardy recognition of the college's responsibilities in the matter. Later he became Hulsean Professor (1878) and finally, for the last five years of his life (1887-92), Lady Margaret Professor. As a scholar in the narrower sense, Hort was undoubtedly the greatest of the three; but his wide and deep learning was not so available, as a constitutional shyness not only prevented easy intercourse with younger men, but also made him loth to put his thoughts into a printed form. During his lifetime but little was published, though some fourteen volumes, made up from his remains, supplemented by the notebooks of his pupils, have since appeared. His most important published work was *The Way, the Truth, the Life*, the Hulsean Lectures for 1871-2 in which many deep and suggestive thoughts are hinted at rather than fully developed. In Cambridge his learning became a legend and himself almost a "cult" (*Life and Letters*, II, p. 368).

The appointment of Westcott to succeed his younger contemporary Lightfoot, as Bishop of Durham, in 1890, was virtually the end of the regime of the Triumvirate in Cambridge, for Hort's health was so poor that his work was never fully resumed. The departure of Westcott removed a dominant personality, and though he left behind him pupils who carried on his work, they could not attain to the same high level. The combination of spiritual and intellectual insight which Westcott had possessed appears only at long intervals, and to say that his successors fell short of it is not really to disparage them. They themselves were all too fully aware of their shortcomings, and perhaps a little glad of their freedom; for though there had been no "dragooning" the presence of such outstanding figures had been a little oppressive. "We grew up under Westcott and Hort like plants under a cedar tree"— said one Cambridge professor.[1] Here the fundamental weakness of the Triumvirate is exposed. They had worked together so long in conscious co-operation that they had been prevented from keeping in sufficiently close touch with younger men. Though always willing to give advice when consulted they did not go out of their way to set their pupils to work. Hort, with his sublime humility, was actually afraid of exercising influence on his juniors and his shyness proved a barrier which was hard to surmount.

Swete

Westcott's successor as Regius Professor was H. B. Swete. His appointment came as a great surprise, for he had not been a success as a college don (*Henry Barclay Swete*, pp. 31 f., 37), and it aroused considerable misgiving. Swete himself had not sought election and yielded only to the pressure of his friends. Their action was fully justified, and Bishop Chase could say of him: "his professorship stands out as a great professorship, justly memorable, and fruitful of the highest good; and he himself gradually gained an almost unique influence over the undergraduates who crowded his lecture-room, and over a very wide circle of students of theology" (*op. cit.*, p. 57). Swete had the faculty which was denied to his greater predecessors of training younger men by finding "big books" upon which they might prove their metal;[2] he was, indeed, ever on the look-out for work to be done and for the men to do it. His own actual contribution to theological learning was very considerable and has been well assessed by Dr. Bethune-Baker (*op. cit.*, pp. 91 ff.); whilst the bulk of matter published and edited by him can be seen from the Bibliography, prepared by Dr. C. H. Turner for the *Journal of Theological Studies*, and since reprinted (*op. cit.*, pp. 163–92).

[1] Quoted by Armitage Robinson, *Lightfoot of Durham*, p. 135.
[2] The present writer can bear his testimony to this faculty, for he was not yet an M.A. when Dr. Swete suggested to him that it was time he was settling to some big task. Eventually he arranged with Dr. Lock for him to edit "Jeremiah" in the Westminster Commentaries.

THE CHARACTERISTICS OF THE CAMBRIDGE SCHOOL

The Cambridge school was hardly a school in the strict sense of the word, that is in the sense of being a definite body propagating a set of doctrines—that would have been alien to the independent Cambridge mind—rather was it a number of scholars who approached theological problems from a similar angle and sought their solution by the application of similar methods. It is true that certain common influences had moulded most of them and certain common beliefs inspired them; but that was not the sole factor which united them. The following seem to me to have been outstanding characteristics.

(a) Historical Outlook

When Creighton gave his inaugural lecture as Dixie Professor of Ecclesiastical History he made special reference to the work of the Cambridge school of theologians in leavening theological learning with the historic spirit and at the same time allowing history its own special field. "Theology," he said, "has become historical, and does not demand that history should become theological."[1] This historical point of view was characteristic of them all; the great exception being Maurice, to whom they owed so much in other ways. Maurice certainly was weak on the historical side; to him the "idea" was more than the "fact," and he has even been accused, though quite unwarrantably, of minimizing the historical figure of our Lord.[2] The importance of this approach to theological questions is manifestly great and it enabled them to study the documents of early Christianity, not in isolation, but against the background of the contemporary world of thought and of action.

(b) Recognition of the Value of Greek Theology

We have seen already that much of the similarity in the teaching of Maurice and Westcott was due to their common interest in Greek theology. It was well for Theological thought in England that this was so; for one of the great weaknesses of the Oxford Movement had been its strange neglect of this side of tradition. Hort, after pointing out the significance of

---

[1] *Historical Lectures and Addresses*, p. 2.
[2] See his own clear statement in *Theological Essays*, p. 128.

their neglect, went on to assess the place of Greek Theology in the thought of the great English divines of the century between 1550 and 1650. He saw in it the source of their "largeness of mind" (*Life and Letters*, II, p. 38). One consequence of this renewed interest in Greek theology was a shifting of emphasis from the Atonement to the Incarnation as the most important aspect of our Lord's life and work.

(*c*) *Conception of Revelation*

In view of the tendency of modern criticism to identify Revelation and Discovery, it will be well to make it clear that the Cambridge school, whatever its present-day successors may hold, was quite emphatic on the "givenness" of Christianity. It was not merely the fruit of man's discovery. Inspiration was, in Westcott's own words, "partly the insight of holiness and partly its divine reward." Whilst Hort pointed out that man's search had to precede the answer of God (*The Way, the Truth, the Life*, p. 1). Thus both parts of Revelation were safeguarded; the "initiative of the eternal," as A. E. Taylor has called it, and the effort of man himself to find out God. The divine and the human sides, as in the doctrine of the Incarnation, both need recognition, and the antithesis between them must not be made too sharp, for God is not only the object of our seeking, but is Himself present in those who seek. He is the Way as well as the Goal which crowns the journey.

(*d*) *Practical View of Religion*

The Cambridge school did not believe in learning for its own sake, and would never have merited the condemnation which W. B. Yeats passed on one of his friends that he "loved his learning more than mankind." Their studies were illuminated by a knowledge of life as it was lived around them, and from their studies they gained a practical sagacity which shewed itself in the discharge of responsibilities in high stations of the Church. It was remarkable that three successive Bishops of Durham—Lightfoot, Westcott, and Moule—had been Cambridge Professors. The practical outlook of the Cambridge school is well seen in the sermon which Hort preached on the consecration of Westcott. Its theme was the application of St. Paul's teaching in the Epistle to the Ephesians to the needs of the modern world—a plea for a new and more complete realization of the meaning of membership in the Church. Of Hort himself, at first sight not a very "practical" person, it has been said: "His theology has a quality too often wanting in the systems of learned men; it is in touch with the world of men, as well as the world of books" (quoted *Life and Letters*, II, p. 373). To the two great problems which confronted the Church in their day—the Social Problem at home and the Expansion of Christianity abroad—the learning of Cambridge attempted to rise. Kingsley found in the Old Testament prophets clues to the Church's attitude in the one case: in the other Westcott helped to found the Cambridge Mission to Delhi and gave his sons to India.

(e) Churchmanship

All the members of the Cambridge school were Churchmen, and convinced Churchmen. In origin they were Evangelicals; but all of them found that school of thought too narrow. As early as 1846 Westcott noted in his journal that the undue exaltation of the minister to which Evangelicalism, as he knew it, tended, was a proof of its insufficiency (*Life and Letters*, I, pp. 44 f.). Whilst Hort, who moved further away still, regarded it as "sectarian" (*Life and Letters*, I, p. 41), unphilosophic (*op. cit.*, I, p. 61) and not sufficiently Catholic (*op. cit.*, I, p. 75). He even felt the Roman Catholic view of Baptism more true than the Evangelical (*op. cit.*, I, p. 76). Later he came to regard "The positive doctrines of the Evangelicals" as "perverted rather than untrue" (*op. cit.*, I, p. 400). As it is not generally realized that Hort stood apart from Westcott and Lightfoot in the matter of Churchmanship—being much nearer to Benson—it may be well to illustrate his position. He wrote in 1858: "I have a deeply rooted agreement with High Churchmen as to the church, ministry and Sacraments" (*op. cit.*, I, p. 400); whilst a little later he shocked his two colleagues by expressing his belief that "Protestantism" was only "parenthetical and temporary" (*op. cit.*, II, p. 31). When Lightfoot's *Christian Ministry* appeared, he could only regretfully accept their different standpoints: "I wish," he wrote, "we were more agreed in the doctrinal part; but you know I am a staunch sacerdotalist, and there is not much profit in arguing about first principles" (*op. cit.*, II, p. 86). In accepting the universal priesthood of all Christians, he also demanded the "representative priesthood of the apostolic ministry, without which the idea of any priesthood vanishes into empty metaphor" (*op. cit.*, II, p. 158). In view of these quotations, and they could be multiplied, it is a little strange to find a Nonconformist writer saying that "Dr. Hort surprised Free Churchmen by proving to them their own principles."[1] I think that the surprise would have been mutual.

But it was not only Hort's position which was misunderstood by Nonconformists, but Lightfoot's as well. We saw above that Harnack confessed his inability to make out what Lightfoot made of the sub-apostolic age; Protestants in England were equally at a loss, to judge from their notion of the practical consequences which they hoped would come of it. They were disappointed and hurt at the refusal of the broad-minded Cambridge bishops to take part in distinctively Nonconformist functions. One who was especially disappointed was W. F. Moulton, between whom and Westcott and Lightfoot a close alliance of scholarship had long existed. To him Lightfoot wrote: "Between yourselves and ourselves there is, so far as I know, only the question of Church order which keeps us apart, and yet even I, whose views are supposed to be very broad on this point, could not see my way to waiving this for the sake of reunion" (quoted in *W. F. Moulton*, p. 267).

METHODS

A little may now be said of the methods which distinguished the Cambridge school. The first task upon which they insisted was the fixing of the text of any Documents upon which they had to work—were they the New Testament writings, the Septuagint, or the Apostolic Fathers. This followed from their belief in the value of language. Then all external evidence had to be amassed—this, of course, followed from their belief in the value of history. For this, immense industry and wide

[1] Silvester Horne, *Nonconformity in the Nineteenth Century*, pp. 127 f.

learning were required, and so high was the standard set for example, by Hort, that he refused ever to publish anything; since he was never satisfied that he had all the necessary data at his disposal. To the text thus ascertained and placed in its proper historical setting there was applied a judgement which was at once balanced and enlightened. The Cambridge scholars would accept no easy conclusions or facile conjectures. All had to be worked out in the sweat of the brow; the true grain of established results separated from the chaff of mere speculation. Here their practical good sense and Churchmanship was of value; for it kept them in touch with the real world which is so different from the imaginary world of the lecture room and the study, and made them value the traditions of the past and the fruit of the long experience of the Christian society. Above all they believed in the Apostolic maxim that spiritual things are spiritually discerned. "The only way to know the Greek Testament properly," said Lightfoot, "is by prayer" (quoted in *Lightfoot of Durham*, p. 14 n.). Perhaps the very different results obtained by some modern scholars, who claim to follow the methods and to be the disciples of the Cambridge leaders, are due to the forgetfulness of this, the most fundamental of those methods.

THE LIMITATIONS OF THE CAMBRIDGE SCHOOL

The limitations of the Cambridge school may be considered under four headings: they were (*a*) too Classical: (*b*) too Conservative: (*c*) apt to lose themselves in details: (*d*) lacking in philosophical and theological sympathies. About each of these something more may be said.

(*a*) *Too Classical*

When Westcott and his fellows were at school their training was predominantly classical and their knowledge of Greek was that of the best age of the language. The day of papyri had not yet come in. So in attempting to discover the exact force of words or of grammatical usages in the New Testament they turned instinctively to classical authors. Westcott never recovered from the sixteen years during which he taught Greek prose to Harrow boys; otherwise he would hardly "have been so insistent in pursuing the ghost of a purposive force in ἵνα throughout the Fourth Gospel."[1] Lightfoot in his later days, when papyri and collections of non-classical inscriptions were being made available, took some interest in them. Whilst still at Cambridge he had made a forecast of the effect of such discoveries which reveals his extraordinary insight; for in a lecture delivered in 1863, referring to some New Testament word which occurred elsewhere only in Herodotus, he said: "You are not to suppose that this word ... had fallen out of use in the interval, only that it had not been used in the books that remain to us: probably it had been part of the common speech all along. I will go further, and say that if we could only recover letters that ordinary people wrote to each other without any thought of being literary, we should have the greatest possible help for the understanding of the language of the New Testament generally."[2] This forecast is, as I say, a piece of extraordinary foresight; but unfortunately such materials were not sufficiently available, and too great a reliance on classical meanings and classical usages has taken from the value of the work of the Cambridge scholars. Even in Swete's *Apocalypse*, published in 1906, there is the same fault, as Sanday pointed out in his review in the *Journal of Theological Studies*, VIII, p. 483. Under this heading it is appropriate to point out that the Triumvirate, except Lightfoot, had no sufficient knowledge of Semitic languages. Neither Westcott nor Hort had much more than a good working knowledge of Hebrew; whilst the former's account of the Peshitta (Syriac) version in his *Canon of the New Testament* is lamentably misleading.

(b) *Too Conservative*

This aspect of the Cambridge school was well brought out in a paper on "Edwin Hatch" delivered at a Conference of Modern Churchmen by the late Professor Sanday.[3] Sanday regarded Hatch as "bolder and more disinterested than even

---

[1] J. H. Moulton in *Cambridge Biblical Essays*, p. 499.
[2] Quoted by Milligan, *Selections from the Greek Papyri*, p. xx.
[3] Published in *The Modern Churchman*, X, pp. 378 ff.

the great Cambridge trio. . . . Not one of the three, not even Hort—unless it was in unpublished work—can be said to have really launched out into the deep. Would it be very wicked if I were to say that Westcott dabbled in fundamentals? I must confess that . . . I used to find that the most irritating thing about him was his incurable optimism. Everything seemed to work out just as he wished. But the way in which all this came out so neatly was just by means of little ingenuities and not by any broad scientific grasp. . . . The *Introduction to the Study of the Gospels* is, I am afraid, a very poor book; and the words that I have just used seem to me to describe it. It is only fair to add that *The Gospel of the Resurrection* is distinctly better. . . . Lightfoot was honest as the day; but he carefully, and even scrupulously, abstained from what I have called 'dabbling in fundamentals.' We remember that Hort said of him that his masculine good sense was 'unaccompanied by either the insight or the delusion of subtlety.' Hort himself knew only too well these temptations and dangers, and he was at bottom a daring thinker." It was not, however, only in "fundamentals" that Conservatism was shewn. In matters of less vital significance they clung to traditional beliefs. Lightfoot held the "North Galatian" theory; both he and Westcott accepted the Johannine authorship of the Fourth Gospel (for which I still feel there is much more to be said than many modern critics allow); Hort held that both the Apocalypse and the Gospel were by John, who was exiled, so he concluded, not under Domitian, but under Nero (see *Apocalypse*, I–III, pp. xi ff.: so also Lightfoot, *Philippians*, p. 200); whilst Swete's *St. Mark*, published in 1898, practically ignores the Synoptic Problem.

Their followers, it need hardly be said, were much more drastic in applying what they believed to be the same methods. One of the most distinguished of them has allowed us to know his own feeling in the matter. He tells us that he regarded Westcott as "incomparably the most revered and inspiring teacher I have ever known; one to whom I thankfully trace back many a principle of study and thought which has had developments and growths that it would not have had perhaps with him, yet which I am fain to believe he would not have deemed illegitimate divergences from the main line of his own convictions."[1]

(c) Too much Absorbed in Details

The attention which scholars of the Cambridge school paid to the exact force of language and style had its dangers; for they tended to become too much absorbed in such details to the neglect of wider interests.[2] When Handley Moule was appointed Norrisian Professor of Divinity in 1899, as successor to Armitage Robinson, he announced his intention of treating "books of Holy Scripture in such a way as to bring out the drift and purpose of the whole document and of its several parts, as living utterances bearing upon living problems." This proposal was welcomed by many and Professor Gwatkin wrote: "Thanks for the Inaugural. It is the right note, and I am further glad of it, because I think our Cambridge school is getting too much absorbed in prolegomena and literary details and needs a call to higher and wider things, which it is in some danger of leaving undone."[3]

(d) Lack of Philosophical and Theological Sympathies

It would be true to say that the main strength of the school lay in its historical and exegetical achievement rather than in its theological or philosophical discoveries. In those who may be called the pioneers, Coleridge and Maurice, these interests were strong, but of the Triumvirate Hort alone was a great or deep thinker. Lightfoot, in some ways the greatest of the three, was primarily, as we have seen, a historian and his treatment of doctrine or theology subordinate to his historical interest.

[1] J. F. Bethune-Baker in *Henry Barclay Swete*, pp. 91 f.

[2] One is reminded of Ruskin's paradox, "the study of anatomy is destructive to art" (see *The Eagle's Nest*, p. v); because the artist is apt to be overcome in "the ghastly toil of bone-delineation" (*op. cit.*, p. vii).

[3] Harford and Macdonald, *Bishop Handley Moule*, pp. 152 ff. Gwatkin himself did something to counteract this tendency by delivering "amazingly suggestive Greek Testament readings," as Bishop Woods has called them (*Theodore, Bishop of Winchester*, p. 32), and as the present writer can also testify.

ACHIEVEMENT

In addition to a number of volumes of Sermons and Addresses the Cambridge school is notable for contributions to (*a*) the Exegesis and (*b*) the Textual Criticism of the New Testament; and, in addition, for bringing fresh light to bear on (*c*) the history of the Early Church.

(*a*) In 1854 Daniel Macmillan, the publisher, suggested to the three friends that they should undertake a Commentary on the whole of the New Testament. Westcott and Hort were to revise the Text, Lightfoot was to compile a Grammar and Lexicon, and Westcott was to do the more strictly exegetical part of the joint venture.[1] In 1860 the Commentary was assigned to the different members of the partnership as follows: Lightfoot, the Pauline Epistles and Hebrews; Westcott, the Johannine writings; Hort, the Synoptic Gospels, Acts, and the remaining General Epistles.[2] A great part of this programme was actually carried out. Lightfoot produced Galatians, Colossians, and Philemon, Philippians, and a volume of *Notes* on 1 and 2 Thessalonians, with portions of other Epistles. Westcott did St. John's Gospel and Epistles; but the Apocalypse was done by Benson, who had no part in the original scheme. Hort's contribution was but meagre in the end, and posthumous, consisting of four slim volumes, Apocalypse i–iii, 1 Peter i–ii. 17, James, and Introduction to Romans and Ephesians.

(*b*) The achievement in the matter of Textual Criticism was even more epoch-making. The whole subject was built up from the foundations, and on a truly magnificent scale.[3] In the original plan a mere few years had been set apart for its accomplishment; in the end it was not until 1881 that the new text and the accompanying introduction and appendix saw the light. At the time it was attacked fiercely by Dean Burgon and others, but their criticisms are now forgotten. The

---
[1] See *Life and Letters of Hort*, I, pp. 240 f.
[2] *Op. cit.*, I, pp. 417 f.
[3] Until the nineteenth century the Textual Criticism of the New Testament was almost an English monopoly—one recalls the names of Walton, Fell, Mill, and Bentley. For an appreciation of the work of Westcott and Hort see Kenyon, *The Textual Criticism of the New Testament*, pp. 274 ff.

THE CAMBRIDGE SCHOOL

discovery of fresh material and further work has no doubt made some modifications necessary, but on the whole the work of Westcott and Hort has stood the test of time, and remains a permanent contribution to the subject which stands almost unrivalled. Alongside the New Testament text there was begun, at Hort's suggestion, the shorter edition of the Septuagint by Swete. This appeared in three volumes between 1887 and 1894. It was a useful forerunner of the great Cambridge edition edited by Brooke and McLean now in course of publication.

(c) In Early Church history the supreme accomplishment was, of course, Lightfoot's edition of the *Apostolic Fathers*. This was hailed by Harnack as the greatest patristic monograph of the century, and it did much to make firm the ground beneath the shifting sands of the sub-Apostolic age. In addition there were Hort's *Christian Ecclesia* and Benson's *Cyprian*, as well as the numerous articles in Smith and Wace's Dictionaries for which the friends were responsible.

INFLUENCE

In addition to its achievement in the realm of scholarship, the Cambridge school exercised a profound influence on Religion in the Victorian Era; this was effected not through the Triumvirate, but through Coleridge and Maurice. The extent to which their influence spread is difficult to gauge; but it can be traced sometimes in unexpected places. Church, for example, in the period between his early Evangelicalism and the coming of Newman, wrote: "There is something in Maurice and his master Coleridge, which wakens thought in me more than any other writings almost" (*Life and Letters*, p. 17). Whilst the respect which Maurice aroused received testimony, after his death, from Mr. Gladstone (by no means a sympathizer with his views as a whole): "who applied to him Dante's description of St. Dominic, as a spiritual splendour" (Morley, *Life of W. E. Gladstone*, I, p. 338). Maurice was also in some sense one of the forces which inspired the "Forward" Movement among the Methodists in the last quarter of the century (*Hugh Price Hughes*, p. 166). The extent of his influence has not always been recognized owing to the supposed obscurity of his style.[1] It was exercised for the most part through the teaching of those whom he had influenced; in certain directions by Kingsley and Hort (the latter had been greatly helped by him), and also in Social Work by Westcott. To Stewart Headlam the one thing which had made Cambridge a power in his life was Maurice. He it was who relieved him of a nightmare and opened up to his ardent soul a new world of service.[2] It was Westcott who influenced Gore, when a school-boy at Harrow; as he also influenced H. F. Pelham, the Camden Professor of Ancient History at Oxford, and by his example gave him a new and "lofty conception of the duties and responsibilities of the scholar."[3] But the Triumvirate themselves made their effect felt in other regions than mere scholarship, though some of those who were influenced by them did not exactly adopt their type of Churchmanship, but advanced further even than Hort in a Catholic direction. Such were Swete, Armitage Robinson, and A. J. Mason. But in another direction also their power was felt. This can be seen in a letter which Dale wrote to Westcott in May 1883. "You may not be much in the way of hearing with what affection and honour you are regarded by Nonconformists. . . . Forgive me for saying—do not let them make you a bishop. I do not know what Dr. Lightfoot may have done for Durham; for those of us who are outside he has done nothing since his elevation."[4]

These are but a few almost haphazard references to the men and movements who came under the attraction of the Cambridge school. The full extent of its influence can be known to God alone, who inspired and directed it—so we believe. But something more can be learned by reading the ample and adequate biographies which have been written round the leading figures, and by recalling the enormous circulations which were gained by their writings.

[1] Yet Martineau could say: "for consistency of thought, and precision in the use of language, it would be difficult to find his superior among living theologians" (*Essays, Reviews, and Addresses*, I, p. 258).
[2] F. G. Bettany, *Stewart Headlam*, pp. 19 f., and 22.
[3] Jackson, *Ingram Bywater*, p. 43.
[4] A. W. W. Dale, *R. W. Dale*, pp. 524 f. See also *Hugh Price Hughes*, p. 476.

16

EDUCATION FROM 1843

IN his Funeral Oration on the dead William IV Sydney Smith had declared that the most pressing task of his successor was the educating of her people. In the early years of the reign but feeble progress was discernible in this most pressing field of demanded activity. Macaulay in a speech on education delivered in 1847 stated that of 130,000 couples married in 1844 a third of the bridegrooms and nearly half of their ladies were unable to sign their names (*Speeches on Politics, etc.*, p. 359). But even then there was no public demand for education. Many regarded it as a fad of the Prince Consort's; "fit perhaps for industrious foreigners in Central Europe who had not our other advantages of character and world position."[1] The business men of the North, for the most part "self-made," could hardly be expected to rate at a high figure advantages without which they themselves had achieved fortune and power. It must be said, however, that some of them realized the value of what they had missed, and recognized that there were other things in life besides the mere ability to amass wealth.

THE COMING OF A NATIONAL SYSTEM

One body there was which pressed for an educated people and did all it could to bring it about—the clergy of the Church of England. Before the Reformation, so Frederick Temple claimed, the Church treated the laity as mere children; the Church now regarded them as men, with responsibilities of their own (*Frederick Temple*, I, pp. 330 f.). Much of the self-denying labour on the part of the clergy in both town and country, and especially in the latter, was simply taken for granted by their parishioners and no gratitude expressed or felt.[2] But there were those who had positions which enabled them to assess such contributions and they have given their

[1] G. M. Trevelyan, *History of England*, p. 648.
[2] See Hughes, *James Fraser, Second Bishop of Manchester*, p. 142.

testimony to the value of the Church's work. Matthew Arnold, who as an official of the Board of Education had opportunities of judging in this matter, gave his opinion that "if there is a class in English society whose record in regard to popular education is honourable, it is the clergy. Every enquiry has brought this out."[1] But the task was proving too great for the Church to undertake; it had shewn the way, it was now the duty of the whole community, through Parliament, to undertake a complete system of national education in which the Church should have its place.

The grants under the Act of 1839, although they greatly increased the number of schools for children being educated, did not prove really adequate to meet the situation in either quantity or quality. In order to improve the quality of the teaching, Robert Lowe began the method of payment by results. This was unfortunate for it encouraged "cramming" and as no count was taken of religious knowledge the Church was opposed to the system and its sponsor. In the end Lowe had to resign.

The first real attempt at a national system was that contained in the Education Bill of 1870. This endeavoured to put a school within the reach of every child at a low cost. The leaving age was to be ten. Further modifications were made by the Act of 1876 which introduced the idea of Compulsory Education, and that of 1893 which made it free. The remaining modifications during the reign were concerned with the progressive increase of the school-leaving age, to eleven in 1893, to twelve in 1899, and to thirteen in 1900.

The Education Bill of 1870 was the work of William Forster, a Quaker. But he had married Jane Arnold, the daughter of Arnold of Rugby, and it is probable that some of the ideas of that great schoolmaster went to the making of the Bill.[2] The Bill caused great difficulties to the Nonconformists because it recognized and subsidized Denominational religious teach-

[1] In *The Reign of Queen Victoria*, II, p. 264.
[2] Such was the opinion of Mrs. Humphry Ward, who was the niece of Mrs. Forster: "It has always been clear to me that the scheme of the Bill was largely influenced by William Forster's wife, and through her, by the convictions and beliefs of her father." *A Writer's Recollections*, p. 35.

ing.[1] In spite of their opposition Forster determined to persevere, for he saw that the only alternative was to leave religion outside the educational scheme; this was equivalent to declaring that in the eyes of the State it was a thing of no account.[2] In the end the Bill, which was supported by Mr. Gladstone, became law. It had as a safeguard what was known as a Conscience clause, to which the name of Cowper-Temple was attached. Such a clause had been first suggested by the Education Department in 1853, but owing to Church opposition it had then been dropped. It was, however, enforced in 1864 and the new clause was intended to make it still more effective. By it "no catechism or religious formulary distinctive of any particular denomination" was to be taught in provided schools.[3]

COMPULSORY EDUCATION

The idea of Compulsory Education was not novel for it had been suggested by Adam Smith (*Wealth of Nations*, Bk. V, ch. i). None the less, it proved distasteful to many Englishmen; as did indeed the whole idea of additional government action. Even when the police were first instituted by Sir Robert Peel in 1829 they were regarded as an intolerable interference with the liberty of the subject, and one likely to have deplorable consequences. But it was the Nonconformists who were especially alarmed at the notion of Compulsion being applied to education; in fact it seemed to them almost as disastrous as government interference in religion.[4] The clause in the Act of 1876 by which Compulsion was first applied was itself optional in the sense that it was enforced only in such areas as chose to adopt the special bye-laws. None the less, it formed

---

[1] Clause 25, which allowed School Boards to pay for poor children in Church Schools, was an especial stumbling-block.
[2] See *Life of William Forster*, I, p. 407.
[3] Elementary Education Act, 32 and 33 Vict., clause 14.
[4] Herbert Spencer also objected to government interference in education, but Dale was in favour of it (see *R. W. Dale*, pp. 267 ff.). So far as I know there was at this stage no realization of the fact that Compulsory Education gives the State the opportunity of controlling in the long run the minds of its members. It is thus a step towards the methods of Fascism or Communism.

a dangerous precedent, since it was recognized, and justly, as the future was to shew, as a step to complete Compulsion. But Compulsory Education was the logical sequel to the Reform Act of 1867 which gave votes to working men. The country dared not hand over power to an uneducated proletariat. "We must educate our masters," as Robert Lowe said.[1] The same course, adopted for the identical reason, was followed about this time in both France and Italy. There was no other choice.

The obvious sequel to Compulsory Education is Free Education and this was introduced by the Act of 1891 which made a new grant of 10s. per head. Incidentally this grant was a great boon to Roman Catholic schools and the passing of the Act was regarded by A. W. Hutton as a triumph for "clerically controlled education."[2]

NONCONFORMITY AND EDUCATION

The disputes which arose over Religious Education were bad for both Education and Religion; but it has to be admitted that there were real grievances under which Nonconformity suffered, especially in areas where there was only a Church school. Furthermore, the Act of 1870 went against their principles by making grants of public money without public control, and even the conscience clause was held to be inadequate. The passing of the Act was a signal for a fresh attack on the Church and a demand for its Disestablishment and Disendowment. This was natural; but it gives support to the opinion of an unprejudiced observer that the whole outcry over education was inspired by religious rancour. "At bottom the battle of the schools," wrote Lord Morley, "was not educational, it was social, and quarrels about education and catechism and conscience masked the standing jealousy between church and chapel—the unwholesome fruit of the historical mishaps of the sixteenth and seventeenth centuries that separated the nation into two camps, and invested one of them with all the pomp and privilege of social ascendency.

[1] Tennyson put the thing in a nutshell: "No education, no franchise." *Alfred, Lord Tennyson*, II, p. 108.
[2] *Cardinal Manning*, p. 170.

The parent and child, in whose name the struggle raged, stood indifferent" (*Life of W. E. Gladstone*, II, pp. 306 f.). Certainly Mr. Gladstone was exceedingly annoyed with his Nonconformist allies. They seemed to assume that he ought to have sacrificed what he considered to be the welfare of the country in order to obtain their support (*op. cit.*, II, pp. 304 f.).

There is probably a good deal of truth in these judgements, and a recent learned Nonconformist historian has confessed that in the dispute over Religious Education the Nonconformist attitude was far from dignified. "To protest and protest, but never to produce any alternative policy for which any sacrifice was made, and after abundant words of defiance to submit."[1] The real difficulty was that the Nonconformists were themselves divided, and so no entirely consistent or continuous policy could be adopted. Some wished to have the Voluntary System maintained, others favoured a State System, and even purely secular education.

Those who supported the Voluntary System did so because of their fear of endowing a form of religious education which was distasteful to them. These were forced in the end to see that the Voluntary System was inadequate. The lack of experience on the part of the teachers, the absence of regular inspection, and the difficulty of raising funds; all these were against it. In November 1867 a meeting of Congregationalists, the Denomination which had been the most determined in resisting government grants, passed a resolution in their favour, with the proviso that there should always be a conscience clause.[2]

The younger men, such as Dale, were for an out-and-out State System. The National Education League, founded at Birmingham in 1869, of which Bright and Joseph Chamberlain were prominent leaders, had this as its end. Religion was to be excluded from the schools. Dale himself had no "use" for undenominational religion, and although at one time he would have allowed the Bible to be used, it was to be read not as a religious book, but as an English classic.[3] But this point of

[1] Whitley, *History of British Baptists*, pp. 289 f.
[2] A. W. Peel, *These Hundred Years*, p. 184.
[3] See A. W. W. Dale, *R. W. Dale*, pp. 478 f., 583.

view was not acceptable to many Nonconformist leaders. Paton was anxious that some common form of Christianity might be discovered on which all could agree; for he saw that to look to the home as a training ground in religious education was no longer possible (*Life*, pp. 145 ff.). Another great Nonconformist leader, Hugh Price Hughes, rather than admit the solution of a purely secular system was willing even to accept the Anglican monopoly. He once said to Dr. (later Sir Henry) Lunn: "If men of our thinking begin to care more for wretched party and sectarian issues than for the whole Church of Christ and the teaching of the Christian religion in our schools, we must go over in this matter to those who do care, however much we may disagree with them on other issues" (*Life*, p. 495: cf. pp. 505 f.). This was a big sacrifice to contemplate; but perhaps it was justified, for as Creighton used to say, to belittle religious education is to drop out the one thing which answers the child's question "Why should I learn at all?" (*Life and Letters*, II, p. 249). It must be remembered that the mere acquirement of knowledge is not necessarily a good thing in itself, and any system of education which fails to train character will produce a race of superficial people—without any power of judgement and a prey to every skilful agitator.

The struggles over the Education Bills did shew one thing very clearly—that if the people of England differed over matters of religion, they were exceedingly anxious that some form of religious teaching should be included in the education provided by the State for their children.

SECONDARY EDUCATION

Thus steps were taken during the Victorian Era to make Elementary Education more efficient and widespread and at the same time, in spite of grave difficulties, to preserve its religious character. Secondary Education, however, was allowed to remain in that state, verging on chaos, in which the opening years of the reign had found it. A Commission to enquire into the subject in 1867 reported that there were few secondary schools that were really efficient and that many parents who desired to obtain such an education for their children were quite unable to do so, as no suitable schools were within their reach. The Endowed Schools Act of 1869 provided for the rearrangement of educational trusts by a special Commission which after being absorbed by the Charity Commission has had its duties handed over to the Board of Education. After the passing of the Reform Act in 1867 all grammar schools were opened to Dissenters, with a conscience clause, and all endowed schools, unless the trust deed stood in the way, were freed from religious restrictions.

The Nonconformists were, in the meantime, making fresh provision for their own children. This was an important piece of work from their point of view since the growth of wealth among them made secondary education well within the means of many of them; to send them to the public schools often meant that they were lost to Nonconformity. So alongside Mill Hill there was founded a public school intended mainly for Methodists, the well-known Leys School.[1] A further step was taken in May 1891 when a Council was established, of which Fairbairn was a prominent member, to endeavour to get religious equality in the public schools, or even to establish Nonconformist hostels in connexion with them.

The defective Secondary Education in England was a serious matter, for it meant that the middle classes who formed "the backbone" of the country, especially at this epoch, were not receiving a training adequate to their responsibilities and their opportunities. In local government, in trade and commerce, and in education itself leadership had to be undertaken by those who were not fully competent because they had missed the appropriate training in their youth. The defect was not merely educational in the narrow sense, for the character, as well as the mind, was robbed of formative influences.

The children of the upper and upper middle-classes went, as before, to the great public schools of the land. And there they received a training which tended to produce a certain "type," rather than to cultivate the mental powers. J. H. Skrine, himself a public schoolmaster, once wrote: "A chivalrous boy from an English Public School is one of the

[1] See W. Fiddian Moulton, *William F. Moulton*, pp. 112 ff.

beautiful things in God's world of men."[1] But already questions were being formulated as to whether it was good to take boys so completely and so early out of their homes. Bishop Percival, himself an outstanding headmaster, declared that "his experience at Clifton led him to the conclusion that the best education in English life was not to be had in a boarding school, but was obtained by the boy who lived in a good home and attended a good school near his home" (*Life*, p. 37). The religious influence in these schools varied enormously. In an interesting note Scott Holland said of his Eton days: "the only stable religious result that I carried away with me from school came entirely from what I should call the denominational side. The shadowy teaching of the sermons ran off me, like water off a duck's back" (*Life*, p. 15). Probably the chief difference lay in the use that was made of the opportunity of preparing boys for Confirmation.

In 1868 there was a small measure of government "interference" in the public schools; seven of the leading schools, in consequence of the report of a Commission, were given power to alter their constitutions and to establish new governing bodies. Such freedom to change was all to the good, for the real weakness of the public school was that it had fallen far behind the needs of the times, and by concentrating too exclusively on the classics as a medium of education for all and sundry was sending out boys into positions of prominence for which they were but poorly prepared. It was not until 1862 that Natural Science was included in the curriculum of an English Public School. In that year Percival, having been appointed headmaster of the new foundation of Clifton, although not himself a scientist, had the insight to recognize its coming importance (*op. cit.*, p. 33).

Before leaving the subject of the Public Schools something ought to be said of the attempt to provide a definite Church education for boys and girls of the middle classes. It was begun in 1847 by Nathaniel Woodard, then curate of New Shoreham. Many schools were founded of varying grades; some cheaper and some dearer. The most famous of them is the "mother house" of Lancing.

[1] See Introduction, p. xvi, to Harford Battersby's *Pilkington of Uganda*.

EDUCATION FROM 1843

One notable thing about the Woodard Schools was that as finally developed they included provision, not only for boys, but for girls as well. Up to the second half of the century the education of girls had been sadly neglected. It was usually left in the hands of governesses who might or might not be competent. Some were sent to small boarding schools. The books used were generally "catechisms" such as *Mangnall's Questions* which contained much miscellaneous knowledge, but knowledge "fragmentary, multifarious, disconnected; taught not scientifically as a subject, but merely as so much information, and hence, like a wall of stones without mortar, it fell to pieces."[1] Some girls of wealthier parents were sent abroad to schools kept by foreigners or by English ladies. Miss Beale, to whose *History of the Cheltenham Ladies' College* I am much indebted, was a pupil in one of the latter: "Mrs. Trimmer's was the English History used in the highest classes. We were taught to perform conjuring tricks with the globe, by which we obtained answers to problems, without one principle being made intelligible" (*op. cit.*, p. 5).

The opening of Queen's College in 1848 provided a supply of women with a higher education who were capable of conducting schools for girls which might rival the public schools of their brothers. Both Miss Beale and Miss Buss were among its members. Miss Buss opened the London Collegiate School in 1850 and three years later the Cheltenham Ladies' College was founded. In 1858 Miss Beale was appointed Principal. As the opening of Queen's College had stimulated the education of girls in secondary schools, so the fact that considerable numbers were being educated in them stimulated in turn the demand for greater provision for the education of women in universities.

THE UNIVERSITIES

The most important events of this period were the appointment in 1850 of Royal Commissions to enquire into the state of the Colleges and Universities, and the Abolition of Tests in 1871. The Dissenters had had something to do with the appointment of the Commissions and they were felt to be an

[1] Report of the Schools Inquiry Commissioners, 1864-8.

attack on the Church by some; but though many academic authorities did their best to make the work of none effect, others co-operated by giving information and, in general, making the enquiries as easy as possible. They recognized that changes were inevitable and that opposition would not help to make them less drastic. The Reports of the Commissions when they appeared were such vast and comprehensive documents that even a summary would demand considerable space. Their recommendations, however, followed two principal lines; they endeavoured to make the government of the universities and colleges more representative, and to render them more readily available to a wider class of students. Nothing really revolutionary was contained in them, but to old-fashioned university men they seemed to be utterly subversive of all that was of value in the system. Even so broad-minded a man as Dr. Moberly, Headmaster of Winchester and later Bishop of Salisbury, could write in his Journal under May 21, 1852: "The Oxford Commission Report is out: sweeping confiscation and revolution are what it means" (quoted in *Dulce Domum*, p. 98). But it left some fragments of religion in the universities, for Liddon could say of a later Commission held under Roundell Palmer, Lord Selborne, that "what the locust had left the palmer-worm had eaten."

By means of various reforms, external and internal, the universities now began to fit themselves for carrying out, in a more adequate manner, the task of educating the youth of the nation. A wider curriculum was gradually introduced, not without opposition. By the Extension Movement some of the benefits of a university education were conveyed to those who were unable to come into residence.[1] Whilst for the poorer men the Non-collegiate system was started. About this time also colleges, later to reach university status, were being formed in many provincial towns. These modern universities definitely and deliberately excluded ecclesiastical influence, presumably to avoid religious entanglements and quarrels. The result is that religion has come to have a low value in

[1] On the Extension Movement see J. Bass Mullinger, *History of the University of Cambridge*, pp. 217 ff., *Life and Letters of Benjamin Jowett*, II, p. 298, and W. H. Draper, *University Extension (1873-1923)*.

the minds of students. This epoch saw also the establishment of the Women's Colleges: Girton in 1874 (after an earlier experiment elsewhere); Newnham in 1871; Lady Margaret and Somerville in 1879.[1]

But the great blow to the older people and to the narrower type of Churchman came with the Abolition of Tests in 1871 and the opening of the ancient universities to students without regard to their religious views. This measure seemed to some the end of the Church's power and influence in the universities; no more could be done. To remain and make the best of things would be a vain effort, "combing the hair of a corpse" as Liddon, who despaired utterly, once put it.[2] Others were more faithful and felt in their hearts that the Church would still be capable in its inherent, God-given strength, of holding its own even when deprived of privilege and prestige. Some even went so far as to welcome the change. James Fraser, afterwards Bishop of Manchester, wrote: "I venture to think that our Colleges will be very much improved by the admission of Nonconformists; and that such admissions will be a gain to the nation, to the Nonconformists, and to the Church of England, which has suffered by the exclusive possession of these privileges and prerogatives" (*Life*, p. 205). Whilst the saintly Edward King was able to say on looking back: "When I was an undergraduate at Oriel, the College was full of resident priests, and we had one Celebration, late in the Term. Now, the Provost and all the resident Fellows are laymen, and there is an early Celebration every Sunday" (quoted G. W. E. Russell, *Edward King, Bishop of Lincoln*, p. 233).

On the other hand, the ambitious hopes of the Nonconformists as to the results which would follow their admission were by no means realized. In fact, as T. H. Green wrote to Dale, it had serious detriments: "The opening of the National

---

[1] The earlier establishment of Queen's College in London should not be forgotten.

[2] Keble College, Oxford, which Liddon had been instrumental in founding, was not affected by the Abolition of Tests, as it was by its deeds a purely Anglican foundation. In Cambridge a similar institution was founded in memory of George Augustus Selwyn, who died in 1878. At first, on account of its denominational restrictions, it was dubbed a "Public Hostel," and not a college.

Universities to Nonconformists," he said, "has been, in my judgement, an injury rather than a help to Nonconformity. You are sending up here, year after year, the sons of some of your best and wealthiest families; they are often altogether uninfluenced by the services of the Church which they find here, and they not only drift away from Nonconformity—they drift away and lose all faith" (quoted *R. W. Dale*, p. 496). To meet this danger Spring Hill, the Congregational College near Birmingham, was closed down, and Mansfield College built at Oxford to be a centre of influence on the University and a place of training for the ministry.

None the less, even if the fears of Churchmen and the hopes of Nonconformists were equally groundless, a great revolution had been wrought, for the Abolition of Tests meant, as Lord Salisbury once said, "turning what has been an institution for the education of youth in the principles of the dominant religion into a simple institution for grinding Latin and Greek into young brains" (quoted Cecil, *Life of Robert, Marquis of Salisbury*, I, p. 326).

Religion in the Universities

We turn now to glance at the state of religion in the universities in the days before the Abolition of Tests had allowed Nonconformists to be admitted on practically equal terms.

In the 'forties Liberal influences were exceedingly strong. As in the country at large, Emerson and Carlyle were carrying all before them among the growing generation. Another name which seems to have had, for many years, a strange attraction for Oxford men, was that of George Sand.[1] "*Consuelo* in particular," writes Mrs. Humphry Ward, referring to the experiences of her father, the younger Thomas Arnold and his more famous brother Matthew, "was a revelation to the two young men brought up under the 'earnest' influence of Rugby. It seemed to open to them a world of artistic beauty and joy of which they had never dreamed" (*A Writer's Recollections*,

[1] Hort tells us that in 1848 the sister University was full of disciples of Froude and George Sand (*Life*, I, p. 85); whilst in a later generation Creighton (*Life and Letters*, I, pp. 80, 102, 126, 184) and Addington Symonds both experienced her influence.

p. 12). It is significant that in 1858 Stanley could write to J. C. Shairp deploring the fact that none of the Balliol youth came to his lectures, presumably because "none of them go into orders, a feature in the prospects of the Church of England far darker than any of those about which our agitators and alarmists are so wild" (*Life*, II, p. 3).

One note of this period, at any rate in Oxford, was the dislike of any connexion with Dissent. For an undergraduate to attend a Nonconformist chapel was an unpardonable sin. A change came when a member of a noble house, who had been saved from an evil life by Benjamin Gregory the Methodist, defied the proctors and threatened to carry the matter further if he were interfered with.[1]

At the time when Nonconformists were entering the universities, religion, especially at Oxford, was at a low ebb. Pusey lived a retired life, but Liddon had some influence. This side of things was strengthened when in 1873 Edward King returned from Cuddesdon. The Evangelicals also were weak. Their leader was Canon Christopher at St. Aldate's, an ex-Cambridge blue and wrangler, who gave the famous "missionary breakfasts." The opening of Wycliffe Hall in 1877, however, and the coming of F. J. Chavasse brought renewed life. But things did not much improve until the 'eighties with the rise of the group of dons who produced *Lux Mundi*, and of Fairbairn, with his massive learning, at Mansfield. Meanwhile the intellectual current ran strongly against any definite faith—the reaction against Tractarianism had not yet spent itself—Comte and Mill were the accepted prophets. The position has been well described by H. Scott Holland in a Memorial Sermon on Bishop Creighton. "He took his stand for God and made his great decision at the extreme hour of intellectual tension, when the panic roused by the new criticism was at its height, and when the victorious efficacy of the scientific and critical methods appeared to have swept the field. It is difficult for us now to gauge the dismay of that bad hour. At the close of the 'sixties it seemed to us at Oxford almost incredible that a young don of any intellectual reputation for modernity should be on the Christian side" (quoted in *Life and Letters of Mandell Creighton*, I, p. 75).

[1] See Benjamin Gregory, *Autobiographical Reminiscences*, pp. 407 f.

Among the dons many might have said as Ingram Bywater was supposed to have done, though without his lisp: "When I wath a child I wath vacthinated and Chrithened; neither of them took."[1]

R. F. Horton, the famous Congregationalist leader, came up to New College soon after the opening of the universities to Dissenters. He had been at Shrewsbury, where he had acquired enough classics to enable him to take a Double First, and a knowledge of rowing which helped to raise his college boat seven places on the river in 1877. His other gifts may be adjudged from his being elected President of the Union. He tells us that "undergraduates in Hall sneered at the Hebrew mythology, and if any scholar of Balliol or a University prizeman was a Christian, and contemplated taking Orders, he was regarded as a freak" (*Autobiography*, p. 31). Dr. Horton says that there was no attempt on the part of Anglicans to proselytize, but "an honourable determination to receive Dissenters on equal terms, and not to molest them" (*op. cit.*, p. 46). Further light on the position of religion in Oxford can be gained from an interesting account of a visit which Alexander Beresford Hope paid to Newman in Birmingham about this time. Newman said that "he had been told that though the former generation at Oxford had been agnostic and continued so the younger one was growing up Christian.... I confirmed this for Cambridge and he listened with evident sympathy" (quoted H. W. and I. Law, *The Book of the Beresford Hopes*, p. 236).

At Cambridge things were obviously very much better at this epoch, and the boast of G. L. Pilkington that "the religious movement in Cambridge was leaving poor old Oxford a long way behind" (*Pilkington of Uganda*, p. xiv) was justified by the testimony of Horton and others who went over there in connexion with the Christian Unions: "We were amazed with the far richer religious life at the sister university," he said (*op. cit.*, p. 36). But Cambridge had never had a Tractarian

---

[1] This anecdote hardly does justice to Bywater's real position: see W. W. Jackson, *Ingram Bywater*, pp. 82 f. He had a high opinion of the value of religion and never desired to weaken it, although he was opposed to "privilege" and intolerance.

Movement against which to react, and the old tradition of Simeon and the great Evangelical leaders still persisted. Its leaders in theology were men of a profounder faith than Jowett or Stanley, and the work of the Cambridge school to which reference has already been made was bearing its appropriate fruit. Hence Cambridge was ready for an aggressive movement, and when Moody and Sankey went there, to the amazement of all who did not know the true state of religion in that University, they met with abundant success.[1]

Later Religious Movements

Perhaps the most famous of all University Religious Societies, the Cambridge Inter-Collegiate Christian Union, or C.I.C.C.U., was founded in 1877 as a result of the Revival Movements. Its origins may be traced still further back to the initiation of the Daily Prayer Meeting or D.P.M. (the undergraduate loves initials!) which began in 1862. Although the C.I.C.C.U. is really undenominational in character, like Keswick it has largely been controlled by Evangelical Churchmen of the Conservative wing. Its members have shown themselves ardent and unselfish in every good work; but their burning zeal and devotion have often outrun discretion. A sad lack of balance, wisdom, and judgement—natural enough in such young and inexperienced Christians—has sometimes led them into eccentricities and to a foolish neglect of the educational advantages of the University. This failure to develop the mental side of their religion has been lamented by the wisest and greatest of them in after years when the opportunity was past for ever. Bishop Woods, looking back on his own days, warned boys going up to the University against this danger, pointing out what a serious handicap it is for those who may, in later years, be called to positions of responsibility and leadership to be deficient in mental training and equipment (see Woods and Macnutt, *Theodore, Bishop of Winchester*, p. 22).

From the account of the University years of this same Bishop (he was at Cambridge from 1892 to 1897) a good idea can be gained of the strength and weakness of religion in Cambridge in that period as seen in C.I.C.C.U. circles. It reveals much

[1] See above, p. 219.

that is admirable and splendid, much that is amazingly immature and foolish, in particular that spiritual pride which is not unfairly described as "bumptiousness." "Tales were told of men who, being hauled by the Dean for cutting chapels in favour of other religious meetings, turned the tables on their persecutor by haranguing him on the state of his soul, and even kneeling on the floor of his room and interceding for his salvation" (*op. cit.*, p. 16). They were, indeed, critical of all older people and a little suspicious of the genuineness of any spiritual experience except their own. Bishop Gwynn recalls Theodore Woods himself as a youth in his father's parish, and doubtful even of that father's full experience. He goes on to say that he got over this phase in time; "but while he was undergoing that necessary youthful malady we had amusing and interesting times" (*op. cit.*, p. 24). It is apposite to notice that whilst Woods was still at Ridley Hall he hung up in his room a portrait of his father, then recently dead, with the painted inscription beneath it: "Whose faith follow." This portrait was hung on the walls of each of his successive studies until the end of his own life.

At Oxford the O.I.C.C.U. was never quite so strong or flourishing, but about the time that Woods was at Cambridge it underwent a revival. This has been described by Miss Padwick in *Temple Gairdner of Cairo*. Symptoms similar to those described above revealed themselves in Oxford, both for good and evil. Gairdner himself, writing to his son who had been "put off" by this intrusive type of Evangelicalism, turned back to those days and wrote: "Was not I in the midst of them, and one of them at Oxford? And as I look round the world I see everywhere that it is *these* men (perhaps mellowed and developed now) who are doing the big things in the world —the big things for mankind, and God, and the Kingdom of Christ: A. G. Fraser, J. H. Oldham, W. E. S. Holland, to take only those known to yourself" (*op. cit.*, p. 21).

Rather more prosaic, perhaps, but not less effective was the Student Movement. This had begun in 1886 in America as the Student Volunteer Missionary Union in the house of Mr. Wilder, a Presbyterian Minister, and the father of R. P. Wilder. The latter was a speaker at Keswick in 1891, and in the following February he started the S.V.M.U. in England at a meeting in Cambridge. A great international missionary Conference was held in Liverpool in 1896. Its youthful chairman was Donald Fraser, who had been converted from Agnosticism at Keswick in the year that Wilder spoke. He shrewdly declared that Europe had probably never seen a more international meeting than the gathering of students over which he presided. It was at this Conference that the watchword, "The Evangelization of the world in this generation" was boldly adopted. In its early years the Student Movement owed much to the wise and sympathetic treatment which Bishop Creighton accorded to it.[1] But soon other leaders, Anglican and Nonconformist, were recognizing its value. Its chief difference from the C.I.C.C.U. and O.I.C.C.U. is to be found in a much less rigid doctrinal outlook and in links with students in other lands.[2]

[1] See an interesting letter quoted by Padwick, *Temple Gairdner of Cairo*, pp. 62 f.
[2] See Tissington Tatlow, *The Story of the Student Movement*, for the official account by one who has been in the Movement from its early days.

17

THE PRESS

ONE of the most remarkable phenomena of the Victorian Era was the growth in scope and influence of the printed page. This had a profound effect upon the religious life of the country, even when it took a secular form.

GROWTH OF THE SECULAR PRESS

There is in man a universal thirst for news; once the means for satisfying it have been discovered an immense circulation and wide influence are bound to follow. For a time, however, the high price of paper and the illiteracy of a large part of the population prevented this. In addition there was a tax on newspapers introduced probably from a fear of allowing news to spread too freely. But in 1836 the tax was reduced from 4d. to 1d. Then in 1855 it was removed entirely, to be followed in 1861 by the abolition of the duty on paper. The reduction in taxation naturally resulted in a corresponding reduction in the price of newspapers. Up to 1836 *The Times* cost 7d.; but after the removal of the last tax it fell to 3d. This marked a great stage in the spread of news. But a greater was to come, for about the same time the *Daily Telegraph* appeared at 1d., and the end of the era saw the *Daily Mail* at half that price. It has been calculated that at the accession of the Queen there were in England 479 newspapers; by the Diamond Jubilee this number had grown to 2,396.[1]

Its Power

Such an increase in circulation and number was the means of the Press obtaining vast power over the thoughts and opinions of the people. As early as 1831 this coming power had been foretold by Thomas Carlyle.

"There is no Church, sayest thou? The voice of Prophecy has gone dumb? This is even what I dispute; but in any case, hast thou not still Preaching enough? A Preaching Friar

---

[1] T. H. S. Escott, *Social Transformation of the Victorian Era*, p. 381.

328

settles himself in every village: and builds a pulpit, which he calls Newspaper. Therefrom he preaches what most momentous doctrine is in him: and dost not thou listen, and believe?" (quoted R. Garnett in *The Reign of Queen Victoria*, II, p. 509).

At the beginning of the era the Press was venal and corrupt and its instruments and agents despised and avoided. There was something of a scandal when a Lord Chancellor invited the editor of *The Times* to dinner. Fortunately with the growth of power and importance there was a growth of the sense of responsibility and moral worth. But the Press was still a danger. In a superficially educated democracy sparks flung out by a designing Press may easily provoke a conflagration. It is said that the Crimean War was largely brought about by the influence which Palmerston, who, according to the Greville Memoirs, "would always see any newspaper man who called upon him," exercised by its means.[1] The Press itself was perfectly aware of its power and one great English newspaper claimed for itself that it discharged in the modern world the function of the medieval Church.[2]

The influence which was thus exercised on the country in general by the newspapers was supplemented, in the case of the more cultivated, by that of the great reviews. Of these *The Edinburgh* had been founded in 1802 at the suggestion of Sydney Smith, who gave it the motto—"I have a passionate love for common justice and common sense." Early editors and contributors, in addition to Smith himself, were Jeffery, Brougham, and, rather later, Lord Macaulay. If *The Quarterly* did not actually kill John Keats its influence was so great that men could believe it possible. An old Lincolnshire squire assured Tennyson in 1832 that it was the next book to God's Bible (*Alfred, Lord Tennyson*, I, p. 94). For those who could not afford reviews there soon appeared popular magazines. At the beginning of the reign no respectable periodicals for the working class were known except *Chambers's Journal* and *Knight's Penny Magazine*. With the increase of railway travel a new type of reader emerged and cheap magazines with illustrations and short stories began to flourish.

[1] Trevelyan, *History of England*, p. 650.
[2] James Bryce, *Studies in Contemporary Biography*, p. 380.

Its Effects

Such matter tended to create superficiality both in those who provided it and those who read it. Congreve, after referring to "the sleet of words which oppresses the world in the shape of magazines and ephemeral literature," pointed out that "The great books of the world might easily be read through, if people would consent to miss the drifting mass of light literature." He added, with undue optimism, that "Magazining is but a temporary disease" (quoted H. F. Brown, *J. Addington Symonds*, p. 129). The extent to which English people were given up to this kind of literature was criticized by the sympathetic German observer to whom I have had occasion to refer before. Carl Peters says: "Nothing gives me a clearer impression of the shallowness of modern English society, than the character of this magazine literature; which provides for many millions of Englishmen the sole spiritual nourishment" (*England and the English*, p. 188). More than a generation earlier Lord Shaftesbury had written (in 1868): "It is curious and instructive to observe what a prodigious effect newspapers and magazines, but newspapers more especially, have produced on the social and political condition of England already. . . . They have diffused an amount of knowledge . . . that never would have been effected in any other way. . . . Hence a mass of information is acquired, alike abundant and superficial" (*Life*, III, pp. 242 f.). Another effect which the same observer had noted with regret was that it revealed to the common people the misdeeds of their social betters and thus tended to rob them of respect and belief in "aristocracy" and hereditary rank (*op. cit.*, III, p. 243).

Perhaps one of the most disquieting effects of the power of the Press, an effect which is connected with the creation of superficial habits of mind, is the extent to which it is able to control and "dragoon" public opinion and to reduce its readers to a low and dull level by the loss of their individuality. This has been even more marked since the end of the Victorian Era. A. J. Toynbee, a shrewd observer of national as well as international affairs, has even declared that "In the latter-day perversion of our Western Press we see the 'drive' of Western industrialism and Democracy being employed to keep the mass of Humanity culturally depressed at, or perhaps even below its pre-industrial and pre-democratic level" (*A Study of History*, III, p. 241).

The creation of a population which was superficial in its mental habits and willing, if not anxious, to be dragooned was bad for religion and the Church, even in the absence of any direct opposition or attack by the Press. But such attacks were not lacking, sometimes on political, sometimes on religious grounds. However, they are now a thing of the past, having disappeared with the occasion. In their day, however, they were serious. That was why Kingsley could speak of journalists (he had actually in mind more particularly those of France) as "men who, having failed in regular work of any kind, establish themselves as anonymous critics of all who labour, under an irresponsibility and an immunity which no despot ever enjoyed" (*Life*, p. 312). But there was another side, and the immense influence for good, for example, of *The Spectator* under R. H. Hutton (1861–97) must not be forgotten. Hutton had been led from Unitarianism (he was editor of the Unitarian *Inquirer*) to orthodox Christianity by the influence of F. D. Maurice, and he made *The Spectator* a means of affecting many whom the pulpit could not reach. His advocacy of mercy and justice and of the "fundamental truth of human redemption through God made Man" was unceasing (see G. W. E. Russell, *Fifteen Sketches of Autobiography*, p. 332).

THE RELIGIOUS PRESS[1]

At the beginning of the century religious publications were by no means novel. In 1793 *The Evangelical Magazine* had been started by a group composed of Churchmen and Nonconformists, several of whom had been associated in the foundation of the Bible Society and the London Missionary Society. Earlier still John Wesley had founded *The Arminian Magazine*—later to be known as *The Methodist Magazine*. With the new century such periodicals began to multiply. In 1802 Zachary Macaulay and other members of the Clapham Sect started *The Christian Observer*, and

[1] I wish to express my obligations to an article by H. W. Peet in the Supplement to *The Times* for January 1, 1935. It supplied me with fresh material and enabled me to check what I had myself collected.

three years later followed *The Eclectic Review*, of a slightly more "high-brow" tone and intended for Dissenters as well as Evangelical Churchmen; of this periodical more will be said later. The Orthodox, or moderate High Churchman, had *The British Critic* (1812), which appeared as a quarterly from 1824 to 1843 when its existence came to an end. There was also *The Christian Remembrancer*—the first of that name—intended to stimulate the clergy to take a deeper interest in theological learning. Although its promoters were High Churchmen, it was not intended to be a party organ. Its career, a somewhat disappointing one, ended in 1830. The religious activity and the controversies which grew out of it in the decade before the accession of Victoria bore fruit in an increased number of periodicals. By the end of the reign the Religious Press had swollen to immense proportions, even apart from the considerable literature represented by the organs of the various religious societies, missionary and otherwise. The conditions which made for the growth of the Secular Press gave also the opportunity to the Religious.

An important date was 1828, when a small group of Evangelical Churchmen, of which J. H. Newman was a member (see *Apologia*, p. 47), founded *The Record*, the earliest religious newspaper, for such it was at its inception. At first it appeared twice and sometimes three times a week and soon acquired a position of enormous influence. Its success was due to the editorial and controversial skill of Alexander Haldane; but the bitterness which marked it, though a common feature of the journalism of the times, was regrettable in a religious periodical. He died in 1882 and the same year it became a weekly, and also slightly more moderate. For violence and aggression towards those who differed from it *The Record* was, if possible, excelled by *The Rock*, which did not spare even trusted Evangelical leaders like Ryle and Hoare. From 1884 its place as a decided and aggressive "Protestant" journal was taken by *The English Churchman*.

It is impossible for the present generation to realize the immense and often malignant power exercised by the religious Press in the first part of the last century. *The Record* actually challenged the authority of the Bishop of London in his own diocese and forced him to give way. This influence was in reality a species of tyranny and was ruthlessly exerted, especially against young clergymen who seemed to be taking their own line. Its persecution led to the dismissal of F. D. Maurice from his chair at King's College, London, in 1853, and one is not surprised that after his experience Maurice did all he could to end what he called an "immoral and godless" domination. In 1860 he succeeded in breaking its power when it got up a protest against his appointment to St. Peter's, Vere Street. The protest was an utter fiasco (see *Life and Letters of F. D. Maurice*, II, pp. 362 ff.). Before this its attacks on Bishop Wilberforce had led that prelate to address a letter (in 1853) to the editor, in which he said: "There is indeed a day coming when to have lived by stirring up strife between Christians will be no better a profession than to have lived upon the wages of prostitution."

Other Church papers were *The Guardian*, founded in 1846 by those who remained true to the English Church after Newman's secession. It was the organ of the older Oxford Movement group and owed much to the regular contributions of R. W. Church. When he became Dean of St. Paul's in 1871 these came to an end, though he still wrote for it from time to time. The newer Anglo-Catholic has, since 1863, had *The Church Times* to represent his point of view and to direct his steps. It may be taken as the high-water mark of Anglican journalism which for some reason or other has never really been able to rival that of Nonconformity or to attain to circulations which bear any real comparison with papers such as *The British Weekly*. The youngest of the Church papers is *The Church of England Newspaper*, to give it the title which it now bears, but from its foundation in 1894 until a few years ago it was known as *The Church Family Newspaper*. Of more substantial Anglican reading there is *The Church Quarterly Review*, founded in 1875.

Before leaving the subject of Anglican newspapers a word must be said on the Parish Magazine, which now finds a place in nearly every parish in the country. Its inventor was Canon Erskine Clarke, who in 1859 produced the first number in the parish of St. Michael's, Derby. The form which it takes is that of a central inset, supplied by some society or publisher; with which the local matter is bound up; and so a considerable amount of reading matter is provided. The circulation of all the various Parish Magazines in the country must go into hundreds of thousands; for they penetrate into humble homes in town and country alike, and are often read "from cover to cover." In days when cheap literature was not so common as it is to-day they were a real boon; and even to-day their usefulness still remains.

We come now to undenominational periodicals, and of these the first to demand notice is *The Christian World*, which appeared in 1857 as an "undenominational and progressive religious weekly." Its success was assured three years later when James Clarke took over the management. He was the first editor of a religious weekly to arrange a telegraph and cable service.[1] Next in order came *The Revival* (1859), which in 1870 changed its name to *The Christian*. Seven years later *The Christian Herald* (1866) appeared, to cater for those interested in "prophecy"; its original style was *Signs of our Times*. In 1878 there came the monthly organ of the Keswick Movement under the title *The Christian's Path to Power*. But this clumsy name was dropped for the well-known *Life of Faith* when the journal became a weekly.

The outstanding journal among the Undenominational Press is *The British Weekly*. This periodical first appeared in 1886 as a "journal of Christian and Social Progress." Under the brilliant editorship of W. Robertson Nicoll it became a power, not only among Nonconformists, but even in literary circles. It is even whispered that the Liberal party owed not a little to its advocacy. Among those who were "discovered" through its pages were J. M. Barrie and "Ian Maclaren." *The British Weekly* and similar undenominational journals have the advantage over papers which are connected with specific religious bodies, as they are preserved from having to descend to the petty personal details which seem inseparable from a Denominational organ.

Among undenominational magazines may be mentioned

[1] The appearance of the serials of Emma Jane Worboise in the pages of *The Christian World* did much to overcome Nonconformist prejudice against fiction.

Good Words, in which many of Mrs. Henry Wood's stories first appeared; *The Leisure Hour*; and *The Sunday Magazine*, to which George Macdonald was a contributor. These periodicals no longer survive; but *The Sunday at Home*, founded by the R.T.S. in 1854, and *The Quiver*, which dates from 1861, are still popular.

Among theological magazines *The Eclectic Review*, to which reference was made above, attained wide influence and reputation under Josiah Conder, who had amongst his contributors John Foster, Robert Hall, and Dr. Chalmers. But in the 'fifties it gradually lost its position, in spite of the recruitment of rising young men such as Dale of Birmingham and Paton of Nottingham.

On the verge between Undenominational and Congregational periodicals stood *The Nonconformist*, which appeared in 1841 under the editorship of Edward Miall, who was also its proprietor. Miall, who was M.P. successively for Rochdale and Bradford, represented, as someone has said, "the dissidence of Dissent and the protestantism of the Protestant religion."[1] His paper was a means to this end. In the middle years of the century it had enormous influence, but like many other similar productions it failed to keep pace with the change of thought and outlook and in 1875 was absorbed in *The Independent*. Another periodical, *The British Quarterly Review*, was started in 1845 by Robert Vaughan and soon made a place for itself among Nonconformists in general. One of the outstanding figures of the earlier period, however, was John Campbell, who had been a member of the staff of *The Patriot*, an Independent organ with the avowed policy of being "radically republican and anti-church." He was very successful with *The Christian Witness*, begun in 1843, and then with *The British Banner*, intended to counteract the Sunday Press. Troubles over the "Rivulet" Controversy (see pp. 141 f. above) led to his cutting

---

[1] Dale had a very high regard for Miall. He describes him as "a man who in enlightenment, conviction, and breadth of view, stood without a peer or rival among the Nonconformist journalists of his day" (*Life*, p. 63). In another place he said of him: "He looked upon the perpetual flux of human affairs from the everlasting hills. His thoughts did not wander through eternity—they dwelt there" (*op. cit.*, p. 369).

loose from denominational control and starting *The British Standard* entirely on his own account. In 1872 *The Congregationalist* was started with R. W. Dale as editor. This was a monthly magazine intended to uphold and defend the principles of the Independents.

Among the Baptists there was *The Baptist Magazine*, founded by Thomas Smith of Tiverton in 1809 (which just failed to live a century as it expired in 1904); *The Baptist Messenger* (1854-99); and *The Freeman*. This journal was founded in 1855, but as its name clashed with that of the Irish Nationalist organ it changed it to *The Baptist Times*. It still survives, having absorbed *The Baptist* in 1872. Among the publications of this denomination there should be included Spurgeon's *The Sword and the Trowel* founded in 1865.

The Methodists, in addition to *The Methodist Magazine*, founded by John Wesley himself, had *The Watchman* 835) and *The Methodist Recorder* (1861). But in 1885 a new star came above the horizon of the Methodist world in the shape of *The Methodist Times*, the organ of the Forward Movement initiated by Hugh Price Hughes. It was remarkable for its wide intellectual outlook and for what in those days was an unusual interest in social problems. Among reviews were *The London Quarterly* and *The Holborn Review*.

Among other bodies which may be noticed here the Quakers had *The Friend*, begun as a monthly, but changing into a weekly in 1893; while the Salvation Army had its famous *War Cry*, begun in 1879 and sold for the sum of only a halfpenny.

The various publications of the Roman Catholic Church in these islands demand a passing notice. The most substantial of them was *The Dublin Review*, founded in 1836 by Wiseman (later to be Cardinal) and Daniel O'Connell; this excellent review carries weight far beyond the frontiers of its own communion. Some ten years later appeared the famous weekly *The Tablet*, founded by Frederick Lucas, who had been a Quaker. 1860 saw the rise of both *The Universe* and *The Catholic Times*. Four years later came *The Month*, which took its place alongside the much older *Blackfriars*, begun in 1820 as a monthly magazine.

A final and separate word must be said of *The Expository*

Times, a journal unique in its way, for it seeks to provide clergy and ministers of all denominations with information on the latest developments of thought and learning in a simple way. It was founded in 1889 by Dr. James Hastings, the editor of so many Dictionaries and Encyclopaedias.

LITERATURE AND ART

THEIR VALUE FOR THE HISTORIAN

For the observer of any period its literature and art have a double importance, since not only do they reflect the conditions of the times, they also had their part in moulding them. Great literature is never content merely to reflect life, it must also impress life; although it scarcely ever adopts the didactic tone, it must teach life. The student of Victorian Religion certainly cannot afford to neglect either of these aspects of contemporary literature. His survey, moreover, must not be confined to that literature which definitely calls itself religious; for literature forms a background to the life of religion and of religious people as of people in general. For just as literature itself is subject to manifold influences, some of which are derived from regions but remotely connected with letters; so its own influence, if unobtrusive, is so potent that it demands examination.

In the eighteenth century literature and art had been, as someone has said, "an intimate and thrilling virtuosity," the interest of the aristocracy and the country gentlemen. Every big house must have its picture gallery and its library, and even the smaller country-houses followed the lead. The culture which was thus engendered was of a mild and pleasing variety and affected only a narrow circle; but something was done to keep it alive when the universities of the land were neglecting this aspect of their duty.

The new era with its widespread educational system and its free libraries[1] and public art galleries gave literature and art an altogether vaster influence on the life and thought of the community in all its ranks and classes. This was realized by the artists and men of letters who began deliberately to make art subserve life, and endeavoured to influence the world around them. Foremost among them were the popular novelists; "who more and more assumed the place from which drama

[1] The first free library was opened in Manchester in 1852.

had fallen, and became the mirror and censor of contemporary manners."[1] But if the novelists were foremost in the attempt to exert influence on their contemporaries they were equally useful as mirrors to reflect contemporary life. The poet may often be a prophet and have the gift of piercing through the shallow thought of his day to something deeper beyond, to ideas that have eternal validity. But this faculty takes from his usefulness as a guide; and indeed the less imagination there is in the recorder the greater will be his usefulness. That is why a writer like Trollope is a more important source than novelists of higher imaginative gifts such as Dickens and Thackeray. In fact it has been said that in his works and those of Mrs. Humphry Ward for a later generation we have "the whole Victorian civilization dissected and preserved."[2]

The eighteenth century had been the great age of English prose writers, but at its end the way seemed suddenly to open upon a new and fruitful world of poetry; a world which produced a harvest recalling the rich beauties of the Elizabethans. The emergence of the great English poets was parallel to the growth of the Romantic school on the continent, for alongside Goethe and Schiller we can place Wordsworth and Coleridge, Byron and Shelley, and the tragic splendour of the youthful Keats. This same generation included Sir Walter Scott, the poet who was to become the first modern novelist.[3] It was also rich in women novelists; whether writers of popular romantic fiction such as Mrs. Radcliffe (d. 1823); or of novels of manners, a class in which Jane Austen (d. 1817) stands supreme, though it includes Fanny Burney (d. 1840), Maria Edgeworth (d. 1849), and Susan Ferrier (d. 1854). This group of women writers was to be followed by a group of men, all of whom, except Thackeray, found fame before they were thirty; it included in addition Lytton, Disraeli, Ainsworth, Dickens, as well as others.

The writers of the early years of the era had certain strong characteristics; although they were markedly individualistic

---

[1] R. Garnett in *The Reign of Queen Victoria*, II, p. 464. "It is the Novelists rather than the Poets who have left the deepest imprint on the popular imagination": said Lord Oxford, *Some Aspects of the Victorian Age*, p. 11.
[2] A. Conan Doyle, *Memories and Adventures*, p. 263.
[3] *Waverley* was published in 1814.

they were sufficiently the children of their age to preserve that reticence on certain topics which public taste in England then demanded; they had, too, a certain ideal tendency—hope and love for their fellows,[1] and the desire to "restore to rectitude the warped system of things," as Charlotte Brontë put it in her address to Thackeray, prefaced to the second edition of *Jane Eyre*. In writers of our own day, it may be worth while to remark, both these tendencies are lacking; there is no restraint in sexual matters (save that provided by the censor) and there is no desire to see the lovely and the hopeful in contemporary life.

If the Victorian Era was fruitful in great novelists, as it progressed there was undoubtedly a decline in all branches of literature. At the beginning there were great men, though their best lay behind them; at the end a number of competent writers and verse makers, but little that seemed inspired. The atmosphere pervaded by Industrialism and Rationalism was not suited to the growth of the highest art, especially in poetry. The poet found himself cut off from life and forced within too narrow a range of inspiration, forced too to seek it in the artificial and the unnatural. A scientific view of the universe, tending as it does to materialism, if it is unfavourable to religion, is also unfavourable to all other activities of the spirit. The intellect can buy its freedom at the price of enslaving the soul. A recent critic has said that: "The degree of assurance with which serious poetry can be written at any period depends upon the prevailing state of certainty about ultimate issues." Thus religion and letters act and react upon one another.

There can be but little doubt that as there was a gradual decline in literature during the era, so also was there a decline in general culture; that is among those classes which may claim to be cultivated. There was much less leisure and much more to read. Hence the habit of "skimming," of getting one's ideas from reviews rather than at first hand, came to prevail. Books were no longer mastered and made part of the mind itself. But the demand for a supposed culture was still strong, and not to know about the latest work was to admit to a damaging meed of ignorance. The early Victorians and the generation

[1] F. S. Marvin, *The Century of Hope*, pp. 80 f.

before them were not always talking about culture, but very often they had the thing itself.

THE VICTORIANS AND RELIGION

The Victorian literary men were not so anxious to reveal the innermost thoughts of their hearts as are their successors to-day; but so far as we can discern their religious views they were in a surprisingly large number of cases separated from orthodox Christianity by a considerable gulf. Such men as Macaulay, Froude, Tennyson, Browning, and Matthew Arnold, though they might have a belief in God and in Immortality, and even a passionate belief in these things, would not have committed themselves further. In some, of the poets especially, there was even a feeling of hostility, though it never reached the passion of a James Davidson in the present century.[1] This hostile feeling is seen in the earlier efforts of Swinburne. In *Poems and Ballads* (1866) Greek Paganism is the prevailing note; in *Songs before Sunrise* (1871) the idea of God is attacked. But it is hard to take Swinburne seriously; there is always something of the undergraduate or the child about him; one feels that he is trying to shock you, to curdle the blood of his elders. It is perhaps in James Thomson's *City of Dreadful Night* that the height of opposition is reached. To him the "good tidings of great joy" were that there is no God and that man has but one life to endure. Others found in Orthodoxy a burden and a hindrance to the belief in God: so Emily Brontë, protested that she still believed, in spite of all:

[1] See Figgis, *The Gospel and Human Needs*, pp. 6 and 8. Two quotations may be given:

"To purge the world of Christianity,
The sacrifice of every human life
That now enjoys or nauseates the sun
Would not be too exorbitant a price!"

and again:

"In flames and crimson seas we shall advance
Against the ancient immaterial reign
Of Spirit, and our watchword shall be still
Get thee behind me, God—I follow Mammon."
Mammon and His Message, pp. 103 and 135.

"Vain are the thousand creeds
That move men's hearts, unutterably vain,
Worthless as withered weeds
Or idlest froth amid the boundless main

To waken doubt in one
Holding so fast by thy infinity
So surely anchored on
The steadfast rock of Immortality."

Browning and Christianity

As the attitude of Browning towards religion and Christianity has been widely misunderstood—largely because opinions have been based on a partial and too narrow survey of his works—it will be well to examine the matter more fully. This is more important, as Browning was ever a potent force in the Nonconformity in which he had been reared. Silvester Horne, for example, suggests that he exercised more influence on Nonconformist religious thought than theologians and preachers: "Out of Puritan England Browning spoke to the nineteenth century as Milton had spoken to the seventeenth" (*Free Church History*, p. 421).[1]

In youth Browning was "passionately religious." But as he grew older he began to feel the narrowness of Nonconformity. It has been said of him and his wife, herself brought up in a Nonconformist home, that they "disowned the Puritan narrowness, and the grey aridity of certain schools of dissent" (Dowden, *Life of Robert Browning*, p. 86). They retained, however, to the end a certain impatience, almost contempt, for Ritualism, and regarded "Puseyism" as "a kind of child's play which unfortunately had religion for its playground" (*op. cit.*, p. 121). When their only child was born in Florence, they had him baptized with Lutheran rites. Later Browning

[1] Lascelles Abercrombie, in his study of the poet in *Great Victorians*, thinks that Browning never got away from the narrow outlook of his early years, in spite of his true greatness, both as a man and a poet. It comes out in *Christmas Eve and Easter Day*, where "the thought is a doggerel rendering of abysmally dull secretarian theology, futile, small, profitless" (*op. cit.*, p. 90). He concludes that "Browning's intellectual life was spent in a backwater" (*op. cit.*, p. 91).

came to attach less and less value to religious dogma; but his belief in the great Christian doctrine of love never faltered, rather it grew stronger; though he was never the "optimist" of those who know only *Pippa Passes*, with its "God's in His heaven, All's right with the world." His own experience had taught him that "Sorrow did and joy did nowise . . . preponderate"; but that it was man's task bravely to face all adverse circumstance. His abandonment of strict orthodoxy probably accounts for the "thundered No" with which he greeted Robert . Buchanan's question whether he was a Christian. Perhaps Dowden has got as near to the truth of the matter as anyone when he says, speaking of Browning's last days: "His early Christian faith has expanded and taken the non-historical form of a Humanitarian Theism, courageously accepted, not as a complete account of the Unknowable, but as the best provisional conception which we are competent to form" (*op. cit.*, p. 364). He never lost his interest in religious questions, which he would eagerly discuss. In the last period of his life, after the return to Italy, he attended regularly, with his sister, the Waldensian chapel in Venice; this was a change from his habit in London, where, according to Mrs. Orr, he went to church but seldom.

The Novelists

We come next to the novelists. T. S. Eliot has recently pointed out that three distinct stages can be traced in their attitude to Christianity. In the first the Faith is taken for granted, but omitted from their picture of life; in the second it is contested or worried about; in the third (which was reached with the present generation) it is treated as an anachronism ("Religion and Literature" in *Faith that Illuminates*, p. 39). There is certainly much insight in this division, and the first two stages may clearly be discerned in our period, though perhaps the extent to which religion was left out has been exaggerated.

If we take the three great novelists of the early Victorian Era, Scott, Thackeray, and Dickens, we find a considerable interest in religion. It may be noticed that all of them were a little unfair to Nonconformity and Evangelical Christianity in general. Scott could see romance "in knights and fair ladies, tournaments, and wandering Scots abroad"; but he did not fully comprehend it in the heroism of the Cameronian and Covenanter preachers whom he failed to understand.[1] Whilst Thackeray in *The Newcomes* and Dickens with his Mr. Stiggins created prejudice against such views. Even Charles Kingsley, to go down a little later, was felt by Hugh Price Hughes to have given in *Alton Locke* a vulgar and materialistic account of Nonconformity (*Hugh Price Hughes*, p. 95). If we wish to see this side of the religious life of the country dealt with more justly, we must turn to the women novelists, George Eliot and Mrs. Gaskell; the latter the child of one Unitarian minister and the wife of another.

By the end of the century all was changed; the novelists reflect the moral and spiritual conflict in the world around them. Thomas Hardy and George Meredith, though the former conformed to the Church of England, depict a scene in which religion is a problem, and possibly an intrusive one. Perhaps one of the strongest solvent forces was Samuel Butler with his ironic and aggressive writings. If there are not many open attacks, there is the creation of an atmosphere in which religion is felt to be out of place. Above all, the sense of responsibility, and with it the sense of sin, is weakened. Man is represented as in the grip of agencies so powerful that his own will is unable to make head against them. It is not always the immoral and the materialistic writers who do the gravest damage.[2]

RELIGIOUS LITERATURE

We come now to literature which was produced definitely for a religious purpose, that is to serve the cause of Christianity in general or some particular denomination within it. The output was simply enormous. Much of it came from the great societies, such as the S.P.C.K. and R.T.S., in response to the demand for books suitable for presentation as prizes in Day and Sunday Schools. Such literature was, it need hardly be said,

---

[1] See Selbie, *Life of A. M. Fairbairn*, p. 5.
[2] Robertson Nicoll thinks that Oliver Wendell Holmes did much harm in this connexion: see *Letters of a Bookman*, p. 143.

excellent in tone and well adapted to its purpose (though sometimes it verged too nearly on the sentimental and even the "goody-goody") but from its very nature and office not destined for survival. Even the more ambitious, full-length efforts of religious writers will probably prove equally ephemeral; for the fate which seems inevitably to cling to literature "with a purpose" will scarcely avoid them. Most of them are already forgotten, the rest will hardly outlive the century. It may be true, as Mr. Dobree has recently affirmed, that literature "has to be judged by its value to humanity" (*Modern Prose Style*, p. 157); but that value, if it be but for the moment, though genuine, will not survive the period of its usefulness. Literature survives, not because it enshrines certain ideas or attempts to propagate specific theories, but because of its form; because, in other words, it is a work of art and so worthy of admiration and preservation in its own right. The Victorian Era, in spite of the revival of general literature which it saw, produced but few writers on religion and theology who will live. In this department of literature England was strangely lacking. It is true that we have the prose writings of a supreme master in J. H. Newman, but he stands almost, if not quite alone; though possibly his disciple, R. W. Church, produced matter which deserves lasting memorial. Others there were who earned fame as preachers, with them we shall deal in a later chapter;[1] but among pure theologians and thinkers there was no Hooker and no Andrewes. The quality of their thought may have been high and the medium through which it was presented perfectly adequate, but as literature it did not reach the highest rank and so it calls for no mention here.

Novelists

The novel was out of favour with the early Victorian religious disciple, especially if he were an Evangelical. Hannah More, in the days immediately before the era, had made tentative efforts to produce a type of religious novel, and even of religious drama, which might fill the gap. Other attempts, along similar lines, were made by Legh Richmond, Edward Bickersteth, and Basil Woodd. The two latter were so successful

[1] See below, pp. 458 ff.

that their works continued to enjoy a wide circulation well into the century. Later there came Miss Sewell with *Laneton Parsonage*, *Amy Herbert*, and other works; Samuel Wilberforce with *Agathos*; the numerous writings of J. M. Neale, whose historical knowledge was extraordinarily wide for his day. But the really outstanding figure in this type of literature was Charlotte M. Yonge.

Charlotte Yonge was the disciple and neighbour of John Keble, and she did much to spread his teaching far and wide by her wonderful gift of story-telling. This gift was so striking that many stories are told of great men, Tennyson and others, who were so fascinated by it that they were unable to put down her novels until some particular crisis in the narrative had successfully been dealt with. Her best-known work is perhaps *The Heir of Redclyffe*, which appeared in 1853 and was taken by the growing school of Pre-Raphaelites almost as a gospel. The rise of George Eliot and the change in the atmosphere which followed the spread of scientific thought robbed her of some of her prestige; but even in the present century cheap editions of her collected novels, going into many volumes, have appeared and been welcomed. But perhaps the Great War put a final bar to her popularity. One reader at least must confess that he can no longer read *The Daisy Chain* and *The Heir of Redclyffe* with the zest that persisted even into early manhood.

Other earlier writers who deserve mention were Miss Bevan, whose *Peep of Day* and *Line upon Line* were household favourites; so too were the writings of Hesba Stretton with circulations reckoned in millions. One interesting authoress was A.L.O.E. (A Lady of England); initials which concealed the heroic name of Charlotte Tucker. This lady at the age of fifty-four went out to the Punjab as a missionary and there poured out the remnant of her days in devoted service.

One of the most popular writers of fiction which must be classed as mainly written for religious propaganda was Charles Kingsley. His vigorous and manly expositions of "Muscular Christianity" under the guise of novels found a ready public. Their literary merit is very considerable as is the historical knowledge and research which lie behind them. They are marred by the writer's utter inability to understand the "Catholic" point of view, a defect which also came out in his disastrous controversy with Newman, which led him into such partial representations as, in a writer less honest, would be reckoned as deliberate misrepresentation rather than lack of understanding.

One extraordinarily interesting attempt at religious fiction must not be passed by—Shorthouse's *John Inglesant*. Shorthouse was by upbringing a Quaker, but later he joined the Church of England. He was a business man and his attempts at writing were but a side activity, at least in his earlier years. The novel which made him famous is probably the only one which reaches a high standard, and much of its charm is due to the very considerable extracts which have been made from contemporary writers. *John Inglesant* gives a picture of the English Church in the days of Charles I and his son which is at once romantic and mystical, and calculated to appeal to the reader of mildly philosophical tastes and interests. The standpoint of the writer is seen in the long *apologia* for Anglicanism—placed on the lips of the hero after his many adventures, material and spiritual, in Italy and Rome—which closes the book. "The English Church, as established by the law of England," he says, "offers the supernatural to all who choose to come. It is like the Divine Being Himself, whose sun shines alike on the evil and on the good. Upon the altars of the Church the divine presence hovers as surely, to those who believe it, as it does upon the splendid altars of Rome. Thanks to circumstances which the founders of our Church did not contemplate, the way is open; it is barred by no confession, no human priest. . . . I am not blind to the peculiar dangers that beset the English Church. I fear that its position, standing, as it does, a mean between two extremes, will engender indifference and sloth; and that its freedom will prevent its preserving a discipline and organizing power, without which any community will suffer grievous damage; nevertheless, as a Church it is unique; if suffered to drop out of existence, nothing like it can ever take its place" (*op. cit.*, pp. 442 f.).

The later years of the era saw the sudden rise to fame of Mrs. Humphry Ward, whose novel *Robert Elsmere* became for a season a considerable storm-centre after its publication in February 1888. Together with her other novels it conveyed Liberal ideas in theology into the homes and minds of English people infinitely more widely than even the writings of her uncle, Matthew Arnold, had done. Perhaps, as with Zola, the "tendency" element in her work may prevent it from being of quite first-rate value to the historian; both as reflecting and influencing English life on its religious and cultivated side it stands alone.

Tracts

The most famous tracts of the century were, of course, the *Tracts for the Times*; so famous, or even notorious were they that some amusing mistakes were made as a consequence; as when a complaint was made of a certain incumbent by a parishioner that he was a terrible Tractarian on the grounds that he circulated in his parish tracts issued by the R.T.S.[1] But if the Tractarians made this form of literature more popular than it had been they were by no means the pioneers. We have already had occasion to notice the activities in this direction which led to the formation of the Society just referred to;[2] they were an equally ready means of religious propaganda in the hands of Hannah More. Her evidential tracts were works of real merit—Bishop Porteous, no mean judge, said of one of them: "Here you have Bishop Butler's 'Analogy,' all for a halfpenny!"[3] Some of her more popular tracts reached circulations of over a million copies. Another prolific writer of a later period was J. C. Ryle, sometime Bishop of Liverpool. It has been calculated that his tracts, which were composed for the Evangelical school of thought, reached the astounding circulation of more than twelve million copies. For the older school of Churchmen, in addition to the writings of the Oxford Movement—in spite of the name these were hardly tracts, some indeed were weighty theological treatises—there was a steady issue from the S.P.C.K.

[1] See Mason, *Life of G. H. Wilkinson*, I, p. 42.
[2] See above, p. 37.
[3] Quoted by Overton, *English Church in the Nineteenth Century*, p. 172, together with other favourable judgements.

But the foremost agency in the production and circulation of this useful form of religious propaganda has yet to be mentioned—Drummond's Tract Depository at Stirling. From this single source tracts numbering hundreds of millions were put into circulation. It was a son of this house who issued perhaps the supreme example of this type of literature—Professor Henry Drummond's *Greatest Thing in the World*. This little tract within six months of its appearance had reached the surprising circulation of 185,000 copies—and it still sells extraordinarily well and makes appeal to many who would normally be left untouched by that particular form of religious approach.

VICTORIAN ART

As in the case of Literature we are not here concerned with Art as such, but merely as mirroring and influencing the ideas and tendencies of the period. The subject matter of Art is life; but life as seen by a particular individual; for life itself is formless, and in art form is given to it by the imagination and craft of the artist. As such, when the work of all the artists of a particular epoch is taken into account, it constitutes as certain and subtle a test of a civilization or society as we are able to apply. The longer the period and the wider the area the more valuable will be the results obtained; but even applied to the narrow span of a century much is disclosed. For art reveals not only the ideas working in men's minds, but also throws light on the social and economic conditions from which it arises.

Decay of British Art

During the generation which preceded the coming of Victoria English craftsmen seem to have lost the secret of making beautiful things, and though we had a school of water-colour painters which was probably without equal, in all other branches of pure and applied art we were woefully deficient. It was long before this state of things was improved; for the Great Exhibition of 1851 was to reveal, to the shuddering gaze of those who had true artistic sensibilities, the terrible deficiencies of English design and decoration. These deficiencies were the offspring of the spirit of the age.

The Victorian Age desired above all else mental ease and material comfort; hence its hatred of anything which seemed likely to disturb the one or the other. Beauty itself, since so often it was allied with passion, came into the category of the potentially disturbing; it could, indeed, make devastating raids into a secure and self-sufficient world. The hideous domestic furniture of the period was hideous because it was an expression of this selfsame desire for security and solidarity. Painting, by a kind of reaction, often descended into the "pretty"; it was content to be merely decorative. As there existed no real artistic tradition to give it strength and distinction it was at the mercy of all manner of outside influences, and questions of morals, and even of politics played over its surface. Art was in the main fulfilling a reflective office, and ceasing, from its own weakness, to guide and mould the nation. At the same time there was a growing interest in beautiful things and a willingness to make the attempt to understand them. In many this was, of course, a mere pose. "The century expects every man to understand and worship art," wrote Canon Barnett in 1872, "so we all talk a little about it" (*Canon Barnett, His Life, Work and Friends*, p. 50).

John Ruskin and William Morris

But a people which had been so thoroughly "industrialized" as the people of England, and had come to trust so confidently in the "mechanical," could arrive at the meaning of art, and produce it, only after gigantic labours, or by the unexpected presence of some genius sent by the pity of Heaven to guide and direct them. But the lot of such a genius when he was sent was a hard one. The nearest approach to such in the Victorian Era was John Ruskin, and his task was perforce mainly one of denunciation. No other remained open to him. But he did not shrink from it and, for those who were able to receive it, exposed the artistic and moral deficiencies of the age. A single passage may be quoted as an example. "Almost the whole system and hope of modern life are founded on the notion that you may substitute mechanism for skill, photograph for picture, cast-iron for sculpture. That is your main nineteenth-century faith, or infidelity. You think you can get everything

LITERATURE AND ART

by grinding—music, literature, and painting. You will find it grievously not so; you can get nothing but dust by mere grinding" (*The Eagle's Nest*, p. 95).

The work of Ruskin and others was not entirely vain, for in the last part of the era there was much aesthetic discontent in England. Our deficiencies were recognized as a reproach to the civilization which we had founded; that new industrial, mechanical civilization which looked so strong and so hopeful when judged by its own standards of profit-making and increased ease of production; but which seemed so poor and thin when the rod of the Spirit was placed against it. Those who possessed clear insight saw that artistic failure was but a symptom of an indwelling disease which affected the whole of society. It was no accident which led both Ruskin and William Morris to turn from aesthetic deficiencies to study social evils.

Ruskin, though possessed of a careful and conscientious copyist's gift, was a critic rather than an artist, and had come into prominence by his championship of Turner. At the time the painter was seventy years of age and nearing the end of his days; his defender, a young man of twenty-three, recently "come down" from Christ Church. The need for a champion was certainly great, for Turner's exhibits in the Academy of 1842 had been described as "produced as if by throwing handfuls of white and blue and red at the canvas." From this youthful championship of a great and neglected genius Ruskin went on to become the aesthetic preceptor of the nation; until his reputation was tarnished by what people regarded as his "unfortunate" venturing into the field of economics. But he fulfilled an office, and no doubt multitudes could have said with Henry Drummond: "Ruskin taught me to see" (*Life*, by Cuthbert Lennox, p. 14).

The influence of William Morris was exerted to the same ends, but by ways that were different. He was a poet, and his verses stirred the hearts of many who were not reached even by Ruskin's magnificent prose; he was a craftsman, who made and manufactured beautiful fabrics—who has not heard of Morris wallpapers?—who printed beautiful books; he was an agitator, who did not disdain to stand at street corners haranguing the mob—though in return they thought him, as Arthur Benson has said, a slightly inebriated seaman. For him the supreme need was that beauty should be brought back into the whole of life, and joy into every department of labour.

Both Ruskin and Morris, the one by his encouragement and the other by direct participation, did their part in furthering the schemes of a noteworthy effort to improve English art and give it a tradition of its own. This was the Pre-Raphaelite Brotherhood. It was in some sense a continuation, in the realm of art, of that outbreak of restlessness and revolt which gave England the Romantic poets of the preceding era. It had its beginnings in 1848, the year be it noted of the revolutionary outbreaks on the continent, when three young artists, Holman Hunt, Millais, and Rossetti, met in the rooms of the first named. So long as his health was equal to the post Rossetti was the leader and inspirer of the Movement. To Burne-Jones and Morris, who came into the Movement a little later, he seemed to be "transfiguring the art of painting, giving to it that purpose and intensity which, they hoped, were soon to quicken the whole of society."[1] Morris and Burne-Jones had been together at Oxford in the 'fifties, both had been intending to take Orders, but the devotion to art gripped them instead. It was they and others who, under the direction of Rossetti, undertook to paint the Oxford Union in 1857.

The Pre-Raphaelites held to certain fundamental and portentous truths; above all the worth of simplicity and hard labour; with a strongly ethical standpoint, they believed, as Mr. Chesterton has put it, that "purity is the only atmosphere for passion" (*G. F. Watts*, p. 40). Their influence, exercised through "an orgy of parable, intense symbolism and legend,"[2] was wide and persistent and the "serious sincerity" which they brought to English art told, and told for good, on all their successors. One may mention in this connexion the lonely figure of G. F. Watts, perhaps "the noblest ideal painter that England has ever seen."

---

[1] A. Clutton-Brock, *William Morris*, p. 46.
[2] Mary MacCarthy, *A Nineteenth-Century Childhood*, p. 10.

ARCHITECTURE

We have already seen that the nineteenth century, and that greater part of it which fell within the reign of Queen Victoria, was a time of activity in Church-building; indeed, since the Reformation no period can compare with it. Unfortunately, many of the buildings were quite unworthy of the object for which they were intended, at least from an artistic point of view, in spite of the vast sums spent or squandered upon them. Canon Overton goes so far as to say: "There are probably no churches which are more of a puzzle and a despair to architects and clergymen than the churches built in the early part of the nineteenth century. Unmitigated ugliness and hopeless inconvenience are their chief characteristics" (*The English Church in the Nineteenth Century*, p. 155). Even those who aimed at some kind of artistic achievement were unsuccessful, and it has been said of the churches erected in 1838 that they "possessed externally an irritating pretentiousness." Some there were who in building, and still more in restoration work, kept in view the great end of the structure—the promotion of the spirit of worship. Lord Shaftesbury, in this as in so many other respects an outstanding figure, when he restored the parish church of Wimborne St. Giles claimed that he had made it "look like a church, and cease to wear the appearance of an old ball-room" (*Life*, II, p. 370).

The Gothic Revival

Mistakes were natural, for at the beginning of the century architecture in England was in a state of chaos. The great tradition which had filled the land with wonderful parish churches in the late Middle Ages had been lost; we no longer had a style of our own and other styles were misunderstood in theory and degraded in practice. Then came the era of the Gothic Revival. This Revival, like the Pre-Raphaelite Movement in painting, was really part of the great movement which began with the Romantic poets and was continued, in the sphere of religion, by the Oxford Movement. On the theoretical side it was propagated by the writings of Rickman and others, who expounded to a generation which had forgotten them the principles upon which genuine Gothic is based. In the world of performance the two Pugins led the way. But the revived style, even in the hands of a Pugin, seemed to many foreign and unnatural. Mark Pattison, querulous as usual, condemned Gothic churches as imitative, copies after originals, "no longer expressions in stone of the faith and sentiments of the builders" (*Essays*, II, p. 172). After the Pugins came other great architects in the same style, which had by then become itself a tradition. Sir Gilbert Scott was among the foremost, though he was lacking in imagination. Mr. Humphry Ward has said of him:

"His original work has too much the air of a copy of some type bequeathed by a far-off century, and in his restorations he was deficient in that sense of historical development which no man who has authority over an ancient building ought to be without" (*The Reign of Queen Victoria*, II, p. 549). G. E. Street, in power of imagination if in nothing else, was his superior. Other architects of note were Bodley, and Butterfield who built Keble College and All Saints, Margaret Street. To one architect was given the supreme task of building the first cathedral to be erected in this island since the Reformation, and he was worthy of the responsibility—J. L. Pearson who built Truro Cathedral.

In the *Life of G. H. Wilkinson*, then Canon under Benson, there has been preserved an account of Pearson's approach to his great task. "Before he would put pen to paper, or even begin to imagine what sort of building he should design, he made his Communion in the little old church of St. Mary, which had been assigned to the Bishop as his cathedral by the Act which founded the see. Mr. Wilkinson had the opportunity of praying with Mr. Pearson then and there. No doubt it was under such influences as his that Mr. Pearson gave a memorable answer to someone who offered a criticism upon his design before he had fully worked it out. 'My business,' he said, 'is to think what will bring people soonest to their knees'" (A. J. Mason, *op. cit.*, II, p. 120).

People often forgot this side of the function of an ecclesiastical building, as they forgot that there is a grim force in Gothic which makes some of the stained glass inserted in the walls of

Gothic churches look "finicking" and mild.[1] But the work of the builder, and of the designer of stained-glass memorials, was not the only work to need supervision. We have seen already that so great an architect as Sir Gilbert Scott has been condemned as deficient in knowledge when faced with the delicate task of restoring an ancient building. If such a criticism has to be made, what of the hundreds of nameless "restorers" up and down the country who, with the best will in the world, lightly set about their task? Some check was put to their activities by the formation of the Society for the Protection of Ancient Buildings in 1877, of which William Morris was the secretary.[2]

If the churches which were erected in the country during the early and middle years of the Victorian Era were an offence, in some cases, to the artistic eye, the numerous chapels which were so lavishly scattered over its face were almost uniformly appalling disfigurements. In early days Nonconformists had been too poor to put up worthy structures, and also afraid, as Dale pointed out, "to invest their money in buildings, of which new political convulsions might deprive them" (*Life*, p. 170). But with the coming of quieter times and vastly increased wealth they had the means at their disposal, but unfortunately not the taste or experience; and what made so many Dissenting chapels hideous was the prodigal ornateness and contempt for all known styles which made them characteristic. Dale may again be quoted as an apologist: "If we sometimes make queer blunders," he says, "if 'Dissenting Gothic' affords amusement, as well it may very often . . . we can only say that we are inexperienced hands at this work, we are improving already, and hope to do better still by and by" (*op. cit.*, p. 170).

MUSIC

In the course of the eighteenth century a great change took place in Western Art, the sceptre passed from Architecture to

---

[1] Cf. Martin Armstrong in *Great Victorians*, p. 104.

[2] A. Clutton-Brock, *William Morris*, p. 137. Morris had been moved to a state of tremendous indignation by the "restoration" of Lichfield Cathedral in the previous year.

Music; and Western artistic impulse was, "as it were, translated from the grosser medium of stone into the subtler medium of sound."[1] At this point therefore it might seem well to enquire into the effect of music on religion in the era, and to canvass its value as a means of revealing the tendencies and ideas underlying the society in which it flourished. But music is not a good revealer because it is cultivated, even more than other arts, for such diverse reasons, and may therefore be supposed to have such diverse effects. To some it affords purely sensuous enjoyment, in some it is the intellect which reacts most strongly. Certain types of music which have behind them a distinct philosophy and view of life may therefore pass quite harmlessly through the ears of those who listen to them; because such a philosophy is not so much rejected as unperceived. Music may therefore be left for consideration until we come to the subject of Worship, and then only considered in its directly religious form.

ART AND RELIGION

Art and Religion have this much in common, that the end of each is to convey a new revelation to man. Furthermore, each of them fails in part because no perfect medium is available. The artist has his vision, but what appears on the canvas is but a suggestion of what he has seen. The man of God, too, has his vision, of "unspeakable things," but he too can find no language adequate to describe it. In each case the vision is of God; for the beauty and joy of the earth are part of the eternal beauty and joy of the universe which God has made. Beauty is also a revelation of God, in fact one might even dare to say that God Himself is beauty, as well as righteousness and truth. Otherwise He would hardly have made the world such a beautiful place. There must be behind all the wonders of Nature, the glow of the sunset, the restless loveliness of the sea, the stately march of the clouds, what Bishop Gore has called "a spirit of beauty which communicates with and

---

[1] A. J. Toynbee, *A Study of History*, III, p. 185. He quotes an illuminating passage from Spengler, *The Decline of the West*, in illustration.

corresponds with the faculty of beauty in man."[1] This was why Charles Kingsley in one of his strange letters to working men wrote: "*Never lose an opportunity of seeing anything beautiful. Beauty is God's handwriting—a wayside sacrament; welcome it in every fair face, every fair sky, every fair flower, and thank for it Him, the fountain of all loveliness, and drink it in, simply and earnestly, with all your eyes; it is a charmed draught, a cup of blessing*" (*Life*, p. 68).

It is by the contemplation of beauty, so Plato perceived long centuries ago,[2] that the soul at last succeeds in regaining the freedom which (so he thought) it forfeited at its birth. And though this may not be a doctrine which, in its entirety, is possible for the Christian, its positive side has been tested and found to be true. There is an aesthetic activity of the soul which can lead to God, and this activity, as Clutton-Brock used to teach us,[3] is something which we are to value for its own sake. For beauty is an end in itself just as much as goodness or truth.

But in the pursuit of beauty we have to beware of a double danger. It may become merely a means for creating pleasure, of stimulating the senses; or it may, on a higher level, be the means of creating an inner harmony which will be a substitute for religion itself. This last may not be a temptation to many, for artistic contemplation with its effortless pleasure is beyond the capacity of all but the few. Such sustained exaltation may come into their lives, if at all, but at supreme moments. In such moments we get "the direct and immediate apprehension of an absolutely satisfying object";[4] time and space cease to exist, and there comes the nearest approach to forgetfulness of his existence which the grown man ever knows, save in his communion with God. Lessing once made the strange remark that "only religion misconceived can draw us away from

---

[1] *Belief in God*, p. 53. Bishop Gore in this very important passage argued that beauty, in so far as it has no "survival" value, is an argument for the existence of God, and, of course, for a God who loves beautiful things.

[2] See James Adam, *Religious Teachers of Greece*, p. 387. A similar thought has been expressed by W. B. Yeats, the Irish poet: "If beauty is not a gateway out of the net we were taken in at our birth, it will not long be beauty" (*The Celtic Twilight*).

[3] *The Ultimate Belief*, pp. 65 ff. [4] W. Temple, *Mens Creatrix*, p. 97.

beauty"; I should like to reverse the substantives and affirm that "only beauty misconceived can draw us away from religion." None the less, it is only too true that religion and beauty have often proved to be incompatible, and the Puritan and the Aesthete have gone their several ways not realizing all that they, respectively, have lost, nor that such loss was not inevitable. There is an interesting testimony to the true Christian conception of art contained in the *Life of Henry Martyn*, by Sargent. "Since I have known God in a saving manner," he remarks, "painting, poetry, and music have had charms unknown to me before. I have received what I suppose is a taste for them; for religion has refined my mind, and made it susceptible of impressions from the sublime and beautiful. Oh how religion secures the heightened enjoyment of those pleasures which keep so many from God" (*op. cit.*, p. 53).

There are those who in times of confusion and doubt find in beauty the only stable thing:

"Under the arch of life, where love and death,
    Terror and mystery, guard the shrine, I saw
Beauty enthroned."

So sang Rossetti, and many have echoed his words. Such a one was William Morris, who found in art a substitute for the religion which he could no longer accept, a consolation for the failure to discover any other more certain approach to God. Clutton-Brock says of him: "The humblest work of art was to him a sign of divinity ... and he was moved by it as other men are moved by noble unexpected actions" (*William Morris*, p. 219).

It would seem that for the artist the only way of safety is that of dedication. To find in religion an inspiration, something that makes life more beautiful and gracious; and something that calls out of him the highest that he knows. "What a gift is Art, music above all," once wrote Jenny Lind, who well knew what this meant, "when we understand, not to make it an idol, but to place it at the foot of the cross ... (The Saviour) alone ... is the goal of all our intense longing, whether we know it or not."[1] In such a way is the danger of making art a substitute

[1] Quoted H. Scott Holland, *Personal Studies*, pp. 28 f.

for religion to be avoided by the artist to whom the temptation is most subtle.

The other danger, that of reaching a purely sensuous outlook on life, is one which affects all alike who contemplate beauty and lose themselves in it. Beyond it lies a further danger; that the sensuous outlook may become the sensual. "The love of beauty," wrote Dr. Inge, "will lead us up a long way—up to the point when the love of the Good is ready to receive us. Only we must not let ourselves be entangled by sensuous beauty. Those who do not quickly rise beyond this first stage, to contemplate 'ideal form, the universal mould,' share the fate of Hylas; they are engulfed in a swamp, from which they never emerge" (*Christian Mysticism*, p. 93). The fears of the Puritan have therefore their justification, but at the same time there is a higher way.

The Puritan Attitude

The mistake of the Puritan is to suppose that man is a purely moral creature; this, incidentally, may lead to the subordination of truth as well as beauty, the doing of evil that good may come. By a kind of reaction certain people of extreme aesthetic sensibility follow beauty in defiance of the moral law, which they come to regard as a purely negative thing, a restriction on their freedom. Both the Puritan and the "aesthete" are surely wrong; for both morality and beauty are ends in themselves worthy of pursuit—for both, as we have seen, are characteristics of the divine nature. But the Puritan acts often through fear of the unknown and his attitude is the fruit of ignorance. This sometimes takes amusing forms, as all actions based on fear of the unknown are apt to do. When F. B. Meyer was driven to resign the charge of Victoria Road Baptist Chapel, Leicester, he and his supporters began to hold services in the Public Museum. One old lady among the helpers was so shocked by the statuary and some of the pictures in the room where they met that she brought down sheets to cover them. This proved an unintentional advertisement and people flocked in to see the figures in their new coverings.[1] In a similar vein the evangelist who was taken into Temple

[1] Fullerton, *F. B. Meyer*, p. 50.

Gairdner's rooms at Oxford stared fiercely at the Greek statues in which Gairdner delighted, and exclaimed: "Smash 'em! smash 'em!"[1] It is certain, I think, that the older Evangelicals with their narrow views of what was meant by the "world" avoided much that was beneficial and condemned needlessly many innocent amusements and recreations. This came largely from an inadequate grasp of the full implications of the doctrine of the Incarnation. But there are many difficulties in the way of those who would decide what is and what is not lawful. Even Bishop Westcott could never make up his mind about theatre-going (*Life and Letters*, I, p. 361), though Bishop Lightfoot was in favour of trying to raise its tone by attendance; he even went so far as to say, in a sermon, that "the emotions aroused by the Drama are from God and of God."

But there have been many who, brought up in a Puritan home, have found that their Puritanism need not come between them and their love of beauty. R. F. Horton, after his first visit to Italy, records that "From that time forward Art took its place in my life alongside Religion, an interpretation of life, a revelation of God" (*An Autobiography*, p. 62). While Hugh Price Hughes wished that a course on Art might be included in the curriculum of all Methodist Training Colleges. "It is high time," he wrote, "that those of us who represent the glorious Puritan tradition should remember that there is such a thing as the 'holiness of beauty' as well as 'the beauty of holiness' " (*Life*, p. 406).

Before leaving the subject of Art and Morality it may be well to expose an idea which is still held here and there, especially amongst religious people, and for which they quote the revered name of John Ruskin as their authority—the idea that great art cannot exist along with low morals. This unfortunately is disproved by experience. There have unquestionably been supreme artists whose lives fell far below the Christian moral standard; even Ruskin's own favourite, Turner, was not impeccable in this matter. What Ruskin did affirm was that "in order to be a good natural painter there must be strong elements of good in the mind, however warped by other parts of the character" (quoted by Collingwood, *Life of John Ruskin*, p. 145).

[1] Padwick, *Temple Gairdner of Cairo*, p. 21.

WORSHIP

ITS IMPORTANCE

WORSHIP of some kind or another is found in every religion, however primitive. It may therefore be said to be natural to the human soul. Worship thus constitutes perhaps the most convenient and searching of all the tests that can be applied to a religion. It stands, indeed, higher than morality; for, as Dr. Kirk has recently reminded us, the principal duty of even the Christian moralist is "to stimulate the spirit of worship in those to whom he addresses himself" (*The Vision of God*, p. x). Now worship, as the Scriptures themselves shew quite clearly, may be that of the individual or of the community. Both are needful; for so long as we live in a material universe and possess bodies, some institutional expression of religion, and the highest expression of religion is worship, will always remain a necessity.[1] Private prayer, though it may differ greatly with individuals, does not differ much from age to age; in this chapter, therefore, only the corporate aspects of worship will receive attention.

At the beginning of the Victorian Era corporate worship and the arrangement and care of the public services of religion were at a very low ebb; this we have already observed (see above, pp. 44 f.). But during the epoch itself, in response to a revived sense of man's needs and of God's dignity, there was an enormous improvement. This deepening of the sense of holy things was in part a result of the efforts of the best of the Tractarians, and was often unaccompanied by any attempt to introduce elaborate ritual. The priest's own consciousness of the unseen was enough to bring it vividly into the hearts of sympathetic fellow worshippers. This is well brought out by the testimony of one of R. W. Church's parishioners at Whatley. "The first thing," he says, "that impressed us all was the extreme solemnity and devotion with which Mr. Church celebrated the Holy Communion. We had heard

---

[1] Cf. Storr, *Spiritual Liberty*, p. 95.

nothing then about the Eastward position, but I can see now his slight figure bent in lowly reverence before the altar, giving the whole service a new and higher and holier meaning by his bearing and entire absorption in the act of worship" (*Life and Letters of Dean Church*, p. 168).

Apart from Tractarian influences, however, there would almost certainly have been a revived interest in worship; but in them first of all it became vocal and active. The century in which we are now living was to see even further developments. These are all to the good, for as von Hügel has said: "The first and central act of religion is *adoration*, sense of God" (*Selected Letters*, p. 261). The act of adoration is capable of drawing to it all man's faculties and demands all his powers, to the exclusion of whatever is selfish and earthly. This has been well brought out in a quotation from William Löhe, made by Heiler: "I know nothing that is higher or more fair than the worship of my Lord; there all man's arts combine in the service of adoration; there is his countenance transfigured, his very form and voice made new; there he giveth God the glory; yea, the holy Liturgy of the Church surpasseth all the Poetry of the world" (*The Spirit of Worship*, p. viii).[1] Even Comte, who recognized no God, had to make provision for worship, and he set forth as the object of his disciples' adoration—the colourless concept of Collective Humanity. In its honour a highly elaborate ritual, borrowed mainly from Roman Catholic sources, was devised.

It is important to emphasize this growing sense of the importance of adoration and worship; since so often it has been forgotten, or rather obscured, by Protestants, being subordinated to instruction and other necessary acts. But this was not universally the case for Henry Venn Elliott could say: "I have always gone to church expecting to derive greater benefits from the prayers than the sermon" (*Life*, p. 38); and James Martineau, the great Unitarian thinker and teacher, held that the primary object of the gathering together of the

[1] The Bishop of Chichester (Dr. Bell) has also emphasized this: "The growth of interest in worship," he says, "implies most certainly the lifting up of the heart from ourselves to God, a hunger for the objective, the real, which only God can satisfy" (*The Modern Parson*, p. 82).

congregation was worship rather than any other thing.[1] The wonderful power of the Roman Church, whatever opinions may be held of its methods and the teaching underlying them, is due largely to the recognition of this need on the part of man for realizing the Presence of God, and of offering to Him the adoration of the whole being. An incident in the life of Hugh Price Hughes shews how one of a generous and sympathetic spirit, although his own training and beliefs were in many ways so different, could grasp and appreciate this aspect of a Roman service. "On entering a Roman Church in Italy on the evening of Christmas Day, he was visibly moved by the prostration of the congregation, their manifest belief that Christ was in their midst, however material and crude to his thinking the interpretation might appear. When he got outside he said in a low voice to my mother, 'I understand this—I understand this. They have it—the root idea.' By this he meant that worshippers were there for the right reason, to feel the presence of Christ, and to meet Him there, not to have a learned discourse or even sing hymns, but to realize their Saviour as they could not elsewhere" (Dorothea Price Hughes, *Life of Hugh Price Hughes*, p. 222).

The public services of the Church should form the central activity of every Christian community, not only because they are intended to promote the fellowship of the body, but because in them God can best be realized. This is the aim which every Christian clergyman or minister should set before him. When Charles Kingsley wrote to his future wife on the eve of entering on their joint labours, he said: "We will not let public worship become 'dead bones.' We will strive and pray, day and night, till we put life into it, till our parish feels that God is the great Idea, and that all things are in Him, and He in all things" (*Life*, p. 43). In a similar vein the Barnetts undertook their stupendous task in Whitechapel. They set themselves to "teach the people that to worship was a privilege, and that prayers and praises were personal actions for which men were only responsible to their Maker." This was to be "the first step towards reality in religious life" (*Canon Barnett*, p. 77).

---

[1] See J. Estlin Carpenter, *James Martineau*, p. 416.

TRAINING IN WORSHIP

Worship, although the instinct itself may be found in every human soul, is a thing that needs training and drawing out. It requires, indeed, a long lifetime to bring it near to perfection; perfection itself can only come when the soul finds itself sharing in the adoration of the heavenly host in the visible presence of God. But here on earth there have been chosen servants of God who have come very near to this state. Such a one was Charlotte Yonge, of whom it has been said: "No one could accompany her twice daily to the church services in the last years of her life and fail to realize that her life's work had consisted in learning to worship. The Psalms, Lessons, Creeds, and Prayers were the paramount interest. All her cultivation, and the experiences of an intensely lived long life had been the means for entering more deeply into their meaning. The loud, thoughtful, joyous tone with which she was accustomed to repeat the Apostles' Creed, and especially the triumphant 'The Life Everlasting. Amen,' revealed the breadth and depth of her intellectual and spiritual life" (C. A. E. Moberly, *Dulce Domum*, p. 19).

From such an ideal as this one has to descend a long way to contemplate some of the "bright" and "popular" services which attempt to cater for what are believed to be the people's needs. The attempt often ends in degrading the whole idea of worship with unworthy hymns, and "prayers" which treat the Deity as if He were unwilling to hear and help unless addressed in terms which no man would use to an equal. There can be but little doubt that much of this irreverence, to give it its proper name, is due to a defective theology. God is reduced to such human proportions that all sense of awe is lost; and this reducing of God to human proportions comes from an unorthodox idea of the Incarnation.

Arnold of Rugby used to hold that one great object of God's revealing Himself in Christ was to furnish us with an object of worship and so to meet the need shewn in idolatry (*Life*, p. 305). This is a dangerous doctrine and Hort, one of the greatest and most orthodox thinkers of the nineteenth century, has laid his finger on its central defect. "I have been persuaded for many years," he wrote to Westcott in 1865, "that Mary-worship and 'Jesus'-worship have very much in common in their causes and results." He pointed out that one has "In Protestant countries the fearful notion 'Christ the believer's God.' ... In Romish countries the Virgin is a nearer and more attractive object, and not rejected by the dominant creed" (*Life and Letters*, II, p. 50). In the same way a contemporary thinker has seen the main danger of the advanced Liberal Protestant in his giving to Jesus the value of God, and thus seeming "to deify a man, by taking a mere man, Jesus, for his God."[1]

One of the great arguments in favour of a set form of service and set prayers, apart from the difficulty of having "public worship" when the congregation does not know the prayers, is that it avoids occasions for irreverence and "false doctrine." Charles Simeon, the great Evangelical leader, has expressed what may be called the Church point of view on the subject. His opinion is the more valuable as it was the fruit of mature consideration and finally expressed after a number of visits to Scotland, where he joined in worship in Presbyterian Churches. "I have on my return to the use of our Liturgy..." he says, "felt it an inestimable privilege that we possess a form of sound words, so adapted in every respect to the wants and desires of all who would worship God in spirit and truth. If *all* men could pray at *all* times as *some* men can *sometimes*, then indeed we might prefer extempore to pre-composed prayer" (quoted Moule, *Charles Simeon*, p. 166). The same sentiments were expressed by an Evangelical of a later generation, Henry Venn Elliott, who recorded his feelings after attending a service at the chapel of the famous Mr. Jay of Bath. (This must have been an exceptional thing as the Evangelicals were careful, as a rule, to avoid Nonconformist places of worship.) "I returned from the *élite* of Dissent," he says, "thankful to God for His mercy in assigning my place in our Church, and thankful above all for the Liturgy" (quoted Bateman, *Life of H. V. Elliott*, p. 3). Coming down to a later period we find that Stopford Brooke had an intense dislike of Nonconformist services with their "extemporary prayers, like leading articles

---

[1] O. C. Quick, *Liberalism, Modernism, and Tradition*, p. 51.

addressed to God." He considered that "Style, which is so right in a sermon, is undesirable in a prayer. It is the minister who prays, not the people" (*Life and Letters*, p. 595).

The Nonconformist preference for a freer and more varied form of worship is based on the knowledge that forms so often become dead and meaningless from constant repetition—and there was much, especially in the early years of the Victorian epoch, to justify their conclusion—and that they fail to meet new needs which may emerge. Among the Methodists, in this as in other things careful to preserve their closer link with the Church, the use of the Prayer Book was often continued. The ministers especially were anxious, in not a few cases, to have a full liturgical service.[1] This led to the idea that they wished to return to the Church and had the effect of alienating other Nonconformists. But on the other hand, as very elaborate services were introduced in some Anglican Churches, those Churchmen who preferred a simpler form and could not find it in their neighbourhood, took to attending the Methodist Chapels where it was still available.[2] Towards the end of the century the need for improving Nonconformist services was widely recognized. Signs of it are to be seen in the volumes of liturgical services for the use of Congregational Churches produced by Silvester Horne and T. H. Darlow. (See *Silvester Horne*, p. 102.) Earlier still the convenience of learning from Anglican sources, apart from the Prayer Book itself, had been recognized by R. W. Dale, who in sending to his assistant, the Rev. George Barber, a *Manual of Intercessory Prayer* by Father Benson of Cowley, wrote: "These High Churchmen, with the use they make of the liturgical and devotional literature of many centuries, have much to teach us" (*Life*, p. 635).

RITUAL

In the matter of the buildings and other accessories of public worship mankind seems to be sharply divided into two classes; those who see in them a hindrance, and wish so far as is possible to be rid of them: and those who find them a help and an

---

[1] See Dorothea Price Hughes, *Life of Hugh Price Hughes*, pp. 103 f., 112.
[2] *Op. cit.*, p. 115.

opportunity. These two classes are not new. In the Middle Ages the division was found, and alongside the elaborate ritual and buildings of the Church and most of the other Orders, the Cistercians, at least in their earliest days, stood out for simplicity and restraint.[1]

The first class demands the uttermost plainness in the necessary accessories of public worship and eliminates all that may prove distracting. A whitewashed building and the smallest amount of furniture is its ideal; so that the mind may have nothing upon which to dwell save God alone. Anything material comes between Him and the soul. It should be remembered that it was from people of this class, and not only from the vulgar agitator, that protests were raised against ritual in the Victorian Era. Bishop Percival, for example, whilst admitting that aesthetic and symbolic worship was natural to a materialistic and luxurious age, declared that it ought to be constantly and vigorously tested "not by its general acceptance or popularity, but by its moral and spiritual fruits." He saw in it a great and ever-present danger "that being sensuous, it is very liable to deteriorate into an emotional worship, which satisfies a mood, but does not regenerate and sanctify the life" (*Life*, p. 148). So too Hastings Rashdall, the late Dean of Carlisle, recognized materialism not only in "a philosophy which denied the creative faculty of reason," but also in "a theology which laid emphasis on ritual regularity and practice rather than on religious life and conduct" (Matheson, *Life of Hastings Rashdall*, p. 254).

In ancient religions the ritual was the important thing; the ideas behind it could be taken or left, or explained away. Ritual as such was therefore a useful binding force.[2] But in the nineteenth century it was just the opposite, a means of division

[1] The endeavour of the Cistercians "was to avoid all ostentation and to live and worship in surroundings of the greatest simplicity. They were, for example, to have no rich vestments or decorated churches and even the books in the library were not to be illuminated": Elliott-Binns, *The Decline and Fall of the Medieval Papacy*, p. 92.

[2] "Renan once visited the rationalist Jew Bernays, and, to his surprise, found him celebrating the Passover with full ritual. Bernays explained that ritual was a principle of union, but that dogma had come to be a principle of disunion": Wilfred Ward, *Last Lectures*, p. 289.

rather than of union. We saw above the disturbances and rioting which followed the introduction into English churches of ritual which was regarded as Roman; but it was not rioting only which followed, but a general spirit of disquiet. When the clergy attended the funeral of Mr. Perceval in 1874 in surplices, their action was regarded by some as "a vast conspiracy to subvert the principles of the Reformation."[1] Even attempts to promote decency and order in the churches themselves were often regarded with suspicion. Edward Stanley, Bishop of Norwich, a liberal and tolerant prelate, who had suffered much for his views, was attacked because he advocated the abolition of high pews and urged that churches should be made more beautiful. In the Victorian Era any new thing was liable to be condemned as Roman or Puseyite. Dr. Arnold had already seen the foolishness of this spirit which cut men off from what might have been a help to them, because it had been previously used by a Church with which they were not in sympathy. He lamented the "absurd confusion in so many men's minds between what is really Popery and what is but wisdom and beauty, adopted by the Roman Catholics and neglected by us" (*Life*, p. 763).

Alongside those who saw in ritual and ornament either a distraction or a danger there were—in addition to those who valued them—others who simply regarded them as beneath their notice one way or the other. In his journal Archbishop Tait wrote down that he was amused at the entire lack of interest displayed by Jowett in ritual and the controversies which it aroused. This remark was published by Davidson and Benham in *Archibald Campbell Tait*, II, p. 430, and came to Jowett's notice. He simply replied: "He was quite right, and I wonder how he or anyone else could take an interest in them" (*Life*, II, p. 394).

It is often supposed that English people, like the famous Master of Balliol just referred to, are not interested in ritual. But this seems to be a mistake, as the history of the various Friendly Societies ought to prove. Rudyard Kipling is surely expressing a typically English point of view when he makes one of his masonic characters say: "All Ritual is fortifying.

[1] See *Life and Letters of Brooke Foss Westcott*, I, p. 334.

Ritual's a natural necessity for mankind. The more things are upset, the more they fly to it. I abhor slovenly ritual anywhere" (*Debits and Credits*, p. 61). One of the first occasions on which the natural love of the English people for pomp and ceremony was revealed was in the Thanksgiving Services for the Recovery of the Prince of Wales in 1872. The various Jubilee Ceremonies in 1887, 1897, and 1935 all shew the same thing. If National life requires outward ceremonies and symbols, so does the life of the Church. "The man who tries to do without symbols is a prophet so austere and isolated as to be dangerously near to a madman," says G. K. Chesterton (*William Blake*, p. 173).

The buildings in which men worship and the fittings with which they adorn them are an opportunity of offering of their best to God and of expressing in outward form, by the aid of every device at their disposal, that inward beauty which is part of the Divine. To worship God in "the beauty of holiness" is indeed the first and essential requirement, but in addition we may worship Him in "the beauty of the sanctuary," as the words may also be rendered. The church, God's house, should be at least as dignified and as beautiful as the houses of His worshippers. Hence we have need of noble and stately buildings and lovely decorations. "The pure and incorruptible Gospel," said E. H. Bickersteth, "will not sound the less sweetly because the House of God in every part of it, within and without, bears witness to the loving earnest care with which we regard all things connected with His service and worship" (quoted by Balleine, *History of the Evangelical Party*, p. 234).

This is a truth which is not always realized and needs to be pointed out. When W. Boyd Carpenter went to Christ Church, Lancaster Gate, in 1879, he was shocked by the fittings and furniture of the sanctuary. "The want of harmony," he wrote in the parish magazine, "is an offence not only against good taste, such as would not be tolerated in a private house, but it is out of keeping with the simple, but good material, which alone ought to find a place within the House of God" (quoted by Major, *Life and Letters of W. Boyd Carpenter*, p. 23).

Sometimes men and women like to make costly offerings to God for use in His service. One example of this is the "Bishop's

Chalice" in Truro Cathedral. "Upon it are mounted . . . 143 diamonds, 6 rubies, 16 emeralds, 6 amethysts, 93 turquoises, 15 corals, 15 pearls, 5 opals, 7 carbuncles, 9 topazes, 1 sapphire, 4 other stones. . . . Beneath the foot is inscribed: 1887. All Saints' Day. This sacred vessel is a memorial before God of the spirit of devotion which in these latter days He has quickened in the Church of England. The gold and 'precious stones of beauty' are the gifts of a large number of persons, who have severally offered that which they most value, for the glory of God and the service of His Holy Table" (A. J. Mason, *Life of G. H. Wilkinson*, II, p. 131).

MUSIC

The reign of Queen Victoria witnessed much activity in the musical world in England; here we are concerned with sacred music only. Even before the Queen came to the throne changes in this department were already taking place and Sydney Smith could speak of the "prodigious" effect of good music in some of the London churches in increasing the congregations (Lady Holland, *Memoir of Sydney Smith*, p. 87). It was indeed time that something was done, for English music was in no healthy condition. Up to the end of the seventeenth century this art had been a necessary part of culture, but in the following century native art was crushed beneath the weight of Handel and, in the early nineteenth, Mendelssohn. The latter, it may be remarked, paid a visit to London to produce "St. Paul" in the year of the Queen's accession.

Englishmen suffered from lack of system and a real knowledge of their art. With Sterndale Bennett there was promise of better things; but the new era really began with Parry and Stanford. With them, however, no great heights were attained and there was little recognition from the continent. "Englishmen wrote church music for the stage, stage music for the Church, organ music for the orchestra, and, as far as we had any orchestral ideas at all, orchestral music for the organ."[1] The typically English music of Purcell and Gibbons tended to be driven out by the rather sentimental compositions of Stainer, Barnby, Dykes, and their fellows. This was a response to popular

[1] D. F. Tovey in *Encyclopædia Britannica*, XVI. p. 15.

taste, but did not make for dignity in Church music, though there can be no question of the religious spirit which underlay it.

If the music provided for Church services was thus of no surpassing merit, the instruments upon which it was produced certainly shewed a vast improvement. At the beginning of the reign services were still being accompanied by a variety of instruments—violins, hautboys, bassoons, and so forth. In the country often there was no music at all or only a barrel-organ. The custom of saying the psalms alternately by the clerk and people persisted, while hymn-singing was not encouraged. Much of the improvement was due to the introduction of Choral Societies and Musical Festivals which set a higher standard of performance and revealed fresh possibilities in the way of material. The care of the Tractarians for every detail of the service did not overlook the musical side of it, and to them most of all must be attributed the revival of Church music in the ordinary parish church. Among Evangelical Churchmen the custom of holding musical services spread but slowly, and it was not until 1891 that the responses were sung at Holy Trinity, Cambridge, Simeon's old church; Handley Moule noted that they were "very sweet and reverent" (*Life*, p. 136). The ideal of Anglican worship was well put by Creighton, when he was Canon of Worcester. It must be "catholic, dignified, simple, free from sensuous excitement, appealing to the whole man, to the head as well as to the heart, quietly stimulating and invigorating, without calling for undue effort, fostering reflection and gradually heightening the spiritual consciousness; this is expressed and cherished in the historic services of the cathedral" (*Life and Letters*, I, p. 315).

Among Nonconformists the improvements usually took the form of somewhat ambitious attempts to render oratorios; the ordinary service, apart from the hymns, not lending itself, save in the case of the Methodists, to elaborate musical efforts.

Unfortunately, musical gifts and spiritual attainments do not always go together and often enough the clergyman or minister finds himself out of sympathy with the organist and the choir. Some fervent natures even regard all music as detrimental if it is produced by a choir and not by the efforts of the congregation alone. F. B. Meyer, before a meeting, was once heard to pray: "Help me to be patient while the choir sings, and let them not distract the people from the message we want them to get" (*Life*, p. 33). But in general there is a high spirit among choirmen and organists and their help can be extremely valuable.

Hymns

I pointed out above that hymn-singing had not been encouraged at the beginning of the era in Anglican churches. This was because it was thought to savour too much of Methodism. Hymn-singing was indeed a feature of Methodist services and one that proved very attractive. William Vincent, later to become Dean of Salisbury, calculated, just before the end of the eighteenth century, that "for one who has been drawn away from the Established Church by preaching, ten have been induced by music" (*Considerations on Parochial Music*, pp. 10 and 14). In spite of this, prejudice was so strong in the minds of the stricter Churchmen that they would not consent to use the same device. Even Marsh, Bishop of Peterborough, a man of much enlightenment and liberality, save where Nonconformity was concerned, inveighed against the use of hymns.[1] But gradually they invaded the services of the Church, and many of them came, not only from antiquity, but from the Methodists themselves, or at least from Evangelical Churchmen like Charles Wesley and Cowper and Newton.

The singing of hymns in the services of the Church is the one point, apart from the sermon, at which novel or false teaching can be introduced. It was, therefore, not unreasonable that the innovation should be regarded with some suspicion. Actually it is probably illegal. Bishop Gore held that "none of the practices objected against High Churchmen were more illegal than the modern habit of hymn-singing. . . . The services were flooded with evangelistic and revivalistic hymns, many of which were good and even necessary at times, but all of which were alien to the spirit of the Prayer Book and to antiquity. By the use of metrical forms any kind of doctrinal

[1] See Overton, *The English Church in the Nineteenth Century*, p. 192.

innovation could be introduced" (Prestige, *Life of Charles Gore*, p. 295).[1]

In 1819 Reginald Heber, the future Bishop of Calcutta, compiled a collection for his parishioners at Hodnet; but even he had "some High Church scruples about using it" (Taylor, *Life of Bishop Heber*, p. 90). It was naturally among the Evangelicals that hymn-singing first became popular, and in 1833 Edward Bickersteth published his *Christian Psalmody*, which had an immense sale, both under its original title and as *The Hymnal Companion*. Other Anglican collections in wide use were *Church Hymns*, which first appeared, from the Society for Promoting Christian Knowledge, as *Psalms and Hymns*; and *Hymns Ancient and Modern*. This last collection, which attained a position of great importance, was first published in 1861 under the editorship of a very influential committee. Stopford Brooke once condemned it as full of "terrible follies and vanities . . . and poetic villainy" (*Life and Letters*, p. 611); but it did good service in its day.

There were also other collections of hymns issued by the various denominations—but they are so numerous that space will not allow any detailed mention of them; for not only did they include collections for Church services but also for Sunday Schools and so forth. A great impetus was given to hymn-singing by the visits of Moody and Sankey and by the hymn book they published. The Salvation Army and the "Keswick" Movement also had their own hymn books.

Hymn-singing was certainly a popular item in the services of both Church and Chapel. Stopford Brooke, who gave much thought to such matters, was of the opinion that congregations liked long hymns and to hear the sound of their own voices; he even ventured to suggest that one reason why young people preferred the Church of England services to those of Nonconformity, was that they had more chance of taking part in them

---

[1] The innovations of doctrine were not all on one side. *The English Hymnal* of 1906, for example, included hymns which directly requested the saints for their prayers. As Bishop Gore considered that the practice of "direct invocation" had been deliberately excluded from the English services, he refused to allow the book to be used in his diocese, although he himself held the doctrine (*op. cit.*, pp. 300).

(*Life and Letters*, pp. 409 f.). Dale considered that hymns had a great influence on the thoughts of those who sang them: "Let me write the hymns of a Church," he once said, "and I care not who writes the theology."[1] But this was surely an optimistic view, for common experience suggests that those who sing hymns take but very little notice of the words they are using. Archbishop Benson was much more accurate when he said: "The habit of hymn-singing in chorus has weakened the sense of truth" (*Life*, p. 374). On the whole, it is well that this should be the case, otherwise, if the words of hymns were taken as a literal expression of the thoughts and desires of those who sing them, there would be a vast and unhealthy increase in sentimentalism. Many of the most popular hymns are really quite unfitted for singing in public; they are suited much more for the closet and the bedchamber where the soul is alone with its Maker. This reveals the weakness and danger of this type, so very popular, of hymn. Liddon in a letter to Scott Holland once condemned it on the ground that "the subjective hymn is either an ode to self, or an assertion of self disguised in religious language" (*Life*, p. 145). Jowett, too, was very critical—"How cocky they are," he once broke out:

'When upward I fly
Quite justified I.'

Who can say such a thing as that?" (*Life and Letters*, II, p. 203). Many would share the opinion of Fairbairn, who wrote: "I am grateful that my childhood was nurtured on the Book of Psalms rather than on the jingling verses that celebrate the 'Sweet Saviour,' or protest how I love 'my Jesus' " (*Studies in Religion and Theology*, p. 272). Hymn writers may rise to great heights or sink to considerable depths; the canonical writers stand alone.

[1] Quoted Silvester Horne, *Free Church History*, p. 250.

THE CALL OF THE WORLD

EARLY MISSIONARY EFFORTS

To carry out the Lord's command to preach the gospel to all nations (Matt. xxviii. 19) was, for the first disciples, a stupendous task; but its full extent could not be known to man until "time and history had lifted him to a position high enough to overlook humanity."[1] Now the extent of the world that has to be won is fully known and the full burden of the responsibility. But this only came to pass in the Victorian Era and in the century of which it occupied the greater part. If that century saw the unveiling of new lands and people, it saw also the greatest advance in propagating the gospel and the widest diffusion of the missionary spirit that Christendom had ever known. Even the early centuries of the Church's existence did not achieve so much.[2]

The discovery of new lands and child races, if at first they seemed destined merely to benefit the dominant white races, soon roused in the Church a sense of new responsibilities laid upon it and the need, in Christ's name, to understand and sympathize with them. Above all, these weak peoples, for whom He had died, needed protecting from the traders who had seized their countries and now sought to exploit their labour. "We have taken Naboth's vineyard," wrote Frank Lenwood, "but nowadays we do not kill Naboth; Ahab needs his labour" (*Social Problems and the East*, p. 115).

But this renewed sense of responsibility for evangelizing the heathen had already been aroused at the beginning of the century; a conspicuous sign of the rising tide of spiritual life in England, and a revival of the tradition, once so strong in the English Church, by which the gospel had been carried from this island to the continent of Europe. To remember this

[1] Fairbairn, *Studies in Religion and Theology*, p. 10.
[2] Such is the opinion of the American expert, R. E. Speer, *Missionary Principles and Practice*, p. 421 : cf. also Bishop Lightfoot on "The Comparative Progress of Ancient and Modern Missions" in *Historical Essays*, pp. 72 ff.

is important for, as the Dean of Manchester has said, "We cannot rightly estimate the nature and development of modern missionary effort unless we examine its links with the past and treasure that past" (In *The Future of the Church of England*, p. 199). None the less, it was a singularly unpropitious moment for a new undertaking since the country was at this time plunged in war, its resources strained, and its manhood engaged.

The Eighteenth Century

Even in the eighteenth century there had been some interest shewn in Missions and operations attempted on a small scale. Its achievement, apart from the great outburst of energy in its closing years, may have been meagre, but at any rate a start had been made. In 1701 the Society for the Propagation of the Gospel had its beginnings. The principal care of the Society was for British settlers abroad and among the chaplains it employed was John Wesley. The preaching of the gospel to the natives in British possessions came also within its scope; but by the end of the century, save for a small mission on the Gold Coast, little had been done. In 1800 it had less than 200 subscribers, and their contributions amounted only to £457. Endowments and legacies brought the total income to nearly £5,000, and with this it maintained some 43 missionaries and 32 catechists and schoolmasters.[1] An even older institution was the Society for the Promotion of Christian Knowledge, founded in 1698, but, as its title suggests, the business in which it was mainly engaged was the supply of literature. Actually it supported a few missionaries (Lutherans) in South India which was not yet British territory and so outside the sphere of S.P.G.

In 1733 the Moravians began their magnificent work in Greenland and Labrador. They had also stations in South and Central America as well as in South Africa. A few years later occurs the heroic name of David Brainerd, who laboured among the Indians of North America from 1744 to 1747. He was supported by funds from Scotland, and his memoirs were published a year before his death by the Society for Propagating

[1] Figures from Overton, *English Church in the Nineteenth Century*, p. 254.

Christian Knowledge of Edinburgh. This man was without distinction either as explorer, scholar, or preacher: yet the flame of his devotion inspired Carey, Henry Martyn, and countless others.

The last decade of the eighteenth century was a time of extraordinary progress in the history of Missions overseas. In 1792 William Carey preached to his fellow Baptists at Nottingham on the theme: "Expect great things from God; attempt great things for God." Soon afterwards the Baptist Missionary Society was founded in the back parlour of a house belonging to a widow at Kettering named Beebe Wallis. There were only a dozen present, including Andrew Fuller, and they raised £13 2s. 6d. to start the new society on its way. Next year Carey sailed for India after immense difficulties in a Danish ship.[1] Three years later came the London Missionary Society, an undenominational organization in whose formation the Evangelical clergy under the leadership of Dr. Haweis, Rector of Aldwinckle, had taken their share. But they soon felt that they wanted their own society and in 1799 the Church Missionary Society was founded. Thus England, at any rate, was awakening to hear the call. But in America there was as yet no response; and the great Church of Rome seemed to have forgotten the glorious days of the early Franciscans, and the names of Raymond Lull and Francis Xavier.

Opposition to Missions

But if there was a response to the call there was also much opposition. The Calvinism of many among the Evangelicals, of whom the famous Dr. Hawker, Vicar of Charles, Plymouth, was highly notorious, made them oppose any attempt to convert the heathen. Belief was the work of the Holy Spirit and it would be presumptuous for man to interfere.[2] Although considerations of space restrict the present study to England, it is interesting to notice, at this point, that a similar, if not

[1] He had originally taken a passage in an East Indiaman, but when the object of his journey was discovered he was turned out of the ship.
[2] See Stock, *The History of the C.M.S.*, I, pp. 281 f. Exactly the same argument had been used in 1786 to crush Carey when he began to agitate for missions to the heathen: see Stock, *op. cit.*, I, pp. 59 f.

even more fanatical, feeling existed to the north of the Tweed.

In the General Assembly of the Church of Scotland in 1796 the following amazing declaration was made by Dr. George Hamilton. "To spread abroad the knowledge of the gospel among barbarous and heathen nations, seems to me highly preposterous, in as far as it anticipates, nay, as it even reverses, the order of nature. Men must be polished and refined in their manners before they can be properly enlightened in religious truths. Philosophy and learning must, in the nature of things, take precedence. Indeed, it should seem hardly less absurd to make revelations precede civilizations in the order of time, than to pretend to unfold to a child the *Principia* of Newton, ere he is made at all acquainted with the letters of the alphabet. These ideas seem to me alike founded in error; and, therefore, I must consider them equally romantic and visionary."

John Erskine made a famous reply, beginning, "moderator, rax me that Bible." But even then Alexander Carlyle expressed his opinion of the "high absurdity" of such an enterprise, adding that it was the first time he had come across it. Christ's kingdom would come "in the course of providence."[1]

Amongst Churchmen there was also a good deal of opposition. To some this sudden outbreak of a desire to minister to the heathen seemed to be a kind of Methodism and as such to be discouraged and, if possible, suppressed. Others were undisguisedly scornful of the whole business and Sydney Smith let his powerful pen play round the notion of "consecrated cobblers" (Carey had been a shoemaker) and the attempt to convert the heathen world.

Early Missions in India

In India the idea of preaching to the heathen was frankly regarded as dangerous and likely to raise up violent opposition on the part of the natives.[2] Even the bishops, before Heber went to Calcutta in 1823, were unfriendly; their business was with Englishmen only. Fortunately there was at Serampore, only fifteen miles from Calcutta, a Danish settlement and there

[1] See R. E. Speer, *Missionary Principles and Practice*, pp. 18, 421, 533 f.
[2] See Overton, *English Church*, etc., pp. 267 ff.

the Baptist missionaries were able to find a refuge and to establish the famous station which was adorned by the names of Carey himself and Marshman and Ward. From this little group the East India Chaplains, sent out by Charles Simeon and Grant, who desired to reach the heathen in the intervals of ministering to their own people, received abundant encouragement and sympathy. Among these chaplains the great name was that of Henry Martyn. Henry Martyn had originally intended to go out under the newly founded C.M.S., but as the way was blocked he did the next best thing and took an East Indian Chaplaincy. He sailed in 1805. Behind him lay a brilliant career at Cambridge, and in his heart he carried a hopeless human love. In health he was exceedingly delicate —I suppose no present-day medical board would have passed him—and after only seven years of service, spent mostly in translational work, he died on his way home at Tokat in Asia Minor on October 16, 1812.[1] The example of his life has been an inspiration to countless others and his name is still venerated in the Cambridge which he loved by the Henry Martyn Hall; and in his native county the Baptistry in Truro Cathedral, as well as the yearly observance of the anniversary of his death, serves to keep his memory alive.[2]

Fresh Advance

The coming of peace in Europe led to a great advance in the work overseas. Two years before British India had been opened to the missionary when the East India Company's charter had been renewed, and advantage was now taken of the opening. But elsewhere there was even more striking advance. The Wesleyan Missionary Society was founded in 1816 following the expedition of 1813 when the Conference had allowed Dr. Coke to proceed at the head of a body of six to Ceylon; he himself died before the end of the long voyage.

---

[1] Tokat is not in Persia as Dr. Carpenter, possibly misled by Sargent, seems to think (*Church and People*, p. 35). It had been the scene of St. Chrysostom's banishment.

[2] Several good lives of Henry Martyn exist; by Sargent, George Smith, and Miss C. E. Padwick.

The London Missionary Society had sent out Knott and John Williams, who had begun a work which already shewed marvellous promise; whilst in Africa Van der Kemp, the pioneer among the Kaffirs and Hottentots, had been labouring since 1798. When Henry Martyn was on his way to India in 1806 he was much refreshed by a meeting with him at Cape Town. In another part of Africa, Bechuanaland, Robert Moffatt and his devoted wife were now starting a work which was to be theirs for nearly fifty years. Another famous L.M.S. missionary, Robert Morrison, had been sent out in 1807 to try and enter China. He went out by way of America, and in New York a scoffing shipowner asked him if he really imagined that he could make any impression on the people of that great country. "No, sir," he replied, "but I expect God can." Morrison was never destined to enter China proper but worked from the East India Company's factory at Canton; there he translated the New Testament in 1814 and vainly waited a further twenty years for the gates to open. He died on July 31, 1834, the day on which slavery ended in the West Indies.

In West Africa the freeing of the slaves had provided work for the missionary societies and in the West Indies themselves the further act of Liberation made abundant openings. The Church Missionary Society began its Sierra Leone Mission in 1816. Up to 1809 the C.M.S. had sent out only five agents, all of them Lutherans. It was not until the end of the war that the first party of English clergymen, three in number, was sent by this society. The S.P.G. did not awaken to new life until three years later, and then most of its work was done, as heretofore, in the colonies and among our fellow countrymen. In 1825 Islington, the C.M.S. college for training missionaries, was founded and soon afterwards the Evangelical Bishop, Henry Ryder, ordained the first men for work abroad. Another notable date was 1826 when Henry Martyn's only convert, Abdul Massih, was ordained by Bishop Heber for work among his countrymen in India.

A type of missionary work which has borne abundant fruit in India saw its beginnings in 1830. Alexander Duff, the Presbyterian missionary at Calcutta, finding that his work was being hindered by the presence of a Hindu college (founded in 1817) in which the writings of Tom Paine and Hume were studied, began a college of his own to meet the needs of Young India in its search for light. It was a bold venture as he had been only a short time in the field and had but a slight acquaintance with the language. None the less, it met with immediate success, and within a short time several Brahmins were converted. He committed one great, though pardonable mistake—since it was later made by Lord Macaulay—he substituted English for Indian culture.

MISSIONS FROM 1837 TO 1872

Thus at the beginning of the Victorian Era the tradition of Evangelization was hardly recovered; but tentative and experimental efforts, not unaccompanied by grievous mistakes and waste of life, had been made. The chief service of such efforts had been to set an example and to furnish a few shining names. Not yet could enthusiasm for Missions overseas be regarded as a gauge of the spiritual life of the Church at home.

The year 1841 was one of importance in the development of the work. Up to this point, although the income of the C.M.S. had doubled during a period of sixteen years and the fruit of past efforts had slowly been garnered, there had been little expansion. "Consolidation rather than extension is the note of the period" (Stock, *op. cit.*, I, p. 251). But in 1841 the Colonial Bishoprics Fund was started, the Red Sea route to India was opened up by the Peninsular and Orient line, and, perhaps most important of all, Livingstone reached Africa.

Africa

David Livingstone had been influenced by Robert Moffatt, whose daughter he was afterwards to marry. In 1840 Moffatt had described to him how he had often seen the smoke of a thousand villages rising in the morning air, and the gospel had not been preached in one of them. This picture Livingstone never forgot, and the various expeditions which gave him a deathless name as an explorer were undertaken in order to open up ways along which the gospel might travel.

Soon after Livingstone's arrival the C.M.S. began work in

Africa using as its agents two Germans, Krapf and Rebmann. Krapf had gone originally to Abyssinia, but in 1844 he responded to the call of the work in East Africa. A few months after he had landed he stood by the newly made grave which contained his wife and child. This to him was a challenge and he flashed it back to the Church in England: "There is now on the East African Coast a lonely missionary grave. This is a sign that you have commenced the struggle . . . the victories of the Church are gained by stepping over the graves of its members." Rebmann did not arrive until 1846, but once there he remained without any furlough for thirty years. The geographical discoveries of these two men and their pioneer work became an inspiration to others to follow through the gap which they had made.

In other parts of the Dark Continent, as it has been well called, work was also going forward. Bishop Gray of Cape Town, famous for his decided stand against Bishop Colenso, did a very effective work in organizing Missions among the natives in South Africa where the L.M.S. and W.M.S. also flourished. The Industrial Mission of the Free Church of Scotland at Lovedale was epoch-making. On the west coast the climate wrought havoc among the white missionaries; but the Niger Mission, begun in 1857 under Samuel Crowther, an ex-slave and future bishop, was crowned with much success. In the year following, many remarkable events combined to give encouragement to Mission work not only in Africa, but throughout the whole vast field. The rule of the British Crown was established in India, inland China and Japan were both opened up to missionary enterprise, the Victoria Nyanza was discovered, and the Universities Mission to Central Africa was founded.

Although the Universities Mission (U.M.C.A.) has been notable as an organ of the advanced Anglo-Catholics, it owed its origin to the challenge issued by Livingstone at meetings held in Oxford and Cambridge in 1857. The first bishop was C. F. Mackenzie, Fellow of Caius College, Cambridge, who had gone to Natal to work under Bishop Colenso in 1854. (It is interesting to notice that Henry Martyn had been among the forces which inspired him to undertake the life of a missionary.) But Mackenzie's time in Central Africa was to be but short, for within just over a year after his consecration he had died of fever, a fate which overtook many others of the first missionaries of the U.M.C.A. His successor, Bishop Tozer, was, however, more fortunate and succeeded in laying the foundation of a great work before his retirement in 1874 when he was followed by Bishop Steere.

India

The annexation of the Punjab in 1849 brought a huge stretch of territory under the control of a group of noble Christian soldiers and administrators—the two Lawrences, Robert Montgomery, and Herbert Edwardes. They openly supported Missions, though in their administration they were strictly impartial. The rest of India was thrown open to Missions when, after the Mutiny, the Crown took over from the East India Company the responsibility of government. But before that event much work had been done here and there. H. W. Fox and Robert Noble had started work among the Telugus in 1841: "the crisis of their decision was at Brighton," records Henry Venn Elliott (*Life*, p. 145), where Hudson Taylor, a generation later, was also to come to a great decision. Noble followed in the steps of Alexander Duff as an educational missionary; a similar work, also in South India, being started by Anderson of the Free Kirk. About this time the first Medical Missions were established in India; Elmslie (C.M.S.) in Kashmir and Valentine (Scottish U.P.) in Rajputana being the pioneers. Other notable figures of this epoch were William Arthur (W.M.S.), who worked in Mysore before going home to make a reputation as a preacher, and William Oakley (C.M.S.), who remained in Ceylon from 1835 to 1886 without a single break for furlough. In North India there were two supremely great missionaries—Pfander and Thomas Valpy French. They once held a famous controversy with a number of Mohammedan sheikhs at Agra. Though both sides claimed the victory it is significant that two of the sheikhs, Imad-ud-din and Safdar Ali, later became Christians. Pfander was the author of the well-known apologetic work for Moslems, the *Mizan-al-Haqq*. French's activity extended from 1850 to 1891 (he became Bishop of Lahore in 1877) and he conceived many schemes for work in India, including a theological college on new lines; but the necessary means and men were not always available. In 1887 he resigned his bishopric to go as a simple missionary to Arabia and there he died at Muscat. In the same year, to anticipate later events, Ian Keith Falconer died at Aden.

The Far East

China was opened up in part by the Opium War of 1840-2; but this war and the second of the same name in 1857-8 were not likely to commend Christianity to the Chinese, since they were the means of forcing upon an unwilling people a traffic which they dreaded. The Treaty of Tientsin in 1860 made many parts available for mission work, but full advantage could not be taken of the opportunity until after the suppression of the Tai-ping Rebellion in 1865.[1] In that year George Moule began work in inland China and Hudson Taylor founded the China Inland Mission.

The L.M.S. had been the first to undertake work in China and their men made a great reputation as linguists. Among them were John Stronach of Amoy and James Legge, afterwards Professor of Chinese at Oxford. The work of the C.M.S. was made possible by an anonymous gift of £6,000. The first stations were opened at Shanghai (1844), Ningpo (1848), and Fuchow in Fukien (1850). The work in the last province was interesting as an illustration of the value of perseverance. For ten years no apparent effect was made by the most devoted efforts on the part of the missionaries. The closing down of the Mission was only narrowly averted when quite suddenly the harvest began to ripen. A great work was also done by the English Presbyterians among whom W. C. Burns was an outstanding figure.[2] He had already won fame as an evangelist at home and in Canada before going to China in 1847, where he laboured until 1868. It was said of him: "All China

---

[1] This movement had as its leader Hung Siu-ch'uan, who professed to be a Christian and had regular worship in his camp. Later he claimed for himself almost divine honours.

[2] See Islay Burns. *Memoir of the Rev. W. C. Burns.*

knows him. He is the holiest man alive." Amongst those whom he inspired was Hudson Taylor. To this famous missionary we must now return.

Hudson Taylor had gone out to China in 1853, but after a short time had been compelled to return owing to a breakdown in health. But the burden of the country and the many unoccupied provinces weighed heavily upon him. One Sunday night at Brighton it became acute. He has described how the sight of a congregation of a thousand and more Christian people "rejoicing in their own security while millions were perishing for lack of knowledge" moved him to the determination to undertake the task of evangelizing them himself. It seemed a foolhardy task; but in 1866 he made a start, sailing for China once more with fifteen companions. The principles of the society which he founded, the China Inland Mission, or C.I.M., are peculiar. The workers have no guarantee as to the sum available for their support, no personal solicitation for funds is undertaken, but all is left to faith in God. The Society accepts workers of any Protestant denomination, but so far as possible it groups them on denominational lines.

In 1858, as we mentioned above, Japan was thrown open to Western influences. The first missionaries, all Americans, landed there in the following year. Their work was made difficult by the low idea held by the Japanese of Western civilization and the Christian religion gained from the Dutch merchants who had been living in Deishama from 1641 under most degrading conditions. In order to retain their trading rights these wretched men had annually been compelled to trample on a cross in the presence of Japanese officials. But by 1868, when the revolution made religious liberty possible in Japan, things were improving and the demand for Western education gave the missionaries a unique opportunity.

The South Seas

The formation of the see of Melanesia in 1855 did much to stimulate Anglican work in these regions. Its famous mission ship, *The Southern Cross*, was built largely by the proceeds of *The Daisy Chain*, which Charlotte Yonge devoted to this purpose. The roll of its bishops is made glorious by the name of John

Coleridge Patteson, murdered in 1871. Others who worked in the South Seas were John Williams, the great L.M.S. pioneer, murdered in 1839; J. G. Paton, the Presbyterian, who in twenty-four years enrolled 20,000 converts; Mr. and Mrs. Gordon, murdered at Erromango in 1861; and James Chalmers, murdered in New Guinea in 1901.

South America

Before leaving the story of Missions in the first half of the Victorian Era mention must be made of the work of the heroic Captain Allen Gardiner, who died of starvation in 1851. His work was taken up by the South American Missionary Society, which numbered among its regular supporters the scientist Charles Darwin, who had been impressed by the results of its efforts on one of his voyages.

MISSIONS OVERSEAS FROM 1872 ONWARDS

The year 1872 is a convenient landmark, for not only is it situated about halfway through the reign of Victoria, but in it there was a definite revival in the work of Missions overseas. After the enthusiasm of the early years of the reign there had come a sad period of relapse. The first pioneers had their devoted followers, but after a time interest seemed to languish and enthusiasm to be well-nigh dead. When Bishop Wilkinson was Vicar of Seaham Harbour in 1859 he worked hard to get a representative missionary meeting, employing all the best devices by way of advertisement and personal appeal. In the end the audience consisted of the schoolmaster, his wife and father and mother (Mason, *Life of G. H. Wilkinson*, I, p. 53). This is but an example to show the state of suspended animation to which the cause had been reduced. Had the Evangelicals taken a greater share in the revival of 1859, no doubt fresh life might have come into the missionary cause, but they chose for the most part to stand aside, and in consequence Missions suffered. By the 'seventies the supply of both men and money seemed to be gradually drying up, and even in the field itself little real progress was being made. Bishop Moule quotes a Roman Catholic periodical as triumphantly (but a little mistakenly) prophesying that "Ere long the sectarian societies will be looking in vain for missionaries, as heresy dies out."

The turn of the tide can perhaps be traced to the institution in 1872 of the Annual Day of Intercession. This step was taken at the suggestion of the S.P.G., and the date chosen was St. Andrew's Day. In 1879, in order to avoid possible offence to Nonconformists, it being thought that the choice of a Saint's Day might be unwelcome to them, the day was changed to the Tuesday before the Ascension. A somewhat humorous sequel was the protest of the Presbyterians against the slight passed upon the Scottish national saint. After trying the new day for six years, it was decided to go back to St. Andrew's Day once more, and that season is still the great time for Missionary Intercession.

Signs of growing life and fresh opportunity abroad can be seen in two other events of the same year—the holding of the first Protestant Missionary Conference in India and the withdrawal of the Proclamation against Christianity in Japan. The next year, however, was to bring severe losses, for in January Henry Venn, who had been secretary of the C.M.S. from 1841 and who was one of the wisest and greatest missionary statesmen the Church of Christ has ever known, left the scene of his earthly labours; and in the following May Livingstone was found kneeling beside his bed at Ilalu. Death to him was no hardship, for had he not said that "Death is a glorious thing to one going to Jesus"? But what was to be the effect on the work? The effect was all that could have been wished; the lonely old man dying there by himself in the centre of Africa struck the imagination of the Christian world and fresh enthusiasm was at once aroused.

Africa

Just a month after Livingstone's death a treaty with Zanzibar was concluded. By it the slave trade was restricted and the market closed; as a consequence, three different missionary efforts were launched in East Africa: the Roman Catholics at Bagamoyo, the C.M.S. at Mombasa, and the U.M.C.A. in Zanzibar itself. A special interest is attached to this last enterprise for the Cathedral which Bishop Steere began to erect was actually on the site of the old slave market. The U.M.C.A. sent forth many noble and self-denying missionaries into the field, bishops like Smythies and Chauncy Maples, clergymen of lower rank like Archdeacon Johnson and A. F. Sym, as well as many lay-men and women. Quite a large proportion of them laid down their lives in the land of their adoption.

Africa meanwhile was being opened up in various directions. The travels of H. M. Stanley made possible two famous developments—the C.M.S. Mission in Uganda (1876) and the Baptist Mission to the Congo (1878). The latter Mission experienced a great movement in 1886 when converts came in by the hundreds, it has been called "Pentecost on the Congo"; of the former more may well be said.

In November 1875 Stanley wrote a letter to the *Daily Telegraph* challenging the Churches to do something for Central Africa. Among those who responded and volunteered to the C.M.S. was Alexander Mackay, a young engineer—later Stanley was to describe him as the best missionary since Livingstone. A party was sent out to Uganda, where in spite of difficulties from climate, from native suspicion, and sectarian rivalries, a great work was done and a growing Church established. But in 1884 following the accession of Mwanga a time of persecution fell upon the infant Christian community. Bishop Hannington, when on his way to Uganda, was met and murdered by order of the king; his dying cry: "I have purchased the road to Uganda with my life," was prophetic, but many Christians were to meet their death before it was fulfilled. Throughout the persecutions Mackay stuck to his post—he was too valuable to the king, for his engineering skill, to be put to death—and did his best to protect the natives. At last the persecution stopped and better times came in. Then the Mission was threatened with another blow for the British East Africa Company decided to withdraw. They were persuaded to postpone their decision on condition that £15,000 was raised to enable them to carry on for a time. The C.M.S. at once took up the matter and at a meeting of the newly founded Gleaners' Union in October 1891 in response to the challenge of Bishop Tucker more than half the sum was promised in half an hour, and the rest within a fortnight. Thus one of England's most valuable possessions was saved for her and one of the most signal of the Church's achievements made possible.

In West Africa during the latter years of the period there was a good deal of quiet progress, the native Churches were gaining strength and experience, and were learning to care for their fellows who still remained heathen. Many of them by this time were almost self-supporting. In Livingstonia the Free Kirk Mission had great success, whilst the work of the Established Kirk at Blantyre is famous throughout the world.

In North Africa the C.M.S. restarted work in Cairo in 1882 in order to influence Mohammedans. This work, one of exceeding difficulty and with little to shew in the way of actual converts, has produced several missionaries of outstanding power and gifts; though their greatest work was done outside the period, the names of Douglas Thornton and Temple Gairdner are known to all workers among Moslems and to many others as well.

India

In India during the latter years of the era there was development mainly in two opposite directions—among the low-caste peoples and by way of Higher Education. The low castes did not fail to notice the difference of attitude towards them, especially in times of famine or plague, exhibited by the Brahmins and by the Christian missionaries. This drew them to the Church. One striking instance may be quoted from Madras, where an exceptionally severe famine in 1877 caused the natives to lose faith in the power of their gods; the missionaries of the S.P.G. and C.M.S. worked heroically to relieve their distress and as a result there was what is known as a "mass movement" into the Church; some 20,000 converts were received by the former, and some 10,000 by the latter Society. Caste, however, remained a problem even when baptism should have made all equal, and the vigorous line taken by some of the bishops caused the loss of many highcaste converts. Its difficulty was not to be lessened when natives began to be ordained, a wise step which had been advocated by Bishop Milman of Calcutta, who thought that the native Churches should provide their own clergy of every grade.

Meanwhile Educational Missions were going from strength to strength—special mention may perhaps be made of Dr. Miller's College at Madras which was worthy of the great traditions, in this kind of work, of Scottish Presbyterianism. One notable feature was the establishment of special missions in connexion with British Universities; the Cambridge Mission to Delhi was the pioneer in 1877; to be followed by the Oxford Mission to Calcutta in 1880 and the Trinity College, Dublin, Mission to Chota Nagpur in 1891. The value of the work done by this type of mission can scarcely be exaggerated. The Mission to Delhi was particularly impressive as it came to reinforce the S.P.G. Mission refounded after the mutiny had swept away, with blood and slaughter, an earlier and strikingly successful station. "The Delhi Mission," as Bishop Lightfoot has said, "was baptized in blood. It was literally murdered. But here, as elsewhere, the blood of the martyrs was the seed-plot of the Church. The work of evangelization has revived. A memorial church, bearing the name of the first martyr, St. Stephen, commemorates the death of these, his latest successors."

China

The progress of Missions in China was noteworthy, and it owed itself to the work of a large band of missionaries from many lands and members of many different religious communions. Among these workers certain names stand out; some of them were survivors from the earlier period, some of them began their labours after 1870. Among the former mention must be made of John Nevius (1854–93), who was the author of an important study of Demon Possession and the compiler of a manual of *Methods of Missionary Work*; of Griffith John of the L.M.S., whose writings helped mission work in the whole of China, though his own work was mainly confined to Hankow; of Bishop G. E. Moule, the first European missionary to penetrate inland China, for he settled in Hangchow in 1864 immediately after the suppression of the

Tai-ping rebellion; of David Hill (1865-96), who did a great work for the W.M.S. at Hankow. Then of later missionaries there was the striking figure of James Gilmour, whose name will ever be associated with Mongolia. He went out in 1870, and, like Henry Martyn, in spite of heroic devotion and ceaseless labours had but little outward success. Though he succeeded in gaining the trust and confidence of those among whom he worked, the harvest was delayed. Gilmour was much in advance of his times in many ways and held views on missionary work which were shared by few contemporaries. He felt strongly, for example, that the Bible alone is of little value as a missionary agent, unless there is someone to explain its meaning (cf. Acts viii. 31). He also opposed the hasty baptism of converts without a considerable period of probation. His ideas on this subject were strengthened by what took place in Shantung in 1877, where there was a kind of "mass movement" on a small scale and many were baptized. Gilmour expressed his anxiety over them and pleaded that baptism should be delayed; his fears were justified, for the movement dwindled and left little permanent benefit.[1] Another who deserves mention is Dr. J. K. Mackenzie (1875-88), who worked for the L.M.S. at Hankow and later at Tientsin. A great medical school was erected for him by the celebrated Chinese statesman, Li Hung-Chang. Another missionary who had great influence with the ruling class was Timothy Richard of the B.M.S., he also did much literary work.

Meanwhile the newly founded C.I.M. was pushing into the interior of China with boldness and persistence, and God was crowning their labours with many blessings. The going forth of the Cambridge Seven in 1885 did much to popularize and stimulate their work. Their women missionaries, with those of other societies such as the C.E.Z.M.S., were penetrating everywhere with commendable courage.

On the whole the missionaries were well received in China. The more enlightened of the local rulers recognized that their influence was all for good, and though the conservatives among them may not have been altogether happy about such

[1] See Lovell, *James Gilmour of Mongolia*, pp. 92 and 116, for further details of his opinions on these two points.

conversions as took place, there was little opposition. In 1895, however, there was a sudden massacre of a body of C.M.S. missionaries, the Rev. Robert Stewart and his party, at Hwasang in the Fuh-Kien province. When the news of this disaster reached England a great Prayer Meeting was held in Exeter Hall for the safety of other missionaries and for the success of their work. The Chinese government offered compensation to the C.M.S., but they wisely refused to accept it and received instead an expression of "profound respect and esteem." Although this outbreak was a surprise Stewart himself seems almost to have expected something of the kind, as an incident at Keswick in 1893 seems to suggest.[1] A number of the members of the Convention were out on Derwentwater when suddenly "a tall, rather majestic figure, standing bareheaded at the prow of one of the boats, uttered an unforgettable call. His hands outstretched, his face with a shining in it that Gairdner never forgot, he cried to that company of happy youth, 'AGONIA is the measure of success . . . Christ suffered in agony: so must we. Christ died: so perhaps may we. Our life *must* be hard, cruel, wearisome, unknown. So was His.' The figure was that of Robert Stewart, and his call did not fall on deaf ears."

Five years later came the terrible Boxer massacres, when some 180 missionaries, wives and children lost their lives. Of this number 78 belonged to the C.I.M. The story of their bravery in the face of death has been often told; but it should not be forgotten, and those who wish to recall it can consult Edwards, *Fire and Sword in Shanshi*, and Broomhall, *Martyred Missionaries of the C.I.M.*

Japan

In Japan much progress was also made, chiefly by American Societies. One outstanding figure was that of Verbeck, the educationalist. He exercised immense influence over the men who were laying the foundations of the New Japan. At one time it almost looked as if the whole nation might become Christian; largely because Christianity was regarded as one of the many Western institutions which seemed to promise

[1] See Padwick, *Temple Gairdner of Cairo*, p. 31.

national progress, but after 1890 a rather less favourable attitude began to prevail. There were, however, sufficient Japanese Christians to make it worth while to establish native churches. The various Presbyterian Societies amalgamated their converts into a single body; while the Anglicans, who included not only the converts of the S.P.G. and C.M.S. but also those of the American Protestant Episcopal Church, formed in 1887 the "Japanese Holy Catholic Society." Anglicans in 1883 had only numbered about 500, but by the end of the century there were some 10,000 of them. This was a striking increase, which was shared by other Christian bodies,

	Men	Wives	Single Women	Total
C.M.S.	558	349	331	1,238
S.P.G. (not including work among white people)	250	200	80	530
C.E.Z.M.S.	—	—	234	234
U.M.C.A.	64	—	42	106
South American Missionary Society	54	17	17	88
Scottish Episcopal Church	42	6	16	64
Total Anglican Missionaries	968	572	720	2,260
C.I.M.	327	196	288	811
L.M.S.	202	160	74	436
United Free Kirk	183	114	109	406
W.M.S.	222	126	54	402
B.M.S.	145	109	75	329
Brethren	124	87	61	272
North Africa Mission	32	23	50	105
Zenana Bible and Medical Mission	—	—	95	95
English Presbyterians	36	23	29	88
South Africa General Mission	36	22	30	88
Friends	30	26	23	79
United Methodists	49	28	2	79
Church of Scotland (Presbyterian)	41	25	2	68
	2,395	1,511	1,612	5,518 [1]

[1] The complete total of missionaries from all societies in Great Britain and Ireland was probably nearly 7,000.

but it fell far below what had been expected and hoped for But if the number of Christians in Japan is not so great as could be wished, they carry a weight and exert an influence far beyond their proportion of the population.

The extent and progress of Missions during the Victorian Era can perhaps best be realized by the table on page 393 of those engaged in propagating the faith through the principal British Societies. It is based on the figures given in Stock's *Short Handbook of Missions*, p. 98, and does not include Roman Catholics.

THE CARE OF OUR OWN PEOPLE OVERSEAS

One of the most striking phenomena during the reign of Queen Victoria was the immense increase in the number of the British people living in the colonies. At the beginning of the reign this had been a mere 4,000,000 including all the colonies and dependencies; by 1900 it had multiplied fourfold. The spiritual needs of many of these new colonists had to be met by the Church at home. In the case of Non-Anglicans, who are accustomed at home to be self-supporting, the colonists formed their own independent communities overseas, and it is with the work of the Anglican Church only that we are here concerned. This was supported in early days by both men and money from England. The chief agencies were the Colonial and Continental Church Society, as it came to be called after 1861, and the S.P.G. The S.P.C.K. also helped by making grants.

Perhaps it would be well at this point to make clear the relationship of the Church at home, as represented by the Archbishop of Canterbury, and the Churches in lands overseas. It can best be done by quoting some words spoken in 1898 by Archbishop Davidson. The Archbishop states that the authority of his see "is almost universally recognized, but it is undefined; it is moral not legal, and its effective exercise depends in no small degree upon the personal weight, tact, and courtesy of the Primate."[1] The various members of the Anglican Communion send their bishops at regular intervals to Conferences at Lambeth for mutual consultation and

[1] F. Warre Cornish, *The English Church in the Nineteenth Century*, II, p. 424.

encouragement; but they are virtually independent, though in communion one with another.

The oldest colonial bishopric is that of Nova Scotia founded in 1787, and the next that of Quebec founded in 1793. A great impetus to the development of the Colonial Episcopate was given by the formation of the Colonial Bishoprics Fund in 1841. At this date the following dioceses were in existence: Calcutta (1814), Jamaica (1824), Barbados (1824), Madras (1835), and Australia (1836). All the other colonies were under the jurisdiction of the Bishop of London, who also exercised control over Anglican communions on the continent of Europe as indeed he does at the present day. The following is the order in which the various dominions proceeded to develop their organization.

Canada

Until 1793 Canada was under the Bishop of Nova Scotia; but in that year John Jacob Mountain was appointed Bishop of Quebec. The next development was the appointment of his son, George Jehoshaphat Mountain, as co-adjutor Bishop of Montreal in 1836. Bishop George Mountain was a great traveller and pioneer, and in 1844 he made his way into Rupertsland at considerable risk and so established the Church in the Prairies.[1] A diocese was established in 1844. In the meantime Toronto had been made a separate see with John Strachan, an ex-Presbyterian, as its first occupant. It was Bishop Strachan who founded Trinity College, Toronto, for the training of the Canadian clergy. Work among the Indians and settlers in the Far West was for a time carried on by the C.M.S., but eventually the Canadian Church took this over.

In 1861 the First Provincial Synod of the Canadian Church was held; but the bishops who attended it came from the civil provinces of Ontario and Quebec only. A Synod of Bishops drawn from a wider area was held in 1874 (the Dominion of Canada had been formed in 1867), and finally in 1893 a General Synod united the whole Church in Canada.

[1] A vivid description of his journey will be found in *What Our Church Stands For*, a volume written by Canadian Churchmen under the editorship of Canon Bertal Heeney. I owe my knowledge of it to the courtesy of the Rev. R. Mercer Wilson.

Australia

Up to 1836 when the first bishop was consecrated for the whole continent, including the South Seas, Australia had been an archdeaconry under the see of Calcutta. The separate diocese was made possible by grants from the S.P.C.K. and S.P.G. During the reign such progress was made that New Zealand became a separate province with seven bishops of its own and the number of sees in Australia proper was increased to twenty. But the work was carried on under exceedingly great difficulties, for many of the settlers were descended from transported criminals. The gold rushes of 1850 and later years did not bring the best type of colonists. In 1847 the title Australia was exchanged for that of Sydney and new sees were founded at Melbourne, Newcastle, and Adelaide. The first Bishop of Melbourne was Bishop Perry, a disciple of Charles Simeon. The see of Adelaide was made possible by the generosity of Frances Burdett Coutts. In 1859 the colony of Queensland was founded and with it the see of Brisbane.

New Zealand had its first bishop in 1841, when the saintly G. A. Selwyn was appointed. He remained there doing an extraordinarily effective work until 1867 when much against his will he was translated to Lichfield. He and the band of friends who went out with him joyously seized the chance presented to them by the virgin soil of the South Seas to plant there "apostolical doctrine untainted by Roman or Puritan error. They were inspired and instructed by the *Library of the Fathers*, in which they found the ideal of patristic Christianity, fierce against heresy, strong in apostolic order and ecclesiastical organization, autocratic with St. Leo, militant with St. Ambrose, dogmatic with St. Augustine; a dominant clergy, an obedient laity; and this ideal they hoped to realize in a missionary Church planted among a simple race."[1] Thus the work at first was not among white settlers—these came later—but among the natives.

[1] F. Warre Cornish, *The English Church in the Nineteenth Century*, II, p. 412.

South Africa

Up to 1847 South Africa, like Australia, had been part of the vast diocese of Calcutta. Its first bishop was Robert Gray, to whom reference was made above. Gray was a man of tremendous energy and power of work. He was a strong and even narrow Churchman, but he succeeded in keeping on good terms with the numerous representatives of other types of Christianity whom he found in his diocese. These included L.M.S. and W.M.S. missionaries, as well as Dutch and German, and members of the Moravian Church. When he became bishop there were but thirteen English clergymen in the whole of South Africa. By the end of the period there were nine bishops and about four hundred clergymen, twenty-three of the latter being natives. A very great part of the work and its success is due to the S.P.G.

THE CHURCH AT HOME AND MISSIONS OVERSEAS

The last thirty years of the nineteenth century saw a noticeable change in the attitude of the country and of the Church towards foreign Missions. This could be seen even in the press. It is hard to believe now that when the Days of Intercession were started a responsible paper like *The Times* could scoff at them. Newspapers of lesser consequence generally ignored such high-flown notions as the conversion of the heathen; they were not "news." In government circles there was also a change of attitude. There had always been Christian officials who had supported Missions and made public their belief in them as an auxiliary to their own work of administration; but this now came to be recognized on a much larger scale. The work of the missionary in education and in dealing with backward peoples was seen to have an immense social value and to be a help to the work of the official. Mission schools had not then revealed one serious weakness: that referred to by Canon Barry, who points out that "despite all their glorious record" Mission schools "have nevertheless been in danger of producing a semi-educated proletariat dissatisfied with handicraft and agriculture and intent on finding clerical employment, which in the nature of things is not available."[1] Finally, there was a distinct change in the attitude of Christian people them-

[1] *The Relevance of Christianity*, p. 43.

selves. It is true that interest in Missions was still confined to a minority even of these, but the circle was gradually widening. There was also a much greater understanding of missionary methods and difficulties. This was due to the improved literature which now began to enjoy a wide circulation and to the formation of numerous agencies for pressing the claims and interest of Missions in various quarters. In this matter the C.M.S. was the pioneer. It founded the Lay Workers' Union in 1882, the Gleaners' Union in 1886, and four years later the Sowers' Band for work among young people. It was a C.M.S. supporter, the Rev. John Barton, Vicar of Holy Trinity, Cambridge, who first thought of Missionary Exhibitions. This was in 1882. Two years later the first Missionary Mission was held.

People in general began to find that their imagination was being captured by outstanding missionary figures; there was David Livingstone and later the Cambridge Seven; about the same time came the murder of Bishop Hannington and the heroic martyrs of Uganda. All these things brought Missions prominently before the attention of the country. But if the Home Church was thus taking a greater interest in Missions and doing more for their support both in men and money, it was itself gaining from the foreign field, often in ways that it did not realize.

It was something in the days before a cheap press and the "wireless" to have some outlet into wider fields and to have the attention drawn to foreign lands and strange customs. The meetings which were held from time to time could be extraordinarily stimulating. From the first the deputations, of the C.M.S. at any rate, made it their business to help those to whom they came, not only pleading the cause of the work abroad, but striving to reach the sinful and indifferent at home. In many cases their visits were a real blessing and encouragement to both the pastor and his flock, especially in lonely and difficult parishes where visiting preachers were much rarer than they have since become with improved means of travel. Edward Bickersteth, the second secretary of the C.M.S., was especially noteworthy for the work which he did. His fervour stirred the hearts of many and gave a new impulse to the spirit of prayer in countless souls.

The missionary cause brought into the life of the Church that element of romance which is not readily discerned, even in the work of a slum parish. There was something attractive in the story of efforts entirely free from convention and of the breaking of new ground in far-off lands. The influence, too, of the saints scattered in lonely stations came back to the Church at home like a fragrance; such as had come from the quiet of "some Bemerton or Hursley" at home.[1] The long roll of heroes and martyrs was an inspiration in days when persecution had become a thing of the past at home. The Church here was so "snug" and comfortable, and its members sat so staid and placid in their warm pews. And to them came the stories of lives laid down and sufferings endured for the faith which they themselves professed.

The very sacrifices, of time and money, which people at home found themselves prepared to make reacted on their own spiritual lives; for, as Dr. Pierson has said, "Religion is a commodity of which the more we export, the more we have remaining." It is a remarkable fact that revivals of spiritual life and missionary activity have always gone together. The Cambridge Seven, for example, were dedicated to missionary work before they roused among the students of England and Scotland the flame of devotion. But perhaps it is not so remarkable after all that it should be so, for the condition of receiving spiritual power is obedience, and since it is the express wish of the Master that all men should be evangelized no Church can expect an enduement of power, pray it never so earnestly, unless it is endeavouring to carry out that wish. Again the faith and devotion of workers at home is fired anew by hearing of the achievements of the gospel in lands overseas. They find there fresh evidence of the power of the Cross to save and transform in new lands and among strange folk. This gives them a fresh confidence in the ability of the Saviour to reach even the most degraded at home.

But great as have been the achievements of the Church in the foreign field during the nineteenth century, the instruments through whom God worked were perhaps an even greater means of stimulating the devotion of workers at home. The glad and eager spirit in which lives were laid down could not

[1] Cf. Padwick, *Temple Gairdner of Cairo*, p. vii.

fail to move those who remained at home. There is a very early instance of this, for Charles Simeon always had a portrait of Henry Martyn hanging over the fireplace in his dining-room. "He used often to look at it in his friends' presence, and to say, as he did so, with a peculiar loving emphasis, 'There, see that blessed man! What an expression of countenance! No one looks at me as he does; he never takes his eyes off me, and seems always to be saying, "Be serious—be in earnest —don't trifle." ' Then smiling at the picture and gently bowing, he would add, 'And I won't trifle—I won't trifle.' "[1]

Thus the devotional life of the Church at home is helped and fostered by the work abroad. But it is not only the devotional life of the Church which is thus helped; it receives fresh light on its problems, intellectual and social, from the same source. For these problems are world-wide and every piece of fresh knowledge which can be collected concerning them is of value. J. H. Oldham has given it as his opinion that "the battle for Christian faith and Christian ideals must be joined along the whole indivisible front of the world's life" (*The World and the Gospel*, p. 198). There are those indeed who think that Christianity may even die out in Western lands, but will find a home among the simpler peoples of less sophisticated outlook. This has been brought out in a beautiful poem, *At the Crib*, by A. S. Cripps, who worked in Mashonaland:

"Freezing doubts have nipped the flowers where the Child reposes,
Good-bye, Grecian violets! Good-bye, Gothic roses!
Bring, now northern blooms are dead—nipped by northern rime—
Rough brown southern grass of ours, flowers of summertime!
Shepherd, Whom Thy sheep refuse, rule Thy goats to-day,
Wear our lilies of the field, mount our throne of hay."

So too social problems cannot be solved in one country only; they are international in scope. "The social order which we have to Christianize," again to quote J. H. Oldham, "is a world order" (*op. cit.*, p. 70).

[1] Moule, *Charles Simeon*, p. 140.

21

SOCIAL CHANGES

THE manners and habits of a people, and the changes which they have undergone during any particular period, may be ascertained from the laws passed to regulate them, from such descriptions as are preserved in its literature, and, in the case of recent periods, from the recollections of survivors. After scrutinizing these various sources of information we are bound to conclude that the social changes experienced by the Victorian Era, and in particular by the latter part of it, were more rapid and vaster than those of any age of which we have record. But they all took place within a single system. The different social groups might fulfil their functions, might seize or neglect their opportunities, might claim their rewards; but the system under which they did so, unfair though it might be, was the same. The changes were only changes in detail. Behind them all was a sense of continuity; for the English people possesses, so Croce has remarked, a "sense of change and of continuity at the same time which [is theirs] not indeed as a gift of nature, but through historical development" (*History of Europe in the Nineteenth Century*, p. 159).

THE REDISTRIBUTION OF WEALTH

The cause which underlay these changes—whether we name them political, educational, or social in the narrower sense—was the amazing redistribution of wealth which formed so significant a feature of the era. The changing scene and the changing influences were due ultimately to the vagaries of the industrial system; a system which could, on the one hand, throw up Hudson, the railway king, and his like, to the enjoyment, sometimes but brief, of wealth and power; and, on the other, eject an ancient family from the lands which it had cultivated almost since time began and plunge its members into poverty and insignificance. The effect of this process was bad; for it transmuted values and gave an enhanced position to mere wealth. It would not be quite true to say that money was substituted for birth as a hall-mark of aristocracy; but wealth soon came to be overvalued as a sign of consideration, whilst wisdom and culture were pushed into the background. There was, as someone has said, a gradual substitution of quantitative for qualitative standards. This was a step back to barbarism.

The rise of "tradesmen" was no new thing in England; many a "noble" family, if its origins were traced out, would find its source in the counting-house of the merchant or the office of the lawyer.[1] Thus the newcomers, after a generation or so, settled down comfortably among those who were of an origin very much the same as their own. There was in any case no special caste of nobility as on the continent. The English custom of vesting family property in the eldest son meant that the younger sons and their descendants, gradually sinking in the social scale, finally mingled their blood with that of the common people.[2] Thus it had been in the past; but the sudden influx of wealthy families into the aristocracy at this juncture was on such an infinitely larger scale that the social system was unable to absorb them; and they themselves failed to rise to their new responsibilities, or to save their heads from being turned by their elevation. The result was unsettlement and the encouragement of class hatred. The sudden "pushing in" of the rising merchant class aroused both the resentment of the older families among whom they tried to take their place, and the bitter envy of those from whom they had risen. Many of them coming suddenly into the possession of great wealth, having no sense of responsibility and no traditions upon which to fall back, entered into a senseless competition with others like themselves, and even drew down their betters into the same

---

[1] See Sir Bernard Burke, *Vicissitudes of Families*, III, p. 213, where a list of noble families is given with their commercial ancestry. T. H. S. Escott points out that in recent centuries ten Lord Mayors of London have founded between them fourteen noble houses, all out of trade (*Social Transformation of the Victorian Age*, pp. 14 f.). There are no old families among the nobility, though many existed, until taxation began to crush them, among the country gentry.

[2] In the Middle Ages the lesser nobility had thrown in their lot with the "commons" and so made possible the rise of a strong middle class in England.

rivalry of ostentation. Shameless luxury among the rich was in consequence met by the discontent of the poor, who were conscious "of the golden shower flying about them without a gleam of gold" for them.

CLASS DISTINCTIONS

In the pre-Victorian Era, especially in the country, social distinctions had been well defined and accepted as a matter of course. There was no jealousy and no striving, since gradations were admitted. Thus intercourse was possible without class-consciousness, and society, if not a unit, was at least coherent and stable. The Industrial Revolution changed all this, for it not only introduced new classes, such as the wealthy manufacturer and the city clerk, but even in the country itself by industrializing farming it raised a barrier between the farmer and the agricultural labourer. In many European countries, alongside the landlord and the tenant farmer, there existed the land-owning peasant. But in England when villeinage was practically abolished in the fourteenth century, freed serfs were not given a share in the land. Up to nearly the end of the eighteenth century, however, the farmers had been on much the same social level as their labourers, alongside whom they often worked. The new scale on which farming was to be conducted and the new commercial methods forced the less adaptable farmers down to the level of their labourers, whilst the successful rose above them to form a separate class. The position of the labourers, it need hardly be stated, was still further depressed. There was, moreover, no room any longer for the small, part-time cultivator of the soil; he disappeared almost entirely until the revival of the allotment system. Capital was demanded and high technical skill; for the business of agriculture was no longer to supply the needs of the village, but to reach out to the growing markets in the large towns. In these towns themselves the Factory System was leading to a similar division of class from class, and to the growth of suspicion and resentment between them. There was a consciousness on the part of the more intelligent of the workers that their labour was being exploited for the private gain of their masters; whilst the latter were determined to keep labour "in its proper place" to cling to their profits and the means of making them at all costs.

Class bitterness in England, however, thanks to the less rigid divisions of society, had never been so violent as on the continent. The "class war" which conditions abroad had provoked was not at all suited to this country. It became less and less applicable as the middle classes gradually extended their sphere in either direction until they now comprehend the vast majority of citizens. But class feeling, even of a milder kind, did emerge; sufficiently disquieting. This was unfortunate, for there had been, in the previous era, a drawing together of the different social groups. The French Revolution had aroused Englishmen to a new appreciation of the seriousness of life which had led to some reform of manners among the upper classes; it had also led to a diminished insistence on privilege. An outward manifestation of this can be found in the gradual simplification of men's clothing, and in a preference for more sober hues. This process continued until there came about a certain approximation of clothing between the different classes; an approximation which has become almost complete, at least to the superficial eye, in our own day with its mass production of cheap clothing. No longer are the lower classes content to go about in drab, squalid garments; but desire to look as well-dressed, on occasion, as their so-called betters.

THE USE OF LEISURE

The improvement in the dress of the lower orders was but one manifestation of the general improvement in the conditions of life. In the earlier years of the period the poor were shut out by their long hours of employment and scanty wages from the enjoyment of almost all that we mean by art and beauty. The working day began at six and went on till eight at night. When the labours of the day were ended little energy was left for amusement or recreation; the labourer was glad to doze by the fireside and then creep off to bed. Even if conditions had been more favourable, the lack of education—the ability to read was by no means common—would still have been a barrier. William Morris has put the disabilities of the poor very strongly:

"The singers have sung and the builders have builded,
The painters have fashioned their lines of delight;
For what and for whom hath the world's book been gilded
When all is for them but the blackness of night?"

This deplorable state of things was being slowly remedied all through the era, and to-day a keen observer can go so far as to say that "We are in the middle of a very interesting experiment. For the first time in history we are trying to extend the best gifts of civilization to the whole nation instead of confining them to a privileged class" (Inge, *Vale*, p. 87).

But even when hours and wages became slightly better poor houses and overcrowded conditions were apt to drive out the men and the wage-earning children to seek their pleasure in the street or the public-house. A Select Committee of the House of Lords actually discussed in 1879 the question of providing counter-attractions; but as no funds were apparently available to finance any schemes which they might suggest, their discussions were important chiefly as showing that the right use of leisure was beginning to be realized as a national problem. Here and there rather dull and unattractive experiments were made, but on a scale quite inadequate to provide a solution. In London things began to improve with the foundation of the London Recreative Evening Schools Association and the Polytechnic. Then the experiment of the Social Institute was tried at Islington in 1894 and proved sufficiently successful for similar Institutes to be opened in other large towns (see J. L. Paton, *Life of J. B. Paton*, pp. 228 ff.). Thus small attempts were made to face a problem which will become increasingly urgent as the years go by; for if the first phase of the Industrial Revolution robbed the working classes of their accustomed leisure, the second phase, with its abundance of cheap power, seems likely to restore it in such abundance as to embarrass society unless some adequate discipline is applied and accepted.[1] The need for guidance and direction in the use of leisure is certainly urgent. For the use of leisure is the test of a civilization. A comparison of the way in which the average English-

---

[1] See further P. E. T. Widdrington, "Religion and Leisure," in *Faith that Illuminates*, pp. 57 ff.

man spends his spare time and the activities of an ancient Greek is very disquieting.[1]

TOWN AND COUNTRY

One of the greatest changes achieved by the Industrial Revolution was that which transferred large numbers of the population from the country to the town. In the words of the *Communist Manifesto*: "The bourgeoisie . . . subjected the country to the rule of the towns . . . created enormous cities, . . . [and] greatly increased the urban population as compared with the rural."[2] Men and women were driven in like flocks and herds from the pleasant countryside to which they were accustomed, and shut up in the dark and narrow streets of the towns. In their villages they had had an assured position and the constant guidance and control of others—the squire, the parson, the farmer. Now they were without either security or direction and so formed admirable material for the agitators who quickly sprang up amongst them. The spread of a superficial education soon came to make things if anything worse. Creighton tells of a shoemaker who on hearing it suggested that yearly Parliaments were not long enough for a man to learn his business, replied: "If I were sent to Parliament, do you think there is any question upon which I should not be fit to pronounce an opinion after a night's thought?" (*Life and Letters*, II, p. 28). The change from town to country certainly raised many problems and brought much dissatisfaction. Well might Bishop Watson at the close of the previous century declare that he loved agriculture, "because it makes good citizens, good husbands, good farmers, good children; because it does not leave a man time to plunder his neighbours, and because by its plenty it bereaves him of the temptation."

CHANGES IN GOVERNMENT

The redistribution of wealth and the movement from the country to the town brought about great social changes; they

[1] "When one thinks of the trashy amusements of England and America —the flicks and talkies and music-hall songs—and realizes what songs and what poetry the Athenian carried in his heart, we may wonder whether we have progressed as far as we suppose": Glover, *The Ancient World*, p. 124.

[2] Quoted by Christopher Dawson, *Religion and the Modern State*, p. 62.

also abolished the last traces of the old feudal system which had been the basis of Local Government in England for centuries.[1] The old landed families, rooted in the soil and looking after their tenants with a kind of paternal oversight, had served a real purpose and had been possessed by a real sense of responsibility. But such a system was ill-calculated to meet the needs of the growing towns and country districts, and in any case the old families, failing to maintain themselves in days of financial stress, were everywhere being displaced by a new class with no traditions of government. As Dr. Inge once wrote "there is no reason why a successful brewer or tobacconist should ape the style of a grand seigneur" (*Vale*, p. 118).

If extensive changes took place in Local Government, those connected with National Government were even more so. The political system which had been hammered out in the eighteenth century was, during the nineteenth, still further developed in order to make it more suited to the requirements of a democratic age. Up to 1832 the landlords alone had votes; in that year the franchise was extended to the upper middle classes and the tenant-farmers; in 1867 the working classes in the towns and in 1884 those in the country also became eligible. This extension of the vote threw very serious and novel responsibilities on sections of the community who were perhaps not yet equal to the burden, either intellectually or morally. The change certainly produced some striking results. After the Liberal defeat in 1895 Scott Holland wrote: "Down goes the middle-class Radicalism and the Nonconformist conscience. They lie smashed in ruins. How shall we do without them? It will be an immense and most perilous shifting of centres" (*Life*, p. 205). The change in the electorate was accompanied by a change, though not so rapid, in the type of Member of Parliament. Dr. Glover has put it in a striking way by suggesting that when Mr. Gladstone gave up politics Horace lost his seat in the House of Commons.[2]

---

[1] Municipal Councils had been established in 1835; elective County and District Councils followed in 1888. See further *A Century of Municipal Progress, 1835-1935*: edited by Laski, Jennings, and Robson.

[2] In *Cambridge Ancient History*, X, p. 536.

STATE INTERFERENCE AND PUBLIC OWNERSHIP

By many the Victorian Era is regarded as the age of Individualism; it was, however, in its later decades, increasingly the age in which the individual was subjected to restraints and deprived of full liberty of action. The tendency towards co-operation and organization had been seen in the establishment of the Religious Societies whose rise characterized the pre-Victorian Era, and in the comparative success of the Oxford Movement. The establishment of the Police and the slow development of a National Educational System were further instances of the same tendency on a larger scale. In these Society itself, by means of an elected government, began to exercise control over its members. The docile citizen of the twentieth century was still in the far future; but he was well in sight. Perhaps the growth of railway travel with its necessary regulations and demands for submission to fixed times and arrangements did something to prepare the way.

The closing years of the century saw vast developments in public ownership, a foretaste of what was to come; and already municipal trams, municipal gas, electricity, and water could be found. In the matter of social welfare there was also much development along similar lines. G. M. Trevelyan indeed regards the "creation of social services by public action and at the public expense" as the chief contribution of the era in this connexion (*History of England*, p. 614). Such efforts really had their origin in Germany, where Bismarck in a quite unsuccessful attempt to circumvent the Social Democrats tried to shew that a paternal government could provide all that they promised. Between 1883 and 1889 measures were passed establishing Sickness and Accident Insurance systems and an Old Age Pension scheme. In this he led the way in that unhealthy competition in bribing the electors which results from one party trying to outbid the other. By such methods Democracy is discredited and democratic government becomes the means of drawing out the lowest, instead of the noblest, characteristics of the people.

State action may eliminate social injustice and remove the terrible insecurity which preys upon so many of the poor; but it carries with it a threat to individual liberty and tends to abolish the feeling of personal responsibility. Pressed to its extreme, it may claim not only to provide for and control the bodies of the people, but to regulate their thoughts and beliefs as well. It then becomes a menace to religious as well as political and economic freedom.

EFFECTS OF POPULAR EDUCATION

The spread of education has undoubtedly and inevitably had far-reaching consequences; increased wealth and political power on the part of the working classes have been amongst them, and also increased opportunities for attaining to higher social levels. The intellectual and cultural divisions which marked off class from class have largely disappeared. At the same time there has been a considerable change in the subjects taught to the sons of the wealthy and the middle classes. Mr. Gladstone might say that "modern European civilization [was] the compound of two great factors, the Christian religion for the spirit of man, and the Greek, and, in a secondary degree, the Roman discipline of his mind and intellect" (*Life*, II, p. 647); but before the end of his life the classics were beginning to lose their exclusive rights and the education of the upper classes to be approximated a little more nearly to that given in the Church schools and those provided by the Boards.

But the gradual breaking down of cultural barriers and the more equal division of political power have not been the only consequence of popular education. It has brought upon the scene an entirely new figure—the elementary school teacher. In the early days of education teachers were drawn from the labouring and small shopkeeper class; gradually the tradesmen and the more ambitious artisans began to send their sons and daughters into the ranks of the new profession, and in the next generation the children of the teachers themselves; for teachers, unlike H. G. Wells's butlers and lady's maids,[1] do tend to reproduce their kind. It would be difficult to exaggerate the importance, from a social point of view, of the consequence of this new type of teacher; from it trained and natural leaders are drawn for every kind of activity, of a religious,

[1] See *Bealby*, p. 1.

educational, and social character.[1] Mr. Christopher Dawson has even suggested that, owing to his expert knowledge of psychology and his experience in training minds and character, the schoolmaster may take the place of the clergyman "as the spiritual power of the future" (*Religion and the Modern State*, p. 55). But the bulk of school teachers are women, and their occupancy of such important and influential positions is a sign and token of the new position which women have come to take in the life of the nation. This is a topic so important as to demand separate treatment.

THE POSITION OF WOMEN

At the close of the reign of Victoria, Dean Vaughan, looking back, expressed the opinion that its leading features had been "the approximation of man to man, class to class, peer to peasant, Churchman to Nonconformist."[2] This is an interesting list, but it does not represent the whole truth, for the Dean failed to record another "approximation"—in the position of woman to that of man. More than a generation before the Queen came to the throne Condorcet had foretold that "the equalization of the rights of men and women would be one of the most important and beneficial features of progress in the future." When she died this prophecy was well on the way to an almost complete fulfilment; and one of the most striking advances in recent social and political history has been the recognition of woman's true place in the commonwealth as the comrade and equal—though diverse—of man. The consequences of this recognition have not yet fully been worked out, nor the limitations to which it must be subject.[3]

It has been stated by a leading authority, the late Dr. Verrall, that the radical disease which more than anything else brought about the collapse of ancient civilization was an imperfect ideal for women. Every student of the classics would, I think, agree that the position given to women by the Greeks and Romans was deplorably low and that it undoubtedly helped

[1] Cf. C. F. G. Masterman, *The Condition of England*, p. 83.
[2] Quoted W. F. Moulton, *Life of W. F. Moulton*, p. 263.
[3] Part of the above paragraph is taken, with some slight alterations, from my Hulsean Lectures, *Erasmus the Reformer*, pp. 23 f.

to undermine their civilization; and admitting this he would draw the further conclusion that the position assigned to women in any epoch is a touchstone by which it may be judged. For the womanhood of an age, as it has recently been pointed out, "not only does a great deal to set the tone of its culture, but also the pitch of its creative and intellectual life. . . . Partly whimsically and partly truthfully, one might find the explanation for so much frustrated idealism of the Victorian Age in the real inequality between the sexes during the period."[1]

From the very first Christianity, in striking contrast to the secular world in which it grew up and the Jewish Church from which it took its origin, gave a very high place to women, as it also did its best to protect children. In this may be found perhaps its greatest achievement; such, at least, is the opinion of R. E. Speer, the famous American missionary expert. "If anybody," he says, "should ask me to risk Christianity on one single cast, to stake everything on one argument, I sometimes think I should almost be willing to select, of all the positions of Christian apologetics, the attitude of Christianity towards women and children" (*Missionary Principles and Practice*, p. 458).

But in spite of many centuries of Christianity in England it still remained in the days of Victoria "a man's country,"[2] and women had to submit to innumerable restrictions, both conventional and legal, which now seem to be absurd and unjust. It is true that women could wield immense power in politics and in the domestic circle; there were indeed many, according to Laurence Housman, who "accepted convention mainly because they believed that it gave them power."[3] But there can be no doubt that in quite a large number of women the power and energy which could find no outward expression was turned inward; hence the tale of nervous wrecks and hysterical spinsters for which the age was noteworthy.

In these days of freedom it is hard to realize that until well into the second half of the nineteenth century women were not supposed to attend public meetings. When the S.P.G. was holding meetings in Chester as late as Bishop Blomfield's days

[1] H. J. and H. Massingham in *The Great Victorians*, p. xvi.
[2] Rebecca West in *Great Victorians*, p. 55.   [3] *Op. cit.*, p. 359.

the presence of a few devout, though daring, ladies threatened to cause embarrassment until by a happy thought places were found for them behind the organ![1]

The legal disabilities under which a married woman laboured at the beginning of the era are now almost forgotten; but they were exceedingly heavy. She had, for instance, as against the father no right to the custody of her children, and after his death she was excluded from guardianship; she was not allowed to own property, even her personal earnings belonged to her husband, a great hardship to working women; and in the matter of divorce she was at a grave disadvantage.

In sexual offences the scales were heavily weighted against the woman. The whole blame was often thrust upon her and after one offence she was left in her degradation. Josephine Butler and other women who worked to raise the fallen were passionately indignant at this injustice of treatment. The women of the street seeking male victims had been, as they pointed out, in most cases themselves the victims of men.[2] Their manner of life was not self-chosen, it was all that society left to them. So, too, other women living in circumstances almost equally degrading had been forced, often enough, to accept them by their dependence.

Attempts to improve the position of women had not been unknown even in the eighteenth century. Mary Godwin's *Vindication of the Rights of Women* had appeared in 1792; but improvement when it came was not to be the consequence of propagandist literature, but of a realization through practical example of what women could do to help the community. When G. M. Trevelyan described the work of Florence Nightingale as giving "a new conception of the potentiality

---

[1] *The Christian Observer* (January 1861), p. 40. Attendance at public meetings might have brought discomfort to their neighbours from the habit of women in that age of fainting on every occasion. When a memorial service was held at St. Andrew's, Well Street, for Adrian Beresford Hope, a friend of the family sat on the women's side of the church "to look after the fainters": H. W. and I. Law, *The Book of the Beresford Hopes*, p. 195.

[2] See her letter printed in R. F. Horton, *Autobiography*, pp. 17 f. Mrs. Butler quaintly remarks that if the Old Testament Canon had been fixed by women the story of Potiphar's wife would have been excluded and that of Susannah and the elders brought in.

and place in society of the trained and educated women" (*History of England*, p. 653), his words are capable of application, on a smaller scale, to the achievements of many other less gifted women.

Legal disabilities could, of course, be removed only by Act of Parliament; but of them there was a good crop. Measures in 1839, 1857, and 1878 gave mothers additional rights to the custody of their children; the last two Acts also improved the position of the wife against an unworthy husband. But perhaps the most important piece of legislation was the passing of the Married Women's Property Act in 1870, which, together with a supplementary Act in 1882, gave to married women the right to possess property of their own and to retain whatever they might earn, even though living with their husbands.

Higher Education

One disability under which women laboured in the early years of Victoria was that of being cut off from Higher Education. They were, of course, at liberty to pursue their own studies, and in not a few cases they read both widely and deeply; even to the extent of arousing the envy of their male friends whose reading, at the same age, was much more confined;[1] but they had little guidance and no opportunity of sharing in the corporate pursuit of learning afforded by colleges and universities. Even in the 'seventies and 'eighties a London season was for the daughter of wealthy parents a substitute for the university.[2] It was only gradually that women's colleges were founded and degrees in some universities opened to them.[3] The inferior education of women was a source of evil, for it tended to suggest that they were mentally incapable of deriving benefit from what was a commonplace privilege of the male. But many were strong in their disapproval of the entire notion of the higher education of women, and especially of men and women thus obtaining opportunities of meeting. The Tractarian leaders in Oxford were divided on this matter. The thought of the establishment of a Hall there for women filled Liddon with alarm, in spite

[1] See *Life of Charles Kingsley*, p. 15.
[2] Beatrice Webb, *My Apprenticeship*, p. 45.   [3] See above, p. 321.

of the interest which Talbot and King were taking in the enterprise. He wrote to Mrs. Sidney Lear in March 1877: "Think of sending —— and —— to places like Oxford and Cambridge, where there are two thousand young men—to be met out for walks, in Lectures, at Church, to be discussed and observed, and everything else! Dr. Pusey deplores it every day, but his influence has no weight in checking the enterprise" (*Life of Henry Parry Liddon*, p. 268).

Political Disabilities

Another direction in which women seemed to be placed in a position of definite inferiority was the refusal of the parliamentary franchise. The first petition to Parliament was made in 1866 by Miss Garrett and Miss Emily Davies. In the year following, John Stuart Mill tried to get votes for women included in the Reform Act. But among women themselves there was a wide division on the matter, and in *The Nineteenth Century* for June 1889 there appeared an Anti-suffrage appeal signed by a number of highly distinguished ladies. Prominent in this group was Mrs. Humphry Ward, a woman, it need hardly be said, of advanced and Liberal ideas. She, and those who thought with her, desired "the fullest possible development of the powers, energies, and education of women," but had no wish for them to undertake any part in running the machinery of State.[1] To the Queen herself any question of the rights of women was simply horrifying and corporal punishment the best method of dealing with its advocates. The subject made her, as she did not scruple to admit, "so furious that she cannot contain herself."[2]

The removal of their disabilities and the opening of opportunities to women was undoubtedly a wise policy, since it abolished a sense of grievance and to a large extent ended the necessity for the practice of those arts—chiefly feline, as an unsympathetic observer has called them—by which many of them had become accustomed to gain their ends. But on the positive side the results of the emancipation and higher education of women have been strangely disappointing,

---

[1] See Janet Trevelyan, *Life of Mrs. Humphry Ward*, pp. 225 ff.
[2] Sir Theodore Martin, *Queen Victoria as I Knew Her*, pp. 69 f.

especially in literature. Lord Acton thought that the writings of George Eliot were "the high watermark of feminine achievement" and certainly no woman since her day has risen above it. Mr. A. W. Benn sums up very pessimistically: "If anything," he says, "the effect of their more favoured position has been to stop the former supplies. Not only are the Sibylline books rapidly decreasing in number, but their contents are less interesting, and the price paid for them has risen" (*Modern England*, pp. 490 f.).

THE VICTORIAN HOME

From the position of women in the Victorian Era to the home life of the period is an easy transition; and no doubt the increased opportunities enjoyed by women had some effect upon it.

The home was one of the most typical elements in the social life and system of the era; with its ordered serenity it was a kind of miniature of the outer world to whose ideals it stood as a kind of stronghold and power house. But even in the Victorian age itself, in spite of the approving notice of some great writers —Thackeray, Trollope, and Mrs. Gaskell among them—the home had many critics. They condemned its excessive restrictions and unnatural reticences, its over-discipline and over-intensity, so baulking of spontaneity. There certainly was something oppressive and almost inhuman in the sternness with which it ignored childish feelings and childish fears, those "subtle, grim, and secret fears" which seized upon tiny minds in their dark and silent nurseries. "Amongst all the pomp, the lavish love and downstairs luxury of those 'good Victorian homes,'" wrote Margaret Vaughan, "there remained in the background a curious and sometimes a grimmer sphere . . . the upstairs nurseries, which were ruled over by a horde of uneducated 'old women.' . . . Some of them were of a beneficent, indeed of a blessed, influence in old-fashioned nurseries; others the reverse" (*Out of the Past*, p. 17). What, however, the critics failed to allow for was the part which it played in training character and adding to the happiness of mankind. The Victorian home, in spite of serious limitations and unnecessary inhibitions, certainly produced men and women of deep culture, of wide and varied interests. Since every home is in its way unique, originality and self-reliance were natural products. Our present rather lax system has so far not succeeded in producing characters of a similar greatness on anything like the same scale. Dr. Major suggests that "fifty years hence we shall probably discover that the secret of Victorian greatness is to be found in the purity and affection of its home life" (*Life and Letters of Boyd Carpenter*, p. 5).[1]

The proud and predominant position of the Victorian home, however, was being slowly undermined as the century drew to its close; for increased wealth and leisure, and the multiplying opportunities for outside amusement, tended to rival its attractions and to lessen the influence of parental authority.

THE VICTORIAN SUNDAY

Closely connected with the Victorian home was the Victorian Sunday. Did not Bishop King once say that Sunday ought to be called the Home Day? The idea behind it was largely that of the Jewish Sabbath rather than a Christian festival; or at least so it seemed to small people who were conscious of inhibitions on every hand. They could understand the denial of pleasures which entailed labour for others, but not the comprehensive prohibitions to which they were subjected. On Saturday night all toys and secular books disappeared, not to come out again until Monday morning. During Sunday the dolls' house remained tightly sealed and in their cardboard barracks the leaden soldiers rested from mimic warfare. It was all very puzzling. To fill up the day there were special Sunday books and games (often connected with missionary work), there were family walks, and as a constant background a succession of religious exercises. The multiplication of services often brought on a kind of spiritual indigestion in those who were not yet capable of assimilating so rich and abundant a feast; with strong reaction in later life.[2]

Some one has said that the enemy of the Sabbath is the

---

[1] It is perhaps necessary to add that the Victorian home must not be judged by absurd caricatures such as *The Barretts of Wimpole Street*.

[2] Cf. the description of Sunday in E. F. Benson, *Our Family Affairs*, pp. 41 ff.

enemy of the poor. On this point the Victorians were very sound; they recognized Sunday as a day of rest, not only for themselves but for their servants. Lord Frederick Hamilton says of his parents: "Neither my father nor my mother ever dined out on a Sunday, nor did they invite people to dinner on that day, for they wished as far as possible to give those in their employment a day of rest. All quite hopelessly Victorian! for, after all, why should people ever think of anybody but themselves?" (*The Days before Yesterday*, p. 45).

This was true of many other households.

The Victorian conception of the way in which Sunday should be spent may have been a little severe and even harsh; but it was certainly better than the present way, held by so many, of regarding it as purely a day for pleasure, with no thought of God at all. The rush and turmoil of the week create an atmosphere in which it is hard to realize the presence of God; to do so the soul must have quiet and peace. This was continually being urged by Canon Barnett: "Religion depends on the Sabbath," he would say, "for unless people have the time and opportunity for thought and quiet they will forget all about God" (*Life*, p. 490).

THE EFFECT UPON RELIGION

The changes hinted at rather than described above were such as to affect the whole structure of society, and through it to challenge those fundamental moral and religious beliefs which, in spite of questionings here and there, carried with them the approval or at least the toleration of the age. That age saw but the beginning of the process of change—we cannot, however, pursue its course into the twentieth century, much less down to the present day—and was, if critical of the mechanism of society, sufficiently secure and complacent to dismiss the possibility that it would ever not merely be regarded as unsatisfactory and capable of improvement, but be condemned out of hand as obstructive and entirely obsolete. So also there was as yet no influential attempt to exalt any political faith as a substitute for religion. There were, it is true, socialists; but no one dreamed of Soviet Russia, or regarded the idea of a Totalitarian State as practical politics.

The changes in society as a whole brought with them a shifting of balance or rather of emphasis; and new figures appeared drawing to them influence and achieving importance. This has been vividly and concisely stated by Mr. Sidney Webb: "The typical figure of the England of the Middle Ages was the lord of the manor; the dominant types of the England of a century ago were the improving landlord and the capitalist mill-owner; the most characteristic personages of the England of the twentieth century are the elected councillor, the elementary schoolmaster, the school-doctor, and the borough engineer" (quoted by Bishop Bell, *The Modern Parson*, p. 8). Stated thus in terms of persons the changes are revealing. In the same way just as Christianity as a whole was affected, so were the clergy and ministers who were its official exponents and representatives. The Church in particular suffered in this respect, for it had formed part of the landed interest; the parson was often the younger brother of the squire or related to him by marriage, and shared with him the government of the countryside. The decay of the landed interest involved the Church in an equal loss of prestige. When Van Mildert, the last Prince Bishop of Durham, died in 1836, his staff of office as Count Palatine was broken and thrown into his grave. It was a symbol of the passing of an ecclesiastical era.

The social position of the clergy, however, continued to be fairly high; in fact the Church probably reached its highest point of social influence in the middle years of Victoria; for it drew on the newly rich families who had risen in the social scale, and now began to offer their sons for the priesthood. But these new families, as I have already pointed out, lacked the sense of responsibility which comes from a traditional connexion with the land; this also told against the Church, though it must gladly be admitted that in not a few cases, no doubt at the urging of the parson, the new class of landowner was often extraordinarily generous to the Church in his parish.

In the towns Christianity was weakened by being too much equated with respectability. The Industrial Revolution had made men come to believe that the real business of life was to make money; religion, so far as it was cultivated, was a thing for one day of the week. The very possession of wealth and a good position was evidence, moreover, of the divine favour and of the status of the possessor in the spiritual as well as in the material sphere. To Nonconformity the Revolution brought increased power and prestige. Shut out until 1828 from public life Dissenters had given their time and energies to business, which in the eyes of the upper classes, who were the leaders and mainstay of the Church, was looked down upon as slightly vulgar. The extension of the franchise worked in the same direction, and the political power of Dissent increased at an even higher rate of progression than the financial.

Dissent as a matter of fact had had a great deal to do with training the working man as a citizen and a potential force in politics. In the chapel "he learned to discuss with his fellows, to organize a society, to administer its affairs. If in the day he was ground down by greed or tyranny, yet in the evening he met with those who looked at the world with other eyes."[1] Thus the social changes had a double effect—within Christendom they increased the power of Nonconformity; outside it they presented a challenge to meet the new conditions. There was thus a call for the use of new methods. With the attempt to devise them we shall deal in the next chapter.

[1] Whitley, *History of British Baptists*, p. 263.

22

NEW METHODS

THE immense change which took place during the Victorian Era in the social and economic life of the country imposed a strain of incalculable severity upon all branches of the Christian Church. It is a remarkable testimony to their vitality that they were able to develop on a quite considerable scale new organizations and to devise new methods through which to meet this tension.

THE NEEDS OF THE TOWNS

From the point of view of the Church of England the biggest problem was to adjust her system, based as it was upon the parish, to the changes consequent on the migration of vast numbers from the country to the town. Almost as soon as men came to perceive the problem suggestions were not wanting as to the way in which it ought to be met. Hurrell Froude, for example, put forward a scheme which, in the somewhat gradiloquent manner of his time, he dubbed a "Project for Reviving Religion in the Great Towns." The mainspring of it was the establishment of colleges of unmarried priests in various centres; this he considered would be the cheapest and most effective way of providing for the rapidly growing populations.[1] But beyond plans to erect new churches and to create new parishes not very much was done to meet the need. A serious attempt to awake the Church to the importance of the matter was made by G. L. Cotton, Master of Marlborough, when he preached at the Consecration of A. C. Tait to the see of London on November 23, 1856. He drew attention to the danger to religion which was looming from the increased secularization of the great towns,[2] and called upon the Church

---

[1] Church, *Oxford Movement*, pp. 53 f.
[2] In 1852 Florence Nightingale, in a letter to Monckton Milnes, deplored the fact that "All the moral and intellectual [working men] seem going over to atheism, or at least a vague kind of theism": see *Life and Letters of R. M. Milnes*, II, p. 475.

to abandon party disputes in order to face the task of coping with it. A similar problem, though not on a scale of such overwhelming vastness, had faced the Church in Italy in the thirteenth century. The growth of trade and some measure of security had resulted in the spread of the towns outside the narrow circuit of their walls into new suburbs for which no spiritual provision had been created. The need of these new suburbs was met, in part at least, by the rise of the friars.[1] In the last century the new auxiliary to the Church's work was found in the quickening of life among the Nonconformists, who resembled the friars in their zeal and energy, as well as by their being outside the parochial system.

The secularization of the big towns was due, in part, as we saw above, to the improvement in the education of the working classes which laid them open to the attacks of Anti-Christian writers and speakers. The task of meeting these attacks was left largely to local initiative. But societies like the Christian Evidence Society and the various tract-distributing agencies provided useful literature for combating unbelief and its agents. The best of the leaders in the campaign against the Church and its teaching, after a time, grew tired of so negative a business and took up various positive lines. Mrs. Annie Besant, for example, by a strange reaction, went to the far extreme of theosophy; other leaders became absorbed in the growing Socialist Movement.

THE NEEDS OF THE UPPER CLASSES

Before turning to the various organizations which were established to meet the spiritual needs of the poor and outcast it may be worth while to glance at the more comfortable classes. These too have their needs and they are often inarticulate; for religion to them is often a matter of inheritance and has no deep root in the soul; the very comfort and security of their lives may also have come between them and experiences which might have driven them back on God. The frequency of missions to reach the degraded and poverty-stricken and the rarity of such enterprises amongst the upper classes might suggest that the former had a monopoly of the need for salva-

[1] See Elliott-Binns, *Decline and Fall of the Medieval Papacy*, pp. 95 ff.

tion. But in the middle years of the Victorian Era the needs of the better classes began to be realized and efforts were put forth to meet them. In 1865, just before the Salvation Army was started, Mrs. Booth invaded the West End and made a great impression; a woman preacher was a novelty and her earnest addresses were such as to appeal to rather jaded audiences. Moody and Sankey, also, were not without their effect on the West End and the meetings held in the Opera House, at which the youthful Henry Drummond first revealed his power of dealing with educated people, were the occasions of many pathetic revelations of spiritual hunger on the part of those who were regarded by the world as fortunate and even distinguished. One of those who realized the need of reaching the educated classes was Benjamin Jowett. He wrote in 1865: "A real religious movement among the educated would be more permanent than any revival. What is wanted just now is not preaching for the poor, but teaching in schools, better and more of it, and preaching to the clergy and educated classes" (*Life and Letters*, I, p. 413). He himself proved quite a successful preacher in the West End and drew numbers to hear him; so J. Addington Symonds testifies in the very next year.[1]

HOME MISSIONS

To meet the needs of the poorer classes something outside the ordinary services was required. Such people have not had the necessary training to appreciate the worship of the Church; they are shy and feel that they will not be welcome where everybody is so respectable and comfortable-looking. Their need was met by the establishment of countless mission rooms and mission halls, some connected with the Church, some with Nonconformist bodies, and some the effort of free-lance missioners. In addition there were societies established for attending to this very matter—of which the greatest was the London City Mission. This organization had very modest beginnings, for it was started in May 1835 by David Nasmith and two companions in a small house on the banks of the Regent's Canal. Now it brings help both material and spiritual to thousands yearly and finds occupation for a considerable

[1] See M. Vaughan, *Out of the Past*, p. 91.

band of experienced missioners. Even earlier than this the enthusiasm kindled for missions overseas had made Christian people feel the reproach of the many heathen at home and efforts were made to reach them by means of definite organizations. The Baptists, as early as 1794, had felt the need for this and in 1799 an association for evangelizing the villages and towns was started. In 1819 the Congregationalists founded a Home Missionary Society of their own.

But those who wish to reach the outcast and poor cannot be content to await their attendance in halls and mission rooms; they must go out and "compel them to come in." Preaching in the open air had been one of the great features of the Methodist Revival—although John Wesley himself had only undertaken it with great reluctance—and had never entirely died out. It received a great impetus as a means of evangelization from the example set by A. C. Tait when Bishop of London. He went everywhere, giving addresses in omnibus yards and at dock-gates, in fact wherever there was the chance of getting an audience. In many parishes open-air services were a novelty, and as such put down to the Puseyites; this at least was the experience of G. H. Wilkinson in 1868 when that great missioner tried the experiment of singing hymns in the streets (*Memoir*, I, p. 217). Another ecclesiastical dignitary who shewed himself not ashamed to proclaim his faith in the open air was Cardinal Manning; like Bishop Tait he would speak anywhere and would stand on a van or a cart as occasion served. He shewed a surprising ability in adapting himself to his varying audiences. The value of open-air preaching is undeniable; but it needs careful supplementing and following up. Francis Underhill, a former Bishop of Bath and Wells, and a missioner of wide experience, has given his opinion as follows: "I have never been able fully to make up my mind as to how much good is done by out-of-door preaching. . . . It is useless to attempt to substitute [it], however well done, for regular parish visiting" (in *Northern Catholicism*, p. 299).

One of the earliest pioneers in open-air work was Robert Aitken. On being rebuked by Bishop Sumner of Chester for preaching in the streets "like a Methodist"—the rebuke came strangely from the lips of a leading Evangelical Bishop—he resigned his living and gave himself up to preaching tours. After a time he came under the influence of the Oxford Movement, from which he gained a deep love of the sacramental system, but without abating his zeal as an evangelist. He settled in the little parish of Pendeen in Cornwall and there did amazing work among the tin-miners. He died in 1873 after taking his part in the founding of the Parochial Missions Society.

The system of holding parochial missions was Roman in origin, but in the English Church it came into prominence mainly through the experiments of G. H. Wilkinson, to whom reference was made above. In 1869 there was a twelve days' mission in London, but it was practically confined to High Church parishes. The High Churchmen certainly produced a number of exceedingly gifted missioners, for in addition to Wilkinson himself there were Twigg, Body, and Furse, to name but a few.[1] But after a time the Evangelicals took up the method, and among the foremost was William Hay Aitken, the son of the Vicar of Pendeen. He was himself Vicar of Christ Church, Everton, when the call to devote his life to Home Missions came through the mouth of Moody. The new movement was abundantly successful and seemed admirably fitted to meet the special needs of the age. About this time E. W. Benson, in his new diocese of Truro, made the experiment of appointing a Diocesan Missioner, the first in the country; his choice fell on A. J. Mason, a famous and beloved name. Soon afterwards Lightfoot, on going to Durham, attached a Canonry in that ancient foundation to the office.

Experiments in the way of holding special services were held up until the passing of the Religious Worship Act of 1855 removed restrictions on meetings for worship. Until it was passed the numbers at such meetings were limited to twenty persons unless, of course, they met in a church or a duly licensed chapel. Taking advantage of the opportunity a series of Special Sunday Evening Services was begun in the spring of 1857 in Exeter Hall. Large crowds, including many who did

[1] Missions became so popular that in 1877 Wilkinson issued a warning against holding them unless there had been adequate preparation. The Church, he felt, needed to avoid such unwise efforts (*Memoir*, 1, p. 341).

not normally attend any place of worship, were attracted by them. Unfortunately, the incumbent of the parish in which the hall was situated issued an inhibition which prevented their continuance. The effect of this act was to turn them over to the Nonconformists who, naturally, were not affected. They shewed great delicacy and forbearance in the matter and did not engage the hall until the impossibility of the Church's being able to use it had been demonstrated; even then they offered to give it up at any time the inhibition should be raised. The success of these services led to the starting of similar services in St. Paul's and Westminster Abbey, as well as in a number of London theatres. This last method of trying to meet the needs of the masses was the occasion for a Roman Catholic lady to pour out her scorn to Disraeli in 1860. "Four theatres hired every evening, for 'divine service,'" she said. "A Bishop preaching at Sadler's Wells, I believe! If theatres will do, what is the use of Churches? And why not one of the usual performers to preach instead of an ordained priest?" Disraeli confessed that he thought her remarks unanswerable (*Life*, II, p. 89).

THE SALVATION ARMY

Humanly speaking the creation of this great organization was the work of one man and his gifted wife; and she was, from a medical standpoint, an invalid. So God uses the weak things of earth to confound the mighty. William Booth[1] had been a Methodist, but the refusal of the Methodist Conference of 1861 to sanction certain of his schemes led him to leave that body and strike out a line of his own. He was not a man of great intellectual force nor of many ideas. It was, in fact, his simplicity and singleness of aim that gave him his power. "Blood and fire," that was the motto of the "Army" and it revealed the directness and flaming zeal of its founder. He was not even a theologian. "Had he been," says Mr. St. John Ervine, "it is inconceivable that he could have founded the Salvation Army. Religious societies are not founded by theologians." So great was his simplicity, however, that it led

[1] There is an excellent and recent study: St. John Ervine, *God's Soldier: General William Booth*.

him to look upon himself as acting under divine inspiration; that seems to be the explanation of his autocratic methods in ruling his followers. Three things were required of them: belief in the possibility of instantaneous conversion, even for the most degraded; courage; and absolute obedience. Courage was certainly required of them in the early days when, like the Christians under the Roman Empire, persecution swept down upon them. It was this persecution which helped to make them more loyal to one another and to their leader.

In recent years it has been the social work of the "Army" which has attracted the greatest attention and gained for it the largest amount of support from those outside. But at first Booth had no idea of undertaking such work; it seemed to him a waste of time and energy. Later on he came to see its value as an act of Christian witness; Christ's representatives shewing forth His love to the outcast; and in 1890, just before Mrs. Booth's death, he issued his great programme and revelation of the need—*Darkest London and the Way Out*. It seems probable that he owed a good deal to J. B. Paton for his changed outlook as he held many consultations with him on the matter of the social aspects of the gospel.[1]

The work of the Salvation Army was not confined to the outcast and degraded at home. Long before social work was undertaken it had spread to the Mission Field, and India was entered in 1882. Unfortunately, its work in this field was conducted on very unsound lines and a desire for "results" led its agents to "steal sheep" from other folds rather than to convert the heathen. The use of publicity and advertisement, not perhaps so objectionable at home, was repugnant to other missionaries, especially when they suffered from its effects. In one case a "convert" stolen from the C.M.S. was taken to England and paraded down the Strand seated on an elephant.[2] Perhaps the simplest, though not the most edifying, explanation of the methods employed was that they were due to the financial organization of the "Army," which throws the responsibility for raising money on the various units.

[1] See J. L. Paton, *Life of J. B. Paton*, pp. 484 f.
[2] See Stock, *History of the C.M.S.*, III, p. 494.

This came out in 1889 when a body of Salvationists began a mission in the C.M.S. district of Palamcotta. "The fact, frankly acknowledged, was that the Tamil Salvationists had to live; that they could not get money from the Heathen; that they could get it from the C.M.S. Christians: hence the selection of Palamcotta." Later they moved on to South Travancore and gathered a large following from among the L.M.S. Native Christians.

As the Salvation Army became prominent, naturally it aroused the suspicions and even the dislike of the stricter type of Churchman. Robert Gregory tells of a girl, in whom his sister was interested, who joined the "Army." After a time she lost her reason and Miss Gregory was approached to provide for her. "No!" she replied, "you took her away to squall and bawl for you, and now she's squalling and bawling on her own you can keep her" (*Autobiography*, p. 51). But it was not Churchmen of the stricter type only who were "put off" by the methods adopted. Lord Shaftesbury, although doubtless he sympathized with the objects of the "Army," protested against its "haughty title" and military constitution.[1] He felt, moreover, that by its "excesses" it was producing "great irreverence of thought, of expression, of action, turning religion into a play, and making it grotesque and familiar." Although many of his friends were supporters of "General" Booth duty compelled him to launch a public attack on the "Army" and its methods. From this position he never retreated and in the last years of his life he condemned "its travesty of religion" (*Life*, III, p. 433 ff.). Another sympathizer who was alienated for the same reason was Stevenson Blackwood. It must be confessed that much of the enthusiasm which the Salvation Army aroused was, if intense, not well regulated.

But there were other Churchmen who approved of the Salvation Army; perhaps because they had no first-hand knowledge of its methods, but only of its results. Benjamin Jowett wrote in November 1882: "I am assured . . . by the police that about twenty of the worst characters in Oxford

[1] The military constitution of the "Army" was not Booth's own idea. He had been working on his own lines from 1865 until the adoption of this basis in 1878. The actual title came two years later.

have been reformed or 'converted' by them. It seems as if religion was leaving the educated classes, and taking up its abode among the poor, and especially among the vulgar" (*Life and Letters*, II, p. 262). A still more august member of the Church of England was also interested in the work of the Salvation Army, no less than the Queen herself. When William Booth brought out his scheme for social work in 1890 the Queen viewed it with some uneasiness and consulted Bishop Walsham How on the matter. He was decidedly critical in his report, but the Queen came to hold a rather more favourable view of the matter through the influence of Boyd Carpenter, who was at Windsor Castle when the Bishop's letter was received. Boyd Carpenter preserved the heads of his comments, which are described by his biographer as judicious and charitable. They are too long to insert here but they may be found in Dr. Major's *Life and Letters of William Boyd Carpenter*, pp. 228 ff.

The greatest testimony to the work of the Salvation Army on the part of the Church, however, was the formation of the Church Army in 1882. This was the work of Wilson Carlile, who died at a great age in 1942. Carlile had come under the influence of Moody and he saw the need for the Church to possess an organization run on the lines of the Salvation Army though avoiding its excesses and, of course, working under the direction, not solely of its "general," but of the duly constituted authorities of the Church itself. The great success which has attended this effort, both in evangelistic, pastoral, and social work, is a testimony to the foresight and devotion of its founder and to the ability of the Church to make use, though perhaps not on a sufficiently adequate scale, of unusual means of carrying on its mission, to employ working men and women to carry the gospel to people of their own class.

SETTLEMENTS

The Settlement Movement began as an attempt to meet the partial segregation of the rich and poor into different districts through the change in social customs brought about by increased wealth and improved means of transport. In older days rich and poor lived side by side, the suburb and the slum were not yet arisen; but by the middle of the Victorian Era the separation had already taken place in the large towns; thus leaving the overcrowded and down-trodden in one locality, the leisured and educated in another. It was thus impossible to get a sufficiency of workers in poor parishes, whilst in the wealthy parishes there were often well-disposed and pious persons who could find no outlet for their energies. To right this condition of things the Settlement Movement came in. Its pioneer was really Edward Denison, the son of the Bishop of Salisbury, who established himself in a small house in the parish of St. Philip, Stepney (of which J. R. Green, the historian, was vicar), with the object of finding out the real state of the necessitous and to do something to help them. But it was not until the foundation of Toynbee Hall in 1885 that the Movement can be said to have begun.

Toynbee Hall, so named after Arnold Toynbee,[1] one of Ruskin's disciples and a devoted worker for the good of his fellow men, was a product of Oxford—like so many movements of one kind and another. In 1884 a motion was brought before the Union to the effect that "in the opinion of this House the condition of the dwellings of the poor in our large towns is a national disgrace and demands immediate action on the part of voluntary associations, municipal authorities, and the Legislature." The motion was supported by a speaker specially invited for the occasion and his earnest and persuasive utterances, so different from the dazzling effusions to which the House was accustomed, made a profound impression. He pleaded for the establishment of a "settlement" in his parish in Whitechapel where men from the universities could live and work among their less fortunate fellows. The speaker was Samuel Barnett.

In due time the Settlement was opened at a meeting in which the Church of England, represented by Bishop Walsham How, and Nonconformity, represented by the Rev. E. S. Reaney, joined in sponsorship. Sir John Seeley was also there to lend the support of Cambridge. Barnett became the first warden

---

[1] Toynbee wore himself out in his efforts to stem the influence among working men of the ideas of Henry George. There is a sympathetic sketch of him, under the name of Edward Hallin, in Mrs. Humphry Ward's *Marcella*.

and at once set out to realize ideas which had been struggling in his thoughts for many months, if not years. In his biography we are told that the objects of the Settlement were: "To provide education and the means of recreation and enjoyment for the people of the poorer districts of London and other great cities; to enquire into the conditions of the poor and to consider and advance plans calculated to promote their welfare. To acquire by purchase or otherwise and to maintain a house or houses for the residence of persons engaged in or connected with philanthropic or educational work" (*op. cit.*, p. 311). The ideals of the Movement were definitely religious, though on no narrow or denominational basis. Barnett himself, who was Vicar of St. Jude's, Whitechapel, was a man of very distinctive religious convictions. His one never-sleeping desire was to help people to live their lives in relation to God (*op. cit.*, p. 76). But he met with a double disappointment. On the one hand he found it very difficult to get the residents in Toynbee Hall to respond; and on the other, similar settlements but on very definite religious and denominational lines were established. A little more may be said of each of these. (*a*) Every morning in Toynbee the warden had family prayers of a simple kind at which he always gave an address over which he had taken much pains; yet few troubled to come, and "his hearers were rarely personally gripped or even interested," writes Mrs. Barnett, with devoted candour (*op. cit.*, p. 490). At first the Settlement had attracted a good many men who were preparing for Holy Orders; but these gradually ceased to come, preferring a more distinctive atmosphere. In the end the majority of the residents were mainly interested in politics and hoped to gain an insight into conditions which would be of service to them later on. (*b*) As to the foundation of "rival" settlements, such as Oxford House, on definitely Church lines. Barnett was much hurt by these and felt that they were a reflection on his own efforts. But they were unavoidable when High Churchmen became really interested in social problems and desired their own organizations. In the end the rivalry was good, for it increased the amount of work accomplished and any sense of indignation on Barnett's part was kept in check by his intense self-mastery and "meekness." Barnett was a truly great man although he never attained to positions of prominence. It is said that Clemenceau, on a visit to England, went down to inspect the Settlement and came away much impressed. Later he wrote: "I have met but three really great men in England, and one was a little pale clergyman in Whitechapel."

Barnett's example has been taken up in all parts of London and in many provincial towns. The universities, their separate colleges, and many public schools have each its own mission; but it is to him that they look back.[1]

An enterprise somewhat on the lines of Settlements was the establishment of what were known as Central Missions. This was the contribution of the Wesleyan Methodists to the solution of the problem of the separation of the rich and poor. The first Central Hall was opened in a derelict chapel in Oldham Street, in the centre of Manchester. There the Rev. S. F. Collier did a noble work.[2] That the Methodists should have been the pioneers in this type of work was unexpected, since it cut right across the Circuit System and involved a breach of Trust Deeds. The great name in connexion with the extension of the Central Mission idea is Hugh Price Hughes, who established the West London Mission in St. James's Hall in 1887 with the help of Mark Guy Pearse.[3] Before this there had been started, in addition to Manchester, Missions in East and Central London; later were to follow South London (1889), South-West London (1899), and Poplar and Bow (1900).

THE REVIVED USE OF THE CATHEDRALS

Alongside the improvision of new methods went, in this season of reviving life, the restored use of some which lay ready to hand, though ignored and forgotten. In the forefront of these, both for their availability and for their neglect, must be placed the cathedrals of the land, and especially the two great churches of London, St. Paul's and Westminster Abbey.

[1] See further Knapp and others, *The Universities and the Social Problem*; and for Toynbee Hall, *Canon Barnett*, pp. 311 ff., and J. A. R. Pimlott, *Toynbee Hall: Fifty Years of Social Progress*.

[2] Fullerton, in his *Life of F. B. Meyer*, pp. 54 f., suggests that the Manchester Central Hall was really copied from Melbourne Hall in Leicester, which Meyer had put up.

[3] See Dorothea Price Hughes, *Hugh Price Hughes*, pp. 196 ff.

We saw above that the holding of Evening Services in Exeter Hall suggested the use of these sacred buildings for similar purposes; and it was high time that they should so be used, though many difficulties had to be overcome before anything like their full capacity for service could be utilized. Charles Kingsley in *Yeast* has left a description of the deadness of a service at St. Paul's in 1847. "The afternoon service was proceeding. The organ droned sadly in its iron cage to a few musical amateurs. Some nursery-maids and foreign sailors stared about within the spiked felon's dock which shut off the body of the cathedral, and tried in vain to hear what was going on inside the choir. As a wise author—a Protestant too —has lately said, 'the scanty service rattled in the vast building like a dried kernel too small for its shell.' The place breathed imbecility and unreality and sleepy life in death, while the whole nineteenth century went roaring on its way outside."

Before this, however, the epoch of Cathedral Reform, which was perhaps to reach its zenith when Benson built the new cathedral of Truro in 1878, had already begun with the work of Walter Kerr Hamilton at Salisbury from 1841 onwards. But even at Salisbury it was only a beginning of things, for Samuel Waldegrave (later to be Bishop of Carlisle) wrote to A. C. Tait on his appointment as Dean of Carlisle in 1849 (Waldegrave was then Canon of Salisbury) urging him to try and make some use of his cathedral and describing how he himself often used to walk in the nave of Salisbury and wish that it could be used for some kind of popular service (see *A. C. Tait*, I, p. 150). When Tait went to London he tried to get both the Abbey and St. Paul's to start popular services. Trench, then Dean of Westminster, was agreeable and on January 3, 1858, a great Sunday Evening Service was held. At St. Paul's, although evening services had been held during the Great Exhibition in 1851, Milman and the Chapter were more difficult. They pleaded that there was no demand in the city and that it would mean additional expense. Tait met this latter objection by raising a fund for the purpose, to which he himself subscribed £100. A service was held on Advent Sunday 1858 and caused such a sensation that Ludgate Hill was for a time completely blocked by those wishing to attend it. The number who failed to obtain entrance into the Cathedral was variously computed at from 10,000 to 100,000 by the newspapers. Although the services were continued during the winter months the Chapter refused permission for them to be restarted in the following year (*op. cit.*, I, pp. 259 f.).

There was no real hope that the Cathedrals would rise to their opportunities until an entirely new set of canons had gained control. When Gregory went to St. Paul's in 1868 he was told that he must not expect to make changes or improvements; every new canon took that line, but he was always outvoted (*Autobiography*, p. 158). But changes were to come quickly at St. Paul's. In 1870 Liddon was appointed a canon, and in the next year, Lightfoot; and, best of all, Richard William Church became Dean.[1] When Liddon was offered his canonry things did not look very hopeful and in discussing the matter with Dr. Pusey he emphasized the need for drastic reformation. "Yes," said Pusey, "it is, in fact, an Augean stable." Commenting on these "strong words," J. O. Johnson wrote: "they expressed what was felt by good Churchmen about many of our Cathedrals of that time. There was a great work which Cathedrals, and Cathedrals only, could do; but there was also first a great work to be done in them."[2]

So was it in London, and so was it also in the Cathedrals up and down the country; it was only when the old Chapters disappeared, or rather were transformed by the entrance into them of younger men, that progress was possible. A good example can be seen in Bristol, where it was not until 1882, when Percival was appointed to a canonry, that Nave services were begun. Even so he had to have a pulpit made at his own expense, and though the Nave was crowded each Sunday evening during the periods of his residence, the services were not continued by the other canons when their turns came round.[3]

A testimony to the vast change that took place in the years about the 'seventies can be adduced from a somewhat unex-

---

[1] See *Life of R. W. Church*, pp. 248 ff., for an account of the great awakening which followed his appointment.
[2] *Life of H. P. Liddon*, p. 135.
[3] See W. Temple, *Life of Bishop Percival*, p. 80.

pected quarter. Dean Stanley on a Sunday evening in 1876 took Lord Beaconsfield to hear Canon Farrar in Westminster Abbey. Beaconsfield was immensely impressed and on coming out exclaimed: "I would not have missed the sight for anything; the darkness, the lights, the marvellous windows, the vast crowd, the courtesy, the respect, the devotion—and fifty years ago there would not have been fifty persons present" (*Life of Dean Stanley*, II, p. 447).

PAROCHIAL ORGANIZATION

In what may be said about the methods employed in the smaller units, the parish may be taken as the norm, for it experienced the same changes as other units, such as the circuit of the Methodist or the "congregation" of denominations organized on a non-geographical basis. One means of promoting greater efficiency in parochial life and organization was to divide and subdivide the existing parishes. In some instances this meant the creation of quite a considerable number of new parishes. West Ham, of which the writer was at one time vicar, is especially interesting in this connexion. The ancient parish was actually split up—not by a single measure, but gradually beginning with the creation of St. John's, Stratford, in 1836—into more than twenty. In the meantime, West Ham had increased from a small country town with a population of a few thousands to one of the largest in England with over 300,000 inhabitants. In such cases the process of division was absolutely necessary, or so it would seem. Canon Barnett, however, felt that the method was wrong because it deprived men of personality and organizing power of a sufficiently wide scope. "There are no adequate places for the best men unless they consent to become Bishops," he said, "and then they are apt to be strangled by their own gaiters" (*Life*, p. 194).

The extraordinary nature of the organizations inside a parish is not always grasped; for in nearly all cases they are both parochial, and yet parts of wider associations. There is thus a dual control; within the parish, the incumbent, and outside it, the leaders of whatever association may be involved. This might seem to give occasion for misunderstanding and the clash of jurisdictions. In practice, however, it seems to work quite efficiently. But the power of the parish priest within his own area is absolute; this is sometimes forgotten, especially when interdenominational societies are concerned. The number of these new organizations is remarkable, both for extent and variety. The majority of them are designed for young people, these will be dealt with later in this chapter; but those that remain are a goodly number. It is a testimony to the public spirit of Christian congregations that the workers in them are almost entirely voluntary. Thus a parish or other similar unit tends to become, by the multiplication of its machinery, a kind of business concern. In this there is grave danger, and especially in the Church of England where the laity have a much smaller share in the management of affairs, that the clergyman or minister may be turned into a sort of managing director to the loss of spiritual power and insight. Efficiency becomes the watchword, but it can be purchased at too high a price. Neville Figgis once said, in his paradoxical way: "If the Church should become really efficient, its days as a spiritual power would be at an end" (*The Gospel and Human Needs*, p. 66).

There is another danger, akin to this. That of trying to attract people to join the Church or congregation by the provision of amusements, and in general, making out that Christianity is a pleasant and easy thing. This policy is not as novel as some may think, for as early as 1868 it was denounced by Lord Shaftesbury as a wrongful substitute for preaching the gospel and "going out into the streets and slums to bring them in" (*Life*, III, p. 8). A recent writer has described the state of affairs in the present time; by the end of the Victorian Era things if not quite so bad, were well on the way to it. He writes: "A common occurrence in town parishes is to find three or four hundred people dancing, or enjoying some other amusement, in the church schools on Saturday night, followed by three or four communicants at the early service next morning, with thirty or forty people at midday and perhaps a hundred at night. These are not all the same people. Most of the dancers rarely, if ever, attend church, though a few are regular worshippers. It is worthy of notice that since the churches provided these amusements their congregations have dwindled. The reason is simple and was foreseen by many Christians: that the two things are totally different; the keenest people on the amusements are not the keenest Christians. The latter have no time to waste nor desire to waste it. This state of affairs has nearly broken the hearts of the spiritually minded ministers of all denominations."[1]

Even when the energies of the clergy and other Christian workers are not expended in the provision of mere amusements, and the buildings intended to be used for more or less sacred purposes are not being devoted to this end, often the activities are more of a social than a religious nature. This is no bad thing, but it is not the highest method of employing such resources. The late Lord Salisbury was once asked to support some Church scheme for promoting purely secular and educative work in one of the poorer districts of London. He refused with the brief comment, "They are asking you for bread and you are offering them stones" (*Life*, I, p. 120).

Even the Pleasant Sunday Afternoon, the invention of Arthur Mursell, a Baptist Minister in Manchester, which had such great popularity for a time and did much to draw men together, had its weak points. Fullerton says: "Their success was only partial and scarcely permanent, while the idea underlying the title, that only something pleasant would attract men, and the half-hint that the other services . . . were not pleasant, made it desirable that something different should be attempted" (*F. B. Meyer*, p. 108).

The methods referred to above were common to practically all parts of the Christian Church, except possibly the Roman Catholic, in this country. Other methods, the revival of those anciently practised here before the Reformation and allowed to drop—again with the exception of the Roman Catholics—were typical of the Church of England, or rather of a school of thought within it. About them there has been much controversy, and in order to avoid entering into it I must be content with a bare record of the steps by which they came in: they were the use of Confession and the revival of Religious Orders.

When Confession was revived as a general method of dealing

[1] J. G. Hayes, *Institutional Christianity*, p. 247.

with souls in the Church of England is not very certain—its use in the Office for the Sick in the Book of Common Prayer presumably means that it never entirely died out—but even as early as 1859 a married woman wrote to *The Christian Remembrancer* acknowledging the benefits which she herself had derived from it since her girlhood. By 1873 the practice had become sufficiently general for a petition to be sent to Convocation asking the Bishops to consider the appointment and training of priests specially qualified to hear confessions. Four years later there was grave scandal owing to the denunciation of a volume of advice to such persons called *The Priest in Absolution*. This work had been privately printed and was intended solely for the use of priests. It contained much about moral questions which was obviously not suited to a wider public; its defenders compared it to a treatise for a medical man. The publicity attaching to the case was very unfortunate; but Archbishop Tait went so far as himself to condemn it. Confession, like many other "Catholic" practices, has suffered from suspicions attaching to it from its origin, and even those who are not interested in religion as such have a very present fear of the growth of priestly influence. An instance of this, not without its amusing and even pathetic side, is told by F. G. Bettany in *Stewart Headlam*. Headlam was giving a public lecture on "The Priest in Absolution" when he was interrupted by one of the audience shouting out: "Atheist that I am, sir, no man shall stand between my soul and my God" (*op. cit.*, p. 87). The interrupter's subconscious mind was still affected, no doubt, by Protestant teaching which he had acquired in childhood, when the deeper matters of the faith had been repudiated.

The revival of Religious Orders in the Church of England began amongst women, and so far as they concerned them will be dealt with later. For men the first Order was that of the Society of St. John the Evangelist at Cowley in 1866. Its first Superior, Father R. M. Benson, was a man of the most holy life and his devotional addresses and writings have been used by Christians of many denominations. Next came, after an interval of twenty-five years, the Society of the Sacred Mission, now at Kelham, for the training of Ordinands—Father

Kelly was the founder. In 1892 seven priests, with Charles Gore at their head, made their profession in Pusey House, Oxford, and so the Community of the Resurrection now at Mirfield was founded. In addition there were attempts, associated with the name of Father Ignatius at Llanthony, and with the island of Caldey, to revive the Order of St. Benedict in the English Church.[1]

WOMEN'S WORK

The changed position of women which came about in the Victorian Era, their gradual emancipation from hampering restrictions, and the gaining of freedom to live their own lives, was not so much a challenge to the Church as a fresh opportunity. The Church had always made considerable use of the services of women; in the days immediately before the period there had been Selina, Countess of Huntingdon, Hannah More, and we must not forget Mary Thorne, who startled the congregation at Shebbear Parish Church by publicly testifying after a service, and so led to the foundation of the Bible Christians, and the ministry of many saintly women evangelists. There was also later Elizabeth Fry. Her work, even when it was social and philanthropic, was inspired by religious motives; the same may be said of that of Florence Nightingale. The latter once said: "If I could give you the story of my life, it would be to show how one woman of ordinary ability had been led by God in strange and unaccustomed paths to do in His name what He has done in her. And, if I could tell you all, you would see how God has done all and I nothing. I have worked very hard, that is all, and I have never refused God anything."

In the Roman Church women who had the vocation could always find a way of exercising it through the Religious Orders, and the revival of the Roman Church in England made this type of work more prominent. In 1844 W. F. Hook speaks of the effects of "Dr. Wiseman's nuns" in Birmingham in gaining converts (*Life of Dean Hook*, p. 414). Even before this, actually in July 1819, a writer in *The Quarterly Review* had openly regretted that the nunneries, instead of being swept

[1] For fuller details see *Northern Catholicism*, pp. 336 ff.

away, had not been turned into Protestant establishments for women. He felt that no one could regard the then state of society "as it affects women, without regretting that an opportunity for alleviating so much evil should have been neglected" (XXII, p. 90). The establishment of Sisterhoods and Deaconesses' Institutions in England was anticipated in Germany, where in 1833 Pastor Fliedner, the founder of the Kaiserwerth Institution, had revived the work of Deaconesses. The members of his community did not take vows, but they received only their keep and a small sum for "pocket-money." Their work was carried on overseas as well as in Germany.[1]

It was in 1845 that Sisterhoods were revived in England by the agency of Dr. Pusey;[2] first at Christ Church, Albany Street, and under Miss Sellon in Devonport in 1849. By the end of the Victorian Era the number of Sisterhoods and similar organizations had increased enormously. Among the most famous of them were the Sisterhood of St. John the Baptist at Clewer, and that of St. Peter at Kilburn. The work done by these women was so impressive that they overcame much of the prejudice that attached to the early days of the movement. Both Sisterhoods sent out nurses to the Crimea during the war and their self-sacrificing labours in the cholera epidemics were known very widely. Another famous foundation was that of John Mason Neale, the hymn-writer, at St. Margaret's, East Grinstead. The work of several of these sisterhoods is carried on both at home and abroad. All these institutions belonged to the Anglo-Catholic party; but the Evangelicals, who had been among the first in the Church of England to give to the work of women its true value, were not inactive. At the Church Congress of 1862 Dean Howson sketched as an ideal the giving of themselves by all classes of women to the work of the Church as the one business of their lives, though he did not commend the Roman or High Anglican system of taking vows. In recent years the Evangelicals have largely failed to enlist the services of women of education for work at home; and one looks in vain for any to correspond to Miss Sellon, with her long years

[1] Florence Nightingale had spent three months at Kaiserwerth.
[2] See Liddon, *Life of E. B. Pusey*, III, pp. 1 ff., and *Northern Catholicism*, pp. 387 ff.

of devoted labour in Plymouth, or with the women whom T. T. Carter was able to gather round him at Clewer. One is tempted to ask. Is it necessary that educated women should be organized on a conventual basis if they are to devote themselves utterly to the service of the Church? Women's work has never been neglected by Evangelicals, however, but the efforts put forth have resulted in the establishing of inter-denominational institutions like the Ranyard Biblewomen and the Mildmay Deaconesses founded by William Pennefather,[1] Vicar of Christ Church, Barnet, and afterwards of St. Jude's, Mildmay Park. These efforts undoubtedly gave to the Church very devoted women workers, but they were not highly educated nor drawn from the best ranks of society.

Outside the Church of England there were also movements which made an increasing use of the services of women. Prominent among them was the Salvation Army whose "lasses" did work of an extraordinarily difficult and self-denying nature; to them, indeed, much of the Army's success was undoubtedly due. In view of the large share which a woman, Mrs. Booth, had had in its foundation this was only natural. Among the Methodists there was also a striking development. This was the establishment in 1885 by Mr. and Mrs. Price Hughes of a Sisterhood copied deliberately from the Religious Orders of the Roman and Anglican Churches. This organization was intended to be a means whereby educated women could find a vocation and devote their special gifts to the service of Christ. There were, of course, no vows as in the case of the Religious Orders, and members were received from any Protestant Evangelical Denomination.[2]

In concluding this section it may be helpful to quote the opinion of Mr. Warre Cornish on the best way of utilizing the service of women in Christian work. His view is that: "The experience of more than half a century among Church people,

---

[1] We need hardly to-day feel that St. Paul has precluded discussion of the question, for though he did undoubtedly forbid women to speak in the congregation (1 Cor. xiv. 34 f.), he also proclaimed that in Christ Jesus there was neither male nor female (Gal. iii. 28), a principle which seems to have very definite corollaries.

[2] See Dorothea Price Hughes, *Hugh Price Hughes*, pp. 201 ff.

High and Low, Roman Catholics and Nonconformists, teaches the same lesson: that the business of evangelizing, civilizing, and nursing is best carried on by women devoted to the work, whether permanently and by consecration, or without conditions; living in communities and under the rule of which obedience forms a part, wearing a distinctive dress, and more or less under clerical supervision. Social distinctions may be recognized or neglected; where the institution is in most thorough working they are least regarded. The practical side of the work depends upon its spiritual side, partly because direct religious teaching is a civilizing influence, but more because spiritual enthusiasm more than any other motive makes the work possible, and supplies the strongest bond of sympathy and encouragement among the members of the community."[1]

So far we have been considering the work which women may do for the Kingdom of God. Something must also be said of the special organizations established to interest women and to draw them into that Kingdom. Foremost among them is the Mothers' Union. This was founded in 1876 by Mary Sumner. It began in the parish of Old Alresford in Hampshire, spread into the diocese of Winchester, and thence throughout the whole Anglican Communion. Its ideals are very high and not all can even pretend to keep them. They are "a holy and unbreakable marriage," Christian education for the children, and personal witness by each individual woman to her Lord and Master.

For younger women the Church has the Girls' Friendly Society. This also came from Hampshire, being started by Mrs. Townsend, the wife of a squire in that county. Like the Mothers' Union it has very stringent rules and aims at a high standard of membership rather than large numbers. Queen Victoria became a patron; but only after satisfying herself that the Society did not interfere between mistresses and maids.

The Young Women's Christian Association was not actually founded until 1887; but it grew out of two organizations, both of which had been started in 1855. One was a prayer union begun by Miss Robarts, the other an association for providing

[1] *History of the English Church in the Nineteenth Century*, II, p. 81.

young business women and others with homes and institutions in which lodging and recreation can be found. The Y.W.C.A. is intended for young women of all denominations and its rules are less strict than those of the G.F.S. Its branches are very numerous and its membership over half a million in various parts of the world.

WORK AMONG THE YOUNG

In order to exert an entirely effective influence on the individual it is necessary that society should be moulded by the same spirit in its religion, its institutions, and its laws. Such a condition has never been realized, except ideally; certainly the influences to which individuals were exposed in the nineteenth century were the products of very various agencies. It is during the early years of the life of the individual, it need hardly be emphasized, that such influences can most effectively be brought to bear. This fact was fully recognized by the Christian societies of the kingdom. But the social changes taking place during the period, and in particular the decay of home life, made the task more difficult. The home is, after all, the most suitable place for the implanting of religious ideas, and the mother's knee the place for learning to pray. As Dale used to say of the young, "if they have no Church in the home, they have no home in the Church" (*Life*, p. 147). At the same time too great an insistence on religion may produce that premature and precocious religiosity which Edmund Gosse has described from his own pathetic boyhood in *Father and Son*. Zeal in dealing with the young, more perhaps than in any other sphere, needs to be tempered with discretion, and it is the example and the atmosphere that counts much more than definite instruction and the attempt to "force" the tender plant and to bring out in it experiences which are the life of its elders.

Sunday Schools

In training the young the chief agency was the Sunday School. Sunday Schools are of very ancient lineage; Cardinal Borromeo, Archbishop of Milan, had introduced them into his diocese in the sixteenth century; and about the same time

John Knox was using them in Scotland. There was an obvious need and they sprang up to meet it quite independently in different parts of the country. In England Robert Raikes of Gloucester is often regarded as the pioneer, but there were many before him and he himself was inspired by a Baptist, William King of Dursley. Raikes began by hiring four "decent women" to teach the children of the streets to read and to learn their catechism. The children were rewarded by buns and hot potatoes. This was in 1780. From that time Sunday Schools spread rapidly and have gone on spreading.

Up to the middle of the reign of Victoria they were concerned largely with secular education, teaching children to read and write as a step to gaining religious knowledge for themselves. But the increased means of education during the week made this side of their work unnecessary, and they were able to concentrate on religious instruction exclusively. But they set the model for the day schools, and often provided the actual building in which it was held. By the end of the period the organization of Sunday Schools and the training of the volunteers who staffed them with such unselfish sacrifice of their time had become a vast undertaking. The provision of suitable literature and courses alone required much thought and effort. The need for co-ordination, however, had been recognized from the first, and in 1785 William Fox, a Gloucester lad who came to live in London, founded the Sunday School Society, with a committee half of Churchmen, half of Dissenters. In 1803 the Sunday School Union was founded by W. Brodie Gurney with the special object of improving methods and providing training. There are also definitely denominational societies like the Church of England Sunday School Institute and the Wesleyan Sunday School Union.

Somewhat similar to the Sunday Schools were the Ragged Schools. In this enterprise Charles Dickens took a deep interest and often showed his sympathies with efforts made by the movement to instruct and raise the very poorest children. But the great name connected with this as with so many other charitable and philanthropic efforts was Shaftesbury. He himself when in London used to take a personal part in the work, visiting the vilest rookeries and getting into personal touch with the most ignorant and degraded (see *Life*, I, pp. 485 ff.).

Work among Older Boys and Girls

One of the great difficulties in connexion with work among the young is the tendency of growing boys and girls when once they go to work to drift away from all religious organizations. Something like four out of five children in the Sunday School never get linked up to the Church. In the Church of England Confirmation helps to keep many in touch and to lead them on to becoming regular worshippers and communicants. Its value was felt by Hugh Price Hughes as a means for bringing young people face to face with the obligations of their baptism (*Life*, p. 389), and if well and carefully used it certainly is the most helpful method for bridging the gap; especially if the newly confirmed are looked after by older communicants or made to join some kind of Guild or Fellowship.

Such Guilds and Fellowships are, of course, not a monopoly of the Church of England. In 1882 a movement in Bristol led to the formation of the Congregational Guilds Scheme for the education of young people in the principles of that denomination. In the previous year a great International Society, for such it became, was started in America by Francis Clark of Portland, Maine—the Christian Endeavour Movement. One Movement has been of great service in keeping boys and young men in touch with their Church, that is the Boys' Brigade. By the end of the century it had no less than 3,000 officers and 40,000 boys on its roll. The Boys' Brigade is, of course, interdenominational; it has a "rival" in the Church Lads' Brigade of the Church of England.

We have already considered the G.F.S. and Y.W.C.A., which work among young women and girls; for young men there is the even better-known Y.M.C.A., with activities extending to men who are no longer young. It was founded in 1844 by George Williams (afterwards Sir George) a young draper's assistant who had come up to London from Somerset. The first meetings were held in his bedroom.

Before leaving this brief sketch of work among the young something must be said of the Children's Special Service

Mission or C.S.S.M. The beginning of this enterprise was a series of services held at Mildmay in 1886 when Mr. Josiah Spiers and Mr. T. B. Bishop gathered in the children from the neighbourhood for definite evangelistic rather than instructional addresses. The next development was the starting of services on the seashore during the summer holidays, the activity with which the Mission is especially connected. In this Mr. Edwin Arrowsmith took the lead. The services became a means of getting into touch with and influencing children from the public schools and grammar schools, a class for which perhaps less was being done than for any other. The services also provided, and this was perhaps not their least important office, an opportunity for young university men and women to make their first essays in preaching the gospel. An off-shoot from the C.S.S.M. was the Scripture Reading Union, which owed much to Mr. Bishop and his devoted labours.

Thus new organizations grew up for reaching and training the young in the knowledge and fear of God. Increasingly they have become better organized and more scientific in their methods. In this as in the work of the Church in general lies a danger. For the real secret of influencing children, and indeed of all Christian work, is still the same—there must be personal knowledge before there can be propaganda; given this and a humble desire to serve the Master and a sympathy with other people, special training and elaborate organization may be a help; without it, it is merely a futility.

23

THE MINISTRY

CHARACTERISTICS

HAVING considered the new methods and devices which the Church adopted for meeting the changing conditions of the era we now come to the living agents through whom they were carried out. In them the change was as great as in the age itself, especially in the Church of England. There was a striking increase in activity and in zeal; but it was apt to descend into "fussiness." The example which Bishop Wilberforce gave, of tireless energy, became in lesser men a "spurious imitation or caricature." It was probably Archbishop Tait who coined the aphorism that "the modern ideal of a Bishop is of a man in a chronic state of perspiration" (*Life*, II, p. 563). The temptation of the age was to multiply activities and to pile up engagements; until these became almost an end in themselves. This was not the least harmful manifestation of a tendency to substitute quantity for quality which the age exhibited. Just before the era came to an end Samuel Barnett wrote: "It seems to me sometimes that we are wasting the clergy in calling on them to 'do' so much; we ought to recall them to their teaching function. The world is poor for want of thought" (*Life*, p. 572).[1] Much of this overactivity and incessant "busyness," was due to the new facilities for locomotion. Did not Claudius Clear (Sir W. Robertson Nicoll) once write an article in *The British Weekly* entitled "The Devil disguised as a Railway Train"? In it he warned ministers of the dangers of overwork and breakdown.

Another characteristic of the newer generation of clergymen was what for a better term one may call "clericalism." It grew in part out of the Oxford Movement with its insistence on the separateness of the clerical Order and its emphasis on the priesthood. Even among the bishops this spirit was not absent,

[1] Mark Pattison has a scathing denunciation of the "active clergymen" of his day, of their ignorance and their complacent superiority (*Essays*, II, p. 199).

and Bishop Boyd Carpenter, who disliked the whole attitude of mind and the professionalism which, to him, it symbolized, shewed his dislike by refusing to wear the conventional gaiters of his office. This same reaction to clericalism and its outward expression by the use of special dress was also found among Nonconformists. Some ministers it is true outrivalled even the clergy in their clerical garb, others went to the opposite extreme; Dale of Birmingham, for example, even abandoned the white tie and conventional black coat, and in strong contrast to those ministers who demanded the title "Reverend" refused to allow it to be used of himself. This recalls a well-known and amusing story which R. F. Horton tells against himself. On his ordination he avowed his intention not to adopt any different title or clothing; he would wear no clothes to distinguish him from his fellow Christians. The insertion of a comma after clothes gave an obvious opportunity for the caricaturist, and a picture appeared of Dr. Horton soaring to the skies tearing off his clothes, piece by piece. The legend underneath ran: "I shall wear no clothes, to distinguish me from my fellow Christians" (*Autobiography*, p. 61). There were those, however, who took a different view. It is said of J. B. Paton that he "delighted to magnify the office of minister. He refused to approve those who, in their reaction against sacerdotal claims, stripped themselves of the title and distinguishing marks which express reverence for the position of those set apart for the Master's special work" (*Life*, p. 106).

SELECTION AND TRAINING

To the man in the street, or perhaps one might better say the man in the pew, preaching is the most important function of the clergyman or minister. But before coming to this activity it will be convenient, without undertaking a detailed survey, to say something of the selection and training of candidates for the ministry. In both respects the Church of England, although conditions gradually improved from what they were in the pre-Victorian Age, was sadly defective and behind most of the other Christian bodies of the country. The clergy were at first practically untrained in the duties of their sacred calling and, in consequence, hardly capable of dealing with the new needs of the growing town populations. But the system, or lack of system, worked extraordinarily well considering all things; those newly ordained, especially if they went into a parish with a conscientious vicar, obtained their training during their diaconate. The Church certainly did nothing to help them before acceptance. In all this it was typically English.

The ordinations themselves began to be better conducted. Hort, who was ordained deacon by Wilberforce in April 1854, wrote of his experiences as follows: "His arrangements were most admirable; from the time I reached Cuddesdon on Thursday till I said good-bye . . . there was nothing whatever to meet one's eye or ear that was not harmonious with the occasion" (*Life and Letters*, I, p. 274). But every bishop was not a Wilberforce and Hort did not meet with such congenial surroundings on his ordination to the priesthood two years later at Ely. He said of it: "Nothing could well be more frigid and perfunctory without being absolutely offensive" (*op. cit.*, I, p. 322). Westcott had a similar experience, which was all the more distressing since it was at the hands of his beloved Headmaster, James Prince Lee, then Bishop of Manchester (see *Life and Letters*, I, p. 116). The idea of using the Chancellor of the Cathedral as the "organizer of ordination candidates" occurred to Bishop Hamilton of Salisbury as early as 1850,[1] and it was put into practice when Bishop Wordsworth of Lincoln appointed E. W. Benson to be Chancellor in 1873.

In these circumstances it is not to be wondered at that the clergy of the Church of England lost their title to be the wonder of the world for learning. Disraeli wrote in 1852 that they were "more ignorant of theology than any body of men in the world, the natural consequence of being tied down to Thirty-nine Articles, and stopped from all research into the literature which they are intended to illustrate" (*Life*, I, p. 1145). This was a quaint statement, but no doubt there was truth behind it. A much more knowledgeable judge, Benjamin Jowett, in the eighties sarcastically remarked of a University Sermon that it "talked about the want of education in the clergy, which was illustrated by the sermon itself" (*Life*, II, p. 225).

[1] See Hughes, *James Fraser, Second Bishop of Manchester*, p. 87.

The explanation of the Church's neglect to provide for any training of its ordinands can be found in the fact that the great majority of them were drawn from wealthy or comfortable homes and had the means of paying for their own training, such as it was. The ancient universities, being Church institutions, were supposed to give all the necessary facilities. In the reign of Victoria it was not considered "the thing" for a "gentleman" to engage in trade; so the Church, the Army, and the Navy divided between them the bulk of younger sons who wished to engage in a career of usefulness. For many of those who took Orders there was waiting a family living, or the nomination of some influential friend; and they had no high ideals beyond the usual English virtue of doing their duty. Much of their work was very successful, but in a social, rather than in a religious sense. They had no high spiritual ambitions, either for themselves or for their flock. The latter, too, were to do their duty in the station to which they were to be called. This whole point of view comes out well in a description by Liddon of a walk which he took with one of his Cuddesdon pupils in March 1855. "He seems greatly in earnest, but quite ignorant of the scope of the religious life. He said that giving himself up to the work was quite a new view to him; his friends had looked forward to his being a gentleman" (*Life*, p. 35). Twenty-one years earlier Hurrell Froude had written to Keble, "Few men can receive the saying that the clergy have no need to be gentlemen" (*Life*, p. 137). It was a common mistake and accounts for the low spiritual tone of many parishes.

G. A. Selwyn was anxious to encourage young men of the lower classes to take Orders. He wrote to John Frere in 1837: "Let the Church take root downwards. Let every peasant in the land have an interest in the Establishment in the person of a son, a brother or a cousin. We have the best materials for the formation of a plebeian ministry that ever were possessed by a nation" (*Life*, I, p. 41). Such ideas, however, were not popular and every parish expected that its incumbent should be a "gentleman." Ingram Bywater, looking back from a much later standpoint, regarded it as fortunate that the clergy in England were recruited from so good a class of society. He also admitted that he was much impressed by the useful and unobtrusive work done by the parochial clergy (*Life*, p. 186).

From such sources the Church of England drew its candidates for the ministry. In the early years of the century the source was so bounteous that ordinands often had difficulty in getting a curacy. Trench, the future Archbishop, wrote to his wife in 1832: "Curacies are just now very scarce and we may have to wait two or three months or more" (*Life*, I, p. 123). The growth of population and the establishment of new parishes in the industrial areas, however, increased the demand for clergymen, and Pusey, in July 1845, began to have doubts as to the possibility of finding men enough to go round. "It is useless," he wrote, "to build new churches without an enlarged supply of clergy. What is wanted everywhere and for everything is not funds, but men" (*Life*, III, p. 79). But his fears were groundless, candidates duly presented themselves, and the shortage of clergy is quite a modern problem.

One source of ministry the Church of England has never used to the full—that of the lay-man. Bishop Lightfoot pointed this out in addressing a meeting of Junior Clergy in 1884. His words are so important as coming from such a leader that they demand quotation:

"There is another problem of the day, which I earnestly commend to your serious attention. I refer to the employment and organization of lay-work in the service of Christ. I feel absolutely certain that in this lies the great hope of the future. We shall only thus secure that strength and diffusion of ministerial agency which will enable us to reach the masses: and what is hardly less important, we shall only thus bind to the Church that large body of men, who at present hang loosely to it, and will certainly drift elsewhere if the Church fails to find employment for their spiritual energies. Incorporate them into the *life* of the Church by entrusting to them the *work* of the Church. Then, and then only, will they feel what they owe to the Church. Keep this problem ever before you. It must have a solution somehow."

"But your evangelist, it may be said, bears a strong likeness to the Wesleyan local preacher. I am not ashamed of the resemblance; I freely confess my admiration of the marvellous capacity of organization which distinguished John Wesley, and which he has bequeathed to his followers. The truest Churchmen are those whose minds are most open to the lessons which can be gathered from all quarters. I believe that the Church of England has a greater power of utilizing the evangelistic zeal of her lay-members than any other Christian community, though hitherto it has been latent. Certainly this ought to be the case, for the sense of corporate unity with her, if she is true to her principles, is built upon a stronger and deeper foundation than accidental association for religious purposes. Most assuredly she will be wise to find employment for this zeal, for an untold mine of missionary power is here, which alone can cope with the spiritual destitution" (*Lightfoot of Durham*, pp. 65 f.).

One noticeable feature of the period was the large number of Scotchmen who came South to find their place in the ranks of the ministry. In the Church itself there were outstanding examples in Archbishop Tait and the present Archbishop of Canterbury; among Nonconformists there were, to mention two names only, Andrew Fairbairn and J. B. Paton. In this connexion the achievement of a small district in Aberdeenshire is worth recording. From three Free Kirk manses in this neighbourhood three men went forth who were destined, in very different spheres, to exercise outstanding influence. From Kieg, Robertson Smith; from Insch, Professor Elmslie; from Rhynie, Alexander Mackay, the famous C.M.S. missionary to Uganda.[1]

THEOLOGICAL COLLEGES

The kind of training which a man receives in his Theological College will depend largely upon the ideal of the ministry which prevails in it. The object of the Catholic is to produce a good priest, one who will speak as the mouthpiece of the Church; the object of the Evangelical is to produce an evangelist and preacher, one who will be able to win souls; the

[1] See Robertson Nicoll, *Life of Professor Elmslie*, p. 11. It is worth noting that Robertson Nicoll himself was born in the same district in the Manse of Lumsden.

object of the Liberal is to produce the teacher, one who will be able to instruct his people and to lead them to fresh fields of knowledge. All these ideals are no doubt combined in every Theological College, but there is a very different emphasis. The Liberal is certainly right in his exaltation of sound learning, for there is no doubt that where this is lacking only superficial success is possible, and in the long run the Church which turns its back on knowledge must perish. Sir Edward Tylor, the famous anthropologist, once brought this out very forcibly: "It needs but a glance through history at the wrecks of old religions to see how they failed from within. The priests of Egypt, who once represented the most advanced knowledge of their time, came to fancy that mankind had no more to learn, and upheld their tradition against all newer wisdom, till the world passed them by and left them grovelling in superstition. The priests of Greece ministered in splendid temples and had their fill of wealth and honours, but men who sought the secret of a good life found that this was not the business of the sanctuary, and turned away to the philosophers. Unless a religion can hold its place in the front of science and of morals, it may only gradually, in the course of ages, lose its place in the nation, but all the power of statecraft and all the wealth of temples will not save it from eventually yielding to a belief that takes in higher knowledge and teaches better life." There is, however, another side; and this is well expressed in Professor Elmslie's conception of the true function of the Theological College set forth in an article in *The British Weekly* for September 16, 1887. He wrote, and coming from the pen of such a man of rare learning and erudition the words had greater weight, "Theological colleges are not in the first instance shrines of culture or high places of abstract erudition, but factories of preachers and pastors. They are not so much fountains of pure scholarship, but are rather to be classed with schools of medicine and institutes of technical education. Their function is not to produce great theologians, but to train efficient ministers—though they will hardly do that without possessing all that is essential to do the other."[1]

[1] Quoted W. Robertson Nicoll, *Professor Elmslie*, p. 117.

Anglican Colleges

We have seen already that the only training which Anglican Ordinands received in the early part of the reign was that of Oxford and Cambridge. Even at the end of the era it was still the normal thing for them to do their theology at the Universities and to leave to the Theological Colleges training in devotional life and more specialized knowledge. The system worked much better than might have been supposed, and one secret of its success was that ordinands were not segregated in seminaries, but were forced to mix with men doing other subjects and to discuss things in general. On the other hand ordinands of the Church of England were often almost entirely ignorant of the conditions of the great towns and of the habits of life and thought of the people whose whole lives have been passed in them.

In the establishment of Theological Colleges the Church of England was behind the Nonconformists, who indeed had, until the establishment of the newer universities, no other place to which to send their students. Even in the present day the Anglican Theological College is organized, or rather staffed, in an entirely different manner from the Nonconformist. The latter type is staffed by a body of learned and experienced teachers, to whom the title of Professor is quite worthily given, men whose names are known in many cases beyond the limits of their own denomination and carry weight with the students and the outside world. In the Church College the Principal is as a rule a man of some standing, though often he has had but a meagre training in parochial work. His staff usually consists of a number of young men who in some cases are actually ordained to their posts. Many of these young men, who are chosen for their promise, in after life attain to positions of prominence. The most striking examples can be drawn from the staff of Cuddesdon, whose Vice-Principals included Liddon and Bishop Gore. In fact some witty person made the *bon mot* that Cuddesdon owed its reputation to its Vices rather than its Principles![1] Probably a combination of the two methods of staffing Theological Colleges would be the ideal, for young

[1] I owe this *mot* to the kindness of Professor Whitney. It is cited by Prestige, *Life of Charles Gore*, p. 39.

men are better able to get in touch with the students, whilst older men have a wider experience and a bigger reputation.

The number of Theological Colleges belonging to the Church of England is too great to allow a separate mention of them all. The oldest was St. Bees, founded in 1816 for non-graduates; later came for the same type of student St. Aidan's, Birkenhead (1846), and St. John's, Highbury (1863). For the work overseas there were the C.M.S. College at Islington (1825), St. Augustine's, Canterbury (1848), St. Boniface's, Warminster (1860), Burgh and Dorchester were founded in 1878. The oldest colleges for graduates were Chichester, founded by Bishop Otter in 1839 with Charles Marriott as its first Principal, Wells (1840), Cuddesdon (1854), Lichfield (1857), and Salisbury (1860). Of Cuddesdon, in view of its great fame, a little more may be said. When Samuel Wilberforce became Bishop of Oxford in 1845 he determined to start a Diocesan Training College and on June 15, 1854, it was duly opened at Cuddesdon. Its ambition was "to form character and to mould habits"; and it has nobly fulfilled it in the lives of many of its numerous students. Lincoln followed in 1874 and two years later Ely, Leeds, and St. Stephen's House, Oxford. At the end of the 'seventies came the two great Evangelical Colleges, Wycliffe Hall, Oxford, and Ridley Hall, Cambridge. They were definitely an attempt to provide for Evangelical Ordinands a fuller and more complete training in view of the growth of Rationalism —the publication of *Supernatural Religion* in 1872 especially revealed the need. Ridley was opened in 1881 with Handley Moule as its first Principal and its objects were declared to be: (*a*) to set forth the sound Scriptural and Theological foundations of the Evangelical faith and practice of the Church of England as seen in the Prayer Book and Articles; (*b*) to combat Rationalistic propaganda. In 1881 was founded the Clergy Training School at Cambridge, Westcott House, run on slightly different lines in its early days.

It will be seen at once from the above list that Church of England Theological Colleges follow the lines of party. This is one of their dangers. In the case of the later "seminary" type of college, such as Kelham (1891) and Mirfield (1902), there is the further danger that priests may be produced who are too conscious of their separation from the laity. Those who are taken into such colleges are often of a not very high state of education and are more easily "moulded" than some other types. When complaints were made to the late Archbishop of Canterbury of the kind of men who were being turned out by the Theological Colleges, he replied: "Yes, indeed, but you should see those men when they go in."[1]

Before leaving the subject of Anglican methods of training something must be said of the work of C. J. Vaughan. Vaughan had been Headmaster of Harrow, which he had raised "from a broken-down, ill-disciplined school of some sixty boys to a thronged, a carefully organized, and, according to the requirements of the day, a most efficient place of education."[2] Later he devoted himself to the training of ordinands whom he gathered round him in a kind of informal Theological College. In order to give himself up to the care of his "doves" (as they came to be called) he refused many offers of preferment, including several bishoprics. He is said to have had a hand in preparing some four hundred men of gifts higher than the ordinary for the ministry of the Church of England. Stewart Headlam was for a time a "dove," though not a very tame one. He apparently received his training free of charge, though it included several hours of tuition daily. For practical work he had to do systematic visiting in St. Clement Danes which was divided up into small districts with a "dove" in charge of each.[3] In a similar way Bishop Lightfoot, when he went to Durham, gathered a number of graduates round him at his palace of Bishop Auckland and had them trained for the work of his great diocese. In the opinion of Bishop Westcott his "greatest work was the brotherhood of clergy whom he called to labour with him in the diocese, and bear his spirit to another generation—greater than his masterpieces of interpretation and criticism, greater than his masterpieces of masculine and yet passionate eloquence."[4] The foundation of this body was the group of men at Auckland.

[1] See Major, *W. Boyd Carpenter*, p. 160.
[2] Sir G. O. Trevelyan in *The Harrow Life of Montague Butler*, p. xix.
[3] See F. G. Bettany, *Stewart Headlam*, p. 25.
[4] Quoted *Lightfoot of Durham*, p. xi.

Nonconformist Colleges

We now come to Nonconformist Theological Colleges and methods of training. The colleges went back in several cases to a much earlier date than the corresponding Church institutions. Many of them developed out of the older academies in which a minister would gather round him a number of men for training. This system often produced powerful preachers, but it was hardly adequate to meet the needs of the changed conditions of the nineteenth century. So regular colleges were established, and when Nonconformists began to attend the older universities Theological Colleges were opened at Oxford and Cambridge.

Perhaps the pioneers in Theological training were the Congregationalists. From the days of the Commonwealth the denomination had prided itself on the intellectual qualities of its ministers, from whom a high standard was demanded, and even the emphasis on the emotional side of religion which followed the Methodist Revival did not cause them to relax. In the early years of the century students in Congregational Colleges were trained in religious knowledge before proceeding to the academic side; this was held to be the reason for the freedom from heresies which the body then displayed.[1] They had at this time many academies, such as Homerton, with a training extending over a period of five or six years. In 1858 there were ten colleges, including the Western, Cheshunt, Hackney, and the Independent College at Manchester. There were also a number of private academies as well as certain pastors who received students for a more personal training. A new stage in Theological training was inaugurated, and not for Congregationalists only, by the appointment of A. M. Fairbairn to be Principal of Airedale College in 1877 (the forerunner of the United College at Bradford). Fairbairn, as Dr. Selbie has said, "not only set before the churches a new and higher ideal of what a theological college should be, but gave practical expression to it" (*A. M. Fairbairn*, p. 161). Later on Fairbairn again made history by becoming the first Principal of Mansfield College, Oxford. This venture was made possible by the closing down of Spring Hill College, Birmingham,

[1] See A. W. Peel, *These Hundred Years*, pp. 24 f.

which had been endowed by the generosity of George Mansfield and his sister—hence the name of the new college. Temporary premises were secured at 90 High Street—where Charles I had lodged during his residence in Oxford—in 1886.[1] The College itself was opened on October 15, 1889, amidst much blowing of trumpets; even *The Times* recognized the event as beginning "a new epoch in the history of the University of Oxford." This aroused the indignation of certain of the members of the University, with which of course Mansfield had no connexion, and Professor Case wrote to point out "that Mansfield College is a Congregationalist seminary built within the precincts of the borough of Oxford."[2] Many old-fashioned Congregationalists were suspicious of the new venture and thought Oxford likely to pervert the men, even *The British Weekly*, then recently founded, considered that it "would become in a short time a pillar of the Church of England."[3]

The Baptists also set a high standard for their ministers in the way of education and training. Their college at Bristol even claims to date back to 1679, when it began as an "academy." The present Rawdon College, Leeds, was founded in 1804 at Bradford; Regent's Park College, at Stepney in 1820; and a college founded at Bury in Lancashire in 1866 was moved to Brighton Grove, Manchester. An institution of a slightly different character was the Pastors' College which Spurgeon started in connexion with the Metropolitan Tabernacle in 1856. It has trained many young men for the Baptist ministry.

Among the Methodists Richmond College, Surrey, was one of three, later to become four, colleges which went to make up what they called the Theological Institution. Under the Rev. Alfred Barrett it set up a high standard of learning, and produced a great scholar in W. F. Moulton. This was a little strange to the older Methodists who regarded the preaching of the "gospel" as the only necessary activity of the minister. The high standard of intellectual attainment, however, has

---

[1] An interesting description of these early days is contained in the *Life of Silvester Horne*, pp. 30 ff.
[2] See Selbie, *A. M. Fairbairn*, p. 180.
[3] *Op. cit.*, p. 181.

been well maintained in Handsworth, Didsbury, and Headingley.[1]

At Oxford Mansfield College was not the only Nonconformist Theological College, for the Unitarians transferred Manchester College there in 1893. This college had been founded in Manchester in 1786 with the threefold dedication "to truth, liberty, religion." In 1803 it was moved to York, and then back again to Manchester before its presumably final settlement in Oxford. At Cambridge there has been since 1899 Westminster College, the Theological College of the English Presbyterians, originally founded in 1844; and also Cheshunt College, belonging to the Congregationalists; and still more recently Wesley College has been opened. Both these colleges were moved to Cambridge in the present century and are mentioned here only for completeness. Cheshunt had been founded by the Countess of Huntingdon in 1768, moved to Cheshunt four years later, and to Cambridge in 1905.

In addition to these more regular methods of training candidates for the ministry there were also others intended to supplement them. Such was the Institute which J. B. Paton founded at Nottingham in 1863. It was intended, amongst others, for those who were called late in life to the ministry, and had definitely in view the work of evangelization, both at home and overseas.

THE PREACHING MINISTRY

The Victorian Age loved oratory, from platform and pulpit alike; and it produced many great preachers. Perhaps the preacher had a better chance of exercising his art than in the present for there was no objection to long sermons. This seems to have been the general rule, though the Vice-Chancellor of Oxford in 1861 said that there were four types of University Sermons distinguished respectively for Altitude, Latitude, Platitude, Longitude. All were tolerated except the last.[2] In

[1] On the Methodist Colleges see W. Bradley Brash, *The Story of Our Colleges, 1835–1935*.
[2] Davidson and Benham, *Archibald Campbell Tait*, I, p. 307. In 1843 Monckton Milnes had said of Pusey's Eucharistic Sermon: "It deserved to be condemned for its length, and if the sentence was interpreted in this way it might do good" (*Life*, I, p. 305).

other respects the fashion of pulpit oratory has considerably changed, and so it is difficult to judge of the merits of the different orators whose reputations and works have survived into the present. So much of preaching is personality that in many cases the printed word is no effective medium for conveying the power and attractiveness of the preacher. Some indeed of the preachers of the past must be accepted purely on the evidence of their contemporaries, so little do their printed sermons succeed in testifying to their skill; all charm and force seemingly have evaporated from the printed page. Others perhaps receive greater praise from the modern judge because their technique more nearly anticipated the style of later days. As F. S. Oliver once wrote of Gladstone: "Posterity is not attuned to his wavelengths, and consequently it knows nothing of the famous orator at first hand."

Dr. Major considered that the six greatest preachers of the Victorian Age in England were Newman, Robertson of Brighton, Liddon, Spurgeon, Magee, and Boyd Carpenter. The last three were the greatest orators and had to be heard rather than read for their merits to be appreciated (*Life of W. Boyd Carpenter*, p. 115). Of Newman's right to appear in such a list there can be no doubt;[1] for the printed page has preserved his charm as well as tradition. So, too, Robertson of Brighton is still read and his right would hardly be challenged. R. F. Horton regarded him as the greatest preacher of the century (*Autobiography*, p. 211); but this did not prevent his appreciating others, for he ventured to forecast that Spurgeon might be "finally ranked with Chrysostom, Bossuet, Liddon, in the very front of the masters of the Christian pulpit" (*op. cit.*, p. 88). Queen Victoria thought Magee was the greatest preacher she had ever heard, though she added the qualification, "out of Scotland."[2] Of Boyd Carpenter Matthew Arnold once wrote, after hearing him in a country church: "There got up into the pulpit a small man in shabby Bishop's attire, and I thought I wonder what's coming now?

[1] A. W. Hutton says that in the early forties only three preachers could fill St. Mary's, Oxford, on a week-day: Newman, Goulbourn, and Manning (*Cardinal Manning*, p. 218).

[2] Quoted Monypenny and Buckle, *Life of Disraeli*, II, p. 404.

and I never heard anything like what I heard then, and I listened as I had never listened to anything before in my life."[1] Another Anglican who might, perhaps, have a claim for inclusion was Henry Melvill, "the Evangelical Chrysostom," who was regarded by Gladstone as the greatest preacher of his day. Other outstanding Evangelicals were Hugh McNeile, Hugh Stowell, and Francis Close; but none of them can be considered to be in quite the same rank as Melvill. Bishop Moule has described the effect of his University Sermons. "As each magnificent paragraph rolled to its close there came an audible sigh from the dense congregation, a sigh of tension relieved and attention renewed" (*Life*, p. 24). Another great Anglican preacher was Samuel Wilberforce, Bishop of Oxford and then of Winchester. John Morley considered that he excelled any speaker, ecclesiastical or secular, "in the taking gift of unction. . . . The only rival within my experience," he wrote, "unless it were Guthrie of Edinburgh, was Spurgeon" (*Recollections*, I, pp. 8 f.). But amongst Anglicans the name of Liddon was outstanding. He succeeded in drawing the "smart set" in crowds to St. James, Piccadilly, in 1870 and his sermons at St. Paul's were listened to by thousands; they were seldom less than forty minutes in length. In spite of a few outstanding names the Anglicans were decidedly below the Nonconformists in the possession of great preachers, and it is even possible that Liddon's pre-eminence was partly due to his appearance which had something in it of the Nonconformist divine.[2] He certainly appealed to very different types of mind, for even James Martineau the Unitarian was impressed by him in spite of their fundamental difference of outlook. "He is a *great* preacher," he once said to Catherine Winkworth, "and I was surprised to find how much I agreed with him" (*Life of Catherine Winkworth*, II, p. 620). Whilst Lord Acton, the Roman Catholic, wrote to Mary Gladstone: "Assuredly Liddon is the

---

[1] Major, *op. cit.*, p. 123.

[2] Thomas Arnold the younger described him as "a dark, black-haired little man . . . with that shiny, glistening appearance about his sallow complexion which one so often sees in Dissenting ministers, and which the devotees no doubt consider a mark of election": see J. P. Trevelyan, *Life of Mrs. Humphry Ward*, p. 20.

greatest power in the conflict with sin and in turning the souls of men to God, that the nation now possesses" (*Letters to Mary Gladstone*, p. 160). Canon Scott Holland, himself a great preacher of a later generation, has suggested the secret of Liddon's excellence in a general judgement. "The preachers," he says, "who produce the deepest effects are those who, having fast hold of the elemental religious principles which their hearers already hold hesitatingly . . . vividly manifest the reality of their application to heart and conduct" (*Personal Studies*, p. 145). Last we must mention Frederick Farrar, Canon of Westminster and later Dean of Canterbury, who made a great name for himself at the Abbey. His sermons were notable for their dazzling rhetoric, though spiritual power and high ethical ideals were part of their substance. A writer quoted by Jacks, *Life and Letters of Stopford Brooke*, pp. 291 f., complains that he had "one of those cast-iron voices, strong and clear, but *seemingly* heartless."

Nonconformist Preachers

The number of Nonconformist preachers of merit was so considerable that it is exceedingly difficult to select names from among them for mention. One may perhaps begin with Thomas Binney, who was Minister at the Weigh House Chapel from 1829 to 1869. He was the author of many controversial pamphlets attacking the Establishment and was indeed the political Nonconformist *par excellence* (of this side of his activities I shall have more to say in the next chapter); but he had other and more positive accomplishments. Dale considers that he, "perhaps, helped more than any other man to modify the traditional method and style of preaching among Nonconformists. . . . He represented a movement—a departure from the limits of conventional orthodoxy; not a revolt against Evangelical doctrine so much as a repudiation of the formulas and phrases in which Evangelical doctrines were generally stated" (*Life of Dale*, pp. 49 f.).[1]

[1] Dr. Vaughan foretold a new era of preaching in the 'fifties; its harbingers were Binney and Spurgeon. "They pioneered the liberation of preaching from the polished fetters and dignified but crippling traditions of the past" (James Marchant, *Life of Dr. John Clifford*, p. 30).

Another preacher of note was Baptist Noel, who had been an Anglican and his secession caused as much sensation as that of Newman, so Silvester Horne, who mistakenly connects both events with the Gorham Case, has claimed (*Nonconformity in the Nineteenth Century*, pp. 123 f.). He first preached in St. John's Chapel, Bedford Row, and then moved to the John Street Baptist Chapel.

Birmingham for some fifty years listened to the voice of John Angell James, the minister of the famous Carr's Lane Chapel. He was the author of *The Anxious Enquirer*, a volume which was sometimes apt to make the enquirer a little too anxious, at least that was the experience of Henry Drummond in later times, though it played a large part in bringing peace to the youthful R. W. Dale (*Life*, p. 16). As Dale grew in mental and spiritual stature he found James's lack of deep thought repellent (*op. cit.*, p. 50), though he still admired his perfect elocution and use of gesture (*op. cit.*, p. 54). His own favourite preacher at this time was George Dawson, a somewhat eccentric preacher who had left the Baptists to carry on his own chapel on lines which approached Unitarianism (*op. cit.*, p. 51).

Another great light of the Nonconformist world was William Jay of Bath. Jay was the son of a mason and he drew vast crowds to the Argyle Chapel. Just as Whitefield had received the praise of Foote and Garrick for his oratory, so did Jay receive the praise of Sheridan. But perhaps the extent of his reputation can best be gathered from an anecdote. He was staying on one occasion with a well-known Evangelical lady and accompanied her to church. The lady was very proud of her vicar's preaching and, on her return, asked Jay to give his opinion of the sermon which he had just heard. "Modesty," he replied, "forbids me to answer, for the sermon was one of my own."

Dr. Raffles of Liverpool was an unusual phenomenon amongst Nonconformist divines, for he was "a man of aristocratic connections as well as of polished manners."[1] His preaching was not deep, but it was very telling and he reached the hearts of his hearers if he did not greatly edify their minds.

[1] J. Guinness Rogers, *Autobiog. Recollections*, pp. 148 f.

The number of people who have been willing or anxious to give their views as to the greatest preacher of their day is almost exactly the number of those whom they selected; for few agree in their selection. I have already quoted several expressions of opinion; they by no means exhaust the list of suggestions. Benjamin Gregory held that Dr. Harris the Methodist of Great Queen Street Chapel, London, was the greatest preacher of the middle of the century; Mark Rutherford (W. Hale White) in his Memoirs states that "Having heard continuously all the most noteworthy speakers of my day—Roebuck, Cobden, Bright, Gladstone, Binney—I affirm unhesitatingly that Caleb Morris was more eloquent than any of them."[1] But the majority of critics would, I imagine, have regarded Spurgeon as the greatest Nonconformist orator of his times.

Spurgeon was born in 1834 in Essex, and when little more than a boy began to display those oratorical gifts which were to place him in the very forefront of his contemporaries, and give him an influence which was almost without a parallel. Not only was he a great preacher, filling week by week the vast Metropolitan Tabernacle with its five thousand and more of an audience; but he superintended a Pastors' College (to which reference has already been made) and edited a magazine *The Sword and the Trowel*. His outstanding position made him a kind of High Priest of Nonconformity, and he interested himself in the affairs of other denominations besides his own Baptists. During the famous dispute in the Congregational Union in 1877, on the terms of religious communion, he adopted an attitude which was almost patronizing, and when it was ended on lines which he approved he wrote to Dr. Allon: "I fear I shall never see your brethren up to my standard, but it is a joy to me to feel that at least the great facts of our religion are heartily believed."[2]

Another great preacher whose head was a little turned by his success was Joseph Parker of the City Temple, who like Jay of Bath was the son of a mason. For thirty-three years

---
[1] Caleb Morris was a Welsh preacher who had a chapel in Eccleston Square.
[2] Quoted A. W. Peel, *Letters to a Victorian Editor*, p. 345.

he carried immense weight in his denomination and amongst Nonconformists in general, both by his preaching and his numerous writings. But he was very critical of others. In 1876 he attacked the Congregational Union and tried to prevent any kind of organization of Congregationalists. In a moment of irony he suggested that the Assembly of the Union should include in its announcement: "The usual speeches will be delivered by the usual speakers."[1] His cruel attack on W. J. Wood in 1890 caused him to be decisively condemned by the Assembly and even to be hissed off its platform. For years afterwards he took no part in its affairs, though later he was reconciled and even acted as Chairman.[2]

These preachers, though not without intellectual gifts, were chiefly notable for their ability to appeal to the emotions and for rhetorical powers. In fact Nonconformist preaching in the middle years of the era was not of a very high intellectual level. This is openly declared by George Eliot. As a young woman she had nourished her heterodoxy when in Geneva by attending orthodox sermons; in later life she regarded the immense popularity of a certain Calvinist preacher (whom she calls A) as a sign of the low mental pitch of society in England. She was not only exasperated by his "superficial grocer's-back-parlour view of Calvinistic Christianity," but by his lack of reverence. He said, 'Let us approach the throne of God,' very much as he might have invited you to take a chair" (*George Eliot's Life*, I, pp. 200 f., and II, p. 273).

There was one Nonconformist preacher, however, who would probably have satisfied the exacting standard of a George Eliot—that was Dale of Birmingham. The authority which he exercised in Birmingham, both in the civic and educational life of the city, was unequalled. His preaching, the outflow of an original and forceful personality, exhibited a combination of the political and the spiritual which was then very unusual. In addition to being a preacher and an organizer of the life of the city he was also a theological thinker of original and deep powers. His views indeed, on such subjects as Conditional Immortality and his "High" notions of the sacraments, caused distress and suspicion in many of his fellow Congregationalists.

[1] A. W. Peel, *These Hundred Years*, pp. 263 f.   [2] *Op. cit.*, pp. 327 f.

His fame was early made by the publication in 1866 of a volume of sermons with the title "Discourses on Special Occasions." This volume was noticed in *The Contemporary Review* by Dean Alford, the editor, together with several others under the heading "Recent Nonconformist Sermons." In his review the Dean took occasion to commend to his fellow Churchmen the merit of Nonconformist preaching and the foolishness of neglecting the lessons to be learned from it. In this connexion it is interesting to notice that Dale towards the end of his life, in recommending models for sermons to his assistant at Carr's Lane, the Rev. George Barber, put into his hands the works of Dean Church and Bishop Paget (the late Bishop of Oxford) with the words: "Read them—read them over and over again, and you will see the kind of sermons I like" (*Life*, p. 642). Thus the different sections of Christ's army may learn lessons from one another in method and in charity.

Another preacher whose sermons reached a very high intellectual level was, of course, Stopford Brooke. A course of lectures which he gave at St. James's Chapel during his Anglican days on the "Theology of the English Poets," "gave him a position unique at the time, as a reconciler of things secular and sacred."[1] In 1880 he left the Church of England, but continued to preach in Bedford Chapel until his retirement in 1895. He drew through all those years congregations of thoughtful men and women, many of them distinguished in their own walks of life, who had found it impossible to worship elsewhere. To Stopford Brooke preaching was a form of self-expression, hardly the proclamation of a message. Hence his occasional feeling of boredom and his practically complete abandonment of the art during the last years of his life.

Closing Years of the Era

In the last generation of the Victorian Era the standard of preaching scarcely retained its high level. Most of the great men were dead and their successors were not, in most cases, quite big enough to take their places. Perhaps, however, they are too near to us for their real value sufficiently to be realized.

[1] Jacks, *Life and Letters of Stopford Brooke*, p. 247.

An acute observer "Mark Rutherford" is almost harsh in insistence on the decay of modern preaching which he attributes to its failure to give sufficient place to "ethical science." "The orthodox churches are given over to a philosophy of rags, and 'Free' pulpits do nothing but mince and mash up for popular ears commonplaces upon books and passing events."[1] But even so there were some great names. Among Anglicans, G. H. Wilkinson, Bishop of Truro; Bishop Boyd Carpenter; Scott Holland, to whom reference has already been made; Father Stanton, and others. Amongst these others the name of Charles Gore must not be forgotten. His preaching at Westminster Abbey marked, perhaps, the highest point in the influence of that historic building in the whole of the era. Among Nonconformists there were F. B. Meyer, Campbell Morgan, Newman Hall at Christ Church, Westminster Bridge Road, R. F. Horton, and Alexander McLaren. Of these last two preachers something more must be said. Horton exhibited a combination in which the mystical and the rational elements were nobly blended. In this he has been but rarely excelled. By some of the younger Congregationalists he was regarded as "the personification of the genius" of their denomination.[2] McLaren[3] of Manchester owed much as a young man to the advice and kindness of Thomas Binney. Long afterwards he would say: "It was Binney taught me to preach." A testimony to his powers as a preacher has been given by Bishop Moorhouse, who was in Manchester during part of McLaren's ministry. "In an age which had been charmed and inspired by the sermons of Newman and Robertson of Brighton, there are no public discourses which for profundity of thought, logical arrangement, eloquence of appeal and power over the human heart, exceed in merit those of Dr. McLaren."[4] But though he was a great preacher McLaren "lacked many of the qualities which make a successful pastor. . . . The deep

---

[1] Quoted Robertson Nicoll, *Letters of a Bookman*, p. 407.
[2] See C. Silvester Horne, p. 151.
[3] This is the correct spelling, though the spelling Maclaren was used by him in his published volumes: see E. T. McLaren, *Dr. McLaren of Manchester*, p. 28.
[4] *Op. cit.*, p. 154.

vein of shyness in his nature made what is called 'personal dealing' difficult to him; but indeed in addressing large gatherings he seemed to deal personally with each."[1] Thus his ministry was almost entirely a pulpit ministry and by that it must stand. One of the secrets of his power lies behind the advice which he once gave to a startled assembly of Nonconformist divines telling them always to burn their MSS. Freshness was his aim, and to preach an old sermon robs the preacher of this appeal. One recalls the opposite practice in Whitefield, who never felt that he had really got the best out of a sermon until he had preached it forty times. But Whitefield was a kind of rhetorical genius and only saved from pure acting by his deep sincerity.

[1] *Op. cit.*, p. 75.

24

REUNION AND FEDERATION

THE CHANGED ATTITUDE

WHEN Victoria came to the throne Christianity in England was represented by a number of different Denominations between whom a state varying between friendship and enmity might be said to exist. Towards the Church of Rome, then beginning to rouse itself from its long sleep, the enmity in many quarters verged on definite hatred. Much the same state of affairs was to be found when the long reign was over; but with certain striking differences. In 1837 divisions were acquiesced in, were taken for granted; in 1901 the conscience of Christendom was stirred on the matter. In 1837 again, divisions followed a denominational line; in 1901 there were, in addition, many cross divisions.

To deal with this latter point first. Since the Oxford Movement and its developments the Church of England has included members who are much nearer to the Roman point of view than to that of their fellow members of the extreme Evangelical wing; and these in turn have little to distinguish them from Nonconformists without the Church. So, too, in regard to scholarship; those who share the same point of view will be found in many different denominations. Thus the real dividing lines no longer coincide with denominational barriers; the lines of division are now vertical as well as horizontal. This has its advantages as well as its drawbacks for it makes denominational barriers less rigid, since they can, in certain matters, be so easily overstepped.

A similar change has taken place in regard to the Church's acquiescence in its divisions. The question of reunion, although not considered so vital as it is to-day, was already beginning to trouble men's minds. They no longer accepted the easy-going standpoint of Selden, who in his *Table Talk* cxxi had expressed the view that "Religion is like the fashion; one man wears his doublet slashed, another laced, another plain; but every man has a doublet; so every man has his religion. We differ about the trimming." One reason why Selden's point of view no longer prevailed was that no longer did every man have his religion. The Church was faced by the "revival of pagan ethics and the destruction of faith in the unseen."[1] This was a call to close its ranks and rid itself of internal divisions, to abolish waste and overlapping. It was this practical reason for reunion which appealed to Evangelicals and Nonconformists. The older Evangelicalism, within and without the Church, Dale has pointed out, "regarded almost with indifference all forms of Church polity, it cared nothing for the Church as the august society of saints" (*The Old Evangelicalism and the New*, p. 17). Some even, with W. F. Moulton, held that "a plurality of independent Christian communities in the same country (was) the ideal state of things, not merely a present necessity."[2] They seem to have had the same point of view in this as the devil himself! For he accepts the service of all and sundry, insisting on no distinctive livery or conformity to any set ritual. Milton, and the older traditions which he followed, was surely wrong in representing the powers of evil as a vast organization. The devil leaves that to his opponents, knowing that a spirit when organized has, together with its freedom, lost the half of its power. Insistence on any particular form of organization is at present the most difficult barrier to reunion. On the other hand, those of a Catholic mind deplored the sin of schism, the parting of the seamless robe of Christ. To them had come, as it came to Gladstone in St. Peter's at Rome,[3] the vision of one great united Church and the longing for its visible attainment.

THE QUESTION OF THE ESTABLISHMENT

If the question of organization was a barrier to the reunion of Christian bodies in England, so too was the Establishment. The desirability or otherwise of having a National Church is a matter for debate and opinions on the subject are many

[1] Wilfred Ward, *Last Lectures*, p. xxv.
[2] See *Life and Letters of Hort*, II, p. 428. Moulton seems to have imagined that Westcott thought the same.
[3] This was on March 31, 1832: see Morley, *Life of W. E. Gladstone*, I, p. 87.

and various. Its advocates have much to say for their belief in it and its opponents also have their arguments. Amongst those who were strongly in favour of the Establishment was Disraeli. He went so far as to say that "There are few great things left in England, and the Church is one" (*Life*, II, p. 83). One of his tasks was to strengthen it and to secure it from internal disruption and external assault. He believed in the Church, partly because as a great historic institution it was a conservative force, but also as a bulwark of the Christian religion in which he saw the highest development of Judaism. Others valued a National Church because it seemed to sanctify the whole of life. This was the point of view of A. M. Fairbairn as a young man in Scotland, and comes strangely from him in view of later developments. Although not a member of the Established Kirk he often spoke in its defence, "Believing that a national church is the ideal church, consecrating the state and connecting religion with all the forms and phases of its life" (Selbie, *A. M. Fairbairn*, p. 75). Tennyson held much the same view and declared that "Any severence of Church and State is . . . above all things to be deprecated, as fostering the common tendency to look upon parts of man as man instead of his whole being" (*Life*, II, p. 57). It is because of this belief that advocates of the Establishment declare that its abolition would mean the secularization of the State. Among the most fervent of these was Dean Stanley, and so firmly did he cling to it that his habitual toleration for views divergent from his own found in this matter a limit. He could not away with those who, whether Nonconformists or Ritualists, desired to end it (*Life*, II, p. 175).

A National Church can give shelter, as a sect cannot do, to those whose views are vague and unformed; who are perhaps feeling their way back to Christianity, or who cannot accept it in its orthodox form. Both J. A. Froude and Matthew Arnold continued to conform, even after their abandonment of orthodoxy; and this surely was to the good. An interesting expression of opinion on this point is contained in Mrs. Beatrice Webb's very interesting description of her early life. After speaking of having shaken off the influence of Herbert Spencer, which for a time had dominated her thinking, she writes:

"And in later years even the attitude towards religion and towards the supernatural which I had accepted from him as the last word of enlightenment, have been replaced by another attitude—no less agnostic but with an inclination to doubt materialism more than I doubt spiritualism—to listen for voices of the great Unknown, to open my consciousness to the non-material world—to prayer. If I had to live my life over again, according to my present attitude I should, I think, remain a conforming member of the National Church" (*My Apprenticeship*, p. 38). Perhaps the presence in the National Church of those who were not in the full sense believers and of many whose membership was little more than a sop to respectability may have inspired Charles Buller's witticism: "Destroy the Church of England, sir? Why you must be mad! It is the only thing which stands between us and real religion."[1]

One evil consequence of the Establishment, in the eyes of those who dissented from it, was that it placed a large part of the Christian community in a position of definite inferiority —even though that position was their own choice, following their conscientious convictions. Nonconformists were apt to regard themselves as treated unjustly and their whole position as being misrepresented. They had their own traditions and a record of which they were proud. This feeling became all the keener with the growth among them, to which I shall refer presently, of the sense of a Catholic Church. Fairbairn especially resented the terms Dissenter and Nonconformist being "used as if they denoted an attitude to the Catholic Church of Christ, when all they denote is an attitude towards a civil institution" (*Life*, p. 257). Difficulties also arose from time to time over the use by Nonconformist ministers of the title Reverend as if they had been clergymen—but in course of time this usage came to be accepted. So also the title Church as applied to a Nonconformist Society was a matter of dispute. At the Church Congress of 1893 at Birmingham, Professor G. T. Stokes of Dublin, who was not an Anglo-Catholic, protested against the practice. Handley Moule, the noted Evangelical leader, who afterwards succeeded Westcott at Durham, got up to make a reply. He explained that whilst

[1] Quoted in Abbott and Campbell, *Life of Benjamin Jowett*, I, p. 433.

glad to co-operate with individuals, he could not do so with organizations "actually competing and sometimes colliding with the National Church" as such. At the same time he could not refuse the name of "Church" to great organizations of living Christians, developed under circumstances to which ancient Church History presents no real parallel" (*Bishop Handley Moule*, pp. 147 f.).

A great French thinker has expressed his opinion that the real religious views of the English people were to be found, not in the Establishment, but in Dissent.[1] There is a certain amount of truth behind this—did not J. M. Neale, the Tractarian, sorrowfully admit that England's Church was Catholic, but not England itself. On the other hand the vast bulk of the nation would call itself "C. of E." Probably the truth of the matter is that the religion of the Englishman is a kind of Protestantism, in spite of the progress of Anglo-Catholicism and the Church of Rome in these lands, and that the Evangelical Party and the Nonconformists really represent the norm. But this is sufficient to cause distress and the feeling of injustice among the latter.

This feeling of undeserved inferiority was bound to produce outbreaks of hostility from time to time, especially if any public event or actual dispute happened to arise to draw attention to it. In the late eighteenth century Dr. Priestley in his controversy with Edmund Burke had denounced the Establishment as a fungus growth on true Christianity which ought to be abolished. He added that once it was abolished no one would ever seek to restore it (*Letters to Burke*, pp. 84, 113 f.). We have already seen the violence of the attacks of Thomas Binney and his use of paradoxical language (see above, p. 70). A further example, this time an extract from the prospectus of *The Christian Witness*, may be added to show the bitter feeling which existed towards the union of Church and State: "The human mind cannot even approximate the formation of a

---

[1] "L'anglicanisme n'est qu'une combination d'hommes d'état, une église plutôt qu'une religion, et l'église d'une caste. C'est chez les dissidents qu'il faut chercher l'âme de la nation." Émile Boutmy, *Psychologie politique du Peuple anglais au XIXe siècle*, p. 76.

true estimate of the calamity and evil which flow from this most unscriptural and most baneful union."[1]

Fresh fuel was provided for the flames by the celebration in 1862 of the Restoration Ejections and this was followed by Spurgeon's unprovoked attack over the matter of Baptismal Regeneration (see above, pp. 206 f.). The Education Acts were a further source of quarrelling and in 1875 it really looked as if Disestablishment was imminent. Bishop Selwyn said that he would not give seven years for his seat in the Lords, and the Nonconformists themselves, a little later if not at this actual epoch, were already looking forward to the next stage of the struggle. For it was not only the Establishment with which they had to make up their account, but with the spirit of "sacerdotalism" entrenched in the Church. This is stated quite plainly by A. M. Fairbairn. "The time is at hand when, one great ecclesiastical conflict over, we shall be face to face, not with the Establishment, but with the Anglican Church. Let us then make it manifest that we claim every man in England for Christ, and that we mean every man to feel what the grace of God signifies for him. If we so interpret our mission, then we shall accomplish a work that will make it impossible for the sceptre that controls English destinies ever to pass into the hands of a disestablished sacerdotal church, and we shall help to keep it for ever in the hands of the risen and reigning Christ" (quoted Selbie, *A. M. Fairbairn*, p. 148). This passage contains two great errors; it anticipated the speedy triumph of Nonconformity, a triumph which failed to mature owing to the passing of political power from the lower middle-classes to the working man; it identified the Church of England with one party within it—the Nonconformists had no monopoly of the desires expressed in Fairbairn's passionate outburst.

The friends of the Establishment meanwhile regarded the attacks upon it with misgiving. Disraeli wrote of the efforts of the Liberation Society in 1868: "As I hold that the dissolution of the union between Church and State will cause permanently a greater revolution in this country than foreign conquest, I shall use my utmost energies to defeat their fatal

[1] Quoted A. W. Peel, *These Hundred Years*, p. 130.

machinations" (*Life*, II, p. 365). But the danger, as Disraeli and his royal Mistress saw well, was not only from Nonconformists, but also from High Churchmen. He wrote to the Queen in January 1879, after the appointment of Lightfoot to Durham, of "the deleterious designs of Canon Lyddon (*sic*) and the Dean of St. Paul's, who wish to terminate the connexion between the Crown and the Church, and ultimately unite with the Greek Church. The Church Union is entirely under their control" (*op. cit.*, II, p. 1279). This is not true of Dean Church who did not even belong to the English Church Union, and was, indeed, "rather afraid of it" (*Life*, p. 301); moreover he did not believe in Disestablishment (*op. cit.*, p. 309).[1] Perhaps he had in view all the time his great opponent, for Gladstone, especially after the failure of the Church of England, in contrast with the Nonconformists, to share his moral indignation at the policy of the government in supporting Turkey, favoured Disestablishment. He felt that the connexion with the State hampered the Church's freedom; yet he hesitated, as well he might, to cut it. The Church was so closely bound up with the national life that many fibres would be severed in the process.

In the later half of the century things began to improve and sentiments of wider toleration to spread among both Churchmen and Dissenters. Dean Stanley had something to do with this, but perhaps, at least so far as the softening of the attitude of Dissenters was concerned, the chief credit is due to Mr. Gladstone. We have already noted the strange fate which made this convinced, even rigid, Churchman, the leader of a political party whose rank and file was made up largely of Nonconformists; but their political relations involved continual meetings and out of them came understanding. To this we have the testimony of Dr. Allon, a leading Congregationalist. In a letter written to Mr. Gladstone himself he wrote: "The kind of intercourse that you have kindly permitted with nonconformists, has helped more consciously to identify them with movements of national life, and to diminish the stern

---

[1] Both Keble and Hurrell Froude had disliked the Establishment; the former once said: "the union of Church and State as it is now understood is actually sinful."

feeling of almost defiant witness-bearing that was strong a generation or two ago. It is something gained if ecclesiastical and political differences can be debated within a common circle of social confidence and identity. . . . Their confidence in you has made them amenable to your lead in respect of methods and movements needing the guidance of political insight and experience."[1] It was about this time that deputations of Anglicans began to appear at Nonconformist Conferences; the first Congregational Union Assembly to be so attended was in 1882,[2] and when in 1877 the Burials Bill allowing Dissenting services in churchyards was introduced, in spite of its having been condemned by Convocation, it was supported in the House of Lords by the Archbishop of Canterbury.

The removal of various Nonconformist disabilities should have made for better feeling; but many of the effects of these disabilities still persisted. There was, too, the social barrier, itself in part a result of the legal and scholastic discrimination against Nonconformity. Dr. Vaughan, whilst admitting the practical disappearance of legal disabilities, in his volume on *English Nonconformity*, went on to say: "But let not our Episcopalian neighbours account it strange, if there are still signs of discontent among us. The many forms of *social* disparagement, disownment and wrong to which Nonconformists are exposed as such, it would require large space to describe" (*op. cit.*, p. 472). But gradually as the older generation, which had known at first hand the burden of disabilities, began to die out conditions changed. A feeling of friendliness towards the Church actually shewed itself; and Nonconformists with a modern outlook like Hugh Price Hughes tried to get the whole question of the Establishment kept in the background, lest it should be regarded as an act of hostility towards valuable allies. In private he was not averse from declaring that Anglicanism itself would obtain the chief benefit from Disestablishment (*Life*, p. 483). But here and there a good deal of "tub-thumping" still went on and even some of the responsible leaders allowed themselves to descend to vulgar attacks

[1] Morley, *Life of W. E. Gladstone*, II, p. 135.
[2] A. W. Peel, *These Hundred Years*, p. 290.

on the Church and its bishops. As late as 1899 Creighton could write: "It may be that I am thin-skinned, but I do not like, after I have been talking intimately and frankly with a man one day as a brother in Christ, to find that a week after, upon a public platform, he has found it necessary to talk about 'purse-proud prelates,' and to denounce the Bishop of London" (*Life and Letters*, II, p. 397).

ATTEMPTS AT REUNION

Efforts to reunite Christendom arising in these islands were not so novel as is generally supposed. As long ago as 1689 Lord Nottingham had brought a Bill for "Comprehension" into Parliament; and in more recent times more than one attempt had been made to bring about a better understanding with Rome and the Orthodox.[1] But in the reign of Victoria the question was much as it had always been. The problems connected with it can best be surveyed from the central vantage point of the Church of England. They then resolve themselves under three headings, each representing a direction of possible progress: Reunion with Rome; Reunion with the Orthodox Churches of the East; Reunion with Protestant Nonconformity at home.

Reunion with Rome

Since the Church of England is a daughter Church of the great Mother of the West the consideration of attempts to restore unity between them demands the first consideration; they make but a melancholy story. We noticed above (pp. 115 f.) the attempts of Father Ignatius to promote, by prayer and other means, the reunion of the two Churches. In 1858 the Association for the Promotion of the Union of Christendom was formed with a few Roman Catholic members, the most prominent of whom was Phillips de Lisle. But the revived Roman hierarchy was unfavourable to such flirtation with heretics and in 1864 Manning put his foot down decisively to stop it. Two years later in a pastoral letter entitled *The Reunion of Christendom* he definitely rejected the attempts of

---

[1] See Wickham Legg, *English Church Life from the Restoration to the Tractarian Movement*, pp. 393 ff.

certain Anglicans to approach the subject. In 1868 the Pope himself shewed the official attitude by issuing a document inviting all non-Catholics to submit to his jurisdiction. In the meantime Dr. Pusey had issued his original *Eirenicon*, to be followed by two others, and had got into touch with a number of French ecclesiastics. There seemed to be some faint hopes of possible negotiations. But the acceptance of Papal Infallibility in 1870 by the Roman Church seemed to shut the door once and for all to any such possibility. There were, however, private negotiations between a number of Anglicans, led by Lord Halifax and the Rev. T. A. Lacey, and certain French Roman Catholics, led by the Abbé Portal and Monsignor Duchesne, between 1890 and 1897. But once again there was a Papal pronouncement, condemning Anglican Orders, to prevent their going any farther. To this the Archbishops of Canterbury and York addressed a dignified and learned reply setting forth the case for English Ordinations. It had been written by John Wordsworth, Bishop of Salisbury, in consultation with Bishop Creighton of London, Bishop Stubbs of Oxford, and others.

Reunion with the Eastern Churches

With the Eastern Churches the position was much the same. In 1840 William Palmer had made some tentative attempts to get the Russian Bishops to consider the claims of the English Church ; but his advances met with a contemptuous rebuff. A. P. Stanley had paid visits to Russia in 1857 and again in 1874, but he was not interested in reunion with the Orthodox, and though something may have been done to increase interest in the Church of England no definite advance had been made. Liddon was also in Russia in 1867. The man, however, who did the greatest work in promoting mutual understanding between the two Churches was J. M. Neale, who wrote the *History of the Holy Eastern Church*. In 1864 the Eastern Church Association was founded. Benson in his years as Archbishop, it may be mentioned, took considerable interest in the Christians of the East, including the unfortunate Assyrians, but no steps towards reunion were undertaken. There were occasions, however, when Anglicans and Orthodox came into contact; these were the famous Bonn Conferences in 1874 and the year following, held chiefly to explore the possibilities of some kind of union with the Old Catholics, as those Romans who refused to accept Papal Infallibility called themselves. The Anglican representatives, although they were headed by Bishop Harold Browne and included Liddon, had no real scholars among them and compared unfavourably with the representatives of the other Churches; the fact that proceedings were conducted in German must also have been a serious handicap. Liddon himself confessed that "We English Churchpeople were as poorly represented as it is possible to imagine" (*Life*, p. 188); whilst a sympathetic Nonconformist who watched the proceedings also noticed the inferiority of the Anglicans in erudition and historic judgement, without appreciating the unrepresentative character of the Anglicans who were present. He hoped that one result of the Conference would be the formation of a school of scientific theology in the Anglican Church.[1]

Reunion with Nonconformity

We come now to the relations of Anglicans and Nonconformists, the division of our subject where most has been done. During the whole period there was much co-operation, at least by the Evangelicals and the Nonconformists. The great interdenominational societies like the Religious Tract Society, the British and Foreign Bible Society, gave the opportunity for this. But even the Evangelicals, save in a few cases, were not anxious for much more; their churchmanship was of a strict type and they were conscious of the social prestige of the Establishment. There were exceptions, of course, as the following record by T. F. Buxton written in 1839 testifies: "Yesterday I was whipt off to a meeting in the city on the subject of Bethnal Green, and had to tell the Bishop of London that I was ready to join Methodists or Baptists, or Quakers, or any honest body, in spreading Christianity in Bethnal Green; but he took it very kindly." The bishops themselves, however, were very cautious, and when the Ragged Schools were first started none of them except Stanley of Norwich would support

[1] See J. L. Paton, *Life of J. B. Paton*, p. 144.

the movement on public platforms for fear of having to associate with Nonconformists. As the reign went on a much more tolerant spirit began to prevail and co-operation on a wider scale became possible. But there was always a feeling of slight mistrust on the part of the Anglicans lest they should find themselves in compromising positions. As late as July 1889 Archbishop Benson wrote of joint efforts of Churchmen and Nonconformists: "These mixtures are not amiss but they won't stand stirring about" (*Life*, p. 357). Further co-operation came about in connexion with Social Problems and the work overseas. In connexion with the latter there were Interdenominational Conferences at Liverpool in 1860 and at Mildmay in 1878 amongst others. Though the C.M.S. took part, the S.P.G. was not represented.

One fruitful act of co-operation, though it led at first to scandal and strife, was the Revision of the New Testament. The Committee to undertake it was appointed in 1870 and attempts were made to bring in representatives of all shades of Christian opinion from Dr. Vance Smith, the Unitarian, to J. H. Newman. The latter refused to co-operate, the former accepted. It was from his acceptance that a storm was aroused, for Westcott had suggested to Stanley the idea of having a joint service of Holy Communion to inaugurate the work. That a Unitarian should have been admitted was a grave offence in the eyes of many and it aroused unnecessary opposition to the whole scheme of Revision. Many of the Nonconformists who took part were hopeful that it would do much to bridge the gulf between them and the Church; but though much was done in this direction, their hopes proved to be too sanguine.[1] Dean Burgon in his attacks on the scheme and its product did not forget to emphasize the wisdom of avoiding any contact with Dissenters. On the other hand Bishop Moberly, a High Churchman, wrote: "The feeling of brotherhood remains and will surely never be lost,"[2] and Westcott declared that something more than the Revised Version would be the result of their common labours.

In addition to these spasmodic efforts at co-operation there were definite attempts to promote actual union. The most

[1] See W. F. *Moulton*, p. 265.   [2] Quoted *op. cit.*, p. 104.

famous of these in the early years (actually just before the period began) was that of Dr. Arnold. In 1833, alarmed by the growth of anti-clericalism and the spirit of uncontrolled reform, he had come to the conclusion that nothing could save the Establishment except union with the Dissenters, and so he set forth proposals so drastic as only to be justified, so he himself admitted in 1840, by the extremity of the peril which they were intended to counter. In his pamphlet entitled *Principles of Church Reform* he urged that the Church should "truly and effectually" be made the Church of England by the admission of all Christians, except Roman Catholics, who he explained really exclude themselves, and, in certain cases, Unitarians. His suggestions were everywhere received with disfavour, even by Nonconformists. Perhaps his rather patronizing attitude towards them—he suggested, for example, that their chapels might be rescued from their "utter coarseness and deformity" by the influence of Anglican ideals—may have had something to do with this. But the whole scheme was, to use his own later expression, manifestly chimerical.

Most of the actual efforts to promote reunion during the greater part of the period were on a small scale and of limited scope. In 1874, for example, Bishop Christopher Wordsworth of Lincoln, moved by the prevalence of Methodism in his diocese, held a Conference with some of its leading representatives. Little came of it as the Bishop wished to discuss great principles, the Methodists, practical matters, such as the right of ministers to the title "reverend."[1] Two years later the Archbishop himself (Tait) held a Conference at Lambeth at which six bishops and twenty-two leading Nonconformists were present. The latter included Dr. Allon, Dr. Angus, Dr. Newman Hall, Dr. Morley Punshon, and Dr. Stoughton. The Conference issued no public statement, but it did much, as the Nonconformists gladly admitted, "to allay heart-burnings, to disarm antagonism, and to promote the spirit of unity" (see *A. C. Tait*, II, p. 503).

The year 1888 saw the foundation of the Home Reunion Society, of which Lord Nelson was President. It held small conferences of Anglicans and Nonconformists at the house of

[1] See Watson, *Life of John Wordsworth*, pp. 97 f.

the Rev. George Greenwood, warden of the Guild of St. Luke. The Anglicans included Westcott and Gore, and the Nonconformists Dr. Allon and J. B. Paton. This same year was marked by a very definite step in advance: the issue of the famous "Lambeth Quadrilateral" by the bishops of the Anglican Communion. In introducing the fourfold resolution which gave the title, they stated quite frankly their own desires and convictions on the subject. Their words demand quotation: "We hold ourselves in readiness to enter into brotherly conference with any of those who may desire intercommunion with us in a more or less perfect form. We lay down conditions on which such intercommunion is, in our opinion, and according to our conviction, possible. For, however we may long to embrace those now alienated from us, so that the ideal of the one flock under the one Shepherd may be realized, we must not be unfaithful stewards of the great deposit entrusted to us. We cannot desert our position either as to faith or discipline. That concord would, in our judgement, be neither true nor desirable which should produce such surrender." The four Articles of the Resolution, representing a basis for approaching the subject, were as follows:

(a) The Holy Scriptures of the Old and New Testaments, as "containing all things necessary to salvation," and as being the rule and the ultimate standard of faith.

(b) The Apostles' Creed, as the Baptismal Symbol; and the Nicene Creed, as the sufficient statement of the Christian faith.

(c) The two Sacraments ordained by Christ Himself—Baptism and the Supper of the Lord—ministered with unfailing use of Christ's words of institution, and of the elements ordained by Him.

(d) The Historic Episcopate, locally adapted in the methods of its administration to the varying needs of the nations and peoples called of God into the unity of His Church.

One very fruitful method of promoting understanding between Churchmen and Nonconformists, and so of leading towards reunion, was that adopted by Dr. H. S. (later Sir Henry) Lunn. He conceived the idea of organizing holiday parties of Churchmen and Nonconformists who might in a quiet and friendly atmosphere discuss their differences and discover their agreements. From such intercourse friendship and understanding, and even projects for common work, would certainly arise and so reunion would be brought nearer. The first conference was held at Grindelwald in the winter of 1892, and it was so successful that it was repeated in the following August, and at intervals since. Amongst Anglicans who took part in these conferences were Bishop J. J. S. Perowne of Worcester, Dean Fremantle, Archdeacon Wilson, Prebendary Webb-Peploe, and Professor G. T. Stokes; among Methodists, Hugh Price Hughes and Dr. Stephenson; Dr. C. A. Berry the Congregationalist; Père Hyacinth and Pastor Theodore Monod.

Perhaps the most fruitful field for co-operation and for experiments in reunion is in lands overseas. There the force of tradition is weaker and the opposition so strong that the Christian Churches might seem bound to stand closer together. Such an expectation, which was to see a great measure of fulfilment in the following century, might well be entertained since it corresponds with experience in the secular and political sphere. This is succinctly expressed by A. J. Toynbee as follows: "It is more difficult to achieve political consolidation in the heart and centre of an expanding society than on the periphery" (*A Study of History*, III, p. 121, n. 3).

Probably reunion will have to wait for some time, until the various sections of Christians have decided what really are the fundamental doctrines and the necessary organization, if any. As someone has said: "Before the problem of the Reunion of Christendom can be helpfully solved, we have first to solve the problem of what is the Christian Faith and what is the Catholic Church." The two problems of Restatement and Reunion are intimately connected. Here we may with profit recall the great principles which Dean Church once laid down for dealing with all Theological Differences. He demanded in any attempt to deal with them: (*a*) accuracy of facts, terms, reasoning; (*b*) elevation, breadth, range of thought; a due sense of what these questions mean and involve; a power of looking at things from a height; a sufficient taking into account of possibilities, of our own ignorance, of the real proportions of things" (*Occasional Papers*, II, p. 461). Certainly without complete candour on either side and complete understanding of all that is involved understanding is impossible. "We may be sure of one thing—no visible unity is worth having," says Dr. Burge, "if it is produced by diplomatic language and is the result of political arrangement. All parties must mean the same thing and know that they mean the same thing" (In *The Contemporary Review* for June 1925).

FEDERATION

We now come to examine the question of reunion and co-operation from the point of view of Nonconformity; leaving aside, of course, their relation with the Established Church which has already received treatment. As in the case of reunion in general the last years of the period saw tremendous advances, the prelude of still more striking progress in the years to come.

Early Dissidence

In the early years of the nineteenth century the Nonconformists had worked together for the removal of their common disabilities, and they had co-operated with one another and with the Church in the great societies; but the basis of their unity, apart from this last aspect, was almost entirely political rather than religious. There was no idea of Federation, much less of a Catholic Church. The multiplicity of Protestant variations shewed no sign of decreasing and the "Dissidence of Dissent" was still apparent. Even from a political standpoint there was not complete unity, for the Methodists were for the great part Tories and in any case they repudiated the term Nonconformist; whilst the older Dissenters looked upon them with suspicion as an upstart body given too much to emotional religion. A good example of this type of Methodist was John Hannah, President of the Conference in 1842 and 1851; he was tutor of Didsbury College for the last twenty-four years of his life. His son, like the sons of not a few leading Methodists, took Orders and eventually became Archdeacon of Lewes.

But if the Methodists refused to co-operate with other Dissenters, they themselves became subject to a number of further splits. "From 1827 to the middle of the century Wesleyan Methodism was subject to a series of convulsions, the consequence of the conflict between the democratic and the clerical parties."[1] This dispute arose from the constitution of the Methodist body which Wesley had left under the control of the Conference, a body selected entirely from the ministry. The district meetings challenged their authority and from 1849 onwards a bitter struggle ensued. An interesting sidelight is thrown on this matter by the experiences of the parents of E. L. Hicks, later to be a very distinguished scholar and Bishop of Lincoln. His mother was a convinced Methodist and after her marriage succeeded in getting her husband, a Churchman, to worship with her. But the latter was a strong Liberal and on the outbreak of the dispute his sympathies were entirely with the reforming ministers who were ejected by the connexion. The claims of the ruling body seemed but a fresh illustration of Milton's saying that the "new presbyter" was but the "old priest writ large." The result was that he returned to the Church, and his wife, weary of religious controversy in her own denomination, went with him (see Fowler, *Life and Letters of E. L. Hicks*, p. 5). The dispute crippled the Methodist body spiritually for at least a generation, and not the least evil was done by the abundant literature engendered by it. "Perhaps there is no parallel in modern ecclesiastical history [in England] to such an overwhelming disaffection. The people left by whole families and congregations all over the country."[2] Those who left were largely of the working classes; some joined seceding bodies, the United Methodist Free Church, Primitive Methodists, Bible Christians, New Connexion, and so forth; but the great majority, Benjamin Gregory says 60,000 out of 100,000, "were lost to Methodism and only too probably to the visible Church" (*Recollections*, p. 396). The various Methodist bodies in Canada united in 1883; their fellow members in England had to wait for another half-century and more before doing the same.

Early Attempts at Organization

Within the various denominations attempts were made soon after the dawn of the century to promote a greater amount

[1] S. Horne, *Free Church History*, p. 294.
[2] D. Price Hughes, *Hugh Price Hughes*, pp. 55 and 191.

of unity and co-ordination. In 1813 the Baptist Union was founded, in 1827 the British and Foreign Unitarian Association, and in 1831 the Congregational Union. These bodies possessed no executive power and were purely voluntary associations. Their usefulness lay in the provision of a means of arriving at a common mind and enabling the denomination, or a considerable part of it, to speak as a whole. For the Congregationalists thus to combine was very difficult in view of their very basis, which regarded each congregation as a separate and entirely independent unit;[1] but it was among the Congregationalists that most progress was made.[2] By 1891 they had actually got so far as to hold an International Council. It met under the presidency of Dr. Dale in the new Weigh House Chapel in London. Horton records with regret his disappointment over the American delegates who were singularly antiquated in their theology (*Autobiography*, pp. 113 f.). But the step was a wise one for it was, as A. M. Fairbairn said, a sign that Independency was "ceasing to be an isolation and learning to be a brotherhood" (*Life*, p. 153).

Rivalry and Isolation

The isolation of the separate congregations of each several denomination was not the only source of weakness; there was also the existence of congregations alongside each other in the same district. Rivalry was bound to arise. R. W. Dale wrote a despairing letter to a Methodist friend in 1889. "I was at Barmouth yesterday. We Congregationalists have a wooden church, holding perhaps 150 people; the Baptists, three years ago, opened a church—stone, however—holding

---

[1] See A. W. Peel, *These Hundred Years*, p. 3, on their dilemma: "We must have increased centralization to make our work and witness effective. . . . We cannot have increased centralization without losing our *raison d'être* and forsaking our distinctive principles." The Congregationalists wished to find the Least Common Measure of Ecclesiastical organization and, like the Greek city states, to be self-centred and to make their own laws (*Thucydides*, 1, cxliv. 2). There is a vivid description in the declaration of the Savoy Conference of Churches "sailing each on its own way in the vast ocean of these tumultuous times and holding out not so much as a light to each other" (quoted Dale, *Life of R. W. Dale*, p. 600).

[2] See Peel, *op. cit.*, *passim*.

about as many; your people have also a church. The Baptists and Wesleyans conduct English services only in the season; it is the same with the Presbyterians. In the winter, I believe, they are all with us. It is no use saying that such a policy as this is hateful—I could swear when I think of it. It exists. It is far too strong. Even the different Methodists . . . can neither combine nor confederate; how can we dream of a more general federation?" (*Life*, p. 396).

Further difficulties were caused by the tendency of individual ministers to "steal sheep" from other folds. The Baptists were especially troublesome in this matter as they found it "easier to allure members from other churches than to win them from the world"—so Benjamin Gregory affirms. He has preserved some of the arguments used by Methodists striving to expose the unsoundness of Baptist arguments in favour of total immersion; they are so ingenious as to deserve quotation, especially as they illustrate the method of using the Bible common in the period. A favourite passage was 1 Peter iii. 20 f., which shewed that if Noah and his family were baptized it must have been by the "sprinkling" of the rain; those who were "immersed" perished in the flood. So also Moses and the Children of Israel were baptized in the cloud (1 Cor. x. 2), which must have been by "sprinkling"; whilst it was the Egyptians who were "immersed" in the Red Sea (*Recollections*, pp. 297 and 405). Still worse than the Baptists were the fresh denominations which arose from time to time, and not least, the Salvation Army. From the days of the Primitive Church novel forms of Christianity have always found it easier to gain converts from among their fellow Christians than by preaching to outsiders. Tertullian has described this as characteristic of the Gnostics and the Marcionites.[1]

Steps towards Federation

Probably the first to contemplate the idea of Federation was John Angell James; whilst an actual scheme was worked out by Dr. Guthrie in 1867. In 1872 a Conference of Baptists, Presbyterians, Methodists, and Congregationalists was held to consider the question of overlapping and of avoiding the

[1] See Harnack, *Mission and Expansion of Christianity*, I, p. 114.

formation of new, weak congregations. During the next eighteen years the idea was floating in the minds of several leading Nonconformists—in 1878 there was an unsuccessful attempt to hold a Free Church Conference—until in February 1890 Guinness Rogers wrote to *The Methodist Times* suggesting a Congress on the lines of the Church Congress. He hoped that it would lead to "a development of the Church idea which at present is hardly realized." In the following year J. B. Paton set out definite proposals in a long letter to the Rev. J. A. Meeson, a Congregationalist Minister of Harrogate. As a result a circular was sent out to all Nonconformist ministers in the country signed by eleven prominent leaders, including, in addition to Paton and Meeson, Hugh Price Hughes, John Clifford, R. F. Horton, and J. Scott Lidgett. This led directly to the first Congress.[1] It was held in Manchester in November 1892 and more than 370 attended it. One result of the Congress was the formation of Free Church Councils up and down the country. At the Congress at Leeds in 1894 plans were made for turning it into a representative body with elected delegates, rather than a Congress with a voluntary membership like the Church Congress. The Rev. Thomas Law and the Rev. J. M. G. Owen were elected as secretaries. At the Congress at Birmingham in 1895, just after the death of Dale, Dr. C. A. Berry presided. Very soon the question of the Unitarians arose. They often co-operated with Nonconformists in local efforts, ought they to be allowed to join the local Free Church Councils and the Central Congress? A strong line against this was taken by Dr. Berry on the ground that no real fellowship was possible unless there was absolute unity in essentials.[2]

Meanwhile the idea of the Church, to which Guinness Rogers had referred in the letter quoted above, was growing in many minds. In the early years of the period this idea, apart from the Church Invisible, would have conveyed nothing to Nonconformists except negatively as a protest against the claims of the Church of England and the Roman Catholic Church.

[1] See J. L. Paton, *Life of J. B. Paton*, pp. 488 ff.
[2] Further details of subsequent developments will be found in Drummond, *Life of C. A. Berry*, pp. 111 ff.

Christianity to them was a purely individualistic thing. Now they were beginning to see that it was something much greater. Dr. Berry himself advocated a Catholic Church as being a divinely ordained institution though, characteristically, he would have retained its congregational basis (*Life*, p. 123). Among the most prominent of those who wished to see a kind of Catholic Church formed out of the various Nonconformist bodies was Hugh Price Hughes (see *Life*, pp. 437 ff.). His ideas, and those of others who thought with him, found expression in the definition of the Church contained in the Catechism issued by the Free Church Council which ran as follows: "It is that holy society of believers in Christ Jesus which He founded, of which He is the only Head, and in which He dwells by His Spirit; so that, though made up of many communions, organized in various modes, and scattered throughout the world, it is yet one in Him." On this definition Price Hughes has the following remarks:

"It will be noted," he says, "that this definition makes no reference whatever to the metaphysical abstraction entitled the 'Invisible Church,' which was invented in the sixteenth century. Of course, we all believe in the 'Invisible Church' in the sense that the Church Triumphant in heaven is a part of the true Church not visible on earth. As we often sing:

> 'One family we dwell in Him,
> One Church above, beneath,
> Though now divided by the stream,
> The narrow stream of death.'

But in Protestant controversy the 'Invisible Church' is used in a totally different sense, to describe some church of which every believer in Christ is a member, even when he totally neglects all the duties and obligations of practical fellowship with his fellow Christians. Anything more entirely opposed to the original purpose of Christ or the best interests both of the individual and of human society, I cannot imagine."

It seems to me that this discovery by Nonconformity of the Catholic Church, even though it was not the historic idea of that body since it ignored Episcopacy, saved it from lapsing into a barren individualism. Had it been content to face the twentieth century with the merely negative policy of the Liberation Society, disendowment and disestablishment, its fate might well have been that of the Liberal Party with which politically it was so closely involved. The vision and power of a number of great statesmen and prophets, for such undoubtedly they were, enabled them to rise above the limitations of their heritage into a clearer air, into what was for them the Catholic Faith. This saved Nonconformity when its political force was spent. For already there were those, themselves loyal to Nonconformity, who were forced to admit the increasing difficulty of remaining in Dissent. I quoted the opinion of Augustine Birrell above (see p. 73); I now add that of one who was much more nearly associated with Nonconformity in its highest attainments, A. M. Fairbairn. In 1897 he wrote: "It is perhaps harder to be a Nonconformist to-day than it has ever been in the history of England. The very decay of the disabilities from which our fathers suffered has made it harder for us than for them to dissent" (quoted W. B. Selbie, *A. M. Fairbairn*, p. 257).

25

THE END OF AN EPOCH

WHEN the great bell of St. Paul's tolled out its iron message "The Queen is dead," it seemed to those who heard it that the foundations of life were being shaken, the great deeps were breaking up. A new century was upon them, a new epoch begun, and a new chapter in their history opened; and they were left to face it bereaved of what long custom had taught them to regard as an enduring stay. In the sermon which Scott Holland preached in St. Paul's on the death of Victoria he expressed in burning words what all were feeling: "She is dead and with her dies an epoch. That mighty period which is commemorated by her name has rolled up as a scroll. That is why we tremble. The ground under us is withdrawn; the world that we have known dissolves; the unknown awaits us."[1]

In English history it would seem, as the late Lord Oxford once pointed out,[2] that only queens have the right to give their names to an epoch—thus we speak of the Age of Elizabeth, the Age of Queen Anne, and the Victorian Era. There may be different judgements of Queen Victoria, but few of those who lived in her reign would deny that she was as worthy as Elizabeth or Anne to lend her name to a great epoch. If at one period of her life, when the loss of a beloved husband left her desolate and mistrustful of herself, she faltered for a moment, that moment soon passed; she rose to meet her responsibilities. Perhaps that much-lamented death was all to the good, for had the Prince Consort lived there might have been a constitutional crisis; if, that is, as some suppose, he aimed at increasing the political power of the monarchy. Victoria was wiser and was willing to accept her limitations, even to see at times her wishes thwarted by her ministers. What

---

[1] *Personal Studies*, p. 12. A similar testimony to the universal dismay comes from the Diary of Arthur Benson, who in conjunction with Lord Esher was to edit her letters: "It is like the roof being off the house to think of England queenless."
[2] Asquith, *Some Aspects of the Victorian Age*, p. 3.

was it that made her so great? She had received no high training by way of education, nor did she read deeply; her outlook and even her appearance were not those of a great lady. Yet she succeeded in preserving her dignity and earning the respect and veneration of her subjects. How was it? There can be no doubt that she had an immense fund of shrewdness and political common sense; a stern determination and sense of duty; and much energy and power of decision. Beneath it all there was genuine religious feeling and a confident trust in the divine aid. This gave steadiness to her purpose and consoled her in times of depression. Strangely enough her religion was not closely akin to that of the Church Established in the southern half of her kingdom. This was admitted by Scott Holland in the Memorial Sermon from which I have already quoted: Her "natural piety was profoundly reinforced by the personal subjective spirituality, so characteristic of Teutonic religion. . . . Such a sentiment did not easily attach itself to the dominant methods and forms of our own worship in the Church of England; it found itself more congenially at home in the simpler rites north of the Tweed" (*op. cit.*, p. 10).

EVENTS AT HOME AND ABROAD

The century had been born amidst war and suffering, and amidst war and suffering it was laid to rest. The great Queen survived it by but a short period; but already there was an undertone of sorrow and anxiety to be heard beneath the still continuing prosperity and comfort of the nation. The long period of unchecked expansion and happy fortune was indeed ended. England would never be the same again.

Political events at home during the last years of the reign were largely conditioned by the split in the Liberal party which had followed Gladstone's adoption of Home Rule in 1886. Ireland still remained a problem and Irish affairs were complicated by the brilliant but tragic career of Parnell. In spite of the split in his party Gladstone was to see one more period of power—he was Prime Minister from 1892 until his resignation in 1894. And so there passed from the scene which he had dominated for nearly half a century a great statesman and a great Christian gentleman.

This same period saw the increase of Social Legislation, measures of interference and coercion by the government—for as such they appeared to many—being now introduced. There was also a development in the way of Local government. All these activities and tendencies have already received treatment under the heading of Social Problems and Social Changes respectively. But the need for changes was revealed and hastened by the outbreak of strikes and other symptoms of unrest. One other measure, perhaps, deserves mention—the Budget of 1894 introduced by Sir William Harcourt and denounced for its innovations in the matter of Death Duties.

The great culminating event of the period, however, was the Diamond Jubilee of 1897. In it the world saw with something of amazement the demonstrations by which a democratic people shewed forth its happy belief in a monarchy. The personal qualities of the Queen were, of course, responsible for the veneration in which the institution was held; for loyalty was based on respect and affection. The Diamond Jubilee was also a demonstration of the growing might of the British Empire, and in the processions the Colonial representatives and the Colonial troops received especial notice from the crowds. It was a time of wild enthusiasm and not a little proud vaunting. But in spite of it all there were those who cared to remember that Empires and Trading nations have their end; that power and wealth cannot remain for ever in the same hands—that some day Britain must go the way of "Nineveh and Tyre." The Jubilee phase, as it may be called, ended quite suddenly with the outbreak of the Second Boer War in 1899.

Up to 1899 England had enjoyed a long period of lasting peace. This was largely due to the tact and patience of Lord Salisbury and the skill of his foreign policy. There had been dangerous incidents when war had been close at hand; but he had managed to stave it off. The earliest of these incidents was the dispute with the United States over Venezuela in 1895. Perhaps the Americans remembered too vividly our complaisant attitude over the "Alabama" and so took a line which was highly provocative; certainly feeling in both countries ran very high; but Lord Salisbury refused to be perturbed and in the end arbitration was invoked and an outbreak avoided. "Fortunately for us," said a well-known American statesman, "Lord Salisbury had a very good sense of humour and declined to take the matter too seriously."[1] There followed almost immediately the telegram from the Kaiser on the occasion of the Jameson Raid in January 1896 when again a conflict was only narrowly averted; so too in 1898 Fashoda might have involved us in trouble with the French. But at last war came—and with a small and comparatively weak people. In its early stages there was considerable bungling and "red-tape" was much in evidence. The world looked on and noted, not without satisfaction, that Britain was finding things extraordinarily difficult. The legend of British invincibility, which if it had never been quite accepted abroad, had been held, to their great comfort, by the majority of Britons at home, was disposed of once and for all. This had a sobering and a salutary effect. It certainly revealed our weaknesses, not only to our neighbours, but to ourselves. Had there been no Boer War one wonders what would have been the state of the British Army in 1914.

But the outbreak of war proved more than the aged Queen could stand and there can be but little doubt that it hastened her end. This has been so well and movingly stated by a contemporary historian that his words may be quoted. "Despite rapidly failing health," writes Sir J. A. R. Marriott, "Queen Victoria's conduct during the Boer War was little short of heroic. . . . She went in and out among her people at home, encouraging the fighter, consoling the wounded, comforting the mourners, warning and stimulating her Ministers. . . . But the strain of the effort was tremendous, and on January 22, 1901, death closed her long reign of sixty-three years."[2]

RELIGION

There are certain general truths concerning religion in the era which have already been the subject of separate chapters; such as the immense activity in the way of providing new

[1] H. Bingham, *The Monroe Doctrine*, p. 12.
[2] *History of Europe, 1815–1923*, p. 380.

buildings and in developing fresh organization; the quickened pirit of devotion in the clergy and ministers and the new care, especially in regard to the former, in their selection and training; the growth of the spirit of toleration and a desire to understand the position of others, and a very tentative move towards closer union and co-operation. Certainly the various Denominations were stronger and more effective than they had been at the beginning of the reign; though no doubt conditions were more difficult and the work less fruitful of results for the same amount of effort. Two testimonies to the improvement of the Church of England may be quoted by way of illustration; they apply equally well *mutatis mutandis* to the Nonconformist bodies. In *The Mind and Work of Bishop King* the following passage occurs: "At the beginning [of the era] the Church seemed effete, worn out, useless; at its end, it had passed through strange and marvellous revivals, and was once more upon its trial, facing a new world with new challenges and new perils" (Randolph and Townroe, *op. cit.*, p. 120). The other passage is from a great Evangelical leader, and refers especially to progress in that party. "Looking abroad over the field of our life and work in general," wrote Handley Moule in 1901, "we see abundant labour and self-sacrifice in many directions. It is my happiness to possess a somewhat wide acquaintance among the younger ranks of the Evangelical clergy, as on the other hand I have inherited some knowledge of a now long-past generation. I can only say that a certain pessimism and misgiving is continually corrected, and transformed into a far brighter feeling, when I think over, in a quiet hour, the host of young missionaries abroad and younger pastors at home whom I am permitted to call friends. I know a great many such men whose lives, I am sure, would have been watched and hailed with delight by the fathers of an elder day; lives in which the Spirit of God lives and works, energizing them for a firmness of conviction, a sacrifice of self, a multiplicity of method and labour, a manifestation of our Lord Jesus Christ, which is indeed a cheering and animating spectacle" (*The Evangelical School of Thought, etc.*, pp. 101 f.). But there was another side to the picture, as I have already hinted; the growth of new knowledge and the spread of education, as well as the numerous and extensive changes in social conditions, made the work of the Church more difficult. Its point of view could no longer be taken for granted. Mrs. Sidney Webb records her opinion, and it is that of a shrewd and enlightened observer, that the last decade of the nineteenth century formed "the watershed between the metaphysic of the Christian Church, which had hitherto dominated British civilization, and the agnosticism, deeply coloured by scientific materialism, which was destined, during the first decades of the twentieth century, to submerge all religion based on tradition and revelation" (*My Apprenticeship*, pp. 54 f.). The new point of view, in its anti-Christian attitude, suffered, as Mrs. Webb herself admits (*op. cit.*, p. 57), from making two great assumptions: (1) that physical science could solve all problems, and (2) that everyone by means of a few small text-books could be his own philosopher and scientist. None the less, in spite of its obvious limitations and errors, the new point of view placed difficulties in the way of the Church's activity, especially in the big towns and among artisan populations.

From remarks on the state of religion and its problems in general we come now to consider the Denominations in particular. Of the Nonconformists nothing need be added to what has already been said under the heading of Federation—for in this lay their principal development in the last decades of the century. Of the Church of England more requires to be noticed. In this period its strength was undoubtedly being much increased by a steady stream of adherents from among the growing class, Nonconformist by birth and upbringing, which was accumulating wealth and regarded membership of the Church as a kind of social hall-mark.[1] This accession of numbers more than counterbalanced the small trickle of

[1] The progress of the "Forsytes" was typical of a general social migration. "Originally, perhaps, members of some primitive sect, they were now in the natural course of things members of the Church of England, and caused their wives and children to attend with some regularity the more fashionable churches of the Metropolis. To have doubted their Christianity would have caused them both pain and surprise. Some of them paid for pews, thus expressing in the most practical form their sympathy with the teachings of Christ." John Galsworthy, *The Forsyte Saga*, p. 20.

those who left the Church for that of Rome. The motive which inspired these converts was certainly dubious; but once received into the Church they took their place among those they found there before them—probably no better and no worse than the rest, yet different. And in this difference lay their contribution. They brought fresh blood into the Establishment and their children often developed unexpected loyalties and usefulnesses. Such accessions were, of course, no new thing, and it would be interesting to trace in the ancestry of some of the great figures of Anglican leaders the influence of early Nonconformist strains—Dean Church, to take but one example and that a great one, was the son of a Quaker who had conformed on his marriage.

Within the Church, the historic parties still kept to their traditional names, but they were very different from their predecessors who had existed when Victoria ascended the throne. The Evangelicals, though many would have been loath to admit it, were much more Liberal and were moving steadily in that direction. The Tractarians were on the way to becoming Anglo-Catholics, with an emphasis on Ritual and a disregard of authority which would have been deeply painful to their forefathers; nor would these latter have appreciated the new attitude towards Rome, towards Biblical Criticism, or towards social questions, which their successors were displaying. The Liberals had advanced greatly, and were now sufficiently bold and secure to come out into the open in definite organizations and to express their views in such a form as would, at the beginning of the reign, have caused the most tremendous outcry and their own immediate expulsion from the Church of England.

The Churchmen's Union was founded in 1898 and its chief aim was to preserve the right of speculation and to support "those who were dissatisfied, in one way or another, with the traditional apologetic . . . against episcopal persecution"—so writes Dr. Inge, who is in a position to know (*Vale*, p. 72). The first President was Hastings Rashdall and its declared principles can be seen from the first report, issued in October 1899. They run as follows:

"1. To defend and maintain the teaching of the Church

of England as the historic Church of the country and as being Apostolic and Reformed.

"2. To uphold the historic comprehensiveness and corporate life of the Church of England and her Christian tolerance in all things non-essential.

"3. To give all the support in their power to those who are honestly and loyally endeavouring to vindicate the truths of Christianity by the light of scholarship and research, while paying due regard to continuity of work for such changes in the formularies and practices of the Church of England as from time to time are made necessary by the needs and knowledge of the day.

"4. To work for the restoration to the laity of an effective voice in all Church matters.

"5. To encourage friendly relations between the Church of England and all other Christian bodies."

These aims and objects, supplemented a little on the social side, are the same as those professed by the Union to-day. But if Liberalism was thus coming out into the open its success has not been nearly so striking as either its friends hoped or its enemies feared. That is if success or failure is assessed by the counting of heads. As a leaven working in the lump of the Church Liberalism has undoubtedly exercised an exceedingly great influence, but as a definite party it has made but little progress. This can be accounted for by its too purely intellectual outlook. "A devout Christian may be a Liberal Protestant or a Liberal Catholic," writes Dr. Inge, "he can hardly be a Liberal without any qualification" (*op. cit.*, p. 74).

In the closing years of the reign the Church of England was fortunate in the possession of a number of great Bishops. Men who were capable of taking their due position in the public life of the nation and of receiving recognition for their intellectual qualities as well as for their ecclesiastical office. Foremost among them were Lightfoot and Westcott, bishops in succession of the ancient see of Durham. Their success as administrators was looked upon with surprise by many; but it was not really so novel as they supposed. That the leader of a school of thought when faced at some sudden crisis, with the necessity of handling practical affairs, should succeed beyond men's expectations is not an uncommon event. And the reason is not far to seek; for the qualities which make a leader of men in the sphere of action are those which are required in the world of thought—a daring and sanguine spirit, an ardent and imaginative temperament. Others who deserve mention were the great historians—Stubbs at Oxford and Creighton at London. As to the latter, Mrs. Humphry Ward speaks of "that remarkable London episcopate, which in four short years did so much to raise the name and fame of the Anglican Church in London, at least for the lay mind" (*A Writer's Recollections*, p. 316). In those days the Church was still able to draw to its service men of high gifts and character in considerable numbers; the outlets and opportunities for such were much more limited then than they are to-day. The new century has altered all that, and in conjunction with a less settled state of belief, has robbed the Church, except in a few outstanding cases, of the men who were fitted to be her rulers. That the Church has still some few who can take their place beside the leaders of other professions and hold their own is fortunately true; many of her dignitaries, however, have little qualification for high position, save an immense energy and a gift for catching the eye of those in authority. Among the greatest of the Church's problems in the present day is to gain the service of men who will be capable of exercising leadership in the future, and giving them the right experience and training. This problem will not be solved by lavish grants and subsidies, for the type of man who will prove a leader will himself be capable of making his own way without such assistance. The Dean of Exeter (Dr. Carpenter) in a recent number of the *Exeter Cathedral Monthly Bulletin* tells how a group of people were discussing, in the presence of Bishop Gore, the increase of the episcopate. Someone said that if there were many bishops the problem would be to find men of sufficient calibre. Gore interposed with the remark "I do not think it would be difficult to maintain the present standard."

THE END OF AN EPOCH

CHARACTERISTICS OF THE ERA

The peculiar characteristics of the era were in large measure the product of the conditions which formed its background—peace abroad and increasing prosperity at home. The age was complacent, regarding respectability as the highest of moral virtues, and inclined to take comfort as the standard of progress and achievement. That it was increasingly humane was also to be expected; though its intensity and gravity were not quite such obvious fruits, but they were the marks of the men who had lived in earlier generations when prosperity had not been so all-enfolding.

The Victorian complacency was certainly a thing to marvel at. It was so placid and undisturbed by any thought of its own limitations; so certain that Englishmen were always right, so condescending to the unfortunate foreigner. It was, if the fruit of wealth and ease, the fruit also of isolation and of that insular situation which had been Britain's safeguard during the Napoleonic Wars and her opportunity when they were ended. But not all Englishmen were blind to the national weaknesses. There were many self-appointed prophets, such as Carlyle and Ruskin, to offer up their denunciations; whilst John Morley's *Essay on Compromise*, published about 1875, was "a ruthless unveiling of some characteristic Victorian insincerities."[1] But the Victorian held on his way through it all, unaffected. Not because, as his neighbours thought, he was a supreme hypocrite; but because he had certain standards of his own and judged other people by himself. Hence his self-satisfaction and assurance. "It is as easy to close the eyes of the mind as those of the body" had been Bishop Butler's warning in the previous century;[2] but the Victorian Englishman had never heard of it.

The standards of the Victorian were in matters of conduct very high, but they were almost entirely negative; they aimed at the avoidance of outward offence. To the disciples of Aristotle, since virtue consisted in following the mean, morality might almost be equated with respectability. In this, if in nothing else, the middle classes of Victorian England were

---

[1] Asquith, *Some Aspects of the Victorian Age*, p. 15.
[2] *Sermons*, X, "Upon Self-deceit."

unconscious Aristotelians; in fact they went even farther and almost identified respectability and religion. Nowadays it is possible to be "respectable" without "religion"; a circumstance which has had a devastating effect in reducing the number of nominal Christians. Much of their attitude towards offences was still due to inherited idea. To the Hindoo a public exhibition of temper is a grave outrage; the Victorian reserved such a designation for offences of the flesh. As Mr. W. J. Turner has put it: "The Puritan conception of the body as separate from and hostile to the spirit is the source of all the Victorians' fear, both of pleasure and of God, and also of their restricted conception of sin" (In *Great Victorians*, p. 501). This is an enlightening statement; if not an entirely exact one; for in this as in other things a materialistic outlook was characteristic of the age. In fact its gravest dangers came from the inequality which results when moral progress lags disastrously behind material advance.

But the comforts, religious and material, of the Victorian Age were largely the possession of a class; the outward peace and security kept the ring for much mental and social turmoil within the nation's life, and if in the last years of Victoria there was a period of quiescence, it was but on the surface. The working classes were determined to get their share of the good things of life; which unfortunately they so often identified with wealth and material comfort.

Beneath all the naïve optimism of the era there was always an undertone of pessimism; of apprehension in face of the unknown. It can be caught in much of the poetry of the time —in Matthew Arnold, in Christina Rossetti, in Swinburne, above all in FitzGerald's paraphrase of Omar Khayyám. In all of them there is a kind of "moan of lost battles," and their sufficient popularity is a sign that they found something in the heart of the people to respond. The later Victorians were a little more outspoken in their pessimism. It was not that they were ashamed of the achievements of their era, or that they really doubted their own capacity; but the doubt was beginning to creep in and they were more critical than their fathers and apt to be disillusioned more readily.

The love of comfort, which was a mark of the age, made

men averse to having their feelings disturbed by the sight or knowledge of the sufferings of others. Hence there was a growth of humanitarianism and an increased realization of the value of human lives. The temperature of civilization was undoubtedly rising. In this there was a strange contrast with the ancient Athenians which Dr. Inge has noticed. "The extreme sensibility to physical suffering which characterizes modern civilization arose together with Industrialism, and is most marked in the most highly industrialized countries. It has synchronized with the complete eclipse of spontaneous and unconscious artistic production, which we deplore in our time. . . . The explanation of this extreme susceptibleness must be left to psychologists; but I am convinced that we have here a case of transferred aesthetic sensibility. We can walk unmoved down the streets of Plaistow, but we cannot bear to see a horse beaten. The Athenians set up no Albert Memorials, but they tortured slave-girls in their law-courts and sent their prisoners to work in the horrible galleries of the Laureion silver-mines" (In *The Legacy of Greece*, pp. 39 f.).

This increased Humanity was part of the growth of Liberal opinions which was a feature of the period, and was seen in the increase of tolerance and also in the appeal to the Mind as a decisive factor in all matters. The Victorian Age was sincere in a rude kind of way and did not deliberately suppress or pervert truth; its prejudices, however, were so strong that truth itself was seen only through the appropriately coloured spectacles. It unquestionably had a pathetic belief in the power of logic to convince, and of the Lamp of Reason as the most illuminating of all the lights of the spirit. It was this belief which gave to the Victorians something of their certainty, a certainty which now is sought in many European countries by carefully placing the Lamp of Reason under a bushel, and bidding the people follow blindly in the steps of self-appointed guides. The most naïve tribute to the power of reason and the value of the concensus of educated opinion is to be found in a passage from the elder Mill: "Every man possessed of reason," he wrote, "is accustomed to weigh evidence, and to be guided and determined by its preponderance. When various conclusions are, with their evidence, presented with equal care and equal skill, there is a moral certainty, though some few may be misguided, that the greatest number will judge right, and that the greatest force of evidence, wherever it is, will produce the greatest impression."

Thus much of the Victorian self-confidence was based on Reason, at least among the educated; though their neighbours might, in their sphere, make its foundations rest upon prosperity and security. They certainly believed in themselves with an ardour which recalls the later Elizabethans. As Mr. Young has said: "they were not ashamed; and like the Elizabethans, their sense of the worth-whileness of everything —themselves, their age, and their country: what the Evangelicals called seriousness; the Arnoldians earnestness; Bagehot, most happily, eagerness—overflowed in sentiment and invective, loud laughter and sudden reproof." They possessed a secret which perhaps we have lost, they knew that the only sure way of enjoying life is to take it seriously. This saved them from the idle acceptance of the gifts which fortune had showered upon them and a hedonistic standard of living. They had a realized sense of their responsibility and the hardness, which at first sight seems repellent, was really a noble denial of self and the spirit in which they stooped to patient and earnest labours. It was in the Arnolds, father and son, that, with some considerable difference of emphasis and change of dogmatic background, this spirit can best be found. In the case of Thomas Arnold it is usually associated with Rugby; but already during the Laleham period, when he took private pupils, it was fully developed. This can be seen from Bonomy Price's description of the Laleham circle: "Everything about me," he wrote, "I immediately found to be most real; it was a place where a new comer at once felt that a great and earnest work was going forward. Dr. Arnold's great power as a private tutor resided in this, that he gave such an intense earnestness to life. Every pupil was made to feel that there was a work for him to do—that his happiness as well as his duty lay in doing that work well. Hence an indescribable zest was communicated to a young man's feeling about life; a strange joy came over him on discovering that he had the means of being useful, and thus of being happy; and a deep respect and ardent attachment sprang up towards him who had taught him thus to value life and his own self, and his work and mission in the world."[1] This intense feeling for the seriousness of life and of the immense significance of the effort of the individual was not unnatural in one who at the end of his not very lengthy life could contemplate the possibility of the generation in which he lived being "the last reserve of the world" and that if the then existing nations did not do God's work it would be left undone.[2]

To Matthew Arnold everything can be forgiven for the sake of that wonderful testimony of a son to his noble father, *Rugby Chapel*. He might scoff, as we saw above (p. 85), at the "intensity" of Rugby, but it was in his veins; how else could it be with one who saw in conduct three-fourths of life? He might be pontifical, or to an unfriendly eye, pompous; but he cared much for ethical attainment, even if he divorced it from the Christian dogma which had given it power in the eyes of his father.

To our own generation this perpetual concern over conduct, this ever present realization of responsibility is hard to understand. It seems so priggish and unnatural, to make life a perpetual burden. But we have gone to the opposite extreme, and live in "an age which looks more gladly on passion than on work," which is apt to scorn solid achievement and be caught by the superficial and the exciting.

The final characteristic of the Victorian Age to which I would refer was its possession of great men. Like the thirteenth century there arose in it a number of dominating personalities in almost every department of life; there were great poets and men of letters; great statesmen and administrators, both at home and abroad; great scholars and bishops; great preachers. It is possible that the tendency to hero-worship which was abroad in the nineteenth century has exaggerated the stature of some of its children; but perhaps the common expectation

---

[1] Quoted Stanley, *Life of Dr. Arnold*, p. 37.
[2] *Lectures on Modern History*, p. 31. This quotation is sometimes used as if Arnold definitely contemplated his generation, without any qualification, as the "last reserve." This is to give to him too large a measure of Victorian earnestness and self-conceit!

that men would behave in an heroic manner helped them to do so. Certainly the tradition of greatness is one that can be cultivated, since it inspires noble and ambitious natures with the desire to be different from their fellows, to be, what the slave Epictetus called, "the purple thread which gives beauty and lustre" to the texture of life. They may fail in their endeavour and realize no splendid and starry aims; but if they have remained true to themselves, their efforts will not have been entirely in vain, and the example of their striving will have given courage and incitement to unknown spectators. For as York Powell has said (referring to Sir Philip Sidney): "A nation's most valued citizens are those who set a high standard of living and culture and do it in such a manner as to make their fellows desirous of imitating them" (*Frederick York Powell*, II, pp. 118 f.).

The reign closed with no prophet and no poet of outstanding merit to make it commemorable. Even in the world of rulers there had been a sad decline. The fall of Bismarck in 1890 had removed the one great controlling figure of Europe and left power in the hands of "three of the most inept rulers in history—William II of Germany, Francis Joseph of Austria, and Nicholas II of Russia."[1] It may be that we are still too close to those days for the great men to be sufficiently prominent for us to recognize them for what they truly were. But perhaps the average standard of character and attainment had risen so high that no one of adequate force and inward energy was then living to raise himself above it. The many great and outstanding figures which stand out like beacons in the earlier years of the era did so largely because they had to make their own way, to develop their own powers, to rely upon themselves. They were outstanding because they were detached, at least in part, from the world around them; strong in legitimate self-reliance and confident in their own developed powers and judgement. Now opportunities are so multitudinous that any one of ordinary ability may achieve a career and attain to a respectable eminence. This makes it harder for any decisively to emerge above the common level.

[1] Hugh Massingham in *Great Victorians*, p. 477.

THE END OF AN EPOCH

THE VICTORIAN ACHIEVEMENT

Time may not yet suffer a complete judgement on the individuals who played their part in the drama of the period, but it has allowed some bubbles to rise to the surface and disperse, though the full work of precipitation has not yet been accomplished. So too in regard to the period itself. All attempts at generalization must still be premature ; but that does not absolve the historian from the attempt to make them. If he can do this with wisdom, and upon a basis of all the facts available, his generalizations will be a stimulus rather than a hindrance; and those who come after and can see the period with greater detachment and fuller knowledge will deal kindly with his failures. But he must not attempt to foreclose the subject and prevent further enquiry; nor must he multiply generalizations; for the unnecessary generalization is only a distraction.

There are two points of view from which the Victorian Era may be judged by those now living; the point of view of those who were born in it and know it from first hand, and the point of view of those who know it only by report. In each case prejudice must be discounted. On the one side it is difficult for us of the older generation to judge an epoch in which we have ourselves been immersed. Unconsciously its standards —intellectual, social, economic, and religious—have been imbibed and by reference to them our own training was acquired. Even if there is an absence of complacency and obscurantism, we are apt to emphasize them unduly and regard them as factors more important than actually they were. We cannot throw off entirely the effects of the atmosphere in which we once lived and moved and had our being; nor crawl out of our skins. But the Victorian Era is now removed from us by a generation and we have the criticisms of that generation to modify our own ideas and memories. But they too have prejudices which require discounting; for each generation invariably takes up a critical attitude towards that which immediately preceded it. This is due not only to close proximity, which forbids any true perspective, but also to the younger generation's imperfect acquaintance with the facts of life. To the present generation looking back the Victorian

Era seems a succession of halcyon days, a golden age of security and peace. To the ardent spirits who lived in its middle years it can never have been any such thing. They had to face the rude shock which comes when new and old are fighting for the mastery; to them, as to us, the age was one of confused transition, when old values were being abandoned for values that had yet to prove their worth. To us the idea of change is familiar; to them, before the coming of evolution, it was novel.

An age, like an institution or an individual, must be judged by its resolved purpose rather than by its actual attainment; for the latter so often depends upon a favourable conjunction of circumstances. What then was the characteristic purpose which gave to the Victorian Era its unity and meaning, gathering up the early years of the reign and shewing them completed and fulfilled in those which followed? Can we trace any such purpose? Was there any consistent, if unconscious design, being worked out, if not by man, by a Divine Hand? What was God trying to teach mankind during that era?

The predominant note of the period was one of struggle, of adaptation. We have seen it already in the world of thought, where the spirit of reform and the spirit of reaction, of tradition and progress were antagonistic. But that struggle permeated the whole structure of the age. Two tendencies, which we may call the centrifugal and the centripetal—or with Bertrand Russell the desire for Freedom and the necessity for Organization—were perpetually at war.

The Centrifugal tendency makes for variety; it is a spirit versatile and eager to follow every thought and impulse; it is the very personification of the "myriad mind" of the Greeks. Above all it is supremely individualistic. It found expression in the Liberalism which was the great characteristic doctrine of the Victorian Age. In economics it shewed itself in Free Trade, *Laissez-faire,* and the toleration and development of the whole Capitalist system; in politics by the encouragement of Democratic institutions and parliamentary government; in philosophy by the demand for freedom of thought (in this the new scientific outlook played its part), by the indulgence, especially in the middle and most brilliant years of the era, of a rather vague idealism, to this belonged the humanitarianism to which reference was made above; in religion by the growing spirit of toleration, the fruit possibly of growing indifference to the truths which underlie it, by an acceptance of Biblical Criticism, by an Ultra-Protestantism, in the sense of a reaction against Catholicism which tended perhaps unconsciously to a complete secularization of life.

The Centripetal tendency, on the contrary, is a spirit breathing a more social air; but it is restrained and even severe, a lover of proportion and of continuity, a lover, too, of order; linking together not only "individuals to each other, and states to states, but one period of organic growth to another" (W. Pater). It can be seen at work in the movement towards Institutionalism; that impulse which manifested itself in the formation of the Religious Societies, in the Oxford Movement, and in the desire for Reunion and Federation. Perhaps behind it all was the Industrial Revolution itself; for the huge scale upon which it developed demanded organization and subordination as a necessity of its existence. From it the same spirit may have passed out into regions apparently remote.

This then was the great, underlying, dual mainspring of Victorian activity and achievement—the endeavour to combine these two tendencies. It mingled in all the multiple activities of men and movements within the period, giving to them variety and richness. If the era did not fully meet the challenge which confronted it, there was an admirable attempt on its part to do so; indeed R. Garnett considers that the great secret of its strength lay in its power of "adaptation to the needs of its own day" (in *The Reign of Queen Victoria*, II, p. 493). But such a quality makes no striking appeal to posterity which has to deal with its own far different problems. Perhaps this is why we have tended to decry our fathers.

EPILOGUE—THE FUTURE

Thus Christianity in the Victorian Era responded to the various challenges which confronted it. Those challenges and the problems in which they consist still face us; though on a scale more vast and of a complexity more alarming, since they arise from a greater variety of life and experience. It is well for us that they do so; for were there no problems and no challenges we might well sink down into stagnation and self-satisfaction; and that for a Church, as for a nation, or any other society, is only another name for death, and the denial of its mission.

The Victorian Era, with all its achievements and all its failures, its opportunities and challenges, lies behind us. It has left us to face a future uncertain and perplexing. But we cannot in justice blame the Victorians and the Church of their age for failing to provide solutions in advance for the problems which beset us. The attempt to anticipate the future may amuse the amateur prophet, but his forecasts seldom find realization in the realm of fact. Certainly we cannot from the achievements of the past find full assurance for the future; so frequently an age of splendid achievement heralds one of decline and dissipation of power. Thus the Age of Elizabeth was followed by the Stuarts and the Civil War; that of Queen Anne by the commonplace drudgery of the Georges, and, in the distance, by the Napoleonic Wars. So the passing of Victoria led to a time of distraction and bloodshed, a time of searching after vague new values and a repudiation of the standards which had given to it its greatness. We have come out into rough waters and we know not whether the principles which guided the Victorians were fully true or merely delusive. Certainly many of the philosophic and secular ideas which gave meaning to the era are dead and dying; we stand on the verge of a new stage of civilization, a vast new epoch. For it seems likely that the wider age which included the reigns of the three great English queens is itself drawing to a close. Humanism, the gift of the Renaissance, with its naïve belief in man and his creative ability and power to meet his own needs, is a decaying force. In politics men are searching for some power above themselves; it may be a dictator, the superman of Nietzsche, or the Totalitarian State, or even a collective Internationalism. The times cry out for a new birth —not of artistic or intellectual life, but of spiritual—and for that ethical achievement which it alone can make actual; for society is in danger of breaking up, and needs remoulding.

But do not the vain searchings of man in art, in philosophy, and even in politics, unconsciously betoken his need of God? He is the only force of potency adequate to the task. Peace can only emerge from the convulsions of the present by a revived spirituality, by the dawn of a new era of faith. But of that dawn there is at present but little sign; that is in the sense of a renewed desire for Orthodox Christianity, or even for Chiistian ethics.

The sadness which marked a past generation when reluctantly it parted with the historic faith is found no longer. "Men have for the most part," said Dr. Figgis, "done with lamenting their lost faith. Sentimental tears over the happy, simple, Christendom of their fathers are a thing of the past" (*The Gospel and Human Needs*, p. 152). So too with Christian ethics. Even in the Victorian Era there were signs already, here and there, that a great deal of Christian morality might be discarded and disowned. Such a repudiation was not at all common, but it was sufficiently so for A. M. Fairbairn addressing the Congregational Union in 1883 to declare that "Society approves what it could not bear were it sensitive in conscience and reverent in heart. The atmosphere around it is becoming less favourable to belief; religion is losing its old sanctity because without its old supremacy" (*Studies in Religion and Theology*, pp. 73 f.). None the less, much of practical Christianity has been woven into the texture of the mind of the race. This is an opportunity for fresh advance, if nothing more.

A historian of religion is apt to become *laudator temporis acti*, to look wistfully at the days that are gone and to confess that they were greater days than these. For though we may not realize it the rationalism of the world around us is deep in our bones, and chills the very breath of our souls. The vision of the painter, and the voice of the poet we pass by unheeding, and the glory of God in natural things. So we sink down into carelessness and sloth, "sit at home by the fire and fatten a lazy body"—as W. B. Yeats has put it in *The Celtic Twilight*; or spend our powers in a restless activity—often meaningless, often quite harmful—seeking we know not what. Luxury and comfort, the munificent products of applied science, lead only to a concentration on the things of the senses. To rescue the world from this mundane materialism men must be made to realize that presence of the unseen which gave depth and refinement to the lives of an earlier generation. Man has the ability to realize the unseen and he can never be content without it. Religion must not be looked upon as a thrifty housewife might look upon a labour-saving device, useful doubtless, but by no means essential. Religion is necessary to the human soul for its completion. "Remove God from the universe," wrote Mr. Middleton Murry in *Keats and Shakespeare*, "and you may very well remove a faculty from the human soul." But it can't be done. The faculty is there and must be satisfied. So in the face of confusion and difficulty there is a turning back to "Fundamentalism" and a "going over to Rome" on the part of some; the giving up of the struggle and the acceptance of an infallible authority, be it Church or Bible, which may stunt the growth of the soul. What we need is a faith which will combine Reason and Insight, Intellect and Emotion, Rationalism and Mysticism.

How we are to reach such a faith does not yet appear; we can but search the heavens for the signs of its coming; and in our own lives and surroundings strive to realize it. Perhaps I can best end by quoting the opinion of one who has, I suppose, exercised a greater influence over English religious thought in this post-Victorian Age than any of his contemporaries. Dr. Inge thinks quite definitely that a choice lies before us, "between the great international Catholic Church and what Auguste Sabatier called the religion of the spirit. . . . Like most other great philosophical problems, this question is largely one of temperament. Christianity has found room for both types. I believe, however, that the aberrations or exaggerations of institutionalism have been, and are, more dangerous, and further removed from the spirit of Christianity than those of mysticism, and that we must look to the latter type, rather than to the former, to give life to the next religious revival" (*Outspoken Essays*, I, pp. 239 and 242). Thus the two tendencies which marked the Victorian Era, the centrifugal and the centripetal, are with us still, to give variety and richness to this age as to that. There is life and there is struggle; and we can thank God that our lot is not cast in a day when ardent souls grow weary because of the spent forces around them. The future lies in His hands, He can build up and He can pull down. The civilization in which we live, like every civilization before it, exists on a knife edge, its "stability is but balance";[1] and if it should go down in blood and ruin, we believe that God has prepared some better thing for us. For we seek no earthly kingdom, but the *Civitas Dei*, that pilgrim city of Christ the king,[2] which is confined by no material walls or foundations because its builder and maker is God.

---

[1] Bridges, *The Testament of Beauty*, I.16.
[2] Augustine, *De Civ. Dei*, I.xxxv, *peregrina civitas regis Christi*.

INDEX

Abercrombie, Lascelies, 342
Acton, Lord, 283, 415, 460 f.
Adam, James, 357
Adderley, J. G., 268
Additional Curates Society, 39
Aeschylus, 282
Aids to Faith, 147
Aitken, Robert, 423 f.
Aitken, W. Hay, 424
"Alabama" Dispute, 194, 492
Alford, Dean, 42 f., 190, 203, 293, 465
Allon, Dr., 191, 463, 474, 480 f.
A.L.O.E., 346
Andrewes, Bishop, 46, 108, 345
Archaeology, 175 ff.
Architecture, 353 ff.
Aristotle, 155, 499 f.
Armstrong, Edward, 8
Arnold, Matthew, 85, 322, 459 ff., 500, 503; on Education, 312; and the Church of England, 470; Theological Writings, 277, 282 f., 348
Arnold, Thomas, Dr., 40, 45, 111, 116, 150, 298, 364, 368, 502 f.; and Rugby, 83–5; on the Church, 106, 480; on Social Conditions, 243, 254; Influence, 48, 181 f., 298, 312
Arnold, Thomas, Junior, 322, 460
Arrowsmith, Edwin, 445
Art and Religion, 356 ff.
Asquith, H., Lord Oxford, 195, 339, 490, 499
Athenians, The, 19, 406, 501
Atonement, The, 210, 280 f.
Augustine, St., 100, 179, 263 f., 396
Austen, Jane, 39, 339

Bacon, Francis, 153
Bagot, Bishop, 99
Bain, Alexander, 287
Baptismal Regeneration, 93, 142, 206, 227 ff., 473
Baptist, The, 336
Baptist Magazine, The, 336
Baptist Messenger, The, 336
Baptist Times, The, 336
Baptists, The, 54 f., 91, 208, 336, 423, 457, 486
Barber, George, 366, 465
Baring, Bishop, 68, 203
Barnett, Canon, 137, 350, 363, 417; Social Work, 257, 429 ff.
Barrett, Alfred, 457

Barrie, J. M., 334
Barrington, Bishop, 114
Barry, F. R., Canon, 261, 397
Barry, W., Canon, 105
Barton, John, 220, 398
Bate, Dean, 250
Bateman, Josiah, 76, 110
Baur, F. C., 183 f.
Baxter, Richard, 205
Baynes, Hamilton, Bishop, 186
Beale, Miss, 319
Bell, Dr., 87
Bell, G. K. A., Bishop, 362, 418
Benn, A. W., 281, 415
Bennett, W. J. E., 233
Benson, A. C., 48, 120, 130, 352, 490
Benson, E. F., 416
Benson, E. W., Archbishop, 48, 295, 302, 308, 309, 374, 448; and Cambridge, 286, 294, 295; Bishop of Truro, 204, 214, 354, 424, 432; Archbishop of Canterbury, 186, 196, 204, 479
Benson, R. M., 222, 366, 437
Bentham, Jeremy, 82, 134 ff.
Beresford Hope, Alexander, 230, 324
Bergson, 17
Berry, C. A., Dr., 192, 482, 487
Besant, Annie, Mrs., 421
Bethune-Baker, J. F., Professor, 299, 307
Bettany, F. G., 210 f., 268, 310, 437
Bevan, Miss, 346
Beveridge, Bishop, 108
Bible, The, 55 f., 155, 277, 315
Biblical Criticism, 141, 146, 175 ff., 210, 239 f., 273, 278
Bickersteth, E. H., Bishop, 369
Bickersteth, Edward, 345, 373, 398
Bingham, H., 493
Binney, Thomas, 70, 461, 463, 466, 472
Birrell, Augustine, 73, 489
Birrell, C. M., 73
Bishop, T. B., 445
Bismarck, 198 f., 408, 504
Blackfriars, 336
Blackwood, Stevenson, 222, 427
Blake, William, 35, 248, 288
Blomfield, Bishop, 44, 66, 77, 230, 233, 411
Bloxam, M. H., 232
Body, Canon, 222
Bonn Conferences, 478

Bonney, T. G., 154, 191
Booth, Charles, 137, 198
Booth, William, 425 f.
Booth, William, Mrs., 422, 426, 440
Borromeo, Cardinal, 442
Bosanquet, Bernard, 241
Boutmy, Emile, 137, 472
Bowden, J. W., 76, 117
Boys' Brigade, 444
Boys Smith, J. S., 35
Bradlaugh, Charles, 210 f., 273
Bradley, F. H., 241, 273, 276 f.
Bradshaw, Henry, 286
Brainerd, David, 376
Bray, Charles, 151
Bridges, Robert, 511
Bright, John, 84, 126, 194, 196, 255, 315, 463
Bristol Riots, 41, 186
British Association, 163, 168, 169
British and Foreign Bible Society, 31, 37 f., 478
British and Foreign School Society, 87, 89
British Banner, 141, 142, 335
British Critic, 332
British Magazine, 107
British Standard, 142, 336
British Weekly, 192, 333, 334, 446, 452, 457
Broadlands, 225
Brodrick, G. C., 80, 82
Brontë, Charlotte, 340
Brontë, Emily, 288, 289, 341 f.
Brooke, A. E., Canon, 309
Brooke, Stopford, 140, 207, 278, 281, 365 f., 373 f., 465
Brougham, Lord, 82, 88
Brown, H. F., 283, 330
Browne, E. H., Bishop, 147, 203, 478
Browning, E. B., 286, 342
Browning, Robert, 52, 141, 286, 342 f.
Bryce, Lord, 43, 84, 275, 329
Buchanan, Robert, 343
Buckland, Dean, 154, 168
Buckle, H. T., 173
Buller, Charles, 471
Bunsen, Baron von, 116, 183
Burder, G., 37
Burge, Bishop, 483
Burgon, Dean, 147, 148, 308
Burke, Bernard, Sir, 402
Burke, Edmund, 11, 472
Burne-Jones, E., Sir, 352
Burns, W. C., 384
Buss, Miss, 319
Butler, Abbot, 130

Butler, Bishop, 132, 170, 348, 499
Butler, Charles, 115
Butler, Josephine, Mrs., 257, 412
Butler, Samuel, 166, 344
Buxton, Thomas Fowell, Sir, 23 ff., 32, 255, 478
Byron, Lord, 339
Bywater, Ingram, 324, 449 f.

Cagliostro, 35
Caird, Edward, 131
Calvinism, 54–5, 209, 377, 464
Cambridge Inter-Collegiate Christian Union, 325 ff.
Cambridge School, The, 48, 132, 292 ff.
Cambridge Seven, The, 220, 391, 398 f.
Cambridge University, 38, 187, 286, 379; Religion in, 212, 219 f., 324 ff.; and Dissenters, 74 f.
Caius, 382
Emmanuel, 298
King's, 80
Queens', 38, 80
St. John's, 293
Selwyn, 321
Trinity, 80, 81, 143, 144, 294
Camden Society, 230
Campbell, Dr., 141 f., 335 f.
Campion, W. J. H., 240
Canning, 32
Carey, William, 377 ff.
Carlile, Wilson, Preb., 428
Carlyle, Thomas, 29, 173, 178, 251, 273, 499; and German Thought, 132; on the Press, 328; on Social Conditions, 29, 250; Influence, 138 ff., 322
Carpenter, J. Estlin, 96, 135, 139, 274
Carpenter, Lant, Dr., 71
Carpenter, S. C., Dean, 8, 43 f., 47, 207, 228, 240, 379, 498
Carpenter, W. Boyd, Bishop, 369, 428, 459 f., 466
Carter, T. T., Canon, 440
Casson, Stanley, 175
Cathedrals, 431 ff.
Catholic Times, The, 336
Cecil, Gwendolen, Lady, 65, 201, 226
Chalmers, Dr., 335
Chamberlain, Joseph, 260, 315
Chambers, R. W., 155
Champneys, William, 67 f.
Channing, Dr., 149, 151
Charity Organisation Society, The, 256 f.
Charles, Thomas, 57
Chartism, 62 ff.

INDEX

Chase, F. H., Bishop, 299
Chateaubriand, 123
Chavasse, F. J., Bishop, 323
Cheltenham Ladies' College, 319
Chesterton, G. K., 35, 59, 84, 104, 352, 369
Children's Special Service Mission, 444 f.
Chillingworth, 55
China Inland Mission, 384 f., 391 ff.
Christian, The, 218, 334
Christian Endeavour Movement, 444
Christian Herald, 334
Christian Observer, The, 331, 412
Christian Remembrancer, The, 41, 332, 437
Christian Social Union, 268 f.
Christian Socialists, The, 64, 250, 266 ff.
Christian Witness, 335
Christian World, The, 334
Christian Year, The, 40
Christopher, Canon, 323
Church Army, The, 428
Church Association, The, 235
Church Attendance, 77 f.
Church Building, 75 f., 207, 353 ff., 450
Church Congress, 237, 241, 439
Church Lads' Brigade, 444
Church Missionary Society, 25, 30, 377 ff., 387 ff., 479
Church of England Newspaper, 333
Church of England Zenana Missionary Society, 391
Church Pastoral Aid Society, 39, 67, 206, 236
Church Quarterly Review, 333
Church Rates, 72 f.
Church, Richard William, Dean, 21, 99 f., 104, 109, 112, 123, 127, 187, 203 f., 226, 280, 295, 361 f., 420, 465, 496; Schooldays, 41, 119; and Newman, 120 f., 309, 345; and St. Paul's, 333, 433, 474; and *The Guardian*, 333; Tolerant Outlook, 142, 164, 182, 208, 240 f., 482
Church Times, The, 333
Churchmen's Union, The, 496 f.
Churton, Archdeacon, 232
Clapham Sect, The, 47, 331
Clapton Sect, The, 47
Clark, Francis, 444
Clarkson, Thomas, 23
Clifford, John, Dr., 140, 150, 487
Close, Francis, Dean, 67, 259, 460
Clough, A. H., 150, 209
Clutton-Brock, A., 17, 244, 252, 352, 355, 357 f.
Cobbe, Frances Power, 288

Cobbett, William, 15, 27
Cobden, Richard, 84, 196, 463
Cogan, Eli, 52
Coke, Dr., 379
Colenso, Bishop, 148 f., 185 f., 382
Coleridge, S. T., 11, 138 f., 288, 307, 309, 339; and German Thought, 132; on Social Conditions, 250; Influence, 103 ff., 135, 144, 181, 292 f., 309
Collier, John, 166
Collier, S. F., 431
Collingwood, W. G., 251, 360
Colonial and Continental Church Society, 394
Comte, Auguste, 136 ff., 269, 323, 362
Conan Doyle, A., Sir, 287, 339
Condorcet, 410
Congregationalist, The, 336
Congregationalists, The, 51, 54, 91, 423, 456, 463 f., 485
Congreve, R., 137, 330
Contemporary Review, The, 279, 483
Convocation, 237
Conybeare, W. J., 190, 293
Cook, F. C., 147
Cook, S. A., Professor, 175
Copleston, Bishop, 40, 43, 46, 48
Cornhill Magazine, The, 251
Cornish, F. Warre, 36, 37, 50, 74 f., 77 f., 394, 396, 440 f.
Cornish, F. Warre, Mrs., 120
Cotton, G. L., Bishop, 420
Coulton, G. G., Dr., 130
Coupland, Professor R., 23, 26
Cowper, William, 372
Cowper-Temple Clause, 313
Cowper-Temple, William, 225
Crabbe, George, 86
Creed, J. M., Professor, 35
Creighton, Louise, 56, 112, 174
Creighton, Mandell, Bishop, 68, 92, 130, 170 f., 246, 279 f., 316, 323, 406, 476 f.; as Historian, 174, 300; as Bishop, 498; on Education, 316; on Worship, 371; and the Student Christian Movement, 323
Cripps, A. S., 400
Croce, B., 401
Cromwell, Oliver, 82
Cross, F. L., 159, 287
Cross, J. W., 139, 151
Cross, Richard, 198
Crowther, Bishop, 382
Cuddesdon College, 230, 449, 453, 454
Cunningham, J. W., 222
Curtis, Lionel, 261

515

Daily Telegraph, 328, 388
Dale, R. W., Dr., 279, 295, 310, 321, 335 f., 355, 366, 374, 461 f., 469, 485 ff.
Dalton, John, 153, 168
Dante, 309
Darby, J. N., 57
Darlow, T. H., 212, 366
Darwin, Charles, 153 ff., 164, 167 ff., 386
Daubeny, Archdeacon, 47, 76, 114 f.
Davidson, James, 341
Davidson, R. T., Archbishop, 394, 455
Davidson, Samuel, 142
Davies, J. Llewellyn, 297
Davison, John, 181
Davy, Humphry, 168
Dawson, Christopher, 244, 248, 253, 406, 410
Dawson, George, 462
De Maistre, J., 123
De Quincey, Thomas, 54
De Vere, Aubrey, 106
Dearmer, Canon, 268
Denison, Edward, 429
Derby, Lord, 195, 203
Dickens, Charles, 29, 254, 339, 343 f., 443
Didsbury College, 458, 483
Digby, Kenelm, 115
Disraeli, Benjamin, 125, 135, 163 f., 198; Education, 52, 84; as Statesman, 195, 199; on Social Conditions, 90, 244, 254; use of Patronage, 203, and the Church, 235, 425, 434, 448, 470, 473 f.
Dobree, Bonomy, 345
Dods, Marcus, Dr., 284 f.
Dolling, Father, 112
Döllinger, Dr., 118
Donaldson, F. L., Canon, 268
Dorner, 183
Dowden, E., 62, 277, 286, 342 f.
Drama, The, 338 f., 360
Draper, W. H., 320
Driver, S. R., Professor, 192
Drummond, Henry, 146, 212 f., 219 f., 349, 351, 422, 462
Drummond, J. S., 192
Dublin Review, The, 336
Duchesne, 477
Duff, Alexander, 380 f., 383
Duncan-Jones, A. S., Dean, 127
Durham Letter, The, 125 f.
Durham University, 82 f.

Ecce Homo, 185, 221
Ecclesiastical Commission, The, 69

Ecclesiastical Titles Bill, 126, 235
Eclectic Review, The, 332, 335
Ede, Moore, Dean, 296 f.
Edgeworth, Maria, 339
Edinburgh Review, The, 329
Eliot, George, 151, 183, 344, 346, 415, 464
Eliot, T. S., 276, 343
Ellicott, Bishop, 147, 203, 293
Elliott, Henry Venn, 67, 76, 214, 362, 365, 383
Ellman, E. B., 44 f.
Elmslie, Professor, 183, 451, 452
Emerson, R. W., 139 ff., 322
Emery, Archdeacon, 237
Engels, 243, 247
English Church Union, The, 235
English Churchman, The, 332
Episcopate, The, 42 ff., 68, 202 ff., 303, 446, 481, 488
Erasmus, 53, 115, 142, 187
Erskine of Linlathen, 282, 292
Ervine, St. John, 425 f.
Escott, T. H. S., 64, 82, 328, 402
Essays and Reviews, 142, 146 ff., 185, 238
Establishment, The, 70, 206 f., 469 ff.
Eternal Punishment, 55, 280 f.
Evangelical Magazine, The, 331
Evangelicals, The, 48 ff., 107 ff., 141, 204 f., 469, 496
Ewald, 177, 187
Exhibition, The Great, 65, 125, 349, 432
Expository Times, The, 336 f.

Fairbairn, A. M., 182 f., 275, 278, 317, 374, 375, 451, 485, 509; and Mansfield College, 323, 456 f.; on the Oxford Movement, 112, 241, 473; and the Establishment, 470, 471, 473, 489
Faraday, Michael, 168
Farrar, Dean, 183, 281, 434, 461
Feurbach, 137, 151
Figgis, J. N., Dr., 180, 262, 282, 283, 341, 435, 509
Fisher, H. A. L., 194
Fitch, Joshua, Sir, 85
FitzGerald, Edward, 500
Forster, William, 312 f.
Fortnightly Review, The, 273
Foster, John, 55, 335
Fowler, J. H., 94, 259, 484
Fox, George, 162
Fox, H. W., 383
Fox, William, 443
France, Anatole, 190

INDEX

France, Catholic Revival in, 103, 123
Fraser, A. G., 326
Fraser, Donald, 327
Fraser, James, Bishop, 202, 321
Freeman, Austin, 246
Freeman, E. A., 173 f.
Fremantle, W. H., Dean, 257, 482
French Revolution, The, 11 ff., 23, 105, 172, 404
French, T. Valpy, Bishop, 383 f.
Friend, The, 336
Froude, J. A., 114, 119, 174, 251, 322, 470
Froude, R. Hurrell, 23, 40, 92 ff., 108, 118, 420, 474
Fry, Elizabeth, 53, 256, 258, 438
Fuller, Andrew, 377
Fullerton, W. B., 359, 431, 436
Fust, H. Jenner, Sir, 228 f.

Gairdner, W. H. Temple, 286, 326, 360, 389, 392
Galsworthy, John, 495
Gambling, 245
Gardiner, Allen, 386
Gardner, Percy, Professor, 282
Garnett, R., 329, 339, 507
Gaselee, S., Sir, 230
Gaskell, Mrs., 344, 415
George, Henry, 198
George III, 13, 17, 31, 87
George IV, 14
German Thought, 38, 74, 132 ff., 182 ff., 293
Gibbon, Edward, 76, 173
Gidney, W. T., 39
Gilmour, James, 391
Girls' Friendly Society, 441 f.
Girton College, 321
Gladstone, W. E., 13, 39, 61, 83, 97, 129, 194, 257, 309, 409, 459 f., 463, 469; as Statesman, 73, 195 ff., 313, 407, 491; use of Patronage, 203 f.; and Dissent, 197, 315, 474 f.
Glover, T. R., Dr., 181, 406, 407
Godwin, Mary, 412
Goethe, 7, 131, 155, 339
Golightly, C. P., 111
Gooch, G. P., 172, 175
Good Words, 335
Goode, Dean, 228
Gordon, Charles, General, 201
Gordon, George, Lord, 31
Gore, Charles, Bishop, 356 ff., 372 f., 438, 453, 466, 481, 498; and *Lux Mundi*, 238 ff.; on Social Conditions, 268

Gorham Judgement, The, 120, 206, 227 ff., 462
Goschen, Lord, 254
Gosse, Edmund, 211, 442
Goulburn, E. M., Dean, 148, 459
Gowen, H. H., Dr., 157, 178
Graham, James, Sir, 90
Grammar Schools, 86, 317; King Edward's, Birmingham, 294
Grant, Charles, 396
Gray, Bishop, 186, 382, 397
Green, J. R., 174, 184, 278, 429
Green, S. F., 236
Green, T. H., 136, 241, 274, 288, 321 f.
Greenwood, G., 481
Gregory, Benjamin, 56 f., 86, 215, 228, 323, 484 f.
Gregory, Robert, Dean, 95, 101, 121, 232, 427, 433
Greville Memoirs, 70, 125, 329
Grey, Lord, 21, 70
Grimm, The Brothers, 178
Grote, George, 82, 89, 134, 194
Guardian, The, 333
Guiney, L. I., 23, 94
Gurney, Edmund, 286
Gurney, Elizabeth, 53, 258
Gurney, W. Brodie, 443
Guthrie, Dr., 460, 486
Gwatkin, Professor, 174, 293, 307

Haddon, A. C., 148
Hadleigh Conference, 95
Haldane, Alexander, 332
Haldane, J. S., 170
Halifax, Lord, 130, 477
Hall, Newman, 466, 480
Hall, Robert, 27, 53, 54, 56, 335
Hamilton, Frederick, Lord, 245, 417
Hamilton, W. Kerr, Bishop, 50, 202, 432, 448
Hammond, J. L., 196
Hampden, Bishop, 75, 96 f.
Hannah, John, 483
Hannington, Bishop, 388, 398
Harcourt, William, Sir, 492
Hardy, Thomas, 344
Hare, Julius, Archdeacon, 48, 80, 138, 143, 182, 293
Harford-Battersby, T. D., 222 f.
Harnack, Adolf von, 296, 303, 309, 486
Harris, Dr., 463
Harris, John, Sir, 24 f.
Harris, Reader, 224
Harrison, Frederic, 137, 147
Hastings, James, Dr., 337
Hatch, Edwin, 305

Haweis, Dr., 377
Haweis, H. R., 278
Hawker, Dr., 377
Hawkins, Edward, 87
Hayes, J. G., 436
Headlam, A. C., Bishop, 296
Headlam, Stewart, 211, 267 f., 437, 455
Heber, Bishop, 373, 378
Heeney, Bertal, Canon, 395
Hegel, 136, 155, 183, 227, 273 f., 276, 288
Heine, 248
Hengstenberg, 183
Hennell, Charles, 151
Herbert, George, 107, 399
Herder, 172
Herford, C. H., 74, 138, 248
Herodotus, 305
Herschel, John, Sir, 154
Heurtley, Professor, 148
Hicks, E. L., Bishop, 94, 259, 484
Highbury, St. John's Hall, 454
Hill, David, 391
Hill, Octavia, 257
Hill, Rowland, 38, 53
Hoare, Canon, 67, 216, 332
Hodder, Edwin, 38, 195, 213
Hodgkin, Thomas, 112, 214 f.
Holborn Review, The, 336
Holland, H. Scott, Canon, 59, 241, 274, 318, 323, 358, 374, 407, 461, 466, 490, 491; and Social Conditions, 262, 265, 268; Writings of, 167, 170, 240
Holland, W. E. S., 226
Holmes, O. W., 344
Holyoake, G. J., 267
Homer, 84, 165
Homerton College, 164, 456
Hook, Dean, 42, 66, 68, 438
Hooker, J. D., Sir, 167
Hooker, Richard, 46, 167, 228, 237, 345
Hope-Scott, James, 120
Hopkins, Ellice, 257
Hopkins, Evan, 222
Horace, 407
Horne, Silvester, 27, 33, 53, 213, 258, 303, 342, 366, 374, 457, 462, 466, 484
Horsley, Bishop, 36
Hort, F. J. A., 145, 148, 164, 212, 228, 265, 286, 292 ff., 364 f., 448
Horton, R. F., Dr., 137, 191, 221, 224, 324, 360, 447, 459, 466, 485, 487
Housman, Laurence, 411
How, Bishop Walsham, 428, 429
Howley, Archbishop, 66, 76

Howson, Dean, 190, 293, 439
Hudson the Railway King, 402
Hughes, Hugh Price, 143, 196 f., 223 ff., 280, 344, 360, 363, 444, 475; and the "Forward Movement," 309, 336, 431, 440; and Reunion, 482, 484, 487 f.
Hughes, J., 37
Hughes, Thomas, 43, 266, 311, 316, 366
Hume, David, 173, 381
Hume, Joseph, 41
Hunt, Holman, 352
Hunt, John, 146 f., 164, 293
Huntingdon, Selina, Countess of 438, 458
Hutton, A. W., 114, 120, 125, 127, 129, 314, 459
Hutton, R. H., 331
Hutton, W. H., Dean, 106, 174
Huxley, Aldous, 135
Huxley, T. H., 138, 151, 163, 166, 170, 272 f., 275
Hyacinth, Père, 482
Hymns, 371 ff.

Ignatius, Father, 241, 438
Ignatius, Father; *see* Spencer, George
Illingworth, J. R., 238 f., 241
In Memoriam, 149, 157
Independent, The, 335
Industrial Revolution, The, 16 ff., 62 ff., 175, 193, 243, 403 ff., 418 f.
Inge, W. R., Dr., 111, 127, 162, 246, 272, 292, 496 f., 501; on the Oxford Movement, 102, 113; on Social Conditions, 156, 209, 264, 405; and Mysticism, 288 f., 359, 510
Irish Church, The, 206
Irvine, Canon, 102
Irving, Edward, 54, 57
Irvingism, 51, 54, 57 f.
Islington College (C.M.S.), 454
Islington Conference, 221 f., 236

Jacks, L. P., 461, 465
Jackson, W. W., 310
James, J. Angell, 77, 462, 486
James, William, 169
Jay, William, 365, 462
Jeremie, Dean, 203
Jewell, Bishop, 228
Jews, The, 33 f., 38, 210
John, Griffith, 390
Johnson, J. O., Canon, 119, 230, 433
Johnson, Samuel, Dr., 84
Jones, Mary, 37

INDEX

Jones of Nayland, 46
Jourdain, Eleanor, 291
Journal of Theological Studies, The, 299, 305
Jowett, Benjamin, 149, 275, 325, 368, 374, 422, 427 f., 448; and Liberal Theology, 143, 146, 241, 279 ff.
Jubilee, The, 193, 201, 369
Jubilee, The Diamond, 328, 369, 492

Kaiserwerth Institution, 439
Kant, 132
Keats, John, 329, 339
Keble, John, 45, 109, 150, 240, 297, 346; on Church and State, 32, 92, 474; and the Oxford Movement, 92 ff., 226, 229; as Poet, 40, 104, 107, 167
Keble, Tom, 121, 232
Keith-Falconer, Ian, 384
Kelham, 437 f., 454
Kelly, Father, 437 f.
Ken, Bishop, 46, 93
Kenyon, F. G., Sir, 308
Kenyon, Ruth, 242
Keswick, 223 f., 325, 327, 334, 373, 392
King, Bryan, 234
King, Edward, Bishop, 112, 236, 321, 414, 416
King, William, 443
King's College, London, 82, 281, 333
Kingsley, Charles, 42, 65, 145, 150, 281, 288, 297, 310, 331, 363, 413; and Social Conditions, 41, 266, 357; and Nature, 164 f.; Novels of, 344, 346 f., 432
Kipling, Rudyard, 368, 492
Kirk, K. E., Professor, 361
Knox, John, 443
Knutsford, Lady, 23
Krapf, J. L., 382
Kuenen, 187

Lacey, T. A., Canon, 477
Lady Margaret Hall, 321
Lambeth Conferences, 237, 269, 394 f., 481
Lammenais, 123
Lancashire Independent College, 142, 456
Lancaster, Joseph, 87
Lang, Cosmo Gordon, Archbishop, 451
Lansbury, George, 247
Law, H. W. and I., 230, 324, 412
Law, Thomas, 487
Lawrence, Archbishop, 227
Lecky, W. E. H., 16

Lee, J. Prince, Bishop, 48, 202, 294, 448
Legg, Wickham, 110, 476
Legge, James, Professor, 384
Leisure Hour, The, 335
Lenwood, Frank, 375
Leo XIII, Pope, 130
Leopold, King of the Belgians, 13, 45
Lessing, 172, 179, 357
Liberal Theology, 47 ff., 93, 97, 105 f., 134, 138 f., 143 ff., 207 ff., 297 f., 348, 496 ff.
Liberation Society, The, 473, 489
Liddell, Robert, Hon., 233
Liddon, H. P., Canon, 71, 93, 105, 117 ff., 189 f., 203, 228 f., 240, 433, 449, 453, 474, 478; on the Evangelicals, 49, 107 f.; and Dissent, 70, 212; and Ritual, 230, 232; on Education, 83, 320 f., 413 f.; as Preacher, 213, 459 ff.
Lidgett, J. Scott, Dr., 487
Life of Faith, The, 334
Lightfoot, John, 162
Lightfoot, Joseph Barber, Bishop, 148, 279, 292–6, 298, 302 ff., 433; and Foreign Missions, 375, 390; no Theologian, 174, 295; as Bishop of Durham, 295, 301, 310, 424
Lilley, A. L., Canon, 268
Lincoln Judgement, The, 236
Lind, Jenny, 358
Liverpool, Lord, 76
Livingstone, David, 381 f., 387, 398
Lloyd, Bishop, 32
Loch, C. S., Sir, 257
Lock, Walter, Professor, 32, 46, 121, 239, 299
Locke, John, 35, 134
London City Mission, 422 f.
London Collegiate School, 319
London Missionary Society, 377 ff.
London Quarterly Review, The, 336
London Society for Promoting Christianity among the Jews, 38 f., 210
London University, 81 f.
Longley, Archbishop, 66, 203
Louis Philippe, 62
Loveless, George, 27 f.
Lovett, William, 63
Lowder, Charles, 234 f.
Lowe, Robert, Lord Sherbrooke, 312, 314
Lucretius, 154
Ludlow, J. M., 266
Lull, Raymond, 377
Lunn, Henry, Sir, 316, 481 f.
Luther, Martin, 50

519

Lux Mundi, 142, 237 ff.
Lyell, Charles, 154
Lynch, T. T., 141
Lyra Apostolica, 107
Lyte, H. C. Maxwell, 83
Lyttelton, Albert, Bishop, 239
Lytton, Bulwer, Lord, 339

Macaulay, T. B., Lord, 24, 84, 149, 173, 256, 311, 329, 381
Macaulay, Zachary, 23, 37, 82, 331
MacCarthy, Mary, 352
MacDonald, J. Ramsay, 64, 259
Mackay, A. M., 388, 451
Mackenzie, C. F., Bishop, 382 f.
Mackenzie, J. K., Dr., 391
Macmillan, Daniel, 308
McIlvane, Bishop, 213
McLaren, Alexander, Dr., 466 f.
McLean, N., 309
McLeod, Fiona, 288
McNeile, Hugh, Dean, 68, 203, 460
Machiavelli, 245
Magee, Archbishop, 459
Major, H. D. A., Dr., 9, 68, 416, 428, 454, 459
Maltby, Bishop, 71
Manchester College, 56, 458
Manchester University, 82
Manners-Sutton, Archbishop, 43, 44
Manning, H. E., Cardinal, 118, 122, 127 ff., 231, 423, 459, 476; Secession, 93, 128, 228
Mansel, H. L., Dean, 147, 274, 275
Mansfield College, 322 f., 456 ff.
Mant, Bishop, 227
Marchant, James, Sir, 208, 243, 461
Marriott, Charles, 189, 226, 454
Marriott, J. A. R., Sir, 62, 493
Marsh, Herbert, Bishop, 37, 80, 132, 293, 372
Martineau, Harriet, 78
Martineau, James, 96, 135, 140, 148, 149, 151, 171, 182, 214, 274, 362 f., 460
Martyn, Henry, 93, 97, 358, 377, 379 f., 382, 391, 400
Marvin, F. S., 17, 29, 35, 85, 179, 251, 271, 340
Marx, Karl, 200, 247, 253
Mason, A. J., Canon, 214, 310, 348, 354, 370, 424
Massingham, Hugh, 411, 504
Masterman, C. F. G., 18, 144 f., 260, 262
Materialism, 158, 165 f., 271 f., 286
Matheson, P. E., 275, 292, 367

Maurice, F. D., 48, 50, 56, 65, 81, 293, 307, 333; Joins the Church of England, 75, 294; Teaching, 144 f., 178, 265, 281 f., 300; and Social Problems, 250, 266 f.; Influence, 138, 145, 241, 297, 309 f., 331
Maurice, Michael, 56
Mazzini, 62
Meeson, J. A., 487
Melbourne, Lord, 28, 60, 87, 96
Melvill, Henry, Canon, 216, 460
Mercer Wilson, R., 10, 395
Meredith, George, 344
Merz, 154
Methodist Magazine, The, 331, 336
Methodist Recorder, The, 336
Methodist Revival, The, 36, 51 f., 54 f., 215 f.
Methodist Times, The, 336, 487
Methodists, The, 53, 56 f., 91, 109, 111, 215, 228, 309, 336, 366, 457 f., 483 f., 486
Metternich, 13
Meyer, F. B., 218, 224, 290, 359, 371, 466
Miall, Edward, 335
Michaelis, 293
Middleton, Conyers, 178
Mildmay Conference, 217, 222
Mildmay Deaconesses, 440
Mill, James, 82, 134, 136, 501 f.
Mill, John Stuart, 113, 135 f., 138, 195, 249, 273 f., 323, 414
Millais, John, Sir, 352
Miller, J. C., 68
Miller, John, 163
Milligan, G., 305
Milman, H. H., Dean, 186, 432
Milner, Bishop, 115
Milner, Isaac, Dean, 38, 80, 106
Milnes, R. Monckton, Lord Houghton, 16, 106, 420, 458
Milton, 159 f., 469, 484
Mirfield, 438, 454
Moberly, Anne, 291
Moberly, C. A. E., 85, 112 f., 291, 364
Moberly, George, Bishop, 42, 66, 85, 320, 479
Moberly, R. C., 239
Modern Churchman, The, 156, 170, 175, 247, 285, 296, 305
Moffatt, R., 380 f.
Moll, W. E., 268
Monk, Bishop, 43
Month, The, 336
Moody and Sankey, 211, 212 ff., 325, 373, 422, 424, 428

520

INDEX

Moore, A. L., 158 f., 161, 164, 239, 241, 288
Moore, George, 246
Moorhouse, Bishop, 289 f., 466
Moravian Missions, 376, 397
More, Hannah, 345, 348, 438
Morgan, Campbell, Dr., 217, 466
Morley, John, Lord, 18, 61, 88, 113, 125, 146, 149 f., 194 f., 197, 204, 211, 237, 273, 283, 314 f., 460, 499
Morris, Caleb, 463
Morris, William, 17, 244, 251 ff., 351 f., 355, 358, 404 f.
Morrison, Robert, 380
Mothers' Union, The, 441
Moule, George, Bishop, 384, 390 f.
Moule, Handley C. G., Bishop, 49, 108, 150, 165, 216, 219 f., 223, 301, 307, 371, 386 f., 460, 471 f., 494
Moule, Henry, 49, 216, 265
Moulton, J. H., Dr., 305
Moulton, W. F., Dr., 182, 303, 317, 457, 469, 479
Mountain, G. J., Bishop, 395
Mountain, J. J., Bishop, 395
Mozley, J. B., Professor, 94, 96, 100, 121, 127, 142, 226, 228, 280, 293
Mozley, J. K., Canon, 281
Mozley, Thomas, 98
Müller, Max, Professor, 178
Mullinger, J. Bass, 81, 320
Murphy, T., 87, 124
Murry, J. Middleton, 510
Mursel, A., 436
Musgrave, Archbishop, 75
Music, Church, 355 f., 370 ff.
Myers, F. W., 223
Myers, F. W. H., 286 f.

Napoleon I, 12 f., 32, 176
Napoleon III, 63, 193
Napoleonic Wars, 11 ff.
Nasmith, David, 422
National Society, The, 47, 87, 89
Neale, J. M., 230, 346, 439, 472, 477
Neale, Vansittart, 266
Nelson, Lord, 23
Nettleship, R. L., 241
Nevins, J. L., 390
Newman, F. W., 102, 152
Newman, J. H., 45, 46, 48, 55 f., 117, 127 ff., 222, 231 f., 277, 287, 288, 294, 309, 324, 332, 345, 347, 479; and the Oxford Movement, 92 ff., 103 ff.; Secession, 99 ff., 120 ff., 184, 227; on Science, 156, 157 f., 169; as Preacher, 40, 101, 226, 459

Newnham College, 321
Newton, B. W., 57
Newton, Isaac, Sir, 35, 153, 378
Newton, John, 24, 372
Nicoll, W. Robertson, 140, 250, 334, 344, 446, 451, 452, 466
Niebuhr, 143, 182
Nietzsche, 508
Nightingale, Florence, 412 f., 420, 438 f.
Nineteenth Century, The, 414
Noble, Robert, 383
Noel, Baptist, 462
Noel, Conrad, 268
Nonconformist, The, 335
Nonconformists, 26, 51 ff., 69 ff., 182 f., 202, 205 ff., 227, 483 ff.; and Education, 86, 90 f., 312 ff.; and Politics, 196 ff.; Disabilities of, 29 ff., 52, 71 ff., 321 ff.
Norris, H. H., 46, 87

Oastler, R., 243
O'Connell, Daniel, 32 f., 336
Oldham, J. H., 326, 400
Oliver, F. S., 459
Ollard, S. L., Canon, 43
Origin of Species, The, 146, 155, 163, 185
Orthodox, The, 45 ff., 76, 106 f.
Oscott, 117
Otter, Bishop, 454
Ottley, R. L., 240
Overton, Canon, 50, 51, 80, 115, 348, 353, 372, 378
Owen, Robert, 27, 267
Oxford Movement, The, 34, 45, 46, 92 ff., 172, 226 ff., 300, 348
Oxford University, 48, 75, 79 f., 82, 203, 273 ff., 323 f.
Balliol, 80, 98 f., 143, 149, 279, 323 f.
Christ Church, 80, 95, 351
Corpus Christi, 92
Exeter, 294
Hertford, 289
Keble, 321, 354
Magdalen, 46
New College, 324
Oriel, 48, 80, 85, 92 f., 143, 321
St. John's, 99

Padwick, C. E., 326 f., 379, 399
Paget, Francis, Bishop, 109, 239, 242, 465
Paget, James, Sir, 171
Paget, Stephen, 274, 283
Paine, Tom, 36, 89, 381
Paley, Archdeacon, 47, 74, 160, 161
Palmer, William, Sir, 32, 477

Palmerston, Lord, 203, 225, 329
Papacy, Temporal Power of, 128, 193
Papal Infallibility, 128 ff., 193 f., 477
Paradise Lost, 159 f.
Parish Magazines, 333 f.
Parker, Joseph, Dr., 463 f.
Parnell, C. S., 491
Parochial Missions Society, 424
Parr, Samuel, Dr., 47, 52
Pater, Walter, 248, 507
Paton, J. B., 259, 335, 405, 426, 447, 451, 458, 478, 481, 487
Paton, J. G., 386
Patriot, The, 335
Patteson, J. C., Bishop, 386
Pattison, Mark, 50 f., 122, 131, 146, 156, 182, 205, 227, 237, 288, 354, 446
Paul, Herbert, 174
Peacock, Dean, 75
Pearse, M. G., 431
Pearson, Hesketh, 48, 81
Pearson, J. L., 354
Peel, A. W., Dr., 27, 70, 116, 142, 187, 191, 208, 258, 315, 456, 463 f., 473, 475, 485
Peel, Robert, Sir, 16, 32, 61, 69, 88, 91, 154, 313
Peet, H. W., 331
Pelham, Bishop, 68
Pelham, H. F., Professor, 310
Pennefather, W., 216 f., 222, 440
Pericles, 19
Percival, Bishop, 246, 265 f., 318, 367, 433
Perowne, J. J. S., Bishop, 182, 190, 482
Perry, Bishop, 396
Peters, Carl, 18, 209, 330
Pfander, Dr., 383
Phillips, Ambrose, 115 f., 476
Phillpotts, Henry, Bishop, 43, 99, 115, 227 ff.
Picton, J. Allanson, 208
Pierson, Dr., 399
Pilgrim's Progress, 69
Pilkington, G. L., 188, 220, 324
Pitt, William, 26, 31, 84
Pius IX, Pope, 123, 477
Place, Francis, 26, 63
Plato, 176, 357
Plymouth Brethren, The, 51, 56, 57
Polybius, 234
Portal, Abbé, 477
Porteus, Bishop, 36, 37, 348
Powell, F. York, 107, 140, 504
Prayer, Book of Common, 38, 106, 206, 230 f., 234, 365 f., 437

Prayer, Power of, 25, 217 f., 285, 361, 387
Pre-Raphaelite Brotherhood, The, 346, 352 f.
Presbyterians, The, 55 f., 387, 458
Prestige, L., Dr., 372 f., 453
Price, Bonomy, Professor, 502 f.
Price, Dr., 52
Priestly, Dr., 52, 472
Priestley, J. B., 260
Prince Consort, The, 60, 193, 311, 490
Pringle-Pattison, Professor, 292
Psychic Research, 286 f.
Psychology, 287
Public Schools, 83 ff., 317 f.
  Clifton, 246, 318
  Eton, 83, 199, 226, 318
  Harrow, 83, 84, 199, 242, 255, 294, 304, 310, 455
  Lancing, 318
  Leys, The, 317
  Marlborough, 420
  Mill Hill, 86, 317
  Rugby, 83, 85, 98, 187, 276, 298, 503
  Shrewsbury, 324
  Winchester, 84, 85
Pugin, A. W., 116, 354
Punch, 126
Punshon, Dr. Morley, 480
Pusey, E. B., Dr., 22, 30, 39, 46, 100 ff., 128, 133, 183, 203, 208, 240, 297, 414, 433, 439, 450, 458, 477; and the Oxford Movement, 95, 105, 172, 226, 229; and Ritual, 231 f., 237; and the Roman Church, 118 ff.; and Scholarship, 127, 132, 189 f., 281
Pusey House, 240, 438

Quakers, The, 31, 53, 56, 57, 209, 336
Quarterly Review, The, 43, 329, 438
Queen's College, London, 319, 321
Quick, O. C., Canon, 271, 365
Quiver, The, 335

Raffles, Dr., 462
Ragged Schools, 443 f., 478
Raikes, Robert, 443
Ranke, 175
Ranyard Deaconesses, 440
Rashdall, Hastings, Dean, 71, 160, 292, 367, 496
Rashdall, John, 71
Rationalism, 133, 138 ff., 273, 340, 501 f.
Raven, C. E., Canon, 267
Rebmann, J., 382

INDEX

Record, The, 332 f.
Religion, Comparative, 177 ff.
Religious Orders, 437 f.
Religious Tract Society, The, 37, 335, 344, 348, 478
Renan, Ernest, 184 f., 367
Reunion, 303, 468 ff.
Review of Reviews, The, 128
Rhodes, Cecil, 84
Richard, Timothy, 391
Richmond, Legh, 37, 345
Rickards, Edith, 290
Ridley Hall, 219, 326, 454
Ritual, 27, 229 ff., 342, 366
"Rivulet" Controversy, The, 141 f., 335
Robarts, Miss, 441
Robert Elsmere, 274, 347 f.
Robertson, F. W., 145 f., 207 f., 459
Robinson, J. Armitage, Dean, 174, 293, 295, 299, 307, 310
Rock, The, 332
Roebuck, J. A., 89, 463
Rogers, J. Guinness, 52, 71, 86, 126, 211, 258, 462, 487
Roman Catholic Emancipation, 31 ff., 119
Romanes, G. J., Professor, 156, 284
Romanticism, 104 f., 226, 339, 352 f.
Rose, H. J., 80, 95
Rosebery, Lord, 32
Rossetti, Christina, 107, 500
Rossetti, Dante Gabriel, 352
Rousseau, 132, 150
Routh, Martin, Dr., 46, 82
Royal Institution, The, 153
Ruskin, John, 84, 137, 286, 429, 499; on Art, 307, 350 ff., 360; on Social Conditions, 250 f.
Russell, G. W. E., 83, 110, 114, 225, 245, 258, 267, 331
Russell, John, Lord, 28, 71, 72, 124 ff.
Rutherford, Mark, 463 f.
Ryder, Bishop, 44, 381
Ryle, J. C., Bishop, 332, 348

St. Matthew, Guild of, 267 f.
Salisbury, Robert, Marquis of, 34, 264, 322; as Churchman, 203, 226, 436; Foreign Policy of, 492 f.
Salmon, George, Dr., 130
Salter, A., Sir, 136
Salvation Army, The, 336, 373, 422, 486
Sand, George, 322
Sanday, W., Professor, 192, 305 f.
Sandoz, Frederick, 39
Santayana, 158

Sargent, John, 379
Schelling, 155, 288
Schiller, 339
Schleiermacher, 143, 293
Schliemann, 176
Schopenhauer, 272, 274
Scott, Gilbert, Sir, 354 f.
Scott, Thomas, 93
Scott, Walter, Sir, 84, 104 f., 339, 343 f.
Scripture Reading Union, 445
Secessions—
  To Rome, 97 f., 102, 115, 119 ff., 495 f.
  To Dissent, 52, 57, 111, 462
Secularism, 210 f., 420 f.
Sedgwick, A., 168
Seeley, J. R., Sir, 185, 221, 429
Seeley, Robert, 39
Selbie, W. B., Dr., 112, 344, 456
Selborne, Lord, 320
Selden, John, 468
Sellon, Miss, 439 f.
Selwyn, G. A., Bishop, 321, 396, 449
Settlements, 428 ff.
Sewell, Miss, 346
Shaftesbury, Lord, 61, 82, 185, 213, 237, 257, 330, 353, 427, 435; at Harrow, 83 f., 255; as Philanthropist, 255 f., 259, 264, 443 f.; on the Evangelicals, 204 ff.; and the Jews, 33, 210; and Liberal Thought, 185, 190, 191 f.; and Church Patronage, 50, 203
Shairp, J. C., 138, 168, 323
Shakespeare, 84
Sharpe, Granville, 23, 37
Shaw, Bernard, 242
Shelley, P. B., 14, 41, 156 f., 339
Shorthouse, J. H., 347
Sidgwick, Henry, Professor, 276, 286
Sikes of Guisborough, 46 f.
Simeon, Charles, 109, 371, 379, 400; as Churchman, 110, 365; Influence, 80, 325, 396
Skrine, J. H., 317 f.
Slavery, Abolition of, 23 ff.
Smiles, Samuel, 209, 246
Smith, Adam, 313
Smith, John, 24
Smith, Payne, Dean, 190
Smith, Pearsall, 223, 225
Smith, Pye, 164
Smith, Stanley, 220
Smith, Sydney, 22, 33, 47 f., 53, 256, 329, 370, 378; on Education, 81, 83 f., 311
Smith, Vance, Dr., 479

523

Smith, W. Robertson, Professor, 178, 187, 451
Social Emancipation, 22 f.
Social Problems, 198 ff., 241 f., 243 ff., 266, 492 f.
Society for the Promotion of Christian Knowledge, The, 37, 69, 86, 191, 344, 348, 373, 376, 394, 396
Society for the Propagation of the Gospel, 30, 37, 47, 376, 380 ff., 411, 479
Socrates, 88
Solon, 19
Somerville College, 321
Southey, Robert, 41, 104, 249
Spectator, The, 331
Speer, R. E., 375, 378, 411
Spencer, George (Father Ignatius), 115 ff., 476
Spencer, Herbert, 166, 179, 272, 275, 287, 313, 470 f.
Spens, Will, 166
Spiritualism, 58, 286 f.
Spring Hill College, Birmingham, 322, 456
Spurgeon, C. H., 336; as Preacher, 227, 459-61, 463; as Controversialist, 206, 208, 463, 473
Stanley, A. P., Dean, 48, 203, 279, 434, 470, 474, 477, 479; and Liberal Thought, 100, 186 f., 280, 325; Pessimism of, 208, 323
Stanley, Edward, Bishop, 48, 368. 478
Stanley, H. M., 388
Stanton, Father, 466
Stead, W. T., 128
Steere, Bishop, 383, 387 f.
Stephen, Leslie, 82, 174
Stephens, W. R. W., Dean, 66 f., 174
Stevens, William, 47
Stewart, Robert, 392
Stillingfleet, Bishop, 114
Stock, Eugene, Dr., 51, 217, 236, 377 ff., 426
Stockmar, Baron, 13
Stoics, The, 134
Stokes, G. T., Professor, 471, 482
Storr, V. F., Archdeacon, 133 ff., 143, 146, 155, 159, 162, 172, 180 f., 274 f., 279, 361
Stoughton, Dr., 69, 480
Stowell, Hugh, 25, 68
Strachey, Lytton, 13, 60, 87, 122, 125, 245
Stretton, Hesba, 346
Strauss, 151, 183 ff.
Street, G. E., 354

Stubbs, C. W., Bishop, 268
Stubbs, William, Bishop, 173 f., 184, 204, 477, 498
Studd, C. T., 220
Student Christian Movement, 263, 326 f.
Student Volunteer Missionary Union 326 f.
Sturge, John, 25
Suez Canal, 199
Sumner, C. R., Bishop, 44, 67
Sumner, J. B., Archbishop, 44, 68, 93, 202, 423
Sumner, Mary, Mrs., 441
Sunday at Home, The, 335
Sunday Schools, 344, 442 f.
Supernatural Religion, 279, 454
Swedenborg, 35
Swete, H. B., Professor, 185, 293, 299, 305 f., 309 f.
Swinburne, Alfred, 1, 341, 500
Sword and the Trowel, The, 336, 463
Sybil, 90, 244
Symonds, J. Addington, 283, 322, 422

Tablet, The, 336
Tagore, 144
Tait, A. C., Archbishop, 44, 203, 204, 229, 298, 420, 446, 451; at Oxford, 98 ff., 111; and Ritualism, 234 f., 237, 368; as Evangelist, 423, 432
Talbot, Edward, Bishop, 239, 414
Tatlow, Tissington, 327
Taylor, A. E., 301
Taylor, Hudson, 383, 385
Taylor, Jeremy, 46, 228
Teignmouth, Lord, 37
Temperance, 245, 257
Temple, Frederick, Archbishop, 63, 109, 118, 160, 189, 204, 311; and *Essays and Reviews*, 146, 208
Temple, William, Archbishop, 161, 357, 433
Tennyson, Alfred, Lord, 13, 16, 71, 146, 273, 280, 314, 329, 346; and Thought, 149, 273, 341; and Science, 156 f., 161
Tertullian, 486
Thackeray, W. M., 251, 339 f., 343 f., 415
Themistocles, 19
Theological Colleges, 451 ff.
Thirlwall, Bishop, 48, 75, 96, 143 f., 182, 186, 279, 293
Tholuck, 183
Thomson, Archbishop, 147, 203
Thomson, James, 341

524

INDEX

Thorndike, Herbert, 46
Thorne, Mary, 438
Thornton, Douglas, 389
Thornton, Henry, 47
Thornton, P. M., 83
Thorogood, John, 72
Thucydides, 199, 485
Times, The, 29, 246, 328 f., 331, 397, 457
Tindal, Matthew, 114
Tolpuddle Martyrs, The, 27 f.
Tomline, Bishop, 32
Townsend, Mrs., 441
Toynbee, A. J., 330 f., 356, 482
Toynbee, Arnold, 429
Toynbee Hall, 429 ff.
Tract 90, 96, 99 f., 111, 147, 288
Tracts for the Times, 95 f., 102, 106, 116, 348
Trade Unions, 27 f., 253 f.
Treitzsche, 61
Trench, R. C., Archbishop, 81, 203, 432, 450
Trevelyan, G. M., Professor, 17, 50, 311, 329, 408, 412 f.
Trevelyan, G. O., Sir, 24, 174, 455
Trevelyan, J. P., Mrs., 414, 460
Trinitarian Bible Society, 38
Trinity College, Dublin, 390
Trinity College, Toronto, 395
Trollope, Anthony, 339, 415
Tübingen School, 183 f.
Tucker, Bishop, 388
Tucker, Charlotte, 346
Turner, C. H., Professor, 299
Turner, J. M. W., 351, 360
Turner, W. L., 500
Tylor, E. B., Sir, 154, 452
Tyndall, J., Professor, 166
Tyrrell, George, 127

Underhill, Francis, Dean, 423
Unitarians, The, 54 ff., 71, 151 f., 458
Univers, L', 98
Universe, The, 336
Universities, The, 73 f., 79 ff.
Universities Mission to Central Africa, 382 f., 387 f.
Ussher, Archbishop, 228
Utilitarianism, 134 ff.

Van der Kemp, 380
Van Mildert, Bishop, 40, 82, 179, 418
Vaughan, Cardinal, 122, 130
Vaughan, C. J., Dean, 410, 455
Vaughan, Margaret, 415, 422

Vaughan, R. A., 208
Vaughan, Robert, Dr., 187, 335, 461, 475
Venn, Henry, 67, 76
Venn, Henry, Junior, 216, 387
Verbeck of Japan, 392
Verrall, Professor, 410
Vestiges of Creation, The, 155, 157
Vicar of Wakefield, The, 39
Vico, 275
Victoria, Queen, 45, 71, 91, 116, 199, 428, 441, 474; Accession, 59 f.; and Parliamentary Reform, 195; and Social Changes, 245, 414; Protestantism of, 203, 235, 491; Death, 490, 493; Character, 491 f.
Vincent, William, Dean, 372
Voltaire, 132
von Hügel, Baron, 122, 157, 167, 362
Voysey, Charles, 143, 151

Wakley, Thomas, 28
Waldegrave, Bishop, 68, 203, 235, 432
Walpole, Spencer, 27
War Cry, The, 336
Ward, Humphry, 201, 354
Ward, Humphry, Mrs., 151, 274, 312, 339, 414, 429, 460, 498; and Liberal Theology, 283, 347 f.
Ward, James, Professor, 271
Ward, W. G., 98 ff., 102, 120
Ward, Wilfred, 169, 367, 469
Watson, Bishop, 74, 406
Watson, Joshua, 47, 69, 76, 87
Watts, G. F., 352
Watts-Dunton, Theodore, 288
Webb, Benjamin, 230
Webb, C. C. J., Professor, 172, 230
Webb, Sidney, 418
Webb, Sidney, Mrs., 257, 267, 275, 413, 470 f., 495
Webb-Peploe, H. W., Prebendary, 222, 482
Wellbeloved, C., 56
Wellhausen, 187
Wellington, Arthur, Duke of, 21, 32, 63
Wells College, 454
Wells, G. P., 155
Wells, H. G., 200, 409
Wesley, Charles, 372
Wesley, John, 55, 109 f., 204, 228, 331, 336, 376, 423
Wesleyan Missionary Society, 379 ff.
West, Rebecca, 411

525

Westcott, B. F., Bishop, 127, 148, 150, 164, 191, 201, 212, 232, 286, 360, 368, 448, 469, 471, 479, 481; at Harrow, 269, 294, 304, 310; at Cambridge, 292, 294–310; Bishop of Durham, 265, 298, 301, 497; on Social Conditions, 137, 265, 268 f.; Optimism of, 170, 306; Influence, 241 f., 310
Westminster Review, The, 135, 147
Whately, Archbishop, 48
Whewell, William, Dr., 80, 154, 164, 168
Whichcote, Benjamin, 292
Whitbread, Samuel, 88
White, Blanco, 96
Whitefield, George, 24, 462, 467
Whitley, W. T., Dr., 87, 126 f., 315, 419
Wicksteed, P. H., 74, 136, 247 f.
Widdrington, P. E. T., 405
Wilberforce, Henry, 231
Wilberforce, R. I., 120, 228
Wilberforce, Samuel, Bishop, 84, 97, 147, 163, 186, 229, 333, 346, 460; Energy of, 66, 202; and Ordinands, 448, 454
Wilberforce, William, 23 ff., 36, 255
Wilder, R. P., 326
Wilkinson, G. H., Bishop, 148, 225, 354, 386, 423 f., 466
William IV, 14, 21, 311
Williams, F. Garfield, Dean, 376
Williams, George, Sir, 444
Williams, Isaac, 95, 100

Williams, Rowland, 147
Willoughby, D., 149
Wilson, Daniel, 110, 222
Wilson, H. B., 99, 147, 149
Wilson, J. M., Archdeacon, 482
Wiseman, Cardinal, 115, 117, 123 f., 336
Women, Position of, 63, 410 ff.
Women's Work, 438 ff.
Wood, Henry, Mrs., 335
Woodard, Nathaniel, 318 f.
Woodd, Basil, 345
Woods, Theodore, Bishop, 307, 325 f.
Worboise, Emma Jane, 334
Wordsworth, Christopher, Bishop, 148, 448, 480
Wordsworth, Christopher, Dr. 80, 143
Wordsworth, John, Bishop, 192, 204, 477
Wordsworth, William, 21, 156, 249, 339; Reaction from Liberalism, 11, 138; Influence, 104, 288, 292
Wycliffe Hall, 454

Xavier, Francis, 377

Yeats, W. B., 301, 357, 509
Yonge, Charlotte, 225, 346, 364, 385
Young, G. M., 502
Young Men's Christian Association, **444**
Young, Thomas, 153, 169
Young Women's Christian Association, 441 f.

Zola, 348